Welcome to ICAEW

I am delighted that you have chosen ICAEW to progress your journey toward becoming the chartered accountancy profession. It is one of the best decisions I also made.

The role of the accountancy profession in the world's economies has never been more important. People making financial decisions need knowledge and guidance based on the highest technical and ethical standards. ICAEW Chartered Accountants provide this better than anyone. They challenge people and organisations to think and act differently, to provide clarity and rigour, and so help create and sustain prosperity all over the world.

As a world leader of the accountancy and finance profession, we are proud to promote, develop and support over 142,000 chartered accountants worldwide. Our members have the knowledge, skills and commitment to maintain the highest professional standards and integrity. They are part of something special, and now, so are you. It's with our support and dedication that our members and hopefully yourself, will realise career ambitions, maintain a professional edge and contribute to the profession.

You are now on your journey towards joining the accountancy profession, a profession that offers a highly rewarding career with endless opportunities. By choosing to study for our world-leading chartered accountancy qualification, the ACA, you too have made the first of many great decisions in your career.

You are in good company, with a network of over 20,000 students around the world made up of like-minded people, you are all supported by ICAEW. We are here to support you as you progress through your studies and career, we will be with you every step of the way, visit page x to review the key resources available as you study.

I wish you the best of luck with your studies and look forward to welcoming you to the profession in the future.

Michael Izza
Chief Executive
ICAEW

Contents

1 Introduction

ACA Overview

The ICAEW chartered accountancy qualification, the ACA, is one of the most advanced learning and professional development programmes available. Its integrated components provide you with an in-depth understanding across accountancy, finance and business. Combined, they help build the technical knowledge, professional skills and practical experience needed to become an ICAEW Chartered Accountant.

Each component is designed to complement each other, which means that you can put theory into practice and can understand and apply what you learn to your day-to-day work. The components are:

Professional development

ICAEW Chartered Accountants are known for their professionalism and expertise. Professional development prepares you to successfully handle a variety of different situations that you'll encounter throughout your career.

The ACA qualification improves your ability and performance in seven key areas:

- Adding value
- Communication
- Consideration
- Decision making
- Problem solving
- Team working
- Technical competence.

Ethics and professional scepticism

Ethics is more than just knowing the rules around confidentiality, integrity, objectivity and independence.

It's about identifying ethical dilemmas, understanding the implications and behaving appropriately. We integrate ethics throughout the ACA qualification to develop your ethical capabilities – so you will always know how to make the right decisions and justify them.

3-5 years practical work experience

Practical work experience is done as part of a training agreement with one of our 2,850 authorised training employers or authorised training principals around the world. You need to complete 450 days, which normally takes between three and five years. The knowledge, skills and experience you gain as part of your training agreement are invaluable, giving you the opportunity to put what you're learning into practice.

15 accountancy, finance and business modules

You will gain in-depth knowledge across a broad range of topics in accountancy, finance and business.

There are 15 modules over three levels. These can be taken in any order with the exception of the Case Study which has to be attempted last. You must pass every exam (or receive credit) – there are no options. This ensures that once qualified, all ICAEW Chartered Accountants have a consistent level of knowledge, skills and experience.

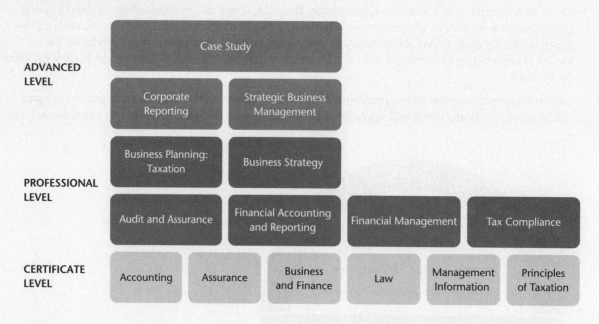

Certificate Level

There are six modules that introduce the fundamentals of accountancy, finance and business.

Each module is examined by a 1.5 hour computer-based assessment which can be sat at any time. You may be eligible for credit for some modules if you have studied accounting, finance, law or business at degree level or through another professional qualification.

These six modules also provide a stand-alone certificate, the ICAEW Certificate in Finance, Accounting and Business (ICAEW CFAB). Once you have completed all six Certificate Level assessments, you can apply for the ICAEW CFAB certificate of completion, visit icaew.com/cfab for more information.

Some of the issues in this exam were introduced at the certificate level in Business and Finance and, to a lesser extent, in Management Information. These two areas are the foundation of Business Strategy.

Professional Level

The next six modules build on the fundamentals and test your understanding and ability to use technical knowledge in real-life scenarios. Each module has a 2.5-3 hour exam, which are available to sit four times per year. These modules are flexible and can be taken in any order. The Business Planning: Taxation and Business Strategy modules in particular will help you to progress to the Advanced Level.

The knowledge base that is put into place at Certificate Level is developed further in this Professional Level exam Business Strategy. Here, the aim is to ensure students can utilise and combine theoretical frameworks to provide advice to management on the strategic management of their businesses. The exam questions are practical scenarios and it is for the candidate to decide which framework or model will provide the most useful analysis of the situation.

Advanced Level

The Corporate Reporting and Strategic Business Management modules test understanding and strategic decision making at a senior level. They present real-life scenarios, with increased complexity and wider implications from the Professional Level modules.

The Case Study presents a complex business issue which challenges your ability to problem solve, identify the ethical implications and provide an effective solution. The Case Study tests through contextualisation the ability to apply your knowledge, skills and experience.

The Advanced Level exams are fully open book, so they replicate a real-life scenario where all the resources are at your fingertips. The Corporate Reporting and Strategic Business Management exams are

3.5 hours and the Case Study is 4 hours. The Strategic Business Management exam will consist of two scenario-based questions, forming a stepping stone to the Case Study.

Access further exam resources and support at icaew.com/dashboard

2 Business Strategy

The full syllabus and technical knowledge grids can be found within the module study guide. Visit icaew.com/dashboard for this and more resources.

2.1 Module aim

To provide candidates with an understanding of how businesses develop and implement strategy.

2.2 Specification grid

This grid shows the relative weightings of subjects within this module and should guide the relative study time spent on each. Over time the marks available in the assessment will equate to the weightings below, while slight variations may occur in individual assessments to enable suitably rigorous questions to be set.

	Weighting (%)
Strategic analysis	35
Strategic choice	35
Implementation and monitoring of strategy	30
	100

Your exam will consist of three questions

Time available	2.5 hours

3 Key Resources

Student support team

Our student support team are here to help you as much as possible, providing full support throughout your studies.

T +44 (0)1908 248 250
F +44 (0)1908 248 069
E studentsupport@icaew.com

Student website

The student area of our website provides you with information on exam applications, deadlines, results and regulations as well as applying for credit for prior learning (CPL). The study resources section includes advice from the examiners, module syllabi, past papers and sample papers, webinars and study guides. The study guides are designed to help put the learning for each module into context and highlight the practical significance of what you'll learn. They also include the syllabus, technical knowledge grids and learning outcomes for each module, enabling you to gain an overview of how your learning links to the qualification. Visit icaew.com/dashboard for these resources and more.

If you are studying for the ICAEW CFAB qualification, you can access exam resources and support at icaew.com/cfab

Online student community

The online student community is a forum to ask questions, gain study and exam advice from fellow ACA and ICAEW CFAB students and access our free webinars. There are also regular Ask a Tutor sessions to help you with key technical topics and exam papers. Access the community at icaew.com/studentcommunity

Tuition

The ICAEW Partner in Learning scheme recognises tuition providers who comply with our core principles of quality course delivery. If you are receiving structured tuition with an ICAEW Partner in Learning, make sure you know how and when you can contact your tutors for extra help. If you are not receiving structured tuition and are interested in classroom, online or distance learning tuition, take a look at our recognised Partner in Learning tuition providers in your area, on our website icaew.com/dashboard

Faculties and Special Interest Groups

Faculties and special interest groups support and develop members and students in areas of work and industry sectors that are of particular interest.

Our seven faculties provide knowledge, events and essential technical resources. They cover Audit and Assurance, Corporate Finance, Finance and Management, Financial Reporting, Financial Services, Information Technology and Tax. As an ACA or ICAEW CFAB student, you are entitled to register to receive either complimentary factsheets from the Financial Reporting Faculty or an e-newsletter from one faculty of your choice each year throughout your studies.

Our 12 special interest groups provide practical support, information and representation within a range of industry sectors including Charity and Voluntary, Entertainment and Media, Farming and Rural Business, Forensic and Expert Witness, Healthcare, Insolvency and Restructuring, Interim Management, Solicitors, Tourism and Hospitality, Public Sector, Valuation and Non-Executive Directors. As an ACA student you can receive free provisional membership of one group each year throughout your studies, apart from the Public Sector group, where a subscription charge is required.

Find out more about faculties and special interest groups at icaew.com/facultiesandsigs

Library & Information Service

The Library & Information Service is ICAEW's world-leading accountancy and business library. You have access to online and print facilities which include company information, country and sector resources, economic forecasts and eBooks, with services that include book loans, document delivery and help with research queries. Visit icaew.com/library for more information.

CHAPTER 1

Introduction to the Business Strategy paper

Introduction

Examination context

Topic List

1. Business Strategy and the ACA exams
2. Knowledge
3. Skills
4. Professional experience and common sense
5. Developing business awareness
6. A guide to the marking process
7. Examination technique

Learning objective

- To become familiar with the context of the Business Strategy paper

Syllabus links

The purpose of this chapter is as an initial help to approaching the Business Strategy paper. The knowledge, skills and business awareness that you will develop in relation to Business Strategy will be of great benefit when you progress to the Advanced level of the ACA syllabus.

Examination context

Whilst an appreciation of models and theories underlying business strategy is important, the focus of your examination is a practical one. You will be required to interpret business scenarios and to provide professional advice to clients and management on what to do. You will not be required to reproduce names and models for the sake of it – knowledge will always need to be applied.

The strategic models and theories you will cover in this Study Manual are to be used in three ways in the examination:

1   To **analyse and interpret**: Applying the appropriate models and perspectives to the situation and issues in the scenario will help you see underlying causes better.

2   To **generate solutions**: Many of the models include recommendations or approaches to resolving problems. You may wish to pass this advice on to management.

3   To **substantiate your comments**: The models and their authors are recognised by management who may have studied them too. You would be expected to refer to them as a framework in a real business report. You will get some marks for doing the same in your Business Strategy exam.

At the beginning of every chapter the examination context comments are there to illustrate how certain topics have been tested in previous sittings. It is important that you take the time to read through this guidance in preparation for your own exam. You may notice that some of the comments made relate to examinations reaching back to 2008/09. Although these questions were set some time ago, they are still very relevant to your studies and have been used within this pack to help you understand how your knowledge may need to be applied. As the examiner highlights, the fundamental concept behind the Business Strategy examination as a practical, scenario based paper has not changed and therefore students are strongly advised to take notice of the points raised. The reference to previous exam questions is particularly useful and questions set more recently have been included in your Question Bank for you to attempt.

1 Business strategy and the ACA exams

As a chartered accountant you will one day find yourself involved in helping an organisation 'find its way' in the world: taking its resources and capabilities and using them to exploit opportunities in markets and industries in order to satisfy its stakeholders over time. To 'find its way' the organisation must have an idea of what it wants to achieve and how it is going to achieve it. At its most basic, this is what business strategy means. The purpose of the Business Strategy paper at the Professional level of the ACA exams is to help you develop and demonstrate the knowledge and skills necessary to ensure an organisation with which you are involved can find its way.

All Professional level exams require both factual knowledge and analytical skills, plus the ability to apply knowledge in real-life scenarios. It is important to distinguish between what we mean by 'knowledge' and 'skills', and to see how the exam assesses each.

2 Knowledge

The knowledge required to do well in Business Strategy is primarily built on that acquired at Certificate level in the Business and Finance and Management Information exams. Your knowledge is extended, enhanced and developed at this level but it is assessed very differently, in a written exam rather than an objective test. Each question in the exam consists of a written 'scenario', often with a numerical element, followed by two or more 'requirements', to which you must prepare answers.

The other major difference between Certificate and Professional level is that knowledge is only assessed in the context of how it is applied to the business scenarios set out in the exam. Thus you would NOT expect to see a requirement like this:

'Describe the factors incorporated in Porter's Five Forces model'.

But you would expect to see a requirement like this (Q1 June 2008 paper, which has a detailed scenario describing the tyre manufacturing industry and a participant in the UK tyre market):

'Using Porter's Five Forces model, identify and evaluate the factors affecting the overall profitability of the UK tyre manufacturing industry.'

While you can assume one or two marks will be available just for the basic knowledge of what each of the five forces is, most of the marks will be for how that knowledge is used to analyse the scenario and explain the pertinent points under each heading.

3 Skills

To be successful in the Business Strategy paper you have to demonstrate a range of skills in applying knowledge. The table below describes the four categories of skill and gives you an example of how you can expect to have each skill tested in the Business Strategy exam.

Skill at Professional level	How the Business Strategy exam might test this skill
Assimilating and using information	
Understanding the subject matter and identifying issues	Reading a large amount of material in the scenario and distinguishing the parts that are relevant to each requirement
Accessing, evaluating and managing information	Taking both written and numerical information and combining them to understand and explain a situation more fully
Using technical knowledge and professional experience	Identifying which pieces of information in the scenario relate to what you already know eg identifying that information about economies of scale is relevant to the 'threat of new entrants' in Porter's model

Skill at Professional level	How the Business Strategy exam might test this skill
Structuring problems and solutions	
Using analytical tools	Calculating ratios relating to performance, using numerical data in the scenario, or using the headings in a model such as Five Forces, PESTEL or SWOT to break down the information in the scenario
Analysing and evaluating problems	Drawing together ratios or categorised written information to get a clearer picture of the situation, highlight the key issues and begin to identify possible solutions
Applying judgement	
Assessing quality of information	Identifying deficiencies in the information available and identifying what may be needed to address them
Assessing options and priorities including ethical issues	Using the analysis to date to identify feasible actions that could or must be taken, and their likely consequences
Considering other perspectives	Standing back from the available analysis and information and establishing whether all the possible angles have been considered
Conclusions, recommendations and communication	
Drawing conclusions and making recommendations	Making a choice between possible actions or viewpoints and providing a reasoned explanation of that choice and its potential consequences
Presenting data and written work	Being professional in producing material for the required purpose and audience

4 Professional experience and common sense

Technical knowledge and professional skills are vital to success in Business Strategy, as we have seen, but the value of your common sense and professional experience should not be underestimated. Your analysis of a situation should always be tempered with your awareness of the 'real world', however this has been obtained. This applies in particular to answers where you make a recommendation: you should think twice for instance about asking for every conceivable piece of additional information before reaching a firm conclusion, or recommending a global overseas expansion to a firm with only 10 employees.

There may be occasions where you do not feel you have any technical knowledge to bring to bear on a scenario. In such a situation you may have to adopt a 'common' sense' approach to one or more requirements. While this is never going to earn you full marks it is better than not providing an answer at all.

A key aspect of professional experience that you need to develop is professional scepticism, that is looking at information that you have been given with a questioning eye. Information that is provided in-house by the management of a company desperate to raise finance, for instance, should be looked at with some scepticism, on the basis that the management may seek to overplay good news and underplay bad news in order to secure their objective. Information provided by a professional firm as an independent reviewer of a business on the other hand may be taken with far less scepticism.

ICAEW

5 Developing business awareness

Throughout this Study Manual we will be building up your knowledge and skills, and demonstrating how these apply to exam questions in a large number of topic areas. Each chapter begins with an example of the type of requirement you might expect for that topic area, so you become familiar from the beginning with the context of the exam.

The variety of scenarios and case examples that you will see in this Study Manual will also help you to build up your business awareness. This is a vital element in developing the combination of knowledge, skills, professional experience and common sense that will help you to do well in the Business Strategy paper, and progress to Advanced level.

You can help yourself further in this respect by taking advantage of resources that are available online in the form of 'real world' case studies. Particularly useful are the case studies on the *Times 100 Business Case Studies* website at http://businesscasestudies.co.uk. These case studies describe and analyse issues in a number of key businesses in the UK and are categorised under the following topics:

- The external environment
- Finance
- Marketing
- Operations
- People
- Strategy

You can browse these case studies at any time. At various points in this Study Manual we will refer you to particular case studies that are pertinent to that topic.

6 A guide to the marking process

6.1 The distinction between Knowledge and Skills

Business Strategy (BS) has the highest skills content of all the Professional level papers and as the BS paper is leading on to Advanced level, there may be some relatively open requirements,. This is reflected in the marking process where the available marks for each requirement are divided into two pools: Knowledge marks (K) and Skills marks (S), with more marks awarded for skills than knowledge. Normally there will be a knowledge: skills split of approximately 30%:70%, although there may be some variation from paper to paper.

Broadly speaking the K marks are for demonstration of accurate knowledge and understanding from the Learning Materials that is relevant to the requirement i.e. the answer is developed using recognised models, tools and frameworks, not just common sense. This demonstration may be explicit or implied. This means that you do not have to set out your knowledge in the abstract before then applying it to the scenario: you can demonstrate your knowledge in the process of applying it to the scenario.

The S marks are for evidence of the skills discussed in the table in section 3 of this chapter.

6.1.1 Example: K and S marks

Requirement: 'analyse the competitive forces within an industry'.

K marks would be awarded for selecting the right model and knowing the key headings, in this case that 'competitive forces' suggests Porter's Five Forces model should be applied under its five headings.

S marks would be gained by:

- Applying the model to the context in the question

  eg identifying information from the scenario under each of the five headings

- Analysing the information

  eg to evaluate the significance of each force

- Reasoning and judgement

  eg summarising the key forces within the industry and their impact on the business in question

6.2 Marking

For any particular exam paper there are three marking documents:

- A detailed mark plan for the paper which is a full answer, containing all the likely points that candidates may make; it is not a model answer as it is highly unlikely that any one candidate could produce it in the time allowed;

- A marking grid which breaks the paper down into the K and S mark pools available for each requirement;

- A separate marking guidance document issued to markers, giving an overview of the typical K and S points for each requirement, to be used in conjunction with the detailed mark plan.

Note that some requirements are marked out of more marks than are actually available, for instance there may be a maximum of 7 skills marks but the total pool is treated as being 9 marks. This headroom increases the chances of a good answer scoring maximum marks.

The marking grid and marking guidance are reproduced below for the December 2009 paper, together with an overview of the key issues and knowledge content.

6.3 December 2009 paper

6.3.1 Overview of key issues and knowledge required:

Q1 – Green Cards (43 marks)

UK retailer of greeting cards, considering two alternative strategies for growth

- Mini case, including data analysis

- Key issues: industry analysis, analysis of competitive position and performance, ethical practices, deciding on strategy to pursue

Q2 – Efficiency Systems Ltd (32 marks)

Small business seeking funds for expansion with a business plan for the bank

- Key issues: mission statement and critical success factors, quality/viability of business plan, risks

Q3 – Total Equipment Hire Ltd (25 marks)

Established plant hire business facing cash crisis and questionable joint venture opportunity

- Key issues: going concern, divestment, cost reduction, part-closure, attractiveness of joint venture

Marks split 27% knowledge, 73% skills

Specific knowledge required:

- Porter's Five Forces: suppliers and substitutes
- Competitive positioning eg niche, BCG, price/quality grid
- Ethical issues
- Critical success factors
- Mission statement
- Structure of business plan
- Risks
- Performance measurement
- Joint ventures

6.3.2 The marking process

The following is one of the requirements in the paper, which will serve as an example of the marking process:

For 6 marks D09 Q1(c) asked candidates to 'discuss the ethical and business implications of GC's participation in, and withdrawal from, the environmentally friendly cards market.'

The available mark pool was K2, S5 – a total of 7 marks with a maximum possible score of 6.

Knowledge: 2 marks

These were for recognising the difference between 'ethical' and 'business' implications and dealing with them separately in the answer:

- Business issues related to things like profitability
- Ethical issues related to the environment and also the transparency or otherwise of GC's behaviour

Skills: 5 marks

The skills that could be demonstrated here included:

- Identifying information from the scenario and analysing it into ethical issues (supporting the environment) and business ones (making a decent margin)
- Using the price and cost data, and the floorspace information, from the question to support comments
- Demonstrating reasoning and judgement in discussing the issue, for instance questioning the company's motives for withdrawal
- Spotting the possibly transparency issue as the percentage of recycled paper and the amount of donation per card were very small
- Making an attempt at some form of conclusion or recommendation

6.3.3 Marking grid BS December 2009

	Available		Awarded			
	K	S	K	S	Max mark	Total awarded
Q1: Green Cards Ltd						
(a)(i) Power of suppliers	1	4				
(ii) Substitutes	1	3			7	
(b)(i) Competitive position & threats	3	7				
(ii) Performance & comparison	2	9			18	
(c) Withdrawal – ethical & business	2	5			6	
(d) Briefing note	1					
Strategy 1	1	4				
Strategy 2	1	4				
Advice	1	2			12	
Total	13	38			43	
Q2: Efficiency Systems Ltd						
(a) Critical success factors	2	3				
Mission statement	1	3			8	
(b)(i) Business plan assessment/additional information	4	12			15	
(c) Key risks	3	7			9	
Total	10	25			32	

		Available		Awarded			
		K	S	K	S	Max mark	Total awarded
Q3: Total Equipment Hire Ltd							
(a) Divestment and cost reduction		2	7			8	
(b) Closure – measuring perf.		3	6			8	
(c) JV – benefits, problems and clarified		3	7			9	
Total		8	20			25	
Overall total		31	83			100	

6.3.4 Marking guidance issued to markers for BS marking December 2009

Q1: Green Cards	Knowledge	Skills
(a) Power of suppliers	• Identify suppliers • Generic descriptions of power of suppliers (without application) • Focus on industry not company	• Analysis of the factors affecting suppliers • Distinguish power in different circumstances (switching, differentiation, international) • Application to scenario and use of information provided • Identify a range of suppliers of different types (ie not just greeting cards) • Conclusion on power
(a) Substitutes *Max of 2 out of 4 if only covered e-cards (1k 1s)*	• Identify general nature of substitutes	• Identify specific types of substitutes in the greeting card market • Discussion of nature of each substitute • Conclusion on effect of substitutes
(b)(i) Competitive position and threats *3 for threats* *3 for data but only give all 3 if include niche market*	• General description of competitive position • Porter • BCG matrix • Price/quality • Identification of threats • (SWOT)	**NB all data treated as skills marks (max 3)** **Data analysis** • Market share • Growth in market • Use of data **Explanation** • Assessment of GC's position in the market • Identification of economies of scale as an issue • Discussion of market positioning • Discussion of threats • Use of BCG matrix • Range of comparisons to: Mood Cards, Cardworld, and handmade card retailers.

Q1: Green Cards	Knowledge	Skills
(b)(ii) Assess and explain performance with data analysis and comparisons with Moon *Data marks are all skills marks (ie no knowledge)* *5 For data* *Max 2 out of 5 if do not include some relative measure (per shop, per employee, per sq metre)*	• General description of movements in data without identifying underlying causes • General comparison with Mood	**NB all data treated as skills marks (max 5)** **Data analysis** • Table of appropriate calculations • Growth (revenue and operating profit) • Relationships per shop (revenue and operating profit) • Relationships for floorspace (revenue and operating profit) • Relationships per employee **Explanation** • Cause-effect relationships (facts from Q) • Link discussion to numerical analysis • Conclusions • Comparisons with Mood Cards
(c) Business and ethical issues – environmentally friendly cards	• General identification of business issues (profitability) • General identification of ethical issues (environmental)	• Transparency issue – recycled paper minimal • Minimal amount paid over • Motivation for actions • Reference to price-cost data for ethical cards • Floorspace comparison • Balanced argument (eg pros v cons) • Conclude
(d)(i) Strategy 1 *Max 3 if no calcs (1k 2s)*	• Description of strategy issues in generic terms • Synergy and cross branding	• Reputational effects • Use of data • Analysis of additional income • Contingent fee risks
(d)(i) Strategy 2 *Max 4 if no calcs (1k 3s)*	• Description of strategy issues in generic terms • General description of implications	• Link with level of service quality • Use of data
(d)(ii) Advice	• Basic assertion	• Rationale and reasoning for recommendation

Q2: Efficiency Systems	Knowledge	Skills
(a) Critical success factors *Max 4 if not for inclusion in business plan*	• Definition of CSFs (implicit or explicit), not just strength	• Identification of specific CSFs • New product development • Customer issues

Q2: Efficiency Systems	Knowledge	Skills
		• Staffing issue
		• Finance issues
		• Reads as though part of a business plan
Mission statement	• Description of MS • Generic mission statement	• Writing specific mission statement • Inclusion of product based issues • Inclusion of market based issues • Reads as though part of a business plan
(b) Critical assessment of business plan	• Identify shortfalls in business plans generally eg need exec summary • Generic additional information • Structured headings per question • More detail suggested but nature of information not specified	• Management weaknesses, and age – level of detail • Product – more detail on Comax functions and legal rights • Fees – more details (eg client list) • Marketing plan • Competitors – detailed analysis • Financing requirements – growth assumptions, analysis of contracts • Realistic additional information requests • Risk and sensitivity of estimates being wrong • Need to convince bank (BP's fitness for purpose) • Wider perspective beyond headings
(c) Risks	• Listing of risks without identifying key risks • Describing risks with minimal application to scenario	• Focus on scenario with finance in place • Investment risk to directors • Future financing risks • Product risks • Personnel risk • Marketing risk • Industry risks

Q3: Total Equipment Hire	Knowledge	Skills
(a) Divestment and cost reduction	• Key headings • Generic descriptions of divestment/cost reduction • Both given reasonable and clear emphasis	• Link with strategy of differentiator • Utilisation computations • Long term issues arising from divestment • Reputational issues • Link to liquidity requirement and interest payment

Q3: Total Equipment Hire	Knowledge	Skills
		• Liquidity v profitability • Going concern • Proceeds > interest payment
(b) Performance measurement for purpose of closure *Max 3 for BSC or other performance measures if not linked to closure* *Max 3 for discussion of closure of no performance measures*	• Performance measures without linking to the closure issue • Recognition of joint cost issue and allocation	• Financial v non financial performance • Interdependence of revenues • Interdependence of costs • Benchmarking • KPIs • BSC if focused on closure • Linking closure and performance • Relate to timing of cash inflow
(c) Joint venture arrangement	• Description of JV arrangement • General advantages and disadvantages of a JV	• Application to scenario • Critical analysis of imbalance in the proposal • Risk issues • Issues for clarification – reasonable and constructive items • Calculations of size of contract (exceeds spare capacity and therefore may be opportunity costs) • Calculation of margin on new contract compared to old contract • Cutting into core business

7 Examination technique

The Business Strategy examiners have the following advice for candidates sitting this paper:

- Read the requirements carefully and select appropriate analytical tools.

- Complete the requirements for each question in the order set out in the question, since very often analysis in the later requirements can be linked back to that in earlier requirements.

- A brief definition of a model is welcomed before going on to apply it in the context of the question.

- Sometimes candidates over-rely on the use of models, as they apply them but do not develop them sufficiently – inclusion of models where not appropriate, and their over-use, can often lead to time-wasting. For example, some candidates will apply a full SWOT analysis to a question which asks them to only identify strengths. Similarly a long list of points for PESTEL analysis, without considering the implications for the particular business in the scenario or the priority of the points, will score limited marks.

- Numbers in a scenario help to tell the story, and are backed up by appropriate narrative; candidates should try to adopt a similar approach in their answers.

- Responding to the scenario and requirements by addressing the major points will score more highly than a scatter-gun approach. Identifying key points in answers is important, and overall it is the quality of an answer's content, rather than its volume, that is key to gaining marks.

- In the context of the requirement, markers award marks for scripts that are properly presented and they have no objection to appropriate use of bullet points, tables, diagrams, and any technique that helps to present information clearly. However, when making points in bullet form, it is important for candidates to write in sentences and to identify causal relationships, elaborating when necessary and applying the information to the scenario.

- Marks are not awarded specifically for the use of headings, but their use will help candidates to structure their answer, leading to a better performance.

7.1 Key tips for exam technique

- Answer all parts of all requirements.

- Identify clearly which requirement is being attempted.

- Demonstrate/apply appropriate knowledge.

- Identify the key issues in scenarios.

- Make use of any numbers in the scenario, presenting any supporting numerical analysis in table format.

- Prioritise issues in answers.

- Use systematic analysis, reasoning and judgement, in particular of cause and effect relationships.

- Conclude/recommend even when not specifically required to do so.

7.2 Key things to avoid

- Ignoring numbers in the scenario and not including any in your answers

- Simply restating facts from the question without any development, often in the context of models, eg SWOT, PESTEL, Five Forces

- Answering requirements in random order

- Throwing models randomly at a situation, especially as a result of confusing the various ideas of Porter

- Producing messy, unprofessional answers

- Failing to use a report or other specified format for your answer when required to do so

CHAPTER 2

Strategy and business

Introduction

Examination context

Topic List

Summary and Self-test

Answers to Interactive questions

Answers to Self-test

Learning objectives

Tick off

- Evaluate a business's purpose

- Evaluate omissions, inconsistencies and weaknesses and the different objectives of stakeholders

The specific syllabus reference for this chapter is 1a.

Syllabus links

In the Business and Finance paper you will have covered the basic objectives and processes of strategic management. This chapter revises these topics and provides a range of alternative perspectives on the role of management in the strategic process.

The following topics, revised and expanded here, were introduced in your Business and Finance paper:

- General objectives of strategic management
- The strategic management processes
- Nature and purpose of strategic plans, business plans and operational plans

The framework of the rational planning model will be employed in subsequent chapters.

Examination context

This chapter reviews some of the leading theories of strategy formulation and provides the names of many authorities on strategy. The remaining chapters of this study manual also provide coverage of names and theories.

In a previous exam (Q1 March 2008 *DA plc*) the scenario contains a lot of information on how the company, which provides information solutions, has used its skills in providing certain products for business customers to develop new, related products. The first requirement is:

'(a)   Explain the factors that may have contributed to DA's competitive advantage.   **(6 marks)**'

Because of the information in the scenario and the fact that the requirement asks about 'competitive advantage', you are put on notice that the material in this chapter on the resource-based view of gaining competitive advantage is relevant, focusing on products and core competences.

1 What is strategy?

Section overview

- Strategies are about the long term development and survival of the business.
- Strategy takes place at several levels ranging from the corporate centre down to strategies for functions such as marketing, human resources and finance.

1.1 Approaches to strategy

There are probably as many different definitions of 'strategy' (or 'corporate strategy') as there are textbooks on the subject.

Definitions

'**Strategy** is the direction and scope of an organisation over the long term, which achieves advantage for the organisation through its configuration of resources within a changing environment, to meet the needs of markets and to fulfil stakeholder expectations.' (Johnson, Scholes and Whittington).

'**Corporate strategy** is concerned with an organisation's basic direction for the future, its purpose, its ambitions, its resources and how it interacts with the world in which it operates' (Lynch).

From these we can say that strategy is therefore concerned with:

- The long-term direction (objectives) of the organisation
- The environment in which it operates
- The resources at its disposal
- The return it makes to stakeholders

Theories of strategy and of strategic management must be used with caution. They don't apply in all situations and the evidence for them is not always clear cut. Therefore this text draws attention to the limitations of some to help you decide how far you can apply them in the exam.

This chapter reviews two broad approaches to strategy: the **rational planning (traditional) approach** and the **emergent approach**. It also considers whether an organisation can achieve competitive advantage by orientating its strategy around its external environment (**positioning-based approach**) or around its internal competences (**resource-based approach**).

1.2 Levels of strategy

Strategy can exist at several levels in an organisation as shown in the diagram below:

1.2.1 Corporate strategy

Corporate strategy is generally determined at head office/main board level. This covers the business as a whole – its overall mission and objectives, product/market decisions, major investment decisions, financing decisions and relations with external stakeholders.

1.2.2 Business strategy

This normally takes place in strategic business units (SBUs). **Competitive** strategy is normally determined at this level covering such matters as how advantage over competitors can be achieved and marketing issues, such as the marketing mix.

1.2.3 Functional (operational) strategies

This refers to the main functions within each SBU, such as production, purchasing, finance, human resources and marketing, and how they deliver effectively the strategies determined at the corporate and business levels.

2 Overview of strategic planning approaches

Section overview

- There is a contrast between the formal rational approach to strategic planning and the emergent approach to the strategy process.

- The rational planning model, originated by Ansoff involves strategic analysis, strategic choice, implementation of the chosen strategy, then review and control.

- Mintzberg criticises it as a failure in practice and of dubious validity as an explanation of what does and should happen.

- The emergent approach views strategy as continuously and incrementally evolving.

- Many businesses succeed through the actions of the founder or CEO.

- Ohmae identified the importance of strategic thinking and focussed attention on a triangle of corporate-based, customer-based and competitor-based strategies.

2.1 Contrast between rational planning and emergent approach

Rational approach also called • Top down approach • Formal approach • Traditional approach	• Strategy involves setting goals first and then designing strategies to reach them • Some prediction of the future is possible • Outcomes of strategic choices can be predicted and controlled • Possible to separate the planning and selection of strategies from the implementation of strategies
Emergent approach also called • Bottom up approach	• Builds management team with right strategic skills • Managers of divisions granted significant autonomy • Empowerment of mangers to develop and adapt strategies as circumstances change and opportunities and threats arise • Strategic choice and implementation happen concurrently

2.2 Benefits claimed for strategic planning

Strategic planning can achieve several benefits:

- Creates a management process to detect and respond to changes in market and environmental forces and so improve performance

- Provides a framework for SBUs to produce plans with clear, long term goals thus avoiding short termism

- Enables derivation of milestones for achievement of goals and monitoring progress by stages

- Mechanism to ensure harmony of objectives, both between SBUs and over time ('goal congruence')

- Improves stakeholder perceptions, for example a clear strategy may improve the share price

- Investing in the planning process develops future management potential and can aid continuity planning

2.3 Mintzberg's criticisms of strategic planning

Strategic planning has fallen from popularity and has been criticised. Mintzberg's critique below is amongst the most insightful. Mintzberg argues that planning doesn't work out in practice.

Problem	Comments
Practical failure	Empirical studies have not proved that **formal planning** processes contribute to success.
Routine and regular	Strategic planning often occurs as an **annual cycle**, but a firm cannot allow itself to wait every year for the month of February to address its problems.
Reduces initiative	Formal planning discourages **strategic thinking**. Once a plan is locked in place, people are unwilling to question it. Obsession with particular performance indicators means that managers focus on fulfilling the plan rather than concentrating on developments in the environment.
Internal politics	The assumption of 'objectivity' in evaluation ignores political battles between different managers and departments. The model doesn't describe reality therefore.

Problem	Comments
Exaggerates power	Managers face limits to the extent to which they can control the behaviour of the organisation. The plans may be ignored by subordinates.
Impractical	The hierarchy of objectives, budgets, strategies and programmes does not reflect the reality of most organisations who prefer simple, more easy to apply programmes such as capital budgeting.

2.4 The role of the leader or entrepreneur in strategy

Many businesses have been successful through the actions of their founders, chief executives or entrepreneurial individuals within the organisation rather than through formal strategic planning.

Interactive question 1: Famous business leaders [Difficulty level: Easy]

Name some corporations which have been made successful by the business leadership given by a famous individual.

See **Answer** at the end of this chapter.

Entrepreneurs are individuals who build new businesses. An entrepreneur is not just the owner/manager of a small business but is best regarded as a manager who pursues opportunity and drives change to create value.

Entrepreneurship is a style of management, with a particular mix of innovation and risk.

2.5 Ohmae's strategic thinking as an intuitive process

Ohmae (*The Mind of the Strategist* – 1982) blames formal strategic planning processes for having withered strategic thinking. Ohmae says strategy is essentially a creative process in which the strategist must pay attention to a **strategic triangle** of 3 Cs.

1. **Corporate-based strategies** build competitive strength by focusing on the *superior competences* which the corporation has in comparison to rivals. He cites Sony's skills in miniaturisation of electronic circuitry and Coca Cola's control over distribution channels as examples of this.

2. **Customer-based strategies** gain superior market position by segmenting markets closely and ensuring products and service are closely tailored to requirements of each segment. The ability of Mercedes-Benz or BMW to cornering a particularly valuable segment of the car industry might be an example of this.

3. **Competitor-based strategies**. Close identification of the methods of rivals and exploitation of any weaknesses in them, such as absolute cost differences or flexibility of supply. Ohmae cites the example of Toyota utilising its superior R&D and quality assurance systems to launch Lexus to exploit the executive limousine market at prices unattainable to Jaguar and Mercedes-Benz who relied on more traditionally engineered cars and car plants.

3 A rational (prescriptive) approach to strategy formulation

Section overview

- The rational planning model starts with strategic analysis, which involves internal and external analysis then corporate appraisal. This informs the business's choice of mission, goals and strategic objectives.

- Any resulting gap in where the business wants to be and where it is currently headed is addressed by identifying and evaluating strategic options and selecting the most appropriate.

- Implementing strategies involves planning the appropriate resources and operations, structuring the business effectively and monitoring using appropriate control systems.

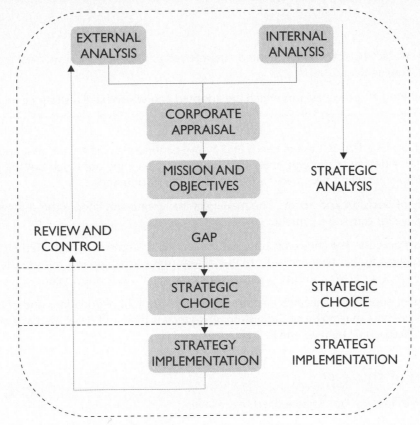

The main stages in the rational approach are:

1. **Conduct a corporate appraisal**: This involves assessing both the present business environment and how it may develop over the planning timescale (typically five + years), and the internal position of the business (such as staffing levels, product quality and financial position).

2. **Set mission and objectives**: Management will assess whether the long-term interests of the business are best met in its present industry and competing in its present way or whether the business needs to strike out in a new direction. This is called its mission. Objectives will be set for the coming years. The job of strategy is to attain them.

3. **Gap analysis**: Involves comparing forecast performance with the strategic objectives set by management. If forecast performance is below the objectives set then this exposes a gap which must be filled by new and better strategy.

4. **Strategic choice**: Management generate new business options for the firm, such as new products or markets, and evaluate these to arrive at a set of potentially successful and affordable strategies to help the firm reach the objectives set.

5. **Strategy implementation**: Management carries out the strategy at corporate, business and functional levels by developing organisational structures, policies and programmes to carry it out.

4 Deliberate and emergent strategies (Mintzberg)

Section overview

- Mintzberg provides a framework that describes how strategic plans and incrementalism combine in practice to form strategies.

- The key point is to allow managers to craft strategies from events as time progresses.

- The conclusion is that a mixture of a strategic plan and management initiative will provide control but also organisational learning.

4.1 Deliberate and emergent strategies

Definitions

Intended strategies (which, if implemented, are referred to as deliberate strategies) are conscious plans imposed by management.

Emergent strategies are behaviours which are adopted and which have a strategic impact.

Emergent strategies adapt to human needs and evolve continuously. The emergent approach can involve the same degree of strategic analysis as the rational planning approach but the processes of choice and implementation take place together. This is for two reasons:

1. **Identity of decision and action.** The managers that create and choose the strategies are also responsible for carrying them out.

2. **Learning process.** The choice of strategies interacts with implementation. Rather than having a grand scheme for the next five years management tries something out this year, learns lessons from where it succeeds and fails, and develops new initiatives for next year.

In the emergent approach, objectives and strategies are a result of negotiations and discussion, taking into account the human element of the system. A strategy is tried and developed as it is implemented. Alternative strategies will be tried where it fails.

4.2 Five types of strategy

Mintzberg (*The Strategy Process*) identified the following.

- **Intended**: The result of a deliberate planning process.
- **Deliberate**: Where the intended plans have been put into action.
- **Unrealised**: Not all planned strategies are implemented.
- **Emergent**: Strategies are created by force of circumstances.
- **Realised**: The final realised strategy results from a balance of forces of the other types of strategies.

The interaction of these strategies is illustrated in the following diagram.

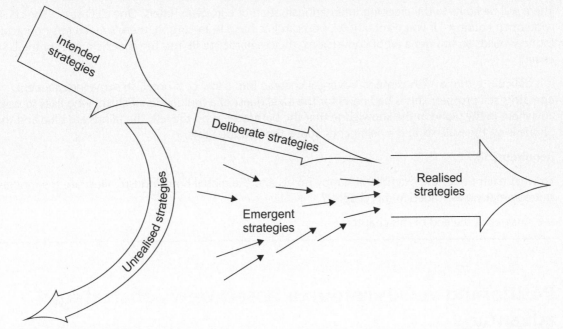

Strategies must still have **purpose** and this will be set by senior management. No actual strategy will be **wholly deliberate** or **wholly emergent**.

The task of **strategic management** is to control and shape these **emergent strategies** as they **develop**.

Interactive question 2: Happy hotels [Difficulty level: Intermediate]

Global hotel chains

The hotel industry is embracing globalisation. International chains are encircling the world, swallowing local operations on an almost daily basis.

John Oliver, chief executive of Happy hotels plc (formerly Thomas' hotels and pub holdings), says: 'Brands are everything – as travel becomes increasingly trans-border, hotels which aren't carrying international brands simply don't deliver the same rate of revenue per room'. The company was unwittingly pushed into the hotel trade by the then UK Trade Secretary, who thwarted the group's ambition to become a global brewer by blocking the purchase of two well known international drink producers.

The market is changing. In the US, 75% of hotels have a well-known brand, compared with just 35% in Europe. Lesley Ashplant, a hotels expert, says: 'Europe is the single largest tourist destination in the world. It has 6m hotel rooms under fragmented ownership. There are clear opportunities in scale, in taking advantage of branding and advanced technology.'

Scale

Size is becoming important as expectations rise – international business travellers want internet connections, widescreen televisions, and push-button blinds in every room. All of this required investment. Servicing the demands of business customers requires employing more staff than most independent operators can afford.

Technology

Hi-tech reservation systems are also emerging as a crucial factor. In an industry where 75% of costs are staff wages, any savings elsewhere are precious. Between a third and half of hotels' revenue comes from food and drink, but these only contribute 20% to 30% of profit. Attempts to make hotel restaurants more attractive have generally failed.

Much more profitable are the rooms themselves. The main thrust, therefore, for most operators, is on improving occupancy. Loyalty card schemes are becoming increasingly elaborate.

Branding

There will be limits to the creeping internationalisation of European hotels. One CEO says: 'The US is a wide-open country – if you want a hotel, you can just build it. In Europe, there's much less opportunity for new-builds so you get a lot of conversions, they're harder to fit into the specific model of the US chain'.

It is difficult to turn a 17th century Provençal château into a low cost hotel, so some independent operators still prosper. This is bad news for the ideal guest of a multinational chain, who likes to wake up anywhere in the world in the knowledge that the bathroom is on the left, the blinds are blue and the phone is on the wall, six and a half inches above the bedside table.

Requirements

To what extent does the example of Happy hotels and the global hotel industry illustrate the models of strategy-making described in this chapter?

See **Answer** at the end of this chapter.

5 Positioning versus resource-based views of strategic advantage

Section overview

- Early prescriptions for strategy emphasised that success lay in 'fitting' the organisation to its environment better (eg satisfying shareholders and customers and staying on the right side of the authorities). This is known as the positioning approach.

- Modern resource-based views emphasise that long-term success lies in organisations, 'playing to their strengths' or '**competences**'.

- For competences to be capable of leading to **superior competitive performance** they must **fit** the present environment, **stretch** the firm to innovate and able to admit **leverage** to gain extra value in new lines of business.

5.1 Positioning view of strategic advantage

A firm or industry faced with the imminent obsolescence of one of its core products, must decide whether to orientate strategy around external customer needs or rather orientate strategy around its internal resources and competences. Choosing the first is an example of a positioning approach. Choosing the second applies the resource-based approach.

Characteristics of the positioning approach are:

- A **focus on customer needs** and adapting products, and the process of making them, to any changes in these needs

- The **gaining of a superior position against rivals** through analysis of the industry and marking and adopting strategies to gain relative market share or reduce relative costs

- The **assessment of relations with stakeholders** such as government, shareholders, suppliers and distributors to use better relationships as a source of advantage

- **Seeking to gain preferential access to resources** such as materials, low cost labour and scarce skills

The significant feature is the belief that successful strategy involves the business **adapting to its environment.**

The positioning view will be seen in this text in the work of Michael Porter (notably his five forces model of industries and his three generic competitive strategies) and in the sections dealing with marketing.

No writer will seriously question the need for successful products and good relations in assisting in making a firm successful from one year to the next. However, the positioning approach has been criticised as inadequate as an approach to sustainable success over decades with particular regard to the following:

- Product life-cycle means particular products will become obsolete so today's successful market position will become a liability in the future.

- Stakeholder groups, such as political parties, will decline in influence so relations with them will not sustain the firm.

- Long-term technological changes will eliminate cost advantages or technical superiority of a given product.

Perpetual change of the organisation's skills base and products will be disruptive and eventually leads the firm into fields in which it has little expertise.

Worked example: Mobile phones

By the mid 2000's Blackberry had established itself as the mobile phone of choice among users, finding popularity among business professionals. Blackberry's popularity was driven in part by the ability of users to access their emails on the go, while the devices QWERTY key pad resembled the keyboard many users were familiar with using in the workplace. At its peak the company even developed a celebrity following with many celebrities claiming to own a Blackberry.

However, in 2007 Blackberry's dominance came under threat when Apple unveiled its first iPhone device. Apple's offering with its innovative touchscreen technology made the Blackberry appear dated. The iPhone's advanced iOS (operating system) meant users could experience high quality graphics and a new range of applications available for download through the Apple App store. By contrast, Blackberry's operating system was principally engineered as a communication tool. Senior management at Blackberry were convinced that the popularity among business professionals would be sufficient to help reduce the threat posed by the iPhone.

However, by 2013 Blackberry's fortunes had reversed. The iPhone had become the number one selling mobile device. Blackberry had overestimated the appeal of its own offering and its ability to continue to attract members of its target market, with many professionals switching allegiance to the iPhone. In response Blackberry switched its focus towards people using their phones for social and private use, rather than business use and unveiled its own touchscreen smart phone, producing the Blackberry Z10. In a bid to rival the iPhone the Z10 provided users with the ability to access popular integrated apps such as Facebook and Twitter. The development of the Z10 took a number of years and resulted in significant expenditure on developing the technology to produce a functioning touchscreen mobile device, as Blackberry struggled to make-up the ground lost to Apple.

The introduction of the Z10 did little to reverse Blackberry's fortunes, as the device failed to take off as anticipated. The launch of the Z10 was hit with reports that stockists were unable to obtain sufficient inventory of the device. Blackberry's problems were further compounded when the Z10's operating system required an urgent 'fix' prior to its full launch. In September 2013, Blackberry reported a significant fall in sales which triggered a drop in the company's share price and left the company's shares trading at a fraction of their 2007 value. Following the announcement the company declared that it was shedding 4,500 workers (40% of the workforce).

5.2 Resource-based view of competitive advantage

Technological changes can destroy industries:

- Downloads damage CD and DVD manufacturers, distributors and retailers
- Electronic methods of communication have threatened the traditional postal system
- Genetic modification of organisms can compromise the pesticide and pharmaceutical industries

The **resource-based view** is an **inside-out** view of strategy. Firms do not look for strategies external to them. They develop or acquire resources and **competences**, create new markets and exploit them.

Johnson, Scholes and Whittington say successful strategies require **strategic capability**.

Resources and competences are needed for the successful execution of defined strategies.

Fit	Resources must be available to fit with the current product-market demands and current needs.
Stretch	This means being at the leading/shaping edge of **new strategic** developments in the industry. This suggests that the organisation's ambitions cannot be met with current resources and competences. Ambition should outpace resources.
Leverage	Existing resources are used in many different ways, so that extra value is extracted from them.

Creation of new markets

A fundamental point made by Prahalad and Hamel (*Competing for the Future*) is that markets are not 'given'. They can be created by corporate action. Companies do not merely 'satisfy' customer needs: they 'create' them.

For example, mobile phone ringtones drew on the mobile phone as a fashion accessory, not just a communication device. Prior to the launch of ringtones there was no ringtone market in existence.

Interactive question 3: Apple and the chicken and egg question [Difficulty level: Easy]

Apple is often cited as an example of a firm that creates industries through leverage of core competences in technological innovation and design of mobile devices. This has created markets such as:

- Personal audio: Through its portable iPod MP3 player enabling users to download the latest music via Apple iTunes.

- Personal computers: Via the original Apple Macintosh 128K which at the time of its release revolutionised the computing industry by becoming the first mass-market PC. The evolution of Apple's computing division has led to the introduction of tablet computers, eg iPad.

- Mobile phones: Apple's first iPhone helped to raise the bar in the standard of mobile technologies when introduced in 2007 heralding the introduction of a new generation of devices. Users are able to synchronise and connect Apple devices to one another due to the products innovative design.

Was it these technologies that built a whole new industry or was the industry already there?

See **Answer** at the end of this chapter.

5.3 Comparison of positioning and resource-based views

According to the **resource-based view** of strategy the role of resources is **more than simply to execute** strategies determined by desired positions in product markets. Rather, the focus of the strategist should be on **resources and competences**. These are **assets** for the long term. Such a combination of resources and competences takes years to develop and can be hard to copy.

Some of the implications are explained in the table below.

Factor	Positioning-based view	Resource-based view
Profitability	Industry profitability determined by the five competitive forces. Position of a company in the industry determines its profitability.	Corporate profitability is based on sustainable competitive advantage achieved from the exploitation of unique resources.
Approach	Outside-in, ie consider outside environment and markets then the company's ability to trade in these conditions.	Inside-out: consider key resources first, then how to exploit competitive advantage in available markets.

Diversity	Maintain diversified portfolio of products (see BCG matrix) to spread risk and generate cash in changing market conditions.	Focus only on products where company has a sustainable competitive advantage.
Key focus	Industry orientation and positioning in the market.	Focus on core competences which competitors do not possess and will find difficult to copy.

6 Planning horizon

Section overview

- Strategic management and strategic planning are often distinguished from operational issues by the length of time concerned: the horizon.

- Most managers have the need to deliver short-term results which can take priority over longer term strategic development of the business.

- The pressure for shorter term results and shorter planning horizons can come from the ownership of the organisation, its capital structure, the industry it is in, its environment and the nature of its management.

6.1 Short, medium and long term planning

There terms are often used but remain ill-defined. A rule of thumb is:

- Short term: Horizon of 1 – 3 years
- Medium term: Horizon of 3 – 10 years
- Long term: 10 + years

6.2 Short run/long run trade off

Managers and businesses are frequently evaluated on short term successes such as profits. Strategic thinking requires that managers consider the long term growth and survival of the business.

Therefore management is required to balance short- and long-term considerations.

6.3 Influences on planning horizons

- **Nature of ownership**
  Firms with shareholders are obliged to ensure some financial return each year to their shareholders. Making sufficient profits each year will normally be needed in order to promote shareholder value. State-owned organisations do not have this obligation (but they will have different ownership issues to contend with, such as the changing nature of political agendas, different governments' attitudes to funding and state control).

- **Capital structure**
  Some investors, such as banks or private equity investors (sometimes called venture capitalists) do not require short term profits. Banks will continue to lend providing assets cover the loans and interest is paid. Private equity investors require profits and share values to grow over a 5 – 10 year period to give them a substantial capital gain when they sell their holding.

- **Nature of industry**
  Industries such as aircraft development, satellite communications and oil pipelines require large capital investments that take a long time to build and to pay back. Long-term plans are essential to justify these.

- **Nature of business environment**
  In rapidly changing environments it is likely that long-term planning may be futile. For example, industries such as bio-technology, home entertainment and mobile communications where effects

of technology and legislation are hard to predict, will tend to avoid plans and instead adopt a strategic management approach within a series of short-term plans.

- **Nature of management**
  Long-term planning is a skill and it is time consuming. Some entrepreneurial managers will avoid it, for example because they lack the time or skill, or because they are unwilling to become 'tied down by red tape'. Others, for example the management of family firms, are reluctant to consider changing the 'way it has always been done'.

Interactive question 4: McDonnell Douglas

[Difficulty level: Intermediate]

Consider the following:

With $14bn in sales, McDonnell Douglas was one of the US's largest defence companies. It successfully turned around the C-17 transport plane program, which a few years earlier was nearly cancelled by the Air Force over technical flaws and delays. However, its commercial aircraft arm, Douglas Aircraft, was a disaster, caught in the tailwinds of Boeing and Airbus. In 1994, McDonnell Douglas's board shocked investors by bringing in an outsider – a brash, controversial former GE executive, Harry Stonecipher – as CEO.

At first Stonecipher insisted that the firm was committed to building passenger airplanes. At one point he said the business was so good that if Douglas wasn't already in it, 'we would be looking for a way to get in'. Unfortunately, years of under-investment had resulted in planes with little imagination, and Douglas would need to spend billions to catch up. Ultimately Stonecipher wasn't willing to make that investment, preferring to focus on short-term stock performance. This involved the reduction of discretionary spending on things such as research and development, training and better production equipment. There was also a closer control of costs.

During his tenure as CEO, McDonnell Douglas's stock quadrupled (Stonecipher carried a laminated copy of the stock chart in his briefcase), but critics say the failure to invest in R&D would have been disastrous eventually. 'This is a company that would have gone out of business in five years', says Richard Aboulafia, an analyst at Teal Group, an aviation research firm. 'It was headed to oblivion.'

Eventually, McDonnell Douglas merged with Boeing.

Requirements

(a) What planning horizon would you expect a firm in this industry to follow?

(b) What factors in the competitive environment, pressure from investors or his personal incentive package could explain the incoming CEO's short-term approach to strategy?

See **Answer** at the end of this chapter.

Interactive question 5: Superware products

[Difficulty level: Exam standard]

Superware Products Ltd (hereafter Superware) was formed in 20X9 by three colleagues who had left a major software house to work on the development of accounting software for small businesses. Superware currently (20Y4) employs 18 staff at the company's head office in Swindon, and a further eight regionally-based salespeople in various parts of the UK.

Company structure

The three directors of Superware are Paul Smith (Managing), Karl Lagerfeld (Sales) and Christian Dior (Development). They each have a small team reporting directly to them and they meet on a daily basis if they are in the office, to discuss the business and to brainstorm a little over coffee. All three directors come from a background of software sales to small and medium-sized organisations. Chris is responsible for six product development staff and two administrators. His staff work full time on developing and upgrading the Superware product, and meet regularly with the sales staff to get feedback from customers and users. In addition to the eight salespeople, Karl has two sales administrators and a secretary working for him. The sales staff meet at head office on a weekly basis and the administrators work closely with the financial accountant. Paul takes responsibility for the remaining staff who perform general administration, reception and clerical tasks. His only specialist staff member is Zandra who, with her assistant, maintains a high level of control over the company's financial reporting and accounts.

Planning and control

Once a year the directors, under the guidance of Paul and with assistance from Zandra, agree a full budget for the next twelve months. The budget is always based on the previous year's performance, with adjustments for known changes such as inflation, costs and forecasts of demand from sales staff feedback. During the discussion of the budget Zandra calculates various ratios to illustrate trends in the company's profitability and liquidity, and the budget is normally adjusted to ensure that trends are as desired. When the budget is agreed, a copy is sent to the bank for its records.

Each month throughout the year, Zandra produces a management report which shows performance against budget for every cost and revenue heading. This report, together with a commentary written by Paul, is sent to each director and they pass copies to their key staff after removing any sensitive information. Four times each year the remaining periods are reforecast and the adjusted end-of-year position (or out-turn) is also compared with the budgeted position. Paul writes an additional commentary in these months which identifies key actions to bring performance back to budget.

The current position

The directors are presently involved in finalising the budget for 20Y4 and are concerned that the process of budgeting is becoming increasingly meaningless. The results for 20Y3 show a significant shortfall in both revenue and profitability against both the budget and third quarter out-turn for the year, yet Paul is still insisting that the 20Y4 budget should be the 20Y3 budget uplifted for inflation and known changes. During the 20Y4 audit Zandra mentioned the directors' concerns to the audit manager who suggested that you, as a recently qualified member of the audit team with an interest in strategic planning, might be able to advise the company on how to proceed. The directors have agreed that this would be useful, and have arranged a meeting at which you can meet them and discuss the role of planning within Superware.

Requirements

Prepare briefing notes to present at a meeting with the directors of Superware at which you will be expected to discuss the following:

(i)   The current planning process

(ii)   Weaknesses of the current planning process

(iii) Recommendations for improvement of the planning process. Recommendations should be clearly justified

See **Answer** at the end of this chapter.

7 Strategy and ethics

Section overview

- The desire by management to act ethically affects the scope of strategies adopted but also requires that management keep an eye on the ethical consequences of its operations.

7.1 Impact of ethics on strategy

Ethics impacts at several points in the strategy process:

- In the **formulation of strategic objectives**. Some firms will not consider lines of business for ethical reasons.

- External appraisal will need to consider the **ethical climate in which the firm operates**. This will raise expectations of its behaviour.

- **Internal appraisal:** Management should consider whether present operations are 'sustainable', ie consistent with present and future ethical expectations.

- **Strategy selection:** Management should consider the ethical implication of proposed strategies before selecting and implementing them.

Ethics and corporate responsibility will be covered in more detail in Chapter 16.

Summary

Self-test

Answer the following questions.

1   For each of the following issues facing an airline, identify the appropriate level of strategy.

(a)   The decision whether to use permanent or contract staff to work as ground crew.
(b)   The decision whether to develop a no-frills alternative airline to existing full-service airline.
(c)   Buying aviation fuel futures to hedge against rising fuel costs.

2   List stages in the rational model of strategic planning.

3   What 3Cs does Ohmae say should be addressed by strategists?

4   List the five types of strategy identified by Mintzberg.

5   Define 'fit', 'stretch' and 'leverage' as used by Johnson, Scholes and Whittington.

6   Read the scenario of Question 3 of the **September 2009 Business Strategy** paper *Somborne Zoological Park* at the end of this study manual. Draft an answer for requirement 3a(i) on the Park's strategic planning process.

7   Go online at The Times 100 Business Case Studies and read the Kellogg's case study 'Using aims and objectives to create a business strategy' at http://businesscasestudies.co.uk/kelloggs/using-aims-and-objectives-to-create-a-business-strategy

Now, go back to the Learning objectives in the Introduction. If you are satisfied that you have achieved these objectives, please tick them off.

Answer to Interactive question 1

Mittal Steel	Lakshmi Mittal
Facebook	Mark Zuckerberg
The Trump Organization	Donald Trump
Berkshire Hathaway	Warren Buffett
Far Eastern Group	Douglas Hsu
Tesco	Sir Terry Leahy
Gazprom	Viktor Zubkov
Ryanair	Michael O'Leary
GE (General Electric)	Jack Welch
TWA	Howard Hughes
Dell	Michael Dell
Tata Group	Ratan N Tata
Hutchison Whampoa	Li Ka-shing
Amazon	Jeff Bezos
Virgin Group	Richard Branson
Apple	Steve Jobs
Microsoft	Bill Gates
Sony	Akio Morita
Bannatyne's Health Clubs	Duncan Bannatyne
Amstrad	Alan Sugar
Ford	Henry Ford

Answer to Interactive question 2

Emergent strategy	–	Unwittingly pushed into hotel trade by blocking off purchase of rival
Unrealised strategy	–	Failed purchase of two global drink producers
	–	Making hotel restaurants attractive
Deliberate strategy	–	Upgrading of rooms
	–	Improved cooking systems
	–	Exclusion of independent operator by enhancing service levels and harnessing of brand and economies of scale

Answer to Interactive question 3

Like the chicken and egg question this can't be answered.

- Apple provided a new way to make sales by fulfilling some of the same needs that had previously been satisfied by existing mobile phones and portable music players, books and magazines, conventional television programming and personal conversation. So in a sense these needs were already there and were being supplied by different industries.

- The value extracted from the needs through sales of personal computers and portable devices and the creation of a range of associated products, helped the mobile devices industry grow exponentially.

Answer to Interactive question 4

(a) An aircraft manufacturer should have a long-term planning horizon because the development of a new aircraft will take up to a decade and, given their huge capital costs, will need to remain in service and be fit-for-purpose, for over twenty years. An example of this is the Boeing 747 Jumbo Jet which is still in service and being made, having first flown in the 1970s).

(b) The short term focus could have come from several causes:

- The style of the CEO was better at cost cutting and stealing assets than longer term strategic thought.

- The CEO realised the shareholders would not support growth because all the remaining shareholders required a dividend from their holdings in a mature business.

- It was a deliberate strategy to increase the value of stock ready for takeover by a large aircraft manufacturer in an industry characterised by increased concentration.

- The CEO was incentivised by the value of stock (eg he held stock options, or had bonuses related to earning per share growth, share price growth or level of ROCE).

Answer to Interactive question 5

Briefing notes

To   The Directors
From   The Auditor
Date   Today
Subject   The strategic planning process of Superware Products Ltd

Current planning process

Currently the planning process in Superware can be illustrated by use of the following model.

Weaknesses

This model is commonly used in smaller organisations, and until 20Y3 was perfectly suitable for the purposes of Superware. However, such an 'incremental' model, combined with a 'budget-constrained' management style such as that practised by Paul, does have some weaknesses in a dynamic environment such as the IT industry. These weaknesses, as illustrated by Superware, are as follows.

(i)   **The use of corporate appraisal at the first stage** tends to lead to a blinkered view of strategy, which will necessarily focus on the current products and markets of the company.

(ii) **The lack of environmental analysis** throughout the strategy process, with the exception of known economic changes as a constraint to business, leads to opportunities and threats not being considered until too late.

(iii) **An incremental approach** which led, particularly in 20Y3, to an optimistic plan being formalised which was possibly not achievable.

(iv) **The modification of plans to meet personal objectives** of the directors, regardless of the achievability of those objectives.

(v) **The short-term nature** of the process, concentrating on a twelve month planning horizon, will tend to give a distorted view of the future and lead to a lack of direction and consistency in the goals communicated to managers and staff.

Having said all this, the process does have one significant strength in that the focus on implementation and review is very thorough, particularly in the revision of out-turns and the targeting of performance improvements.

Recommended modifications

It is recommended that the company modify the planning process in line with the following model.

The detailed content and major changes from the current process are explained as follows.

(i) **External environmental analysis** is a formal analysis of the context in which the company does business. It may well include studies of market size, customer needs, competitor behaviour and changes in technology. Such a study should concentrate on major changes which will affect Superware either as opportunities or threats.

Examples of such changes might include an emerging customer need for a tax module to cope with pay and file, demand for an alternative platform such as UNIX, or an opportunity to launch a totally new product line to meet unsatisfied demand.

Internal analysis of the organisation will identify the current strengths and weaknesses, not merely in terms of the financial performance but also some of the qualitative aspects.

Examples might include the organisation and resources of the company.

(ii) **Corporate appraisal** summarised by SWOT.

(iii) **Objectives** should be agreed, taking into account the requirements of all interested parties, which are perceived as achievable by the managers and staff. Objectives should also take into account the risks and opportunities identified as a result of the environmental analysis.

(iv) **Strategies** can then be formulated, based on all the previous stages, to achieve the company objectives, protect against threats and exploit opportunities.

Examples of such strategies might be product or market development, or even diversification into, for example, management software for doctors or schools.

(v) **Implementation and review** of strategy should still take place as currently, but as part of the implementation phase it will be necessary to re-evaluate the organisation structure and such tactical issues as investment.

(vi) **The time horizon** for the planning process should be extended in order to give better strategic visibility and to introduce some consistency between years. Due to the volatile nature of the IT industry, it is probably unnecessary to plan more than three years in advance.

Although the changes outlined seem a radical departure from the process currently carried out in Superware, the benefits in terms of business performance should be significant.

1 (a) Functional strategy: concerns HRM
   (b) Corporate strategy: affects shape and scope of business
   (c) Functional strategy: financial strategy to hedge risk

2 (a) Corporate appraisal
   (b) Mission and objectives
   (c) Gap analysis
   (d) Strategic choice
   (e) Strategic implementation

3 • Company
   • Customer
   • Competitor

4 • Intended strategy
   • Deliberate strategy
   • Unrealised strategy
   • Emergent strategy
   • Realised strategy

5 Fit: Resources able to support current product-market demands and needs
   Stretch: Firm should have resources at cutting edge of the industry or should seek to acquire
              them
   Leverage: Resources can be used in many ways

6 Refer to the answer to Q3ai of the September 2009 Business Strategy paper at the end of this
   Study Manual.

7 There is no answer to this self-test, as it is designed just to help you increase your business
   awareness.

CHAPTER 3

The purpose of an organisation

Introduction

Examination context

Topic List

Summary and Self-test

Answers to Interactive questions

Answers to Self-test

Learning objectives

Tick off

- Evaluate a business's purpose in terms of its stated mission and objectives ☐

- Identify the stakeholders of a business, their likely interests and the level of influence they have ☐

- Evaluate the process of strategic objective setting in Not for Profit (NFP) organisations ☐

Specific syllabus references for this chapter are 1a, 1b, 2c.

Syllabus links

Some coverage of stakeholders and their interests, and the nature and desirable qualities of business objectives, was given in your Business and Finance paper.

Examination context

In the exam you may be required to create a mission statement for a given organisation or to identify the inconsistencies and omissions in an existing one. You may also be asked to suggest appropriate goals and objectives. This will involve balancing the needs of different stakeholder groups, identifying possible conflicts of interest and recognising the priorities for the organisation. One of the scenarios in the exam may be a not-for-profit organisation so you must understand the particular issues such organisations face when determining objectives and strategy.

In a previous exam Q3 March 2008 (*Campaign for Trading Equitably*) the scenario contains information on a fair trade charity which is reviewing its position after a few years of operation. The second requirement is:

'(b) Critically evaluate the content of CTE's mission statement, making recommendations for any improvements.   **(5 marks)**'

From the phrase 'critically evaluate' and from the fact that you are asked for improvements, you are put on notice that there are weaknesses in the current statement that you need to identify specifically and then address. You are not being asked for a general exposition of what a mission statement in theory is for.

1 The concept of mission

Section overview

* The purpose of an organisation may be communicated in a mission statement. The role and value of such statements has been a matter of debate.

1.1 Mission statements

Definition

Mission: the values and expectations of those who most strongly influence strategy about the scope and posture of the organisation (Johnson, Scholes and Whittington: *Exploring Corporate Strategy*).

Johnson, Scholes and Whittington have suggested that 'the mission of an organisation is the most generalised type of objective and can be thought of as an expression of its *raison d'être* (reason for existing).'

1.2 Elements of mission

The Ashridge College model of mission (Campbell *et al A Sense of Mission* 1992) links business strategy to culture and ethics by including four separate elements in an explanation of the **features of a successful mission**.

(a) **Purpose** Why does the organisation exist? Who does it exist for?

* To create wealth for shareholders who take priority over all other stakeholders?
* To satisfy the needs of all stakeholders, including employees, for example?
* To reach some higher goal such as the advancement of society?
* To alleviate the poverty of the needy?

(b) **Strategy:** the competitive position and distinctive competence of the organisation.

(c) **Policies and standards of behaviour:** the policies and behavioural patterns underpinning its work.

(d) **Values:** what the company believes in which is replicated in employees' personal values.

Worked example: Mission of easyJet

EasyJet is a listed company offering a no-frills airline service between UK and other European airports.

The following strategic framework is set out in its 2012 annual report:

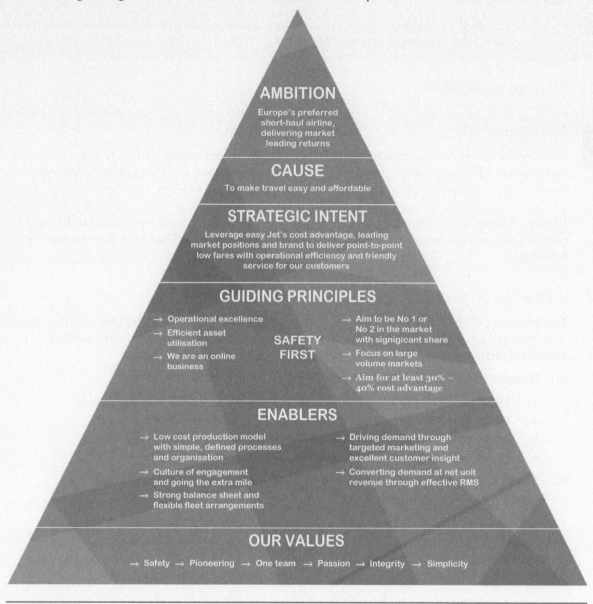

AMBITION
Europe's preferred short-haul airline, delivering market leading returns

CAUSE
To make travel easy and affordable

STRATEGIC INTENT
Leverage easy Jet's cost advantage, leading market positions and brand to deliver point-to-point low fares with operational efficiency and friendly service for our customers

GUIDING PRINCIPLES

→ Operational excellence
→ Efficient asset utilisation
→ We are an online business

SAFETY FIRST

→ Aim to be No 1 or No 2 in the market with signigicant share
→ Focus on large volume markets
→ Aim for at least 30% – 40% cost advantage

ENABLERS

→ Low cost production model with simple, defined processes and organisation
→ Culture of engagement and going the extra mile
→ Strong balance sheet and flexible fleet arrangements

→ Driving demand through targeted marketing and excellent customer insight
→ Converting demand at net unit revenue through effective RMS

OUR VALUES

→ Safety → Pioneering → One team → Passion → Integrity → Simplicity

Worked example: Mission of IBO

The International Baccalaureate Organisation (IBO) is a not-for-profit educational foundation that develops and examines internationally curricula for school-age pupils.

International Baccalaureate Organisation mission statement

'The International Baccalaureate Organisation aims to develop inquiring, knowledgeable and caring young people who help to create a better and more peaceful world through intercultural understanding and respect.

To this end the IBO works with schools, governments and international organisations to develop challenging programmes of international education and rigorous assessment.

These programmes encourage students across the world to become active, compassionate and lifelong learners who understand that other people, with their differences, can also be right.'

1.3 The importance of mission to corporate strategy

The role of mission in strategy is determined by the approach to strategy formulation:

1. **Rational approach**: Mission is the starting-point of strategy formulation. It is the basis on which strategic objectives are set. Any strategy developed must be shown to be consistent with the mission before it is adopted. The culture and values of the organisation must be moulded to serve the strategy.

2. **Emergent approach**: Mission is embedded in the culture of the organisation and used to generate strategic initiatives.

The authors of the Ashridge model claim their model suits either view because, regardless of whether strategy is formulated bottom-up or top-down, all four elements will have to be in place and congruent if the strategy is to be fully successful.

1.4 Mission statements

Mission statements are formal documents that state the organisation's mission. There is no standard format, but the four element Ashridge model of mission is a good basis for writing a mission statement. Mission statements are published within organisations in order to promote desired behaviour: support for strategy and purpose, adherence to values and adoption of policies and standards of behaviour.

Benefits claimed for mission statements are that they:

- Provide a basis for the control of organisations, ie managerial and operational goals can be set on the basis of them

- Communicate the nature of the organisation to stakeholders

- Help to instil core values in the organisation

Some commentators are suspicious of mission statements:

- They are often **public relations** exercises rather than an accurate portrayal of the firm's actual values.

- They can often be full of **generalisations** from which it is impossible to tie down specific strategic implications or develop meaningful strategic objectives.

- They may be ignored by the people responsible for formulating or implementing strategy.

2 Organisational goals and objectives

Section overview

- We assume that the primary aim of profit seeking organisations is to increase the wealth of their owners.

- However in practice it seems likely that other factors may force management to offset profitability goals against other objectives.

- Not-for-profit organisations are likely to have multiple aims, reflecting a wider group of stakeholder

2.1 Purpose of the organisation

A basic division of organisational purpose is:

1. **Profit seeking organisations**: The **primary goal** of these is assumed to be to deliver economic value to their owners ie to increase shareholder wealth. Goals such as satisfying customers, building market share, cutting costs, and demonstrating corporate social responsibility are **secondary goals** which enable economic value to be delivered.

2. **Not-for-profit organisations (NFP)**: The primary goals of these vary enormously and include meeting members' needs, contributing to social well-being, pressing for political and social change. Secondary goals will include the economic goal of not going bankrupt and, in some cases, generating a financial surplus to invest in research or give to the needy. Often the goals of NFP organisations will reflect the need to maximise the benefit derived from limited resources, such as funds. Their objectives may be more heavily influenced by external stakeholders such as the government.

2.2 Shareholder value maximisation

The simple assumption is that profit-seeking organisations seek to maximise shareholder value.

The concept of shareholder wealth maximisation is relied on in several ways:

- As a decision-making criterion: techniques such as NPV and IRR assume this as the goal of the business.

- As a criterion to evaluate divisional managers: using performance measures such as Return on Capital Employed (ROCE) or sometimes Return on Investment (ROI) which should exceed cost of capital and rise from year to year.

- As the basis for financial incentives for managers. Bonuses may be based on improvements in the ROCE, earnings per share (EPS) or share price from year to year.

- As a benchmark against which to evaluate the board. Investment analysts and 'active value' investors use shareholder value measures to evaluate corporate performance and some newspapers publish league tables to name and shame underperforming boards.

2.3 Limitations of shareholder value assumption

Shareholder wealth maximisation may not be an accurate **description** of managerial behaviour and decisions because:

- **Corporate governance is too weak** to give shareholders sufficient information or influence to ensure management maximise shareholder wealth rather than, say, their own emoluments.

- **It ignores the non-financial goals of shareholders**: Family firms, firms with ethical funds holding shares, and firms with substantial shareholdings in the hands of governmental bodies will be also required to satisfy non-economic objectives such as sustainability or employment.

- **It is impossible to verify**: Seen in retrospect a board's decisions may be seen to have failed to maximise shareholder wealth. Yet this is consistent with a board that wished to maximise shareholder wealth but whose decisions were limited by time, information available and their own skills. Also to judge whether wealth was maximised it would be necessary to know the outcomes of all the alternatives the board ignored.

It may not be a suitable **prescription** for management because it:

- **Ignores the nature of the financial return required**: Shareholders receive their wealth from dividends and from capital growth. They are assumed to be indifferent between the two, but may not be in practice due to income needs and the different tax treatments of income and capital growth.

- **Overlooks the power of stakeholders** other than shareholders, eg increasing shareholder wealth at the expense of staff benefits may lead to loss of staff and industrial action.

- **Ignores corporate responsibility** (CR): Many cultures take the view that profits should be balanced against the good of society and the natural environment.

2.4 Setting business objectives

Hierarchically, missions and objectives can be shown as follows.

There should be goal congruence, ie the mission and objectives set at each level should be consistent with each other and not in conflict.

Quantifying objectives

Objectives must be capable of being quantified, otherwise progress towards them cannot be measured.

For a government agency or charity, for instance, to state its objective as 'to improve the welfare of old age pensioners' is not precise enough. It must state how it is going to measure the achievement – in terms perhaps of the number of places in old people's homes, the number of meals-on-wheels served, the number of patients treated in geriatric wards – so that several targets may make up its overall objective.

In other words, for objectives to be of use in practice, they must be SMART – **S**pecific, **M**easurable, **A**chievable, **R**elevant and **T**imebound – eg 'increase online revenues by 25% within one year'.

Objectives specified in this way are often referred to as 'closed' objectives.

2.5 Examples of objectives

In practice objectives vary in attributes and in terms of the precision with which they are specified. The following gives some examples:

- **Corporate objective: open**
  Our primary aims are to provide a sound investment for our shareholders by increasing shareholder value and also worthwhile job prospects for our employees. Our objectives are customer satisfaction, real growth in earnings per share and a competitive return on capital employed.

- **Corporate objective: closed**
  The most important objective remains the achievement of a minimum return of 20% on average capital employed, with a target return of 25%.

- **Business unit objective: open**
  One of the main aims for one of the business areas in which the company is involved is to play a leading role in meeting the requirements of the widening and expanding home entertainments industry.

- **Business unit objective: closed**
  In the UK we are budgeting our house building unit to sell 2,500 homes next year – a figure that will put it among the top ten house builders. Ideally, existing performance statistics should be used to measure objectives; if a new system of data collection or processing has to be instituted in order to measure progress towards objectives, extra cost will be incurred.

Interactive question 1: Gooseberry Farm Ltd [Difficulty level: Exam standard]

The entire share capital of Gooseberry Farm Ltd is owned by Giles MacDonald and his wife. Its business is owning and running a 1,200 acre arable farm located five miles outside the local county town, Norbridge.

A decline in farm income

As a result of a change in the way European Union farming subsidies are calculated, Gooseberry Farm Ltd faces a sharp decline in its annual trading profits, which in recent years have averaged £90,000. Mr MacDonald is therefore considering using 200 acres to establish a new exclusive 18-hole golf course. Local businessmen regard this as feasible, since planning permission will readily be forthcoming and membership waiting lists at the two existing clubs in the Norbridge area exceed 350.

The golf club company

It is proposed that Gooseberry Farm Ltd will sign a 100-year lease with a new company, Millennium Golf Club Ltd, which will pay an annual rent of £25,000 to Gooseberry Farm Ltd for use of the land. The issued capital of the golf club company will be two £1 shares, owned by Mr and Mrs MacDonald, and the remainder of its initial funding will be £1 million in the form of 15% per annum irredeemable loan stock. Fifty local businessmen, including Mr MacDonald, have each agreed to purchase £20,000 of this stock.

Of the funds thus raised £225,000 will be spent on converting the arable land to become a landscaped golf course. A further £25,000 will provide working capital.

The club house company

The remaining £750,000 will be used to purchase a 25% stake in a separate company, Century Club House Ltd, to develop and operate a club house. This will have conference facilities, a sports hall, two bars and a restaurant. A local property company will subscribe the other 75% of the share capital of Century Club House Ltd. Millennium Golf Club Ltd will pay an annual rent of £25,000 for the use of the club house, but Century Club House Ltd will manage and run all facilities offered there, taking the profits that will be earned.

When ready to commence business in January 20X6, the new golf club will be much better appointed than the two existing Norbridge courses, and the only serious competition for comparable leisure facilities will come from three hotels in Norbridge itself and a country house four miles away.

Budgets of the golf club company

Annual operating expenses of Millennium Golf Club Ltd are budgeted at £450,000, comprising the following:

	£
Salaries, wages and professional's retainer	125,000
Course maintenance	50,000
Rent of land and club house	50,000
Administration and other expenses	50,000
Interest on debenture loan stock	150,000
Depreciation	25,000

The terms of the debenture loan stock issue prohibit a dividend being paid on the two ordinary shares, so that any surplus is applied for the benefit of the club and its members.

On the revenue side, Millennium Golf Club Ltd's share of profits on the investment in Century Club House Ltd is expected to total £100,000 in 20X6, the first year of operations. Green fees, chargeable to non-members using the golf course, are expected to amount to an additional £50,000 a year.

On the assumption that target membership levels are achieved, annual subscriptions are initially to be set at £500 for each member. This will be £100 less than for full membership at the two rival golf clubs in the area. In addition, no joining fees will be payable in the first year of operation, but thereafter (as with the other two clubs) they will be equal to one year's subscription.

On this basis Mr MacDonald and his associates are sure that they will be able to recruit around 350 members from the existing two clubs, including a good number of influential local businessmen and low handicap players. In addition, the new club expects to recruit most of those currently on the waiting lists at its two local rivals.

can afford to move out of a FTSE 100 company altogether and therefore remain long term shareholders whether the investment is liked or not.

There is a perceived trend towards greater involvement and communication. To quote one director: 'Investors are much more sensitive to their responsibilities than in the past because they are looked on as the guardians of the corporate conscience.'

3.4 External stakeholders

External stakeholder groups – the government, local authorities, pressure groups, the community at large, professional bodies – are likely to have quite diverse objectives.

External stakeholder	Interests to defend	Response risk
Government	• Jobs, training, tax	• Tax increases • Regulation • Legal action
Interest/pressure groups	• Pollution • Rights • Other	• Publicity • Direct action • Sabotage • Pressure on government

These stakeholders are likely to play a greater role in determining the objectives for NFPs.

3.5 Dependency

A firm might depend on a stakeholder group at any particular time.

(a) A firm with persistent cash flow problems might depend on its bankers to provide it with money to stay in business at all.

(b) In the long term, any firm depends on its customers.

The degree of dependence or reliance can be analysed according to these criteria:

(a) **Disruption**: Can the stakeholder disrupt the organisation's plans (eg a bank withdrawing overdraft facilities)?

(b) **Replacement**: Can the firm replace the relationship?

(c) **Uncertainty**: Does the stakeholder cause uncertainty in the firm's plans? A firm with healthy positive cash flows and large cash balances need not worry about its bank's attitude to a proposed investment.

The way in which the relationship between company and stakeholders is conducted is a function of the parties' **relative bargaining strength** and the philosophy underlying **each party's objectives**. This can be shown by means of a spectrum:

3.6 Stakeholder mapping: power and interest

Mendelow suggests that stakeholders may be positioned on a matrix whose axes are power held and the likelihood of showing an interest in the organisation's activities. These factors will help define the type of relationship the organisation should seek with its stakeholders.

(a) **Key players** are found in segment D: strategy must be **acceptable** to them, at least. An example would be a major customer.

(b) Stakeholders in segment C must be treated with care. While often passive, they are capable of moving to segment D. They should, therefore be **kept satisfied.** Large institutional shareholders might fall into segment C.

(c) Stakeholders in segment B do not have great ability to influence strategy, but their views can be important in influencing more powerful stakeholders, perhaps by lobbying. They should therefore be **kept informed.** Community representatives and charities might fall into segment B.

(d) Minimal effort is expended on segment A.

A single stakeholder map is unlikely to be appropriate for all circumstances. In particular, stakeholders may move from quadrant to quadrant when different potential future strategies are considered.

Stakeholder mapping is used to assess the **significance** of stakeholder groups. This in turn has implications for the organisation.

(a) The framework of **corporate governance** should recognise stakeholders' levels of interest and power.

(b) It may be appropriate to seek to **reposition** certain stakeholders and discourage others from repositioning themselves, depending on their attitudes.

(c) Key **blockers** and **backers** of change must be identified.

Stakeholder mapping can also be used to establish political priorities. A map of the current position can be compared with a map of a desired future state. This will indicate critical shifts that must be pursued.

Interactive question 2: Supavac plc   [Difficulty level: Exam standard]

Supavac plc ('Supavac') is a listed company which manufactures vacuum cleaners. Some 70% of its output is sold to Avold plc ('Avold'), a major UK-based chain of electrical stores. Vacuum cleaners are sold under Avold's own label and are regarded as being in the mid to upmarket range. Manufacturing takes place at Supavac's two factories, both of which are in the UK and are of approximately equal size.

The workforce of Supavac is largely unskilled or semi-skilled and is not unionised.

Avold has been a major customer of Supavac for about 30 years, but a new management team recently took over at Avold. It informed the board of Supavac that a new annual contract is to be arranged which would involve a major reduction in prices offered, and that the volumes purchased next year would be only 60% of previous years. It was also made clear that further price reductions would need to take place in future years if the contract were to be maintained at the new lower volumes.

As employees became aware of the increasingly competitive conditions, the possibility of factory closure emerged.

The board of Supavac identified two strategies:

Strategy 1. Close one factory and attempt to cut costs at the other by a policy of efficiency improvements and redundancies.

Strategy 2. Close both UK factories and open a new factory in Eastern Europe where labour costs are significantly lower than in the UK.

Requirements

Identify and justify the position of each of the following stakeholder groups in Mendelow's power-interest matrix with respect to the two strategies.

(i)   UK-based employees
(ii)   Potential employees in Eastern Europe
(iii)   Shareholders in Supavac
(iv)   Avold

See **Answer** at the end of this chapter

4   Not-for-profit organisations

Section overview

- The number of not-for-profit organisations potentially outweighs the profit seeking ones if we include voluntary sports clubs, interest groups and associations.

- Understanding how strategy is developed in these is important. It is similar to strategy formulation in businesses but without the comfort of the assumption of a single overriding goal of profit.

4.1   Voluntary and not-for-profit sectors

The term **not-for-profit organisation (NFP)** encompasses many different organisations whose only similarity is that they do not seek to make economic returns for their owners.

NFPs include:

- **Volunteer organisations**: providing services such as neighbourhood improvement, assisting the elderly, providing opportunities for children and youth, visiting the sick.

- **Charitable trusts**: set up around clear objectives to achieve some cultural or social goal eg. education of the young, art and music.

- **Governmental bodies**: these range from departments of central government down to local administrative bodies. Obvious examples include Police services, armed forces and education services.

- **Mutually-owned public benefit corporations**: these are effectively companies which do not issue shares to the public but rather whose capital is provided, and debts guaranteed to a certain limit, by others. They are free to raise debt from third parties. Their members are the stakeholder groups they serve and they will have procedures to consult and report to them. In the UK these include rail infrastructure provider Network Rail and Foundation hospitals. A more well-known example is the UK Public Schools which are in fact private schools for fee paying pupils but which have the legal status of a public corporation.

The taxation treatment of the incomes of NFPs is likely to be favourable because their surpluses are not treated as profits. For this reason many NFPs have to work hard to defend their status against accusations that they are merely a tax avoidance device. To do this they need to demonstrate a genuine **public interest**.

Business strategy issues are just as relevant to a not-for-profit organisation as they are to a business operating with a profit motive. The tasks of setting objectives, developing strategies and controls for their implementation can all help in improving the performance of charities and NFPs.

4.2 Objectives

Objectives will not be based on profit achievement but rather on achieving a **particular response** from various target stakeholders.

Here are some possible objectives for a NFP:

(a) Surplus maximisation (equivalent to profit maximisation)
(b) Revenue maximisation (as for a commercial business)
(c) Usage maximisation (as in leisure centre swimming pool usage)
(d) Usage targeting (matching the capacity available, as in the NHS)
(e) Full/partial cost recovery (minimising subsidy)
(f) Budget maximisation (maximising what is offered)
(g) Producer satisfaction maximisation (satisfying the wants of staff and volunteers)
(h) Client satisfaction maximisation (the police generating the support of the public)

There are no buyers in the NFP sector, but rather a number of different **audiences** (or stakeholders):

(a) A **target public** is a group of individuals who have an interest or concern about the charity.
(b) Those benefiting from the organisation's activities are known as the **client public**.
(c) Relationships are also vital with **donors and volunteers** from the general public.
(d) There may also be a need to lobby **local and national government** and businesses for support.

The objective setting process must **balance** the interests and concerns of these audiences, which may result in a range of objectives, rather than a single over-riding one. In order to allow for this balance to be achieved:

NFPs will typically feature wide **participation** in the objective setting process. Indeed it may be a legal condition in their constitution and essential to maintaining their legal status.

Stakeholder power and interests are likely to be more obvious in NFPs than in profit-seeking organisations.

Interactive question 3: Foundry Theatre   [Difficulty level: Exam standard]

The Foundry Theatre is a major regional theatre in Westingham and was built seventy years ago. 30 years ago the Arts Council awarded the theatre a grant for the first time 'to allow the theatre to undertake more prestigious productions than their own resources allow'. This grant (of £5,000) was very significant in that it marked the transition from **commercial** to **subsidised** theatre.

A few years after the Arts Council grant was awarded, the theatre was refurbished extensively with money from Westingham City Council at a cost of £884,000. Despite this, the theatre was soon in difficulties and heading for considerable financial losses. In a report published at the time the council's treasurer stated that the theatre should 'slash costs and attract bigger audiences in order to improve its financial position'. In addition, the theatre was criticised for not staging enough popular shows, for inadequate use of the building and for having a 'top heavy' management structure.

Again the council offered to step in with financial assistance providing the theatre cut its costs and implemented a review of its management structure. The theatre administrator refused the council's terms, indicating that many of the council's proposed savings would severely compromise the theatre's artistic standards.

Changes were eventually made and the theatre survived.

The objectives of the theatre were enshrined in the memorandum of association of the Foundry Theatre Trust as follows.

- To promote, maintain, improve and advance education, particularly by the production of educational plays and the encouragement of the arts of drama, mime, dance, singing and music.

- To receive, educate and train students in drama, dancing, music and other arts and to promote the recognition and encouragement of special merit in students.

The company (and the theatre) has enjoyed varying degrees of success over the last 10 years (attendance figures are given in Appendix I).

The current position

In a recent article in the *Westingham Gazette* the following comment was made.

'The Artistic Director has resigned, attendances are down by 50%, productions planned for the new year are cancelled, the company is heading for a £250,000 deficit – but there is no crisis at the Foundry, said Stephen Appleyard, Chief Executive, Westingham Theatres Committee.'

In carrying out an internal analysis for Westingham Theatres Ltd the following comments have been made.

James Knowles-Cutler (newly-appointed Artistic director)

'The objective of the theatre is clear to me. We should aim to increase our audiences through a programme of challenging plays. Rehashing populist plays is not our role. We should attempt to attract well-known (in theatre terms) classical actors and seek to stimulate debate and interest in theatre through a programme of good classics (for example, *The Caretaker* by Pinter, *Waiting for Godot* by Beckett, etc) and challenging modern plays. My ultimate objective is to establish ourselves as the leading "serious" theatre outside of London.'

Thomas Sutherland (Finance director)

'We are still dependent for a large amount of our funding on central government grants. The percentage of our funding coming from this area looks to be about 50%. This is misleading because the actual amount of this funding has been growing very slowly. The fact that it represents up to 50% is due to a reduced proportion of revenue coming from box office receipts. Therefore, we really have one objective – to boost our sales or receipts from the box office. Our current revenue includes £1,171,856 (20X9) down from a high of £1,596,245. Thus I estimate our ideal objective is to increase our box office receipts by 30% over the next three years. I believe there are a number of ways we can achieve this.

(1) We can reduce the price of our "Foundry Card". This is a membership card which allows the holder to attend five peak performances (ie Friday and Saturday) for the price of four performances. By reducing the price we would encourage demand.

(2) We should also reduce our prices on an individual performance basis. I believe this would increase attendances by such an amount as to increase total revenues overall.

(3) The restaurant/café side could be improved. The theatre occupies a first rate position in the city and has an excellent atrium space in the entrance hall. This is already used at lunchtimes, etc, but could be profitably used in the evenings for pre-theatre dinner.'

Brian Johnson (Westingham City Council, appointed to board of trustees of the Foundry Theatre)

'The trustees for the theatre believe the objective is to broaden the audience. The current composition of our audience is shown in Appendix II. Clearly the greater proportion of the audience comes from A/B income groups. We need to push more into other market segments. By boosting attendances in this manner we can go some way to achieving increased revenue figures. We think focusing on the production of highbrow theatre will only alienate a large group of the very people we are trying to attract.'

Requirements

You are part of a consultancy team appointed by the Westingham Council to investigate the theatre's position.

(a) In the light of information provided in Appendix II discuss the use of price reductions as a means of achieving the objectives as stated by the finance director.

(b) Draft a memorandum to the trustees of the theatre explaining the objectives of the theatre as expressed by the artistic director, the finance director and the trustee. You should comment on their compatibility and suggest a possible prioritisation of these objectives.

See **Answer** at the end of this chapter.

Appendix I

Attendances at Westingham Theatre 20X0 to 20X9

Year	Theatre	Studio	Total
20X0	159,700	16,600	176,300
20X1	168,800	12,900	181,700
20X2	167,900	8,000	175,900
20X3	167,700	18,000	185,700
20X4	210,300	21,200	231,500
20X5	206,869	14,902	221,771
20X6	175,064	16,533	191,597
20X7	159,966	13,491	173,457
20X8	175,435	4,903	180,338
20X9	100,807	9,510	110,317

Appendix II

Demographic characteristics of theatre-goers and local population

		Total population in metropolitan county around Westingham	Foundry audiences	Foundry mailing list 2005	Foundry card holders 2005
(1)	Social class (% A/B/C1)	29%	80%	50%	71%
(2)	Education (% completing full-time education, age 19 or over)	3%	50%	N/A	N/A
(3)	Age (% under 35)	37%	Main theatre 55% Studio theatre 75%	25%	7%
(4)	Sex (% females)	51%	50% apiece in main theatre and studio	66%	64%
(5)	Westingham post code	N/A	80% (estimated)	70%	91%

Appendix III

Revenues

Year	Box office £'000	Government grant £'000
20X3	1,144	927
20X4	1,306	1,072
20X5	1,330	1,054
20X6	1,446	1,095
20X7	1,596	1,065
20X8	1,117	1,103
20X9	1,172	1,157

Summary

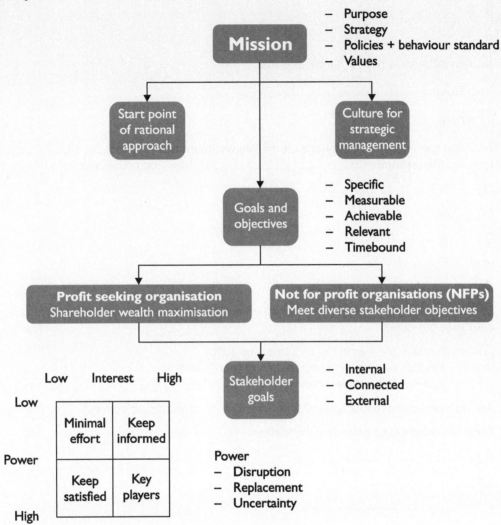

Mission
- Purpose
- Strategy
- Policies + behaviour standard
- Values

Start point of rational approach

Culture for strategic management

Goals and objectives
- Specific
- Measurable
- Achievable
- Relevant
- Timebound

Profit seeking organisation
Shareholder wealth maximisation

Not for profit organisations (NFPs)
Meet diverse stakeholder objectives

Stakeholder goals
- Internal
- Connected
- External

	Low	Interest	High
Low			
	Minimal effort	Keep informed	
Power			
	Keep satisfied	Key players	
High			

Power
- Disruption
- Replacement
- Uncertainty

CHAPTER

3

Self-test

Answer the following questions.

1 What are the four elements in the Ashridge definition of 'mission'?

P ....

S ....

P ....

V ....

2 Mission statements have a standard format.

☐ True

☐ False

3 Fill in the gaps: Most organisations set themselves quantified (1) .... in order to enact the corporate (2) .... Many objectives are:

(3)   S ....

(4)   M ....

(5)   A ....

(6)   R ....

(7)   T ....

4 Some objectives are more important than others. These are called .... corporate objectives.

5 (a)   'Increase the number of customers by 15%'
  (b)   'Produce reports within three days of month end'
  (c)   'Achieve 35% market share'

Are each of the above examples of unit objectives or corporate objectives?

6 There are three broad types of stakeholder:

(1)   ....

(2)   ....

(3)   ....

7 Define an NFP.

8 Read the scenario of the **March 2008 Business Strategy** paper in the Question Bank entitled *Campaign for Trading Equitably*, which we mentioned at the beginning of this chapter. Draft an answer for requirements (a) to (c) on the objectives, mission statement and stakeholders of the Campaign for Trading Equitably.

9 Go online to The Times 100 Business Case Studies and read the IKEA case study 'Meeting the needs of the consumer' at http://businesscasestudies.co.uk/ikea/meeting-the-needs-of-the-consumer

Now, go back to the Learning objectives in the Introduction. If you are satisfied that you have achieved these objectives, please tick them off.

Answer to Interactive question 1

(a) **Mission statement**

For Millennium Golf Club Ltd, a suitable mission statement might be:

'Our mission is to become the premier golf club in the Norbridge area by offering excellent value for money. We will achieve this by charging low fees, having high quality facilities and restricting the membership numbers of the club to ensure exclusiveness. At the same time we will protect the environment and help to preserve the local countryside.'

Suitable key objectives might include:

1. To hit the membership target of 750 members in the first year.

2. To recruit at least 350 members from rival clubs.

3. To ensure 30% of golf club members have a low handicap.

4. To attempt to win an award for golf club design and facilities by 20Y0.

5. To hold a local golf championship at the club by 20Y0.

6. To monitor the wildlife around the golf club and make sure that numbers of breeds of wildlife are maintained.

(b) **Mission, objectives, strategic tactical and operational plans**

The relationship between the elements of planning can be shown in the following diagram.

Mission

The mission attempts to define the purpose of an organisation. It usually mentions the organisation's long term strategy (ie the principles of business it will employ to compete, survive and prosper) as well as its policy and values and behavioural standards. The mission must pay some attention to the environment and markets in which the business operates.

Objectives

Once an organisation has decided its mission, then the objectives should follow from it. Objectives are usually quantified and have a time limit for completion. For the Golf Club, if its mission statement includes 'to become the premier golf club in the Norbridge area' then its objectives should be set to try to achieve this. Hitting membership targets for the first year is one possible objective, or making sure that a certain percentage of golf club members have a low handicap is another. Either would help to achieve the mission.

The strategic, tactical and operational plans of an organisation will be formulated with the mission statement in mind. The strategic plans (ie the detailed things the organisation should do over the next few years to succeed) should follow from the strategy outlined in the mission statement. The tactical plans (very short term plans to achieve limited goals, such as a marketing campaign to raise awareness of the golf club initially) should support the overall strategy of the business. Operational plans deal with those day to day issues of the business. All the operational plans should agree with the overall strategy of the business. There is no point in trying to be the premier golf club if the people employed are not of suitable calibre and the course is not well maintained.

In short, everything should follow from the mission statement: the plans to run the business on the various levels as well as the objectives set to ensure those plans work.

Answer to Interactive question 2

Interest

	Low	High
Power Low		UK employees — Strategy 1 (-/+) — Strategy 2 (-/+) Eastern European employees — Strategy 1 (-/+) — Strategy 2 (-/+)
Power High		Shareholders — Strategy 1 (-/+) — Strategy 2 (-/+) Avold — Strategy 1 (-/+) — Strategy 2 (-/+)

(i) **UK-based employees**

The power of employees to stop or moderate any closure decision is limited. If the entire UK workforce is united, then significant costs can arise from disruption. However, once the decision is announced the employees at the site that is not to be closed have a much lower negative interest in the decision. Indeed, from the perspective of self interest their employment might even be more secure as a result of the closure of the other plant; hence they could develop a positive interest.

In general, however, UK employees would favour strategy 1 as there are fewer redundancies.

Perversely, if the redundancy payments are sufficiently high some employees may favour redundancy to continued employment and thus have a positive interest in strategy 2 (eg if they were going to leave anyway).

(ii) **Potential employees in Eastern Europe**

Potential employees have probably not yet been specifically identified but they would have no power to influence the decision in either case.

Clearly, once selected, they would have a strong positive interest in strategy 2, particularly if local unemployment is high and/or Supavac is offering better pay and conditions than local employers.

(iii) **Shareholders in Supavac**

The ability to maintain the Avold contract is essential to Supavac shareholders as it counts for 70% of sales. The strategies under consideration appear necessary to reduce costs and thus maintain the Avold contract, even if not at volumes previously attained. The shareholders would favour the strategy that best achieves this, having regard to all other factors (such as quality, certainty of supply, transport costs, labour costs).

The shareholders have the ultimate power to determine the direction of the company. While in the short term the directors are empowered to make the relevant decisions, they can be displaced if these are not in the interests of shareholders.

(iv) **Avold**

Given that Avold takes 70% of Supavac's sales, it has considerable power over Supavac and is likely to be in a position to influence the decision of where production should take place. It will undoubtedly need assurances, if vacuum cleaners are to be manufactured overseas, as to quality and delivery schedules. The ability of Supavac to cut costs will have an impact on its ability to deliver price reductions.

Avold is interested in the reorganisation as vacuum cleaner manufacture is a competitive market, with a range of alternative suppliers available if Supavac fails to deliver cost reductions. (Alternatives are possible as there is an element of judgement involved, given the information available.)

Answer to Interactive question 3

(a) **Effectiveness of price reductions**

The finance director has a stated objective of increasing sales revenue as far as possible and suggests reducing prices to achieve this.

As a means of enhancing sales the following comments are relevant.

(i) Given the information on the population in Appendix II, 80% of the audience comes from social grouping A/B/C1.

It could be argued that going to the theatre represents a small amount of total expenditure for such groups, and therefore a rise in price may be possible to increase sales revenue.

Alternatively, in order to attract a wider audience (students, children, unemployed), price reductions may help to raise sales revenues.

(ii) The pricing structure needs to be much more precise, ie it needs to take into account

- Time of week and performance (students, cheap mid-week seats)
- Ability of audience to pay and their income bracket

(iii) It also assumes that the demand for theatre seats is driven largely by price. This is a very strong assumption. Non-price factors which would influence the demand would include the programme of plays itself, actors involved, time of year, etc. The implicit assumption made by the finance director is that, *ceteris paribus*, reducing price will increase demand. One badly chosen programme of plays could reduce overall demand in a given season.

(b) **Memorandum**

To	Members of the Westingham Council
From	ABC Consultants
Date	Today
Subject	The Foundry Theatre – Objectives and role

1 The nature of objectives

Objectives differ dramatically between organisations and in the way they are expressed. The most obvious distinction is between open and closed objectives.

Open objectives contain no reference to a quantified target for the objective. For example, a statement such as 'we aim to increase our market share' is open. Thus there is no guidance on by how much to increase the target of the objective nor over what timescale.

Closed objectives contain some quantified target value for the objective in question. The following is an example of a closed objective: 'Our objective is to increase our market share (by volume) by 12% over the next three years.' This contains a criterion by which to assess the target volume. It gives a target (12%) and a timescale (three years).

The final point to be made about objectives is that as far as possible they must be consistent. It is important to have a principal objective in agreement with supporting objectives. It is the duty of senior management to ensure that objectives are consistent and avoid dysfunctional behaviour.

2 The objectives for the Foundry Theatre

2.1 Introduction

Examination of the objectives for the Foundry Theatre are best undertaken from a 'stakeholder' viewpoint.

From the information given it can be seen that two of the objectives are 'open'. It is difficult to see how to assess the theatre against such open-ended objectives.

Clearly, in following the trust's objectives audience surveys could be carried out to determine

- Income bracket
- Residential area
- Frequency of attendance, etc

Thus, given the data in Appendix II on audience composition, this objective will be achieved if, *ceteris paribus*, more C1/C2 males under 35 attend plays and concerts.

The objective can thus be clarified and become closed.

2.2 Compatibility of objectives

Clearly the objectives put forward by the artistic director and the trust are mutually incompatible. If either objective is to be pursued to the exclusion of the other, stakeholder conflict is assured. If so, two possible (there may be more) outcomes become apparent.

- The artistic director becomes disgruntled and resigns.

- The trustees become disaffected and attempt to make changes at the theatre (in the absence of more information on the memorandum of association of the trust, it is difficult to say what power they have).

The next issue is to see whether the objective of the finance director is compatible with the other two.

The objective of increasing box office receipts is compatible with either of the other two.

(i)   From the viewpoint of the artistic director, increasing audience figures (and therefore receipts) will come from a small percentage of the metropolitan area's population (29% are A/B/C1) and these already provide 80% of the audiences of the Foundry Theatre.

(ii)   Given the increased ability to pay of the A/B/C1 income groups, increasing the attendance price of tickets and a more challenging series of plays may satisfy both the finance and artistic directors.

(iii)   From the trust's viewpoint, putting on less 'difficult' plays and increasing the number of popular touring reviews/plays may well boost audiences. Therefore reducing price may well enhance demand in volume terms, thus increasing box office receipts overall.

2.3 Prioritisation of objectives

There is an additional important element here and that is the amount of government grant. Appendix III shows the amount of government grant the theatre has received since 20X3.

The percentage of revenue accounted for by government grants is less important than the amount. It can be seen to have grown very little (compound annual growth of just 1.5% between 20X3 and 20X9). In real terms this has almost certainly fallen.

A critical issue facing the theatre therefore is its role as a subsidised theatre.

The current government is not disposed towards subsidies. There appears little hope of the grant increasing as a source of revenue.

The most important objective therefore is for the theatre to increase its box office revenues. Failure to do so (given no growth in subsidy) will eventually diminish the theatre's ability to stage its own productions.

The reduced ability to stage its own productions means that the artistic director's objective cannot be achieved.

3   Conclusions and recommendations

The main conclusions are as follows.

- Increasing box office revenue is the primary objective for the theatre.

- The finance director's assumptions on how this may be achieved are questionable.

- Audience research should be carried out re frequency/preferences, etc. This will provide information as to programmes and willingness to pay.

- The increased revenue appears likely from three principal sources.

    - Increased prices to current A/B/C1 theatre-goers and a challenging programme.

    - Lower prices to C1/C2/D income groups with a change in programme emphasis to 'popular' plays/musicals.

    - Perhaps a combination of both of these could work with plays/shows at varying prices during the week.

- Using the atrium space to provide a restaurant/café would probably increase non-theatre audience and thus provide an additional source of revenue.

1   Purpose
     Strategy
     Policies and standards of behaviour
     Values

2   False

3   (1) objectives (2) mission (3) specific (4) measurable (5) achievable (6) relevant (7) time bound

4   Primary

5   (a) Unit
     (b) Unit
     (c) Corporate

6   (1) Internal
     (2) Connected
     (3) External

7   An organisation whose attainment of its prime goal is not assessed by economic measures. Their first objective is to be a non-loss operation in order to cover costs. Profits are made only as a means to an end, such as providing a service.

8   Refer to the answer to parts a to c of Campaign for Trading Equitably in the Question Bank.

9   There is no answer to this self-test, as it is designed just to help you increase your business awareness.

CHAPTER 4

The macro environment

Introduction

Examination context

Topic List

Summary and Self-test

Answers to Interactive questions

Answers to Self-test

Learning objectives

- Explain how a business collects and distributes information and data relating to its external economic environment in order to manage its strategy

- Analyse for a given situation the external factors which may impact on a business's performance and position, identifying significant issues in areas such as:

    - Sustainability issues
    - Macroeconomic forces
    - International trade, financial systems and global economic factors
    - Government policies
    - Cultural environment
    - Markets for finance, labour and other resources

- Identify the risks attached to operating a global business

Specific syllabus references for this chapter are: 1b, 1f, 3d, 3g, 3h.

Syllabus links

Environmental analysis was covered in your Business and Finance paper under section 6 of the syllabus. However its coverage was at the level of core knowledge. In the Business Strategy examination you will be required to apply it.

Examination context

The scenarios in the majority of exam questions will require you to absorb and understand information about the external environment in which an organisation operates based on a scenario. You will also need to assess the implications of the environment and changes in the environment for the strategic positioning and strategic decisions of an organisation. To do this you will need to apply your knowledge using the tools and ideas covered in this chapter.

We referred briefly to Q1 March 2008 (*DA plc*) in Chapter 2. The scenario contains a great deal of information about various aspects of the external environment in which the company operates. The third requirement is:

'(c) Prepare a PESTEL analysis on the credit reference industry, clearly explaining the implications for DA's plans to implement the Checksta product. **(8 marks)'**

While the instruction to use the PESTEL model is very clear, you should also pay close attention to the remainder of the requirement. Firstly note that you are being directed towards analysing the 'credit reference industry' as a whole; it is a big mistake to ignore this and simply use PESTEL to consider how the company alone is affected. Secondly however you are asked to explain how these PESTEL developments in the industry as a whole might affect the company's own plans to introduce the Checksta product. This means that you do need to bring the analysis back to what the company is doing. There is therefore quite a lot to do for only 8 marks.

1 The business environment

Section overview

- Strategy is concerned with matching the organisation to the threats and opportunities in its environment.

- The process of gathering and disseminating the necessary knowledge about a firm's external environment is a specific example of knowledge management.

1.1 Importance of management understanding business environment

The environment contains those factors 'surrounding the organisation'. It includes the general macro-economic environment (the political, economic, social, technological, ecological and legal influences in the countries a business operates in); and factors particular to the firm or industry such as competitors, customers and suppliers.

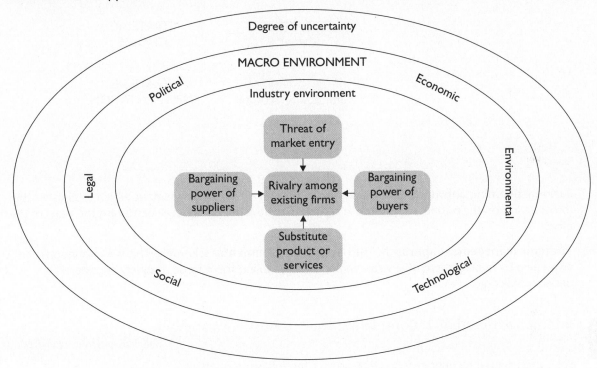

To be viable (eg able to sustain itself through time) the organisation must achieve an appropriate 'fit' with this environment. This includes:

- Results that meet the expectations of its owners (shareholders, government, members etc)
- Products and services that meet its clients' expectations at least as well as rivals'
- Ability to remain within the legal and ethical codes of the societies it works in
- Attractive as a place to work for its staff
- Satisfying the needs of other powerful or influential stakeholders

C H A P T E R

4

Rational planning approach: Environmental appraisal is a **one-off assessment** which establishes the forces acting on the business at present and **forecasts** how these may develop during the years of the plan.

Strategic management approach: The need for **environmental scanning**. This is a continuous awareness by management of environmental issues enabling them to be routinely considered in decision making.

 Interactive question 1: Considering the business environment

[Difficulty level: Intermediate]

For a professional accountancy practice, answer the following questions.

(a) What are the main external factors, in your view?
(b) How do these main environmental/external factors affect the strategies of the practice?
(c) In your view, how do managers perceive the environment of the organisation?
(d) How do you think managers incorporate environmental/external issues into decision-making?

See **Answer** at the end of this chapter.

1.2 Gathering and disseminating environmental information

An effective information system:

*   Gathers environmental information
*   Validates and corroborates the information
*   Disseminates the information so that people who need it can find it

1.2.1 Sources of environmental information

Internal sources include:

- **Employees:** Some will be following developments affecting the firm or their field of work, or have past experiences and networks of contacts that can provide insights.

- **Internal records system:** This will reveal comments of sales teams at meetings, revenue and cost trends at different locations, customer requests or complaints etc.

- **Formal information resources:** Many firms may employ information resources specialists to create current awareness reports eg accountancy firms have technical departments that monitor changes to regulations and the outcomes of adjudications, test cases and appeals.

External sources include:

- **Trade media:** Magazines and journals specific to the industry or to particular business functions.

- **Published accounts of rivals**, suppliers and clients.

- **Government statistical reports.**

- **On-line resources:** Subscriptions to business information vendors, current awareness services (emails from vendors who monitor the media for articles containing keywords specified by management).

- **Market reports:** Published research from investment analysts, market researchers, trade departments of governments etc.

1.2.2 Validating environmental information

Professional scepticism should be applied when considering environmental information. Is it valid and fit for the purpose of analysis? Issues to consider in validating environmental information include:

- Integrity of the source: internet gossip and market rumours lack integrity on their own

- Forecasting and predictive record in the past

- Degree of substantiation: is there more than one report or instance of this from independent sources?

- Age of the information: how up to date is it?

- Motivation of provider: does the provider have something to gain from convincing the firm of this information?

1.2.3 Disseminating environmental information

Dissemination can be assisted by:

- A well designed intranet with clear files and a search facility

- Periodic briefing reports with a digest of the most significant information

- Periodic seminars to brief management

- Annual management development sessions at an internal or external business school to introduce and discuss new environmental issues

2 Environmental dynamics

Section overview

- The ability of the business to plan, and its requirement for information about its external environment, will be influenced by how predictable its environment is.

2.1 Environmental uncertainty

Strategic planning takes place in the context of an uncertain future environment as competitors enter and leave the market, governments and their policies change, technology develops.

Changes in the external environment which have a long-term impact may be dealt with by strategic planning, but dealing with changes that have an immediate short term impact may involve crisis management.

The intensity of environmental issues varies from sector to sector and company to company.

Some businesses exist in relatively **static** environments, where the environment is simple (few competitors, limited products, slow rate of change) but many face environments which are **dynamic** – complex and characterised by rapid change.

In static environments, the business's historic and current environment will be a useful predictor of the future. In dynamic environments this will be of little benefit.

The degree of uncertainty and pace of change will affect the amount of resources devoted to environmental assessment. For example, investment banks employ substantial research departments and each day begins with dissemination of relevant environmental information to traders and managers. Airlines also have research departments which 'red flag' issues on a regular basis and also provide reports and forecasts as inputs into their strategic planning process.

2.2 Scenario planning

Definition

Scenario planning: The development of pictures of potential futures for the purposes of managerial learning and the development of strategic responses.

2.2.1 When is scenario planning useful?

Scenario planning is useful where a long-term view of strategy is needed and where there are a few key factors influencing the success of the strategy, eg in the oil industry there may be a need to form a view of the business environment up to 25 years ahead, and issues such as crude oil availability, price and economic conditions are critical. For example, Shell was the only major oil company to have prepared its management for dealing with the shock of the 1970s oil crisis through scenario planning and was able to respond faster than its competitors.

It is important to understand how scenario planning differs in nature from the normal strategic planning exercise. Scenario planning is a wider exercise than simply viewing the entity's operations at a company level and considering a range of external variables likely to impact on the ability of the entity to achieve its objectives. It tries to take a longer term view of the different ways in which an industry may develop. Ultimately, strategic planning results in an organisation developing a strategy, whereas scenario planning is focused on identifying a range of plausible alternatives which give an indication as to the future state of an industry.

Factors such as technology may cause major uncertainty regarding the future shape of an industry (consider for example the impact that e-mail has had on the delivery of letters and that e-readers have had on the book industry.) So in scenario planning a key question might be to consider where the industry will be in 10 years' time. An organisation that wishes to have a sustainable business needs to ask "what if?" questions and come up with contingency plans.

The nature of scenario planning means that precision is not possible, but it is important to develop a view of the future against which to evaluate and evolve strategies.

Scenario building attempts to create possible future situations using the key factors. The aim is to produce a limited number of scenarios so that strategies can be examined against them in terms of 'what if ...?' and 'what is the effect of ...?'.

A UK-based car manufacturer could assess the impact of a 'Green Scenario'or a 'High Value Sterling Scenario' on its business. Financial models of the firm are often used in conjunction with this approach to assess impact on profit. Although these provide a useful approach, it is important not to become too committed to one scenario; after all, they are only forecasts which might not in the event be valid.

2.2.2 Steps

- Identify key forces which might affect an industry or market, using techniques such as PESTEL analysis (see later).

- Understand the historic trend in respect of the key forces.

- Build future scenarios, eg optimistic, pessimistic and most likely.

The scenarios generated are then 'plots' to be played out making managers consider future possibilities and encouraging them to think about strategy more flexibly. In Chapter 10 we shall explore the role of scenario building and its use in risk management.

Interactive question 2: Oil industry scenarios   [Difficulty level: Intermediate]

Oil producers use scenario planning extensively.

Requirements

(a)   Identify the factors that make scenario planning popular with oil industries.
(b)   Suggest some alternative industry changing scenarios that an oil producer might consider.

3   PESTEL analysis

Section overview

- In your Business and Finance paper, you will have encountered PESTEL factors in your studies of the environment of business.

- This section looks at each PESTEL factor in more detail and identifies how each may impact on the strategy of the organisation.

- Later sections extend analysis to the global business environment.

3.1   Using PESTEL analysis

PESTEL is a handy checklist environmental factors, which was introduced in the Business & Finance paper:

- **P**olitical
- **E**conomic
- **S**ocial/cultural
- **T**echnological
- **E**cological/environmental
- **L**egal

PESTEL identifies the factors in the external environment affecting a particular industry. Depending on the industry, some factors will be more significant, eg legal and ecological issues may have a major influence in the airline industry, whereas political issues will play a major part in the healthcare industry.

The organisation must focus on the key influences currently affecting its business and those that might become significant in the future ie the key threats and opportunities that arise as a result of the PESTEL analysis.

Worked example: Software in India

The rapid emergence of the software industry in Bangalore in India has been made possible by a combination of technology (cheap and relable telecommunications), economics (low labour costs in India compared to industrialied nations) and political/social factors (the high level of education and the widespread use of English).

3.2 Political factors

Political factors relate to the distribution of power locally, nationally and internationally.

Political risk is the possibility that political factors will have an impact on the business's environment or prospects. The impact could be positive or negative, the issue is the uncertainty created.

Types of risk include the following.

- **Ownership risk:** A company or its assets might be expropriated (or nationalised) by the state, normally with compensation. Confiscation is, effectively, expropriation without compensation.

- **Operating risk: Indigenisation/domestication.** The firm may be required to take local partners. There may be a guaranteed minimum shareholding for local investors.

- **Transfer risk** may affect the company's ability to transfer funds or repatriate profits.

- **Political risk:** The government of the host country may change taxes or seek a stake in the business to increase its power or to satisfy local public opinion.

Sources of political risk

Source	
The country	This covers government stability, international relations, the ideology of the government in power, the need for contacts, favouritism for local suppliers, political violence, governments' ability to change the law and operating conditions, governments' need to appease powerful stakeholders.
The product	Consumer/basic products. High-tech components may have national security or armaments implications. Oil extraction in some countries places the oil companies near regions of ethnic or political conflict.
The company	Size, connections, reputation, influence on the environment.

Managing political risk

Companies, especially transnational corporations, might take measures to reduce political risk. These include:

- Detailed risks assessments prior to investing in the country.

- Seeking protection from legal agreements with the host country or from bi-lateral trade agreements between nations.

- Partnering with a local business to increase acceptance of the project and to lobby for political support.

- Raising finance for projects from the host country to put local pressure on politicians to help safeguard investment.

- Operate under the auspices of international bodies eg World Health Organisation, UNICEF etc.

- Share project with other firms to spread the risks between them.

- Avoid total reliance on one country, eg oil companies extract oil from many countries to offset risks of interrupted supplies or spiralling costs.

- Lobbying for political support from home government for projects and to resolve issues.

- Support for political groups in host country that are favourable to the project.

3.3 Economic factors

The economic structure of a country should be considered in strategic decision-making. Countries typically progress from reliance on primary industries (eg agriculture, minerals, forestry) through manufacturing to tertiary services (eg financial and commercial sectors).

Lesser developed countries	Reliant on a small number of products (eg crops or minerals) as the main export earner. Infrastructure is poor.
	Implications:
	Wealth and foreign exchange rate depend on yield of product and world price of product.
	Political actions aimed at securing control over incomes from product either domestically (eg insurgent liberation forces) or externally (eg develop cartels, invasion etc).

Newly industrialising countries	Rapid industrialisation and manufacturing base grows
	Implications:
	Infrastructure struggles to keep pace (eg power shortages, lack of housing, lack of roads, ports etc).
	Large shifts in population towards areas of industry and away from villages.
Advanced industrial country	There is a wide industrial base and a well developed service sector.

These affect overall wealth, financial stability and patterns of demand.

In setting strategy an organisation needs to consider where the economy is currently and where it is heading.

- Long-term exchange rates' behaviour affect the relative competitiveness of imported and domestically produced products and exports. A falling domestic exchange rate makes firm's exports more competitive and imported inputs more expensive. This may be determined by the value of key exports such as oil, minerals, crops, manufactured goods etc.

- Interest rates (long-term and short-term) affect cost of finance and also levels of demand in the economy.

- The economic infrastructure, for example access to payments systems, consumer and trade credit, access to venture and other capital, the quality of the stock exchanges.

3.4 Social/cultural factors

Social factors include

- **Make-up of population**: eg growth rate, proportion of old and young people.

- **Family structure** and size; the importance (or lack of it) of the extended family and relationships with non family members; the extended family provides contacts and work.

- The **role of women** in the labour force and in society as a whole (expectations vary from society to society). In different cultures, gender stereotypes are more sharply drawn than in the industrialised west.

- Extent of **social mobility**: the degree of social stratification and difference within each society and whether people can move between them, the changes in size, wealth and/or status of different groups within the population and the geographical distribution of the population between regions and urban, suburban and rural areas.

Cultural factors are identified in the diagram on the following page.

These factors affect strategy in several ways:

- The **market for products**, eg religious prescriptions on food, financial services

- **Promotional strategies**, eg language of adverts, considerations of imagery and decency

- **Methods of conducting business** in countries, eg conventions of negotiation, giving and receiving gifts, ensuring 'face' for contacts (ie maintaining self-respect and status)

- **Methods of managing staff**, eg language differences, attitudes to managerial authority

- Expectations of **business conduct**, eg extent of engagement with CSR, time horizon of investment, engagement in political matters

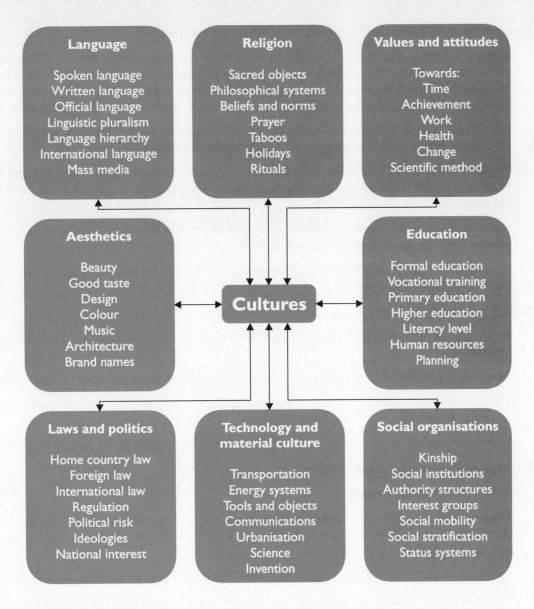

Language

Spoken language
Written language
Official language
Linguistic pluralism
Language hierarchy
International language
Mass media

Religion

Sacred objects
Philosophical systems
Beliefs and norms
Prayer
Taboos
Holidays
Rituals

Values and attitudes

Towards:
Time
Achievement
Work
Health
Change
Scientific method

Aesthetics

Beauty
Good taste
Design
Colour
Music
Architecture
Brand names

Cultures

Education

Formal education
Vocational training
Primary education
Higher education
Literacy level
Human resources
Planning

Laws and politics

Home country law
Foreign law
International law
Regulation
Political risk
Ideologies
National interest

Technology and material culture

Transportation
Energy systems
Tools and objects
Communications
Urbanisation
Science
Invention

Social organisations

Kinship
Social institutions
Authority structures
Interest groups
Social mobility
Social stratification
Status systems

3.5 Technology

The strategic significance of the technological environment includes:

- Technological base, and therefore customer and staff familiarity with it, varies across countries. Operations will have to take this into account.

- Technological change challenges existing industry structure and competitive advantages and so strategies to harness or evade it are necessary.

- Technological change can render existing products obsolete. Therefore continuous R&D and learning is necessary to remain competitive.

- Technological change creates uncertainty which may influence the approach to strategy formulation that is adopted.

3.6 Ecological environment factors

There is an increasing focus on maintaining the world's resources rather than depleting or destroying them, in order to ensure that they support human activity now and in the future.

This desire for 'sustainability' encompasses environmental issues such as:

- Climate change and pollution. The 2007 report of the Intergovernmental Panel on Climate Change (IPCC) forecast that global average temperatures by the end of the 21st century will have risen between 1.4C and 6.4C above the average for 1990. Global warming is forecast to cause polar ice caps to melt, leading to a chain of events including rises in sea levels and climate change.

- Energy gap as fossil fuels diminish while, for example, countries such as Brazil, Russia, India and China (the BRIC economies) are growing rapidly and demand more energy.

- Waste recycling issues as developed countries recognise the forecast use of landfill and also realise that much landfill is hazardous waste (eg Nicam batteries, electronic circuitry, oil and solvents in car engines).

- Bio-diversity issues as growing of cash crops and destruction of forests for grazing or building land also destroys species of plant, insects and animals.

- Introduction of genetically modified organisms into the food chain leading to loss of species and potentially hazardous future effects.

Main government policies are:

- Reduce carbon emissions through targets set in cross governmental accords such as Kyoto agreements.

- Penalisation of carbon creating industries through taxes levied on emissions or on fossil fuels used.

- Investment in non-carbon creating technologies such as nuclear energy, wind and wave power and electric or hybrid cars.

- Making foreign aid dependent on acceptance of environmental policies by recipient countries.

- Regulations covering hazardous waste.

Implications for business strategy

- Need to accept 'polluter pays' costs – taxes on emissions and requirements that firms buy certificates from refuse firms confirming recovery or destruction of materials the firm introduces into the supply chain.

- Increased emphasis on businesses acceptance of CR and principles of sustainable development.

- Potential for economic gain from cleaning-up operations and selling surplus 'permits to pollute' to firms that have not cleaned up.

- Potential competitive advantage from development of products that ecologically conscious buyers will favour.

- Need to monitor ecology-related geo-political and legislative developments closely.

3.7 Legal factors

Legal factors relate to the role of law in society and its role in business relationships. This can be assessed in terms of:

- **Systemic factors**: How effective is the legal system at enforcing contracts? To what extent are legal decisions likely to be interfered with by politicians ie are the courts independent of government? How easy is it to get hold of legal advice? How speedy are the courts? To what extent is regulation delegated? Are rights of private property genuinely enforceable?

- **Cultural factors**: To what extent are business relationships conducted formally or informally? The USA is regarded as a litigious society; in Japan (partly because the small size of the legal profession), business is widely believed to be based more on long-term relationships.

- **Context and regulatory factors**: Cover civil and criminal law, laws relating to consumer protection and advertising, employment, health and safety and so forth. Furthermore, to what extent is competition promoted, regulated and enforced? Intellectual property rights are examples of specific issues which need to be considered.

Interactive question 3: Estate Agent Industry   [Difficulty level: Exam standard]

Estate agents are residential property agencies which act on behalf of individual vendors to assist in the sale of their home. Revenues are derived from financial services, lettings, valuations and surveys. However, the main source of revenue – about 75% – is commissions on the sale of residential property.

Until 2007, estate agents in the UK had benefited from a 13 year housing boom with significant annual increases in house prices and high sales volumes.

The slump in the housing market in 2008 and 2009, despite falling mortgage interest rates, saw the closure of about 4,000 estate agent offices which constituted around one quarter of the UK industry. A report in 2013 highlighted that in the year up to June 2013 , 77 estate agents in the UK went into insolvency compared to 49 in the preceding twelve months. However, the report makes it clear that estate agents in London had suffered less than in other parts of the country. This was primarily due to high demand for property in the capital.

In 2014 two mortgage lenders, the Halifax and Nationwide indicated that house prices in the UK had risen by 7.5% and 8.4% respectively since 2013, with the average house in the UK worth over £170,000.

The fortunes of the housing market appear to be mixed as total mortgage lending topped £12.2bn in April 2014, the highest level since 2008. However, the number of loans approved in April 2014 fell from January.

The increasing use of the Internet has meant that private sales can be made directly between buyer and seller without the use of an intermediary such as an estate agent. This has become an effective competitor, threatening the established business model in the industry. In 2013 the government moved to make it easier for estate agents' companies to operate private sale websites. Websites such as 'The Little House Company' charges private sellers commission fees which are a fraction of those being charged by traditional estate agents.

There are however some reasons for optimism in the UK housing market.

The population in the UK is expected to reach 73m people by 2037, with an increase in the requirement for single occupant households as the demographics in the UK change. This is predicted to increase the demand for houses in the long term.

The policy of the current government is also encouraging to the housing market as there is an intention to increase the number of 'new build' dwellings to accommodate the expected increase in population and replace the older sections of the existing housing stock. The government's 'help to buy' scheme was introduced in 2013 to help first time buyers get onto the property ladder. The scheme provides eligible buyers with a 5% mortgage deposit to take advantage of a government loan to purchase a new build home.

In 2010, shortly after coming to power the coalition government suspended the use of home information packs 'HIP' an initiative introduced in 2007 by the previous government. Home information packs required the seller of residential property to produce a pack at an early stage in the marketing of the property. The scheme was aimed at reducing uncertainty for buyers. Although, good news for sellers, commentators suggest that scrapping the 'HIP' may deter first time buyers as the associated costs for land registry searches will now be picked up by the purchaser.

Making the announcement Housing Minister Grant Shapps, highlighted the government's commitment to green housing and noted that the change in policy will still require sellers to produce a energy performance certificate.

Requirements

Discuss the environmental factors that affected the Estate agent industry, using the following headings.

(a)   Political
(b)   Economic
(c)   Social
(d)   Technological
(e)   Ecological
(f)   Legal

See **Answer** at the end of this chapter.

4 The international business context

Section overview

- Few if any businesses are unaffected by global influences from competition, new markets or, at the very least, cheaper sources of supply.

- The view that certain nations have built-in advantages from low costs or harder-working staff has given way to a more sophisticated view that home factors may configure to give advantages to a handful of specific industries.

- This is illustrated using the Porter Diamond model.

4.1 The importance of the global business environment

The rapid industrialisation from the 18th century was a consequence of early involvement of merchants and businesses in trade. In the 21st century improved transportation and communications and cross-border business ownership have created, for most industries, a global business environment.

Global competition affects firms in several ways. It:

- Provides the opportunities of new markets to exploit

- Presents the threat of new sources of competition in the home economy from foreign firms

- Offers an opportunity of relocating parts of business activity (or **supply chain**) to countries able to perform them better or more cheaply

- May drive cross border acquisitions and alliances

This leads management to make significant strategic investment decisions that rely on assessments of the stability and trends of the global business environment:

- Development of products for international markets

- Advancing credit to clients in international markets or investing in businesses and assets in host countries

- Reliance of international sources for supplies of crucial inputs

Worked examples: Vehicle manufacture and call centres

Case study (1) Global vehicle manufacturing

The history of vehicle manufacturing is an example of internationalisation and, to a degree, globalisation. According to Dicken, world output of motor vehicles in 1960 was circa 13m units. By 2013 this had risen to just over 83m according to the International Organization of Motor Vehicle Manufacturers.

Fuelling the long term increase to 2013 was vehicle production in Asia, Latin America and, in recent years, countries such as China. The Financial Times (January 2013) reported that Chinese car production was set to outstrip the number of cars made in Europe for the first time in 2013, with China expected to make 19.6m cars compared to Europe's 18.3m. In the early 1970's one of every two cars made was produced from a European factory. Today, however, the continent makes one fifth of the world's cars.

European car manufacturer's have suffered in recent years since the 2008 global recession as car sales have reduced significantly.

The global automobile industry is characterised by extended global supply chains and international alliances between manufacturers. Illustrated below is an example of an alliance between two of the world's largest car makers.

In 2012 in a bid to address increasing global competition and a slow down in the European market, American car maker General Motors (GM) and French producer PSA Peugeot Citroen entered into a global alliance predicted at saving $2bn a year. The agreement aimed to create a global purchasing joint venture to allow both companies to buy parts and share vehicle platforms used in car production.

However, by late 2013 GM moved to sell its interest in PSA as the struggling French car maker sought closer co-operation with the Chinese Dongfeng Motor Corp. Reports indicated that only a fraction of the anticipated savings and synergies from the original agreement had been realised. The breakdown in relations moved GM to manage its revival on its own.

Case study (2) Call centres and 'offshoring'

Call centres are being used increasingly by organisations seeking to reorganise their customer service functions. Increasingly call centres are located overseas.

Some firms that locate call centres in India, for reasons of the lower cost of graduate labour, give their staff elocution lessons in the appropriate regional accents, and update their staff on sporting events and soap opera plot lines for the sake of engaging callers in conversation. An example is GE Capital, whose US, UK and Australian arms have set up call centres in India. In some cases, more sophisticated functions are sent offshore.

In an interesting reverse move, late in 2013, the global insurer RSA (formerly Royal & Sun Alliance) announced plans to create 350 jobs in the UK. The announcement follows the decision to shut its offshore Indian call centre operations. Making the announcement, John Elliott, RSA's personal lines customer service director highlighted the need for the company to improve the level of service customers receive when contacting one of the company's call centres. Elliott added 'The missing ingredient has been culture, and that's something we haven't been able to recreate in India'.

4.2 The global corporation

Definition

Globalisation: The production and distribution of products and services of a homogenous type and quality on a worldwide basis.

Levitt (*The Globalisation of Markets* – 1983) described the development of a 'global village' in which consumers around the world would have the same needs and attitudes and use the same products. A global corporation would be one that operated as if the entire world was one entity, to be sold the same things everywhere.

Levitt's focus was on the marketing aspects of globalisation. The global business corporation will also be characterised by

* **Extended supply chains**: Instead of making the product at home and exporting it, or setting up a factory in the host country to make it, the global corporation may factor out production so that different parts of the product (or service) originate in different countries. Womack *et al* (*The Machine That Changed The World*) suggest that the globalisation of the automobile industry led the way for this model.

* **Global human resource management**: This involves pan-national recruitment and development of human resources.

Interactive question 4: A global corporation?   [Difficulty level: Easy]

Some would say that such purely global organisations are rare. Industry structures change and foreign markets are culturally diverse. Even within the USA, there is an enormous variety of cultural differences. Can you think of a global corporation that fulfils the requirements of the definition given above?

See **Answer** at the end of this chapter.

4.3 Ohmae's five Cs: factors encouraging development of global business

Ohmae (*The Borderless World*) has identified a number of reasons which might encourage a firm to act globally arranged into a 'five C's' framework. (Recall in Chapter 2 the discussion of three of these C's under Ohmae's prescriptions for strategic thinking.)

The customer	Are consumer tastes across the world converging upon similar product characteristics?
The company itself	Selling in a number of markets enables fixed costs to be spread over a larger sales volume.
Competition	The presence of global competitors, who are enjoying the benefits of global commitment, could encourage a previously local or regional operator to expand its activities.
Currency volatility	Setting up assembly overseas is a way of reducing the exchange rate risks inherent in exporting and may also help to get around government imposed trade barriers.
Country	Locating business activities overseas may provide cheaper access to labour, materials and finance, along with the goodwill of host governments.

The continuing political acceptance of free-trade by international economies is essential to the success of these strategic investments.

4.4 Porter: *The Competitive Advantage of Nations*

Management developing strategy in a global environment needs to understand the competitive advantages they have over firms from other countries.

Porter (*The Competitive Advantage of Nations*) seeks to 'isolate the national attributes that foster competitive advantage in an industry'.

Porter identifies determinants of national competitive advantage which are outlined in the following diagram. Porter refers to this as the Diamond.

Role of factor conditions	Basic factors	Advanced factors
Human resources skills, (price, motivation, industrial relations) Physical resources (land, minerals, climate, location relative to other nations) Knowledge (scientific and technical know-how, educational institutions) Capital (ie amounts available for investment, how it is deployed?) Infrastructure (transport, communications, housing)	Basic factors include: natural resources, climate, semi-skilled and unskilled labour. Basic factors are inherited, or at best their creation involves little investment.	Advanced factors include modern digital communications, highly educated personnel, research laboratories and so forth. They are necessary to achieve high order competitive advantages such as differentiated products and proprietary production technology.

Role of demand conditions	Comment
The home market determines how firms perceive, interpret and respond to buyer needs. This information puts pressure on firms to innovate and provides a launch pad for global ambitions.	• There are few cultural impediments to communication in the home market. • The segmentation of the home market shapes a firm's priorities: companies will generally be successful globally in segments which are similar to the home market. • Sophisticated and demanding buyers set standards. • Anticipatory buyer needs: if consumer needs are expressed in the home market earlier than in the world market, the firm benefits from experience. • The rate of growth: slow growing home markets do not encourage the adoption of state of the art technology. • Early saturation of the home market will encourage a firm to export.

Role of related and supporting industries	Comment
Competitive success in one industry is often linked to success in related industries. Domestic suppliers are preferable to foreign suppliers, as 'proximity of managerial and technical personnel, along with cultural similarity, tends to facilitate free and open information flow' at an early stage.	This facilitates the generation of clusters. These are concentrations of many companies in the same industry in one area, together with industries to support them. For example, London in the UK is a global financial services centre, with a concentration of banks, legal services, accounting services and a depth of specialist expertise. Silicon Valley is a further example.

Role of strategy, structure and rivalry	Comment
Structure	National cultural factors create certain tendencies to orientate business people to certain industries. German firms have a strong presence in industries with a high technical content.
Strategy	Industries in different countries have different time horizons, funding needs and so forth. • National capital markets set different goals for performance. In some countries, banks are the main source of capital, not equity shareholders. • When an industry faces difficult times, it can either innovate within the industry, to sustain competitive position or shift resources from one industry to another (eg diversification).
Domestic rivalry	• With little domestic rivalry, firms are happy to rely on the home market. • Tough domestic rivals teach a firm about competitive success. • Each rival can try a different strategic approach.

Two other variables, **chance events** and the **role of government**, also play their part in determining the competitive environment.

4.4.1 Interactions between the determinants

The factors in the 'Diamond' are interrelated. Competitive advantage in an industry rarely rests on a single determinant.

- Related industries affect demand conditions for an industry. For example 'piggy-back' exporting is when an exporting company also exports some of the products of related industries.

- Domestic rivalry can encourage the creation of more specialised supplier industries.

Related business and industries are geographically clustered. A cluster is a linking of industries through relationships which are either vertical (buyer-supplier) or horizontal (common customers, technology, skills). Clusters are supposedly a key factor in the competitive advantage of nations.

Within a country, the industry may be clustered in a particular area.

- The Indian software industry is based in Bangalore.
- The UK investment banking industry is largely based in London.

Worked example: Motor industry – cluster effect drives sector's competitiveness

No part of the Basque country's rich industrial heritage can rival its $10bn annual turnover car industry as the driving force of the region's economy.

Generating 18 per cent of the region's gross domestic product, the sector and its associated companies employ more than 76,000 people globally, and account for almost 40 per cent of all car parts exported from Spain.

The Basque car sector has grown over several decades to such an extent that a region of less than 7,800 square kilometres is home to every part of the car production process, from steel factories to engineering companies and technical universities.

More than 30 multinational companies connected to the automotive industry have factories and offices in the region. They include Michelin, the tyre manufacturer, Valeo, the components manufacturer, and Daimler, which has a production plant in Vitoria.

Other companies involved in different stages of the car production chain include ArcelorMittal, the steelmaker, which has six production sites and a research centre in the Basque country, and Saint-Gobain, the French construction materials company.

Exemplifying this integrated approach is the Automotive Intelligence Centre, a business and development hub for the sector located outside Bilbao. The wavy-roofed steel and glass building opened just over three years ago and contains numerous companies, both Basque and foreign, that have operations in the region.

Serving as a research and development centre, industry infrastructure hub and training site, among other functions, the AIC is aimed at forging collaboration between the numerous companies related to the Basque automotive sector to increase their international competitiveness.

'We felt the industry was very vertically oriented, from the final clients downwards,' says Inés Anitua, managing director of the AIC and of ACICAE, the Basque country's automotive industry cluster.

'We wanted to start working more horizontally, to think differently. In Europe we have a strong knowledge [base] and the car industry was born here, so it is important we can sustain that knowledge.'

Originally thought up in 2006, the AIC was funded at first by the local administration and the European Union, but is now sustained by contributions from its industry members.

The industry in the region is very close-knit, with an interesting mix of companies, says Ms Anitua. More than 30 foreign groups have invested in the region, which has its own 'global players', she adds.

Mondragon Automoción, part of the Mondragon co-operative group, supplies parts to Honda, Ford and Renault-Nissan, among others, and is one example of a local company with a wide international footprint, with production plants in Brazil, Mexico and China.

Another is CIE Automotive, which is one of the companies with a base in the AIC and is quoted on the Madrid and São Paulo stock exchanges.

'We have many [opportunities] to work with other companies in our sector on different projects,' says Iñigo Loizaga, a technical operator with CIE Automotive at the AIC. 'We can also work together on certain commercial needs, demonstrate what we do together to clients and look at international expansion more efficiently. There are many synergies,' he says.

Oriel Saperas, director of the AIC's competitive intelligence department, produces sweeping opinion pieces on important developments in the sector, as well as confidential intelligence reports commissioned by members and companies outside the cluster.

'People receive a lot of information. We can organise this into something to suit the strategic objectives of companies, using a global view,' he says.

This collection of companies, a mix of foreign multinationals and indigenous manufacturers, allows the different parts of the production process to be in proximity to each other, and reduces the risk of one part suffering if a large component maker were to close down.

'The mix we have here is quite unique. Other regions may have a vehicle manufacturer, then foreign parts manufacturers. But if the big brand decides to close, the others will then move. We are not as dependent, as we export 80 per cent of production,' says Mr Saperas.

The steps taken by the Basque car industry to internationalise in recent years have produced impressive results.

Now, 80 per cent of total sales are to outside Spain, with a rising proportion derived from countries beyond Europe, and this is expected to result in record total sales for this year.

Sales outside the EU more than doubled between 2006 and 2009 from 14.6 per cent of the total to 32.5 per cent, while sales within the EU, excluding Spain, fell over the same period from 56.6 per cent to 46.2 per cent.

'In the past, we used to talk about exporting by selling to France or Germany. Now, you have to prove you can sell parts to many parts of the world to be able to survive. We have done that, and that is why some of our members have not only survived but have grown,' says Mr Saperas.

During the economic crisis, sales fell in 2010 to $10bn, compared with the $11bn generated in 2009, but the AIC expects an increase in international sales to help total revenues for 2011 come in above, or at least match, the 2009 figure once final numbers are calculated.

'This structure has enabled us to grow together at all levels,' says Ms Anitua. 'We have achieved something unique here that will keep the sector strong.'

(*Financial Times,* 27 March 2012)

Interactive question 5: Why do banks cluster?   [Difficulty level: Easy]

It is easy to see why mining companies should congregate in a cluster around coal seams, or shipping services would congregate around ports, but why should banks and software companies be clustered in the same way, given plentiful IT and broad bandwidth communications?

See **Answer** at the end of this chapter.

4.4.3   Using Porter's Diamond to develop business strategies

Porter claims that firms gain competitive advantage from either of two sources.

- Lower costs of supply to customers which result in higher profitability (cost leadership).
- Differentiated service or reputation resulting in higher prices and sales revenues (differentiation).

Porter advises management to consider the diamond factors in their home country and to compare them with the diamond factors available to rivals from other countries.

He offers the following prescription.

- If the home diamond factors give a comparative cost advantage over those of foreign rivals then management should adopt strategies based on **overall cost leadership**. This may explain the strategies of South Korean car manufacturers like Hyundai/Kia, Daewoo and SsangYong (the latter two being respectively offshoots of General Motors and Daimler Chrysler).

- If the home diamond factors give a differentiation advantage over foreign rivals management should adopt strategies based on **differentiation**. This may explain why car manufacturers Mercedes, BMW and Audi tend to develop and initially produce their limousines in Germany but build vans and utility cars in Spain, South Africa and Brazil.

- If the diamond does not confer advantage over rivals then management must **focus** on sub-sections of the industry which large players may have overlooked or not be able to exploit commercially. This may explain the large number of private banks in Switzerland or the boutique sports car makers in Italy (Ferrari, Lamborghini, Masserati etc).

 ### Interactive question 6: Chinese car industry [Difficulty level: Intermediate]

At the end of the twentieth century China's car production did not match any single large auto company in the developed world. In 2013 the International Organization of Motor Vehicle Manufacturers (OICA) reported China was the world's largest car producer. But it is not just volumes. China's car makers now produce not just low-cost runabouts, but also luxury and sports models, 'concept cars' and even a few hybrid and electric vehicles. Local car makers in the fastest-growing car market would appear to have come of age.

Until recently many Chinese car makers built thinly-disguised copies of vehicles made by Volkswagen, GM and Toyota. In the past few years things have changed. In preparation for a push overseas local firms such as Chery, Great Wall and Geely have proved they can develop their own vehicles too. Buying designs from international specialists and installing robotic production lines has led to an increase in the types of cars produced. Chery was reported to be working on developing more than 100 new models, however this figure was subsequently revised downwards. In April 2014 Chinese car makers held an impressive 37.1% of the market in China for passenger vehicles. By 2015, car maker Chery expects to export 500,000 vehicles to over 100 countries.

For a number of years foreign car makers had been worried by the Chinese firms' ultra low prices, however this has been changing in recent times. The rise of China's affluent middle class has led increasing numbers of Chinese consumers to switch to more expensive Western brands renowned for safety and flair. Chinese domestic car brands have also been damaged by poor safety crash results. Chinese cars exported today mostly go to Africa, south-east Asia and the Middle East, where expectations are lower and price matters more.

The development of China's car manufacturing business has been helped by a number of factors: A lot of early technology was borrowed. The government also offered support to fledgling firms via direct investments, guaranteed loans and a program aimed at supporting Chinese production of electric cars. Universities provided technical help, especially in the development of expensive engines. Future legislation is likely to force foreign firms to do more research and development in conjunction with Chinese partners to ensure continued access to cutting-edge engineering skills.

Requirements

(a) Identify, using Porter's Diamond, the sources and nature of any competitive advantage enjoyed by Chinese car manufacturers.

(b) Recommend a strategy for Chinese car makers based on this analysis.

See **Answer** at the end of this chapter Interactive question text.

5 Limits to globalisation of business

Section overview

- Despite the forecasts there are many impediments to the development of global businesses such as protectionism. These are reviewed here.

- Pursuing a global strategy is a source of risk to a business, either because the forecast opportunity doesn't come about or because host governments change their policies towards 'foreign' investment and render it no-longer valuable.

5.1 Political risks in international business

The development of plans for international business will depend on the following factors:

1. The stability of the government. Rapid changes or political unrest make it difficult to estimate reactions to an importer or a foreign business.

2. International relations. The government's attitude to the firm's home government or country may affect trading relations.

3. The ideology of the government and its role in the economy will affect the way in which the company may be allowed to trade, and this might be embodied in legislation.

4. Informal relations between government officials and businesses are important in some countries. Cultivation of the right political contacts may be essential for decisions to be made in your favour.

Political risk is still relevant with regard to overseas investment, especially in large infrastructure projects overseas. History contains dismal tales of investment projects that went wrong, and were expropriated (nationalised) by the local government.

- Suspicion of foreign ownership is still rife, especially when prices are raised.

- Opposition politicians can appeal to nationalism by claiming the government sold out to foreigners.

- Governments might want to re-negotiate a deal to get a better bargain, at a later date, thereby affecting return on investment.

In addition to expropriation, there are other dangers:

- Restrictions on profit repatriation (for example, for currency reasons)
- 'Cronyism' and corruption leading to unfair favouring of some companies over others
- Arbitrary changes in taxation
- Pressure group activity

Worked example: India's challenge to attract new investment

China's growth as a economic power has been widely reported for many years. As the *Economist* (2014) reported, GDP per citizen has risen from $300 to $6,750 over thirty years. By contrast India one of the so-called 'BRIC' economies expected to achieve exponential economic growth over the next hundred years has struggled to achieve the same level of global dominance in international trade. In the mid-1980s India's GDP per head was the same as China's, however today **it** is now less than a quarter.

According to the *Economist*, India's economic failings have been largely due to a string of weak government administrations which have left the country with a vast population of people underemployed and living in poverty, and an inability to attract new investment from foreign companies.

Historically, India's system of government has deterred foreign investors, as the country is governed on a devolved regional basis, increasing the difficulty for the central administration to enact national business friendly policies.

However, some commentators are optimistic about India's future. In May 2014, Narendra Modi and his BJP party were elected as the country's new prime minister and government respectively. The challenges

Mr Modi faces are vast and include among other issues, dealing with India's debt- burdened banks, improving the tax system, reducing inflation and investing in the country's transport infrastructure.

In 2012 companies including Vodafone and Nokia made the headlines when the then Indian government changed the country's tax rules governing mergers and acquisitions. This move required Vodafone to pay tax on companies it had previously acquired, with subsidiaries of Nokia also being accused of having 'unpaid' tax liabilities.

5.2 Protectionism in international trade

Protectionism is the discouraging of imports by, for example, raising tariff barriers and imposing quotas in order to favour local producers. It is rife in agriculture.

Protectionist measures include:

Tariffs or customs duties: A tax on imports where the importer is required to pay either a percentage of the value of the imported good (an *ad valorem* duty), or per unit of the good imported (a specific duty).

Non-tariff barriers: Restrictions on the quantity of product allowed to be imported into a country. The restrictions can be imposed by import licences (in which case the government gets additional revenue) or simply by granting the right to import only to certain producers.

Minimum local content rules: A specified minimum local content of products should be made in the country or region in which they are sold to qualify as being 'home made' and so avoid other restrictions on imports. This leads manufacturers to set up factories in the country.

Minimum prices and anti-dumping action: To stop the sale of a product in an overseas market at a price lower than charged in the domestic market, anti-dumping measures including establishing quotas, minimum prices or extra excise duties are used

Embargoes: A total ban or zero quota.

Subsidies for domestic producers: Financial help and assistance from government departments that give the domestic producer a cost advantage over foreign producers in export as well as domestic markets.

Exchange controls and exchange rate policy: Regulations designed to make it difficult for importers to obtain the currency they need to buy foreign goods.

Unofficial non-tariff barriers: Administrative controls such as slow inspection procedures or changing product standards which are hard for foreign suppliers to anticipate and respond to.

5.3 Trade blocs and triads

Trading blocs

Currently, a number of regional trading arrangements (or 'blocs') exist, as well as global trading arrangements. These regional trading groups take three forms.

1. Free trade areas – members in these arrangements agree to lower barriers to trade amongst themselves, eg NAFTA (USA, Canada, Mexico).

2. Customs unions – these agree a common policy on barriers to external countries. Tariffs, taxes and duties are harmonised amongst members.

3. Common markets – in effect, the members become one trading area. There is free movement of all factors of production. The European Union (EU) features a common political decision making process and a single currency and has economic union as an aim.

In addition to NAFTA and the EU, other major regional trade organisations include:

Mercosur – Brazil, Argentina, Paraguay, Uruguay and Chile

The Economic Community of West African States (ECOWAS)

The Association of Southeast Asian Nations (ASEAN) – Indonesia, Malaysia, Philippines, Singapore and Thailand

Triad theory describes the international business environment as a limited number of 'superblocs'.

The Triad

Ohmae developed the concept of a global economic triad in 1985, consisting of three main economic blocs: the USA, the EU and Japan, which controlled 75% of world trade.

Triad theory rejects the idea that homogenous products can be developed and sold throughout the world. Multinationals have to develop their products for the circumstances of each triad.

The Triad theory which applied in the latter part of the 20th century may be out of date now. The emerging markets, particularly those of China and India, but also Eastern Europe may give rise to additional trading blocs or a shifting economic triad for the 21st century of China, India and the US.

Summary

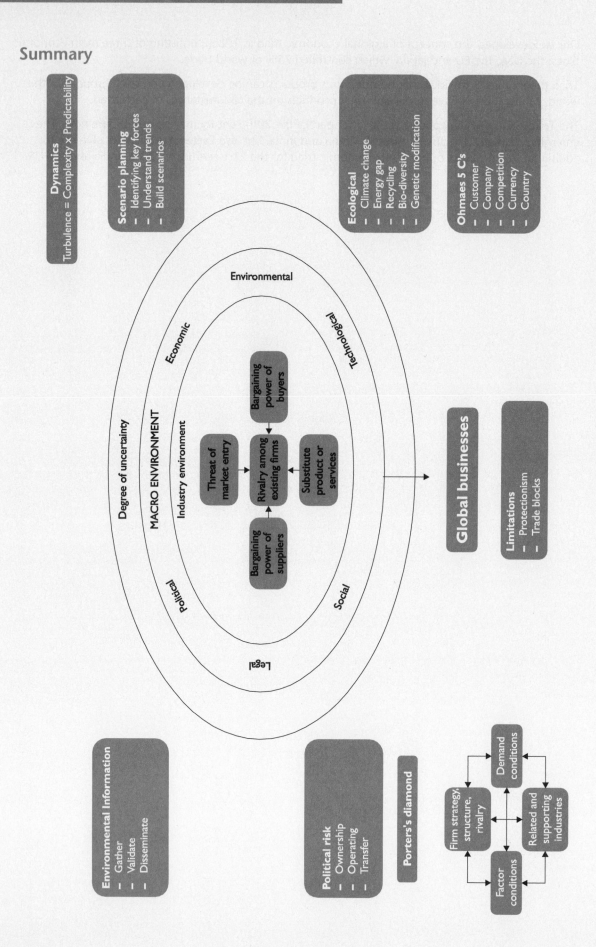

Dynamics
Turbulence = Complexity × Predictability

Scenario planning
– Identifying key forces
– Understand trends
– Build scenarios

Ecological
– Climate change
– Energy gap
– Recycling
– Bio-diversity
– Genetic modification

Ohmaes 5 C's
– Customer
– Company
– Competition
– Currency
– Country

Degree of uncertainty

Environmental

Economic

Technological

MACRO ENVIRONMENT

Industry environment

Political

Social

Legal

Threat of market entry

Bargaining power of buyers

Rivalry among existing firms

Substitute product or services

Bargaining power of suppliers

Global businesses

Limitations
– Protectionism
– Trade blocks

Environmental Information
– Gather
– Validate
– Disseminate

Political risk
– Ownership
– Operating
– Transfer

Porters's diamond

Firm strategy, structure, rivalry

Demand conditions

Factor conditions

Related and supporting industries

Self-test

Answer the following questions.

1   PDB Motors plc is a major UK car manufacturer with plants in the UK and Europe. It is seeking to exploit both the buoyant North American and Brazilian markets for car sales.

Suggest two reasons why it would be a logical strategy for PDB Motors plc to build an assembly plant in Mexico.

2   Social and technological factors always need to be assessed when analysing the environment within which a business operates.

Give two examples of each of these factors which would be relevant to Busline plc, a UK operator of coach tours to Scarborough and Whitby (seaside towns in the North of England).

Suggest how each of your factors may impact future demand.

3   Read the scenario of the **March 2008 Business Strategy** paper in the Question Bank entitled *DA plc*, which we mentioned at the beginning of this chapter. Draft an answer for requirement (c), including a PESTEL analysis and explaining its relevance to DA plc's plans.

4   Go online to The Times 100 Business Case Studies and read the Siemens case study 'Meeting global and local needs' at http://businesscasestudies.co.uk/siemens/meeting-global-and-local-needs

Now, go back to the Learning objectives in the Introduction. If you are satisfied that you have achieved these objectives, please tick them off.

Answer to Interactive question 1

(a) External factors would include:

- Rival accounting firms seeking to take clients themselves
- Other professional practices which may direct work toward us
- Regulations such as tax laws, accounting standards and audit standards
- The labour market for post-qualified and qualified accountants
- The general state of the economy and its effect on business

(b) These factors create opportunities and threats. New regulations create a need for professional advisers to provide guidance to clients. Competitors or a thriving labour market with higher pay create threats (incidentally notice how you changed your perspective on the last point because you would like to have the higher pay but you are calling it a threat for your firm). This illustrates how flawed the distinction between 'internal' and 'external' is when we discuss environmental analysis.

(c) This will depend on the managers psychological make-up. Some will see it as a tiresome bind that makes them have to keep changing things and also which makes it hard to plan or feel certain. Others will see it as invigorating.

A very interesting test of management is the extent to which they see themselves as powerless in the faces of environmental changes or whether they believe they can shape and respond to them.

(d) Again, this varies. Some will avoid making decisions which could be affected by environmental uncertainty, and will wait till it settles down (hence incrementalism). Some will simply ignore environmental issues that cannot be proven. Perhaps a more balanced approach is to adopt strategies that would still deliver benefit under a number of environmental developments or perhaps have several courses of action running at the same time, with each one designed to take advantage of different environments. In another context, energy companies invest in several different technologies because they do not know how oil prices and environmental regulations will develop.

Answer to Interactive question 2

(a) Oil producers adapted scenario planning techniques from their original military applications (notably in planning for the aftermath of thermonuclear war) during the 1970s. This followed the oil price shock when the Arab states then at the centre of OPEC massively increased the price of oil and caused inflation and recession in industrialised Europe and North America. This decision was itself justified in part as a response to the perceived support of oil consuming Western countries for support of the occupation of Palestine and Egypt.

It was a response to the high turbulence (eg political shifts, vulnerability to economic factors etc.) and dynamism (eg speed of change of political landscape) in the oil industry. Furthermore the very long investment periods in the industry necessitated long-term strategic plans based on assumptions about the future.

(b) Possible scenarios would incorporate a combination of:

- War in the oil producing countries of the Middle East

- Aggressive energy politics by countries such as Russia and Venezuela, holders of large reserves of oil and gas

- High energy demand from industrialising countries such as China and India

- Increasing legislation in industrialised nations aimed at reducing use of carbon dioxide producing fuels

- Development of new energy sources such as clean coal, biomass fuel, wave and wind, and re-emergence of nuclear power

- Discovery of new oil or energy reserves

Answer to Interactive question 3

PESTEL analysis

The factors affecting the estate agent industry are very closely linked to prosperity and activity in the residential housing market. The PESTEL analysis therefore needs to consider the wider housing market as well as factors directly affecting the estate agent industry

(a) **Political**

Political influences relate to the extent to which it is government policy to support and promote the housing market (social housing, 'help to buy' scheme owner occupied housing, increased 'new builds') in the form of local and national governments incentives (taxes reliefs, grants) and reductions in regulations (scrapping of the 'home information pack') which are a deterrent to house purchase.

Also, however, given the dependence of the housing market on the prosperity of individuals, the success of a government's economic policies is likely to impact on the housing market.

(b) **Economic**

One of the major factors that has influenced the industry was the recession, as estate agent sales are strongly dependent on house sales, which in turn are closely correlated with economic prosperity for both price and volume.

The housing market suffered severely in the recession as disposable incomes fell and economic confidence to make major financial commitments reduced (eg through redundancies, pay freezes, and general economic uncertainty). However, this pattern now appears to be reversing as total mortgage lending has surpassed 2008 levels.

(c) **Social**

The increasing population and the change in demographics have expanded the long run potential growth of the housing market. In particular the increased proportion of single occupancy dwelling increases the volume, but changes the mix, of desired housing. Unlike the rest of the UK demand for housing in London continued to remain strong during the recession due to the desirability of living in the capital city. This suggests that estate agents based in the London area are likely to be better placed to survive future downturns in the economy.

(d) **Technological**

Increased usage of the internet, and other electronic means of communication, is a threat to estate agents as a substitute sales channel for direct transactions between buyer and seller.

However, internet technology provides an opportunity to advertise the stock of each estate agent more effectively to a wider audience.

(e) **Ecological/environmental**

The requirement for increased energy efficient homes can be both a capital cost to new buyers but also a potential cost saving in energy bills. This may change both the quantity and types of housing sold but also require estate agents to become more knowledgeable about energy issues and imposes more duties and costs on them as a result, ie through dealing with surveyors to complete home energy ratings.

(f) **Legal**

Legal issues can be both a benefit and a cost to the industry. Legislation may directly affect the practices of estate agents, but also impact upon the housing market.

The requirement for sellers to produce an energy performance certificate represents a cost to sellers and thus may deter them from putting their houses on the market. However the certificates may encourage buyers to enter the market by reducing uncertainty.

Answer to Interactive question 4

Levitt cited examples such as Coca-Cola in his article. More recently, examples such as Starbucks, Mercedes Benz, Microsoft and Disney have been called global businesses.

In practice, these corporations offer subtly different products in different markets and their appeal is not global. For example, Coca-Cola has suffered badly from an anti-American sentiment and Disney has not been as successful in Europe as it had hoped.

Answer to Interactive question 5

The reasons cited for geographical clustering of financial and IT businesses are:

- Proximity to educational and research centres. For example, in USA the IT industry clusters around its universities.

- Networking and mutual exchanging of staff.

Answer to Interactive question 6

(a) The scenario suggests the following sources of the Cost Leadership advantages enjoyed by the Chinese car industry:

 1. **Demand conditions**: China is a very large market and fast growing. This enables firms to gain significant economies of scale and also to justify investment in the new models and production equipment. Although demand is still high for domestic brands this appears to be changing as the number of affluent Chinese middle-class buyers continues to grow. Buyers from this group are now preferring to purchase foreign models. Historically, demand in China was driven for low price cars and which had forced car makers to concentrate on reducing costs.

 2. **Related industries**: The only cited example is the assistance from universities in R&D. This provides significant cost advantages compared with in-house development. The low price of the Chinese vehicles suggests that steel and other components are being sourced cheaply too.

 3. **Factor conditions**: China clearly has a good technical education system. It is also known for having abundant cheap labour and land available for building car plants. It has good sea links and freight handling for the purposes of exporting.

 4. **Firm strategy, structure and rivalry**: The scenario mentions that domestic car makers hold 37.1% of the Chinese market. The Chinese government is keen for the market to achieve future growth among Chinese brands and has put in place measures to support local car makers. This will give each significant economies of scale and an incentive to invest in product and process improvement. That foreign-made cars are allowed into China gives a stimulus to product development and the search for competitive advantage.

(b) Any attempt by Chinese car manufacturers to go 'up-market' and develop unique designs and distinctive brands for export may be a mistake. Given the growth in demand for better domestic cars among Chinese buyers they might be better focussing on the domestic market.

 The appropriate strategy for the industry is to influence Chinese buyers to purchase domestic cars. Despite recent changes in buyer behaviour, China still has huge internal markets available to it that value its present offerings. Its low cost position may enable it to focus on export markets such as other developing economies where low cost is also important. However its advantages are location specific and it should access these markets by exporting rather than, say, setting up factories outside China.

 The poor quality of its products should be addressed. It may be cheaper to stop the design faults causing poor crash test results than it is to fix problems with cars once sold. Arguably, this would improve customer perception at home and abroad.

1   Two reasons from the following:

   - This would allow PDB to take advantage of low labour costs in Mexico.

   - The location would be close to potential major markets, cutting transport costs and reducing lead time.

   - The NAFTA will avoid sales to the USA and Canada being subject to import restrictions.

   - It delivers sales growth prospects to a company facing a saturated European market.

2   **Social factors**

   Two examples form the following:

   - Increasing car ownership (lower demand)
   - Higher proportion of older people in society (higher demand)
   - Cheap overseas packages available (lower demand)

   Technological factors

   Two examples from the following:

   - Development of high speed trains (lower demand)
   - More comfortable coaches being developed (higher demand)
   - Greater internet accessibility, creating more awareness of other travel options (lower demand)

3   Refer to the answer to part c of DA plc in the Question Bank.

4   There is no answer to this self-test, as it is designed just to help you increase your business awareness.

CHAPTER 5

The industry and market environment

Introduction

Examination context

Topic List

Summary and Self-test

Answers to Interactive questions

Answers to Self-test

Introduction

Learning objectives

Tick off

- Analyse a business's current markets, drawing conclusions consistent with the data and results and highlighting relevant issues in terms of their likely impact on the strategy of the business

- Analyse the external factors which may impact on a business's performance and position, identifying significant issues in areas such as:

  - Its industry and markets, including competition
  - Supply chain factors

- Explain, in a given scenario, how products and services must evolve in the face of changing consumer demand and industry competition

The specific syllabus reference for this chapter are: 1b, 1c, 2h.

Syllabus links

This chapter covers some of the same objectives as Chapter 4 through the use of additional models. Some of the models covered here will be familiar to you from the Business and Finance syllabus.

Examination context

This chapter looks at techniques such as Porter's Five Forces and life cycle analysis. Applying the appropriate models to the scenario in the exam will help you understand and analyse the wider context in which the organisation is operating and the factors that are likely to impact on business performance.

In Q1 March 2010 (*Blazing Bicycles Ltd*) the scenario contains a great deal of information about the history of the UK bicycle industry in which the company operates. The first requirement is:

'(a) discuss the extent to which the concept of the industry and product life cycle can be applied to the UK bicycle retailing industry and to sales of different types of bicycle.   **(7 marks)**'

The instruction to apply the concept of the life cycle is very clear, but note that it is the life cycles of both the industry and of particular product types within the industry that need to be analysed. In addition, in being asked to discuss 'the extent' to which the model applies, the question is raised as to whether that extent is very far, ie the model may be inadequate and limited as an explanation in this context. If you fail to address all aspects of this requirements when preparing your answer, you are severely limiting the marks available to you.

1 Porter's Five Forces approach

Section overview

- Strategic analysis requires management to consider the competitive forces in the organisation's industry, and Porter's Five forces is one of the most influential models used.

- Long term profitability determined by the extent of competitive rivalry and pressure on an industry.

- By considering the strength of each force and the implications for the organisation, management can develop strategies to cope.

- Like all models of analysis it has limitations particularly in industries that are rapidly changing.

1.1 The basic model

According to Porter, five competitive forces influence the state of competition in an industry. These collectively determine the profit (ie long-run return on capital) potential of the industry as a whole.

Source: adapted from Porter M, Competitive Strategy *(1980) New York: Free Press*

Porter claims that the intensity of the fifth force, that is the rivalry amongst industry competitors, is driven by the intensity of the other four forces. If these other forces are driving profitability down, the firms in the industry will compete more intensely to restore their own profits.

1.2 The threat of new entrants

A new entrant into an industry will bring extra capacity and more competition. The strength of this threat is likely to vary from industry to industry, depending on the strength of the barriers to entry. Barriers to entry discourage new entrants and influence the likely response of existing competitors to the new entrant. These will include:

- Scale and scope economies
- Product differentiation
- Capital requirements
- Switching costs
- Access to distribution channels
- Cost advantages of existing producers, independent of economies of scale
- Response of incumbents

Entry barriers might be lowered by:

- Changes in the environment
- Technological changes
- Novel distribution channels for products or services

The development of e-commerce had a significant impact on traditional retailers. The Internet is good at providing information based services at low cost so new entrants delivering information such as share prices have had a significant impact.

Generally an industry with low barriers to entry will be characterised by a large number of small firms.

Worked examples: Confectionery and brewing

Confectionery

The UK confectionery market is dominated by three organisations – Mars, Nestlé and Cadbury (owned by Kraft) – each with large shares of the market. Some smaller organisations survive, but there are significant barriers to entry, which include:

(a) The minimum efficient size, particularly in the chocolate sector, needed to adequately compete

(b) The advertising expenditure needed to establish brand awareness in a market where advertising spend is huge

(c) The need to penetrate the supermarket distribution network

(d) The experience of the main competitors in production and marketing

In 2010 American food producer Kraft Foods purchased UK confectionery company Cadbury in a £11.5bn deal. Although controversial, Kraft's acquisition of Cadbury helped the company to overcome some of the barriers to entry that would have been experienced had Kraft attempted to enter the UK market directly.

Brewing

The traditional brewer Adnams is based in Southwold, a small town on the Suffolk coast. Within the surrounding area it has held a near monopoly for years, with a sufficiently strong competitive position to withstand the pressure from the large national brewers. This is not solely on account of the quality of its product.

Brewing is subject to considerable economies of scale in manufacture. However, distributing beer over large distances adds considerably to the cost, since most of the cargo is water. Adnams' base in Southwold is sufficiently remote that the production cost disadvantage it suffers from its relatively small scale is offset by its relatively low distribution costs. Major brewers, based for example in Burton-on-Trent, find the cost of transporting beer all the way to the edge of Suffolk to be too high to make it an attractive market for them.

Adnams is thus able to enjoy virtual market dominance in its own area, in spite of being a very small player in the industry as a whole.

1.3 The threat from substitute products

A substitute product is a product/service produced by another industry which satisfies the same customer needs.

Substitutes affect profitability of an industry through:

- Putting a ceiling on prices eg air fares will determine the maximum level of train fares over similar routes

- Affecting volumes of demand

- Forcing expensive investments and service improvements eg CDs + DVDs supplied with booklets, posters and other offers to make them more attractive as artefacts compared to virtual downloads

Threat from substitutes is determined by:

- Relative price/performance eg speed of plane travel against the speed of train travel may be higher but does it justify the higher price?

- Switching costs from one to another eg download may be cheaper than CD but necessitates buying an MP3 player.

Interactive question 1: Blockbuster [Difficulty level: Exam standard]

Launched in 1985, American company Blockbuster became the largest film rental company in the world. It offered customers the ability to rent video games and movies (initially on video cassettes and later DVDs) for a short period, from its owned and franchised stores. A decade ago it employed 60,000 staff and opreated 9,000 stores worldwide. Once a leading provider of home entertainment, the company finally closed down its operations in late 2013.

'Even at its peak, Blockbuster's sticky carpets, sad-looking stock and large pictures of Adam Sandler rarely made visiting the doomed film rental chain worthwhile'.

Source: 'Blockbuster no tears for the film rental giant's demise', by Robbie Collin, *The Telegraph*, November 2013

Requirements

Identify the factors that enabled substitutes to cause the financial decline of Blockbuster.

See **Answer** at the end of this chapter.

1.4 The bargaining power of buyers (customers)

Buyers (customers) may include:

- Industrial customers and distributors seeking to obtain lower costs to boost their own margins, or better inputs and smoother transactions with suppliers

- Governmental or other not-for-profit organisations seeking to gain more benefit for their clients

- Consumers wanting better quality products and services at a lower price

Satisfying their wants may lead them to trade around the industry, forcing down the profitability of the industry. Buyer power is increased by:

- The customer buying a large proportion of total industry output

- The product not being critical to the customer's own business and a lack of proprietary product differences which would otherwise make them favour or be locked into one supplier

- Low switching costs (ie the cost of switching suppliers)

- Products are standard items and hence easily copied

- Low customer profitability forcing them to prioritise cost reductions

- Ability to bypass (or acquire) the supplier

- The skills of the customer's purchasing staff

- High degrees of price transparency in the market

Worked example: Retail pressure

In the UK market for fresh fruit and vegetables, one of the most prized possessions of a grower is a contract to supply Marks & Spencer. Many small farmers commit large proportions of their acreage to such contracts, and subsequently risk huge losses if the resulting produce does not meet the stringent quality criteria of the customer.

Powerful buyers put pressure on industry profits. Buyers are particularly powerful when:

(a) Purchasers are large, relative to suppliers

(b) Purchases represent a significant proportion of the buyer's costs, in which case these costs will be subject to great scrutiny

(c) Purchases are undifferentiated. Customer bargaining power is greatly increased when using the Internet to evaluate products and compare prices. This is particularly true for standardised products

(d) There are few switching costs incurred by the buyer in changing to an alternative supplier, and any change involves few risks. Thus, if the products of alternative suppliers have similar characteristics, then the buyer would not need to switch its own processes to accommodate a different type of input/material. (For example, if a car manufacturer sources brakes from a new supplier, then there are low switching costs if the new brakes are compatible with the cars' existing wheels, tyres, suspension and with the factory's production line machinery)

(e) The buyer earns low profits, in which case it will pressure supplier prices down in an attempt to increase margins

(f) The buyer has the potential to take over the supplier (backward integration)

(g) The buyer's product is not strongly affected by the quality of the supplier's product

(h) The buyer has full information about the supplier's cost structure or the supplier's competitive position

1.5 The bargaining power of suppliers

Suppliers can exert pressure for higher prices but this depends on a number of factors.

- Are there just one or two dominant suppliers to the industry, able to charge monopoly or oligopoly prices?

- The threat of new entrants or substitute products to the supplier's industry.

- Whether the suppliers have other customers outside the industry, and do not rely on the industry for the majority of their sales.

- The importance of the supplier's product to the customer's business.

- Whether the supplier has a differentiated product which buyers need to obtain.

- Would switching costs for customers be high?

- The level of switching costs for their customers.

Worked example: Manchester United

Manchester United is one of the highest earning football clubs in the world, yet its players' wages are comparable to those at other Premier League clubs, and considerably less than those at some leading Spanish and Italian clubs. It is able to do this – despite employing some of the leading players in the world – because the prospect of regularly winning trophies, and the prestige of playing for the club, counters the bargaining power of individual players and their agents. There is a deeply-held perception within the organisation that 'no player is bigger than the club'.

Industry profitability can also be squeezed by powerful suppliers. This is so when:

(a) There are few suppliers and the opportunity exists to establish a cartel

(b) There are few substitutes and switching is not a viable alternative. The Internet tends to lessen supplier power, reducing barriers to different supplier migration

(c) The industry supplied is not an important customer, suppliers may be unwilling to negotiate or discount

(d)   The supplier's product is an important component and the buyer cannot risk a disruption of supply

(e)   The supplier's product is differentiated or unique, and changes would have to be made to the buyer's product in order to switch

(f)   Suppliers threaten takeover (forward integration)

1.6   Competitive rivalry

The intensity of competition will depend on the following factors.

- Rate of market growth

- Level of fixed costs

- Ease of switching for buyers

- Importance of capacity utilisation/economies of scale

- Degree of uncertainty re actions of rival firms

- Strategic importance

- Exit barriers (non-current assets with a low break-up value; redundancy payments, effect of withdrawal on the other operations within the group)

1.7   Using the Five Forces framework

The Five Forces framework should be used to identify the key forces affecting an organisation and hence the opportunities available and threats to be considered. The key forces will tend to differ by industry so, for example, for manufacturers of own branded products the power of the large retail buyers (eg Sainsbury's, Tesco, ASDA, Marks & Spencer, etc) will be very important.

Consideration should be given to whether the forces will change over time and if so, how. Strategies will need to be developed to adapt to these changes.

It is essential for an organisation to determine not only how it stands in relation to the forces but also how its competitors stand.

Competitive strategy will be concerned with how an organisation can influence the competitive forces, eg can competitive rivalry be diminished? Can barriers to entry be created?

The ideal market, in which profits are easiest to make, is one where there is:

- Low supplier power
- Low customer power
- Little prospect of substitutes emerging
- High barriers to entry
- Weak inter-firm competition

1.8   Limitations of the Five Forces model

- **Ignores the role of the state**: In many countries, the state is a positive factor in the industry via ownership, subsidy, or presentation or regulation of competition. The Five Forces model seems to present government as just as a rule setter which is country-specific and reflects the US experience. However, another view is that the government can influence each of the other forces by legislation and economic policies.

- **Not helpful for not-for-profit organisations**: The Five Forces are those which determine industry profitability. If profitability is not a key objective for managers, they might not consider five forces analysis to be helpful.

- **Positioning view and not resource-based**: It assumes profitability will be determined by dealing better with the five forces ie outside-in. Individual business', strategic decision-makers should focus on product-market strategy. This ignores competence building for innovation to enter new industries.

- **Assumes management are required to maximise shareholders' wealth**: In some countries, companies pursue market share objectives instead, as has been the case in Japan, traditionally, and

South Korea, where large groups, with easy access to credit (and low cost of capital) did not overtly pursue profit objectives.

- **Ignores potential for collaboration to raise profitability**: The model underplays the potential for collaboration (eg supply chain collaboration) to build long-term relationships with suppliers, customers or distributors, joint ventures, to avoid substitutes, and so on.

- **Dynamic industries**: The model is less useful in industries that are rapidly changing as it is difficult to predict how the forces may change. Dynamic industries may require a greater focus on risk management.

Worked example: Collaboration in automobile industry

- Supplier/manufacture collaboration over design of parts for new cars and in supply chain management.

- Supplier/buyer collaboration – garages selling the cars also receive assistance with technology to service cars in order to help them resist independent service centres and on-line sellers.

- Manufacture/Manufacture collaboration – many car firms work together to develop models and technologies for each to use. They also join forces to resist legislation aimed at the industry.

1.9 Competition in different types of industry

The intensity of competition varies between industries according to the nature of what is being traded.

Industries can be classified as:

1. **Primary**: involved in agriculture, forestry and extraction of minerals including oil
2. **Secondary**: processing materials by manufacture into final finished products
3. **Tertiary**: industries engaged in the provision of services

Primary industries

Competitive forces tend to be stronger in primary industries for the following reasons:

- Undifferentiated products: this leads to competition upon price (commodity competition)

- Large number of producers

- High level of fixed or sunk costs (eg a crop in a field will rot if not sold so any price is better than none)

- Lack of alternative products available to produce (eg monoculture)

This reduces the levels of profit available to the producers.

Examples include commodities such as tea, coffee and cocoa, timber, vegetables and meat.

Firms engaged in primary industries may adopt the following strategies to raise their profits:

- Form collective marketing bodies to improve bargaining strength against the buyers, eg farmer co-operatives, Association of Oil Producing and Exporting Countries (OPEC).

- Create brand differentiation for their products or for the produce of their country eg *Appellation d'origine contrôlée* (French wine).

- Seek to set up value-adding processing activities to improve the value of the commodity.

Secondary industries

Profits will tend to be greater than in many primary industries due to:

- The possibility of greater differentiation in processing and manufacture owing to the application of design or branding

- Lower number of producers

- Potential to use capital equipment to make alternative products

However, in many secondary industries the power of the five forces is sufficient to reduce profitability to bare long-run minimum levels. High exit barriers in the form of writing off capital equipment and paying redundancy and other costs on the cessation of business may cause firms to continue in loss-making industries for many years.

Tertiary industries

In some tertiary industries high degrees of differentiation allow high profitability. Examples include accounting and business services, football and entertainment and some retailing.

Other tertiary industries feature intense competition and low profitability, eg logistics and parcel delivery, office cleaning, call centre services.

Worked example: Battle of the food chain

The following article demonstrates the shift of concentration from primary industries of crop growing to secondary food processors towards the tertiary industries of retail and the pervasive influence of globalisation.

'In the last half century, nothing short of a revolution has taken place in the world of food. Never has so much power over the global food system been concentrated into the hands of so few.

Until the second world war, it was the farmers who were the major players in food. But no longer is it those who produce the raw food that control the food supply chain. Instead, power is being concentrated at a staggering rate into the hands of a few giant companies who process the raw product and a few known as supermarkets who control the gateways to our mouths. And all are internationalising, most regionally, some globally.

The rise of the big processors has been phenomenal. In the USA just 100 firms now account for 80% of all value-added – that's the increase in price over and above raw farm food prices. Be it in Europe or the US, the concentration of manufacturing power is the same, it is just the names that are different. In the UK it is Nestlé and Unilever, in the USA Altria (created by the merger between Kraft and General Foods). These companies operate on a vast scale.

Concentration is almost entirely a result of manufacturer's buying each other to get their hands on the successful brands. 'National' brands like Kit-Kat – once owned by Rowntree's of York – has been turned by Nestlé into a global brand.

The level of manufacturing concentration is now remarkable whether one looks nationally, regionally or globally. Take meat. In the mid 1970s, the top four US beef packers controlled around a quarter of the American market. Today just 20 feedlots feed half of the cattle in the US and these are directly connected to the four processing firms that control 81% of beef processing, either by direct ownership or through formal contracts. In this sort of food system the farmer becomes a contractor, providing the labour and often some capital, but never owning the product as it moves (as rapidly as possible) through the food system. They never make the major management decisions.

But even the global, household-name, hugely profitable manufacturers can no longer claim control of the food supply chain. That has been wrestled from them by the global, household-name, hugely profitable companies that control access to the consumer: the retailers. In the UK, the top five supermarket chains now account for two thirds of food sales, while half of the country's food is now sold from just 1,000 giant stores.

Even the biggest manufacturers rely on the supermarkets to get their products to the consumer. And to do that they have to agree forward contracts with the retailers, whose logistics systems demand tight specifications, delivery times and margins.

Source: Guardian Unlimited website

2 Industries, companies, markets and technologies

Section overview

- The industry life cycle model describes the stages of development from introduction, through growth and maturity, into decline.

- The phase that an industry is at will affect the behaviour of the competitive firms within the industry and have implications for choice of strategy.

2.1 Industry life cycles

Definition

Industry: A group of organisations supplying a market offering similar products using similar technologies to provide customer benefits.

The concept of life cycle analysis is popular in strategic management and can be used to describe the phases of development that an industry , or market segment within an industry, goes through.

The key stages of the industry life cycle are:

- **Introduction** – newly invented product or service is made available for purchase and organisations attempt to develop buyer interest. There may be significant competitive advantage to those firms who are first in the industry.

- **Growth** – a period of rapid expansion of demand or activity as the industry finds a market and competitors are attracted by its potential.

- **Maturity** – a relatively stable period of time where there is little change in sales volumes year to year but competition between firms intensifies as growth slows down.

- **Decline** – a falling off in activity levels as firms leave the industry and the industry ceases to exist or is absorbed into some other industry.

Each phase has different implications for competitive behaviour and corporate strategy eg if an industry is growing, the organisations operating in that industry can grow as the market develops; in a mature industry, growth can only be achieved by stealing market share from other competitors and typically the market becomes more fragmented.

Some industry life cycles are identical in pattern and timing to that of their product (eg in the hat industry, or steel industry). Others have longer life cycles than the particular products, eg the music industry which has endured from sheet music till MP3 and downloads, merely releasing (and re-releasing) its music as new products as the format changes.

Many businesses will not wish to risk having only a single product or all their products at the same stage of development as they may all decline together. This leads to the concept of a balanced product portfolio which is discussed further in Chapter 6.

The financial returns to firms in an industry vary according to the stage:

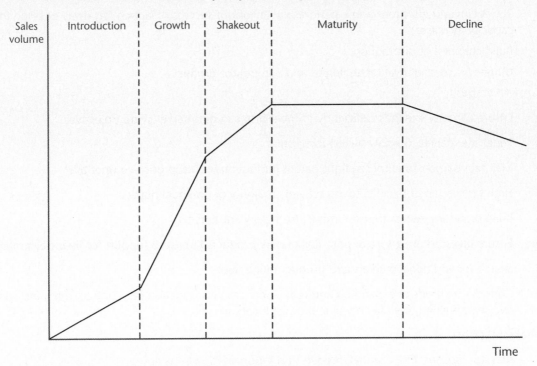

2.2 Characteristics of the industry at different phases

	Introduction	Growth	Shakeout	Maturity	Decline
Customers	Experimenters, innovators	Early adopters	Growing selectivity of purchase	Mass market, for branded	Price competition Commodity product
R&D	High	Extend product before competition	Seek lower cost ways to supply to access new markets	Low	
Company	Early mover Production focused	React to more competitors with increased marketing	Potential consolidation through buying rivals	Battles over market share Seek cost reduction	Cost control or exit
Competitors	A few	More entrants to the market	Many competitors, price cutting but winnowing out of weaker players	Depending on industry, a few large competitors	Price-based competition, fewer competitors
Profitability	Low, as an investment	Growing	Levelling off	Stable, high or under pressure	Falling, unless cost control

2.3 Strategic implications of industry life cycles

Management must pursue different strategies at each stage:

Introduction stage

- Attract trend-setting buyer groups by promotion of technical novelty or fashion
- Price high (skim) to cash in on novelty or price low (penetration) to gain adoption and high initial share

CHAPTER

5

- Support product despite poor current financial results
- Review investment programme periodically in light of success of launch (eg delay or bring forward capacity increases)
- Build channels of distribution
- Monitor success of rival technologies and competitor products

Growth stage

- Ensure capacity expands sufficiently to meet firm's target market share objectives
- Penetrate market, possibly by reducing price
- Maintain barriers to entry (eg fight patent infringements, keep price competitive)
- High promotion of benefits to attract early majority of potential buyers
- Build brand awareness to resist impact from new entrants
- Ensure investors are aware of potential of new products to ensure support for financial strategy
- Search for additional markets and product refinements
- Consider methods of expanding and reducing costs of production (eg contract manufacturing overseas, building own factory in a low cost location)

Shakeout phase

- Monitor industry for potential mergers and rationalisation behaviour
- Seek potential merger candidates
- Periodic review of production and financial forecasts in light of sales growth rates
- Shift business model from customer acquisition to extracting revenue from existing customers
- Seek to extend growth by finding new markets or technologies

Maturity phase

- Maximise current financial returns from product
- Defend market position by matching pricing and promotion of rivals
- Modify markets by positioning product to gain acceptance from non-buyers (eg new outlets or suggested new uses)
- Modify the product to make it cheaper or of greater benefit
- Intensify distribution
- Leverage the existing customer database to gain additional incomes (eg mobile phone operators seeking to earn from content management)
- Engage in integration activities with rivals (eg mergers, mutual agreements on competition)
- Ensure successor industries are ready for launch to pick up market

Decline phase

- Harvest cash flows by minimising spending on promotion or product refinement
- Simplify range by weeding out variations
- Narrow distribution to target loyal customers to reduce stocking costs
- Evaluate exit barriers and identify the optimum time to leave the industry (eg leases ending, need for renewal investment)
- Seek potential exit strategy (eg buyer for business, firms willing to buy licenses etc)
- The response of competitors is particularly important – there may be threats as they attempt to defend their position, or opportunities, eg when a competitor leaves the market

Worked example: Microsoft Xbox One

A company's policy on innovation will be linked to its assessment of how the product lifecycle concept applies to its portfolio.

In late 2013 Microsoft launched its next generation games console: Xbox One. The launch of the Xbox One followed the introduction of Sony's Playstation 4 earlier that year.

The BBC's technology reporter, Leo Kelion, pointed out at the time that Microsoft's Xbox One 'will be more expensive, but includes a higher resolution body-movement sensor in the Kinnect; better voice recognition; and a more ambitious bid to take charge of your living room thanks to its ability to control satellite and cable TV set top boxes'.

Gaming expert Brian Crecente told the BBC 'Where Sony's PlayStation 4 delivers an intensely focused gaming machine, Microsoft's Xbox One promises an entertainment hub, a system just as capable of controlling your cable box as it is delivering a new game for you to play'.

In recent years, there has been an interesting evolution in the relationship between gaming console manufacturers and their customers. Users of game consoles and mobile technologies have in turn become suppliers of content for others to enjoy.

Recognising this, Microsoft announced its intention that in the future every standard Xbox One will work as a development kit, allowing developers to develop and self publish games digitally on the Xbox One. This move follows Google Play and Apple's App Store which have created open markets for all kinds of developers.

Microsoft's decision to introduce the Xbox One was made having acknowledged that its earlier console the Xbox 360 (which had been introduced in 2005) was nearing the end of its lifecycle. In 2011, Computer and Video Games.com highlighted comments made by Microsoft Vice president Chris Lewis who stated that 'Xbox 360 was halfway through its lifecycle'.

Source: BBC and www.computerandvideogames.com

Interactive question 2: Profitability of airlines   [Difficulty level: Intermediate]

The airline industry as a whole is loss making (ie adding profits of successful airlines to losses of unsuccessful ones). Even successful airlines struggle to get an operating margin above 10%.

Using the following models identify contributory factors to the low rates of profits in airlines.

1. Industry life cycle
2. Porter's Five Forces

Identify potential strategies to restore profitability in the light of your analysis.

See **Answer** at the end of this chapter.

3 Product life cycles and international activities

Section overview

*   Global firms recognise that markets develop at different rates.
*   These differences in stage of development mean that products can be managed differently across the world.

3.1 Extending product life cycles through operating abroad

When domestic performance declines, some firms try to close the gap by exporting.

This is possible only if there are **different product life cycle patterns** in different countries as shown in the diagrams below.

Product life cycles in different countries

International business must consider many markets simultaneously, with a view to implementing a global introduction and manufacture. The financial returns to an investment may depend on the roll-out of this strategy.

Worked example: Film industry

Why are UK passengers on transatlantic flights often able to see films before they are released in the UK?

Solution

The product life cycle for a film can be characterised as:

Introduction: Premiere and advance screenings

Growth: General release to major cinemas and available to watch via online channels (eg blinkbox)

Maturity:
- DVD release
- Scheduled television programming
- Sequels and pre-quels

Declines: Sold as multi-package DVD or to television stations.

The international product life cycle for Hollywood films has tended to be

Phase I – to US Market. Films are released to the US market first. This explains why UK passengers on transatlantic flights are able to see films before being released in the UK.

Phase 2 – to other Anglophone countries (eg UK, Eire, Australasia)

Phase 3 – dubbed for non-Anglophone countries for mass release

3.2 International Trade Life Cycle

The International Trade Life Cycle is used in developing long-term product strategy. It postulates that many products pass through a cycle during which high income, mass-consumption countries are initially exporters but subsequently lose their export markets and ultimately become importers of the product from lower-cost economies.

From the perspective of the initiator high income country, the pattern of development is as follows.

- **Phase 1. The product is developed in the high income country** (eg the USA). There are two main reason for this.

    - High income countries provide the greatest demand potential

- It is expedient to locate production close to the market during the early period so that the firm can react quickly in modifying the product according to customer preferences

- **Phase 2. Overseas production starts**. Firms in the innovator's export markets (such as the UK) start to produce the product domestically. Thus, for example, the UK market is then shared by the innovative US firm and the UK firms.

- **Phase 3. Overseas producers compete in export markets**. The costs of the UK producers begin to fall as they gain economies of scale and experience. They may also enjoy lower costs of labour, materials etc than the US firms. The UK firms now start to compete with the US producers in third-party export markets such as, say, Greece or Brazil.

- **Phase 4. Overseas producers compete in the firm's domestic market**. The UK firms become so competitive, due to their lower production costs that they start to compete with the US firms in the US domestic market. The cycle is now complete.

Worked example: Fender guitars

The electric guitar industry is dominated by two main US brands, Fender and Gibson, both trading on their heritages of having developed the earliest commercial electric guitars in the 1950s and having been the guitars of choice for many influential players.

From the 1950s until the late 1970s both guitar brands were sold predominantly in the USA and were expensive as imports into Europe. In the early 1980s a copycat range to Fender was developed by a rival in Japan under the brand name Tokai and sold there. The Tokai was widely held to be superior in build quality and tone to the products being made in the USA and so Tokai guitars began to appear in Europe and USA. In 1983 Fender commenced production in Japan of identical guitars to its USA made models and sold these in Japan and Europe. A further wave of copycat products from South Korea and Thailand in the 1990s led Fender to establish a third factory in Mexico producing a parallel line of products for sale in USA and Europe, still under the Fender name. It also developed a flanker brand 'Squier by Fender' which was initially made in Japan before being put out to contract manufacture across Indo-China later. Gibson took a different route, acquiring a minor rival, Epiphone, in the 1970s and continuing to make Gibson guitars exclusively in the USA whilst also selling copies, made in Japan and later under contract elsewhere, under the 'Epiphone by Gibson' brand.

4 Industry segments and strategic groups

Section overview

- Returning to concepts of an industry it is possible to see segments or strategic groups within the same industry.

- Competitive strategy should be based on choosing the right segments for the organisation to operate in, and achieving success in each chosen segment by defending the firm's position there.

4.1 Industry segment recognition

Assessing the environment at industry level ignores the existence of segments within an industry. A company needs to segment the market, target its customers, and implement a marketing mix to satisfy them. The grid below identifies some of the key issues.

Benefits to management from recognising strategic segments are:

- Better tailoring of products and marketing mix to the wants of customers within a group (this is called market segmentation and targeting and is covered in detail in Chapter 8)

- Closer definition of competitors (ie those within the same segment) as distinct from others in the same industry but serving different sub-groups

- Identification of mobility barriers, ie factors preventing potential rivals entering the segment or preventing management from taking firm into new segments

4.2 Key considerations

The grid below identifies some of the key considerations in identifying strategic segments:

The product	What category of product is it?
	Eg consumer product, consumer service, specialist business product, business service, component, raw material etc
The customer	Who is the primary customer? eg consumer, business, organisation, government
	What is the location of the customer? eg local, national, regional or global basis
	Is the buying decision made centrally or locally?
	Cultural differences might affect buying behaviour, especially in negotiation and necessitate a difference in approach eg the appointment of go-betweens.
Segmentation	Are there different groups of customers with different buying characteristics?
	Is industry divided naturally by country or region? Do trade barriers or tariffs enforce segmentation?
	Does the industry effectively straddle several borders? In a global industry there may be no point in segmenting by country.
	If there are many competitors, a potential supplier might prefer to stay close to one particular market.
	A supplier may, because of its size or because of transportation differences, be unable to serve the entire industry.
Competitors	Where is rivalry strongest?
	Are there any niches with less competition? The identification of industry segments can enable firms to defend niche segments against larger, less focused, rivals.

4.3 Identifying country clusters

In choosing which groups of **countries** to enter, a firm might focus on particular countries or regions or groups of countries with similar characteristics using the following bases.

Basic data	Issues
Level of economic development, infrastructure and so on.	For example, the lack of a fixed line telecommunications network in Africa may encourage take-up of mobile telecommunications.
Cultural similarities (eg for intellectual property, common language).	It is easy to overestimate the similarities between two countries that might be assumed because they speak the same language. For example, despite the common use of English, there are distinct cultural differences between the US and the UK.
Member of economic groupings (eg a strategy for the EU).	Economic groupings such as the EU have tariff barriers for some external goods. They may have common product standards which must be adhered to.
Similar market or regulatory structures.	This suggests similar marketing mixes may be appropriate to more than ones market. American credit card companies have expanded in the UK because UK consumers use credit cards. German consumers tend not to use credit cards as frequently.
Inter-market timing differences: life cycles.	Certain markets have similar demand patterns for similar goods but that one leads and the other lags. For example, it is assumed that Internet penetration will rise in the developed world, but that the US will lead, and other countries will follow as innovations spread.

If countries are deemed to be similar, then it may be possible to use one country to 'predict' the behaviour of another.

4.4 Mobility barriers

These are factors that make it hard for a firm in one strategic group to develop or migrate to another. They function as barriers to entry and, as such, can enable superior rates of profit to be enjoyed by firms within a strategic group.

They relate to the following.

- **Characteristics**, such as branding, user technologies and so on, specific to markets overseas or to geographical regions within a country.

- **Industry characteristics**: To move into a mass volume end of the market might require economies of scale and large production facilities. To move to the **quality end** might require greater investment in research and development.

- The organisation may lack the **distinctive skills** and competences in the new market area.

- **Legal barriers**.

4.5 Buyers in the public sector

Developing business in industrial segments where governmental institutions are significant buyers raises special considerations:

- **Public accountability**: Governmental use of public money is often subject to controls and scrutiny that would be unthinkable in private corporations. This will vary from country to country according to the extent to which public accountability for expenditure is deemed to be important to the political system.

- **Governments are rarely monolithic**: Different government departments may have different cultures, agendas and resources. Regional political variations mean that local government purchasing units may have different processes.

- **Political considerations**: Public procurement will look at the whole social benefit and not merely costs. Therefore employment effects, and factors such as pollution will be considered. Government bodies may also require that its suppliers can show they conform to its own policies in matters of non-discrimination, sustainability etc.

- **Purchasing by tender**: Usual forms of buying procedure are the open tender and the selective tender. For a selective tender process, the firm needs to be accepted on the appropriate list. In some countries, it takes considerable persistence to get to that stage, since it may take several visits to appropriate government officials to establish a good working relationship.

Summary and Self-test

Summary

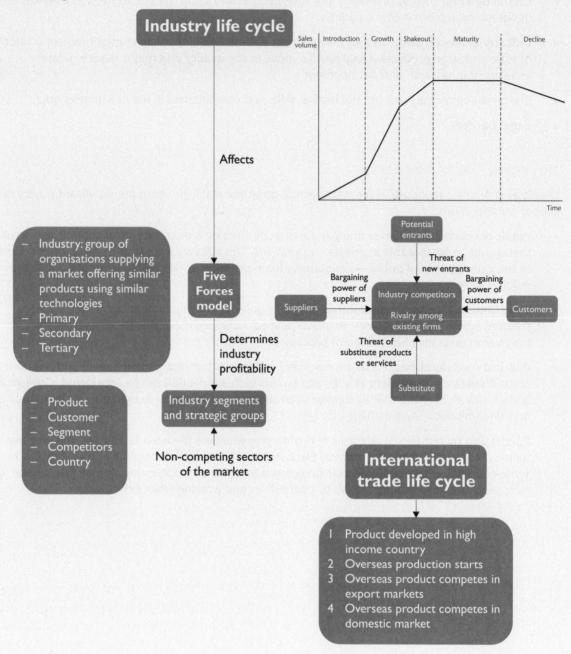

Industry life cycle

Sales volume | Introduction | Growth | Shakeout | Maturity | Decline

Time

Affects

– Industry: group of organisations supplying a market offering similar products using similar technologies
– Primary
– Secondary
– Tertiary

Five Forces model

Determines industry profitability

– Product
– Customer
– Segment
– Competitors
– Country

Industry segments and strategic groups

Non-competing sectors of the market

Potential entrants

Threat of new entrants

Bargaining power of suppliers

Suppliers → Industry competitors

Rivalry among existing firms

Bargaining power of customers

Customers

Threat of substitute products or services

Substitute

International trade life cycle

1 Product developed in high income country
2 Overseas production starts
3 Overseas product competes in export markets
4 Overseas product competes in domestic market

Self-test

Answer the following questions.

1   Mr Mavers runs a small newspaper and sweet shop in the centre of a large city. Will his customers exert a high or low bargaining power over him? Justify your answer.

2   'Large companies often exert a high bargaining power over their suppliers.' What type of suppliers will the following have?

   (a)   A large, mid-price chain of clothes shops
   (b)   A large top division football club

   Discuss the quotation above in the context of these two businesses.

3   'Audit fees for UK companies have fallen by 20% in real terms over the last ten years.' Given the intensity of competition within the industry, why do accountancy firms not withdraw from audit and focus their efforts instead on more profitable areas of work?

4   **Horsley Foods Inc**

Horsley Foods Inc was incorporated in 1891 and is currently established as a leading producer, distributor and retailer of foodstuffs in the USA. It produces its own chocolate which is a brand leader in the USA and recently it has shown interest in expanding its activity to Britain. The project is still very much at the drawing-board stage and you have been engaged as a management consultant to assist in the assessment of its viability and the construction of a strategic plan to achieve its objective.

The chairman's view

Your initial interview with the chairman, Hank Langford, took place two months ago. The chairman was optimistic about the venture as the following summary of his comments shows. 'We're a big player in the US but you can't stand still in this game. We've got to spread our wings and I want to see us playing around the globe. Europe is our first target and establishing in Britain gets us our foot in the door with the single European Market opening the way to the rest.

Our big strength is our chocolate – a lot of our success in the US is based on cracking the chocolate market there. We sell all sorts of branded chocolates. And your big vice is chocolate! Did you know that you Brits are the second largest consumers of chocolate in Europe, behind the Swiss? Last year you ate 8.8 kgs per head.

So taking our chocolates into Britain as the first step makes strategic sense.' Prior to writing your preliminary report you undertake some investigation into the nature of the UK chocolate market.

The products of the chocolate industry

The UK chocolate industry produces three main categories of chocolate.

*   **'Blocks'** which are generally moulded blocks of chocolate with or without any additional ingredients. These products are sold in standard sizes and are distributed mainly through grocery outlets.

*   **'Countlines'** which are chocolate products sold by count rather than by weight, eg Snickers, Kit-Kat and Smarties. These, unlike block chocolates, have a wide range of products which are distinct from each other in size, shape and weight, tend to have a strong brand image and are distributed mainly through non-grocery outlets such as newsagents and kiosks.

*   **'Boxed chocolates'** which are individually branded products, such as Black Magic, and are mostly sold as gifts, about 80% in holiday periods such as Christmas and Easter. During these periods they are mostly sold through grocery outlets, while over the rest of the year sales are mainly through non-grocery outlets.

The main competitors in the UK market

Your research produced the following findings.

Name of firm	Key brand names	Market share	
		UK %	Europe %
Bradbury-Repps (UK)	Dairy Milk		
	Creme Eggs		
	Crunchie		
	Flake		
	Milk Tray	30	10
Restler (Swiss)	Milky Bar		
	Kit-Kat		
	After Eights		
	Smarties	28	20
Venus (US)	Venus Bar		
	Milky Way		
	Galaxy		
	Twix		
	Snickers	26	16
Blosoft (Swiss/US)	Toblerone	2	12
Others		14	42
		100	100

The economics of competition

Companies in the confectionery sector have to be competitive in three key areas to be successful in the long run.

(1) They have to be cost-conscious, both when purchasing raw materials and during the production process.

(2) They have to distribute and market their products in the most effective way.

(3) They have to compete by bringing out new products when possible and desirable. Your analysis of the breakdown of the total costs of the 'Big Three' showed the following components.

Your analysis of the breakdown of the total costs of the 'Big Three' showed the following components.

Component	%	Comment
Raw material and production costs	55	Fluctuating cocoa prices usually absorbed by producers to preserve relatively stable retail prices
Packaging and distribution costs	15	
Marketing costs	20	Venus was the seventh highest UK advertiser last year, spending £33 million, closely followed by Restler with £32 million and Bradbury-Repps £29 million.
Other absorbed costs	10	
	100	

Requirements

Prepare a memorandum for the main board of Horsley Foods Inc which:

(a) Assesses the nature of the competitive forces (using Porter's Five Forces model so far as the information allows) which Horsley would face if it were to expand into the UK chocolate market. **(12 marks)**

(b) Identifies the different competitive advantage strategies which Horsley could pursue if it is to penetrate the UK chocolate market. **(8 marks)**

(c) Recommends a strategic way forward for the company in this matter. **(5 marks)**

(25 marks)

5   **Gizmo Petrol Company**

The Gizmo Petrol Company is a large company selling petrol through approximately 200 petrol stations, half of which are concentrated in the North-West region of England.

It has always maintained a strong presence in residential locations, as the managing director of the firm, Mr Macari, has always felt that people are more likely to purchase petrol as they leave for work or when they return home from work.

Gizmo operates its petrol stations via a five-year agreement with a single petrol supplier. The agreement is such that there is a minimum level of petrol which Gizmo has to purchase; at present the amount purchased is twice the minimum level. There are a number of other suppliers in the market should Gizmo require a new supplier in the future.

The company has been able to fund its expansion policy by borrowing from the bank and at present the company's gearing ratio stands at 32%. The company benefits from a strong positive cash flow which has allowed it easily to meet its repayment requirements and earn a reasonable profit margin. However, this margin has been eroded in recent years with the recession and as consumers become more price-conscious.

The market as a whole has seen consolidation over recent years with small independent petrol stations finding it difficult to compete with the large multi-nationals. The company is now faced with competition from two slightly larger national companies, local independent petrol stations and supermarkets which are supplying cheap petrol to customers in an effort to attract them into their stores.

The product range offered by Gizmo at present is made up of the following items.

Unleaded petrol	44% of company sales
Lead replacement petrol	31% of company sales
Diesel	23% of company sales
Non-petrol sales	2% of company sales

The move towards environmentally-friendly products within society and the taxation system benefiting unleaded petrol have allowed Gizmo to expand its sales of this product at the expense of lead replacement petrol.

The transport system within Britain is still largely dominated by cars, as individuals enjoy the freedom and flexibility of the motor vehicle and the government has maintained its road building policy. Competitors have also taken the lead in the development of improved petrol stations offering more services than selling petrol only. Gizmo has never been at the leading edge of developments within the industry and still largely sees the purpose of a petrol station as merely providing petrol. Gizmo's non-petrol sales are mainly made up of confectionery and cold snacks.

Requirements

Prepare briefing notes for Mr Macari containing an analysis of the external position of Gizmo within the marketplace.   **(16 marks)**

6   Read the scenario of the **March 2010 Business Strategy** paper in the Question Bank entitled *Blazing Bicycles Ltd*, which we mentioned at the beginning of this chapter. Draft answers for requirements (a) and (b) on industry and product life cycles and competitive international advantage.

7   Go online to The Times 100 Business Case Studies and read the Nokia case study 'Building a global telecommunications business' at http://businesscasestudies.co.uk/nokia/building-a-global-telecommunications-business

Now, go back to the Learning objectives in the Introduction. If you are satisfied that you have achieved these objectives, please tick them off.

Answer to Interactive question 1

Substitutes include:

- Supermarkets sell many of the most popular film titles at low prices
- On-line shops such as Amazon provide DVDs
- Downloads from Netflix, Apple iTunes and postal DVD rental from Love Film
- Piracy of movies by unregulated download sites and file sharing

These substitutes predominantly reduced the willingness of customers to visit Blockbuster stores with the consequence that the company's sales revenue fell.

The principal reason is the improvement in price/performance of these substitutes.

Supermarkets may be cheaper but are, importantly, convenient because households shop there each week and so simply add the latest film release to their trolley. Furthermore, purchasing the latest films removes the need for customers to return to a Blockbuster store once the rental period has finished. Where the households are not minded to follow film releases they were unlikely to visit Blockbuster.

Film downloads may be free or cheaper. They are also more convenient because again no special visit to a store is needed, the film trailer can be sampled and be immediately available for watching on various computer platforms.

Amazon may be cheaper but also provides customer film reviews which enable buyers to have more information before buying than could be gained by a visit to a Blockbuster store.

The introduction of new technologies indicates that traditional Blockbuster customers had little loyalty to the company as they were able to easily switch to different substitute providers of film entertainment products.

Answer to Interactive question 2

Industry life cycle

The industry seems to be at the shakeout phase with overcapacity due to many operators and liberalisation of competition (so-called 'open skies') leading to greater competition on profitable routes.

Consolidations (eg Air France with KLM) and failures (eg Swiss Air) have occurred.

Porter's Five Forces

Buyer power	• Increased availability has led to more choice in the market
	• The growth of electronic booking services (eg e-bookers, expedia.com, last minute.com) has restricted ability of airlines to charge full price
	• The change in the nature of the buyer towards short-haul leisure where price is more important than it was to business travellers
Supplier power	• Aviation fuel accounts for 30 – 35% of costs and is determined by oil producer cartels and large oil companies
	• Airframes are provided by two firms (Boeing and Airbus) and engines by three firms (GE, Pratt and Whitney, Rolls Royce)
	• Airport landing plots and services are provided by national monopolies
Substitutes	• Faster trains with better facilities which travel to centre of cities
	• Alternative leisure eg cruises
	• Technologies such as video-conferencing

Entrants	• Low cost point-to-point providers attack by short-haul router
	• Opening up of competition by bi-lateral agreement (eg USA and EU) or under pressure from World Trade Organisations
Competitive rivalry	• Very high fixed cost industry makes competition for volume force prices down towards marginal cost
	• Limited opportunities for differentiator given similarity of aircraft and destinations
	• Volatile demand due to seasons and economic/political factors

Restoring profitability

Consolidation of airline industry to reduce capacity.

Operate alliances to rationalise competition and benefit from economies of scale (ground handling, fuel purchase etc).

Oppose increasing take off and landing slots or greater competition.

Reduce fixed costs, eg by outsourcing, use of operating leases, better capacity planning.

Differentiate service to gain higher yield per passenger.

1   High bargaining power.

Presumably there are many other similar shops nearby, so customers will go elsewhere if he does not stock the products they want.

2   (a) Chain store

- Suppliers will be small independent manufacturers of clothes

- Many suppliers will exist

- All suppliers will have very similar products

- High bargaining power over suppliers is likely, given that if the chain store is dissatisfied with one supplier, there is unlikely to be a problem finding an alternative

(b) Football club

- Main suppliers are players

- Players are highly skilled individuals

- Each player's specific attributes will differ

- Low bargaining power is therefore likely, given that some players will not be easily replaceable

- This contradicts the quotation, but the situation arises because the suppliers, although small, do not offer a standard service

3   Accountancy firms have a strategic need to offer audit in the sense that clients will expect a range of services. The audit is often the loss leader that introduces the client to the firm. Other more profitable services can then be offered.

All large companies are obliged by law to have an audit, so accountancy firms will always have a market.

4   **Horsley Foods Inc**

Memorandum

To	The Board of Directors, Horsley Foods Inc
From	A Consultant
Date	Today
Subject	Proposed entry into UK chocolate market

1   **Analysis of competitive forces within the UK chocolate market**

The UK chocolate market is currently dominated by three companies which between them account for 84% of total sales as follows.

	Market share %
Bradbury-Repps	30
Restler	28
Venus	26
	84

All three firms have wide product portfolios with strong representation in blocked chocolate, countlines and boxed chocolate.

The nature of the competition within this oligopolistic industry is shaped by three key factors:

- The nature of the barriers to entry into the market
- The nature of the competition between the rivals
- The power of the large retail buyers

These will be considered in turn.

(a) Barriers to entry

The most significant barrier to entry lies with the strengths of the established brand names. The chocolate industry engages in extensive advertising geared both to strengthening brand images and to differentiating one company's products from another's, eg a 'Kit-Kat' (Restler) has to be differentiated from a 'Twix' bar (Venus), even though their ingredients are broadly similar.

Both Venus and Restler spent over £30 million last year on promoting their branded products. At the same time as strengthening existing brand images, this level of advertising makes it difficult for new products to be successful.

Other barriers to entry are as follows.

(i) **Economies of scale**
With little scope for cost savings on raw material inputs, companies must try to lower costs through economies of scale from their production. Production is therefore highly automated, particularly with the relatively capital-intensive block and countline chocolates.

(ii) **Distribution systems**
With many of the products, particularly block and countline chocolates, having a high rate of inventory turnover and with the retail outlets for chocolate being so diversified (supermarket, newsagent, vending machine, etc) an efficient national inhouse distribution network is essential.

(b) Competition between the rivals

As with most UK oligopolistic markets (petrol retailing, high street banking and volume car manufacturing being other examples) competition between the rivals is conducted on non-price grounds. Prices are kept relatively stable despite fluctuations in raw material costs.

The non-price competition is intense and can take the following forms.

(i) Massive advertising to establish and reinforce differential brand images (see above).

(ii) Augmenting the actual product by means of

- 10% extra weight free
- Coupon-based competitions

The intensity of the competition is evidenced by the size of the respective advertising budgets.

(c) Power of buyers

Both block chocolate and boxed chocolate are retailed predominantly through grocery outlets – which are increasingly dominated by supermarkets such as Tesco, Sainsbury, Safeway, etc. A firm wishing to break into this sector needs to be aware of the buying clout wielded by such firms at the expense of the producers' margins.

In conclusion it should be noted that chocolate manufacturers do **not** face competitive threats from

- Powerful suppliers – raw materials are purchased at going world commodity prices
- Substitute products

2 **Strategic difficulties to overcome**

The major issue which Horsley Foods Inc must resolve before embarking on a UK chocolate venture is the nature of the competitive advantage it intends to secure over its rivals. There are several possible avenues to explore.

(a) **Low cost strategy**

Competitive advantage is secured by operating at lower unit costs and thus retailing products at lower prices than those of rivals.

It is difficult to see how Horsley Foods Inc could gain an advantage here.

(i) Raw materials (cocoa beans, sugar, etc) are secured at prices based on world commodity markets.

(ii) Bradbury-Repps, Restler and Venus already experience economies of scale with regard to purchasing, production, marketing and finance.

(iii) It is doubtful whether chocolate is a price-elastic product.

(b) **Product differentiation strategy**

Competitive advantage is secured by encouraging a perception among buyers that the products are qualitatively superior to those of rivals.

However, it has previously been emphasised that this is already the basis of competition within the industry. Vast sums are spent on promoting brand images for wide product ranges and many possible angles for the mass market producer have probably already been explored. However, web sites offer the opportunity to reinforce brands encouraging loyalty and repeat purchases.

(c) **Product focus strategy**

Competitive advantage is secured by concentrating on a narrow product range targeted at a specific market segment. An example in the chocolate industry is Ferro Rocher's boxed chocolates.

This is a possible avenue to explore but it would involve Horsley Foods Inc in developing a strategy for the UK at odds with its wide range, mass market US strategy.

3 **Conclusion – a way forward**

The conclusion from the above analysis is that the UK chocolate market is stable and dominated by three large firms which have come close to 'sewing up' the market in terms of

- Successfully establishing a wide range of household brand names

- Obtaining economies of scale which render penetration pricing more viable as a long term strategy

- Operating efficient distribution networks

Given the extent of the entry barriers, it is doubtful whether a fourth player could be successfully established.

It is recommended, therefore, that if the proposed strategy of breaking into the UK chocolate market as a prelude to eventual expansion into Europe is to proceed, Horsley Foods Inc consider an **acquisition** in order to obtain immediate brand power and market share.

To serve the company's longer-term plans, consideration should be given to acquiring Venus Inc, another US firm. Such an acquisition offers

- Greater market power in the USA
- Significant market shares in both UK and the rest of Europe
- Knowledge and experience of breaking into Europe from the USA
- Operating, investment and management synergy

5   Gizmo Petrol Company

Briefing notes

To   Mr Macari
From   Mr Smith
Date   Today
Subject   Analysis of the external position of the Gizmo Petrol Company within the market place

Gizmo's external position

Gizmo's position within the market place can be analysed according to the opportunities and threats that it faces.

(a)   **Opportunities**

(i)   **Product range**

The company should follow the lead of competitors and take advantage of the move by consumers towards convenience shopping. The provision of essential everyday household items, such as light bulbs, should be seriously considered, given the company's location in residential areas.

(ii)   **Expansion**

Gizmo's operations are largely concentrated in the North-West of Britain. Given the company's experience, consideration should be given to moving towards other areas.

(iii)   **Political**

The government's road building policy should provide motorists with improved transport facilities and hence ensure that petrol is still a highly desired product.

(iv)   **Independent retailers**

The increased competition within the market place has already seen many small independent petrol firms ceasing to trade. This situation is likely to continue in the future and therefore Gizmo should use this as an opportunity to purchase petrol stations at a reasonable price to aid its nationwide expansion.

(v)   **Location**

Given that Gizmo has the opportunity to expand, it should look towards locating in areas other than residential, eg sites near towns would provide consumers with convenient places to fill up with petrol.

(b)   **Threats**

(i)   **Substitutes**

The privatisation of the railways may present motorists with an improved rail network, and may lead many of them to abandon the car and use the railways.

(ii)   **Political**

The government may influence the price of petrol by tax rises to aid rail privatisation.

(iii)   **Competitors**

Supermarkets may further drive down the price of petrol or offer cheaper petrol to attract customers in order to improve their sales. As customers are also becoming more price- conscious prices may also generally fall, putting pressure on margins and cash flows.

(iv)   **Technology**

Gizmo's lack of technological development may leave it open to attacks from competitors who may develop improved service stations. At present no scalable alternative power supply for cars has been discovered but in the future, with the move towards green ideas, it may be that petrol will be replaced as the fuel for cars.

(v) **Supplier**

The fact that Gizmo is supplied by only one company may cause future problems with quality and price flexibility if the market price fluctuates.

(vi) **Social attitudes**

Consumers may turn towards public transport as being more environmentally-friendly.

6 Refer to the answer to parts a and b of Blazing Bicycles Ltd in the Question Bank.

7 There is no answer to this self-test, as it is designed just to help you increase your business awareness.

CHAPTER 6

Strategic capability

Introduction

Examination context

Topic List

Summary and Self-test

Answers to Interactive questions

Answers to Self-test

Learning objectives

In the context of a business scenario:

- Identify the significance and effect of internal factors which may affect or influence a businesses ability to achieve its chosen strategy including its current resources, product/service portfolio, value chain and organisational and operational capabilities ☐

- Evaluate the critical success factors for a business ☐

- Explain the nature of capabilities and core competences ☐

- Carry out a resource audit using the Ms model and identify limiting factors ☐

- Understand the value chain model and apply it to scenarios and industries ☐

- Describe the role of networks, including supply chain management, in the development of a business's strategic capability ☐

- Apply the concept of product portfolio analysis ☐

- Explain, in a given scenario, how products and services must evolve in the face of changing consumer demand and industry competition ☐

- Identify and evaluate methods of further developing a specific business which adjust existing strategies or implement new strategies to take account of changing position and risk ☐

The specific syllabus references for this chapter are 1a, 1d, 2h, 3d.

Syllabus links

You will have been briefly introduced to most of the concepts in this chapter in your Business and Finance syllabus.

Examination context

This chapter includes key principles of strategic capability, core competences and resource based strategy. Questions are likely to focus on the linkages between elements and the manner in which, when used together, they can facilitate strategy and leverage competitive advantage.

In Q2 December 2008 (*Taylor-Thorne plc*) the scenario contains a great deal of information about the company's operations which involve handbag manufacturing. The first requirement is:

'(a) (i) Prepare a value chain diagram for TT. It should include brief notes for each of TT's relevant activities within the diagram

(ii) Briefly explain the TT value chain and describe how TT creates value **(13 marks)'**

There are two key skills in answering this requirement: first, to be careful and diligent in presenting the value chain diagram clearly and professionally, accurately capturing the information needed, and second to analyse how the particular combination of activities used by the company actually add value to it.

1 Analysing a business' strategic capability

Section overview

- Having analysed its external environment, an organisation must assess its strategic capability as the next step in strategic analysis.

To develop a strategic plan, a business must be aware of its current position. In the rational approach to strategic planning, having completed an analysis of the external environment, management needs to undertake internal analysis. This involves consideration of:

- Critical success factors and competences
- Resources
- Value chain
- Supply chain
- Product/service portfolio

2 Critical success factors and core competences

Section overview

- Critical Success Factors (CSFs) are the areas at which an organisation must excel if it is to achieve sustainable competitive advantage (SCA).

- Threshold resources and competences are the basic resources and activities required by all firms in the market and which are necessary to stay in business.

- Only by having unique resources and core competences can a firm generate SCA.

- Kay identified three distinct capabilities or sources of core competence: competitive architecture, reputation and innovative ability.

2.1 Critical success factors

Definition

Critical success factors (CSFs) are a small number of key goals vital to the success of an organisation ie 'things that must go right'.

An alternative definition is provided by Johnson, Scholes and Whittington.

Critical success factors 'Those product features that are particularly valued by a group of customers, and, therefore, where the organisation must excel to outperform the competition'

This is more restricted because it deals merely with product features rather than considering additional factors vital commercial success such as product availability, competitive knowledge or cost and performance control.

2.2 Identifying CSFs

The concept of CSFs was originally developed by Daniel in 1962 and refined by the Massachusetts Institute of Technology (MIT) as a device for aligning the information provided by a firm's information systems to the firm's business needs to ensure it is relevant and complete (this aspect is discussed further in Chapter 14).

MIT proposed five areas in which CSFs should be identified.

1. **The structure of the particular industry**: These are the factors shaping the success of the industry as a whole and the factors that will determine the number and profitability of the players within it eg consumer adoption of genetically modified foods is a CSF for any firm involved in developing or growing GM crops.

2. **Competitive strategy and position**: The key elements of the business strategy that must be delivered. For example growth in market share or percentage coverage of target market.

3. **Environmental factors**: Although not directly under the influence of management these must be monitored and action taken if they deviate from the firm's plan. For example a house building firm would regard the state of the economy and lending rates as CSFs and if they were to become adverse would cut back on its new-starts.

4. **Temporary factors**: These could be internal changes that are being made to organisational structure, or cost reductions. The success of these short-term projects is critical to the overall success of the business.

5. **Functional managerial position**: Each managerial role will have CSFs associated with it related to the manager's performance of their role.

Worked example: CSFs for M-Payment firms

M-Payment refers to the use of mobile phone (cell-phone) credits to pay for goods and services. The owner waves their mobile phone handset over the shop's sensor and the transaction fee is charged to the mobile phone operator and billed to their customer in due course. Where goods are purchased using the mobile phone, such as tickets where the handset is used to navigate through an automated switchboard or web-enabled mobile phones accessing websites, the funds can be transferred at the time of purchase.

The benefits are:

- Individuals will not have to carry separate credit cards, cash etc.

- Security will improve because there will be no opportunity to try to capture Personal Identification Numbers (PIN numbers) from terminals.

- Individuals denied credit cards will be able to use virtual payments systems.

- Provides methods of payment in countries that lack the infrastructure of banks etc providing the country has a retail network for 'pay as you go top-up' cards.

According to research carried out in 2005 by Booz Allen and Hamilton M-Payment was proving successful in Japan and Korea, but not USA and Europe.

They outline the following industry CSFs that will determine the uptake of M-Payment.

- Banks and credit card companies must evaluate ways to let mobile telecoms participate in collaborative ventures rather than setting up rival payment systems.

- Mobile operators must consider new mobile payment systems in the context of new ways to open up revenue streams, especially from monthly m-payment subscription charges or per transaction fees. Operators must also take full advantage of the positive side effect of embedding the mobile phone even deeper into the life of the subscribers – a significant motivator in the Japanese model.

- Handset suppliers must embrace new approaches and start to consider active integration of mobile payment capabilities into product road maps and line-ups. Mobile payment capabilities are seen by some as the next big thing to drive handset replacement, making standardisation and compatibility across operators and platforms critical to preserve user attractiveness and scale benefits.

- Merchants must use their vast experience with cashless payments to drive further cost decreases that accrue from giving up cash, and to offset POS technology upgrade costs.

- Finally, it needs to be demonstrated to mobile phone users that mobile payment is much more attractive than other more familiar payment schemes. The bundle of convenience aspects (safe, secure, available, fast, transparent, etc) needs to be packaged and sold to target groups individually.

2.3 CSFs and competitive advantage

CSFs differ from one market segment to another, eg in some price may be key, in others quality, in others delivery, etc.

CSFs concern not only the resources of the business but also the competitive environment in which it operates, discussed in Chapters 4 and 5, ie how will the business achieve a **sustainable competitive advantage (SCA)** over its competitors?

The following diagram shows the relationship between the different **resources** of an entity and the activities and processes which transform those resources into outputs to create added value (**competences**). It also shows the way in which entities can generate a SCA over their competitors by their unique control/ownership of particular core competences in these processes and activities.

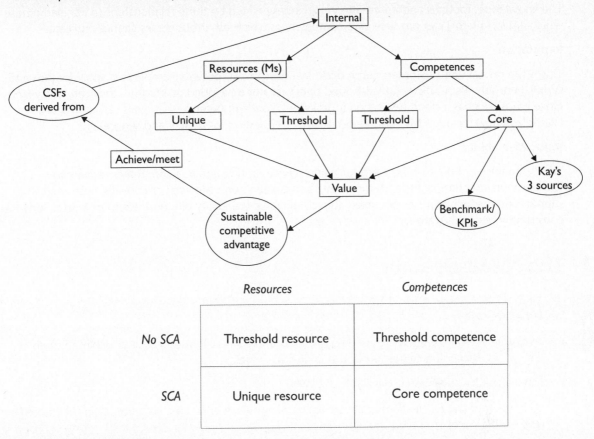

	Resources	Competences
No SCA	Threshold resource	Threshold competence
SCA	Unique resource	Core competence

Threshold resources	The **basic** resources needed by **all** firms in the market.
Unique resources	Those resources which give the firm a sustainable competitive advantage over its competitors, enabling it to meet the CSFs. They are resources which are **better** than those of the competition and **difficult to replicate**.
Threshold competences	The activities and processes involved in using and linking the firm's resources **necessary to stay in business**.
Core competences	The critical activities and processes which enable the firm to meet the CSFs and therefore achieve a sustainable competitive advantage. The core competences must be **better** than those of competitors and **difficult to replicate**.

2.4 Core competences – Kay's three sources

Kay (1993) argues that there are three distinct capabilities a company can develop that add value. These capabilities or core competences can originate from three sources.

Competitive architecture

This is the network of relationships within and around a business. There are three divisions as described below.

- Internal architecture – relationships with employees
- External architecture – relationships with suppliers, intermediaries and customers
- Network architecture – relationships between collaborating businesses

The knowledge, routines and information exchanges created by these relationships (particularly those which are long term) can produce core competences which other businesses cannot replicate.

Reputation

This is the reason why customers come back, investors invest, potential employees apply for jobs and suppliers supply. Reputations (at least good ones) are not developed overnight – they can take years. Once a business has a good reputation it provides a core competence that rivals cannot match. Examples (may) include BMW and Virgin Atlantic (reputation for quality and service).

Innovative ability

This is the ability to develop new products and services and maintain a competitive advantage. Organisation structure, culture, routines, etc. and collaboration between employees, customers and suppliers (ie the architectures discussed above) influence the ability of a business to innovate. Sony has consistently been innovative.

3 The resource audit

Section overview

- A resource audit catalogues the assets by considering physical resources, intangibles, human resources, technological resources and financial resources.

- An alternative and handy checklist is the 9Ms.

- Firms own many assets. Some of these assets will be sources of superior earnings in the future for the business and are called strategic assets.

- Therefore it is not sufficient to simply identify the resources. A business must understand whether they are strategic assets ie unique resources that underlie the firm's SCA.

The **resource-based** approach views the resources of the organisation not just as facilitators to gain competitive advantage from product-market strategies but as sources of strategic advantage in themselves.

In reviewing strategic capability, a first step is to conduct a **resource audit**. This covers physical resources, intangibles, human resources, technological resources and financial resources.

The audit should be comprehensive, but it is useful to identify the unique resources which underlie the firm's sustainable competitive advantage (ie what sets it apart from other organisations) as opposed to those that are necessary (ie threshold) but do not form the basis of SCA.

3.1 Physical resources

These include resources owned by the firm and resources to which the firm has access, for example in a supply chain or network.

- Physical assets should be audited reviewing how cost-effectively they are used. A measure of **capital productivity** is profit per unit of capital.

- **Inventories** and working capital are also resources, but they have to be financed. The focus of just-in-time approaches to inventory management and production (JIT) has been to reduce the need to finance working capital.

- Raw materials. Is the firm vulnerable to sudden changes in prices – are there long-term supply contracts or hedging instruments which can overcome this?

- Finally, are physical resources constraints on strategic activity (ie **limiting factors**)?

3.2 Intangibles and other resources

Brands and other reputational assets are resources created by a firm through the process of transforming inputs into outputs. Patents and other aspects of intellectual property are also intangibles.

These also include customer relationships and relationships with other key stakeholders such as media, and governments.

3.3 Human resources and labour markets

Human resources comprise the productive services people offer to the organisation. Human resources more generally can include the following:

- **Headcount**: Does the firm have enough people to do the task or can the work be done more productively with fewer?

- **Skills base** available to the firm: measured though qualification and training, and the social and psychological aptitudes linking the technical skills to performance.

- **Culture**: The emotional and motivational climate of an organisation is critical to its success particularly in industries where personal service is essential to the 'experience' the company is offering.

- **Knowledge**: A firm's knowledge is partly embedded in people, what they do and how they are organised.

- **Workforce structure** and organisation structure

- **The right mix of labour and capital**

  There is a trade off, in some respects, between using people and using equipment to save money or to increase efficiency. For example, reducing the costs of a call centre can be achieved by:

  - Voice activated software and voice recognition software to process simple transactions
  - Outsourcing it off-shore to a country where labour costs are lower

  The choice will depend on the potential cost savings and benefits and perhaps customer resistance and the firm's attitudes to reputational risk if it cannot achieve its level of service.

- **Service levels**

  Whilst some services can be automated, others cannot – customer service staff are often those who encounter the most moments of truth with the customer. In a service-led economy, the quality of human interaction is an important element of customer satisfaction. To provide good service, those at the customer interface must be supported by a management infrastructure of robust information systems and good training and supervision.

- **Human capital and knowledge industries**

  Knowledge-based industries require the creation and use of intellectual property. The skills and mindset necessary for this may often rely on the education and cultures of the country of operation.

- **Workforce structure**

  The right balance between full-time and part-time staff can provide a variable resource that can be accessed when necessary to achieve flexibility. The flexibility of employment contracts, such as covering other tasks and locations, can add to this.

3.4 Technological resources

Technology is a resource in many different ways. Here we focus on two aspects.

- The organisation's capability to manage technology projects, especially IT projects. The costs and complexities of such projects means there is potential for failure (and success) on a huge scale.

  Implementing a successful technology solution enabled low cost carriers such as easyJet and Ryanair to reduce their cost structures and to open low cost air travel to many people. Alternatively, failed technology implementations can drive away customers.

- The impacts of the technology itself:
  - Enable the development of a new product or service generated by technology
  - Have a disruptive impact on an industry (eg digital music downloads threaten to overturn the traditional music industry business model)
  - Enable increase in productivity
  - Engender additional risks

3.5 Financial resources

The business will need finance for any expansion. One aspect of a resource audit would be to simply look at the different sources of finance available to the firm – internal generation, loans, equity, credit etc. However, it should be noted that each will come with strings attached such as ceding control to other stakeholders, unavoidable interest payments in the future, the need to keep the investment markets informed. Management may prefer to invest from retained profits as there is not the management time (or scrutiny) involved in getting outside parties to invest more.

3.6 The need for integration

Resources considered on their own are inert. **Resources are of no value unless they are organised into systems**, and so a resource audit should go on to consider how well or how badly resources have been utilised, and whether the organisation's systems are **effective** and **efficient**.

Resource	Utilisation
Technical resources	For example, processes for new product development, ability to serve customers efficiently.
Managerial skills	An effective management is a key organisation resource in planning activities, controlling the organisation and motivating staff.
Organisation	Organisation structure is critical. For example product or brand divisionalisation or brand management should facilitate communication and decision-making, at the level of the brand.
Information and knowledge systems	These have a strategic role.

The organisation and transformation of resources to create value is covered in more detail in section 5, which looks at value chain analysis.

3.7 The 9Ms checklist of resources

The **9Ms model**, introduced in the Business & Finance paper, is another way of summarising the resources and sources of competences to be evaluated: **Machinery, Make-up, Management, Management information, Markets, Material, Men and women, Methods and Money.**

3.8 Limiting factors

Definition

Limiting factor: A factor which at any time, or over a period, may limit the activity of an entity, often occurring where there is shortage or difficulty of availability.

In the short term a business must make the best use of the resources available to it.

In the long-term, the company may wish to:

- Reduce the shortfall by obtaining more of the resource

- Economise on use by reconsidering the activities consuming the resource, eg redesign a product to use less machine time

Worked example: Easing limiting factors in banks

Banks have shifted their business from reliance on providing accounts for money transmission and loans to a wider portfolio of products including pensions, home loans, credit cards, and insurances. This presented problems because the floor space of banks is limited, as are staff numbers and staff accommodation. The banks responded to these limiting factors by:

- Increasing the number of Automated Teller Machines (ATMs) which dispense cash and account balances but also can be used to make deposits and pay bills.

- The provision of telephone and on-line banking services to reduce the volume of transactions taking place in the bank branches.

- Reducing the number of cashier places to make room for front-office cubicles housing financial advisers. The resulting queues encouraged customers to use the ATMs and online services.

- Recruitment of staff predominantly to sell financial service products, accompanied by use of distance learning materials to assist them in passing the requisite regulatory exams.

4 Benchmarking competences

Section overview

- Benchmarking compares the use of assets across the firm or across the industry and indicates where they might be used better or where they are already a source of superior performance.

Once a business has identified its CSFs and core competences, it must identify performance standards which need to be achieved to outperform rivals and achieve SCA. These standards are sometimes called key performance indicators (KPIs).

One way of setting KPIs is to use benchmarking. Benchmarking is defined by the Chartered Institute of Management Accountants (CIMA) as: 'The establishment, through data gathering, of targets and comparators, through whose use relative levels of performance (and particularly areas of underperformance) can be identified. By the adoption of identified best practices it is hoped that performance will improve.'

To ensure a balanced and comprehensive range of performance measures are set, the Balanced Scorecard can be used.

4.1 Purposes of benchmarking

Benchmarking encourages improvement and change in order to achieve strategic competitive advantage over competitors, or at least to reduce costs and streamline operations.

4.2 Bases for benchmarking

Internal benchmarking

- Historical comparison looks at performance over time to ascertain trends/significant changes, etc but the danger is that performance against competitors is ignored.

- Branch comparisons within the same organisation may help to identify best practice which can be implemented in all branches. Again, the danger is ignoring competitors.

Competitive benchmarking

This involves comparing performance with other firms in the same industry or sector. This may involve the use of league tables (eg schools, hospitals, universities). The problem with industry norm comparisons is that the whole domestic industry may be performing badly (so international comparisons are better) or the whole international industry is losing out to other industries (so a wider perspective is needed – see below).

Activity (or best in class) benchmarking

Comparisons are made with best practice in whatever industry can be found. British Airways improved its aircraft maintenance, refuelling, turnaround, etc. by studying Formula One motor-racing pit teams.

Generic benchmarking

Benchmarking against a conceptually similar process. Again, Formula One was used by car manufacturers to help reduce changeover times on production lines. (Return to the diagram in section 2.3 to see how resources and competences are related to SCA and CSFs.)

Interactive question 1: Car seats

[Difficulty level: Exam standard]

Y plc manufactures car seats for children. Y's home country, Z land, has extensive legislation on car safety for many years and child seats are compulsory. The company was formed 10 years ago by an entrepreneur who had previously worked as a technical consultant for an industrial foam company. Despite strong competition, Y plc has succeeded largely by careful marketing.

The car seats come in a range of sizes and there are a variety of options from fully integrated seats for very young babies to booster seats for older children. The company's main customer is an accessory manufacturer with a major presence in Y plc's home market. It buys the car seats from Y plc and sells them under its own brand as 'safety approved'. It advertises the car seats in accessory brochures and on its website. The company's second major customer is a large superstore in the home country which specialises in children's clothing and accessories such as prams and pushchairs. The remaining sales are to a varied mix of large and small mainly independent car accessory retailers.

The car seats have historically all been produced on a single site in the north of the home country. The Managing Director uses his connections to source the foam padding from several suppliers with a commitment to achieving the lowest price but complying with safety standards and expectations. Z land has sophisticated economy with efficient capital markets; JIT logistics are common in all forms of manufacturing.

The company is considering possible methods of expansion and is currently considering exports to neighbouring countries.

Requirements

(a) Explain how conditions in Z land could give Y plc a competitive advantage when it starts its export operations.

(b) The Managing Director of Y plc is constantly trying to improve the productivity and quality of his manufacturing operations and is considering a programme of benchmarking. Explain why a benchmarking programme would help Y plc and suggest how it might be carried out.

See **Answer** at the end of this chapter.

5 Transforming resources: the value chain

Section overview

*   Porter's value chain encourages management to perceive of the business as a sequence of activities that add value to inputs in order that the final good or service shall command a profitable price on the market.

*   The crucial activities that sustain competitive advantage are called cost drivers and value drivers.

*   Competitive advantage can be created and sustained by linkages in the value chain which help to co-ordinate and optimise activities.

*   Extending the value chain to an underlying value system of suppliers, distributors and customers makes it hard for competitors to replicate.

5.1 The value chain

Definition

Value chain: the sequence of business activities by which value is added to the products or services produced by an entity.

In overview, value chain analysis sees the firm as an input/output device.

The value chain consists of the organisation's resources, activities and processes that link the business together, and the profit margin. Together these create the total value of output produced by the business, quantified by the price paid by the customer.

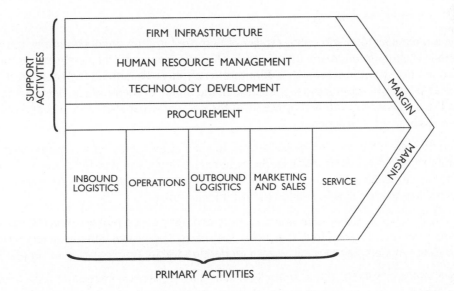

The **margin** is the excess the customer is prepared to **pay** over the **cost** to the firm of obtaining the necessary resource inputs and of performing value-creating activities upon them before selling them to the customer.

5.2 Value chain activities

Primary activities relate to production, sales, marketing, delivery and service, in other words anything directly relating to the process of converting resource inputs into outputs.

Activity	Comment
Inbound logistics	Receiving, handling and storing inputs to the production system (ie warehousing, transport, stock control etc).
Operations	Convert resource inputs into a final product or service. Resource inputs are not only materials. 'People' are a 'resource', especially in service industries.
Outbound logistics	Storing the product and its distribution to customers: packaging, warehousing etc.
Marketing and sales	Informing customers about the product, persuading them to buy it, and enabling them to do so: advertising, promotion etc.
After sales service	Installing products, repairing them, upgrading them, providing spare parts, advice (eg helplines for software support).

Support activities provide purchased inputs, human resources, technology and infrastructural functions to support the primary activities. Each provides support to all stages in the primary activities. For instance procurement where at each stage items are acquired to aid the primary functions. At the inbound logistics stage it may well be raw materials, but at the production stage capital equipment will be acquired, and so on.

Activity	Comment
Procurement	Acquire the resource inputs to the primary activities (eg purchase of materials, subcomponents, equipment).
Technology development	Product design, improving processes and/or resource utilisation.
Human resource management	Recruiting, training, developing and rewarding people.
Management planning and firm infrastructure	Planning, finance, and quality control: these are crucially important to an organisation's strategic capability in all primary activities.

Worked example: Maple plc

Maple plc is a manufacturer and online retailer of bespoke furniture designed entirely to the consumers specification. The furniture is made using high quality materials and skilled craftsmen to produce exquisite one-off items of furniture. Their furniture is considered a high added-value product that sells at a high price. Significant advertising supports the brand image of the product. Every element of the supply to the customer is controlled by Maple as the company manufactures, sells and delivers the furniture directly to the consumer.

An outstanding level of after-sales service is also provided as each piece of furniture is sold with a 10-year guarantee, two years interest free credit, optional treatments to prevent stains or damage and optional furniture cleaning services. Customer satisfaction is a key value of the company and a strict approach is taken to discipline in relation to customer complaints.

The staff are all either skilled or semi-skilled and the company runs a highly respected training programme to ensure they continue to develop their skills. The production machinery has recently been upgraded to the highest standard following a tendering exercise from equipment suppliers.

Inventory is well controlled and the strong links with the suppliers via integrated systems allows the correct materials to be automatically ordered when an order from a customer is confirmed. Strong IT systems also support the finance and marketing functions of Maple.

The company operates online, with no physical presence, which allows it to offer a wide range of choice to the customer allowing them to select different elements and 'build' their furniture from scratch. Once

ICAEW

complete, delivery is made using their own vans and the furniture is carefully installed by experienced staff.

CHAPTER

6

Requirements

Draw the value chain for Maple plc

Firm Infrastructure	Profit-orientated culture, tight financial control				
Technology Development	IT ordering systems, inventory control, payables management		Delivery IT systems		IT credit arrangement systems
Human Resource Management	Training HO supply staff generally and in IT systems	Manufacturing skills training, working practices	Delivery IT systems training	Discipline relating to customer issues	Training of delivery/ Installation staff
Procurement	Managing supplier relationships, payables management	Tendering system for new equipment, significant financing support		Marketing department	Financing and administration of customer credit facilities
Primary activities	Optimal delivery, sourcing high quality materials	Latest equipment, prime site factory, skilled labour	Prime sites for shops, delivery to customers	Installation for customers, advertising	Optional cleaning service, 10-year guarantee
	Inbound Logistics	Operations	Outbound Logistics	Marketing and Sales	Service

MARGIN
MARGIN

5.3 Cost and value drivers

Cost drivers

Using the value chain as a basic analysis tool, it is possible to look at each of the value activities and identify the major influences on the costs incurred. These structural factors which influence cost are the cost drivers. For example supermarkets regard the diversity of products (food, clothes, spirits, audio, etc) stocked as cost drivers because for each additional product line stocked the supermarket incurs the costs of logistics, stocking, stacking, programming electronic point of sale systems (EPOS), product training and promotion costs.

The factors which influence the cost of a given activity may vary, even between competitors in the same industry. An understanding of cost behaviour will allow a firm to assess the possibilities of adopting a least cost competitive stance.

Value drivers

Unlike cost drivers, the potential sources of value are likely to be many and varied. An understanding of the value drivers for a particular key value activity is essential for a firm trying to differentiate itself from its competitors.

For example, if competitive advantage centres on the durability of a product, then this can be supported by the sourcing of components, product design and maintenance services offered (the key value activities). In turn the value drivers for these support activities might be supplier vetting and approval procedures, the use of freelance designers and in-house after-sales service teams.

5.4 Linkages

One of the key aspects of VCA is that it recognises that the firm's resources are not a random collection but are organised in such a way that the firm's products or services are valued by its customers.

ICAEW

Strategic capability   131

Activities in the value chain affect one another. Linkages connect the activities in the value chain. They have two roles.

*   They **optimise activities** by enabling trade offs. For example, more costly product design or better quality production might reduce the need for after sales service.

*   Linkages reflect the need to **co-ordinate** activities. For example, Just In Time (JIT) requires smooth functioning of operations, outbound logistics and service activities such as installation.

These linkages are often unrecognised, especially if there is a rigid functional structure. A value chain analysis can help draw them to management's attention and so improve business performance. Eg Internet technologies can reduce production times and costs by improving information flows as a way of integrating value chain activities, eg by making procurement more efficient or sharing demand information with suppliers.

5.5   The value system

A firm's value chain is connected to what Porter calls a **value system**, ie activities that add value that extend beyond the organisation's **boundaries**.

For example, when a restaurant serves a meal, the quality of the ingredients – although the cook chooses them – is partly determined by the grower. The grower has added value, and the grower's success in growing produce of good quality is as important to the customer's ultimate satisfaction as the skills of the chef.

5.6   The value chain and competitive advantage

Competitive advantage can be **sustained by linkages** in the value chain and also in the wider **value system** of suppliers, distributors and customers. The planning of these linkages can provide the basis for cost advantages or become the basis on which the firm's products are differentiated from those of competitors. **Competitors can often replicate parts of a value chain but it is more difficult to copy linkages**. As businesses outsource more and more activities, the links in the value system become more important. Electronic communications enhance the ability of businesses to outsource.

Here are some examples of how companies – in practice – aim to differentiate themselves. They may not have **consciously** used the value chain but you can see how thinking about various activities of a business can help solve a strategic problem: in this case, commoditisation.

Worked example: Escaping commoditisation

Commoditisation is what many manufacturers seek to avoid: history is full of examples of one-time world-beating products – such as rolling bearings, chemicals and memory chips – that have been copied and have lost their distinctiveness and price advantages. Commoditisation basically results in **price competition** as **products** and **companies** are identical.

Not every firm can pursue 'cost leadership' and many firms seek to add value by escaping from the commodity trap and pursuing differentiation. Here are some examples.

- **Choose the value system**: 'Focus on a niche' is the strategy employed by many of Germany's engineering companies. By selling their products into a small market across the world, they gain the economies of scale and expertise to deter new entrants. They are part of a value system, but have chosen their customers very carefully.

- **Set the standards** which others must adhere to, such as Intel for PC chips. It does, however, suggest the need for **overwhelming competence** in the **technology and marketing areas of the value chain**.

- **Differentiate** commodity products by branding; again this is partly a matter of **customer perception** (an aspect of sales and marketing).

- **Control the process**: Some manufacturers dominate not a product but an operations process that creates a 'cluster' of product opportunities. 'Vacuumschmelze', a German company, makes products for industries including electronics, cars, electricity distribution and retailing. The German company's expertise starts with the techniques it uses to melt and form tiny components made from exotic metals including nickel, cobalt, neodymium and samarium, as well as non-metals such as silicon and boron.

- **Add services**: 'Heidelberger Druckmaschinen', the world's leading maker of printing presses, has set up 'print academies' in nine cities around the world to organise courses on printing techniques for customers and potential customers. This is clearly an example of **after-sales service** being used to build customer relationships.

5.7 Use in strategic planning

The principal use of the value chain is to assist in understanding the business and its strengths and weaknesses, as a form of position analysis. However, the value chain can be used specifically to:

- Identify strategically significant activities (the value activities) as an aid to targeting capital investment

- Compare with the value chains of competitors, to identify sources of differentiation

- Identify opportunities for synergy between the firm and a potential acquisition, for example opportunities to transfer skills or share activities

The value system highlights the relationship between a firm and its customers and suppliers.

- This will assist managers in identifying competitive forces in the system, and targeting potential vertical integration prospects.

- Management of these wider linkages can make it more difficult for competitors to replicate the organisation's value chain and hence contributes to sustainable competitive advantage.

Interactive question 2: Hairdressers [Difficulty level: Exam standard]

X Ltd is a chain of hairdressers with fourteen sites operating in the business districts of the capital and three other major cities. It has a very simple philosophy – quality haircuts for women who are short of time. It operates a no appointment, drop-in system. Customers take a ticket on arrival and wait in a large comfortable seating area until their numbers are called. All staff are multi-skilled and there are no specialists. The company aims to keep waiting times below fifteen minutes.

The salons offer a wide range of services from very simple cuts to more complex styles and treatments. In 50% of their stores X Ltd also offers beauty treatments, such as facials, in a separate salon on site. The company's main publicity comes from personal recommendation by satisfied customers, but they also occasionally advertise in high quality women's magazines.

After a recent period of expansion, the management team of X Ltd feel that their business model is not being applied consistently throughout the organisation and they have decided improvements and adjustments need to be made. However, none of the management team knows how to relate their philosophy to their operations to the best effect.

Requirements

(a) Using the concept of the value chain, explain how X Ltd can adopt the quality and speed approach throughout its activities.

(b) What are the benefits and problems of value chain analysis for a company such as X Ltd?

See **Answer** at the end of this chapter.

6 Outsourcing value activities

Section overview

- Outsourcing is the use of an external supplier as a source of components, products or services previously provided in-house.

- The practice of **outsourcing** may be used to strengthen an organisation's value chain.

Definition

Outsourcing: The use of external suppliers as a source of finished products, components or services previously provided in-house.

Research by PricewaterhouseCoopers (a major provider of outsourced services) has found that when most business processes are stripped down to their basics, about 70% of business processes are common to all firms. This suggests that they could be outsourced without loss of competitive advantage. With the help of technology and telecommunications it is now possible for **one service provider** to devise a common process to deal with **many different local processes in a single location**.

In addition to cost considerations, management may take the view that a chain is only as strong as its weakest link and therefore supply chains can be strengthened by outsourcing weak links to more competent providers.

Interactive question 3: Outsourcing and core competences   [Difficulty level: Easy]

Should a core competence ever be outsourced?

See **Answer** at the end of this chapter.

The issues to be considered in deciding **whether to outsource** include:

- The firm's **competence** in carrying out the activity itself. Low competence implies high cost and risk of poor performance.

- Whether **risk** can be managed better by outsourcing, eg shift legal liability to the provider and possibly also levy charges for breakdowns in performance that will mitigate losses.

- Whether the activity can be **assured and controlled** by the framework of a contract and performance measures, eg outsourcing payroll can normally be done relatively easily but systems development is more open-ended.

- Whether **organisational learning and intellectual property** is being transferred. The in-house operation may be a source of significant learning leading to product and process improvement. This is one reason that in the early stages of the international production life cycle (Chapter 4) firms keep manufacturing in-house rather than outsource to cheaper contract manufacturers.

The issues to consider in deciding **whom to outsource to** include:

- The **track record** of the provider and its experience of similar partnerships

- The **quality of relationship** on offer, eg will they place staff at your premises, hold regular meetings, provide open-book accounts?

- The **strategic goals** of the provider, eg is this their core business, will they operate globally alongside the firm?

- The **economic cost** of using them (including whether they will take staff over and pay for transferred assets)

- Their **financial stability**

Worked example: The London Fire Brigade

In March 2012 the London Fire Brigade (LFB) – the largest fire service in the UK – announced its controversial decision to outsource its 999 control centre to outsourcing giant Capita:

'The deal will see Capita run the call centre on behalf of the fire brigade and also supply the new 999 control system. Existing staff including 999 control officers and back office employees will be transferred to Capita and it is expected that the new systems will go live later in 2012.'

According to the LFB this will save £5m over the 10 year life of the contract and will allow the service to focus on its core business of putting out fires and saving lives.

Other fire brigades in the UK, also under pressure to make savings, are said to be monitoring the LFB initiative to consider whether a similar approach could be taken in their areas.

However, critics have argued that the moves to 'privatise' the handling of the fire service's 999 calls will put lives at risk based on a concern that private companies winning such contracts would not be held accountable for mistakes.

Interactive question 4: Outsourcing R&D   [Difficulty level: Easy]

Give two advantages and two disadvantages of a computer software company outsourcing its research and development.

See **Answer** at the end of this chapter.

7   Supply chain management

Section overview

- Supply chain management (SCM) is the management process, often assisted at the operational level by high power IT applications, of synchronising the networks in the service of the final customer.

7.1   What is supply chain management?

Definition

Supply chain management (SCM): The management of all supply activities from the suppliers to a business through to delivery to customers.

This may also be called **demand chain management** (reflecting the idea that the customers' requirements and downstream orders should drive activity) or **end-to-end business** (e2e). In essence it refers to managing the value system.

The main themes in SCM are:

- **Responsiveness** – the ability to supply customers quickly. This has led to the development of Just In Time (JIT) systems to keep raw materials acquisition, production and distribution as flexible as possible

- **Reliability** – the ability to supply customers reliably

- **Relationships** – the use of single sourcing and long-term contracts better to integrate the buyer and supplier

Example: Tesco information exchange

Tesco Information Exchange (TIE) uses information technology to improve the reliability of its supply chain. Suppliers receive information on actual store demand, depot inventories, weekly sales forecasts, as well as daily point of sale information, to help forecast demand.

7.2 Technology and SCM

Technology is vital to SCM, given the vast flow of information between suppliers, customer and intermediaries.

Technology applications which have facilitated SCM include:

- Email

- Web-based ordering and tracking. This involves outsiders seeing some management information on an *extranet*

- Electronic data interchange (EDI) of invoices and payments, ordering and sharing of inventory information

- Satellite systems able to track positions of trucks

- Radio data tags fixed to pallets or boxes of valuable items to enable them to be located in the supply chain (including within a warehouse)

This has led to:

- Reductions in costs

- Better outsourcing opportunities

- Increased product and service innovation

- Mass-customisation of products: ie customised products made by mass production methods, eg Dell computers, superior car marques

7.3 Supply chain networks

Supply chain management involves optimising the activities of companies working together to produce goods and services. It can involve the following:

- Closer **partnership** relationships with a **reduced number of suppliers.**

- **Reduction in customers served**: For the sake of focus, companies might concentrate resources on customers of high potential value.

- **Price and stock co-ordination**: Firms co-ordinate their price and stock policies to avoid problems and bottlenecks caused by short-term surges in demand, such as promotions.

- **Linked computer systems**: Electronic data interchange and use of intranets saves on paperwork and warehousing expense.

- **Early supplier involvement** in product development and component design.

- **Logistics design**: Hewlett-Packard restructured its distribution system by enabling certain product components to be added at the distribution warehouse rather than at the central factory, for example user-manuals which are specific to the market (ie user manuals in French would be added at the French distribution centre).

- **Joint problem solving** among supply chain partners.

- **Supplier representative on site**.

The aim is to co-ordinate the whole chain, from raw material suppliers to end customers. The chain should be considered as a **network** rather than a **pipeline** – a network of vendors support a network of customers, with third parties such as transport firms helping to link the companies.

8 Networks, relationships and architecture

Section overview

- Network analysis recognises that businesses are frequently webs of networks between internal departments and also with outside contractors, customers, and suppliers.

- This gives rise to the importance of understanding the relationships between the partners and the value of **relational contracts** based on trust and commitment to replace **transactional contracts** in which each side tries to get the greatest gain for itself.

- The virtual firm is introduced and a modern organisational structure which replaces vertically integrated businesses with a high reliance on networks.

8.1 What do we mean by architecture?

The concept of the **value system** suggests a variety of interrelationships between different businesses. We shall now explore the nature of some of these relationships.

Definition

Architecture: the network of relational **contracts**, within or around, the firm.

A **relational contract** contains parties doing business with each other in a long term relationship. Its provisions are only partly specified but it is enforced not by legal process but by the needs the parties have to go on doing business with each other (as opposed to a **spot contract** which is a one-off transaction).

These **relational contracts** may have a **legal basis**, but also include a **pattern of expectations** that the parties have of each other.

Firms may establish these relationships in two ways, internally and externally.

Internal networks ...with and among their employees (internal architecture)	Organisation structure and culture; job descriptions and work patterns to encourage development; employment contracts (eg employer commitment vs 'short term hire'); remuneration structure to encourage 'loyalty', 'creativity' and a willingness to satisfy individual preferences for the collective's benefit.
External networks ...with their suppliers or customers (external architecture) among firms engaged in related activities (Kay, 1993)	Relationships with suppliers – eg long-term supply contracts, detailed design specifications – firms share knowledge and establish fast response times on the basis of relational contracts. Networks are **groups** of firms making relational contracts with each other, who need to do business together in the long term, and who arguably depend on a common skills base.

The type of network relationship can range from the **collaborative** (founded **on commitment and trust**) to mainly **transactional** (just a buy-sell relationship). A **collaborative** network involves a great deal of co-operation, which may be enshrined in joint venture agreements. In a **transactional relationship**, there is no commitment to the long term.

Drivers of collaboration strategies that result in network arrangements can be characterised as follows:

- **Blurring of market boundaries**: Eg convergence of telecommunications and computing. This increases the complexity of technologies.

- **Escalating customer diversity**: Customers are becoming more demanding. In global markets, customers are more diverse almost by definition.

- **Skills and resource gaps**: Firms need to collaborate in technologically demanding markets.

Definition

Asset specificity: Where investments are made to support the relationship which have the effect of locking parties into a relationship to some degree.

An example is the investment by the Anglo-French company Eurotunnel in an undersea rail link that locks Eurotunnel into partnerships with the rail operators using it from either end, (ie Eurostar and SNCF). Both sides required long-term contracts before they would make the commitments necessary.

If a firm makes a **relationship-specific investment,** this implies that it would not make sense to make the investment **outside** the business relationship (eg if the component was so specialised no-one else would buy it).

8.2 Types of external network

The **relationship** between firms in a network can be close or distant, and we can model them as follows.

Distant   Outsourcing – purchase of goods/services

Partnership – co-ordinated/integrated activities

Alliance – joint ventures: shared ownership

Ownership – for example, vertical integration

Definitions

Alliance: An agreement between firms to share a commercial opportunity characterised by each member of the alliance retaining autonomy and pursuing its commercial interests.

Partnership: Joint participation in the serving of a market or project characterised by the close interrelationship of operations, exchange of staff and mutual trust and commitment to working with the other

In many industries, collaborative ventures and strategic alliances are becoming increasingly common. They can be very complex.

Worked example: Rail networks

In 1994 the UK government broke up and sold the national railways provider, British Rail, to private investors. To avoid the possibility of private monopolies exploiting the customer it was sold off in pieces as different companies. On the day following privatisation a typical passenger's journey would have involved the following networks:

- The car park they parked in was operated by a private firm under a license agreement from the firm owning the railway station.

- The station was operated either by Railtrack, the company set up to run infrastructure, or by the rail operator with the greatest use of the station. In the latter case the other rail operators would lease 'slots' at the station for their trains to stop there.

- The platform information on train arrivals was provided by Railtrack because it is based on the signalling systems they provide.

- The timetables of the rail operators were co-ordinated by Railtrack who also operated a telephone National Rail Enquiries service.

- The ticket purchased was sold by the station operator but if there was 'through-ticketing' across rail operators there would be recharges on to another.

- The train was operated by the rail operator.

- The rolling stock was owned by a separate leasing company.

- Cleaning, catering, track maintenance etc were largely contracted out by the rail operators and by Railtrack to private firms.

The success of this network approach has been questioned in the years since it was created.

Following a series of high profile train crashes, the privately owned Railtrack collapsed in 2002. The rail infrastructure was then taken over by Network Rail, a government-backed company.

In April 2012 Network Rail announced the launch of an alliance with South West Trains which would form a joint management team for the franchise which would have responsibility for both the trains and the track of routes out of London Waterloo. This was the biggest step towards integrated running of track and trains since the roles were split when British Rail was privatised and six, less extensive but similar, alliances are expected to follow. These changes follow a wide-ranging review of UK rail which found the system to be much more costly to run than those in other European countries.

As can be seen from the rail example above there are many types of organisational forms that can be developed. Networks display **horizontal** (eg joint ventures) and **vertical** (supply chain) linkages.

8.3 Choosing alliance partners

Firms enter long-term **strategic alliances** with others for a variety of reasons.

- They share development costs of a particular technology.

- The regulatory environment prohibits take-overs eg most major airlines are in strategic alliances because in most countries there are limits to the level of control an 'outsider' can have over an airline.

- Complementary markets or technology.

Strategic alliances only go so far, as there may be disputes over control of strategic assets.

Choosing alliance partners

The following factors should be considered in choosing alliance partners.

Drivers	What benefits are offered by collaboration?
Partners	Which partners should be chosen?
Facilitators	Does the external environment favour a partnership? Relevant factors here would include the availability of suitable providers, legal environment that does not outlaw collaboration as anti-competitive, and high investment costs involved in establishing provision that could not be borne by a single user of the service.
Components	Activities and processes required by the network. What will the alliance partner contribute?
Effectiveness	Does the previous history of alliances generate good results? Is the alliance just a temporary blip? For example, in the airline industry, there are many strategic alliances, but these arise, in part, because there are legal barriers to cross-border ownership.
Market-orientation	Alliance partners are harder to control and may not have the same commitment to the end-user.

Alliances have limitations

1. **Core competence**: Each organisation should be able to focus on its core competence. Alliances do not enable it to create new competences.

2. **Strategic priorities**: If a key aspect of strategic delivery is handed over to a partner, the firm loses flexibility. A core competence may not be enough to provide a comprehensive customer benefit.

8.4 Networks and global business

There are some distinct forms of global business network.

Keiretsu and chaebol

These are business networks common in Japan and Korea, whereby groups of firms are linked in a number of different ways.

- A general trading company exists at the centre.
- A central bank circulates finance from one activity of the network to another.
- Many of them have received favourable treatment from the state.
- There are cross shareholdings between companies.
- They depend on personal relationships and agreements: high trust.

In both countries, such firms have made high investments and typically result in conglomerate diversification. This business model has come under attack, as a number of chaebol have collapsed recently.

Family networks

Networks based on family structures are common in businesses run by overseas Chinese according to Dicken (*Global Shift*). The family – a relatively small group of insiders – is key to decision making, and operates on the following principles.

- The purposes of the firm is 'the long-term interest on family prosperity'.
- Risks must be hedged to protect family assets.
- Key decision makers exist in an inner circle.
- Such firms do not trust non-family members.
- Personal obligations cement and reinforce non-contractual business relationships.

The network is exclusive, but family loyalties mean effective business co-ordination in many countries.

Networks and globalisation

Networks and relationships on any number of levels may be suitable for global businesses. When these are linked to the type of geographic cluster identified in Chapter 4 there is the potential for considerable complexity.

8.5 The virtual firm

An extreme example of networking is the so-called **virtual firm**. It is created out of **a network of alliances and subcontracting arrangements**. It is as if most of the activities in a particular **value chain** are conducted by different firms, even though the process is loosely co-ordinated.

9 The product-service portfolio

Section overview

- Firms with multiple products (eg consumer goods firms like Heinz) or multiple business units (eg GE) are said to be managing a portfolio of businesses in the same way as a fund manager might manage a portfolio of stocks and shares.

- The Boston Consulting Group matrix (BCG matrix) is a technique to assist management to visualise their portfolio and to manage it to improve the financial performance of the corporation as a whole.

- The GE Business Screen is an alternative to the BCG matrix, which takes a broader view of the factors making a business unit competitively strong and its industry financially attractive.

- Treating businesses as investment portfolios was popular in USA and Europe in the 1960s and 1970s but has declined in favour since, with the search for core competences and core businesses. This has led to a re-evaluation of the concept of portfolio analysis.

9.1 The need for a mix of products and services

Many businesses sell more than one type of product or service. For example:

- Accounting firms sell audit services, tax advisory services, accounting services and so on

- Consumer goods companies such as Procter and Gamble sell a mix of products such as soap powder, children's nappies, cosmetics, drinks, dental hygiene products and shaving products (amongst many others)

These are sold in different markets because of technological and social change, the influence of competition, the demands of shareholders that their investments grow and so on.

The product life cycle and BCG models (to be discussed shortly) can help assess the balance of a product portfolio.

Worked example: Apple and portfolio management

American technology giant Apple, maker of the iPhone and iPad actively manages its product portfolio in order to keep ahead of the competition. In March 2014 a report in the *Wall Street Journal* highlighted that the company had taken to hiring engineers from competing technology companies, including HTC. Apple's recruitment drive has been largely driven by the need to produce new products faster in response to growing demand for the latest iPhone and iPad devices. The lifecycle of many of Apple's products has reduced in recent years as competitors such as Samsung have been increasing the speed at which it develops its own range of mobile devices. To date, Apple has taken to releasing a new iPhone mobile phone nearly every year to replace older models which are nearing the end of their lifecycle.

9.2 Product life cycle (PLC) revisited

The concept of a life cycle for an industry or product was explored in Chapter 5, along with the strategic implications for each stage of the cycle.

Many businesses will not wish to risk having only a single product (or group of closely related products) or all their products at the same stage of development as they may all decline together.

The business should seek to maintain a balanced portfolio of products with variety to protect against downturns in the fortunes of individual products and to have products at different stages of development. Thus a business needs:

- A mix of yesterday's products, today's products and the products of tomorrow
- A range of products with different length cycles
- Lots of products in development/introductory stage
- Lots of products in maturity to support others

In the strategic analysis process, a firm should assess:

- The stage of life cycle that any particular product has reached

- Each product's remaining life (how long it will continue to contribute to the portfolio)

- How urgent is the need to develop and innovate new and improved products

- If the life can be extended or the balance of the portfolio improved by targeting other markets? Different markets may be at different stages in the life cycle, so a company can increase the balance of its portfolio by developing overseas markets. Eg the market for luxury cars is mature in the USA and Europe but growing in India and China.

9.3 Boston Consulting Group matrix

9.3.1 The basics

This matrix was developed by the Boston Consulting Group (BCG) in 1968.

BCG analysis can be applied to:

- **Individual products**
- **Whole strategic business units (SBUs)** and business streams

A company analyses its products or SBUs along two dimensions:

This gives the following matrix:

Relative market share

	High	Low
High	STAR	PROBLEM CHILD/QUESTION MARK ?
Low	CASH COW £	DOG

% rate of market growth

The BCG matrix differs from the product life cycle in that it takes account of external market factors, such as growth rate and share.

- Just as a firm might have a portfolio of products at different stages of the life cycle, it can have a portfolio of different products on the matrix.

- The objective (again) is for the company to have a balanced portfolio.

9.3.2 Boston classification of quadrants

- **Stars**

    Stars are products with a high share of a high growth market. In the short term, these require capital expenditure in excess of the cash they generate in order to maintain their market position, but promise high returns in the future.

    – Their market share is big enough to exploit opportunities but high growth rates will attract newcomers/competition.

    – Therefore cash must be reinvested heavily to hold their existing position and build upon it.

    – Overall moderate net cash flow.

- **Cash cows**

    In due course, stars will become cash cows, with a high share of a low-growth market. Cash cows need very little capital expenditure and generate high levels of cash income. Cash cows generate high cash returns, which can be used to finance the stars.

    – Low growth so high market share is unlikely to be attacked by new firms wishing to enter the market.

    – Therefore little investment required to defend position but large enough market share to exploit available opportunities.

    – Large positive cash flow.

- **Question marks (or problem children)**

    Question marks are products in a high-growth market, but where they have a low market share. Do the products justify considerable capital expenditure in the hope of increasing their market share, or should they be allowed to die quietly as they are squeezed out of the expanding market by rival products? Because considerable expenditure would be needed to turn a question mark into a star by building up market share, question marks will usually be poor cash generators and show a negative cash flow.

    – Attractive markets but insufficient market share to exploit them.
    – Choice between getting out or getting big.

- If deciding to stay in the market, must invest heavily to gain market share.
- Large negative cash flow.

- **Dog products**

  Dogs are products with a low share of a low growth market. They may be ex-cash cows that have now fallen on hard times or question marks that never succeeded in gaining critical mass in a market. Dogs should be allowed to die, or should be killed off. Although they will show only a modest net cash outflow, or even a modest net cash inflow, they are 'cash traps' which tie up resources such as stocks and productive capacity and provide a poor return on investment, and not enough to achieve the organisation's target rate of return.

  - Unattractive markets without the market share to really benefit from what could be achieved if bigger.

  - The best strategy may be to exit the market ('divest').

  - Modest cash flow.

  Although the best strategy is often to exit the market, this is not the case for all dogs. They can be a valid part of a product portfolio, for example to complete a range, or to fill a niche market.

  There are also **infants** (ie products in an early stage of development), **war horses** (ie products that have been cash cows in the past, and are still making good sales and earning good profits even now) and even cash dogs, which are dogs still generating cash, and dodos, which have low shares of low growth markets and which are losing cash.

Notes

- Clearly if the company has four cash cows – good. However, if they are a small proportion of the company's total sales then it is not as impressive as it first appears.

- For individual products the objective is to move the product in an anticlockwise direction around the matrix to become a cash cow, ie

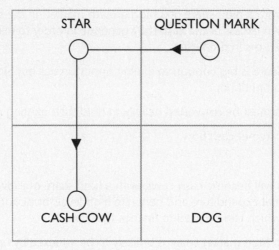

9.3.3 Plotting a BCG matrix

How are products plotted onto the matrix? For each of the company's products, calculate the following:

- Relative market share. A typical method is to use: $\dfrac{\text{Your sales}}{\text{Largest competitor sales}}$

- Percentage growth rate of the market. In excess of 10% growth is often regarded as high, but it will depend upon the type of market.

- Express the sales of each product as a percentage of the company's total sales. Each product is then represented by a circle – the area of which is proportional to the sales of that product.

Worked example: Plotting a BCG matrix

An industrial equipment company has five products with the following sales and market characteristics.

Company's product	Sales £m	£m sales Top 3 firms			Market growth rate %	Relative share
A	0.5	0.7	0.7	0.5*	15%	0.71
B	1.6	1.6	1.6*	1.0	18%	1.0
C	1.8	1.8*	1.2	1.0	7%	1.5
D	3.2	3.2*	0.8	0.7	4%	4.0
E	0.5	2.5	1.8	1.7	4%	0.2

* Company sales within the market

Relative share calculated as Company sales/Top firm sales or Company sales/Sales of next nearest competitor.

This information can then be plotted on to a matrix.

- The size of the circles indicate the contribution the product makes to overall turnover.
- The centre of circles indicates their position on the matrix:

Market share (relative to major competitor)

The evaluation and resulting strategic considerations for the company in the matrix above are:

- There are two cash cows, thus the company should be in a cash-positive state.

- New products will be required to follow on from A.

- A is doing well but needs to gain market share to move from position 3 in the market – continued funding is essential. Similar for B.

- C is a market leader in a maturing market – strategy of consolidation is required.

- D is the major product which dominates its market; cash funds should be generated from this product.

- E is very small. Is it profitable? Funding to maintain the position or selling off are appropriate strategies.

9.3.4 BCG matrix and PLC

The **product life cycle** concept can be added to a market share/market growth classification of products, as follows.

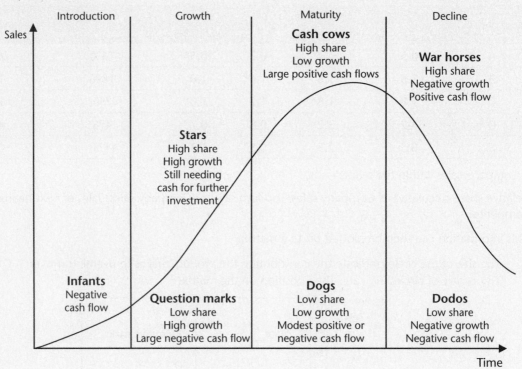

9.4 Shortcomings of the BCG matrix

BCG portfolio analysis is useful because it provides a framework for planners to consider and forecast potential market growth and to evaluate the competitive dimension through an evaluation of market share and the likely changes in cash flow. However, it should not be used uncritically, as follows.

- Factors besides market share and sales growth affect cash flow, eg amount of R&D and investment in new technologies.

- Many firms, anxious to present a good ROCE and EPS to investors, still use return on investment when assessing the attractiveness of a business opportunity, despite the opportunity it gives for accounting manipulation and the fact that it ignores the time value of money. Therefore question marks and stars can look like bad businesses.

- The model provides no real insight into how to compare one opportunity with another when considering which opportunity should be allocated investment resources, eg how does a star compare with a question mark?

- Rates of profit of some small businesses can be very high. Therefore in the right conditions a firm can profit from a low share of a low-growth market. (This point is made by Porter in his criticism of the BCG and he uses it to justify focus strategies to gain competitive advantage. See Chapter 7.)

- The model does not take risk into account, which is a crucial difference from the investment portfolio approach from which it takes its inspiration.

- The matrix focuses on known markets and known products. As a generation tool, it sits firmly in the rational planning model and also within the positioning approach to strategy.

- The model assumes industry and market can be defined for purposes of calculating share and growth. Chapter 5 has shown that this is difficult in practice. Ignoring substitute products can lead management to overestimate the attractiveness of a business unit for investment purposes.

- The model suffers from difficulties in forecasting growth (eg despite high historic growth B&Q and several rival home improvement firms suffered following the decision by television executives to end screening shows featuring home improvements and makeovers).

9.5 GE Matrix

As a result of some of these weaknesses in the BCG model, variations have evolved. **General Electric's Business Screen is a three by three matrix which** compares **market attractiveness (size, growth prospects, competition)** with **business strength (management skill, brand reputation, capacity) to identify appropriate management approaches for different SBUs.**

	Attractive	**Average**	**Unattractive**
Strong	Invest for growth	Invest selectively for growth	Develop for income
Average	Invest selectively and build	Develop selectively for income	Harvest or Divest
Weak	Develop selectively Build on strengths	Harvest	Divest

Business strength (vertical axis) — Market attractiveness (horizontal axis)

9.6 General criticisms of portfolio analysis

Portfolio analysis invites management to view their businesses as a collection of income generating assets which, combined, create a corporation with a financial performance that mixes risk and returns in a way that will appeal to shareholders.

This approach to corporate strategy reflects the prevailing wisdom in USA and Europe of the 1970s and 1980s and led to conglomerates and other multiple businesses. Many of these foundered in the 1990s in the face of more focused competition from Japanese firms, leading to demergers and a search for 'core businesses' (eg Ford Motor Company gave up on its electrical goods producing subsidiary Philco, Phillips withdrew from white goods subsidiary Whirlpool, numerous oil companies sold off shipping and retailing operations).

Drawbacks of portfolio planning approaches:

- Portfolio models are simple; they do not reflect the uncertainties of decision-making.

- BCG analysis, in particular, does not really take risk into account.

- They ignore opportunities for creative segmentation or identifying new niches.

- They assume a market is given rather than something that can be created and nurtured. After all, industries may be unattractive because customer needs have not been analysed sufficiently.

- They rely on identifiable products rather than services, or more nebulous relationships.

- They ignore the profit-generating capability of business relationships.

- Creating a corporation with the financial characteristics of a well-balanced portfolio does not increase the share price. This is because investors can diversify risk in how they construct their own portfolio.

- Recycling cash flows from cash cows to question marks ignores the alternative of paying out dividend and letting shareholders decide where to invest the money.

- Creation of portfolios may cause the business to move beyond its core competences and so lead to diminishing returns on investment through time.

Interactive question 5: Catterall Wentworth   [Difficulty level: Exam standard]

Catterall Wentworth is a large firm of accountants based in London with a number of regional offices. It is divided into four main areas: tax, audit and accounting, corporate finance and management consultancy. However in addition to the provision of these general services, additional specific services have been developed. A partners' meeting has been called to discuss the future strategy of the firm, the accountancy industry and the place of Catterall Wentworth within it.

Over the past ten years the nature of the accountancy industry has changed significantly. Profits are lower than they have been for many years and competition is fierce, especially amongst the larger firms. More is being asked of accountants, and their image has taken a battering following the demise of some important clients (such as Enron and Parmalat) in the US, the UK, Italy and Australia. There has been a knock-on benefit. Business has been growing fast in the field of corporate governance advice and products to assist firms manage the requirements of Sarbanes-Oxley.

Catterall Wentworth has responded by setting up an Assurance division within the Audit and Accounting Section. The division, offering specific advice on corporate governance and Sarbanes-Oxley has shown significant growth and there are plans to recruit more staff to expand it further, as the market for these services continues to develop.

Meanwhile, new accounting standards are being introduced by international accounting bodies. These demand far greater expertise from UK accountancy firms. Catterall Wentworth have earmarked a significant proportion of their training budget to IAS training courses and are beginning to see a payback as they have won a number of new clients recently specifically because of their IAS knowledge.

Margins on audit and taxation services are slim. The industry is growing increasingly concerned about auditor liability. Whilst auditors are hopeful that they should be able to negotiate proportionate liability with clients within the next few years, a number of firms are facing legal cases which could result in significant claims against them, and this situation looks set to continue for some time. Another concern is the Inland Revenue's strict attitude towards tax avoidance. The Inland Revenue has made plain that specific tax avoidance schemes that it has not vetted will result in the accountancy firms that sold the schemes being fined. Aggressive tax plans, of the sort Catterall Wentworth specialised in, are rarely receiving approval.

Another concern is the raising of the audit threshold. Until the end of 2003, any business with a revenue of £1m or more had to be audited. However, since 2012 the threshold for private limited companies has been revised. In order to be exempt from requiring an audit, companies must meet two of the following:

1.   Annual turnover of no more than £6.5m
2.   Assets worth no more than £3.26m
3.   50 or fewer employees on average throughout the year

For many accountancy firms including Catterall Wentworth, the loss of these small clients has had a significant impact on their business. In addition, the rules governing independence have made the provision of non-audit services to audit clients much more problematic which has further reduced the profitability of the audit side of the business.

Although consultancy is seen by some as the most profitable sector, the firm has seen their revenue rise by only a modest amount in the area of general consultancy. In an attempt to generate new business Catterall Wentworth have introduced a new product; tax efficient supply chain planning, which involves multi-disciplinary teams, from consultancy and tax, working together to help larger clients. As more UK companies source and sell across international boundaries, the demand for such services is predicted to grow. Catterall Wentworth are one of the first firms outside the Big Four to offer the service.

Catterall Wentworth's long-established corporate finance department is currently their most profitable area. The division advises clients looking to raise further funds. They have a number of listed clients and many more that may well look to list in the future. To support such firms they have just introduced a pre-list planning service which helps firms prepare for a listing up to eighteen months in advance. It is early days yet and they are not yet sure how many clients will take up the service.

Requirements

You are an outside consultant.

Using the information above, prepare a report for next week's partners' meeting which analyses the product portfolio of Catterall Wentworth using the BCG matrix. Your report should explain the logic behind your reasoning and conclude on the balance of the portfolio.

See **Answer** at the end of this chapter.

Summary and Self-test

Summary

Self-test

Answer the following questions.

1   A major UK chain of betting shops has decided to establish an offshore operation based on the Channel Island of Alderney. This is because such locations do not need to charge punters a tax levy. Bets would be placed by telephone, fax, e-mail or over the Internet.

Describe three key resources that would be required to offer such a service.   **(3 marks)**

2   What is internal benchmarking? Suggest two ways a chain of pubs could use internal benchmarking to improve performance.   **(3 marks)**

3   Rapid Fit UK (RFUK) is a highly profitable listed company specialising in fitting new tyres, brake pads, exhausts etc to cars and vans. It is now seeking to diversify and has decided to offer fixed price servicing on a while-you-wait basis. This would be pre-booked by motorists over the Internet. RFUK's managers believe that they can undercut franchised dealers by offering a quick, no frills service for routine servicing, but are worried about their fitters' ability to tackle complex repair jobs on a wide range of vehicles.

Evaluate the effect of the following four factors on RFUK's ability to deliver this strategy: financial resources, human resources, current services offered, and information systems.   **(4 marks)**

4   Explain what is meant by benchmarking and suggest why organisations might use it.   **(3 marks)**

5   What is a 'cash cow' in the Boston Consulting Group (BCG) matrix? Suggest two examples.   **(2 marks)**

6   Gaddes Ltd is the UK's largest manufacturer of digital radios. Sales for the year ended 31 January 20X4 were £42 million, with an estimate of £48 million for the following year in a market that is expanding by 12% a year. Gaddes Ltd's major competitor had sales of £36 million in the year ended 31 January 20X4.

Explain how Gaddes Ltd's radios would be characterised when applying the Boston Consulting Group (BCG) matrix. Describe how existing competitors are likely to react in this market.

          (4 marks)

7   **Barclays Bank plc**

Below are extracts taken from Barclays Bank Annual Report 2013.

The landscape for banks has fundamentally changed and will continue to evolve in the coming years. We believe these changes are not cyclical but represent a structural shift. Our Transform programme, launched in 2013, will reshape Barclays to generate sustainable returns and to meet the needs of all of our stakeholders.

Market and operating environment

Barclays is a global financial services provider with our home markets in UK, US, and South Africa, and distribution and operations in a further 47 countries. Banks are invariably exposed to the economies and markets in which they operate. This exposure ranges from mortgage lending (dependent on the ability of borrowers to repay and house price valuations) to corporate advisory (which may reflect business confidence in the economy).

Prior to the financial crisis, global growth was supportive with banks well-positioned to benefit from their exposure to the upward trajectory of the global economy. Global economic growth has faltered in recent years. This has prompted unprecedented monetary policies across central banks, for example quantitative easing and near zero interest rates. This policy response has, in turn, posed new challenges for banks such as compressed interest margins.

A further challenge to the banking industry, and indeed to Barclays, in recent years is one of poor conduct, damaging our reputation and causing a loss of trust amongst our customers, clients and stakeholders. We recognise the importance of rebuilding trust in Barclays as well as meeting, and bettering, the developing needs of our customers and clients.

Barclays' sustainable success will be assured by becoming the 'Go-To' bank for all of our stakeholders. If we understand their needs and priorities and ensure that these are at the heart of our decision-making, we will be able to build a bank which is lower-risk, more predictable and higher-performing.

UK retail banking strategy

UK the retail banking division provides a wide range of banking products and services delivered with excellent customer experience. We no longer incentivise our people on product sales but on customer service: our journey to 'Go-To' is focused on making customers lives easier.

We seek to add value to our clients through our end-to-end network, for example an individual retail customer in the UK is able to access current and savings account balances along with Barclaycard data all on the same mobile banking app. Pingit, our peer-to-peer payments service, is seamlessly integrated within our retail banking offering, a further example of this joined up approach to the way we do business.

'Your bank' campaign

As well as getting feedback and sense-checking our ideas, we have created a place where customers can share their ideas and suggestions for how Barclays can be better shaped around their needs and individual life stages, putting them at the heart of everything we do. In the first week we received over 370,000 interactions on the Your Bank site and 2,226 ideas. With all of the ideas that we receive, we are taking a 'you said, we did' approach and have made eight commitments to making real change for our customers.

1. We are undertaking a formal review of our overdraft charges in 2014, with a view to making them simpler and more transparent. We have already started pilots with the launch of text alerts in June to customers who had gone over their overdraft limit and into their personal reserve, which would mean they would traditionally incur a £22 charge. The alerts tell them they have a day's grace to add cleared funds and avoid the charge. In the first three months, over 65,000 customers avoided charges totalling over £1.4m, a response rate of 27 per cent. We are now looking at where else we can roll out text alerts as a next step. Yes it's a cost to us, but it's the right thing to do.

2. We have launched CloudIt through online and mobile banking as a result of customer feedback (CloudIt allows customers to store electronic versions of their bank statements and other important documents on a personal online account). Being able to access your secure documents whilst on the move will really make our customer's lives much easier.

3. Contactless payments have been very well received by customers, so we're now looking at alternative contactless methods of payments which we'll be testing with customers.

4. We're looking to pilot paying-in coin machines in our branches. Our customers told us they'd welcome something that can automatically count coins and credit their account.

5. We will extend our free Barclays Pingit app to the under 16's, subject to developing proper parental controls. Younger customers, being tech savvy, will benefit from the app allowing them to send and receive money simply using their mobile phone number.

6. We are going to allow our mobile banking customers to set up new payees on their mobiles. This will extend the app meaning that customers can really do much more on the move.

7. To further extend our services to a wider range of customers we've made our mobile banking app available on Windows platform and are planning to do the same for Pingit.

8. We have expanded our mobile banking services to include mortgage accounts, so customers can view their mortgage arrangements wherever they are.

A selection of movements in key performance measures 2012/2013:

	2013	2012
Number of customers	16.7m	15.8m
Number of branches	1,560	1,593
Number of employees	32,900	33,000
Operating income	4,176m	4,115m
Adjusted profit before tax	1,195m	1,225m

Source: Barclays Bank 2013 Annual Report

Requirement

You are a junior consultant working for the management consultancy division of a major UK accountancy practice.

Write a briefing note to your managing consultant analysing the competitive strategy being pursued by Barclays UK retail banking division . Include in your report a **value chain analysis** of the bank's operations. **(15 marks)**

8 **APCS plc**

APCS plc is a large international manufacturer of personal computers. Within Europe it sells four main types of PC – those aimed at the home market, those aimed at the commercial market, laptops and PC servers for networks.

After-sales service for the whole of Europe is provided by a call centre in Scotland. For example, a customer in Germany rings a number in Germany and the call is then automatically routed to a German speaker at the Scottish call centre. The customer pays for a local call and will be totally unaware that the call is being dealt with in another country. APCS plc pays the cost of the international call.

The organisation of the call centre is critical, with telephone operators speaking eleven languages. The technology must ensure that the call is routed to the appropriate operator. In addition there are three levels of call taken at the centre. The first level operators deal with routine questions. Second and third levels of operators exist to deal with questions that cannot be answered at a lower level.

The main costs of the call centre are telephone bills and salaries. An important financial measure is the cost per call, which varies from country to country. Non-financial measures are the following:

- Call drop-out rate, ie the percentage of customers who are put in a queue but hang up before reaching an operator

- Average duration of each call

The current focus is on improving these measures from month to month, rather than comparing with other call centres.

The management team is currently reviewing the performance appraisal system and have asked for your advice. In particular they would like some thoughts on benchmarking the call centres.

Requirements

As a member of the accounts department, draft a memorandum to the management team dealing with the following matters.

(a) An appraisal in terms of strengths and weaknesses of the current performance measures used.
(5 marks)

(b) What benchmarking is and how it is done. **(4 marks)**

(c) Whether benchmarking would be suitable for APCS plc. **(7 marks)**

(16 marks)

9 **Gizmo Computer Games Ltd**

Geoff Carter is the managing director of Gizmo Computer Games Ltd ('Gizmo'), a growing software house that specialises in writing computer games.

Recently the firm was visited by Peter Ng, a student on placement as part of his MBA course. An extract from his report is given below.

'I feel that Gizmo's main critical success factors (CSFs) are innovation, command of technology, bug rate and graphics skills and you should look to measure and control key performance indicators (KPIs) in these areas.'

Geoff is completely confused by the jargon in the report and has asked you to prepare a brief memorandum to explain what Peter is talking about before he talks to him on the telephone tomorrow.

Requirements

Write a memorandum to Geoff giving reasons why the CSFs highlighted might be important to Gizmo, and suggestions for a suitable KPI to measure each CSF. **(8 marks)**

10   Read the scenario of the **March 2011 Business Strategy** paper in the Question Bank entitled *MPW Ltd*. Draft answers for requirements (b) and (c) on supply chain efficiency and CSFs/performance measurement.

11   Go online at The Times 100 Business Case Studies and read the Portakabin case study 'Achieving growth through product development' at http://businesscasestudies.co.uk/portakabin/achieving-growth-through-product-development

Now, go back to the Learning objectives in the Introduction. If you are satisfied that you have achieved these objectives, please tick them off.

Answers to Interactive questions

Answer to Interactive question 1

(a) Porter identifies four elements of national competitive advantage that support the export efforts of successful firms.

These elements and how they can be applied to Y are explained below.

Factor conditions are a country's endowment of the inputs to production, such as human resources, physical resources, knowledge, capital and infrastructure. Porter distinguishes between basic and advanced factors. The latter are more important for sustained success, and include modern communication and investment in facilities and highly educated personnel. Z land appears well-endowed with these advanced factors, having sophisticated financial markets and industries using modern systems such as JIT.

Demand conditions in the home market have determined how Y has responded to customer needs. Careful marketing has made this response successful and Y has an enviable reputation at home for quality, innovation, reliability and customer focus that should transfer well to the world market. The success that has been achieved to date has meant that Y has the necessary economies of scale to be able to compete globally.

As the home market has shaped Y's priorities, the company would be well advised to use this experience and seek abroad those segments that have been successfully targeted in the domestic market. This will require an investment in market research, as the company must determine how well the products will be received abroad. This is vital, as there is little point in launching products if the customers do not want them or can see little difference from existing offerings towards which they may already feel very loyal.

The impact on the home market of more international activity must also be considered. Does Y have the resources to be able to support both markets, and continue to maintain its accustomed high standards?

The presence of **related and supporting industries** at home, which have to date supplied Y with the components it has needed for its successful products, will be important in launching those products internationally. The continued support of these suppliers will be vital, at least in the initial stages of international development. Y must assure itself that these suppliers have the resources to provide a higher level of support. Otherwise, international suppliers may need to be sought and this will demand closer and more complex supply chain management.

National firm strategy, structure and rivalry issues create distinctive business environments in different countries. For example, domestic rivalry is important because tough domestic rivals teach a firm about competitive success, and rivals for the home market have to try different strategic approaches.

Y has been successful against strong competition in the domestic market and this has provided good training for the international market, which may feature more, and larger, competitors than Y has been used to facing at home. However Y must ask itself whether its reputation for supplying reliable and good quality products will be enough to guarantee its success in a wider competitive market. It could be that the wider market does not value reliability and quality as highly as Y's domestic customers. This would wipe out its main differentiating factor.

(b) Benchmarking can be very useful for business, both in relation to internal processes and to wider management concerns.

Internally, the adoption of best practice should improve productivity; reduce waste and costs associated with quality failures; and contribute to increased customer satisfaction.

At the **operational** management level, benchmarking is useful if there is any tendency to complacency and it can improve awareness of the processes by which value is currently created and how they could be improved in the future.

At the **strategic** level, benchmarking can be an important contributor to awareness of competition in the changing task environment and how the company is responding to it, both practically and strategically.

There are **disadvantages** to benchmarking. A full programme can overload managers with demands for information, restrict their attention to the factors that are to be benchmarked and affect their motivation by seeming to reduce their role to copying others. It can also undermine competitive advantage by revealing trade secrets. Strategically, it can divert attention away from innovation and the future by focussing it on the **efficiency of current operations**. This is a particularly important point for Y Ltd, with its current move towards exporting: this will require a great deal of attention by managers at all levels.

If Y Ltd were to undertake a programme of benchmarking, firm commitment by the Managing Director would be essential to drive it along. It would then be necessary to identify the areas in which improvement was sought and to decide how such an improvement would be identified and measured. Since benchmarking is about **processes rather than results**, measures would have to be rather more detailed than the usual summary measures used in normal management reports.

It would then be necessary to **identify suitable benchmarking partners**. Some industries, such as printing in the UK, run sophisticated benchmarking programmes; Y Ltd may be able to join such a scheme. Alternatively, trade associations or chambers of commerce may be able to help. Y Ltd need, not, of course, benchmark against competitors, or even against other motor accessory manufacturers. Its distribution operation, for instance, might be compared with a similar operation in a completely different industry.

Once a scheme of measurement and comparison is in place, it is necessary to determine what **improvements** are possible and to implement them. It will be tempting for the Managing Director of Y Ltd to delegate this role to a single manager, but better results will be obtained if the responsibility for making and monitoring the necessary changes is embedded in the normal management structure. Success and failure in making and continuing the agreed improvements can then be monitored as part of the **normal performance review process**.

Answer to Interactive question 2

(a) The value chain is a model of how firms create value for their customers. The value chain describes a number of activities carried out in the firm.

Primary activities are directly related to the processes of production and sales.

Inbound logistics are those activities involved with receiving, handling and storing inputs to the production system.

Operations convert the resource input into the end product.

Outbound logistics relate to storage and distribution.

Marketing and sales inform customers about the product, and include advertising and promotion

After sales service

Support activities obtain purchased inputs, human resources, technology and infrastructure to support the primary activities

Competitive advantage is obtained by configuring the value chain in certain ways. X Ltd can use the value chain to ensure that their philosophy of quick, quality haircuts can be adopted and maintained throughout the business. The main areas that X Ltd needs to concentrate on are Human Resource Management, Procurement, Technology Development, Operations, Marketing and Sales.

Human Resource Management

An important way X Ltd generates value for its customers is by operating without appointments and with multi-skilled staff. This means that whatever a customer needs, she can expect to be attended to quickly and efficiently without having to plan ahead for an appointment.

The company therefore must ensure their staff have the capabilities to meet the objectives of quality and speed. It is clear that they need to be highly trained as they need to be able to work quickly and avoid making mistakes. They need to be multi-skilled so that each member of staff can achieve maximum utilisation and be in a position to deal with any customer and her needs. The company also needs to ensure that they have an adequate workforce of trained juniors to deal with washing hair, cleaning of the salon and general fetching and carrying. This will ensure that the stylists themselves are not wasting time when they could be generating income for the salon.

Technology development

There are many areas in this kind of business where technology can help to achieve the organisation's stated aims. The simple ticket waiting system might be developed to provide an indication of waiting time and an option to prefer a particular stylist, for example. The salons could also use modern technology to make the salon experience more appropriate for their target clientele. This could include computer terminals in the waiting area for busy clients to check email (assuming they do not have email capable devices such as Blackberry).

Operations

X Ltd should consider making the beauty salon business entirely separate from the hairdressing salon as the two businesses seem to offer a mixed message to clients – one of speed but also relaxation. Furthermore the company needs to analyse its current and potential market and determine whether they will require more complex services such as colouring as this kind of procedure would add to the time the stylist needs to spend with each client. They could consider offering a separate area for such services and having dedicated staff working in this area.

There is potentially a new market for X Ltd to explore by considering the people who are just too busy to leave the office for a haircut. They could target large office complexes and offer in-house hairdressing services at convenient times.

Marketing and sales

X Ltd has been fortunate in that its name has become well-known through personal recommendation. However, it would be unwise to reply on this simple recipe. A sophisticated business needs an appropriate marketing communications strategy. This may require the assistance of consultants to develop properly, but X Ltd should certainly consider some kind of targeted campaign, even if only run at a low level of intensity to ensure its services are known to potential customers. Careful advertising in local and even national newspapers might be appropriate, though it would be expensive. A high quality direct mail campaign to business addresses might be more appropriate.

(b) By performing a value chain analysis a company such as X Ltd is forced to look in detail at its activities and identify areas for improvement. This may never be achieved if the company is simply concentrating on external analysis as a source of new opportunities

Businesses need to focus on trying to achieve sustainable competitive advantage; by considering each activity of the business as a potential source of strength or a possible weakness, the company can ensure that maximises the value that it offers. This analysis can also help to identify core competences, which are particularly appropriate source of competitive advantage in the long term.

All companies should concentrate on achieving consistency throughout their operations. That is, if a particular target is set, such as quality or speed or value, then this should be applied to all the activities of the business to ensure that achievement in one area is not negated by failure in another. Examining the business in the light of the value chain is a method of ensuring that value created in one area is not destroyed in another. In the case of X Ltd there is, for example, an element of contradiction between the aim of targeting women who are short of time and the use of a queuing system rather than appointments.

A further aspect of the value chain that needs to be considered is the application of this concept to the entire value system and the linkages between that system. By considering these linkages, a company can achieve better relationships with its customers and suppliers and ensure partners are sought who hold similar values and conduct business in a similar manner ie are compatible.

The value chain also has some limitations in its application. Fairly obviously, it was based on a manufacturing model and it may be difficult to apply to businesses in the service sector such as X Ltd. Companies in this situation need to ensure they are comfortable with general principles of the exercise and not get too caught up in trying to make their business fit within a certain framework. Companies also need to ensure they don't focus on value chain analysis to the detriment of environmental analysis and a consideration of competitive forces.

Answer to Interactive question 3

(a) The firm may effectively be surrendering its source of competitive advantage.

(b) If all the knowledge needed to run a business is held 'outside' it, short-term profit improvements may be made at the (long-term) expense of the ability to innovate.

(c) A current competence may be less relevant in future, in which case outsourcing may be part of an exit strategy.

(d) Managers may disagree as to the business and processes they consider to be core.

Answer to Interactive question 4

Advantages of outsourcing R&D

(a) Potentially less expensive if R&D is used on an *ad hoc* basis
(b) Gain from outside expertise and competence
(c) Flexibility to cope with larger projects or to render cost base more variable
(d) Frees management up to focus on more important or strategic issues

Disadvantages of outsourcing R&D

(a) May be cheaper in-house if R&D is a perpetual and continuing activity
(b) Exposes firm to risk from poor quality or unreliable/unstable provider
(c) Loss of organisational learning
(d) Loss of control over intellectual property (IP). For example, who owns the developments?

Answer to Interactive question 5

Catterall Wentworth

To	Partnership Board
From	ANO Accountant
Date	Today
Subject	Product portfolio analysis for Catterall Wentworth

I have analysed the product portfolio of the firm using the BCG matrix. The matrix is designed to consider the products of the firm from two perspectives – how fast the market for such a product is growing, and what share of the market the firm currently enjoys. In the case of a service industry such as Catterall Wentworth the term product refers to the services they offer to clients.

The logic behind the use of the matrix is that to be successful it is necessary to have a significant market share. It is at that point that economies of scale become achievable and brand strength will become established. However, since all products have limited life spans a firm must also have newer products to take over as the older products decline.

Catterall Wentworth's products can be analysed as follows.

Question marks

These are products for which the market is growing but where the share of the firm is still limited. Although they have the potential to become profitable, services in this category are usually expensive to offer as the firm is not yet operating at full efficiency and share will need defending against other players.

Two of the services offered would fall into this category: tax efficient supply chain planning and prelist planning. Both are newly offered products and Catterall Wentworth do not yet have significant share. However whilst the former sounds very likely to become a star (see below) in the near future, the latter is very much an unknown and it may never get fully off the ground.

Stars

Products in this category are already doing well. Successful market share has been achieved and the long term future of the product seems likely. However the market is still growing and the risk of losing share to other entrants before achieving long term success still exists.

Both the Assurance division and the IAS advice services would be considered stars. In both areas Catterall Wentworth have recently won a number of clients which will have improved their share of the overall market. However the markets are still growing fast, offering real potential only if they can hold their share against their competitors.

Cash cows

Cash cow products are the real money earners. Market share is established and a slow down in the growth of the market should prevent many new players entering. It is the funds from these products that support the investment in the newer product areas.

Catterall Wentworth's corporate finance department is a cash cow. It is well established and profitable. General consultancy is probably also a cash cow. Modest increases in revenues are not unusual in slow growth markets. However if the income from consultancy has been following a downward trend then a new approach will be needed to prevent share being eroded.

Standard taxation services (such as provision of corporation tax returns) are not specifically mentioned in the above analysis. It may be reasonable to assume they are a cash cow, since margins are still being earned from them (albeit slim ones).

Dogs

Dog products are those with a low share of a market with little growth potential. They may be previously successful products that are coming towards the end of their lifecycle, or question marks that never did achieve share. They make little or no contribution to profits.

Aggressive tax planning is clearly a dog product. HM Revenue and Customs has effectively brought it to the end of its lifecycle by insisting on prior approval for tax planning schemes.

Using the BCG analysis, audit services would also be defined as dogs. The market for Catterall Wentworth's audit services is in decline as the smaller firms come within the audit exemption. As liability fears continue to abound in the industry it is seen as higher risk, and insurance premiums eat into profits. In addition, since audit clients cannot now be used as a 'way in' to sales of the higher margin non-audit services, the low returns from audits become more obvious.

Conclusions

Catterall Wentworth has on the face of it a balanced portfolio. It has services in all the key areas. However closer examination suggests a less optimistic picture.

It is the income from the cash cow products that supports the new investment. It is not clear from the information provided what proportion of the firm's turnover their cash cows make up. However general consultancy is only earning limited profits which puts pressure on the corporate finance department to earn enough to fund the whole business.

The star products IAS advice and the Assurance division will make them money in time. However spending on staff and training is probably matching any increase in revenue from them at the moment. In addition the problem children will need to be marketed and developed if they are to be successful and this too takes funds.

Dog products are often a drain on a firm's resources. Whilst the firm may well cease offering aggressive tax planning, if they continue to offer audit services, these may end up being provided at an effective loss.

Catterall Wentworth will need to make some difficult decisions if they are not to run out of the funds they need to support their current product portfolio.

Answers to Self-test

1.
- Staffing will be a major issue, since a small island will not have a large number of available and suitable staff, and relocation from the UK would be costly.

- Technology will also be important, given the variety of ways of placing bets. The company will have to invest heavily to ensure the systems work.

- Finance to acquire and equip suitable premises will be significant.

2.
- Internal benchmarking is the comparison of current results with other results recorded by the same organisation.

- A chain of pubs could compare the performance of individual pubs in the chain to identify best practice. Overall results could be compared year on year to monitor improvements.

3.
- Financial resources: as a profitable listed company RFUK should easily be able to afford what is really only an extension of its current service.

- Human resources: this is a key constraint because the current staff may lack the skills needed. A programme of recruitment and training will probably be required.

- Current services offered: this strategy seems like a sensible addition to the current service and is a logical fit – it is product development.

- Information systems: the service will be unpopular unless RFUK can rely on the Internet booking idea working properly. Again, a key issue.

4. Benchmarking is the establishment through data gathering of targets and comparators, by the use of which can be identified relative levels of performance (and particularly areas of underperformance).

Four sources of comparative data are: internal, competitive, activity (or process) and generic.

By adoption of identified best practices, it is hoped that performance will improve.

5. The BCG matrix is a way of analysing a portfolio of products by considering their market share and market growth.

On this matrix a 'cash cow' is a product with a high market share and low market growth.

A high market share implies that the product is well established. Low market growth implies that it is probably nearing the end of the product life cycle. The product therefore has few serious competitors, and this is unlikely to change in the future.

In the short term this product is a money spinner, but in the longer term sales may well die away.

Examples may include Bic biros and Casio electronic calculators.

6. **Gaddes Ltd**

Company sales are forecast to grow at 14%, whilst the market generally is growing at 12% – according to the BCG model the growth rate is likely to be considered high.

As market leader, Gaddes Ltd's sales are almost 17% higher than their major competitor. Thus they also have a high relative market share.

As a result the radios are likely to be categorised as a star product.

Competitors are likely to be attracted to the market by the high growth rate and the prospect of generating good returns. These factors may give rise to moderate cash investment by competitors.

7 Barclays Bank retail banking division

Briefing note

To	Managing Consultant
From	Junior Consultant
Date	Today
Subject	The competitive strategy of Barclays retail banking division

1 Competitive strategy

The strategy pursued by Barclays retail banking division can be classified as one of differentiation. Differentiation is achieved in several ways.

* Quality of service to customers.

* A reliable service that does not fall below the advertising image.

* A friendly approach to banking.

Barclays as a group appears to be trying to cultivate a fresh image to try and remove it's association with the banking crisis and financial scandals (LIBOR rate rigging). Overall, an image is being projected of a bank which is focused on customers.

It is interesting to note that although the division's profit before tax fell from £1,225m in 2012, to £1,195m in 2013, the number of customers using its services actually increased from 15.8m to 16.7m. This suggests that Barclays focus on enhancing the customer experience of using its services through embracing new technologies may be having some effect, despite the marginal drop in the number of branches being operated.

It is worth noting that on the face of it an increase in customer numbers and a decrease in profits suggests the divisions strategy may not be working as successfully as planned. However, most banks tend to assess the value generated by customers over their entire lifetime as opposed to the profits generated over the course of a year.

Barclays focus on increasing it's online offering to customers may potentially lead to further branch closures in the future as customers process more of their own bank transactions. This move may help the bank to reduce it's operating costs in the long term but may also have a negative impact on the service levels Barclays customers receive, as there will invariably be fewer branches to meet their needs. Not all customers are likely to have access to online banking, and some may be unwilling to exchange the traditional experience of visiting a local branch.

2 Value chain analysis

Value chain analysis is often best applied to manufacturing type entities and provides less insight when used in relation to service based businesses, due the nature of their primary activities. Nonetheless, value chain analysis can provide some useful insights into their support activities, so the following analysis focuses predominantly on Barclays support activities.

2.1 Infrastructure

Although Barclays retail banking division has a national image as the organisation has a branch presence in many UK high streets, it also operates internationally. Furthermore, Barclays places a strong emphasis on innovating its offering, with such developments requiring extensive financial investment.

In order to support such innovations Barclays clearly has significant financial resources at its disposal to fund upgrades to its online banking services and coin paying-in machines.

2.2 Technological development

Technological development would appear to be a key value driver in Barclays retail division. The extract provided indicates a number of initiatives aimed at putting the bank on the cutting edge of technology, clearly as part of Barclays strategy to become the 'Go To' bank. Interestingly over the period 2012-2013 the bank acquired 900,000 customers, this may be part of a greater underlying shift in customer attitudes towards the bank since the global banking crisis.

2.3 Procurement

We have limited detail on Barclays procurement operations. However, the planned pilot of the new coin paying in machines indicates that the bank is likely to have strong connections with suppliers of such technology. Barclays already users suppliers to provide it with ATM's, therefore close co-operation with such suppliers in developing the new coin paying in machines is likely to play a significant role in the success of the pilot.

2.4 Human resource management

Again, little is known about Barclays approach to managing its human resource. Over the period the retail banking division decreased the number of people it employed. As previously mentioned the desire to respond to customer demands as part of the bank's 'your campaign' initiative may help to explain the decrease in employee numbers, as customers can now perform an increasing number of banking transactions themselves using internet based banking.

2.5 Operations management

- Strong focus on improving the range of services available to customers through embracing advances in technology

- No longer incentivise staff to simply sell products to customers, greater focus on providing an 'excellent customer experience'

2.6 Marketing

- Its marketing orientation is revealed by the comments of becoming the 'Go To' bank. Barclays prides itself on its 'your bank' campaign which is focused on engaging with customers to find out how Barclays offering can be enhanced.

3 Conclusion

Barclays retail banking division provides a good example of a strategy of differentiation, while operating in a highly competitive market selling standard, basic products.

FI	National geographic branch coverage. Significant financial resources.			
HRM	Significant human resource. Strong focus on delivering high standards of customer service through staff training.			
TD	Continual technological developments. Strong focus on innovation in banking (online, mobile and contactless payments).			
P	Good supplier relations to deliver new paying in coin machines.			
	Strong focus on customer service. Listening to customers through 'Your bank' campaign		Marketing orientation to become the 'Go To' bank	Strong focus on customer service. Listening to customers through 'Your bank' campaign
	IL OPS	OL	M+S	SER

8 APCS plc

Memorandum – draft

To	The management team
From	An accountant
Date	Today
Re	The current system of performance measurement

Introduction

This memorandum looks at the current system of performance measurement and at how benchmarking could improve matters.

An appraisal of current measures

Strengths	Weaknesses
• The current system looks at three measures and is good in so far as non-financial aspects are included along with financial aspects.	• Difficulties in comparing costs between countries and from month to month as tariffs and exchange rates change.
• Cost per call is vital as the cost of telephone calls is the major cost of the call centre and must be monitored in order to control it.	• The cost per call measure could encourage operators to give customers a shorter (but probably inferior) answer. This is also a problem even with the non-financial measures used.
• Call drop-out rate is a very useful indicator as customer goodwill will be lost if people find themselves queuing for a long period of time. This could also indicate if more operators are needed.	• The main weakness of the approach is that no indication is given as to whether customers actually get a satisfactory response. Some form of customer survey is necessary – perhaps a sample of customers could be called back and views sought.
• Average call duration is probably more useful than cost as if affords better comparability.	• The measures do not seem to be broken down by operator level – one would expect level three queries to take much longer to solve than level one.
	• The lack of some form of comparison with other call centres. It may be that the call centre is very efficient but keeps being asked to improve.
	• The use of last month's figures as this month's target. This could encourage staff to work at less than maximum efficiency to avoid setting a more difficult target for next month.

What is benchmarking and how is it achieved?

Benchmarking involves setting targets by looking at comparable organisations – preferably at 'the best of the rest'. Such organisations could be drawn from any of the following.

- Internal benchmarking: look at other call centres within APCS plc

- Competitive benchmarking: look at competitor companies, such as IBM

- Activity benchmarking: look at any companies with call centres

- Generic benchmarking: look at conceptually similar processes, such as order processing at a large mail order company

The following steps are required to implement and run a system of benchmarking.

1 Gain senior management commitment
2 Decide which processes and activities need to be benchmarked

3   Understand the processes and develop appropriate measures
4   Monitor the process measuring system
5   Choose appropriate organisation against which to benchmark
6   Obtain and analyse data
7   Discuss results with process management and staff
8   Develop and implement improvement programmes
9   Monitor results.

Suitability for APCS plc

1   Management commitment should be forthcoming due to the team leadership style. Once the team has decided on benchmarking, all members will support it.

2   The main process to be benchmarked relates to the answering of customer queries, so this step is fairly easy. However, it must be decided, for example, whether to split the processes into different levels.

3   Developing appropriate measures – as mentioned above, we need measures more focused on whether operators are giving customers satisfactory answers.

4   Monitoring should be straightforward, though calling back customers will involve more cost. There is also the problem that questions which need to be asked are not too vague or subjective.

5   Choosing appropriate organisations for comparison – APCS plc does have other call centres, so non-financial measures can be compared between them. The problem of changing exchange rates could make costs difficult to compare.

6   With competitive benchmarking the main issue will be obtaining data – perhaps they could be called to determine average response times, etc. However, it would not be possible to find drop-out rates.

7   A forum for discussion will need to be set up – a minor problem.

8   It is vital that results will be acted upon for the system to have credibility. A settling-in period would also help.

9   Perhaps a team member should be assigned to take control of the whole process.

In summary, APCS plc is already well on the way towards benchmarking, and the introduction of the approach should not involve much painful change and cost. Internal benchmarking will be much easier but competitive benchmarking will give a much better idea as to whether or not APCS plc has a competitive advantage in this area.

9   Gizmo Computer Games Ltd

Memorandum

To	Geoff Carter
From	An Assistant
Date	Today
Subject	Strategic planning

A competence-based approach to strategic planning involves looking at what we are good at – our core competences. Ideally these are areas that we have to be good at to succeed ('critical success factors' or 'CSFs') and are also difficult for competitors to copy.

Once CSFs have been identified, they need to be measured and controlled. This is done by setting targets for related areas. Each CSF could involve looking at many key performance indicators ('KPIs').

Critical success factors of Gizmo and suggested KPIs

Peter has suggested four areas to consider. My thoughts on these are as follows.

- **Innovation.** Given the rate of change in the industry, it is vital that Gizmo's games are seen to be up to date, even 'cutting-edge'. One way of measuring this is to look at the number of extra features or gimmicks in each new game compared with its predecessor.

- **Command of technology.** With technology changing so rapidly it is vital that programmers are totally aware of what the hardware is capable of doing. It will be difficult to find suitable KPIs for this as it is very difficult to quantify. One way could be to send staff on external specialist update courses that include tests or exams at the end. Scores on these tests could be monitored.

- **Bug rate.** Nothing will alienate customers more quickly than bugs in games that prevent them being played correctly. It is thus vital that games are bug-free. This can be measured easily by looking at the number of bugs found once a game is sold, within say six months. Ideally this would also involve assessing whether or not bugs are serious.

- **Graphics.** Many players are impressed more by the graphics than they are by the complexities of a game, so again Peter has identified a key area. Assessing graphics performance will be difficult – possibly the best way is to look at consumer reviews in magazines which will grade games. We want at least a 4 star score.

In summary, Peter has suggested some important areas that Gizmo needs to consider. However, these should be reviewed along with more conventional measures, such as cost control.

10   Refer to the answer to parts b and c of MPW Ltd in the Question Bank.

11   There is no answer to this self-test, as it is designed just to help you increase your business awareness.

CHAPTER 7

Strategic options

Introduction
Examination context
Topic List
1 Rational planning model revisited
2 Corporate appraisal (SWOT analysis)
3 Gap analysis
4 Generic competitive strategies: how to compete
5 Product-market strategy: direction of growth
6 Other strategies
Summary and Self-test
Answers to Interactive questions
Answers to Self-test

Learning objectives

- Analyse a business's current markets and competitive strategy

- Identify, describe and evaluate, in a given scenario, the alternative strategies available to a business

- Explain, using information provided, how to position particular products and services in a market to maximise competitive advantage

Specific syllabus references for this chapter are: 1c, 2a, 2i.

Syllabus links

The basic concepts of competitive strategy and strategic growth were covered in your Business and Finance paper. The topics are summarised again here as the concepts covered in this chapter form a core area of Business Strategy. As well as developing the ideas further they are also applied to scenario problems of the sort you may face in your examination.

Examination context

This chapter looks at various models which can assist an organisation in developing its products and markets and in choosing strategies for competitive advantage. In the exam these models can be used to assess the strategies already identified in the question or as a way of generating strategic options for the business. Either way, the concepts of SWOT analysis, Porter's generic strategy model and Ansoff's growth matrix are fundamental knowledge for the Business Strategy exam.

In Q3 September 2008 (*DT Ltd*) the scenario, which involves a company providing training for learner drivers, contains a great deal of information about the company's history, environment and hopes for its future. The first requirement is:

'(a) Prepare a SWOT analysis of the current strategic position of DT and clearly identify what you consider to be the major issues.   **(8 marks)'**

Sometimes a question to which you should apply SWOT is not quite so clearly signposted; you may instead be asked to discuss a company's strengths, or the threats to it (in which case application of the new entrants and substitutes elements of Five Forces may also be relevant). Note that the requirement above is asking about the company's *strategic* position, so operational detail is not required, and also that the *major issues* should be highlighted. Too many answers requiring a model such as SWOT are uncritical, giving marginal or totally unimportant points as much weight as core ones.

1 Rational planning model revisited

Section overview

- The development of strategic options involves the final three steps of the rational model.

- Choices involve understanding the present situation, identifying gaps, and developing potential ways to deal with this.

1.1 The rational model

Chapter 2 introduced the rational model.

The present chapter considers three of the stages:

- **Corporate appraisal**: Combining assessment of environment (Chapters 4 and 5) with assessment of resources, competences and capabilities (Chapter 6) to help management identify the strategic position of the business and its forecast performance.

- **Gap analysis**: Management compare forecast performance with the strategic objectives of the business to identify where strategic adjustments are needed to deliver planned performance.

- **Strategic option development**: Management generate and evaluate strategic options to close the planning gap identified.

1.2 Three strategic choices: overview

Johnson, Scholes and Whittington (*Exploring Corporate Strategy*) identify three distinct groups of strategic options. Strategic choice requires that management makes choices under each of the following:

- **Competitive strategy**: The way that the firm will seek to win customers and secure profitability against rivals. This is covered in the present chapter and continued in Chapter 8 where marketing strategy is discussed.

- **Product/market strategy**: The decision on what products to offer over the coming years and the markets to be served. This is covered in section 5 of this chapter and again continued in Chapter 8.

- **Development strategy**: The decision on how to gain access to the chosen products and markets. Discussion of this choice is reserved until Chapter 11.

Worked example: Virgin group

The following extracts have been adapted from the Virgin Website (2014) and illustrate the way this international consumer goods and services corporation applies the 'three strategic choices' approach.

Competitive strategy

Virgin is a leading international investment group and one of the world's most recognised and respected brands. Conceived in 1970 by Sir Richard Branson, the Virgin group has gone on to grow successful businesses in sectors ranging from mobile telephony, travel, financial services, leisure, music, holidays and health & wellness. Virgin employs more than 50,000 people around the world, operating in over 50 countries. Global brand revenues were £15bn (US $24bn) in 2012.

All the markets in which Virgin operates tend to have features in common: they are typically markets where the customer has been under-served, where there is confusion and/or where the competition is complacent.

In these markets, Virgin is able to break into the market and shake it up. Virgin's role is to be the consumer champion, and we do this by delivering to our brand values, which are:

Value for money

eg Virgin Australia – low cost airlines with transparent pricing.

Good quality

High standards, attention to detail, being honest and delivering on promises.

eg Virgin Atlantic Upper Class Suite – on-board bar, large flat bed on board, touchscreen monitor, mood lighting etc.

Innovation

Challenging convention with big and little product/service ideas; innovative, modern and stylish design.

eg Virgin Galactic – space travel experiences.

Brilliant customer service

Friendly, human and relaxed; professional but uncorporate.

eg Virgin Mobile Australia has won awards for its customer service as the company treats its customers as individuals.

Competitively challenging

Sticking two fingers up to the establishment and fighting the big boys – usually with a bit of humour.

eg In 2012, Richard Branson and Virgin Trains successfully forced the UK government to back track on its announcement that the franchise to run the West Coast Main Line had been awarded to FirstGroup a rival train line operator. Virgin appealed the government's decision after it came to light that the process for awarding the route was based on flawed information and passenger projections.

Fun

Every company in the world takes itself seriously so we think it's important that we provide the public and our customers with a bit of entertainment.

eg VAA [Virgin Atlantic Airways] erected a sign over the BA-sponsored, late finishing London Eye saying: BA Can't Get It Up.

Product/market strategy

Travel and tourism	Leisure and pleasure	Social and environment
eg	eg	Eg
• Virgin Atlantic	• V Festival	• Virgin Green fund
• Virgin Balloon Flights	• Virgin Casino	• Virgin Unite
• Virgin Holidays	• Virgin Experience Days	• Virgin Earth Challenge
• Virgin Trains		
• Virgin Galactic		

Shopping	Media and telecommunications	Finance and money
eg	eg	• Virgin Money
• Virgin Books	• Virgin Mobile	
• Virgin Wines	• Virgin Media	
• Virgin Megastore	• Virgin Radio	

Development strategy

We draw on talented people from throughout the group. New ventures are often steered by people seconded from other parts of Virgin, who bring with them the trademark management style, skills and experience. We frequently create partnerships with others to combine skills, knowledge, market presence and so on.

Once a Virgin company is up and running, several factors contribute to making it a success. The power of the Virgin name; Richard Branson's personal reputation; our unrivalled network of friends, contacts and partners; the Virgin management style; the way talent is empowered to flourish within the group. To some traditionalists, these may not seem hard headed enough. To them, the fact that Virgin has minimal management layers, no bureaucracy, a tiny board and no massive global HQ is an anathema.

Our companies are part of a family rather than a hierarchy. They are empowered to run their own affairs, yet other companies help one another, and solutions to problems come from all kinds of sources. In a sense we are a community, with shared ideas, values, interests and goals. The proof of our success is real and tangible.

Exploring the activities of our companies through this web site demonstrates that success, and that it is not about having a strong business promise, it is about keeping it!

Although the Virgin group is a family of businesses with a shared brand, all of the companies run independently. Often the companies are set up as joint ventures with other partners, so they all have different shareholders and boards.'

2 Corporate appraisal (SWOT analysis)

Section overview

- Before dreaming up options, management needs to take stock of the present position of the business.

- A SWOT analysis is an important technique for visualising the situation and is drawn from the environmental assessment and internal appraisal already conducted.

2.1 Role of corporate appraisal

A complete awareness of the organisation's environment and its internal capacities is **necessary** for a rational consideration of future strategy, but it is not **sufficient**. The threads must be drawn together so that potential strategies may be developed and assessed. The most common way of doing this is to analyse the factors into **strengths**, **weaknesses**, **opportunities** and **threats**. Strengths and weaknesses are diagnosed by the internal analysis, opportunities and threats by the environmental analysis.

SWOT analysis is covered in detail in the Business and Finance text.

2.2 Bringing them together – the cruciform chart

A cruciform chart (literally 'cross form') can be drafted on a flip-chart by the person facilitating the strategy discussions. Its benefits are:

- Limitations on space restricts management to focusing on the big points
- Allows mapping of connections between points (see below)

However, effective SWOT analysis does not simply require a categorisation of information; it also requires some **evaluation of the relative importance** of the various factors under consideration. In the exam it is vital that you indicate the relative importance of points that you identify and r provide a summary of the key issues to go with your cruciform.

- **Match strengths with market opportunities**
  Strengths which do not match any available opportunity are of limited use while opportunities which do not have any matching strengths are of little immediate value.

- **Conversion**
  This requires the development of strategies which will convert weaknesses into strengths in order to take advantage of some particular opportunity, or converting threats into opportunities which can then be matched by existing strengths.

2.3 Weihrich's TOWS matrix

Weihrich, one of the earliest writers on corporate appraisal, originally spoke in terms of a TOWS matrix in order to emphasise the importance of threats and opportunities. It has several benefits:

- It provides a clear set of steps to move from SWOT to the formulation of strategic options.

- It makes management aware of the need for **defensive** strategies (WT) in addition to strategies to grasp opportunities.

	Strengths	Weaknesses
Opportunities	SO Strategies	WO Strategies
Threats	ST Strategies	WT Strategies

Note that this is therefore an inherently **positioning** approach to strategy. A further important element of Weihrich's discussion was his categorisation of strategic options:

- SO strategies employ strengths to seize opportunities.
- ST strategies employ strengths to counter or avoid threats.
- WO strategies address weaknesses so as to be able to exploit opportunities.
- WT strategies are defensive, aiming to avoid threats and the impact of weaknesses.

One useful impact of this analysis is that **the four groups of strategies tend to relate well to different time horizons**. SO strategies may be expected to produce good short-term results, while WO strategies are likely to take much longer to show results. ST and WT strategies are more probably relevant to the medium term.

3 Gap analysis

Section overview

- Gap analysis helps management visualise the ground to be made up between their intentions for the performance of the business and its forecast performance without new initiatives (strategies).

- There are three groups of strategies to help close the shortfall of performance (gap): improve efficiency, develop new market and products, and diversify.

3.1 Overview of gap analysis

Gap analysis compares two things:

- The organisation's **targets** for achievement over the planning period

- What the organisation would be **expected to achieve** if it carried on in the current way with the same products and selling to the same markets, with no major changes to operations. This is called an F_0 **forecast,** by Argenti

Definition

Gap analysis: The comparison between an entity's ultimate objective and the expected performance from projects both planned and under way, identifying means by which any identified difference, or gap, might be filled.

3.2 Strategies to fill the gap

The planning gap may originate from a number of causes:

- Ambitious objectives being set by management (or imposed on management by investors)
- Underperformance of existing product portfolio (eg maturity stage approaching)
- Difficult environment (eg industry or economic slow-down)

The gap could be filled by new product-market growth strategies. For example a management team wishing to increase profitability might consider:

- **Efficiency strategies**: reduce the costs of present products and economise on the assets used.
- **Expansion strategies**: develop new products and/or new markets.
- **Diversification strategies**: enter new industries which have better profit and growth prospects.

These are illustrated below.

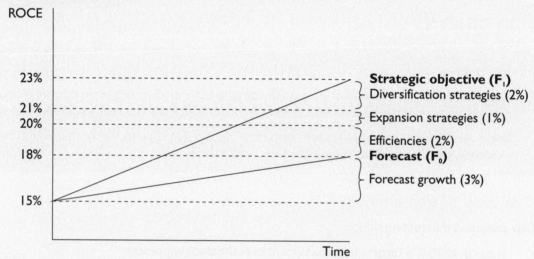

Gaps can also be closed by the simple expedient of setting the objectives lower. Most writers on strategy regard this remedy as an unacceptable admission of defeat by management.

4 Generic competitive strategies: how to compete

Section overview

- Firms must position themselves well in two markets: the market for their products; and in the stock market.

- Porter's concept of competitive advantage states that such positioning can be achieved only in three mutually exclusive ways: cost leadership, differentiation and focus.

- Porter's generic competitive strategies were introduced in the Business & Finance text and are summarised again here as they are a core topic for Business Strategy.

4.1 Competitive advantage

Competitive advantage is anything which gives one organisation an edge over its rivals.

In the 1960s and 1970s this tended to be interpreted solely in terms of the marketing concept of providing the customer with superior benefits and so winning sales.

Porter widened the concept of competitive advantage in 1980 by stating that competitive advantage is the consequence of a successful competitive strategy:

Competitive strategy means 'taking offensive or defensive actions to create a defendable position in an industry, to cope successfully with competitive forces and thereby yield a superior return on investment for the firm. Firms have discovered many different approaches to this end, and the best strategy for a given firm is ultimately a unique construction reflecting its particular circumstances.' (Porter)

Note that Porter defines competitive advantage in terms of 'superior return on investment' rather than simply superior sales or higher sales revenue.

In Chapter 6 we examined the concept of the value chain and discussed how a business can create and sustain competitive advantage using cost or value drivers. The choice of competitive strategy will determine whether the focus of the chain should be cost (cost leadership) or value (differentiation) and will have implications for operational strategies (see Chapter 13).

4.2 The choice of competitive strategy

Porter argued that selecting and implementing one of these strategies is the only way to effectively counter the industry forces identified in his Five Forces model.

The diagram below summarises his argument.

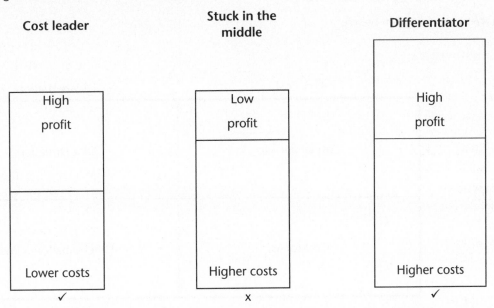

Competitive pressures will increase as a market ages so that once the mature stage of the industry is reached only two competitive strategies will deliver competitive advantage (ie superior ROI).

- **Low cost**: A firm following this strategy will withstand the shrinking margins better and so, as rivals fall away, may be left as a major player with enhanced power against the power of suppliers and buyers.

- **Differentiation**: A firm presenting itself as a superior provider may escape price pressure by avoiding straight-forward price comparisons with rivals.

A **stuck in the middle** strategy is one where the firm has sought to attract many segments at different price points and so is seen as not being as differentiated as the market leader but, perhaps because of the costs of serving the differentiated segment, not able to make good profits at the cost leader's prices.

Worked example: Tesco: Stuck in the middle?

A report in the Economist (2013) highlighted the problems facing UK retail giant Tesco. According to the Economist, in December 2013 Tesco reported that 'same-store sales in Britain had dropped 1.5% in the third quarter', with the company's European and Asian operations falling by 4% and 5.1% respectively.

Spending power among British shoppers has failed to reach the heights that it achieved in 2007 and is predicted to be 10% lower now than six years earlier. By contrast discounters such as Aldi and Lidl have experienced a steady increase in year on year sales with the latter reporting a increase of 14%. Unlike Tesco, retailers such as Lidl are succeeding in offering a 'no-frills' shopping experience, with most produce being wheeled out from the warehouse on pallets straight onto the shop floor. Discounters have worked hard in recent years to shed the 'poor mans' stigma that had become synonymous with their brand, with many increasing advertising spend and improving the quality of the goods sold.

Tesco problem's have been further compounded as up market rival Waitrose has reported an increase in sales of 9% over the last 12 months.

Tesco recently withdrew its supermarket operations in the USA after its 'Fresh & Easy' venture failed to deliver the anticipated returns. In a bid to attract more customers in the UK, Tesco CEO Philip Clarke has focused efforts on enhancing the retailer's online offering and investing in new convenience stores. However analysts are yet to be convinced that such moves go far enough to improve the company's fortunes.

4.3 Porter's three generic strategies

Illustrated in the diagram below:

4.3.1 Competitive basis

	Low cost	Differentiation
Broad	Cost leadership	Differentiation
Competitive scope		
Narrow	Cost focus	Differentiation focus

4.3.2 Cost leadership

A cost leadership strategy seeks to achieve the position of lowest-cost producer in the industry as a whole. By producing at the lowest cost, the manufacturer can compete on price with every other producer in the industry, and earn the higher unit profits, if the manufacturer so chooses.

How to achieve overall cost leadership

(a) Set up production facilities to obtain economies of scale.

(b) Use the latest technology to reduce costs and/or enhance productivity (or use cheap labour if available).

(c) In high technology industries, and in industries depending on labour skills for product design and production methods, exploit the learning curve effect. By producing more items than any other competitor, a firm can benefit more from the learning curve, and achieve lower average costs.

(d) Concentrate on improving productivity.

(e) Minimise overhead costs.

(f) Get favourable access to sources of supply.

(g) Use value chain to streamline activities and reduce non-value adding activities (see Chapter 6).

(h) Relocate operations to cheaper countries.

Classic examples of companies pursuing cost leadership are Ryanair and Lidl. Large out-of-town stores specialising in one particular category of product are able to secure cost leadership by economies of scale over other retailers. Such shops have been called category killers; an example is Toys R Us.

4.3.3 Differentiation

A differentiation strategy assumes that competitive advantage can be gained through **particular characteristics** of a firm's products.

How to differentiate

(a) **Build up a brand image** (eg Pepsi's blue cans are supposed to offer different 'psychic benefits' to Coke's red ones).

(b) **Give the product special features** to make it stand out (eg Mercedes finger print recognition security system).

(c) **Exploit other activities of the value chain** (see Chapter 6) eg marketing and service.

(d) Use **IT** to create **new services** or **product features**.

Worked example: Microsoft

Microsoft Corporation's success is largely attributed to its operating systems and, in particular, the Windows environment it has developed. Windows has undergone a number of significant step changes of version in the past 20 years or so: the original Windows 3.1, Windows 98, Windows XP, Windows Vista, Windows 7 and Windows 8.1. Developers have designed each successive version on the premise that the PC user wishes to turn their machine into a one-stop communication and entertainment device and to work seamlessly between material on the local drive of their machine and other available resources on-line and also able to present documents, show moving pictures and also play sound files. It must also have its own security system. Therefore more and more features are bundled in that previously were bought separately from other providers.

The flagship Microsoft application is Microsoft Office. This too has moved through iterations premised on the belief that users wish to manage their knowledge across many platforms from printed page to spoken word and Internet page.

During the past few years Microsoft has lost ground to two specific applications:

- Linux – a stand-alone operating system developed from Unix systems used on super-computers
- Firefox – a stand-alone Internet browser

Both have the advantages of being free to download (but of course to do so the user has probably already bought Windows and has Microsoft's IE browser). Both are 'open source coding' which means that users are a community and contribute to improving the programmes. The main attractions claimed by supporters of the systems seem to be their superior operational performance; ie differentiation.

4.3.4 Generic strategies and the Five Forces

Competitive force	Advantages		Disadvantages	
	Cost leadership	Differentiation	Cost leadership	Differentiation
New entrants	Economies of scale raise entry barriers	Brand loyalty and perceived uniqueness are entry barriers		
Substitutes	Firm is not so vulnerable as its less cost-effective competitors to the threat of substitutes	Customer loyalty is a weapon against substitutes		
Customers	Customers cannot drive down prices further than the next most efficient competitor	Customers have no comparable alternative Brand loyalty should lower price sensitivity		Customers may no longer need the differentiating factor Sooner or later customers become price sensitive
Suppliers	Flexibility to deal with cost increases	Higher margins can offset vulnerability to supplier price rises	Increase in input costs can reduce price advantages	
Industry rivalry	Firm remains profitable when rivals go under through excessive price competition	Unique features reduce direct competition	Technological change will require capital investment, or make production cheaper for competitors Competitors learn via imitation Cost concerns ignore product design or marketing issues	Imitation narrows differentiation

4.3.5 Focus (or niche) strategy

In a focus strategy, a firm concentrates its attention on one or more particular segments or niches of the market, and does not try to serve the entire market with a single product. Within the niche, the firm can either aim to be a cost leader or pursue differentiation

Porter suggests that a focus strategy can achieve competitive advantage when 'broad-scope' businesses fall into one of two errors:

- Under-performance occurs when a product does not fully meet the needs of a segment and offers the opportunity for a differentiation focus player.

- Over-performance gives a segment more than it really wants and provides an opportunity for a cost focus player.

Advantages

- A niche is more secure and a firm can insulate itself from competition.

- The firm does not spread itself too thinly.

- Both cost leadership and differentiation require superior performance – life is easier in a niche, where there may be little or no competition.

Drawbacks of a focus strategy

- The firm sacrifices economies of scale which would be gained by serving a wider market.

- Competitors can move into the segment, with increased resources (eg Lexus moved into the US luxury car market, to compete with Mercedes and BMW).

- The segment's needs may eventually become less distinct from the main market.

Worked example: Specialised online dating

Internet dating has grown hugely in popularity over the past decade and more recently very specialised online dating services have begun to appear.

Uniformdating.com is one such specialised dating service which was launched to provide a dating platform specifically for individuals working in the uniformed services, including the police officers, firemen and women, soldiers, RAF personnel, pilots, doctors and nurses.

Uniformed personnel typically face a number of restrictions as part of their working lives, including working difficult shift patterns, working away or being on tour. These unique circumstances can place a significant strain on these people and the relationships they attempt to maintain. Uniformdating.com claims to understand these difficult circumstances and provide the solution via its matching services to help its members find their ideal match and form lasting relationships.

The site is not, however, restricted to those working in uniform and they welcome and encourage new members who are not necessarily from these professions, but who are looking to meet someone from the uniformed or emergency services. This allows the company not only to serve the main niche of uniformed personnel, but also to tap into the niche market of 'dating a man/woman in a uniform'.

Since its launch, the site has grown hugely and, as of April 2012, claims to have 'hundreds of thousands of uniformed members'. It has successfully carved out this niche in the UK, USA, Canada and Australia.

Other, perhaps less well known, examples of online dating services targeting niche markets include Farmers Only and Geek2Geek. Farmers Only is a US and Canada dating site aimed at 'down to earth folks only' serving single farmers, ranchers, cowboys, cowgirls and animal lovers. Geek2Geek, also US based, describes itself as 'the safe, friendly, and easy to use site where geeks and their admirers can find each other'. Its advertising explains that 'traditional dating sites just don't work well for them'.

4.4 Conceptual difficulties with generic strategy

In practice, it is rarely simple to draw hard and fast distinctions between the generic strategies as there are conceptual problems underlying them.

- **Cost leadership**

  - **Internal focus**: Cost refers to internal measures, rather than the market demand. It can be used to gain market share: but it is the **market share which is important,** not cost leadership as such.

  - **Only one firm**: If cost leadership applies cross the whole industry, only one firm will pursue this strategy successfully. However, the position is not clear-cut.

    - More than one firm might **aspire** to cost leadership, especially in dynamic markets where new technologies are frequently introduced.

    - The boundary between cost leadership and cost focus might be blurred.

    - Firms competing market-wide might have different competences or advantages that confer cost leadership in different segments.

- **Higher margins can be used for differentiation**: Having low costs does **not** mean you have to charge lower prices or compete on price. A cost leader can choose to 'invest higher margins in R&D or marketing'. Being a cost leader arguably gives producers more freedom to choose **other** competitive strategies.

- **Differentiation**: Porter assumes that a differentiated product will always be sold at a **higher** price.

  - However, a **differentiated product** may be sold at the same price as competing products in order to **increase market share**.

  - **Choice of competitor**. Differentiation from whom? Who are the competitors? Do they serve other market segments? Do they compete on the same basis?

  - **Source of differentiation**. This can include **all** aspects of the firm's offer, not only the product. Restaurants aim to create an atmosphere or 'ambience', as well as serving food of good quality.

Focus probably has fewer conceptual difficulties, as it ties in very neatly with ideas of market segmentation. In practice most companies pursue this strategy to some extent, by designing products/services to meet the needs of particular target markets.

4.5 Bowman's strategic clock

Porter's basic concept of generic strategies has been the subject of further discussion. Bowman's clock model was developed from surveys of practising managers attending MBA programmes who were asked to describe the competitive strategies being followed by their own firms, which represent possible combinations of price and quality across a whole spectrum.

The strategy clock

4.5.1 Price-based strategies

Strategies 1 and 2 are price-based strategies.

- A **no frills** strategy (1) is aimed at the most price-conscious and can only succeed if this segment of the market is sufficiently large. This strategy may be used for market entry, to gain experience and build volume. This was done by Japanese car manufacturers in the 1960s.

- A **low price** strategy (2) offers better value than competitors. This can lead to price war and reduced margins for all. Porter's generic strategy of **cost leadership** is appropriate to a firm adopting this strategy.

4.5.2 Differentiation strategies

Strategies 3, 4 and 5 are all differentiation strategies. Each one represents a different trade-off between market share (with its cost advantages) and margin (with its direct impact on profit). Differentiation can be created in three ways.

- Product features
- Marketing, including powerful brand promotion
- Core competences

The pursuit of any differentiation strategy requires detailed and accurate **market intelligence**. The customers and their preferences must be clearly identified, as must the competition and their likely responses. The chosen basis for differentiation should be inherently difficult to imitate, and will probably need to be developed over time.

The **hybrid** strategy (3) seeks both differentiation and a lower price than competitors. The cost base must be low enough to permit reduced prices and reinvestment to maintain differentiation. This strategy may be more advantageous than differentiation alone under certain circumstances.

- If it leads to growth in market share
- If differentiation rests on core competences and costs can be reduced elsewhere
- If a low price approach is suited to a particular market segment
- Where it is used as a market entry strategy

The basic **differentiation** strategy (4) comes in two variants, depending on whether a price premium is charged or a competitive price is accepted in order to build market share.

A strategy of **focused differentiation** seeks a high price premium in return for a high degree of differentiation. This implies concentration on a well defined and probably quite restricted market segment. **Coherence** of offer will be very important under these circumstances. Johnson, Scholes and Whittington give the example of a department store offering a range of products to a variety of customer types but failing to differentiate such matters as premises, décor and staff according to the particular segment served.

4.5.3 Failure strategies

Combinations 6, 7 and 8 are likely to result in failure as there is little perceived added value to compensate for the premium on price.

Interactive question 1: Eurofoods   [Difficulty level: Exam standard]

EuroFoods is a French-German consumer products group with a revenue of £8 billion a year at 20X2 retail prices. One of EuroFoods' activities is the manufacture of ice-cream.

Medley is an American company. It has worldwide sales of £5 billion a year and these come mainly from chocolate products. Three years ago Medley started to diversify. It did this by selling a new product, ice-cream, in one of its existing markets, Europe. Although Medley had no prior experience of ice-cream, it believed that it could exploit its existing expertise in food products, marketing and distribution in this new area.

The European ice-cream industry revenue is £6 billion at 20X2 retail prices.

Market share	%
EuroFoods	60
Medley	10
Local producers*	30
	100

* These are defined as manufacturers who sell within only one European country.

Distribution has always been a very important aspect of the food industry. However, it is particularly so in the ice-cream business. This is because the product must be kept refrigerated from factory to shop, and also whilst it is stored in the shop.

Many of the shops which sell EuroFoods' ice-cream are small businesses and the freezer which is required for storage is a costly item for them to buy. EuroFoods has therefore developed a scheme whereby it will install and maintain such a freezer in these shops. The shop owner does not have to pay for the freezer. The only condition which EuroFoods imposes is that the freezer must be used exclusively for the sales of its products.

EuroFoods believes that this arrangement has worked well for everybody in the past. EuroFoods' expenditures on the freezers have ensured that its products have reached the consumer in good condition and also enabled it to simplify inventory control. It has also played a part in building its market dominance by enabling shops which otherwise would not be able to do so, to sell its products.

The European ice-cream business

The peak time of year for sales of ice-cream in Europe is from mid-June to mid-August. These summer sales are deemed 'impulse' sales by the trade and are traditionally made from small retail outlets where EuroFoods tends to have its exclusive arrangements. The other sort of sale is the 'take-home', which are purchases made in larger quantities at supermarkets. These outlets do not have exclusive agreements with EuroFoods.

Analysis of European ice-cream sales in 20X2 is as follows.

	Volume	Value	Return on sales – Profit before tax
	%	£ billion	£ billion
Impulse sales	40	4	0.48
Take-home sales	60	2	0.12
Total	100	6	

Medley

Medley would like to obtain its future growth from the impulse sector of the market. It owns 14,000 non-exclusive freezer cabinets, mainly in the UK. However, it is costly to maintain these to sell the eight products which constitute its product range. Another problem is that in many cases small shops have room for only one freezer and this has often already been supplied by EuroFoods. As Medley's UK managing director said:'It means only big competitors with a full range of products can enter the market'.

Medley would like to be able to place its products in the freezers provided by EuroFoods. However, when it tried to do this two years ago in Spain, EuroFoods was successful in a legal action to prevent this.

Medley has now complained to the European Union that EuroFoods' exclusive freezer arrangements restrict competition and are unfair.

You are presently working for Thunderclap Newman, a merchant bank, as a business analyst in its Confectionery Division.

Requirements

Write a report to the head of the Confectionery Division of your bank, which

(a) Identifies strategies which lead to competitive advantage.

(b) Makes recommendations to **both** companies on their possible future strategy options if the EU decides that exclusive freezer arrangements are:

- Anti-competitive and, in future, freezers should be available to any manufacturer
- Not anti-competitive and EuroFoods can continue to protect the use of its freezers

You should include a general explanation of how a firm may attain a competitive advantage.

Note: A billion equals one thousand million.

See **Answer** at the end of this chapter.

5 Product-market strategy: direction of growth

Section overview

- The second strategic choice, outlined in section 1 above, is which products and markets to serve.
- Ansoff classifies the choices on a matrix into market penetration, product development, market development and diversification.
- Each strategy has its particular benefits and drawbacks.

5.1 Product-market growth matrix

Ansoff drew up a **growth vector matrix**, describing how a combination of a firm's activities in current and new markets, with existing and new products can lead to **growth**.

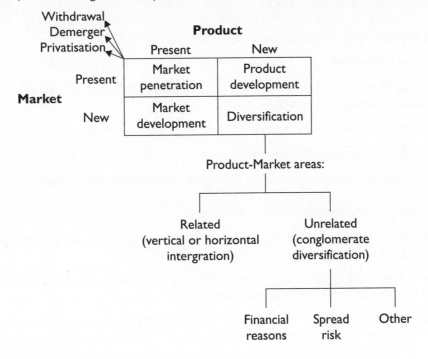

5.2 Growth vectors

Ansoff identifies four directions (or vectors) of growth available to the business which were introduced in the Business & Finance text. Unlike Porter's generic strategies, where only one should be followed, management can pursue all four of Ansoff's vectors if it wishes to, although some eg diversification, are more risky than others. In the Business Strategy exam you may be required to use the Ansoff matrix to analyse the ways in which a business has grown.

5.2.1 Market penetration

The firm seeks to do four things:

- **Maintain or to increase its share** of current markets with current products, eg through competitive pricing, advertising, sales promotion
- Secure dominance of growth markets
- Restructure a mature market by driving out competitors
- Increase usage by existing customers (eg airmiles, loyalty cards)

The ease with which a company can pursue this strategy depends on its market and its competitors. If the market is growing it may be relatively easy to gain share. However if markets are static (mature) it is not.

5.2.2 Market development: present products and new markets

There are many possible approaches. Here are some examples.

- **New geographical areas** and export markets (eg a radio station building a new transmitter to reach a new audience).

- **Different package sizes** for food and other domestic items so that both those who buy in bulk and those who buy in small quantities are catered for.

- **New distribution channels** to attract new customers (eg organic food sold in supermarkets not just specialist shops, Internet sales).

- **Differential pricing policies** to attract different types of customer and create **new market segments**. For example, travel companies have developed a market for cheap long-stay winter breaks in warmer countries for retired couples.

This strategy is likely to be more successful, the closer the characteristics of the new market are to existing markets (or segments).

5.2.3 Product development: new products and present markets

This has several advantages.

- The company can exploit its existing marketing arrangements such as promotional methods and distribution channels at low cost.

- The company should already have good knowledge of its customers and their wants and habits.

- Competitors will be forced to respond.

- The cost of entry to the market will go up and newcomers may be discouraged.

5.2.4 Diversification: new products and new markets

Diversification occurs when a company decides to make **new products for new markets**. It should have a clear idea about what it expects to gain from diversification.

- **Growth:** New products and new markets should be selected which offer prospects for growth which the existing product-market mix does not.

- **Investing surplus** funds not required for other expansion needs, bearing in mind that the funds could be returned to shareholders. Diversification is a high risk strategy, having many of the characteristics of a new business start-up. It is likely to require the deployment of **new competences**.

Because of the extent of the change, diversification normally involves more risk than the other strategies.

5.3 Types of diversification

Ansoff identifies **two classes** of diversification:

1. **Related diversification:** Integrating activities in the supply chain or leveraging technologies or competences. This involves either horizontal or vertical integration.

2. **Conglomerate diversification:** The development of a portfolio of businesses with no commercial similarity or links between them.

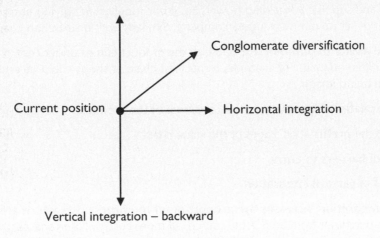

5.3.1 Horizontal integration (related diversification)

Horizontal integration is development into activities which are competitive with or directly **complementary** to a company's present activities. There are three cases:

- **Competitive products**: Taking over a competitor can have obvious benefits, leading eventually towards achieving a monopoly. Apart from active competition, a competitor may offer advantages such as completing geographical coverage.

- **Complementary products**: For example, a manufacturer of household vacuum cleaners moving into commercial cleaners. A full product range can be presented to the market and there may well be benefits from having many of the components common between the different ranges.

- **By-products**: For example, a butter manufacturer discovering increased demand for skimmed milk. Generally, income from by-products is a windfall to be counted, at least initially, as a bonus.

5.3.2 Vertical Integration (related diversification)

Vertical integration occurs when a company becomes its own supplier (backward) or distributor forward).

- **Backward integration**: taking over responsibility for **upstream processes** eg a clothing retailer producing or designing its own clothes.

- **Forward integration**: taking over responsibility for **downstream processes** eg an electrical goods retailer setting up its own installation, servicing and repairs service.

Advantages of vertical integration

- **Economies of combined operations**, eg proximity, reduced handling.

- **Economies of internal control and co-ordination**, eg scheduling and coordinating operations should be better. Information about the market can be fed back to the production companies.

- **Economies of avoiding the market**. Negotiation, packing, advertising costs are avoided.

- **Tap into technology**. Close knowledge of the upstream or downstream operations can give a company valuable strategic advantages. For example, computer manufacturers have instituted backwards integration into semi-conductor design and manufacturing to gain a better understanding of the technology and its potential.

- **Safeguarding proprietary knowledge**. If a firm makes components itself, it does not have to supply specifications to its suppliers; this information therefore stays confidential.

- **Assured supply and demand**. The firm will have first call on supplies in scarce periods and the greatest chance of having an outlet in periods of low demand. Fluctuations in supply and demand are not eliminated but can, perhaps, be better planned for.

- **Reduction in bargaining power of suppliers and customers**. Two of Porter's forces on a firm are customer and supplier bargaining power. So, if our suppliers are giving us a rough time, we take them over or set up our own supply company. Similarly with distribution channels.

- **Enhanced ability to differentiate**. More of the product comes under control so we have a greater ability to differentiate it. For example, a specialist chain of shops could be established with a distinctive brand image.

- **Stronger relationships** with the final consumer of the product.

- A share of the **profits** at all stages of the value chain.

- Creation of **barriers to entry.**

Disadvantages of vertical integration

- **Vertical integration increases the proportion of the firm's costs which are fixed**. For example, if the firm purchases from an outside source, all those costs will be variable. If the input is produced internally, the firm has to bear all the fixed costs of production. Vertical integration increases business risk from this source.

- **Reduced flexibility to change partners**. If the in-house supplier or customer does not perform well, it is not easy to switch to outsiders. You will probably have to get rid of the in-house company first.

- **Capital investment needs**. Vertical integration will consume capital resources. For integration to be a good choice it must yield a return greater than, or equal to, the firm's opportunity cost of capital, adjusting for strategic considerations.

- **Cut off from suppliers and customers**. By integrating a firm may cut itself off from the flow of technology from its suppliers or market research information from its customers. For example, a firm will have to take responsibility for developing its own technology. Other potential suppliers may be reluctant to share their technology as they would be supplying it not just to a customer, but a customer who is also a competitor.

- **Dulled incentives**. The captive relationship between buyer and seller can quickly lead to inefficiencies. These can quickly spread through the group as products produced at too high a cost are passed through.

- **Differing managerial requirements**. Different businesses need different management skills. Because a company is a successful manufacturer, this does not mean that it can turn its hand to retailing with a reasonable chance of success.

- Avoid transaction costs arising from external relationships. Costs arise over contract negotiation, compliance monitoring, redress actions etc.

- **Overconcentration**: A company places 'more eggs in the same end-market basket' (Ansoff). Such a policy is fairly inflexible, more sensitive to instabilities and increases the firm's dependence on a particular aspect of economic demand.

- The firm **fails to benefit from any economies of scale** in the industry into which it has diversified. This is why, in the publishing industry, most printing is subcontracted to specialist printing firms, who can work machinery to capacity by doing work for many firms.

5.3.3 Conglomerate diversification

Not very fashionable in the USA and Europe where its financial returns have been disappointing, however, it has been a key strategy for companies in Asia, particularly South Korea.

Conglomerates

- The characteristic of conglomerate (or unrelated) diversification is that there is no common thread, and the only synergy lies with the management skills. Outstanding management seems to be the key to success as a conglomerate, and in the case of large conglomerates they are indeed able, because of their size and diversity, to attract high-calibre managers with wide experience.

- Two major types of conglomerate can be identified. The **financial conglomerate** provides a flow of funds to each segment of its operation, exercises control and is the ultimate risk taker. In theory

ICAEW

it undertakes strategic planning but does not participate in operating decisions. The **managerial conglomerate** extends this approach by providing managerial counsel and interaction on operating decisions, on the assumption that general management skills can be transferred to almost any environment.

Advantages of conglomerate diversification

- **Risk-spreading**: Entering new products into new markets offers protection against the failure of current products and markets

- **High profit opportunities**: An improvement of the **overall profitability and flexibility** of the firm through acquisition in industries which have better economic characteristics than those of the acquiring firms

- Ability to grow quickly by making acquisitions in diverse fields

- **Escape** from the present business

- **Better access to capital** markets on mergers and acquisitions

- **No other way to grow**

- **Use surplus cash**

- **Exploit under-utilised resources**

- **Obtain cash**, or other financial advantages (such as accumulated tax losses)

- **Use a company's image and reputation** in one market to develop into another where corporate image and reputation could be vital ingredients for success

- Avoidance of the disadvantages of other types of diversification, eg anti-monopoly legislation

The example of Virgin Group above may be an example of conglomerate diversification.

Disadvantages of conglomerate diversification

- The **dilution of shareholders' earnings** if diversification is into growth industries with high P/E ratios.

- **Lack of a common identity and purpose** in a conglomerate organisation. A conglomerate will only be successful if it has a high quality of management and financial ability at central headquarters, where the diverse operations are brought together.

- **Failure in one of the businesses will drag down the rest**, as it will eat up resources.

- **Lack of management experience**: Japanese steel companies have diversified into areas completely unrelated to steel such as personal computers, with limited success.

- **Poor for shareholders**: Conglomerate acquisitions give no additional benefit to the shareholders – since there is no synergy, the individual investor will do no better investing in a subsidiary company through a holding company than he would have done if he had invested in the subsidiary directly. Shareholders can spread risk quite easily, simply by buying a diverse portfolio of shares. They do not need management to do it for them.

- Since there is no synergy there is no operating advantage over several smaller firms

- Earnings of conglomerates and the price-earnings ratios of their shares seem to be particularly badly affected by economic recession (and this may mean that during a recession they are unable to continue with acquisitions).

The methods by which Ansoff's growth strategies can be implemented (eg organic growth, acquisition etc...) will be considered in Chapter 11.

Note: Assume that the current date is March 20X9.

The Blue Jeans Group was floated in March 20X4 on the Alternative Investment Market with a capitalisation of over £22 million. The company was founded eleven years earlier by three Kenyan Asian brothers who began their venture with a stall on the King's Road market.

Eight years prior to flotation, the business had been built up to such an extent that the brothers were forced to choose between the wholesaling and retailing arms of their operation. In the event, they decided to focus their effort on the faster-growing wholesaling activities. The capital released by the sale of the retail outlets was then used to purchase a warehouse near to the King's Road to stock the garments. It was at this time that the decision was taken to develop Blue Jeans as the brand name for the range of jeans and fully co-ordinated casual wear in which they were trading.

When the brothers began their wholesaling operations, the rapid growth in the market for jeans meant that their largest competitors had full order books and were not in a position to satisfy market demand. Therefore there was plenty of 'market room' for a company like Blue Jeans. The brothers decided to concentrate their effort initially on smaller retailers, since many of these were not being adequately sourced by the larger (mainly US) manufacturers.

Eventually contracts were obtained with John Lewis and the Burton Group, among others. The small retailer was not ignored but, as Blue Jeans grew, it was forced to direct its efforts towards the more established shops rather than market traders.

Manufacturing – sourcing policy

In the first instance Blue Jeans turned to Hong Kong to obtain the larger quantities which it required for its expanding business. It generally takes seven or eight months for a new manufacturing unit to attain the standards which are demanded by Blue Jeans. Around 90 per cent of the company's orders are now produced in Hong Kong. Blue Jeans considers that its policy of contracting out the manufacture of its garments has generally been successful. However, recent delays in producing new styles of jeans from new patterns have caused problems.

Currently Blue Jeans is radically restyling part of the BSCO brand and hopes to take the market by surprise. A contract to produce the first batch of 5,000 pairs of the new design is about to be awarded. Two competing tenders are being considered.

Supplier A   An existing Hong Kong based supplier, offering to deliver the garments in three to six months' time at a cost of £10 per pair payable on delivery.

Supplier B   A new supplier to Blue Jeans, which in the past has worked almost entirely for one of its smaller competitors. Supplier B is offering to produce the jeans at £9 per pair payable in advance. It will deliver in nine months and will pay a penalty fee of £0.50 per garment per month for any late deliveries.

On only one occasion has Blue Jeans become involved in the manufacture of its own garments. The outcome of which was near disastrous. The experience led the brothers to make two important policy decisions.

First, they decided not to go into manufacturing themselves but to concentrate on buying and selling. Secondly, they decided to stick with experienced manufacturers and not to attempt to obtain too great a degree of manufacturing process innovation. Recent changes in textile industry technology, eg flexible manufacturing, JIT, etc, have led one of the brothers to question this approach.

Product market strategy

During the past decade considerable changes have taken place in the jeans market. Therefore flexibility and ability to respond to fairly rapid changes in fashion are an essential component of the ability of a company, such as Blue Jeans, to survive in the jeans business.

The current jeans product strategy of Blue Jeans is based upon a portfolio of four brand names, each of which has its distinctive appeal and identity. First, there is the Blue Jeans brand itself. This is the original brand and is the leader in the group's international activities. The Blue Jeans brand, which is targeted at fashion-conscious men and women in the 15-25 age bracket, consists of two main elements. There are basic denim jeans which are offered on an all the year round basis and there is a casual collection offered on a seasonal basis. The jeans brand is from time to time strengthened by the addition of jeans-related products. These have included footwear, marketed under licence, leather jackets and a range of accessories such as belts and watches. It is envisaged that bags, holdalls and grips will also be introduced.

The Big Stuff Company brand (BSCO) is more 'classical' leisurewear with more contemporary fashions. The BSCO brand is aimed at both men and women in the 16-25 age group. The Buffalo brand, which was designed in Bordeaux initially for the French market, has its own distinctive French flavour. Moreover, its sales are biased heavily towards women, although it caters for both sexes in the 16-24 age group. By contrast, Hardcore is tough and masculine, based upon a traditional 'macho' image. Since it was introduced it has developed its own clearly defined niche within the men's jeans market – namely the 16-35 age group.

Company financing

The development of Blue Jeans during its early years was reflected in a steady expansion in its revenue and profitability. However, five years on, losses were incurred due to a number of unfortunate events. By the 20X2/X3 financial year profitability had recovered and had reached a total of almost £1 million. In order to maintain growth in March 20X4 five and a half million shares, representing almost one quarter of the group's equity, were sold at 100p on the Alternative Investments Market (AIM). This sale raised over £5m for investment purposes.

Since the floatation of the Blue Jeans Group in March 20X4, the company has gone from strength to strength, with average sales growth being roughly 50 per cent per annum. (The Appendix contains Blue Jeans' financial details). Turnover in the year ending 31 March 20X9 is expected to be over £100 million with profits of over £10m. The brothers are keen to maintain this record of sales growth, while at the same time providing the highest possible returns to their shareholders.

The jeans market

During 20X4 a revival in the jeans market occurred, stimulated by Levi's successful reintroduction of its five pocket, fly button 501 jeans. This development, backed by a heavy advertising campaign, may be seen in terms of a more general appeal to nostalgia in society which was prevalent at that time. A craze for stone-washed jeans also helped to boost sales temporarily. However, this fad had fizzled out by 20X7, by which time overall sales were again static.

A more important trend during the mid to late 20X0s was for the jeans market to become increasingly fashion conscious. Traditionally the style of jeans has changed relatively slowly and manufacturers have relied on making standardised products at high volume. This has tended to accentuate the importance of production economies of scale.

Jeans market 20X6

United States (490m pairs)	Europe (180m pairs)
Levi Strauss 24%	Levi Strauss 11%
Diesel 14%	Diesel 4%
Lee 10%	Wrangler 3%
Wrangler 10%	Lee 2%
Guess 3%	Lee Cooper 2%
Others 39%	Blue Jeans 2%
	Others 76%

More recently, rapid changes in style have required companies to exhibit greater flexibility. Designer jean companies, such as Blue Jeans, have generally done well. Of the major manufacturers, Levi and Diesel have prospered. By contrast, Wrangler and Lee Cooper have suffered from their 'cowboy' and 'old fashioned' images respectively.

In an attempt to reverse the adverse trend, Wrangler initiated a major TV advertising campaign. This followed an expansion of such activity by Levi and Blue Jeans. Each of the campaigns had one factor in common – targeting of adolescents, the chief consumer of jeans.

A common feature of the strategic response of the major manufacturers to their business environment has been a decision to withdraw from manufacturing and source their output from contract manufacturers in the Far East. The unquestioned European leader in this respect has been Blue Jeans.

Blue Jeans plc financial details

Blue Jeans: Five year trading summary

	20X8	20X7	20X6	20X5	20X4
	£'000	£'000	£'000	£'000	£'000
Revenue	97,461	72,241	50,242	31,113	19,906
Profit on ordinary activities before taxation	12,756	8,399	5,905	4,208	2,633
Taxation	5,019	2,867	2,010	1,718	1,177
Profit on ordinary activities after taxation	7,737	5,532	3,895	2,490	1,456
Minority interests	240	180	160	47	36
	7,497	5,352	3,735	2,443	1,420
Earnings per share	31.9p	22.8p	15.9p	10.4p	7.8p

Requirements

(a) Outline the factors Blue Jeans should consider in awarding the contract to produce the first batch of the new style BSCO jeans.

(b) As a management consultant, prepare a memorandum to the managing director which

    (i) Performs a corporate appraisal of Blue Jeans at March 20X9.
    (ii) Uses Ansoff to analyse its future strategy options.

See **Answer** at the end of this chapter.

6 Other strategies

Section overview

- The growth strategies identified by Ansoff involve essentially successful business divisions.
- Where divisions are less successful there are strategic choices involving letting them go.

6.1 Withdrawal

Withdrawal may be an appropriate strategy under certain circumstances.

- Products may simply disappear when they reach the end of their life cycles.

- Underperforming products may be weeded out.

- Sale of subsidiary businesses for reasons of corporate strategy, such as finance, change of objectives, lack of strategic fit.

- Sale of assets to raise funds and release other resources.

Exit barriers may make this difficult and/or costly.

- Cost barriers include redundancy costs, termination penalties on leases and other contracts, and the difficulty of selling assets.

- Managers might fail to grasp the idea of decision-relevant costs ('we've spent all this money, so we must go on').

- Political barriers include government attitudes. Defence is an example.

- Marketing considerations may delay withdrawal. A product might be a loss-leader for others, or might contribute to the company's reputation for its breadth of coverage.

- Psychology. Managers hate to admit failure, and there might be a desire to avoid embarrassment.

- People might wrongly assume that carrying on is a low risk strategy.

Worked example: The Royal Bank of Scotland sells Citizens Bank

The following example illustrates the importance of considering the business environment and the impact it has on organisational investment and divestment decisions.

In May 2014 the BBC reported The Royal Bank of Scotland's (RBS) planned public share sale of its US subsidiary, Citizens Bank. RBS purchased Citizens in 1988 and 'turned it into one of the biggest regional banks in the US'. At the height of the global recession in 2008 the UK government moved to support RBS as part of a bank 'bail out' programme, since which RBS has 'been under pressure to sell its foreign holdings'. RBS's decision to divest its Citizen Bank operations have in part been driven by claims of fines for mis-selling mortgages in the US.

Citizens Bank has approximately five million customers and assets of $122.2bn, operating nearly 1,400 branches. The share sale is expected to raise £2.75bn. As the BBC reported, CEO of RBS, Ross McEwan said 'The divestment of Citizens is a key component of our plan to continue to strengthen RBS's capital position. The achievement of our plan will allow us to focus fully on the needs of our customers'.

Source: BBC

6.2 Divestment and demerger

Divestment and demerger have become more common as companies seek to reverse the diversification strategies they once pursued. There are several reasons for this.

- To rationalise a business as a result of a strategic appraisal, perhaps as a result of portfolio analysis, where a lack of fit has been identified. Another reason might be to free up management time to concentrate on core competences and synergies.

- To sell off subsidiary companies at a profit, perhaps as an exit route after managing a turn-round or as a management defence strategy to avoid a potential take-over of the whole company.

- To allow market valuation to reflect growth and income prospects. Where a low growth, steady income operation exists alongside a potentially high growth new venture, the joint P/E is likely to be too high for the cash cow and too low for the star. The danger is that a predator will take over the whole operation and split the business in two, allowing each part to settle at its own level.

- Satisfy investors: diversified conglomerates are unfashionable. Modern investment thinking is that investors prefer to provide their own portfolio diversification.

- To raise funds to invest elsewhere or to reduce debt.

Worked example: 21st Century Fox

In January 2014, 21st Century Fox announced that it was selling its 47% share in Chinese television company, Star China to TV channel operator China Media Capital. Reuters reported that the move represented a 'clear sign of (Rupert) Murdoch's waning interest in China due to the various restrictions and limitations on trade in the country'. James Murdoch, CEO of 21st Century Fox's international operations commented 'today's divestment underscores our broader agenda of streamlining our affiliate ownership structures'.

Source: Reuters

Demerger can realise underlying asset values in terms of share valuation. ICI's demerger of its attractive pharmaceuticals business led to the shares in the two demerged companies trading at a higher combined valuation than those of the original single firm.

Worked example: Taylor Wessing

Taylor Wessing, the UK's 18th biggest law firm by revenue, is prearing to spin off its document review business into a separate entity in the latest move by the firm to shake up its business model.

New Street Solutions, which mines and manages documents for due diligence and property transactions, will be demerged from Taylor Wessing within the next six months or so.

NSS wants to be able to offer its services beyond current clients such as banks and commercial landlords to other law firms, which might be put off if the business were not independent of Taylor Wessing.

Document review, which does not have to be done by experienced, and therefore expensive, lawyers, is one area where firms have looked to cut costs since the financial crisis hit.

Source: *Financial Times*, February 2012

Summary

Self-test

Answer the following questions.

1 Define corporate appraisal.

2 How can corporate appraisal be used to guide strategy formulation?

3 What is gap analysis?

4 What is required for a successful cost leadership strategy?

5 How do you differentiate?

6 Draw Ansoff's growth vector diagram.

7 Explain two alternative strategies for existing products or markets that can be pursued.

8 Explain how a producer of natural spring water could attempt to gain a competitive advantage over its rivals giving specific examples.

9 If a tennis racquet manufacturer began selling a line of tennis clothing, what sort of growth would this be in terms of Ansoff's matrix? Suggest two ways in which such development could be achieved.

10 **Hannafords Dairy Ltd**

Hannaford's Dairy Ltd (Hannafords), operates a fresh milk delivery service. The company is one of your firm's clients. Recently the directors have been concerned about the company's future. This is partly because the directors intend to sell the company for the maximum value, and retire, in about five years' time. You have been asked to assess the current position and make recommendations for the future strategic direction of the company. The company's stated objective is 'to provide the best possible service to our customers.'

Hannafords was formed in the early 1960s by two brothers when they inherited a milk delivery business from their father. Immediately before the father's death the business had amounted to three milk rounds carried out by the father and sons. The relatively small amount of administrative work had been undertaken by the father. The business operated from a yard on the outskirts of Avonbridge, a substantial town in the far south west of England.

Hannafords expanded steadily until the early 1980s, by which time it employed 25 full-time rounds staff. This was achieved because of four factors.

(1) Some expansion of the permanent population of Avonbridge
(2) By expanding Hannafords' geographical range to the villages surrounding the town
(3) An expanding tourist trade in the area
(4) A positive attitude to marketing

As an example of the marketing effort, the arrival of a new resident into the area is reported back by the member of the rounds staff concerned. One of the directors immediately visits the potential customer with an introductory gift, usually a bottle of milk and a bunch of flowers, and attempts to obtain a regular milk order. Similar methods are used to persuade existing residents to place orders for delivered milk.

By the mid-1980s Hannafords had a monopoly of door-step delivery in the Avonbridge area. A combination of losing market share to Hannafords and the town's relative remoteness had discouraged the national door-step suppliers. What little locally-based competition there once was had gone out of business.

Supplies of milk come from a bottling plant, owned by one of the national dairy companies, which is located 50 miles from Avonbridge. The bottlers deliver nightly, except Saturday nights, to Hannafords' depot. Hannafords deliver daily, except on Sundays.

Hannafords bought and developed a site, for use as a depot, on the then recently established Avonbridge Trading Estate in 1970. This was financed by a secured loan which the company paid off in 1985. The depot comprises a cold store, a parking area for the delivery vans, a delivery van maintenance shop and an office.

Profits after adjusting for inflation, have fallen since the early 1980s. Volumes have slipped by about a third, compared with a decline of about 50% for door-step deliveries nationally over the same period. New customers are increasingly difficult to find, despite a continuing policy of encouraging them. Many existing customers tend to have less milk delivered. A sufficient profit has been made to enable the directors to enjoy a reasonable income compared with their needs, but only by raising prices. Currently Hannafords charges 40 pence for a standard pint, delivered. This is fairly typical of door-step delivery charges around the UK. The Avonbridge supermarket, which is located in the centre of town, charges 26 pence a pint and other local stores charge between 35 pence and 40 pence.

Currently, Hannafords employs 15 full-time rounds staff, a van maintenance mechanic, a secretary/bookkeeper and the two directors. Hannafords is regarded locally as a good employer. The company pays good salaries and the directors have always taken a paternalistic approach to the employees. Regular employment opportunities in the area are few. Rounds staff are expected to, and generally do, give customers a friendly, cheerful and helpful service.

The two brothers continue to be the only shareholders and directors, and comprise the only level of management. One of the directors devotes most of his time to dealing with the supplier and with issues connected with the rounds. The other director looks after administrative matters, such as the accounts and personnel issues. Both directors undertake rounds to cover for sickness and holidays.

Requirements

(a) Comment on the company's stated objective ('to provide the best possible service to our customers') as a basis for establishing a corporate strategy.   **(2 marks)**

(b) As far as the information given in the question will allow, undertake an analysis of the strengths, weaknesses, opportunities and threats (SWOT analysis) of the company.

You should explain each point you make and provide some indication of the importance which you attach to each.

Indicate what additional information you would need to obtain and why you need it, to enable you to complete your SWOT analysis.   **(16 marks)**

(c) Indicate how the resources of the company could form the basis of its future strategy.

(6 marks)

(24 marks)

11 Read the scenario of the **September 2008 Business Strategy** paper in the Question Bank entitled *DT ltd*, which we mentioned at the start of the chapter. Draft an answer for requirement (a) on SWOT analysis.

12 Read again the scenario of the **March 2008 Business Strategy** paper in the Question Bank entitled *DA plc*, which we mentioned in Chapter 2 and 4. Draft an answer for requirements (a) and (b) on DA plc's competitive advantage and its methods of expansion.

13 Go online at The Times 100 Business Case Studies and read the Bryant Homes case study 'Building a competitive advantage' at http://businesscasestudies.co.uk/bryant-homes/building-a-competitive-advantage

Now, go back to the Learning objectives in the Introduction. If you are satisfied that you have achieved these objectives, please tick them off.

Answer to Interactive question 1

Report

To	Head of Confectionery
From	Business Analyst
Date	Today
Subject	EuroFoods and Medley – the international ice-cream market

1 Terms of reference

This report outlines the strategy options for EuroFoods and Medley under the alternative scenarios resulting from the pending EU decision on exclusive freezer arrangement.

2 Competitive advantage

There are a number of different generic strategies which lead to competitive advantage for a firm's products, and these were identified by Michael Porter of the Harvard Business School.

- **High volume/low cost (overall cost leadership)**
  The cost of manufacture of the product is reduced to the lowest level in the market, thus leading to increased margins. The firm is also able to engage in price wars more effectively than its competitors.

- **Differentiation**
  Significant differences are developed in the quality, features and marketing of the product. Customers are therefore willing to pay a higher price, or the market might fragment altogether, leading to total domination of a niche.

- **Focus**
  Either of the above strategies can be combined with a greater or lesser degree of concentration on a smaller number of potential customers. Use of a focus strategy may defeat competitors using either of the two strategies above, but targeting a wide market. It will also be important in devising strategies for EuroFoods and Medley to consider the effects of the competitive forces in the marketplace.

3 Scenario 1 – EU decision outlaws exclusive freezer arrangements

This decision will have a profound impact on the ice-cream market throughout Europe, as it will directly threaten the strong supplier status of EuroFoods in the impulse market. An indication of how significant this might be can be gained from some analysis of the market data.

Current position

% of European market	Volume	Revenue	Profit
Impulse sales	40	67	80
Take-home sales	60	33	20
	100	100	100

It is not clear from the data given exactly what share EuroFoods has of the impulse sales market, but it is unlikely to be less than its 60% overall share of the market, due to the competitive advantage gained from its exclusive freezer arrangements. Indeed, the commentary suggests EuroFoods to be dominant in this lucrative market segment. The outcome of an EU judgement in favour of Medley would therefore be to remove a significant entry barrier – the control of distribution.

3.1 EuroFoods' strategic options

The threat of new entrants to the market must be considered by EuroFoods as significant when forming a competitive strategy to take account of this scenario. Ideally, the entry barrier to the impulse sector formerly provided by the exclusive freezer arrangement must be replaced by another of equal effectiveness.

It would appear that the greatest current advantage that EuroFoods possesses in the EU impulse sales market, with the exception of the exclusive freezer arrangement, is its scale of production and established position as market leader.

This suggests that barriers to entry are available in the areas of economies of scale and the experience effect, both of which should lower the cost of production. It seems clear that an 'overall cost leadership' strategy may well be open to EuroFoods, which would enable super-profit to be taken.

This profit could be reserved for a future price war, but it is more likely that Medley will continue with its current differentiation strategy. It seems more apposite to recommend that EuroFoods invest heavily in product development and marketing in order to produce, brand and place cheaper products which directly compete with the more exclusive and higher-priced Medley brands.

3.2 Medley's strategic options

The removal of exclusive freezer arrangements by the EU will present Medley with a major opportunity for growth. Although there will be a cost impact, as Medley will have to negotiate a fee for the use of the EuroFoods freezers, this will be far less significant than the removal of a major entry barrier.

The EU is likely to view a punitive fee strategy by EuroFoods as being similarly anticompetitive.

The strength of Medley seems to lie in its ability to demand a higher price by differentiation of the product. As the basic product is the same (ice-cream), this is probably by the use of brand names carried over from the chocolate products.

The profit earned in this way must be reinvested in widening the distribution network into outlets previously dominated by EuroFoods, and in reinforcing the transfer of brand image to maintain the margin, while generating additional sales.

Due to the recent heavy capital investment in the European factory, it is unlikely that Medley can compete under an overall cost leadership strategy, which is the likeliest option for EuroFoods anyway. Maintaining the focus on the impulse sales segment seems preferable to attempting to compete in the take-home market which yields far lower margins.

4 Scenario 2 – Exclusive freezer arrangements remain

This represents a continuation of the current market conditions, which suggests that EuroFoods will find it easier to maintain its dominance of the market. However, Medley has already achieved a 10% market share with a new product and further penetration is likely.

4.1 EuroFoods' strategic options

EuroFoods must continue to exploit its competitive advantage in the impulse segment by entering into more exclusive freezer arrangements in areas of Europe not significantly penetrated.

In the take-home sector, however, EuroFoods is very vulnerable to attack even though margins are lower and branding is probably less significant.

EuroFoods may like to consider supplying major supermarket chains with a low-price 'clone' of the Medley product, possibly under an own brand. This should be supported actively by the supermarkets which will devote more freezer space and force Medley out of the segment.

The cost advantages of EuroFoods will ensure that Medley cannot compete without a significant subsidy from the other (non ice-cream) areas of the business.

4.2 Medley's strategic options

If the exclusive freezer arrangements are to continue, Medley must continue its differentiation-focus strategy by supporting the brand in the impulse segment.

Significant capital expenditure will be required to supply and maintain freezers in competition with EuroFoods, and many small retailers will be unable to provide space for both.

Medley will have to examine opportunities for alternative retail methods which are less expensive and more attractive to the retailers.

It may be possible, for example, to invest in the development of smaller freezers which could be placed on the counter. This would require Medley to limit the number of lines on offer (possibly to the one existing line) to make the best use of the limited display space and avoid stock-outs or heavier distribution costs due to more frequent deliveries.

In the take-home segment, the exclusive freezer arrangements do not apply, and Medley has an opportunity to penetrate the market with multi-buy packs of the same branded product.

However, the brand will have to be heavily supported by advertising to guard against copies from EuroFoods. It may be possible to widen the range of lines using other Medley brand names, if the impulse sale segment seems out of reach.

Medley cannot rely on retailers breaking the exclusive freezer arrangement with EuroFoods, but can make it known that it will supply non-exclusive freezers if retailers have problems with EuroFoods. This strategy may backfire if EuroFoods refuses to supply retailers which break the agreement.

5 Conclusions and recommendations

It can be seen that the decision in the EU is fundamental to the strategy formulation of both companies. The strategies recommended can be summarised as follows.

	Decision pro-Medley	Decision anti-Medley
EuroFoods – impulse EuroFoods – take-home	Overall cost leadership and product development	Maintain entry barriers own-branded clones
Medley – impulse	Differentiation – focus	Differentiation – focus/branding
Medley – take-home	n/a	Branding, advertising new products

Answer to Interactive question 2

The Blue Jeans Group

(a) Choice of supplier

Many factors should be taken into account in selecting a supplier. The main considerations are the following.

- **Cost**

  Supplier A is more expensive but is paid on delivery. Once penalty payments are incurred B becomes even cheaper.

- **Delivery**

  The importance of prompt delivery needs to be considered. Delivery by B is very late whilst A's is earlier but uncertain. Late delivery by B may save cost but it could lead to a loss in profits. Delivery dates quoted on both tenders could be considered to be unacceptably long.

- **Quality**

  Supplier B is new to Blue Jeans and may fail to meet the required quality standard.

- **Reliability**

  Supplier B is new to Blue Jeans and two significant risks are involved.

  (i) **Credit risk** – payment is in advance and Blue Jeans are therefore carrying the credit risk.

  (ii) **Security** – there is some danger that the design of the new jeans may be 'leaked' to Supplier B's existing customers.

In conclusion, Supplier A appears the safer option but delivery dates need to be renegotiated. It would probably be better to test Supplier B on a less important order before allowing it to work on new designs.

(b) **Memorandum**

To   Board of Directors, Blue Jeans plc
From   A Consultant
Date   March 20X9
Subject Strategic position of Blue Jeans plc and future strategy options

1   Current strategic position

- The current financial position of the firm is strong in terms of profit and sales growth. EPS has shown a dramatic increase. Its past profit problems now appear to be resolved. No information is available on liquidity and financial structure and it is necessary to examine these areas before making a final recommendation.

- It has a range of products aimed at particular market segments and a 'designer image' which is important in the current market for jeans. It has a clearly focused strategy based on product differentiation.

- Its share of the European market is low (20X6) and it appears to have no stake in the large US market. However, in Europe it is of similar size to most other companies, apart from Levi Strauss. The jeans market is currently static and intense competition can be expected. Competition from other leisurewear manufacturers (eg track suits, etc) is also possible.

- It is currently supplied almost exclusively from Hong Kong. This could well have cost advantages, but several problems are apparent.

  (1) The unstable political situation in Hong Kong could eventually threaten supplies.

  (2) Exchange rate changes could lead to uncertainty over costs of products to be sold in the European market.

  (3) A danger of forward integration by existing suppliers also exists.

  (4) Long lines of supply and a long lead time in bringing new suppliers up to the required quality standard may hamper Blue Jeans' ability to exhibit the greater flexibility needed to cope with rapid changes of style. Changes in production technology may now be increasing the attractiveness of in-house manufacturing.

- Little information is available as to Blue Jeans' existing customer base and detailed information will be required before a final recommendation can be made.

2   Future strategy options

2.1 Introduction

The objectives of the firm are expressed in terms of sales and profits. To a certain extent these two factors are in conflict as sales can often be increased at the expense of profit although this has not appeared to be a problem in the past. Maintaining past growth in both these areas is a considerable task in the face of a static market for jeans, and unless Blue Jeans can make advances in market share, a gap between objectives and actual performance is likely to develop if it simply continues with its existing strategy.

2.2 Options

The options for future strategy can be thought of under four headings.

Diversification – moving into new areas

Product development – selling new products to existing customers

Market development – selling existing products in new markets

Market penetration/internal efficiency – growth in sales and profits by increasing share of existing market, and/or reducing cost.

2.3 Diversification

- Blue Jeans has no experience of diversification into totally different product markets so this possibility is discounted.

- Horizontal diversification is a possibility, involving the takeover of an existing competitor. Two existing competitors (Lee and Wrangler) are currently experiencing difficulties due to their old fashioned image and could be potential targets. They would both provide footholds in the US market and possibly allow Blue Jeans to generate economies of scale. However, on the evidence available both of these companies are considerably larger than Blue Jeans (see US market share) which could make any takeover difficult (but not impossible).

- Vertical integration. Two possibilities exist here.

  (i) Forward integration into retail. Given the nature of jeans retailing this seems unlikely, however, more detail on existing customers is required before this can be ruled out.

  (ii) Backward integration into manufacture. Although previous attempts have been unsuccessful, this does not mean that the strategy should be dismissed out of hand. It is investigated in detail in the next section.

2.4 Establishment of a manufacturing facility

- **Advantages**

  (i) Savings in transportation costs, search costs, etc.

  (ii) Improved quality.

  (iii) Greater flexibility in design and manufacture if features such as flexible manufacturing, JIT, etc are introduced.

  (iv) More rapid response to changes in styles.

  (v) 'Secrecy' of new designs is also maintained.

  (vi) Avoidance of exchange risk if manufactured in UK. (Exchange risk on exports would still exist.)

- **Disadvantages**

  (i) Blue Jeans will carry the 'volume risk' of manufacture. If demand falls it will still have to cover its fixed manufacturing costs.

  (ii) Subcontracted suppliers, due to their experience or location, may offer cost advantages.

2.5 Product development

- Some attempts have already been made to broaden Blue Jeans' product range by the addition of jeans-related products.

- This trend could be continued by the introduction of other products such as sportswear or similarly related products, which could be sold through existing distributors. Careful analysis of the demand for these new products would be required. Significant marketing expenditure could be required to promote these products.

- The possibility of on-line sales should be investigated. This would avoid the need to find new distributors.

2.6 Market development

- Blue Jeans' coverage of the European market should be reviewed. Information is only available on France and the UK. Other countries, including Eastern Europe states should be investigated.

- Blue Jeans has no stake in the US market which in 20X6 was three times larger than the UK.

- Licensing of the Blue Jeans name to manufacturers in other countries could be considered, although this could detract from quality and hamper any export drive at a later date.

- Online sales could enable Blue Jeans to enter new markets/market segments without the necessity of a physical presence. This could be a first step before any overseas expansion is considered.

2.7 Market penetration

- The situation in the jeans market appears to be changing from one requiring high volume at low cost to one of product differentiation.

- Blue Jeans should therefore continue to differentiate its product through advertising and aiming at particular market segments. New brands for new segments could be introduced. Online sales/website may encourage loyalty and repeat purchases.

- Cost reduction is of course important but this should not be at the expense of the policy of differentiation. This will be a major consideration in the decision to establish manufacturing facilities. The increased flexibility of own manufacture and the ability to introduce new products rapidly may outweigh the benefits of reduced cost and risk from out-sourcing. Alternatively the internet could be used to seek new supplies and reduce costs.

3 Conclusions

- The recent financial performance of Blue Jeans has been strong but in a static jeans market existing growth rates will be difficult to maintain.

- Changes in the competitive nature of the jeans markets may lead to a greater emphasis on flexibility, rather than cost. A detailed financial appraisal of in-house manufacturing is now required. This could either be by a green field start-up or an acquisition.

- Blue Jeans' existing policy of differentiation should be continued.

1 A critical appraisal of strengths, weaknesses, opportunities and threats.

2 Match strengths with market opportunities; convert weaknesses into strengths and threats into opportunities.

3 Comparison of the objective with the outcomes of already-planned activities.

4 Economies of scale; latest technology; learning curve effect; improved productivity; minimised overhead costs; favourable access to sources of supply.

5 Build brand image; create special features in the product; exploit the value chain.

6

		Product	
		Present	New
Market	Present	Market penetration	Product development
	New	Market development	Diversification

7 Using the BCG matrix, one of four strategies can be pursued for each product.

 (a) Building market share: This is an appropriate strategy if

  (i) Market growth rate is high
  (ii) The product is in its growth stage (of the product life cycle)

  Such a strategy is appropriate for stars and some (if not all) problem children but requires considerable cash to fund high marketing expenditure.

  This strategy involves heavy advertising, discounted pricing and intensive use of promotional techniques.

 (b) Holding market share: This is appropriate where both the product and market are mature, as in the case of cash cows, but could be applied to some stars.

  Holding is achieved by ensuring that advertising expenditure and prices are comparable to those of competitors.

 (c) Harvesting: This strategy allows market share to decline, thus allowing the company to maximise its short-term earnings.

  It could be applied to the problem children which the firm does not wish to or does not have the resources to turn into stars.

  Harvesting is typically achieved by cutting marketing expenditure and/or raising prices.

 (d) Withdrawal: This is an appropriate strategy where the product has a lower than viable market share with no realistic hope of an improvement – typically applicable to dogs.

  The product is in an unattractive market, and there is thus little purpose in improving market.

8 Product differentiation:

 • Advertising campaign to stress health giving properties
 • Package in fancy glass bottles
 • Label the bottle using more stylish design

 Cost leadership:

 • Use plastic bottles
 • Bring prices per litre down below competitors
 • Sell in multi-packs to increase volume

9 Product development – sales of a new and different product are made but to the same (original) market or customer base.

This could be achieved by:

- Buying in tennis clothing made by another manufacturer and rebadging it
- Developing their own range of clothes from scratch
- Entering into a strategic alliance with a clothes manufacturer to develop the range together

10 **Hannafords Dairy Ltd**

(a) **Objective**

Objectives need to provide a practical basis for the establishment of a strategy.

Hannafords' objective – 'to provide the best possible service to our customers' – lacks most of the elements in 'SMART', an often-used technique for evaluating objectives.

Specific. 'Best possible service' is rather vague and needs expansion into more specific areas, eg all deliveries by 8 am.

Measurable. There is no readily available scale on which to measure whether 'the best service' has been given.

Achievable. It is hard to say whether the objective is achievable given the comments on specific/measurable above.

Relevant. The objective is very relevant if the business is to survive in the face of increased competition from supermarkets.

Timescale. No timescale is mentioned but is not perhaps necessary. Given the way the objective is expressed and the current position of Hannafords (see (b) below), it is probably a day-to-day objective!

(b) **SWOT analysis**

This analysis looks at the immediate strengths and weaknesses of the company itself and the opportunities and threats presented by the environment in which it operates.

(i) Strengths of Hannafords

(1) The main strength of the company is its monopoly of milk delivery in a fairly isolated area.

(2) It has a good reputation locally so that even with a price more than 50% above that of the supermarket, it is losing business more slowly than the industry average.

Other, less significant strengths include the following.

(3) It has no loans outstanding and owns its premises.

(4) It has a reputation for being a good employer with good wages, and the staff respond to this.

(5) The directors have shown some skill in marketing as all new residents in Avonbridge are targeted with an introductory gift as an incentive to have a daily milk delivery.

(ii) Weaknesses of Hannafords

(1) A significant weakness is the reliance on one source, owned by a national dairy. Although it would seem unlikely the dairy would withdraw supplies, it may be able to force price increases on Hannafords.

(iii) Threats

(1) A significant threat is in relying on one product (doorstep delivery of milk) with reducing sales in a declining market. If it continues to decline this will not be a sustainable position.

(2) Another main threat is that posed by the supermarket and town shops which undercut on price by up to 35%.

(3) A less immediate threat is that the cultural acceptance of the milkman is being gradually eroded, so that for many people all their grocery shopping, including milk, is done at the supermarket. The milkman is therefore not considered.

(iii) Opportunities

(1) The most important opportunity presented is to take advantage of the company's position as the only doorstep delivery operation by diversifying into other products.

(2) A further significant opportunity is to cut the cost base by only delivering every other day. This would require careful handling to ensure it had customer support but would allow for a halving of the delivery fleet. Given the company's employment reputation this may have to be achieved through normal turnover of staff, unless other opportunities for the workforce can be found.

Other, less significant, opportunities include the following.

(3) Free or cheap 'cool boxes' for keeping the milk fresh when people are at work all day.

(4) Carrying advertisements on the milk floats or on the milk bottles.

(5) Considering diversifying into cheese production, which could be marketed to tourists both through local shops and on the milk rounds.

(6) Explore selling milk to the local supermarket as part of a 'buy British' campaign. This is quite topical as a number of supermarket chains now actively purchase goods for resale from local communities.

(7) There may be scope for the brothers to sell the company to the local milk supplier when the time for them to retire comes.

Summary

Overall, Hannaford's Dairy Ltd is performing well. The brothers' experience of the milk delivery market in Avonbridge has been invaluable in helping them exploit the company's position over local rivals, who have gone out of business. The company's position has been supported in part by its remote location which has helped to deter potential competitors.

The continued success of Hannaford's Dairy is likely to depend on the brothers' ability to make its operations more cost efficient in the long term without damaging the company's local image as a good employer and supplier.

Additional information

In order to complete the SWOT analysis it would be useful to have the following information.

(i) The financial statements of the last three years and budgets for the next year, in order to assess its financial strength and cash reserves. This will give an idea of the timeframe within which any changes have to be made.

(ii) How close is the nearest rival to assess the likelihood of the monopoly position being threatened.

(iii) An analysis of past prices from the dairy to see whether it tries to impose price increases regularly.

(iv) The relative remoteness of the outlying villages and the public transport facilities. This would be to assess the usefulness to those without cars of Hannafords offering other products on their deliveries.

(v) A market survey of the likely customer reaction to deliveries on alternate days.

(vi) The demand for local advertising.

(vii) The location of any other cheese makers and their proximity.

ICAEW

(c) **Resources and strategy**

It is important for the company to identify its core competencies from which it can develop its strategies. These appear to be as follows.

Competitive architecture

- Internal: Good (paternalistic) relationships with staff.

- External: Losing customers at a slower rate than national experience so there appears to be some degree of customer loyalty.

Reputation

- Good in terms of home deliveries as it has established a monopoly position. Service regarded as friendly, cheerful and helpful.

Innovative ability

- Marketing innovation, eg flowers for new customers.

Ownership of strategic assets

- Monopoly on doorstep deliveries.

Based on these core competencies possible strategies to improve profits are to use the delivery network to expand the product range, eg fruit drinks, milk drinks, fruit, vegetables, and fresh/frozen meats. Alternatively or in addition the network could be used for deliveries of a different nature, eg mail, parcels, prescriptions (particularly for the elderly), dry cleaning, etc.

11 Refer to the answer to part a of DT Ltd in the Question Bank.

12 Refer to the answer to part a and b of DA plc in the Question Bank.

13 There is no answer to this self-test, as it is designed just to help you increase your business awareness.

CHAPTER 8

Strategies for products and markets

Introduction

Examination context

Topic List

Summary and Self-test

Answers to Interactive questions

Answers to Self-test

Learning objectives

- Explain, in a given scenario, how products and services must evolve in the face of changing consumer demand and industry competition ☐

- Explain how to position particular products and services in the market place to maximise competitive advantage ☐

- Define and understand the key terms and concepts used in marketing ☐

- Understand and be able to apply the concept of market segmentation ☐

- Understand the marketing mix, its roles and limitations ☐

- Explain how a business can collect and analyse financial and other data in order to provide relevant information for strategic decision making ☐

- Explain how to develop a marketing strategy ☐

Specific syllabus references for this chapter are: 2b, 2h, 2i.

Syllabus links

In the Business and Finance paper you will have covered the basic objectives and processes of marketing management. You will also have shown how the marketing function assists in the achievement of business objectives.

This chapter revises these topics and explains how marketing is an essential part of management both in understanding the environment within which the organisation operates and as a means of promoting growth and developing other strategic objectives.

Examination context

This chapter is important for the exam. Questions may test understanding of marketing concepts in a variety of different types of scenarios. An understanding of product and marketing strategy may involve a particular issue, such as pricing, but also a coherent approach should be put forward where the pricing decision is based upon appropriate market research and is supported in a coherent manner by other aspects of the pricing strategy. Moreover, the market strategy in this chapter needs to be seen in the context of the wider business strategy set out in other chapters.

In Q3 March 2010 (*NP Ltd*) the scenario contains information about the company's new energy-efficient washing machine technology which it has developed and wishes to launch. The first requirement is:

'Advise [Nilesh] on the issues to address when selecting the best market for the new technology, using

the following headings:

(i)   Market research
(ii) Segmentation and targeting.   **(10 marks)'**

When answering a question like this the key thing to remember is that to obtain the skills marks you must apply what you know to the scenario in front of you, not just list out theories.

1 Revision of product market strategies

Section overview

- Marketing is one of the functional strategies responsible for implementing the strategic choices of management.

- Marketing can help create Porter's generic strategies of cost leadership, differentiation or focus through how it targets and positions products.

- Marketing strategy identifies and helps develop new products and markets in the Ansoff matrix.

1.1 Marketing terminology

Marketing

Marketing may be defined as the set of human activities directed at facilitating and consummating exchanges. From this it can clearly be seen that it covers the whole range of a firm's activities. Alternatively, marketing could be defined as 'the management process which identifies, anticipates and supplies customer requirements efficiently and profitably' (Chartered Institute of Marketing).

Customer, consumer and targeting

A distinction can be made between:

- The customer, who purchases and pays for a good or service.
- The consumer, who is the ultimate user of the good or service.

Thus if a company makes corn flakes, its customers are supermarkets etc, but the consumer is the individual who eats the corn flakes. Both customer and consumer need to be targeted.

To obtain greater precision a firm may segment its market, ie divide it into smaller parts where the parts can be treated differently for marketing purposes. The firm can then target particular segments. Segmentation is covered in section 2 below.

Marketing orientation

A firm which has a marketing orientation will see the needs of consumers/customers as vital. If it develops and markets products to meet these demands (ie to meet the critical success factors), certain structural characteristics will be apparent within the company, ie:

Function	Activity/department in the company
Identifying customer/consumer needs	Marketing research
Developing products to meet consumer/customer wants/needs	R&D/production
Determining the value of the product to the customers	Pricing
Making the product available to the customer	Distribution
Informing the customer/consumer of the product's existence and persuading them to buy it	Promotion

1.2 Product-market strategy: direction of growth

Chapter 7 demonstrated that to respond to the environment, businesses have to choose:

How to compete: Competitive strategies include cost leadership, differentiation or focus.

Direction of growth: Product/market strategy refers to the mix of product and markets (new or existing) and what the firm should do.

Method of growth (acquisition or organic growth): This will be covered in Chapter 11.

Marketing strategy deals with the first two of these because it enables an organisation to concentrate its limited resources on the greatest opportunities, defining how the organisation will engage customers, prospects and the competition in the market arena, to increase sales and profits and so achieve a sustainable competitive advantage.

1.3 Marketing strategy and Porter

Porter's **three generic strategies** are recipes to create superior long-term profitability.

Overall cost leadership – achieve lowest delivered cost to customer to boost margins and survive market entry and price wars better than competitors.

Differentiation – acquire status of premium perceived value in the market to enable higher prices to be charged and to resist competition from cheaper 'follower' products.

Focus – monopolise a niche segment by provided either a specifically tailored product of very high perceived value or by cutting extraneous costs to gain access to the lowest price segments.

Marketing strategy positions products in the market place according to these generic strategies. This will involve correct tailoring of the main elements of marketing, the **marketing mix**:

- **Product** – the offering the customer consumes
- **Price** – the pricing point and actual cost in use to customer
- **Promotion** – how it's advertised and sold
- **Place** – where it is available, can be accessed or bought from
- **People** – the personnel the customer meets
- **Physical** – the look and feel of the business premises, publicity etc
- **Process** – the way the clients make a purchase or the way the client is dealt with

The final three Ps are particularly important for service companies' marketing

Worked example: Airline marketing strategies

EasyJet – a cost leader

EasyJet was founded in March 1995 as a no-frills airline. It had two leased aircraft and contracted in all ground staff and maintenance. 10 years later, as a listed company with a substantial fleet and another 120 new planes on order it welcomed its 100 millionth passenger. Its marketing strategy consisted of:

- Promotion of its low price position via gaudy posters and full page press advertisements making clear comparisons with rival's prices and naming and shaming corporations which wasted shareholder's money by not using it.

- Ensuring a very high profile for its flamboyant founder, Stelios Haji-Ioannou. This provided many free column inches in the popular press, inevitably against the backdrop of his airline's name.

- Promotion of its low costs base at Luton Airport as 'London's Third Airport' to overcome the latter's previous reputation as merely a holiday airport. The name London Luton Airport was belatedly adopted some years later by the airport itself.

- Basic level of service with no in-flight food or entertainment, basic departure lounges to avoid costs of using airport facilities and delays waiting for passengers. This included no reserved seating and reusable boarding passes.

- Direct sales to save commissions, initially by operating a call centre but, ahead of most other airlines, via its website.

- Dynamic pricing under which the ticket price would rise or fall according to the level of demand for the particular flight.

- Featuring of strong white on orange livery which is very distinctive and visible (even from the ground) and also allowed some piggy-backing from the much larger campaigns being run at the time by mobile phone operator Orange.

- Featuring of telephone number 292929 which emphasised its entry level fare of £29 on its original routes from Luton to Edinburgh – about 10% of the lowest fares of its rivals to the same destination.

- Participation in several series of a fly-on-the-wall documentary showing its daily work.

- In 2014 as part of its 'Generation EasyJet' campaign, the airline increased its marketing spend to £53m in a bid to consolidate its market position. An article in Marketing Week highlighted that despite the increase, EasyJet have maintained a minimum marketing spend per customer with this reported as being low at an average £1.69 per passenger seat. However, benefits have come from targeting the marketing spend much more efficiently. The introduction of allocated seating, improvements to EasyJet's mobile app and enhanced data capability have enabled the airline to roll out special offers on seats at the appropriate moment. EasyJet claim such moves are designed to build brand affinity and loyalty.

British Airways – a differentiator

In the past BA has sought to be 'the World's favourite airline'. Its marketing strategy has included:

- Large scale promotion in magazines, posters and television emphasising its friendly staff, superior cabin accommodation and accelerated check-in procedures.

- Routes to and from major airports from its hub at London Heathrow, the main hub of European and Transatlantic air travel.

- Distinctive red, white and blue livery across planes, uniforms and promotional materials.

- Search for global image via ethnic paintings on its planes, sponsorship of events etc.

- Several classes of passenger service and accommodation to enable premium passengers to remain separate from lower price 'World Traveller' customers.

- Frequent flyer benefits.

Qatar Airways – a focus player

Qatar Airways is one of the world's leading airlines, operating 129 aircraft serving 134 destinations. The airline was set up in 1993 and predominantly served travellers to the Middle east and Asia. Like most major airlines Qatar Airways offers flights for families and groups of 10 or more travellers, however in 2014 the company announced plans to launch its own daily all business class flights from Heathrow airport in the UK to Doha in Qatar. Its marketing strategy includes:

- Running articles in the business press on the new service to attract target users
- All seats convert to beds with the maximum cabin capacity capped at 40 passengers
- Passengers can access over 900 movies and television shows
- Customers can use SMS mobile texting and GPRS technology to connect with business colleagues
- When customers arrive at Heathrow they will treated to priority security screening
- Passengers can arrive at the steps of the plane by limousine
- A return flight is expected to cost over £4,000

Source: *The Telegraph*

1.4 Marketing strategy and Ansoff

Product-market strategy is the mix of products and markets. **Market segmentation** is a tool of marketing strategy that helps management to identify new markets, and to use a **marketing mix** to arrive at a desirable market position. The Ansoff matrix identifies various options (see details in previous chapter).

Product

		Present	New
Market	Present	Market penetration	Product development
	New	Market development	Diversification

Market penetration: Maintain or to increase its share of current markets with current products, eg through competitive pricing, advertising, sales promotion and to increase usage by existing customers.

Market development: Expand into new market segments or geographical areas.

Product development: Launch of new products to existing customers or similar markets.

Diversification: Develop into new industries.

Worked example: Johnson Wax

Johnson Wax

SC Johnson & Son, the multibillion-dollar consumer products company, used marketing strategy to develop from floor wax to candles – and much, much more.

Samuel Curtis Johnson started the company in 1886 when the special wax he used to finish parquet floors became very popular with customers and led Johnson to develop *Johnson's Prepared Wax* and move into consumer products. Then the company discovered aerosol can technology, put the wax and paste mix into pressurized cans, and launched *Pledge* – the first sprayable furniture polish for home use.

From here the company filled aerosol cans with anything sprayable: scented liquid became *Glade*, an air freshener now available in more than a dozen fragrances; an insect repellent *Off!*, which is still the category leader, shaving gel *Edge* took it into a whole new market.

Meanwhile, *Off!* led to plug-in insect repellents and, through another route, to insect repellent candles. The plug-in units are also the basis of newer presentations of Glade fragrances.

1.5 Danger in assuming 'one size fits all'

Market segmentation refers to the practice of looking for sub-groups in a market.

Focus players obviously depend on this, but it is also practised by broader market players too:

- Differentiated breakfast cereal manufacturer Kellogg's segments the market into children's cereals (Rice Krispies, Frosties etc), adult cereals (Corn Flakes), commuters (cereal brands in a bar).

- US-based cost leader supermarket chain Wal-Mart segments the market into geographical locations where its price-conscious positioning will appeal.

The argument for **mass marketing** is that it creates the largest potential market, which leads to the lowest costs, which in turn can lead to lower prices or higher margins.

Critics point to the increasing splintering of the market, which makes mass marketing more difficult and denies the firms that use mass marketing the opportunities of niche markets.

A proliferation of media (Internet, cable TV, mobile phones) and distribution channels (download, direct selling from websites and catalogues) is allowing more personalised shopping and more personalised marketing messages. It is difficult to practice 'one size fits all' marketing and some observers even claim that mass marketing is dying. It is being replaced by **target marketing** and **personalised marketing**.

2 Segmentation, targeting and positioning

Section overview

- Market segmentation divides markets into sub-units to help target the marketing effort.

- Segmentation bases are the methods used to divide consumer and industrial markets.

- Positioning a product involves putting in the market at a point that will attract the interest of its target segments and able to satisfy their requirements.

2.1 Market segmentation

Definition

Market segmentation: The division of the market into homogeneous groups of potential customers who may be treated similarly for marketing purposes.

Segmentation allows the organisation to vary its marketing mix to each segment it chooses to enter.

Alternatives are:

- Mass (undifferentiated) marketing – no segmentation eg sugar

- Niche (concentrated) marketing – concentrate on one or two market segments eg Morgan cars

- Micro marketing – complete segmentation, tailoring products and services to individual needs eg Dell offering customers the opportunity to customise PCs to meet their own needs

2.2 Benefits of market segmentation

- The organisation may be able to identify new marketing opportunities, because it will have a better understanding of customer needs in each segment, with the possibility of spotting further sub groups.

- Specialists can be used for each of the organisation's major segments. For example, small business counsellors can be employed by banks to deal effectively with small firms.

- The total marketing budget can be allocated proportionately to each segment and the likely return from each segment. This optimises return on investment.

- The organisation can make adjustments to the product, price and other elements of the marketing mix to improve returns.

- The organisation can try to dominate particular segments, gaining the competitive advantage from a Focus strategy.

2.3 The bases for segmentation

The methods used to split the market up into segments are called **segmentation bases.** They will seek to segment markets according to factors such as:

- Type of customer, eg business, personal, own use, presents etc

- Different needs and tastes of the customer

- Location of the customer

- Spending potential of customer

- Circumstances of the customer, eg loans targeted at new businesses or those with poor credit ratings

Segmentation can be divided into industrial segmentation and consumer segmentation.

Industrial segmentation includes:

- Geographic: eg as basis for sales force, distribution or because industries cluster
- Purchasing characteristics: eg order size, frequency of order
- Benefit, eg reliability, economy, durability, versatility, safety, value for money
- Company type: eg type of business, sole trader, partnership, limited company
- Company size: eg number of employees, profits, revenue
- Internet eg capable of/willing to buy online

Consumer segmentation includes:

- Geographic: eg as by country, region, city etc

- Psychological: groups sharing common psychological characteristics, eg old people may be security-oriented

- Purchasing characteristics: eg heavy user, medium user, low user

- Benefit: eg soap powders – smell, whiteness, economy, stain removal

- Demographic: divides the market into groups based on such things as age, gender, family size, income, occupation, race etc. One method – socio-economic grouping – is explored further below

2.3.1 Socio-economic grouping

Socio-economic	Social status	Job description	Approx % of UK population
A	Upper middle class	Higher managerial, administrative and professional eg chief executive, surgeon	3
B	Middle class	Middle management, administrative and professional eg teacher, bank manager	11
C1	Lower middle class	Supervisory, clerical, junior management, administrative, non-manual eg bank clerk, sales person	23
C2	Skilled working class	Skilled manual workers eg electrician, carpenter	33
D	Working class	Semi and unskilled manual jobs eg assembly line worker, refuse collector	22
E	Subsistence	Pensioners, widow(er)s, lowest grade workers, unemployed eg casual workers	8

Modern information and communications technology, especially social media, make it possible to create 'segments of one' for personalised marketing.

- Personalised versions of home pages for on-line stores (eg Amazon 'page you made')

- Loyalty cards allowing personalised offers to be given at the check-in (eg screens on shopping carts in supermarkets), check-out or in personalised mailings

- Interactive TV with specifically tailored advertisements in the commercial breaks

- Personalised email and text messages and alerts

2.3.2 Buyer and customer behaviour

A crucial element in the marketing process is understanding **why** a buyer does or does not purchase an organisation's goods or services. If the organisation does not understand the process, it will not be able to respond to the customer's needs and wishes.

Due to the differences that often exist between 'consumer buyers' (those who purchase items for personal consumption), and 'industrial buyers' (those who purchase items on behalf of their organisation and where there are far fewer but larger buyers), it is traditional to split buyers into these two broad groups for analysis.

Consumer adoption model

The people who first buy one type of consumer goods are frequently the same people who first try others. Customers can be divided into groups according to the speed with which they adopt new products.

The **innovators** are relatively young, lively, intelligent, socially and geographically mobile and of a high socio-economic group (largely AB).

Conversely, the **laggards**, who are slow to accept new products, are older, less intelligent, fixed in their job and residence, less well off, and lower on the socio-economic scale. It can be seen that when a company launches a new product, its early customers are likely to be significantly different from its later ones. The consumer adoption model is also consistent with the product life cycle.

This concept can be very useful for marketers trying to assess for example, future Internet demand/uptake, the potential market for WAP phones and other product innovations.

Interactive question 1: Global automobile market [Difficulty level: Intermediate]

(a) Explain the concept of marketing segmentation and the benefits that it can bring to a global automobile business like Toyota, Ford or General Motors.

(b) Identify and illustrate, with examples, SIX criteria that can be used to segment the global automotive market.

See **Answer** at the end of this chapter.

2.4 Targeting

Targeting involves selecting the best market segments.
The attractiveness of a market segment depends on it being:

- **Measurable**: The ability to forecast the sales or market potential of the segment. Knowing this will be essential for production and distribution planning and also for financial forecasting.

- **Accessible**: The ability of the firm to make and distribute a product to and the availability of suitable promotional media.

- **Stable**: The likelihood that the segment will persist for sufficient time to enable a return on the investment of developing a marketing mix for it.

- **Substantial**: The profits available will give an adequate return on capital employed.

- **Defensible**: There should be barriers to entry to allow the firm some measure of dominance.

Issues to consider include:

- How big is the market segment?
- How quickly is it growing?
- How many competitors are there and what is their market share?
- What are the main distribution channels?
- Are there any potential substitute products or services?
- What is the relative power of buyers/suppliers?
- What resources and competences does the company have?

Target marketing tailors a marketing mix for one or more segments identified by market segmentation.

Targeting strategies can be:

- **Single segment** strategies (concentrated strategies): One market segment is served with one marketing mix – suitable for smaller organisations with limited resources.

- **Selective specialisation** (multi-segment strategies): Different market mixes are offered to different market segments. Proctor and Gamble provide Pampers disposable nappies to young families, cosmetics such as Calvin Klein to the youth market and Old Spice to the elder male.

- **Product specialisation**: The organisation specialises in a particular product and tailors it to suit different market segments. Dell and Apple both make computers targeted at homes and at businesses.

- **Market specialisation**: The organisation specialises in serving a particular market segment and offers that segment an array of different products. Harley Davidson aims at the older and born-again biker and sells a range of motorcycles, accessories, apparel and, with less success, cosmetics.

- **Full market coverage**: The organisation attempts to serve the entire market. This coverage can be achieved by means of either a mass market strategy in which a single marketing mix is offered to the entire market, such as Starbucks coffee houses, or by a multi-segment strategy in which sufficient separate marketing mixes are offered to cover the whole market. Many supermarket chains attempt the latter when they offer economy, standard, and premium ranges of own-label products in lines that include food, cleaning products, clothing and light bulbs.

2.5 Positioning

Definitions

Positioning: The overall location of a product in the buyer's mind in relation to other competing products/brands.

Re-positioning: Changing the identity of a product, relative to the identity of competing products, in the collective minds of the target market.

A product or brand can be positioned in a number of ways, eg via a price or emphasis on a particular characteristic or set of characteristics. In other words, positioning means giving a product a place relative to its competitors on factors such as quality, price, image, being exotic, providing status, etc.

Positioning can be facilitated by a graphical technique called perceptual mapping, various survey techniques and statistical techniques like multi-dimensional scaling and factor analysis.

One way of obtaining the information required to draw up this type of matrix would be to ask target consumers to rank the products on a five-point scale on quality. Values could then be attributed to the respective answers as follows: very good score: 5, good score: 4, reasonable score: 3, poor score: 2 and very poor score: 1. The information could be brought together as shown below.

Even such a rather simple product positioning matrix as shown above may give valuable insights in the relative positions of the various brands.

The first conclusion is that the position of brand B is rather precarious. It is more expensive than brand C, but considered to be of lower quality. C is considered to be of better quality, but sells at a lower price. There also appears to be a gap in the market in the middle segment at a price level between D and C.

In Chapter 7 we looked at Bowman's clock as a model that can be used to analyse the position of a business relative to its competitors based on its chosen combination of price and perceived added value.

Worked example: Supermarkets & Watches

In food supermarkets the major competitors are positioned more or less centrally, with Waitrose at the higher end ('quality food, honestly priced') and ASDA towards the lower end. Tesco has gradually moved up the quality scale, with its 'Finest' range, whilst ensuring price competitiveness with it's 'Everyday value' range. Marks and Spencer, as a relative late-comer to food retailing, has always tried to occupy a position of distinctly superior quality. As we saw in Chapter 7, during the recent recession, discount supermarkets Lidl and Aldi have thrived as consumers switch from premium priced products in search of value for money. This has in effect helped to move the likes of Lidl and Aldi into direct competition with established players including Tesco and Sainsbury's. This shift has seen a return to the high street of discount retailer Kwik Save which operates a 'back to basics' convenience store format, which prides itself on its aggressive promotions policy.

Comparable to the UK supermarket sector are the leading global watch brands, with each brand positioned to appeal to particular buyer groups. Swiss brand Omega is over 150 years old, its watches are largely targeted at business professionals and watch collectors. Omega is the producer of quality precision watches and prides itself on its long time association with the Olympic Games having been nominated as the official time keeper on 21 occasions. Fellow Swiss brand TAG Heuer is classed as a luxury watch brand, targeted again at business professionals but also sports fans due to its partnership with the McClaren F1 team. Fossil watches by contrast was established in the USA in the 1980's, its watches are targeted more as fashion items and are sold at considerably lower prices.

Interactive question 2: Rex Ltd
[Difficulty level: Intermediate]

Rex Ltd is a UK-based nationalised car manufacturer that is going to be privatised in the next four years. It has suffered from years of poor management and under-investment. This has resulted in a poor public image and a diverse product range. Details of current models are given below.

Off-road division

Range Rex. A market leader with a strong image as being the off-road vehicle to be seen in around town. It enjoys a high profit margin but is starting to face increasing competition in a growing market.

Land Rex. A leader in the market of 'working' off-road vehicles. Has a huge market share and faces few competitors in a fairly static market.

Family division

Mindless. A revolutionary design – 30 years ago. This is the original small car. It is now competing against many larger models including Rex's Matchless in the small family hatchback market. The Mindless is not a hatchback and, as a result of nil investment over the last 20 years, is regarded as being an anachronism, bought only by enthusiasts. It is totally unprofitable.

Matchless. An economical and fun to drive small family hatchback. The car is well designed but poorly built. It has the potential to become market leader but is held back by its poor reputation. This is a growing but highly competitive market.

Hopeless and Hapless. Two models in the medium-size family market. They are both poorly designed, poorly built and have astonishingly bad reputations. Neither car has a market share of any significance. The market is not growing. It is, however, thought vital to have a car aimed at this market sector.

Executive division

The Rex. What was once a car synonymous with quality has had its reputation somewhat tarnished lately due to its unreliability. Its existing customer base is loyal but increasingly being persuaded to buy more reliable imported cars. This is a growing and highly profitable market.

Requirements

Explain what the terms 'product positioning' and 'market targeting' mean and how these might be applied in developing Rex's strategy.

See **Answer** at the end of this chapter.

---

3 Marketing research

Section overview

- The definition of marketing in paragraph 1.1 emphasises 'meeting customer needs' and also 'efficiency'.

- Marketing research helps management identify needs that can be satisfied at a profit to the firm.

- It also helps evaluate the effectiveness of the component parts of the marketing effort to ensure marketing reaches it objectives efficiently.

3.1 Areas for marketing research

In order to meet the critical success factors in target segments and develop sustainable competitive advantage over competitors, information is needed.

Definition

Marketing research: is the systematic gathering, recording and analysing of information about problems relating to the marketing of goods and services.

Marketing research therefore includes not only market research but also the gathering of any data useful for formulating the seven 'P's marketing mix.

Market research involves looking at specific markets, their size, market trends, information resegmentation, customer characteristics, customer needs and wants, demand curves, competitors' products, etc.

Product research could include laboratory testing to analyse product safety, durability and shelf-life.

Pricing research could include attempts to generate more accurate figures to facilitate cost-plus pricing.

Promotional ('market communications') research might include contacting national newspapers to determine their readership and how much they would charge for advertising.

Distribution research could include contacting potential retail outlets to determine what margins they would expect to make.

3.2 Stages in marketing research

A research programme will involve the following steps:

- Defining (and locating) problems, setting objectives
- Developing hypotheses
- Research – desk and field research
- Data collection
- Analysis and interpretation
- Conclusions and recommendations

3.3 Desk research

Definition

Desk research is the gathering and analysis of existing or secondary data. This may use existing company reports and other information from both internal and external sources.

Information from internal sources

Many companies develop internal databases. Information can come from many sources eg accounts department, production records, orders etc. Supermarkets use loyalty cards to develop databases as a means of segmenting and targeting. The initial information provided is supplemented by purchasing information every time the card is swiped at the till.

Other often neglected sources of information are:

- Management accounts:
    - Analysis of sales/profits by produce or region

- Sales department:
    - More sales analysis – customer complaints

- R&D department:
    - Information about technical developments

Rules for successful desk research

- Assume that the work has already been done – it just needs to be located.
- Think laterally and keep an open mind.
- Follow up leads, however vague.
- Get behind the published data, since often what is published is just a summary.
- Avoid saying 'market research'.
- Avoid asking for 'statistics'.

3.4 Field research

Definition

Field research involves the collection of new (primary) information direct from respondents. As such it is usually more expensive than desk research and so is only performed if desk research fails to answer all questions asked.

3.4.1 Types of research

There are three basic types of field research.

- **Opinion research**: to determine people's opinions on general issues, eg pollution.

- **Motivation research**: to determine why people do what they do, especially why they would buy one product rather than another. Their motives may be complex/subconscious.

- **Measurement research**: to quantify research so that sample results can be extrapolated to the target population, eg how many people are planning a holiday to Italy next year?

Specific techniques

- In-depth interviews.

- Group interviews.

- Trial testing, eg out of three chocolate bars which would you choose?

- Word association, eg 'lager drinkers' – lout?

- Observation, eg use cameras to determine how long on average it takes to serve customers in a restaurant.

- Questionnaires – very common.

- Online – Internet surveys and focus groups (see later).

Sampling

- Ideally one should choose **random samples**, where each person in the target group has an equal likelihood of being selected. If large enough, a random sample will be representative of the target population in every respect, not just those considered important. Consequently extrapolation of results is more reliable and easier to quantify. Unfortunately it can be very difficult to be unbiased in a sampling technique.

- A popular alternative is **quota sampling**, where certain characteristics of the sample are predetermined. People are then chosen specifically to fill the required quotas within the sample.

  For example, suppose the target population is made up of 56% men and 44% women, a quota sample of 200 people would therefore contain 112 men and 88 women. Once 88 women had been questioned no more would be asked.

  The main problem with quota samples is that, while they may be representative as far as preselected criteria are concerned, they are likely to be biased in other respects. Consequently it is more difficult to predict how the population as a whole will behave.

- Opinion and motivation research tend to use small samples, whereas measurement research samples are much larger to facilitate more accurate extrapolation.

- In **panelling** the same sample is retained so that changes/trends in behaviour are easier to identify, eg the British government's National Food Survey was of approximately 2,000 families.

- Sampling may involve personal face-to-face contact (eg door-to-door, intercepting people in shopping centres, etc), telephoning, mailshots and email shots or by putting questionnaires in magazines. The problems with questionnaires are, firstly, a low response rate and, secondly, that the sample picks itself, so may not be representative of the population as a whole as only those wishing to partake in the questionnaire will respond.

  In recent times it has become increasingly common for organisations to run surveys via their websites. In many cases this approach is directed to gain user feedback on using the entity's website, products or services. Companies such as Survey Monkey help businesses and individuals alike to run surveys on various issues through social media sites such as Facebook or Twitter. .

Test marketing

Test marketing involves a trial run of a product in a typical segment of the market before proceeding to a national launch. This could involve just selling a product in selected locations: eg Marks & Spencer may initially try out a new product in 10 representative stores.

At the other end of the scale the test may incorporate all aspects of the marketing mix in a certain area of the country. Such a test market should have the following characteristics:

- Small
- Self-contained
- Representative
- Adequate promotional facilities

Examples include Norwich, Reading, Oxford and the Tyne Tees TV region.

Experimentation

Users of the experimental method attempt to investigate only one variable at a time, keeping all other factors constant.

Examples of the experimental approach can be found in advertisement testing, where alternative advertisement designs can be assessed in otherwise identical marketing situations. It can also be found in package testing, where different packaging styles are used whilst other factors are held constant.

Theoretically, any marketing mix variable could be tested. The method for setting up a test would be similar to that set out below, which describes how to carry out a **sales area test**.

- Select areas which are as nearly identical as possible and which represent the market for the tested product.

- Ensure that all factors except that being tested are as nearly identical as possible. In a sales area test this means using similar distribution outlets in comparable positions within the area.

- Record sales in each area before the variable is introduced.

- Set up the new variable in all except one or two areas. These are the control areas, in which previous marketing mix settings are maintained.

- Measure sales while the tested variable is set up, and afterwards. Differences between the test-variable areas and the control areas are due to the effects of the test variable.

In practice it is difficult to find test areas which resemble each other closely, and non-tested variables tend to alter during the test due to factors beyond the control of researchers.

4 Branding and brand equity

Section overview

- Brands add value to products by making them recognisable and endowing them with associations attractive to the target segment.

- The ability of a brand to do this, to be the basis for future product launches, and to defend a product's market share against incursions makes a brand an asset because it generates future earnings.

- Although difficult to value precisely for balance sheet purposes it is conventional to describe this ability to create future value as brand equity.

4.1 Branding

Brands have three essential features:

- **Name**: This should be legally protected, memorable, and be consonant with the product itself if possible. The names of cosmetic brands like Obsession and Clinique do the latter well, whereas others like Estee Lauder and Helena Rubenstein as names say very little at all.

- **Livery**: Designs, trademarks, symbols, and a range of visual features which should make it identifiable. Brands like Mars and Coca Cola are very recognisable.

- **Associations and personality**: This helps a brand distinguish a company's product from competing products in the eyes of the user. Drinks like Bacardi Breezer are fun drinks whereas Chivas Regal has gravitas.

4.2 Branding policy

There are different branding policies that an organisation can adopt:

- **Single company name**: Examples of companies which use a single label on all products, and describe individual items in a more or less factual way include Crosse & Blackwell and Heinz. This policy has several advantages; the attributes possessed by one product are transferred to another and new product launch is simplified because there is no need to build up new brand awareness. (eg Virgin and derivatives of easyJet).

- **Different brand names for each product**: This is where a company produces a number of products with significantly different positions in the market, or where the market is highly segmented, the brand strategy is often to use different brand names for each product. This policy is very common among manufacturers of soap powders, chocolate bars and breakfast cereals.

- **Own branding**: Many retailers sell grocery, clothing and hardware products under a brand name of their own to help create loyalty to the store rather than to the producer of the product.

4.3 Brand positioning

A basic perceptual map can be uses to plot brands in perceived price and perceived quality terms.

- Cowboy brands: Excessively priced brand for the quality of the product.
- Premium brands: Top of the range quality, but high-priced.

- Bargain brands: Good quality for a relatively low price.
- Economy brands: Cheap brands, low-priced and low quality.

Price and quality are important elements in the marketing mix, but they will not, in the customer's opinion, be considered independent variables. A high price will usually be associated with high quality and equally low price with low quality. Thus, while everybody would like to buy a bargain brand, there is a problem to overcome. This is a question of belief: will customers accept that a high quality product can be offered at a low price? A key question is whether the quality of the product is readily discernable by the consumer.

4.4 Brand equity

Definition

Brand equity: An intangible asset that adds value to a business through positive associations made by the consumer between the brand and benefits to themselves.

- **Financial**: One way to measure brand equity is to determine the price premium that a brand commands over a generic product.

- **Brand extensions**: A successful brand can be used as a platform to launch related products. The benefits include raising brand awareness leading to reducing advertising expenditures and enhancing the core brand. These benefits are more difficult to quantify than are direct financial measures of brand equity.

- **Consumer-based**: A strong brand increases the consumer's attitude strength towards the product associated with the brand, leading to perceived quality, inferred attributes and eventually, brand loyalty.

The benefits of a strong brand equity include:

- A more predictable income stream

- Increased cash flow by increasing market share, reducing promotional costs and allowing premium pricing

- Having an asset that can be sold or leased

- Reduced marketing costs because of high brand awareness and loyalty

- More power in bargaining with distributors and retailers

- Higher prices accepted by the market because the brand has higher perceived quality

- Potential for launching extensions easily because the brand has high credibility

- Defence against price competition

5 The marketing mix

Section overview

- The marketing mix represents the tools marketers have to position products and to obtain sales.

- The traditional four Ps marketing mix was designed for tangible products and has been extended into the seven Ps to apply to service based businesses.

- The seven Ps are introduced briefly here so that you can relate to them better in the detailed descriptions of each in the later sections.

5.1 Seven marketing Ps

Definition

Marketing mix: The set of controllable marketing variables that a firm blends to produce the response it wants in the target market.

In the Business & Finance text you will already have been introduced to the traditional 4 Ps of the marketing mix (Product, Price, Place, Promotion), which is primarily directed at tangible products.

The tertiary sector of a developed economy will typically account for over half its economic activity. This is the service sector.

Services differ from products because of their intangibility and consequent need to provide reassurance to the customer through the visible aspects of service provision. This leads to an extended marketing mix for services and knowledge based businesses, known as the 7 Ps.

In practice, many manufacturing industries will pay attention to the service elements of their offering too as a form of differentiation eg Car makers will pay attention to the showroom and after-sales service to enhance their brands and fast food providers likewise.

The three extra Ps with particular emphasis in service marketing are:

- **People**: The people working for an organisation often say more about that company than any product or service can. They must portray the values of that organisation whenever they contact customers – a restaurant could serve the finest food imaginable, but it counts for nothing if the waiter has poor personal hygiene.

- **Processes**: The way in which a good or service is delivered has an impact on the way in which customers perceive the organisation.

- **Physical evidence**: The elements of 'marketing mix' which customers can actually see or experience when they use a service, and which contribute to the perceived quality of the service, eg the physical evidence of a retail bank could include the state of the branch premises, as well as the delivery of the banking service itself.

5.2 Characteristics of service

A service can include a haircut, an audit, a theatre presentation, the processing of a financial transaction in a bank account or an insurance policy.

There are some basic characteristics of services that distinguish them from purely physical products:

- **Intangibility**: A service is not a physical thing. A bank transaction is performed for you, you have evidence that it has been achieved, but in itself it is what someone does for you.

- **Inseparability**: The delivery of the service occurs often at the same time it is consumed. You do not store a haircut for consumption later. The service is produced by the barber/hairdresser and consumed by you at the same time.

- **Heterogeneity/variability:** Many services face problems in ensuring a consistent standard. For example, the friendliness of flight attendants on an aircraft can affect your enjoyment of the service. This is also true of business services such as auditing or the offering of financial advice: regulatory bodies and the firms themselves go to great lengths to ensure there are procedures in place to ensure consistency.

- **Perishability:** A service cannot be stored. You cannot store a haircut for later consumption.

- **Ownership:** Typically, a service rarely results in a transfer of ownership. The purchase of a service sometimes only confers the right to use something.

Worked example: Disney

Disney theme parks are a good example of service delivery. The processes, including booking, queuing procedures at the attractions, operations of the attractions and design of the customers' walk through the park, are vital to its functioning. So too are the employees or the 'cast' as they are called; their job is to interact with customers. Physical evidence is clear in the branding and thematic coherence as well as the existence of souvenirs to take away, photographs of the people enjoying the ride and so on.

Interactive question 3: Services marketing   [Difficulty level: Intermediate]

(a) Identify four differences between services and products, giving a practical example for each, and discuss the problems that these differences present to the marketer.

(b) Identify the extended marketing mix which a small service company, such as a management consultancy, would need to consider when marketing its services.

See **Answer** at the end of this chapter.

5.3 The extended marketing mix

Mix element	Comment
Product	Quality of the product as perceived by the potential customer. This involves an assessment of the product's suitability for its stated purpose, its aesthetic factors, its durability, brand factors, size, packaging, associated services, etc.
Price	Includes prices to the customer, discount structures for the trade, promotion pricing, methods of purchase, alternatives to outright purchase.
Place	Distribution channels, location of outlets, position of warehouses, inventory levels, delivery frequency, geographic market definition, sales territory organisation, intermediaries and logistics between the producer and the end consumer.
Promotion	Covers the **communications mix** • Advertising • Public relations • Personal selling • Sales promotions, eg contests or limited special offers
People	Staff appearance, service training, technical knowledge, manner etc.
Processes	Efficiency of the service. For example, the ease with which a well-designed loan application form can be completed could be an important element in a bank's loan service.
Physical evidence	Refers to items that give physical substance, such as logos, staff uniforms and store layout/design. However, the purpose of evidence is that a service is intangible: physical evidence enforces the idea by giving something to show for it.

ICAEW

Interactive question 4: Marketing mix   [Difficulty level: Intermediate]

Indicate the main characteristics of marketing mixes which would be appropriate for the following.

(a) A large banking group

(b) A company that manufactures electronic components for computer manufacturers

See **Answer** at the end of this chapter.

6 Product

Section overview

- Products are what the customer is physically buying and experiencing.

- Product strategy decides which features to add to a product, ranging from basic features to the augmented ones that may differentiate it from rivals.

- New product development is a part of this process and is the Product Development strategy identified by Ansoff. It is expensive and risky and so needs to be justified.

- Developing products for global markets, and whether to adapt them to different country markets, is reviewed in connection with Ansoff's Market Development strategy.

6.1 Defining and classifying products

Marketers consider products as not a thing with features but a package of benefits that satisfy a variety of consumer needs.

Products cover offerings that fall into one of the following categories:

- **Goods** – something tangible ie, something that is felt, tasted, heard, smelled or seen.

- **Services** – something is considered a service if it is an offering a customer obtains through the work or labour of someone else. Unlike goods, services are not stored, they are only available at the time of use and the consistency of the benefit offered can vary from one purchaser to another (eg, not exactly the same hair cut each time).

- **Ideas** – the marketer attempts to convince the customer to alter their behaviour or their perception in some way. Marketing ideas is often a solution put forth by non-profit groups or governments in order to get targeted groups to avoid or change certain behaviour.

6.2 Components of a product

The total product offering is made up of three main elements:

- **Basic** (or core) product eg, a car – at the very heart of all product decisions is determining the key or core benefits a product will provide. From this decision, the rest of the product offering can be developed.

- **Actual** product, eg a BMW 5 Series – while the consumable product is, in most cases, the most critical of all product decisions, the actual product includes many separate product decisions including product features, branding, packaging, labelling, and more.

- **Augmented** product, eg BMW 5 Series with lease finance, M3 sports equipped or X5 off-road capabilities – goods and services that provide additional value to the customer's purchase.

6.3 New product development

New product development (NPD) is a generic term which incorporates innovative products and modifications and improvements to existing products.

Not all NPD is blue-skies innovation.

	Novelty to customer	
Novelty to firm	Low	High
Low	Product refinement	Product repositioning
High	New product line	New to the world

The product development strategy of the company can:

- Develop new product features through adapting existing features
- Create different quality versions of the product
- Develop additional models and sizes

Reasons for product development

- The firm has high relative share of the market, strong brand presence and enjoys distinctive competitive advantages in the market.

- There is growth potential in the market. (The Boston Consulting Group recommend companies to invest in growth markets.)

- The changing needs of its customers demand new products. Continuous product innovation is often the only way to prevent product obsolescence.

- It needs to react to or incorporate technological developments.

- It needs to respond to competitive innovations in the market.

However product development strategy carries considerable investment risk. There are reasons why new-product development is becoming increasingly difficult to achieve.

- In some industries there is a shortage of good new product ideas.

- Narrowing market segments lead to low volumes that cannot justify the investment involved.

- A company typically has to develop many product ideas in order to produce one good one. This makes new-product development very costly.

- Even when a product is successful it might still suffer a short life cycle with rivals quick to 'copycat' in the market but with their own innovations and improvements.

- There is a high chance of product failure.

6.4 Global products: standardise versus adapt

Products can be classified according to their degree of potential for global marketing:

- Local products – seen as only suitable in one single market.

- International products – seen as having extension potential into other markets.

- Multinational products – products adapted to the perceived unique characteristics of national markets.

- Global products – products designed to meet global segments.

Factors encouraging standardisation	Factors encouraging adaptation
Economies of scale in production and marketing	**Differing usage conditions**. These may be due to climate, skills, level of literacy, culture or physical conditions.
Consumer mobility	**General market factors** – incomes, tastes etc.

Technology	**Government** – taxation, import quotas, non tariff barriers, labelling, health requirements. Non tariff barriers are an attempt, despite their supposed impartiality, at restricting or eliminating competition.
Image	**History**. Sometimes, as a result of colonialism, production facilities have been established overseas. Eastern and Southern Africa is littered with examples. These facilities have long been adapted to local conditions.

Financial considerations. In order to maximise sales or profits the organisation may have no choice but to adapt its products to local conditions

Pressure. Sometimes suppliers are forced to adapt to the regulations imposed on them (eg the EU) if they wish to enter into the market. |

Keegan has distinguished five adaptation strategies of product and promotion to a foreign market. See the diagram below:

Product

	Do not change Product	Adapt Product	Develop new Product
Do not change Promotion	Straight extension	Product adaptation	Product invention
Adapt Promotion	Communication adaptation	Dual adaptation	

Promotion

- **Straight extension**: Introduce the product in the foreign market without any change. Straight extension has been successful with cameras, consumer electronics, and many machine tools. In other cases, such as some US gas-guzzling vehicles, it has been a disaster.

- **Product adaptation**: Alter the product to meet local conditions or preferences. A company can produce a **regional version** of its product, such as a Western European version, or a **country version**.

  Examples of this are McDonald's producing burgers made of fish and chicken for the Indian market where the cow is sacred, pharmaceutical companies modifying medicines to satisfy different national/state regulations.

- **Communications adaptation**: An adjustment in marketing communications only. This is a low cost strategy, but different product functions have to be identified and a suitable communications mix developed, eg bicycles promoted as a means of transportation, rather than for leisure, in developing countries.

- **Dual adaptation**: Both product and communication strategies need attention to fit the peculiar need of the market, eg different clothing to suit different tastes and different promotion to reflect fashion in certain countries and functionality in others.

- **Product invention**: Creating new products to meet the needs and exclusive conditions of the market.

  For example, the development of clockwork radios to serve needs of villagers in developing countries where batteries are scarce and expensive.

7 Place

Section overview

- The aim of distribution is to position the product where the target consumer can readily access it whilst at the same time maximising the earning to the firm.

- There are many distribution channels available to firms and they are selected on complex grounds including support, margin and market position.

- Distributing to overseas markets involves similar channel selection decisions.

7.1 Distribution strategy

Distribution strategy means deciding on the best way to get your product to your customer. The decision depends on several variables:

- The existing distribution channels for your type of product
- The cost of setting up your own network for your product
- The regulatory environment governing your type of product
- The cost of inventory and how this changes with the different distribution strategies

Distribution strategy should be consistent with the price, product and promotion. The places where the product is available say a lot about its perceived quality and status. The channels of distribution must match the image goals of the product and the customer's perception of the product.

7.2 Points in the chain of distribution

Distribution functions are carried out through a **channel** of distribution which comprises all the institutions or people involved with the movement and exchange of products or services.

Retailers are traders operating outlets which sell directly to households.

Wholesalers are intermediaries who stock a range of products from competing manufacturers to sell on to other organisations such as retailers. Many wholesalers specialise in particular products. Most deal in consumer goods, but some specialise in industrial goods (for example, steel stockholders and builders' merchants).

Distributors and dealers are organisations which contract to buy a manufacturer's goods and sell them to customers. In addition to selling on the manufacturer's product, distributors often promote the products and provide after-sales service.

Agents purchase the manufacturer's goods, but earn a commission on whatever sales they make.

Franchisees are independent organisations which in exchange for an initial fee and (usually) a share of sales revenue are allowed to trade under the name of a parent organisation. Examples include Ikea, McDonald's and some Starbucks shops.

Direct selling includes:

- Mail order
- Telephone selling
- Personal selling (consumer/industrial)
- Computer-shopping or TV shopping

7.3 The choice of distribution channel

Distribution channels fall into one of two categories: direct and indirect channels.

- **Direct distribution** means the product going directly from producer to consumer without the use of a specific intermediary. Direct distribution methods generally fall into two categories: those using media such as the press, leaflets and telephones to invite response and purchase by the consumer and those using a sales force to contact consumers face to face.

- **Indirect distribution** refers to systems of distribution which make use of an intermediary; a wholesaler, retailer or perhaps both.

Considerations in developing efficient channels of distribution

- The reach of the distributor. Can they access the target markets?

- The degree of exclusivity that the channel will offer. Will the firm's goods be sold side by side with rivals?

- The amount of support given by the channel. It may be necessary for the channel to provide an efficient after-sales and repair service, or to agree to an immediate exchange of faulty products, advertising or sales promotion support.

- The economic costs of supplying such as number of delivery drops, the average order size and whether they can return unsold goods.

- Support for combined promotions.

 Worked example: Insurance

Before the Internet many car insurance sales were made through brokers, eg the AA. With the Internet there was the opportunity to sell direct, eg Direct Line via call centres. Now reintermediation has occurred with the creation of online brokers to replace the traditional broker of the past, for example screentrade.co.uk.

7.4 Selling and distribution in overseas markets

There are a number of elements to consider when selling overseas. How the company's **sales presence** in export markets is organised is one of the key decisions.

Depending on the product, it may be sold directly. For example, over the Internet or by exhibiting at local trade shows.

Many businesses look for a **partner** who already understands the local market. For example:

- They can sell to a **distributor** who then sells their products locally.

- They can use a **sales agent** who sells products on their behalf, or puts them into contact with potential customers on a commission basis.

- They can enter into a **joint venture** with a local business. This gives them a share of the management and profits of the joint venture, but is a more complicated and expensive option.

If an organisation wants complete control over sales, it can set up its own **local office**. This is the most expensive option.

8 Promotion

Section overview

- Promotion is more than advertising, it also involves public relations, personal selling and sales promotion. We consider the increasing use of social media as a means of promoting products and services along with the risks it brings in Chapter 14.

- Promotion does more than tell people the product and firm exists. It aims to influence the target customers' perceptions of the product so that they see it as a viable solution to their needs.

- Sales force selection, training and management are therefore as much part of this element of the mix as designing a poster.

8.1 Promotion mix

The promotion mix consists of four elements:

(a) **Advertising**: Paid communications in the media which are designed to influence potential customers favourably regarding a company's products or services. Advertising is sometimes called above-the-line promotion.

(b) **Sales promotion**: Non-media promotional activity aimed at increasing sales. Sales promotion includes a variety of techniques such as give-aways, competitions, trading stamps and exhibitions. It is sometimes called below-the-line promotion.

(c) **Public relations**: The creation of positive attitudes regarding products, services, or companies by various means, including unpaid media coverage and involvement with community activities.

(d) **Personal selling**: The techniques by which a sales force makes contact with potential customers.

The promotional mix is often described in terms of push and pull effects.

- A pull effect is when consumers ask for the brand by name, inducing retailers or distributors to stock up with the company's goods.

- A push effect is targeted on getting the company's goods into the distribution network. This could be by giving a special discount on volume to ensure that wholesalers and retail customers stock up with products that the company is promoting.

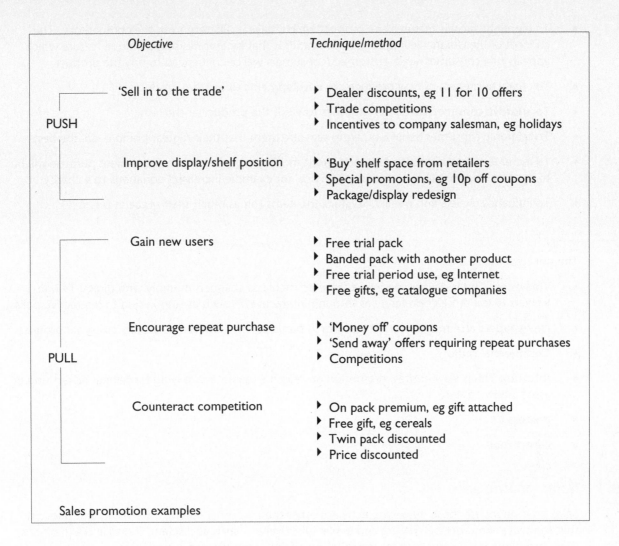

Sales promotion examples

8.2 Advertising

Advertising is an explicit invitation to buy the offering. It also seeks to reinforce the positioning of the product, for example UK department store John Lewis advertises its products with the tagline 'never knowingly undersold', which reinforces the company's brand image of quality and ethical trading. BMW claim its cars are 'designed for driving pleasure'. Advertising is often classed under one of three headings:

- **Informative advertising** – conveying information and raising consumer awareness of the product. Common in the early stages of the product lifecycle or after modification to the product.

- **Persuasive advertising** – concerned with creating a desire for the product and stimulating actual purchase. Used for well established products, often in the growth/maturity stages of the product life cycle. The most competitive form of advertising.

- **Reminding advertising** – reminding consumers about the product or organisation, reinforcing the knowledge held by potential consumers and reminding existing consumers of the benefits they are receiving from their purchase.

8.2.1 The objectives of advertising

The objectives of an advertising campaign may be any of the following.

- To communicate certain information about a product. This is perhaps the most important objective.

- To highlight specific features of a product which make it different from the competitors'. The concept of the Unique Selling Proposition (USP) is that by emphasising a unique feature which appeals to a consumer need, customers/consumers will be influenced to buy the product.

- To create awareness of new products, or developments to existing products.

- To improve customer/consumer attitudes towards the product or the firm.

- To reinforce consumer behaviour, eg to reassure them that their regular brand is still the best.

- To increase sales and profits: for a non-profit-making organisation, the equivalent purpose will be to increase response to the product or service, for example increased donations to a charity.

- To influence dealers and resellers to stock the items (on as much shelf-space as possible).

8.2.2 Advertising media

The principal media are:

- **Television**: This is developing into a targeted media as channels multiply with digital TV and viewers reveal product preferences through interactive TV such as responding to interactive polls.

- **Newspapers and magazines**: Magazines in particular are targeted at specific customer groups.

- **Commercial radio**

- **Internet**: This is via websites, promotion on search engines, and paying for banner advertising on associated websites.

- **Posters**

- **Direct mail**

8.3 Sales promotion

Sales promotions are those marketing activities other than personal selling, advertising and publicity, that stimulate consumer purchasing and dealer effectiveness, such as displays, shows and exhibitions, demonstrations and various non-recurrent selling efforts not in the ordinary routine.

Sales promotional techniques have a more direct effect on usage than does advertising. As such sales promotions can be particularly useful in inducing trials by consumers of rival products.

Examples of sales promotion activities are:

- Coupons to be redeemed against purchase or free gifts.

- Promotions directed to distributors such as 'listing allowances' paid by consumer goods firms to stores so that they will stock the good, or volume bonuses to car dealers.

- Sales force promotions aim to motivate the sales force to sell more. They might include contests.

8.4 Public relations

Public relations has the aim of earning understanding and support and influencing opinion and behaviour. It is the planned and sustained effort to establish and maintain goodwill and mutual understanding between an organisation and the public.

PR encompasses more than customers. It seeks to help the firm build relationships with:

- Customers
- Consumers
- Employees
- Influencers (such as government, regulators and investment advisers)
- Investors
- Suppliers
- Potential employees

There are a wide range of PR activities including:

- Press releases
- Product/service literature
- Corporate relations and sponsorship
- In-house corporate communications
- Design of annual financial reports
- Brochures
- Special events
- Crisis management

8.5 Personal selling

The sales force engages in personal selling, as compared with the non-personal selling of advertising and sales promotion activities. It will include the activities of:

- Delivery and repair staff who may also sell image of the firm or service agreements and upgrades.
- Sales staff within the premises of the sales organisation.
- Travelling sales representatives.
- Call centre staff.

The task of selling

- Communicating the advantages of a product to the customer, to develop the target customer's 'product and market knowledge'.

- Securing a sale.

- Prospecting for additional customers. This involves searching for prospective customers, perhaps visiting them several times, and then making a sales pitch.

- After-sales service. Queries and complaints will arise and must be dealt with to the customer's satisfaction, in order to win repeat sales.

- Gathering information about what the customer wants.

Interactive question 5: Canal Cruises   [Difficulty level: Intermediate]

Canal Cruises Ltd is 60% owned by Captain Salmon. The company has 60 narrow boats and is located just off the Kennet and Avon Canal. There are twenty boats of each of the following lengths, 30ft, 50ft and 70ft. Boats are hired to families and parties of people during the cruising season, which is April to October.

The narrow boats are regarded generally as being of high quality and their hire charge reflects this. All boats have a microwave, stereo and colour TV on board. The boats are currently advertised in *Waterways World*.

Recently Canal Cruises has been approached by the directors of Welsh Cruisers Ltd who wish to sell their business. Welsh Cruisers Ltd is located on the Llangollen Canal and has 30 narrow boats. The boats are of a much lower quality than those of Canal Cruises and over recent years less than half of the boats have been hired out at any one time during the season.

Requirements

Prepare briefing notes for Captain Salmon covering the following areas.

(a) Assuming that Welsh Cruisers is to be acquired and using Ansoff's matrix, comment on the marketing strategies which the company can now pursue, and state with reasons that which you would recommend.

(b) Suggest how the company may go about promoting the newly-acquired Welsh Cruisers and increase the number of boats hired.

See **Answer** at the end of this chapter.

9 Price

Section overview

- Pricing affects sales revenues and profits through affecting margin and volumes.

- Prices should be set with regard to **costs**, **customers** and **competitors**: the 3Cs.

- The sensitivity of volumes of demand and total earnings to price changes is assessed using the economic principles of the price elasticity of demand.

- Although revenues must exceed costs in order that a profit can be made it will be shown that basing price solely on costs is likely to be suboptimal.

- Basing prices on customer perceptions of value will establish the maximum prices that can be charged to a customer, but tends to overlook competition which may put a lower ceiling on maximum price.

9.1 Principles of pricing – the three Cs

Kotler presents the pricing decision as a balance between 3Cs

- Costs
- Customers
- Competitors

Prices must be supported by the remaining elements of the marketing mix. The ability of a firm to charge more than competitors depends on the ability to create differentiation.

A fourth C is corporate objectives.

Corporate objectives

Possible pricing objectives are:

- To maximise profits using demand, elasticity and cost information – the assumed objective in economic theory.

- To achieve a target return on investment (ROI or ROCE). This results in a cost-based approach.

- To achieve a target revenue figure (eg sales maximisation below).

- To achieve a target market share (eg using penetration pricing – see below).

- To match the competition, rather than lead the market where the market is very price sensitive.

9.2 Price elasticity of demand

Economics states that the market demand for a good will increase as the price falls.

Definition

Price elasticity of demand: measures how far demand for a good will change in response to a change in its price.

The price elasticity of demand is used in pricing decisions to:

- Forecast the impact on revenues of a change in the selling price
- Forecast the impact on sales volumes of a change in the selling price

9.2.1 Price elasticity of demand and sales revenue

Consider the following demand schedule which shows the effect of the price of this good on sales revenue the firm receives.

Price	Quantity demand	Total revenue
£10	50	£500
£5	150	£750

In this example the lower price permits a higher sales revenue to be obtained. This is because the fall in price has led to a significant rise in the volume of demand. Demand would be said to be elastic.

If at a price of £5 only 80 units were sold, then total revenue would fall from £500 to £400 and demand would be said to be inelastic.

(a) When demand is **elastic**, a change in price will lead to a change in total revenue in the opposite direction.

  (i) If the price is lowered, total sales revenue would rise, because of the large increase in the volume demanded. This is the case in the worked example above.

  (ii) If the price is raised, total sales revenue would fall because of the large fall the volume in demanded.

(b) When demand is **inelastic** the following will happen.

  (i) If the price is lowered, total sales revenue would fall, because the increase in sales volume would be too small to compensate for the price reduction.

  (ii) If the price is raised, total sales revenue would go up in spite of the small drop in sales quantities.

Information on price elasticity therefore indicates how consumers can be expected to respond to different prices.

9.2.2 Price elasticity of demand and sales volume

Management need to forecast the effects of changes in price on sales volume in two situations:

- Production planning: the level of production will need to be changed to avoid shortages, if the price is cut, or unsold stocks and slack capacity, if the price is raised.

- Rationing demand: where capacity is fixed and in excess demand the price can be raised to reduce the demand.

9.2.3 Influences on price sensitivity of demand

Price elasticity of demand is a measure of the price sensitivity of customers for a good.

Main influences making demand insensitive to price (ie making demand price inelastic) are:

- The product is regarded as a necessity by buyers (eg cigarettes).

- There are few close alternatives available from competitors (ie a lack of **substitutes**).

- The product is highly differentiated and so the customer is brand loyal and will not switch even if prices rises.

- The time since the price changed is short. Therefore customers have not had a chance to notice the price change or to source alternatives.

- The price of the product is insignificant as a proportion of total spending.

9.3 Price discrimination

Definition

Price discrimination: (differential pricing) means setting different prices for a similar product in different parts of the market.

The economic principle behind not setting same price for all is that it may be lower than the keenest (price inelastic demand) customer segments would pay, and so lose revenue, but also too high for less keen (price elastic demand) segments and so lose volumes. Charging high prices to the former and low prices to the latter will maximise revenues.

In order to be successful however there must be:

- Different elasticities in different the markets
- Little 'leakage' between the markets where there are different prices so separation is maintained

Different methods of differential pricing are:

- **Market segment**: In many countries in the world there are discounts for students and young people for certain products and services (eg cinema tickets, rail travel).

- **Product version**: Many car models have 'add on' extras which enable one brand to appeal to a wider cross-section of customers. Final price need not reflect the cost price of the add on extras directly: usually the top of the range model carries a price much in excess of the cost of provision of the extras, as a prestige appeal.

- **Place**: Theatre seats are usually sold according to their location so that patrons pay different prices for the same performance according to the seat type they occupy.

- **Time**: Hotel prices vary according to season. These are all attempts to increase sales revenue by covering variable but not necessarily average cost of provision.

- **Dynamic pricing**: The price of the product varies according to present levels of demand compared with normal demand patterns. Budget airlines will initially set the prices of a future flight low and sophisticated computer programmes will track cumulative sales volume and if it rises more sharply than normal the price will be increased.

9.4 New product pricing: market penetration and market skimming

Market penetration pricing is a policy of low prices when the product is first launched in order to gain sufficient penetration into the market. It is therefore a policy of sacrificing short-term profits in the interests of long-term profits.

- The firm wishes to **discourage rivals** from entering the market.

- The firm wishes to **shorten the initial period of the product's life cycle**, in order to enter the growth and maturity stages as quickly as possible. (This would happen if there is high elasticity of demand for the product.)

Market skimming: The aim of market skimming is to gain high unit profits very early on in the product's life.

- The firm charges high prices when a product is first launched (eg a popular new book may first be published in hardback format, then only later in paperback).

- The firm spends heavily on advertising and sales promotion to win customers.

- As the product moves into the later stages of its life cycle (growth, maturity and decline) progressively lower prices will be charged. The profit is skimmed off in progressive stages until sales can only be sustained at lower prices (eg newly released DVDs and computer games are launched at high prices initially, then the prices are lowered subsequently).

- The firm may lower its prices in order to attract more price-elastic segments of the market; however, these price reductions will be gradual. Alternatively, the entry of competitors into the market may make price reductions inevitable.

9.5 Prices and costs

With the exception of some not-for-profit organisations all organisations will require that in the long run sales revenues should exceed costs.

Therefore management often seek to set prices of each product on the basis of its costs to achieve a **mark-up** on the costs to attempt to earn a profit.

These approaches were covered in your earlier studies. Briefly they are:

- **Marginal cost based**: The price is set as a mark up on the variable costs of the product to give a contribution. This contribution should be sufficient to cover overheads with an additional amount for profit.

- **Full cost based**: The overheads are allocated to the product, eg by absorption costing, and a mark-up added to this representing the profit.

- **Target return based**: The full cost is increased by an amount representing the rate of profit required on the assets used to make the product.

Basing price on costs may have several advantages:

- **Simplicity of operation for distributors**: Stores with thousands of lines of stock and frequent changes will simply set mark-ups for each product class.

- **Control of sales discounting**: Sales teams and distributors will be aware of the mark-up (more likely **margin** ie % of full sales price that represents profit) and will ensure they do not drop price to uneconomic levels to win a sale.

- **Ease of budgeting**: Systems of standard costing and budgetary control require that prices and costs be forecast more than a year in advance. It is easier to make assumptions based on costs and then use variance analysis and reporting to deal with exceptions.

- **Conformity with contracts**: An increasing number of commercial partnerships have followed state procurement methods of cost-plus contracts to ensure fair but not excessive profits for suppliers. Often the supplier is required to offer **open book accounting** so that partners can verify this.

The problems of cost-based pricing are that it:

- **Ignores the effect of prices on volumes**: Most estimates of costs assume a forecast (standard) level of production. If this results in an excessive price then the firm will either not achieve these volumes, and so not recover fixed overheads, or it will suffer the costs of an increasing inventory of unsold goods. In both cases profits would be reduced.

- **Ignores the effect of volumes on costs**: Stimulating demand by accepting low prices and margins on initial production may enable a firm to gain economies of scale over time and also to access a much larger market.

- **Is useless for very high fixed cost industries**: Where variable cost per customer served is low or zero (eg television broadcasting, cinemas, sports grounds and festivals, hotels), the objective of pricing must be to maximise sales revenue. This can only be accomplished by referring to the demand schedule and price elasticity of demand, and not by reference to costs.

- **May not suit positioning of the product**: Successful differentiation will increase potential prices without increasing costs in the same proportion. There is a danger the firm could undersell its product and reduce profits.

- **Ignores competitive conditions:** Where a product is sold in several markets, margins should vary. In less competitive markets margins can be higher, but lower in more competitive markets. Having the same price in all markets is unlikely to maximise profits (see differential pricing above).

- **Does not consider the implications for sales of other products made by the firm:** Selling some products at low or negative margins may generate sales of associated purchases (a so-called **loss leader** approach).

- **Inherent problems in assessing costs:** The approach will focus on production costs and allocate other costs as overheads. The methods of attributing costs to products may not be sensitive enough and hence lead to some potentially profitable products to be priced out of the market.

- **Invites poor cost control:** Increasing costs will be passed on as higher prices resulting in less sales and revenues.

In practice cost-based prices are taken as the starting point for prices but these are then adjusted for considerations of strategic advantage, competition etc, by the management of the firm or by the sales team in the field.

9.6 Basing prices on customer perceptions of value

Effective sales teams are able to negotiate prices to obtain the maximum price the customer is willing to pay. However setting list prices and deciding pricing points for product ranges requires a more general approach.

Recall the 3Cs above. Prices should be set according to the perceived value differences between the product and its rivals.

Methods include:

- **Going rate approach:** Where the product is being launched into an established market the existing market prices are taken as a ready guide to value. A firm launching a new chocolate bar would place its price close to the price of the most similarly positioned product. A house builder would look at the prices of similar established properties in the area.

- **Product comparison approach:** Show a panel of target customers two products: a benchmark product which already has an established market price; and the new product for which a price is needed. Let the panel tell you how much more (or less) they would pay for the new product compared to the old.

- **Factor pricing approach:** Some of the augmented features of a product can have known price potential, eg car manufacturers can assess the price premium gained by having an automatic gearbox, sports styling kit, additional seating etc. Once the price of the basic car is set, the prices of the higher specification versions can be established by adding up the prices of the extra features.

- **Economic value to customer approach:** Some products are bought for the value they give. In business-to-business marketing the price a supplier charges for its products must take account of the price that can be achieved for the finished product. Fleet cars may be sold at a premium if the supplier can show better residual values or lower running costs. In consumer markets prices may be increased to cover the benefits of interest free credit or extended warranties.

9.7 Special pricing decisions

- **Promotional prices** are short-term price reductions or price offers which are intended to attract an increase in sales volume. (The increase is usually short-term for the duration of the offer, which does not appear to create any substantial new customer loyalty.) Loss leaders and money off coupons are a form of promotional pricing.

- **Every day low prices** is a response to customer cynicism about many of the promotional prices being in fact the right price after highly promoted reductions to an artificially inflated price. Firms will maintain low prices on a number of benchmark products to restore customers' faith.

- **Product line pricing** refers to the situation where a firm produces ranges of products of different sizes and qualities. It is essential that appropriate **price differentials** be maintained to stop one product underselling another, say a smaller high specification car robbing customers from a larger low specification one, but also close enough to allow sales teams to trade some customers up to higher value versions.

- **Captive product pricing** refers to the situation where prices of accessories can be inflated because the customer already has the basic product. Examples include ink cartridges for printers, spares for cars, drinks and desserts in a restaurant selling an attractively-priced main product. In these situations the pricing decision is taken to maximise the total earnings from the customer, sometimes over a number of years, rather than the earnings from each particular product.

- **Predatory pricing** describes artificially low prices designed to drive competitors out of the market. In many countries this is regarded as an illegal anti-competitive action and the authorities will scrutinise the costs of the supplier in relation to the price to establish whether the margin being achieved is realistic or deliberately low. In cross-border trade this would be called **dumping**.

Interactive question 6: Pricing methods   [Difficulty level: Intermediate]

The managing director of a small manufacturing company, specialising in industrial packaging tape, is worried that the cost-plus pricing method currently used is not necessarily the most appropriate. She asks you to provide a memorandum that:

(a) Explains the role and importance of pricing to the marketing effort.

(b) Suggests and explains the differences in both competitor-based methods and demand/market-based methods which could be considered as alternatives.

See **Answer** at the end of this chapter.

10   Relationship marketing

Section overview

- Repetitive purchases of a product create the potential for the firm to build a relationship with the customer.

- This leads to a distinction between transactions marketing, which sees product sales as a sequence of independent sales, and relationship marketing under which a transaction is another chance to maintain and deepen the relationship with the client.

- The change in focus has been driven by improvements in ICT which enables better tracking of customers, and the need to retain and increase spend per customer in mature markets where winning new customers is an expensive *nil sum* game for the industry.

10.1   Transactions marketing and relationship marketing

Many marketers say that the marketing mix does not cross product/service boundaries whereas customers do. Customers expect firms to be consistent in how they treat them.

The regular client of a sandwich bar, railway station or hotel will perceive that they have a relationship with the firm. However to its staff the customer is just another transaction in a busy day. This disparity in perception can lead to difficulties when the customer believes their relationship has been breached by some action of staff.

Strategies for products and markets   237

Definitions

Transactions marketing: Management approach that focuses on the product and develops marketing mixes for it according to the needs customers satisfy when they buy it.

Relationship marketing: Management process that seeks to attract, maintain and enhance customer relationships by focusing on the whole satisfaction experienced by the customer when dealing with the firm.

The key characteristics of relationship marketing are:

- Every customer is considered an individual person or unit.

- Activities of the company or organisation are predominately directed towards existing customers.

- It is based on interactions and dialogues.

- The company or organisation is trying to achieve profitability through the decrease of customer turnover and the strengthening of customer relationships.

10.2 Developing relationship marketing

Building up customer relationships requires a change of focus from the 'transaction-based approach' to the relationship approach. The contrast is shown in the table below.

Transaction marketing (mainly one-way communication)	Relationship marketing (mainly two-way communication)
Focus on single sale	Focus on customer retention
Orientation on product features	Orientation on product benefits
Short time scale	Long time scale
Little customer service	High customer service
Limited customer commitment	High customer commitment
Moderate customer contact	High customer contact
Quality is the concern of production	Quality is the concern of all

Instead of one-way communication aimed solely at gaining a sale, it is necessary to develop an effective two-way communication process to turn a prospect into a lifetime advocate.

Payne shows this as a **relationship marketing ladder**. Only repeated good experiences of dealings with the firm will lead to a customer turning from a client into someone willing to tell others they should be buying from us. This is not uncommon in consumer markets such as automobiles, hairdressing, financial services etc.

Partners are principally found in business to business marketing and refers to situations where trust has grown to the point that our customers will seek to tailor their business to us and not to seek alternative suppliers. The exchange of technical information and consultation of design that goes between a major airline and an engine manufacturer is an example of this.

Stronger bonds to build loyalty and retention can be developed by:

- Loyalty schemes, eg supermarket loyalty cards, frequent flier schemes, company clubs.

- Personalisation programmes, eg Amazon.com suggesting films, books etc which might suit returning customers.

- Structural ties, eg providing customers with computer equipment to manage orders.

Relationship marketing has grown in response to several factors:

- **The increasing cost of attracting new customers**: It costs more to win new customers than to keep old ones. In mature markets encouraging customers to switch mobile telephone provider, credit card or home loan involves the firm in giving significant incentives which are readily matched and so the offer has to be raised.

- **Marketing strategies based on product development**: Stores, utility providers and media owners seek to expand by selling wider ranges of products to their existing customers. Therefore the customer may deal with several parts of the business at once. A bad experience with one part could collapse sales in the rest.

- **Increased capabilities of information technology**: Common databases across the firm mean that any point of contact a customer makes can have access to details of the customer and past dealings and also record the present transaction, These applications are generically called **Customer Relationship Management systems** (CRM).

10.2.1 Links to value chain and value system

Relationship marketing is a refocus of the traditional marketing approach, with a greater emphasis being placed on the creation of customer value. This requires a detailed understanding of the customer's value chain and an ability to identify whereabouts in that chain the opportunities for enhancing value arise.

Interactive question 7: Branding and relationship marketing

[Difficulty level: Intermediate]

Your client is a large automobile manufacturer.

(a) Explain the concept and importance of branding to the company.

(b) Explain the way in which relationship marketing can be used by the company to attract and retain its customers.

See **Answer** at the end of this chapter.

11 Marketing and ethics

Section overview

- The way that marketing is carried out may raise ethical concerns.

The way that marketing is carried out may raise ethical concerns. Ethical issues begin with questioning whether marketing exists to sell people things they don't need and so wastes resources and causes envy and dissatisfaction. The nature of products, the means by which they are promoted, the level of prices and the selective way they are made available are also ethical issues. There is also the key ethical question of honesty in marketing. These issues are examined in more detail in Chapter 16.

Summary and Self-test

Summary

Marketing and strategy

Generic strategy
– Differentiate firm and products
– Avoid excessive costs

Orientation of firm
– Marketing ✓

Product/market strategy
– New markets
– Product refinements
– New products

Consumer
– Geographic
– Psychological
– Purchasing characteristics
– Benefit
– Demographic

Segmentation

Sub-groups of buyers with distinct needs

– Define problem
– Hypotheses
– Data
– Research
– Analysis
– Recommend

Market research

Desk research (secondary)

Field research (primary)

Brands

Targeting

Positioning

– Measurable
– Accessible
– Stable
– Substantial
– Defensible

Marketing mix
– Product
– Price
– Promotion
– Place
– People
– Physical
– Process

Relationship marketing

– Focus on keeping customers
– Turn into clients

ICAEW

Self-test

Answer the following questions.

1 What types of segmentation would a paint manufacturer segmenting the market in paint sold to other businesses use?

2 Why might demographic segmentation by itself not be a successful basis for car manufacturers targeting their customers?

3 Explain briefly market segmentation and market targeting, and the relationship between the two.

4 Describe, with examples, two ways in which a market can be segmented.

5 Give four differences between industrial and consumer markets.

6 Why is a brand name important to the following?

(a) Purchasers
(b) Manufacturers

7 Briefly describe the four elements of the promotion mix.

8 Give two reasons why most consumer good manufacturers choose not to distribute and sell their goods directly to the public.

9 Describe the use of targeting in marketing planning.

10 Show the marketing implications for two of the service characteristics.

11 Complete the table below describing the different relationships with a customer or client.

Relationship type	Description
Partner	
Advocate	
Supporter	
Client	
Purchaser	
Prospect	

12 Read the scenario of the **March 2010 Business Strategy** paper in the Question Bank entitled *NP Ltd,* referred to at the beginning of the chapter. Draft an answer for requirement (a) on market research, segmentation and targeting.

13 Re-read the scenario of the **March 2008 Business Strategy** paper in the Question Bank entitled *DA plc,* which we have seen in Chapters 2, 4 and 7. Draft an answer for requirement (d) on marketing strategy.

14 Go online at The Times 100 Business Case Studies and read the Nivea case study 'The use of the marketing mix in product launch' at: http://businesscasestudies.co.uk/nivea/the-use-of-the-marketing-mix-in-product-launch

Now, go back to the Learning objectives in the Introduction. If you are satisfied that you have achieved these objectives, please tick them off.

Answer to Interactive question 1

(a) **The concept of marketing segmentation**

The growth of specialised segments in a market has resulted in firms producing goods and services that are more closely related to the requirements of particular kinds of customers. Instead of treating its customers the same, the firm identifies sub-groups of customers whose precise needs can be more effectively met with a targeted approach. A global manufacturer of automobiles can segment the market into luxury brands including 4x4 leisure vehicles, family saloon car products and small car ranges. The criteria for segmentation will include executive customers where comfort, quality and safety are key issues, high mileage business executives who spend much of their working day in the vehicle and require office specification equipment together with high levels of reliability and low running costs per mile, and family saloon vehicles that have a high utility requirement such as safety and convenience. Each of these segmented customer groups have identifiable needs that are required to be serviced with a matched range of vehicle specifications.

There are three stages of target marketing, which are:

Market segmentation

Identify basis for segmentation

Determine important characteristics of each market segment

↓

Market targeting

Select one or more segments

↓

Product positioning

Develop detailed product positioning for selected segments

Develop a marketing mix for each selected segment

A global automobile manufacturer will need to consider the variables for segmenting the market, such as:

- **Business requirements**: Based on level of vehicle specification, value for money within each segment group, fleet management support including purchase discount policy, and vehicle maintenance, repair and spare parts servicing levels.

- **Demographic variables**: Age, gender, family size, social class and disposable income, and education.

- **Perceived benefits**: Different people buy the same or similar products for quite different reasons such as considering vehicles as fashion statement as a lifestyle option or as a product fulfilling particular functional requirements such as family transportation.

- **Loyalty:** Analysis of brand loyalty can tell a manufacturer about its customers attitude to its current brand and thus where it could stretch an existing brand name to include new products within a range.

- **Lifestyle and cultural considerations**: Understanding how the different consumer groups around the globe spend their time and money, the influence of their cultural attitudes and beliefs will be seen in the take up and targeting of products incorporating our range of vehicles.

(b) **Segmentation criteria**

There are a number of criteria that can be used to segment the global automobile market. We need to understand the performance for each criteria and how effective the targeting and positioning has been from our efforts. These will include:

Fleet car purchases: The UK and Europe has large purchases of fleet cars for business purposes. This is a unique characteristic whereas the rest of the world predominantly uses company lease schemes where the individual purchases the vehicle and the company manage the lease arrangements. Consequently an important segment in the UK and Europe are the business fleet purchasing managers that have responsibility for significant purchasing decisions. Often company executives will select a vehicle from a predetermined list and it is important that the global manufacturer is included in the company car lists.

Engine fuel: This choice of engine fuel is an important criterion. Diesel is very common in Europe with a cost benefit compared to petrol as well as vehicles driving longer distances for each journey and in the car's expected life. Consequently there are more European cars with diesel variants. However the UK still has more petrol fuelled cars, although diesel has become more popular. Alternative engine fuels including LPG and hybrid engines are also included in product ranges.

Disposable income: The purchase price is an important criterion and personal customers can be segmented based on disposable income. This is important for individual customers who have access to sufficient disposable income to purchase a vehicle outright or are able to afford a loan arrangement to pay for the car.

Car performance: This is a good criterion to appeal to sports car enthusiasts where a racing marquee is used to market the car. Performance on a race track can be transferred to an aspirational lifestyle associated with a particular brand of car and global brands can be marketed with global promotions such as with Formula 1 motor racing.

Manual or automatic transmission: This is an important criterion for many international markets. For instance, America and Australia have a high proportion of vehicles with automatic transmission where the UK has a very high proportion of manual (or standard) gearboxes and crucially this is an important criterion to understand in segmenting the marketplace.

Gender: With more females entering the workforce there will inevitably be an increase in female customers with enough disposable income to purchase vehicles. This is a global phenomenon that is a result of harmonisation of job opportunities between male and female employees across the globe. Consequently an important criterion is to understand the requirements of this important segment and include their requirements with tailored products that would appeal to potential female customers.

There is a need to understand the potential for each segment in order for to have the potential to grow. There is a need to assess current competitor activity and the likelihood of future targeting by other businesses to these segments. Understanding the unique selling points within each segment is an important marketing activity.

Answer to Interactive question 2

Positioning and targeting

Product positioning is a technique which carefully targets various product attributes of the (chosen) market segments.

Various factors of the product can be considered (eg quality and price) and the company can in this way decide how to position its product. This will also help to focus on the competition and on what Rex will have to develop if it is to be successful.

Considering quality and price, this might be represented as follows.

High price

BMW
Ⓐ

High quality ——————————————— Low quality

Tata
Nano

Low price

BMWs are regarded as high quality expensive cars; the Tata Nano, branded as the 'world's cheapest car', is regarded as a lower profit inexpensive vehicle. By focusing on the products in this way Rex Ltd can decide where it wants to position itself. As it enjoys a high reputation for its off-road vehicles, it might wish to try to move the whole business more upmarket. A possible position might therefore be at A, ie quality to rival BMW but at a lower price. Market targeting considers how markets can be split into different sectors and then each sector targeted with a specific product. There are three possible approaches.

(i) **Undifferentiated marketing**: One product, one market. No attempt is made to segment the market.

(ii) **Differentiated marketing**: The market is segmented with products being developed to appeal to the needs of buyers in the different segments.

(iii) **Concentrated marketing**: The market is segmented with the product being specifically targeted at a particular segment.

As Rex Ltd has different products aimed at different sectors, off-road, small, family hatchback, etc it is obvious that it has adopted a differentiated approach. This might be developed further to produce a range of a particular model. For example, the new improved Matchless could be produced as a three-door, five-door, GTi etc. This will be necessary if Rex Ltd is going to win the market share it wants.

Answer to Interactive question 3

(a) There are five characteristics of a service, which are described below:

- **Perishability**: A service cannot be stored or saved for later consumption. It has an immediacy that cannot be held over until sometime in the future. For example, a meal in a restaurant has to be eaten at the time it is paid for. This can cause problems with the utilisation of capacity as some occasions in the restaurant, eg evenings and weekends, will be more popular than others, eg lunchtimes. Marketers have to give incentives for customers to purchase at off-peak times to counter this eg happy hour deals.

- **Intangibility**: You cannot touch or feel the service offering as it has an abstract delivery. Unlike a product which you can touch (and smell and see) a service has no physical presence. It is only the paperwork that accompanies the service which has a tangible element, eg The MOT certificate after the car has had its annual service and is deemed roadworthy. This can cause problems since customers cannot see what they are getting for their money and they can only make a judgement based on experience of the service.

- **Inseparability**: A key distinguishing feature of a service is that the provider and receiver of the service are inseparable in the sense that the customer has to be present for the service to take place – unlike a product, where you can buy a can of soft drink but the seller does not have to be present when it is consumed at a later date. This presents a problem for the marketer as they cannot always ensure that the process is enjoyable for the customer.

- **Heterogeneity**: The delivery of the service will vary each time to the customer. This is because a service is dependant on the unique interaction between the provider and the customer which will vary depending on the individuals. The variability is created by the influence of human behaviour in the transaction and consistency can become a difficult problem to manage. Eg a meal in one Pizza Express restaurant may be a very different experience from a meal in the same restaurant in a different town.

- **Non-ownership:** With a product, eg a tyre, ownership is transferred at the point of sale. Ownership of a service typically remains with the provider and payment for the service just confers the right to use something. For instance, gym membership allows the customer to make use of the facilities but they are not owned by the customer.

These are the differences between a service and a product and their associated problems for the marketer.

(b) **The extended marketing mix**

The extended marketing mix comprises People, Process and Physical Evidence and is to be applied to a small independent firm of management consultants in order to derive the following benefits.

- **People**

There should be a strong emphasis on staff training to ensure a consistently high quality of provision. Poor customer service is the most commonly quoted reason for a change in sourcing services and is the most difficult problem to overcome to recover lost custom. The high level of people involvement in management consultancy demands that their customers are treated in a very professional manner throughout the delivery process. As their customers will judge the quality of the service by the conduct of the staff the close proximity of the staff working in a small business magnifies the need to adequately train all employees. This can include such areas as personal presentation, dealing with enquiries, providing quotations and maintaining technical competencies in line with current developments.

- **Physical evidence**

The image of the branches of the consultancy and any correspondence that is sent out in response to enquiries, including from the website, need to be consistent and include company brand identity such as logo or accreditation awards. This is crucial as it is one of the means that current or prospective clients will use to evaluate the consultancy.

The staff uniforms, interior decoration of the branches, tidiness and signage should reflect a common and consistent quality image for the management consultancy. It should believe that the colour scheme and logo reflect its professionalism and trustworthy image which should be maintained to retain its fresh feel. All its literature and website content should be regularly updated to provide an impression of current thinking for its clients that enhances quality perceptions for the offering.

- **Process**

As part of customer service, efficient administrative processes underpin a high quality of provision. For instance if a client has spent an unnecessary amount of time trying to contact a management consultant they would become very frustrated and annoyed at the waste of their valuable time. It sends all the wrong messages concerning the offering and will become a source of friction between the two parties that will have to be recovered. The small business will need to consider putting procedures and resources into place to ensure these problems are carefully managed and that the client's expectations are at least achieved, if not surpassed.

Conclusion

Many companies, large and small, often treat these areas of the marketing mix with limited attention, which results in a poor perceived level of customer service. By paying due attention to the quality of all the people, the physical evidence and the process involved in the management consultancy operation will enhance the service marketing provision.

Answer to Interactive question 4

(a) **A large banking group**

A large banking group, such as Barclays, has to focus on four key sectors.

(i) The consumer market
(ii) The corporate market
(iii) The small/medium business market
(iv) The financial markets

In all these sectors both international and domestic considerations are necessary.

The bank, whilst essentially a service, offers its customers a range of products. Although some of these products are intangible, they are nevertheless perceived by customers as offering specific benefits and meeting specific needs. It is important for a large banking group to engage all the elements of the marketing mix for these sectors.

In the consumer market distribution has become a major issue, particularly with the advent of direct banking. Service is an important element of the bank's response to an increasingly competitive marketplace. New products are being launched as the bank's marketing environment poses new opportunities and threats. Communication is critical both in terms of customer acquisition and retention. The heavy use of advertising and direct marketing are evidence of the importance attached to these components of promotion.

Within the corporate market a different range of tools will be utilised. In particular, relationship marketing and sponsorship become important elements of the mix. A range of financial services is offered to corporate clients particularly with investments. The product mix, communication and distribution structure will vary from the consumer market, with the sales function becoming more dominant.

For the small/medium business the role of the business adviser is important, along with the various services the bank provides to assist the business in managing its financial affairs more effectively. It is not uncommon to see TV advertising targeted at entrepreneurs. Each element has an important part to play in the bank's competitive position.

(b) **Electric component manufacturer**

A company that manufacturers electronic components for computer manufacturers will focus its marketing activities on a relatively few number of customers in the business sector. The need for consumer marketing activity will therefore generally be unnecessary although organisations such as Intel have gained a strong market position in the supply of computer chips by building a strong brand reputation with consumers. The assumption in this case is that this manufacturer is focused upon its business customers.

The predominant marketing mix activities will focus upon product quality and delivery with strong sales force and technical support. It is likely that corporate entertainment and the building up of relationships throughout the customer's organisation will be important aspects of the company's marketing programme. The role of distribution is important particularly in terms of product availability and speed of delivery. There is a danger that this market can become price driven as technological change means new products are copied or become obsolete very quickly. A strong commitment must therefore be made to research and new product development.

Packaging and branding are less critical components as tools of communication, although they can play a role in supporting the manufacturer's overall positioning. Publicity, particularly in the trade press, can be an important tool of communication. The supply of support literature and price structure alongside easy to access order processes will enhance the competitive position of this company. With a focus on fewer customers, direct marketing techniques should predominate. The relationship that the manufacturer has with distributors in the supply chain will also be important to ensure wide availability of component parts.

Answer to Interactive question 5

Briefing notes

To	Captain Salmon
From	J Sayso, Chartered accountant
Date	Today
Subject	Marketing

1   **Marketing strategies**

If Welsh Cruisers Ltd is acquired, this will represent growth in the business of Canal Cruises. The information provided suggests that the quality of Welsh Cruisers' boats is much lower than that of Canal Cruises, as is the level of boat hiring. Four possible growth strategies could be adopted. These are discussed below.

Market penetration

Market penetration involves selling existing products in existing markets. The overall market of Canal Cruises is the narrowboat hire market and is restricted to those who read *Waterways World*. It targets the top end of this restricted market. To sell more of the existing product to this market it would have to convert the lower quality Welsh Cruisers' boats into those of a quality similar to its own (eg installing TVs, microwaves and stereos). Such conversion may be very expensive (complete boat refits and painting may be required) but the company would be operating in a market segment with which it is familiar. However, there may not be the demand for an extra 30 quality boats.

Market development

Existing products are sold in new markets. Again, conversion of Welsh Cruisers' boats is necessary and further expense will be incurred in developing new markets (market research, promotion etc). New markets can be developed by advertising, promotion via channels other than *Waterways World* (see 4 below).

Product development

Canal Cruises could leave the lower quality narrowboats as they are and target the lower end of its *Waterways World* market. Extra promotional expenses would be incurred as would marketing research costs (which would be necessary to gain information about the new stage segment).

Diversification

This involves leaving the lower quality boats as they are and selling to potential customers who are not already in the company's existing market. Marketing research and promotion costs would be incurred as for 'market development'.

Recommendation

Canal Cruises should pursue a diversification strategy, because Welsh Cruisers already has some business gained via its existing advertising and promotional channels; the business needs development. Restricting promotion to *Waterways World* (product development) may result in lower hirings. The other two strategies (converting the boats) are likely to be too expensive.

2   **Promotion**

The main promotional objective will be to increase hirings of Welsh Cruisers' boats to the same level as that of Canal Cruises. The promotional possibilities are discussed below.

Waterways World

The company could promote all its activities through *Waterways World* as it does presently. This policy has been very successful to date. Should the company adopt the diversification strategy above, it is doubtful whether the target market (those looking for a cheap boat) would read *Waterways World*, and the promotional objective would not be achieved.

Adverts could still be placed in *Waterways World* but other channels should also be used (see below). It is recommended that the name 'Welsh Cruisers' is maintained and separate advertisements used for the differing parts of the business, otherwise people may begin to associate the lower quality of Welsh Cruisers' boats with those of Canal Cruises.

Wider promotion

It has already been mentioned that Welsh Cruisers must have existing means of promotion and they should be examined carefully to see if they are reaching the target market.

An advertising message needs to be thought out – for example 'value for money' could be emphasised and this must be communicated to the target market. Advertisements could be placed in the larger circulation daily or Sunday newspapers (and their supplements), radio adverts could be used, travel agents could be approached to stock brochures and so on.

The possibility of online sales should be investigated. A website could be created (either for the company as a whole or for Welsh Cruises alone). Discounts could be offered for online booking, repeat purchases etc to encourage market penetration and development. The site could be used to promote a particular image for the business and reinforce the brand.

Other promotional techniques

In order to increase sales and gain repeat hirings, various other 'non-advertising' techniques could be used. Examples are set out below.

(a) Welsh Cruisers could accept all male or female parties on 'social drinking' holidays (with the option for the customer of taking out damage insurance!)

(b) '20% off' coupons could be issued to customers for use later in the hiring season or '10% off next year's hire charge' coupons.

(c) Drivers could be provided at a small extra charge for those who are wary of taking out a boat for the first time and who would otherwise not hire.

Answer to Interactive question 6

(a) **Memorandum**

To	Managing Director
From	Anne Accountant
Date	6 December 200X
Subject	Report on Pricing Methods

1 **Introduction**

I have been asked to produce a report detailing the importance of pricing in marketing terms and also to explain the differences in competitor-based methods and demand-based methods.

2 **The importance of pricing in marketing terms**

Pricing plays an essential role in the marketing of your product. First of all, you need to cover all of your costs, but the price will help to create an image of your product in the eyes of your customer.

As part of the marketing mix, price will help the perceived quality, value and image. If the price is high, then customers generally take the view that the product is of high standard and is good quality. This of course, needs to be backed up with the other elements of the marketing mix. If the price is low, there is a danger that the perception is of low quality and is 'cheap and cheerful'. This is only a danger, however, if you want to position your product as a high quality item. In general terms, price will help you to position your product in the market. This can be visualised with as 'perception map'.

The above map shows two dots, which demonstrate that in positioning your product by price, it will create an image to your customer.

Price can help to gain market share by using methods such as 'price skimming' or 'price penetration'. Penetration will gain a large marketing share as price is set very low, whereas skimming pricing is where the price is set high, usually for new products launched into a market with few competitors and a smaller market share is gained.

3 **Key factors that concern pricing**

There are four key factors that affect pricing decisions, also known as the 4 Cs:

- Cost – related to the actual costs involved
- Consumer/customer – related to the price the consumer will pay
- Competition – related to competitors prices for substitute or complimentary products

- Company – related to the company's financial objectives

3.1 Financial issues – cost

- This is the lower level of a price – often accountants use cost when deciding on the pricing structure. There are at least four different types of costs in regard to a product or service:

  - Fixed cost – a cost that does not change according to the increase in the number of units produced ie rent and rates for the premises

  - Variable costs – a cost that changes according to the number of units produced such as raw materials

  - Total costs – a sum of fixed and variable cost times the quantity produced

  - Average cost – this is the total cost divided by the number of units produced

- Contribution – allows the accountant to analyse whether the product can be sold at less than cost for a period of time, but making a contribution to the costs

- Breakeven analysis – indicates the amount of units that must be sold at a given price to cover costs

- Company's financial objectives – the company's objectives in terms of profitability also need to be taken into account when considering the price

3.2 Economic issues

Economic issues such as the following also need to be taken into account:

- Customers' demand

- Demand is considered and calculations on how much will be demanded at a certain price using the demand curve will be undertaken

- It is useful to know the shape of the demand curve when setting prices as you can set a high price if your market is inelastic

- Marketing communications serve to influence the demand curve to make it more inelastic

- You must consider inflation year on year, affecting the cost of employment, raw materials and distribution

- This is also a consideration for customers' disposable income

- The possibility of the euro currency in the UK must be anticipated

3.3 Competitors

- Competitors must be taken into account.

- The marketer looks at competitors, macro environment, internal environment, stage in the product life cycle and sets a price at what the market will bear.

All of the above factors and perspectives play a key role in finalising a price.

(b) 4 **Competitor-based pricing**

This method is where the pricing policy is based upon competing prices in the market. This is different to cost-plus pricing in that it takes into consideration how the other competitors are pricing their products and how their products are perceived by their customers. Cost-plus pricing does not do this, and merely covers costs and leaves room for a little profit. The price does not necessarily have to be cheaper than competitors, as discussed before, it depends upon how you want your products to be perceived by your customers, and compared to your competitors.

Some of the methods used for competitor-based pricing include price matching, going rate pricing and predator pricing.

4.1 **Price matching**: This is where the company guarantees that the product cannot be bought for less anywhere. If it can be bought for less, they usually refund the difference. Therefore, the price is very much based on the competitors in the market place.

4.2 **Going rate pricing**: Here the pricing policy is determined by the competitors' pricing strategy and a similar price is set (but not guaranteed as above).

4.3 **Predator pricing**: This is where the pricing policy is set low so that the competition has problems in competing for market share.

5 **Market/demand-based pricing**

The final method is more suitable to take into account market needs and wants and relates to what is in demand. Compared to competitor-based pricing, it takes demand into consideration. As customers are becoming more demanding, this is a more suitable method of pricing. Economic issues and the elasticity of demand are considered here.

There are a number of methods such as penetration and skimming strategies, discount and allowance pricing, segmentation pricing and promotional pricing. I will explain a number of these methods below.

5.1 **Skimming**: This is where a high price policy is undertaken to 'skim the cream' of the market. This is more advisable if you have a product which is new into the market and there are few competitors. It is important that you are able to lower the price once you have established a customer base and need to gain more market share.

5.2 **Penetration**: This is where the price starts off low and market share is gained quickly. It is difficult however, to increase the price once this has been undertaken.

5.3 **Segmented pricing**: Companies will often adjust their basic prices to allow for differences in customers, products and locations. The company sells a product at two or more prices, even though the difference in price is not based on differences in costs. Examples may be where different customers pay different prices for the same product such as rail travel First Class and Standard fares. Another example is time pricing where prices vary by the day or the hour such as telephone companies and 'off-peak' calls.

6 **Conclusion**

I hope that this has helped in your consideration of the pricing policy to adopt for the industrial packaging tape. Please contact me should you require any further information.

Answer to Interactive question 7

(a) **Importance of branding**

One of the most distinctive skills of professional marketers is their ability to create, maintain, protect, reinforce and enhance brands. A brand is a name or term like Toyota, General Motors or Ford, a symbol or design which is used to identify the goods or services of one seller to differentiate them from those of competitors. Thus the brand identifies the manufacturer and supplier of the product. Brands, unlike other forms of intellectual property, such as patents and copyrights do not have an expiry date and their owners have exclusive rights to use their brand name for an unlimited period of time.

A brand has value to the business, known as brand equity. They can reinforce customer loyalty as well as name awareness, perceived quality, strong brand associations and other assets such as channel relationships. Branding also increases innovation by giving producers an incentive to look for new features that can be protected against imitating competitors. Thus branding will result in more product variety and choice for consumers.

The use of branding

A brand conveys a specific set of features, benefit and services to the buyer. The brand has four different dimensions, which are described below.

Attributes

A brand first brings to mind certain product attributes such as build quality, power capability and so on. A large automobile manufacturer would use these attributes in its advertising and promotional activities.

Benefits

Customers do not purchase attributes, they purchase perceived benefits. Therefore, attributes must be translated into functional and emotional benefits. For example, the attribute 'well built' might translate into benefits demanded by our customers, such as reliability or high resale value.

Values

A brand also says something about the buyer's values. The brand marketer must identify the specific group of buyers whose values coincide with the delivered benefits package such as high performance, safety and prestige.

Personality

A brand also projects a personality. The brand will attract people whose actual desired self image match the brand's image. This would be important for the business customer who purchase from the large automobile manufacturer as well as the consumer purchasing an automobile.

A company must define its overall branding strategy which affects all of its products. It is necessary to consider how new products fit into the brand structure particularly as the large automobile manufacturer will have developed a series of marques that identifies each family of its products. Safeguarding the association of quality developed with the large automobile manufacturer's products will be paramount.

(b) **The concept of relationship marketing**

Introduction

Customer relationship marketing is becoming increasingly more important owing to the increase in customer education and expectations. Many large firms now have a dedicated policy for this subject and we need to consider the implications.

Customer lifetime value

For any organisation, the sale should not be considered as the end of the relationship but instead the beginning of the process to retain that customer. Therefore, it is more efficient to keep existing customers happy and delighted with their experience rather than finding new customers. This process should be continued at each sale and be seen as part of a long-term relationship between ourselves and the customer.

Relationship marketing

This is a long-term approach to creating, maintaining and enhancing strong relationships with customers and other stakeholders. Organisations need to view each transaction as part of a long-term goal. If the customer is satisfied with the product or service they have received for the price they have paid, they are more likely to return. A short-term outlook on the other hand will consider only a quick profit and not the more important possibility of a repeat purchase.

There are five different distinguishable levels with the relationship that can be formed with customers who have purchased a product or service. These are:

- **Basic**

  Selling a product without any follow up.

- **Reactive**

  Selling a product with follow up encouraged on the part of the customer.

- **Accountable**

  Having sold a product, the follow up occurs a short time afterwards to confirm the customer's expectations have been met.

- **Proactive**

  The sales person contacts the customer from time to time with suggestions regarding improved products.

- **Partnership**

  The company works continuously with the customer to deliver improved levels of value.

Relationship marketing can contribute to an organisation in a number of ways. It can establish a rapport with customers creating trust and confidence. It allows an opportunity to interact and hence communicate the large automobile manufacturer's commitment to satisfying customer's needs and wants. It can help to improve their experience and adds that personal touch, which links the emotions of both parties. By creating a notional bond as one of its objectives relationship marketing strives to achieve a sense of belonging thereby making the customer feel part of the business. It attempts to tailor products and services to cater for specific needs of customers, therefore reducing the need to switch behaviour. The use of database management and information communication technology helps to address the customer needs in a focused manner and can be manipulated to the individual's requirements.

There are significant benefits that can be derived from relationship marketing. It can contribute to cost savings as it is up to five times more expensive to find a new customer than retain an existing customer. It can help to entice new customers away from competitors as a perceived added value activity. It will also make it more difficult for existing customers to switch, as there is an emotional bond that underpins loyalty to the customer and the company.

1   A paint manufacturer segmenting the market in paint sold to other businesses might use the following types of segmentation:

- Type of business – potential customers may be divided into several different groups such as paint wholesalers, do-it-yourself retail outlets, specialist decorating outlets, housing developers, contracting decorators, and vehicle manufacturers.

- Usage, range and size are all means of segmenting the paint market. The size of container and packaging of the paint will vary according to the user needs of the customer. Contracting decorators may use large containers of a limited range of colours and not be particularly concerned about packaging, while do-it-yourself outlets and specialist stores may require a full range of colours and containers of various sizes with attractive decoration.

- Geographical area is an important segmentation variable for this type of industry. Customers may be domestic or overseas. Paint is exported to many different countries – each will need their own marketing strategies.

2   Reasons why demographic segmentation alone may not be a successful basis for car manufacturers targeting their customers include:

- A car manufacturer may use buyers' age in developing its target market and then discover that the target should be the psychologically young (young at heart) and not the young in age. (The Ford Motor Company used buyers' age in targeting its Mustang car in America, designing it to appeal to young people who wanted an inexpensive sporty car. Ford found to its surprise that the car was being purchased by all age groups.)

- Income is another variable that can be deceptive. One would imagine that working class families would buy a Vauxhall Astra and the managerial class would buy BMWs. However, many Astras are bought by middle-income people (often as the family's second car) and expensive cars are often bought by working class families (plumbers, carpenters etc).

- Personal priorities also upset the demographic balance. Middle-income people often feel the need to spend more on clothes, furniture and housing which they could not afford if they purchased a more expensive car.

- The upgrading urge for people trying to relate to a higher social order often leads them to buy expensive cars.

- Some parents although 'well off' pay large fees for the private education of their children and must either make do with a small car, or perhaps no car at all.

3   Market segmentation is the process of identifying groups of buyers with different buying desires or requirements. Market targeting is the firm's decision regarding which market segments to serve. Markets made up of buyers seeking substantially different product qualities and/or quantities are called 'heterogeneous markets'.

4   For example

• By geographical region	– eg North v South, different countries
• By demographic factors	– eg age, sex, social class, lifestyle, education, income
• By the way the product is used	– eg professional builders or amateur DIY'ers
• By customer requirements	– eg tea granules, bags and leaves are a response to different levels of convenience required.

5 Industrial and consumer markets differ in the following ways.

Consumer markets	Industrial markets
Products purchased to satisfy personal needs	Products bought for use in firm's operations or to make other products
Buying decision may be complex and irrational: 'it caught my eye'	Buying motive linked to improving quality and/or profitability. Technical specifications are a very important element of the product definition
Likely to have many customers with low buying power	Likely to be fewer firms but each has greater spending power
Customers spread out	Customers concentrated, either geographically or by industry
Longer distribution channels	More likely to sell direct
Advertising is main promotional tool	Personal selling extremely important
	More negotiation involved with pricing

6 To the **purchaser** the brand name is important.

- It distinguishes the product from alternatives
- It permits repurchase of a product which has proved satisfactory when previously bought
- The purchaser is familiar with the attributes of each well-known brand
- The problem of making a choice is reduced
- The familiar brand name encourages a feeling of security about the purchase.

To the **manufacturer** the virtues of branding are somewhat different.

- It encourages repurchase (this is effectively the same as 'brand loyalty')

- The brand name is a merchandising asset: it is useful in persuading people to purchase at the point of sale

- The brand name becomes associated with the product's intended attributes, thus positioning it in the customer's mind and the market

- The brand name is used in all promotion effort, and tends to enhance the effectiveness of advertising.

7 The promotion mix consists of four elements.

- Advertising: Paid communications in the media which are designed to influence potential customers favourably regarding a company's products or services. Advertising is sometimes called **above-the-line** promotion.

- Sales promotion: Non-media promotional activity aimed at increasing sales. Sales promotion includes a variety of techniques such as give-aways, competitions, trading stamps and exhibitions. It is sometimes called **below-the-line** promotion.

- Public relations: The creation of positive attitudes regarding products, services, or companies by various means, including unpaid media coverage and involvement with community activities.

- Personal selling: The techniques by which a sales force makes contact with potential customers.

8 There are several reasons for using separate firms for getting goods to the consumer. These include the following.

- Market knowledge is far deeper in an established intermediary.

- Market coverage is larger for a firm with a distribution chain already running; set-up costs of a distribution network are large

- Distribution speed is likely to be much higher in an existing company specialising in this area.

- Distributors may cover a range of complementary products to enhance sales of the principal product.

9   Targeting is where the marketing mix elements are designed to fit an identified segment.

10   For any two characteristics:

Intangibility	Judgemental evaluation
Inseparability	Provider and client impact on quality of service
Variability	Consistency based on delivery process
Perishability	Instantaneous consumption that cannot be stored
Non ownership	Services are used and not owned

11

Relationship	Description
Partner	The most loyal business associate
Advocate	Active recommendation for business
Supporter	Some tacit approval for offering
Client	Some repeat activity
Purchaser	Completed at least one transaction
Prospect	Likely source of potential business

12   Refer to the answer to part a of NP Ltd in the Question Bank.

13   Refer to the answer to part d of DA plc in the Question Bank.

14   There is no answer to this self-test, as it is designed just to help you increase your business awareness.

CHAPTER 9

Strategy and structure

Introduction
Examination context

Topic List

Summary and Self-test
Answers to Interactive questions
Answers to Self-test

Learning objectives

- Describe, in a given scenario, the advantages and disadvantages of alternative business structures

- Evaluate the different types of organisational structure and recommend an appropriate structure for a given strategy

- Analyse the governance and management structures of businesses and identify strengths and weaknesses

- Identify the steps needed for a given business to develop its corporate governance to meet the needs of its strategic objectives and external requirements

Specific syllabus references for this chapter are: 1e,3b, 3c

Syllabus links

The rudiments of organisational structure and governance were covered in the syllabus for Business and Finance.

Examination context

The key element in this chapter is how structure links with strategy. Knowledge of organisational structures in isolation from strategy would not normally be examined. The idea that there is no one ideal structure is important, as it means that issues of structure will need to interact with the strategy according to the particular circumstances of the scenario. Organisations which are structured divisionally face particular issues including the extent of decentralisation, performance evaluation and transfer pricing.

This chapter contains references to a number of named studies. It is desirable to attribute the source of these studies in describing them. However, for examination purposes it is not the intention that the names should be quoted or reproduced without application. Rather, it is intended that the implications and results of these studies can be applied appropriately to practical scenarios to inform applied strategy and organisational structure recommendations.

In Q2 June 2011 (*Henford plc*) the scenario contains a great deal of information about a conglomerate company's organisational structure. The second requirement is:

'(b) In respect of Henford's organisational structure:

(i) Draw organisational charts for both Henford's old structure (ie prior to 2011) and its new structure; and

(ii) Evaluate whether the change from the old functional structure to the new structure is likely to be beneficial for Henford. **(13 marks)**'

As well as having to read and interpret the information provided, you also need to show skill in drawing accurate structure diagrams neatly, incorporating all the relevant information in the right places. You then need to apply judgement as to whether and how the change in structure is an improvement for the organisation.

As drawing structure charts is something that students generally struggle with, it is worth brushing up on your drawing skills prior to your examination! A good answer on structure requires you to be confident in not only applying your knowledge of traditional organisational structures, but also be able to make reference to the works of Mintzberg and Handy, both of which we discuss in the chapter.

In this chapter we also consider the importance of corporate governance. Some of the themes discussed here you should be familiar with from your earlier law and business and finance studies. Governance is mentioned twice in the Business Strategy syllabus so should not be overlooked. It is important that you understand the interaction between strategy and governance.

In Q2, June 2014, Best Fresh Bakeries Ltd (BFB) is a family-run company with five shops, each of which bakes and sells its own high quality, fresh produce. BFB is owned and managed by three directors, Henry the father who owns 80% of the shares and his two sons, who each own 10%. Whilst Henry is content with the status quo, his sons want to expand and are considering setting up a single centralised baking facility. They are threatening to outvote Henry at the Board meeting. Jon, a friend of Henry's, has suggested he appoints some non-executive directors to side with him in the argument.

The second and third requirements are:

'(b) Assuming the expansion strategy is implemented, briefly explain the factors that should be considered in determining transfer prices from the new centralised baking production facility to the five individual BFB shops, and recommend how the transfer prices should be set.   **(9 marks)**

(c) In light of Nigel's and Ralph's voting intentions, and Jon's suggestions, explain the governance issues for BFB.   **(7 marks)'**

1 Strategy and structure

Section overview

- The management team and staff of a firm must be organised to carry out the operations and strategy of the business.

- There is a debate about the direction of influence between strategy and structure. Does management build a structure once it has decided strategy or does the structure determine the strategy through its influence on the flows of information and managements assessment of what is possible?

- The most appropriate structure depends on the stage of development of the organisation and the nature of its competitive environment (**contingency approach**).

1.1 Structure needed to implement strategy

A strategy without effective organisation of the people required to carry it out is doomed. Strategies can only be implemented by, and through, people.

Developing an appropriate structure requires consideration of three areas:

Organisational configuration – the primary groupings of staff into departments or divisions

Centralisation/Decentralisation– where the responsibility for decision making lies

Management systems – this includes the make-up of the senior management team, eg the corporate board, and the methods they use to govern the organisation. This includes the processes used to monitor financial results, to arrive at strategic decisions and to manage risk.

1.2 Impact of strategic choices on structure and *vice versa*

The relationship between strategy and structure is a complex one.

Structure follows strategy

This **top-down approach** says that management decide the strategy then build or revise organisational structure to implement it.

The argument for structure following strategy was put forward by Chandler. He argues that the structure of the organisation must be adapted to fit the strategy adopted by management.

In his analysis any changes to organisation structure were a response to the organisation's stage of growth:

- Geographic expansion called for departmental offices to be set up to administer the new field units.

- Vertical integration required a central office and multi-departmental structure.

- Diversification required a general office to administer divisions operating in different industries.

Strategy follows structure

An alternative **bottom-up view** is that the strategy a firm follows emerges from, or depends on, its structure or that the structure limits the choice of strategy.

For example:

- Organisational structure and the interests of people within it shapes the flow of information to those responsible for strategic management. For example government ministers can only respond to issues they are told about and can select only from the options they are presented with.

- What actually gets done depends on power. The informal organisation may feature quite different power relations than suggested by the formal structure.

- Highly centralised structures tend to stifle innovative strategic solutions

- Divisionalised structures restrict collaboration and 'joined up' strategies

- Bureaucratic structures focus on maintaining the *status quo*.

Both the top-down and bottom-up views are extreme expressions. Managers recognise both forces will be at work.

- Management will restructure to implement new strategies
- Management strategies will be partially unrealised because the structure worked against them
- Structures will develop organically as teams and managers adapt to new challenges and initiatives
- Restructuring will create new initiatives and possibilities at the same time as suppressing others

1.3 Contingency approach to organisation structure

The modern contingency approach takes the view that there is no one best, universal structure. There are a large number of variables, or situational factors, which influence organisational design and performance. The contingency approach emphasises the need for flexibility (Mullins, 2002).

The most appropriate structure for an organisation depends on its situation. It is an 'if then' approach, ie **if** certain situational factors are present, **then** certain aspects of structure are most appropriate.

Typical situational factors include:

- Type and size of organisation and purpose
- Culture
- Preferences of top management/power/control
- History
- Abilities, skills, needs, motivation of employees
- Technology (eg production systems)
- Environment (see below)

Burns and Stalker identified two (extreme) types of structure (and management style).

- **Mechanistic** – rigid structure, bureaucratic management structure/style, applicable in stable environments.

- **Organic** – more fluid appropriate to changing circumstances (ie dynamic environments).

This links with the traditional/emergent approaches to strategy and structure. Both mechanistic and organic elements may exist side by side in any one organisation, eg in a hotel 'production' departments like the kitchens may be suited to a mechanistic structure but 'service' departments like marketing/reception may work better with organic structures.

2 Mintzberg's organisational forms

Section overview

- Organisational structure sets out how the various functions within the organisation are arranged.

- Mintzberg suggested that all organisations can be analysed into six building blocks.

- The particular structure of the business will depend on which of the building blocks is more dominant.

2.1 Components of organisations

In Business & Finance you were introduced to Mintzberg's theory of organisational configuration (sometimes called **the structure of sixes**), characterised by five distinct components that operate within the sixth, the **ideology** of the organisation or **culture**.

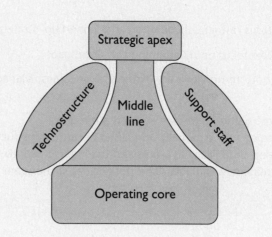

2.2 Configurations of organisations

Mintzberg suggests that each component of the organisation has its own **dynamic**. The precise shape (configuration) of the organisation will be determined by the degree of influence each exerts:

- The **strategic apex** is responsible to the organisation's owners and wishes to retain control over decision-making (centralisation).

- The **technostructure** consists of analysts whose reason for existence is the design of **procedures** and **standards** and wants an environment that is standardised and highly regulated.

- The members of the **operating core** work directly on the product or service. They prefer to work autonomously, achieving what other co-ordination is necessary by **mutual adjustment**.

- The managers of the **middle line** seek to increase their **autonomy** from the strategic apex, and to increase their control over the operating core.

- **Support staff** only gain influence when their expertise is vital.

2.3 Structure and environment

Mintzberg discusses five configurations, which stem from whichever building block is key . Each is characterised by different internal factors (size, type of work and complexity of tasks) and is appropriate in a different external environment (static/dynamic; simple/complex; single product/market or diverse). These are outlined below.

Configuration	Key building block	Environment	Internal factors	Key co-ordinating mechanism
Simple structure (**entrepreneurial**)	Strategic apex	Simple Dynamic	Small Young Simple tasks	Direct supervision
Machine bureaucracy (**functional**)	Techno-structure	Simple Static	Large Old Regulated	Standardisation of work
Professional bureaucracy	Operating core	Complex Static	Professional Simple systems	Standardisation of skills
Divisionalised	Middle line	Simple Static Diverse	Very large Old Divisible tasks	Standardisation of outputs
Adhocracy/ Innovative (**matrix**)	Operating core	Complex Dynamic	Young Complex tasks	Mutual adjustment

ICAEW

Interactive question 1: Organisational configurations   [Difficulty level: Intermediate]

Identify the organisation configurations suggested in the following cases.

(a)   Creation Ltd provides public relations services to clients. It is run by five partners, with a staff of copy editors, designers, party-throwers and people with contacts in the press. Clients contact one of the partners who assembles a team to solve a client's problem, though the partner does not direct the solution.

(b)   Smithers Ltd is a small family company. The chief executive and founder is a strong leader and tends to dominate decision making. He does not believe in discussing his decisions with staff. According to Mintzberg what would be the key building block and the main co-ordinating mechanism in Smithers Ltd?

See **Answer** at the end of this chapter.

We will now go on to consider the structures suggested by Mintzberg in more detail:

- Entrepreneurial
- Functional (or bureaucratic)
- Divisionalised
- Matrix

3   Types of business structure

Section overview

- Generally as a business grows, its structure progresses from entrepreneurial to functional to divisionalised.

- Matrix structures attempt to co-ordinate separate departments to serve joint goals such as particular customers or projects.

- A matrix structure can occur independently or within a functional or divisional structure.

3.1   Entrepreneurial structure (simple)

Typically a single owner-manager in a small business, who has specialist knowledge of the product or service and has total control over the running of the business.

This structure is flexible and quick to adapt to change, but dependent on the entrepreneur and limited in its ability to cope with expansion or diversification.

3.2 Functional structure (bureaucracy)

Functional structure leads to departments that are defined by their functions, that is, the work that they do. Specialism means the firm is more efficient and can benefit from economies of scale, but it can lead to conflict and the bureaucracy can hamper cross functional innovation and creativity. The rigid structure is unsuitably for changing environments.

Functional divisionalisation

3.3 Divisional structure

The business can be divided into autonomous units based on geography, product or market. Divisionalised structures can be adapted for growth and diversification and are most suitable for larger diversified businesses.

3.3.1 Geographic structure

Some authority is retained at Head Office (organised, perhaps, on a functional basis) but day-to-day service operations are handled on a territorial basis. Within many sales departments, the sales staff are organised on this basis.

Geographical structure

Advantages of geographic divisionalisation

- Better and quicker local decision making at the point of contact between the organisation (eg a sales executive) and its customers.

- It may be less costly to establish area factories/offices than to run everything centrally (eg costs of transportation and travelling may be reduced).

- It might be essential for overseas operations to cope with different environments.

Disadvantages of geographic divisionalisation

- Duplication of management effort (eg a national organisation divided into ten regions might have a customer liaison department in each regional office).

- It struggles to cope with large clients who span the divisions.

3.4 Product/brand divisionalisation

Product divisionalisation: The elements of an organisation are grouped by products or product lines. Some functional divisionalisation remains (eg manufacturing, distribution, marketing and sales) but a divisional manager is given responsibility for the product or product line, with authority over personnel of different functions.

Advantages

- Individual managers can be held accountable for the **profitability** of individual products.

- Specialisation can be developed. For example, some salesmen will be trained to sell a specific product in which they may develop technical expertise and thereby offer a better sales service to customers. Service engineers who specialise in a single product should also provide a better after sales service.

- The different functional activities and efforts required to make and sell each product can be co-ordinated and integrated by the divisional/product manager.

- It should be focused on how a business makes its profits.

The **disadvantage of product divisionalisation** is that it increases the overhead costs and managerial complexity of the organisation.

Brand: A brand is the name or design which identifies the products or services of a manufacturer or provider and distinguishes them from those of competitors. Brands may denote different products or, often, similar products made by the same firm.

Product/brand divisionalisation

- Branding implies a unique marketing position. It becomes necessary to have brand divisionalisation. As with product divisionalisation, some functional divisionalisation remains (especially on the manufacturing side) but brand managers have responsibility for the brand's marketing and this can affect every function.

- Brand divisionalisation has similar advantages and disadvantages to product divisionalisation. In particular, overhead costs and complexity of the management structure are increased, the relationships of a number of different brand departments with the manufacturing department, if there is only one, being particularly difficult.

3.5 Customer or market segment divisionalisation

- Divisionalisation by customer is commonly associated with sales departments and selling effort, but it might also be used by a jobbing or contracting firm where a team of managers may be given the responsibility of liaising with major customers.

- Another example is where firms distinguish between domestic consumers and business customers, with different marketing and supply efforts for each.

3.6 Hybrid structures

Very few organisations divisionalise on one basis alone. This was clear in the NHS example above.

Many organisation hierarchies in practice combine elements of a number of these approaches. In the example below, research and development is centrally organised, but the operating activities of the firm are geographically arranged. This is an example of a **hybrid structure**.

Interactive question 2: Erewhon Bank   [Difficulty level: Intermediate]

The Erewhon Bank plc has branches in the UK, Eire, France, Germany and Denmark. It grew from the merger of a number of small local banks in these countries. These local banks were not large enough to compete single-handedly in their home markets. The Erewhon Bank hopes to attract both retail and corporate customers, through its use of home banking services and its heavily advertised Direct Bank service, which is a branchless bank to which customers telephone, email or post their instructions. The bank also specialises in providing foreign currency accounts, and has set up a revolutionary service whereby participating customers can settle their own business transactions in euros.

What sort of organisation structure do you think would be appropriate?

See **Answer** at the end of this chapter.

3.7 Matrix organisation

A matrix organisation structure provides for the formalisation of management control between different functions, whilst also maintaining functional divisionalisation. It can be a mixture of a functional, product and territorial organisation. The matrix structure is most suitable for complex/hi-tech industries.

Worked example: Matrix management

Matrix management first developed in the 1950s in the USA in the aerospace industry. Lockheed-California, the aircraft manufacturers, were organised in a functional hierarchy. Customers were unable to find a manager in Lockheed to whom they could take their problems and queries about their particular orders, and Lockheed found it necessary to employ 'project expediters' as customer liaison officials. From this developed project co-ordinators, responsible for co-ordinating line managers into solving a customer's problems. Up to this point, these new officials had no functional responsibilities.

Owing to increasingly heavy customer demands, Lockheed eventually created programme managers, with authority for project budgets and programme design and scheduling. These managers therefore had functional authority and responsibilities, thus a matrix management organisation was created.

The matrix organisation imposes the multi-disciplinary approach on a permanent basis.

	Production Dept	Sales Dept	Finance Dept	Distribution Dept	R&D Dept	Marketing Dept
UK director						
Netherlands director						
Sweden director						

The product managers may each have their own marketing team; in which case the marketing department itself would be small or non-existent.

In some cases the matrix structure involves the appointment of a special manager responsible for a project or customer. They are charged with ensuring that the necessary departments pull together to achieve what is needed.

Advantages of a matrix structure

- It offers greater **flexibility**. This applies both to **people,** as employees adapt more quickly to a new challenge or new task, and to **task and structure,** as the matrix may be short-term (as with project teams) or readily amended.

- It should improve **communication** within the organisation.

- Dual authority gives the organisation **multiple orientation** so that functional specialists do not get wrapped up in their own concerns.

- It provides a **structure for allocating responsibility to managers for end-results**. A product manager is responsible for product profitability, and a project leader is responsible for ensuring that the task is completed.

- It provides for **inter-disciplinary co-operation** and a mixing of skills and expertise.

- There are many geographic areas with distinct needs, but the firm wishes to exploit economies of scale.

Disadvantages of matrix structure

- Dual authority threatens a **conflict** between managers. To prevent this, the authority of superiors should not overlap and areas of authority must be clearly defined. A subordinate must know to which superior he is responsible for each aspect of his duties.

- One individual with two or more bosses is more likely to suffer **role stress** at work.

- It is sometimes more **costly** – eg product managers are additional jobs which would not be required in a simple structure of functional divisionalisation.

- It may be **difficult for the management to accept** a matrix structure. A manager may feel threatened that another manager will usurp his authority.

- It requires consensus and agreement which may slow down decision-making.

Interactive question 3: Boxer plc   [Difficulty level: Intermediate]

Boxer plc is a company which manufactures dried pasta, produces ready-to-eat meals and is about to start making specialist pasta sauces for distribution to independent delicatessen shops.

The dried pasta revenue and profits have been substantial and stable in the last few years, with sales of the Boxer brand to all large supermarket chains as well as to wholesalers.

The ready-to-eat meals are produced only for Marks & Spencer and Sainsbury's. Products are badged by the retailers under their own name.

Boxer has recently recruited Jake La Motta from Sauce Specialists Ltd. He has considerable knowledge of and contacts within the small delicatessen market. Boxer wishes to pursue a cautious approach to this new area, incurring only limited investment.

Requirements

Design an appropriate structure for Boxer plc.

See **Answer** at the end of this chapter.

4 Span of control

Section overview

- Span of control refers to how many people report to one manager. This will influence the shape of an organisation.

- Wide spans of control create flat management hierarchies whereas narrow spans of control create tall organisational structures.

4.1 Introduction

- The span of control refers to the number of people reporting to one person.

- This influences the shape of the organisation:

Tall and flat organisational structures

- A determinant of whether the organisation is tall or flat is the use of delegation – 'the transfer of legitimate authority without passing on ultimate responsibility'.

Factors influencing span of control

- **Location of subordinates**: The more widely spread, the fewer that can be managed effectively.

- **Complexity/nature of the work**: As complexity increases (and the need for greater teamwork), so the span decreases.

- **Management personality and ability**: The better they are, the more people they can manage.

- **Subordinate ability**: The better they are, the more that can be delegated and therefore managed by the manager.

- **Level of organisational support**: Personnel departments can remove the routine personnel tasks from a manager, enabling him to manage more people.

- **Level of 'danger' involved if delegation takes place**: The more dangerous, the less people that can be managed.

Effects of setting span of control incorrectly

Too wide (flat)

- Loss of contact between superior and subordinates – demoralised subordinates

- Loss of control over subordinates.
- Subgroups form with unofficial leaders.

Too narrow (tall)

- Too many management levels and too much cost.
- Delays in decision-making (because of the length of the chain of command).
- Over-supervision and demoralised staff.

Span and IT

IT can have significant effects on organisational structure in terms of:

- New patterns of work
- Form and structure of groups
- Supervisory/management roles
- Changes in lines of authority
- Job design/descriptions
- Centralisation/decentralisation of decision making and control

New technology (eg the Internet) has often resulted in flatter structures (ie wider spans) with fewer levels of management. Office-based technology can facilitate a greater range of functions and self-checking for staff.

5 Flexible structures

Section overview

- Flexible structures allow firms to adapt to changing circumstances.

- Networks can exist within and between organisations.

- Handy's shamrock structure or flexible firm captures the idea that modern organisations strive to be lean at the core but maintain access to other skills and activities through a variety of networks.

5.1 Network organisations

Network organisations were introduced in Chapter 6. The idea of a **network structure** is applied both within and between organisations.

Within the organisation, the term is used to mean something that resembles both the **organic** organisation discussed earlier in this chapter and the structure of informal relationships that exists in most organisations alongside the formal structure. Such a lose, fluid approach is often used to achieve innovative response to changing circumstances.

The network approach is also visible in the growing field of **outsourcing** as a strategic method. Complex relationships can be developed between firms, who may both buy from and sell to each other, as well as the simpler, more traditional practice of buying in services such as cleaning. These were discussed extensively in Chapter 6.

Writers such as Ghoshal and Bartlett point to the likelihood of such networks becoming the corporations of the future, replacing formal organisation structures with innovations such as **virtual teams**. Virtual teams are interconnected groups of people who may not be in the same office (or even the same organisation) but who:

- Share information and tasks
- Make joint decisions
- Fulfil the collaborative function of a team

Organisations are now able to structure their activities very differently:

- **Staffing**: Certain areas of organisational activity can be undertaken by freelance or contract workers. Charles Handy's shamrock organisation (see below) is gaining ground as a workable model for a leaner and more flexible workforce, within a controlled framework. (The question is: how can this control be achieved?)

- **Leasing of facilities** such as machinery, IT and accommodation (not just capital assets) is becoming more common.

- **Production** itself might be outsourced, even to offshore countries where labour is cheaper. (This, and the preceding point, of course beg the question: which assets and activities do companies retain, and which ones do they 'buy-in'?)

- **Interdependence** of organisations is emphasised by the sharing of functions and services. Databases and communication create genuine interactive sharing of, and access to, common data.

Network structures are also discerned between competitors, where **co-operation on non-core competence matters** can lead to several benefits:

- Cost reduction
- Increased market penetration
- Experience curve effects

Typical areas for co-operation between **competitors** include R&D and distribution chains. The spread of the **Toyota** system of manufacturing, with its emphasis on JIT, quality and the elimination of waste has led to a high degree of integration between the operations of industrial **customers** and their **suppliers**.

5.2 The shamrock organisation

Largely driven by pressure to reduce personnel costs and to adapt to new market imperatives, there has been an increase in the use of part-time and temporary contracts of employment. These allow rapid down-sizing in times of recession or slow growth and can save on the costs of benefits such as pensions, holiday pay and health insurance. The growth in the proportion of the workforce employed on such less-favourable contracts has attracted political attention but continues. It has produced the phenomenon of the **flexible firm** or, as Handy calls it, the **shamrock organisation**.

Handy defines the **shamrock organisation** as a 'core of essential executives and workers supported by outside contractors and part-time help'. This structure permits the buying-in of services as needed, with consequent reductions in overhead costs. It is also known as the **flexible firm**.

The **professional core** are permanently employed staff who provide the core competencies and distinctive knowledge base of the organisation.

The **flexible labour force** are temporary and part-time workers who can be deployed, when required by peaks in demand (eg seasonal tasks or projects).

The **contractual fringe** are external providers (consultants, sub-contractors and freelancers) who can undertake non-core activities and/or provide specialist services more economically than the organisation could arrange internally. Many organisations now **outsource** activities such as IT, logistics, maintenance, call-centre management and so on.

Representation of Handy's shamrock organisation

Customers are a fourth cluster, to whom the organisation may be able to 'sub-contract' some tasks. Information and communication technology (such as the Internet) has allowed sales, service and supply to be conducted on a 'self-service' basis: booking tickets, downloading music/books, getting on-line help and so on. (Even low-tech equivalents, such as home-assembly furniture, enable the organisation to devolve activities to customers and save costs.)

Organisations are increasingly seeking to be lean at the core – where activities are important to their competitive strategy – while maintaining access to a full range of flexibly deployed services at the periphery.

6 Issues for divisionalised organisations

Section overview

- An organisation is centralised when decision making authority is concentrated in its strategic apex.

- Centralisation offers greater control and coordination whereas decentralisation offers greater flexibility.

- Using financial controls necessitates the development of responsibility centres and the use of investment based control measures such as ROCE and residual income (RI).

- Divisional inter-trading requires the setting of appropriate transfer prices.

6.1 Centralisation v decentralisation

Centralisation/decentralisation refers to how much authority/decision-making ability is diffused throughout the organisation.

- **Centralised structures**: Upper levels retain authority to make decisions.

- **Decentralised structures**: Ability to make decisions (ie commit people, money and resources) is passed down to lower levels of the hierarchy.

Factors affecting amount of decentralisation:

- **Management style**: Authoritarian = centralised.

- **Size of organisation**: As size increases, decentralisation tends to increase.

- **Extent of activity diversification**: The more diversified, the more decentralised.

- **Effectiveness of communication**: Decentralisation will not work if information is not communicated downwards.

- **Ability of management**: The more able, the more decentralisation.

- **Speed of technological advancement**: Lower managers likely to be more familiar with changing technology, therefore decentralise.

- **Geography of locations**: If spread, decentralise.

- **Extent of local knowledge needed**: If required, decentralise.

6.1.1 Advantages/disadvantages of decentralisation

Advantages

- Senior management is free to concentrate on strategy: day to day decisions are delegated to lower levels of management.

- Motivation for lower managers from increased delegation/responsibility.

- Local expertise of managers improves decisions based on local knowledge.

- Quicker and more effective responses to local conditions.

- Career paths for managers/employees.

Disadvantages

- More difficult to co-ordinate organisation as lots of people are making the decisions rather then just a few.

- Incongruent decisions, ie different levels of management may pursue different objectives.

- Loss of control by senior management.

- Complicated structures.

- Problems with transfer prices.

- Evaluating divisional performance becomes difficult.

- Duplication of some roles (eg administration).

6.2 Rules for successful divisionalisation

A divisionalised structure:

- Focuses the attention of subordinate management on business performance and results

- Enables greater flexibility in business units to enable them to respond to local competitive challenges

- Enables financial evaluation and comparison of performance of divisions, eg by measures such as return on capital employed

Three key considerations in successful divisionalisation are:

- **Autonomy**: Divisional management should be able to run their businesses otherwise there is little to be gained from having separate divisions.

- **Controllability**: The factors against which divisional managers are evaluated should be within their control.

- **Corporate optimality**: Divisions should follow courses of action that bring the best result for the corporation as a whole.

In practice there can be a tension between these three considerations, for example:

- Corporate centre wishes to implement **group-wide initiatives** on quality, risk management, human resource development or corporate branding which is irrelevant to, or conflicts with, the immediate business needs of a division.

- Inter-trading between divisions is important but there are disputes on the appropriate **transfer price** because each division want to maximise its own profits.

- Allocation of **head office costs** between divisions for central services such as IT, HRM, marketing, corporate treasury mean that many of the divisional costs are uncontrollable.

- **Local competitive conditions** seem to require different products and prices from those laid down by head office, eg in a national marketing campaign.

Worked example: Leisure clubs

The following shows some of the problems that can occur where divisionalisation is operating inappropriately.

A major operator of health and leisure clubs has over 40 centres in a country. The centre manager has profit centre responsibility and is also evaluated on ROCE each year for the purposes of granting a bonus pool to the centre which is shared between the manager and staff. The clubs are ranked into grades according to their size and the range of activities offered. All exercise equipment and facilities are determined by the grade of club and the replacement of equipment is on a strict 5 year basis. Members join a particular centre and pay fees to it. The fees they pay are based on the grade of club they join. However membership of one club entitles them to use other clubs in the chain.

A number of problems have arisen:

- Managers of lower grade clubs situated near higher grade clubs have canvassed members by emphasising that their fees are lower but that members can still use the higher grade club if they choose.

- Some clubs face competition from smaller independent fitness clubs which are able to undercut the national pricing structure.

- Managers of older clubs are complaining that they are being forced to replace equipment that is still perfectly serviceable, and preferred by customers over newer versions which have slick but pointless features, and so are losing out on bonuses because the book value of assets leaps.

- Managers of established clubs are complaining that they get little benefit from the central re-charge for marketing because most marketing activity is being used to launch new clubs.

- Managers of new clubs complain that they are not getting bonuses because they have new equipment and membership numbers are still growing and this is causing staff to leave or become despondent.

6.3 Performance management of divisions

Responsibility centres

Control requires that managers are appointed with clear **domains of responsibility** such as range of activities, geographical scope and resources. As covered above, these are the basis of divisionalisation.

From a financial control perspective responsibility centres are:

- **Revenue centres**: Responsible for revenues only such as a sales department

- **Costs centres**: Responsible for keeping expenditure within limits such as a hospital ward or IT function

- **Profit centre**: Responsibility for revenues and costs (and therefore profit) but not balance sheet

- **Investment centre**: A business within a business responsible for balance sheet and profit

Multi-divisional firms generally assign Investment Centre responsibility to divisions.

The nature of responsibility will influence the way in which performance is managed, since division managers must only be held to account for factors within their control. Divisional performance management is covered in Chapter 12.

6.4 Transfer pricing between divisions

Definition

Transfer price: The price at which one division in a group sells its products or services to another division in the same group.

Divisions buying and selling with each-other leads to transfer prices. Several situations may give rise to this:

- Transfer of finished goods between divisions, eg a car manufacturer selling cars to its sales division

- Transfer of components between divisions, eg engine manufacturing plant selling engines to the car assembly plant

- Transfer of staff or customers between divisions, eg a professional practice seconding staff from one office to work on a project run by another office

- Provision of central services, eg the group IT function selling hardware, training and user support services to divisions

Consider the following example:

Transfer prices have several implications:

- **They determine the profits of divisions**: If the upstream (supplying) Division A charges a high price of £15,000 for its cars then all of the final profit from the product (£30m) will be enjoyed by it and none by the downstream Division B.

- **They affect performance evaluation**: If Division A takes all the profit its manager will look better.

- **They determine the tax to be paid**: If Division A is in a different country does take all the profit for itself then it will be taxed according to the tax rates in its country.

- **They determine the currency in which profits are made**: Suppose Division B is in a country where dividends are subject to punitive withholding taxes. By charging a high price Division A is taking the money out of Division B's country as a payment for the cars and not as a dividend and so avoiding the withholding tax on dividends.

- **They may determine the price and final sales of the product**: Suppose Division B decides to set its market price as a 15% mark-up on costs. If the cars are transferred by Division A at cost, the final price would be £19,550 ie (£12,000 + £5,000) × 1.15. If the transfer price were £15,000 then the final price would be £23,000. This would clearly have a significant effect on volumes sold and therefore profits. Another situation is where the receiving division must pay an **import tariff** on its receipts of the components. Here charging a low transfer price will reduce the amount of the tariff and so avoid the final good being priced out of the market.

- **They can lead to dysfunctional decisions**: If either division believes it can get a better deal from the market it may take it. For example, if division B could obtain supplies of cars elsewhere, say from other dealers supplied by A, it might leave A with unsold stock. Conversely A might supply to alternative channels and leave B with empty showrooms and unabsorbed overheads.

Cost based methods of setting transfer prices

This leads to the inevitable problem of deciding which cost to use:

- **Full cost**: The variable costs plus an amount to cover overheads. This leaves the supplying division in a break-even situation.

- **Variable cost** (or marginal cost): This leaves the supplying division making nil contribution and so enduring losses equal to its fixed costs.

- **Opportunity cost**: The revenue foregone by not selling the item to highest bidder.

Optimal transfer pricing requires that divisions sell components at the higher of variable cost and opportunity cost.

Other methods of setting transfer prices

Managers of divisions will want to record a profit. For this reason the following transfer price setting methods have been identified:

- **Negotiated prices**: The transfer price is established by discussions between the divisional managers in a bargaining process.

- **Two-part transfer prices**: The transfer price is set at variable cost to ensure corporate optimality but in addition to this price the supplying division records an extra amount in its sales ledger to arrive at a profit figure for evaluation purposes.

- **Dual pricing**: The receiving division records the transfer at standard variable cost which may aid decision making. The transferring division reports the transfer at a higher value (eg cost plus) to give a profit incentive. This should lead to goal congruence but may lead to poor cost control as profits are made more easily. The accounting problem makes this method unpopular.

Considerations in transfer pricing

- Impact on group profitability

- Impact on product positioning: Where the internal transfer price is also the price on external markets it will influence the positioning of the product

- Costs of the system: Month ends determining and recording inter-company charges ('chasing wooden dollars') is a non-value adding activity

- Motivational impacts of the system: Transfer prices affect evaluation of managers, bonuses for divisions and the purchasing decisions of the divisions

Interactive question 4: Marble Makers Ltd [Difficulty level: Easy]

Marble Makers Ltd manufactures and sells high-end marble for use in domestic kitchens. The company's customers often pay a premium to purchase marble as part of bespoke kitchen designs.

The company has two divisions, the manufacturing division and the retail division. The manufacturing division is based in a factory in Kent, and it imports marble from overseas and finishes it to the customers' individual requirements. The retail division consists of four small shops located in wealthy areas across the UK. The managing director was keen to locate the shops as close as possible to those areas lived in by members of the target market. He believes that the shops act as a great showcase for Marble Makers' final product. The retail division is the manufacturing division's only customer.

The Head of Finance has provided the following projections for the two divisions for the next 12 months. These projections show external income and costs before any transfer price recharges:

	Manufacturing £m	Retail £m
Estimated retail sales	–	30
Variable costs	12	5
Fixed costs	7	3

Requirements

(a) Calculate the expected profit or loss to be made by each division over the next 12 months. You should assume that transfer prices are based on the current arrangement of retail price less 40%.

(b) Determine the transfer pricing formula (retail price less an appropriate %) which would enable the manufacturing division to break-even in the next 12 months. You should assume that costs are in line with the projections provided.

Interactive question 5: External offer [Difficulty level: Easy]

Unit costs	Division A £	Division B £
Variable	10	15
Transfer price	–	20
Fixed costs	5	10
Profit	5	25
Selling price	20	70

Division A can sell outside at £20 per unit or transfer internally to Division B at £20 per unit.

B receives an offer from a customer of £30 per unit for its final product.

Requirements

(a) Would B accept the offer of £30 per unit given the existing transfer price?

(b) Is this the right decision from the company's point of view if

 – A has surplus capacity?
 – A is at full capacity?

See **Answer** at the end of this chapter.

Interactive question 6: Full cost transfer price [Difficulty level: Easy]

A multi-product company has two divisions.

Unit costs for a particular product

	Manufacturing division £	Selling division £
Variable	20.00	15.00
Fixed (apportionment of costs incurred for all products)	11.00	–
	31.00	15.00

Transfers are at full cost.

Ultimate selling price = £40.00

Requirements

Are the transfers recommended from the point of view

(a) Of the company?
(b) Of the selling division?

See **Answer** at the end of this chapter.

Interactive question 7: Full or variable cost? [Difficulty level: Easy]

A corporate power plant serving divisions A and B:

Power plant

Budgeted fixed cost per month	£10,000
Standard variable cost	£1/kwh
Actual total cost in January	£18,000

Usage of power plant in January

	A	B
Budgeted usage (kwh)	4,000	6,000
Actual usage (kwh)	4,000	2,000

Requirements

How much are A and B charged if

(a) The charge is based on full actual cost?
(b) The charge is based on standard variable cost plus a share of budgeted fixed costs?

See **Answer** at the end of this chapter.

---

7 Organisational structures for international business

Section overview

- International business needs structures based on divisionalised structures but varied to reflect the national cultures of the countries where they are to be based.

- The steps in becoming an international (or transnational) organisation are outlined.

- The appropriate structure for an international business will depend on the stage of its international development and the trade of between local responsiveness and global coordination.

7.1 The development of overseas operations

With overseas operations, business structures are likely to be made complex by distance (geographical and cultural).

Organisational structures for international expansion often start by having a separate division for international activities. As growth occurs the business is often reorganised into divisions by geographical area or alternatively organised by worldwide product groupings. Eventually this may lead to a matrix structure.

The critical issue in devising an appropriate structure for an international business is the extent to which the need for local independence and responsiveness takes precedence over global coordination.

Thus international businesses can follow a **multi-domestic strategy** where activities are located in individual national markets and products/services tailored to local needs, or a **global strategy** where standardised products are developed and produced centrally.

7.2 Multi-national business structures

Bartlett and Ghoshal identify four possible structures for a multi-national business:

		Low	High
Global	High	Global product division	Transnational corporations
Co-ordination	Low	International division	Local subsidiary

Local independence/responsiveness

International division – a stand-alone division added on to the domestic structure, which draws on the products and technology of the home business. Often observed when a business first starts to internationalise.

Local subsidiary – geographically based and operate independently. Local management has a high degree of autonomy. Appropriate for a business following a **multi-domestic strategy**.

Global product division – typical for a company following a **global strategy**, which will have separate world-wide divisions for soft drinks, alcoholic beverages etc.

The transnational approach, which attempts to achieve high local responsiveness and high global coordination, has been used by some international companies to build in strategic and organisational flexibility. The transnational corporation (TNC) is like a matrix. It involves having dispersed and interdependent subsidiaries, integrated into a worldwide operation, with different parts of the organisation specialising in different areas.

The TNC:

* Co-ordinates **various stages** of the **production chain** between different countries

* Can take advantage of differences in geographical distribution in factors of production (eg raw materials, skilled labour, access to capital) and government policies (eg taxes, subsidies)

* Has geographical flexibility; it can switch resources and operations at an international and global scale

8 Governance

Section overview

* At its broadest corporate governance would cover all aspect controlling the organisation including its structure and systems. Here it is restricted to a discussion of the role of the Corporate Board.

* Governance should take the overview of the direction of the business and consider the proper policies to deal with risk and the transparency of the appointment of directors etc.

* The governance of not-for-profit organisations requires greater transparency than the governance of businesses.

8.1 Introduction

Over the last two decades, in the wake of a series of major corporate scandals such as Enron and Worldcom, there has been a growing concern to make board stewardship of public companies more effective.

It is important when deciding on an appropriate structure that practical matters of corporate governance are not forgotten. Areas to consider include:

- The split between executive and non-executive directors
- The possible establishment of an audit committee
- The possible creation of an internal audit function
- Building responsibility for risk management into job descriptions
- Creating a framework for communication with external and internal stakeholders

8.2 Strategy and governance

Definition

Corporate governance: The set of rules which governs the structure and determines objectives of an organisation and regulates the relationship between the organisation's management, its board of directors and its shareholders.

- Corporate governance is about what the board of an organisation does and how it sets the values of the organisation, and is to be distinguished from the day-to-day management of operations by full-time business executives. The powers of executive managers to direct business operations are one aspect of governance, but management skills are not.

- Similarly, corporate governance is not concerned with formulating business strategy, although the responsibility of the board of directors and executive managers is for strategic decisions taken.

Corporate governance and strategic management

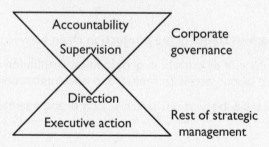

The diagram shows the distinction between governance and the rest of strategic management, with governance mainly concerned with accountability and supervision.

The **two-tier board form of governance** practised in Germany recognises this split. The upper, supervisory board is responsible for monitoring and overseeing the work of the executive board which runs the business, and has the power to hire and fire its members. The management body is responsible for direction and executive action. Thus the supervisory board is responsible for governance.

8.3 Structure of governance

The **UK Corporate Governance Code** is a code of practice embodying a **shareholder-led approach to corporate governance.** The Code is a guide to a number of key components of effective board practice, based on the underlying principles of all good governance: accountability, transparency, probity (integrity) and focus on the sustainable success of an entity over the longer term. The previous edition (known as the Combined Code) was published in 1998 and was revised by the FRC in 2010 and 2012 in light of continued turmoil in the financial world.

The Code applies to all companies with a Premium Listing of equity shares on the London Stock Exchange, regardless of whether they are incorporated in the UK or elsewhere. Listing of shares is run by the UK Listing Authority (UKLA), which is part of the Financial Conduct Authority (FCA). The UKLA's Listing Rules require **all companies listed in the FTSE 350** to apply the Code's main Principles and to include in their annual reports **a statement of compliance** with the supporting principles and provisions of the Code or **an explanation of non-compliance** (which may be justified in certain circumstances provided good corporate governance is still achieved). **Other companies** can apply the Code more flexibly but are encouraged to follow it as an example of '**best practice**' and may experience pressure from their stakeholders if they do not adopt it.

The **key principles** set out in the five main sections of the Code are as follows:

1. **Leadership** – Every company should be headed by an **effective board** which is collectively responsible for the long-term success of the company. The board's role is to provide **entrepreneurial leadership** of the company **within a framework of prudent and effective controls** which enables risk to be assessed and managed.

   There should be a clear **division of responsibilities** at the head of the company between the **running of the board** and the executive responsibility for the **running of the company's business**. The roles of the Chairman and Chief Executive should **not be exercised by the same individual**. The chairman is responsible for leadership of the board and ensuring its effectiveness in all aspects of its role.

   As part of their role as members of a unitary board, non-executive directors should **constructively challenge** and **help develop proposals on strategy**.

2. **Effectiveness** – The board and its committees should have the appropriate balance of skills, experience, independence and knowledge of the company to enable them to discharge their respective duties and responsibilities effectively.

   The board should include an appropriate **combination** of **executive** and **non-executive directors** (and in particular **independent non-executive directors**) such that no individual or small group of individuals can dominate the board's decision taking. (The role of the non-executives is seen as critical in preventing a listed company from being run for the personal benefit of its senior executive directors.)

   There should be a formal, rigorous and transparent procedure for the **appointment of new directors** to the board. All directors should be submitted for **re-election** at **regular intervals**, subject to continued satisfactory performance.

   All directors should receive **induction** on joining the board and should regularly **update and refresh** their skills and knowledge. All directors should be able to allocate **sufficient time** to the company to discharge their responsibilities effectively.

   The board should be supplied in a timely manner with **information** in a form and of a quality appropriate to enable it to discharge its duties.

   The board should undertake a formal and rigorous annual **evaluation of its own performance** and that of its **committees** and individual **directors**, including an evaluation of the **balance** of skills, experience, independence and knowledge of the company on the board, and its **diversity**, including gender.

3. **Accountability** – The board should present a **fair, balanced** and understandable **assessment of the company's position and prospects**.

   The board is responsible for determining the nature and extent of the significant risks it is willing to take in achieving its strategic objectives. The board should maintain **sound risk management and internal control systems**.

   The board should, at least annually, conduct a **review of the effectiveness of the company's risk management and internal control systems** and should report to shareholders that they have done so. The review should cover all material controls, including **financial, operational and compliance controls**.

   The board should establish formal and transparent arrangements for considering how they should **apply the corporate reporting and risk management and internal control principles** and for maintaining an appropriate relationship with the company's **auditors**. The board should establish an **audit committee** of at least **three** or, in the case of smaller companies, **two independent non-executive directors**.

4. **Remuneration** – Levels of remuneration should be sufficient to **attract, retain and motivate directors** of the quality required to run the company successfully, but a company should avoid paying more than is necessary for this purpose.

    A significant proportion of executive directors' remuneration should be structured so as to **link rewards to corporate and individual performance**. The **performance-related elements** of executive directors' remuneration should be **stretching** and designed to promote the **long-term success of the company**.

    There should be a **formal and transparent procedure** for developing policy on executive remuneration and for fixing the remuneration packages of individual directors. **No director should be involved in deciding his or her own remuneration**. The board should establish a **remuneration committee** of **at least three, or in the case of smaller companies two, independent non-executive directors**. The remuneration committee should have delegated responsibility for **setting remuneration for all executive directors and the Chairman**, including pension rights and any compensation payments.

5. **Relations with shareholders** – There should be a **dialogue with shareholders** based on the **mutual understanding of objectives**. The board as a whole has responsibility for ensuring that a satisfactory dialogue with shareholders takes place.

    Nothing should override the general requirements of law to treat shareholders equally with regard to access to information. The board should use the AGM to communicate with investors and to encourage their participation.

8.4   Role of the board and non-executives

Boards of directors in the UK have five principal roles:

*   Accountability – the liability to render account to someone else. A director is accountable to the shareholders, at common law or by statute, and the company's annual report and accounts, for example, should be presented to the shareholders for approval

*   Supervision – monitoring and overseeing management performance

*   Direction – formulating the strategic direction in the long term

*   Executive action – involvement in implementing and controlling strategy

*   Risk assessment and management – determining the nature and extent of the risks the company is willing to take to achieve its objectives and ensuring good practices in risk management

The 'tone at the top' sets the pattern for the way in which a company conducts itself, and board members should give ethical leadership. A board of directors should have the necessary skills, experience and integrity, both individually and collectively, to govern the company effectively. A lack of collective experience among the board members will affect the quality of decision-making by the board.

The board of directors should exercise full control and monitor executive management.

*   There should be a clearly accepted division of responsibility to ensure a balance of power. Where the chairman is also the chief executive there must be a strong and independent element of the board.

*   The board should recruit non-executive directors of sufficient calibre and number.

*   The board should have a formal schedule of matters for decision to ensure that direction is firmly in its hands.

*   All directors should take independent professional advice where necessary at the company's expense.

Non-executive directors (NEDs) should bring an independent viewpoint to the issues of strategy, performance, resources and standards of conduct. They should be independent of management and free of any responsibility that could materially interfere with the exercise of independent judgement apart from their fees and shareholding. Fees should be time-related and reflect responsibilities.

NEDs should be appointed by a formal selection process and appointment approved by the board for a specific term subject to re-election - their re-appointment should not be automatic.

Non-executive directors should scrutinise the performance of management in meeting agreed goals and objectives, and monitor the reporting of performance. They should satisfy themselves on the integrity of financial information and that financial controls and systems of risk management are robust and defensible. They are responsible for determining appropriate levels of remuneration of executive directors and have a prime role in appointing and, where necessary, removing executive directors, and in succession planning.

Director's duties

You should be familiar with the duties of directors from your earlier law studies. As you will recall the UK Companies Act 2006 places the following 'general duties' on company directors:

Duty	Explanation
To act within powers (s171)	Directors must: • Act in accordance with the company's constitution • Exercise powers only for the purpose for which they were conferred
To promote the success of the company (s 172)	Directors must act in the way they consider, in good faith, would be most likely to promote the success of the company for the benefit of its members as a whole
To exercise Independent judgment (s 173)	It does not mean that they are not exercising independent judgment where they act in accordance with • An agreement duly entered into by the company that restricts the future exercise of discretion by its directors, or • The company's constitution
To exercise Reasonable care, skill and diligence (s 174)	ie the care, skill and diligence that would be exercised by a reasonably diligent person with • The general knowledge, skill and experience that may reasonably be expected of a person performing their functions as director • Actual general knowledge, skill and experience
To avoid conflict of interest (s 175)	A director must avoid a situation in which they have or could have a direct or indirect interest that conflicts or possibly may conflict with the interests of the company or another duty.
Not to Accept benefits from third parties (s 176)	A director must not accept a benefit from a third party by reason of their • Being a director or • Doing (or not doing) anything as director Unless the acceptance of the benefit cannot reasonably be regarded as likely to give rise to a conflict of interest.

Duty	Explanation
To declare interest in proposed transaction or arrangement (s 177)	Provided the director is, or ought reasonably to be, aware of the situation, they must declare the nature and extent of any such interest (direct or indirect) to the other directors, unless it cannot reasonably be regarded as likely to give rise to a conflict of interest.

8.5 Reward structures

The remuneration committee exists in public companies for the purpose of demonstrating to shareholders and any other interested parties that there is an objective process for determining the financial rewards of directors and any senior staff who are remunerated on a performance related system. The committee is composed of non-executive directors; members of the firm of external auditors have also sat on the remuneration committee.

The committee has delegated responsibility for setting remuneration (including pension rights and compensation payments) for all executive directors and the chairman. The committee should also recommend and monitor the level and structure of remuneration for senior management. The board of directors implements the necessary recommendations.

Issues considered by the committee would be the following:

- Remuneration levels for non-executives
- Length of service contracts for executive directors
- Performance related systems of reward
- Pension contributions
- Compensation for loss of office
- Share option schemes

It is important to remember that the corporate governance issues on rewards extend to the entire reward package of individual directors, as well as to the reward policy generally. The package may consist of:

- Annual compensation (basic salary, pension contributions by the company for the individual, payments by the company into a personal pension scheme arrangement for the individual, a bonus (often a cash bonus) tied perhaps to the annual financial performance of the company and various perks, such as membership of the company's health insurance scheme, private use of company aircraft or boats, and so on).

- Long-term compensation, consisting of share option schemes or company shares or the award of additional options depending on long-term performance indicators.

- A severance payment arrangement, whereby the company is committed to giving the individual a minimum severance payment if he or she is forced to leave the company.

It is often useful to think of a reward package as a combination of fixed and variable elements:

- The fixed elements are the remuneration received by the director regardless of performance, such as fixed salary and salary-related pension.

- The variable elements are the performance-related elements (cash bonuses, awards of share options or shares depending on performance, etc).

8.6 Risk profiles

An issue in corporate governance is that the directors of companies might take decisions intended to increase profits without giving due regard to the risks. In some cases, companies may continue to operate without regard to the changing risk profile of their existing businesses.

The **moral hazard** to shareholders from the increasing risk profile of a firm is greater than to its directors.

Shareholders stand to lose some or all of the value of their investment in the business. To shareholders, investment risk is important, as well as high returns.

Directors, on the other hand, are rewarded on the basis of the returns the company achieves, linked to profits or dividend growth, and their remuneration is not linked in any direct way to the risk aspects of their business. Risk assessment and risk management is now recognised, particularly in the UK, as an ingredient of sound corporate governance and greater emphasis has been placed on this in the 2010 Code.

The duties of the board of directors must include ensuring that there is an operative and effective framework of prudent controls which enables risk to be assessed and managed. Shareholders should feel confident that the board is aware of the risks faced by the company, and that a system for monitoring and controlling them is in place.

The risk management cycle is an interactive process of identifying risks, assessing their impact, and prioritising actions to control and reduce risks.

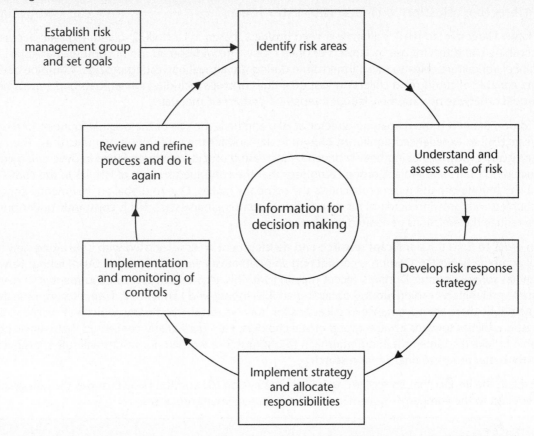

Source: The CIMA risk management cycle, taken from 'Fraud risk management – A guide to good practice'

Once the risks have been identified and assessed, and the organisation's risk appetite has been set, strategies can be developed by the risk management group to deal with each risk that has been identified.

Strategies could include:

- Ignoring small risks (but ensuring that they remain under cyclical review)
- Contractual transfer of risk
- Risk avoidance
- Risk reduction via controls and procedures
- Transferring risks to insurers

Risk management is covered in more detail in Chapter 10.

Interactive question 8: Director's remuneration [Difficulty level: Easy]

Explain and assess the impact of various components of remuneration on a director's behaviour:

- Performance related bonuses
- Transaction bonuses
- Share options

See **Answer** at the end of this chapter.

Interactive question 9: Happy Harvester Ltd [Difficulty level: Intermediate]

Happy Harvester Ltd (HH) is a family-owned business, based in Norfolk, England. HH manufactures combine harvesters for use by farmers of grain crops. The widespread use of combine harvesters in global agriculture helps to save farmers time during the annual harvesting process. Combine harvesters are capable of cutting and collecting vast quantities of crops including wheat, oats and corn, which would otherwise be extremely labour intensive if performed manually.

Gordon Bennett is the managing director of HH, and he is the son of the original founder. In recent years HH has experienced significant growth in demand for the machines it manufactures. The company's growth is being heavily driven by increasing orders from large farms in developing countries including China and India. Gordon recognises that the continued success of HH lies in the company's ability to innovate the types of machines the company makes. Due to global environmental concerns coupled with growing demand for more efficient combine harvesters, HH is constantly under pressure to reduce the emissions generated by its machines.

In order to fund the significant research and development costs associated with innovating new models of combine harvester, Gordon is considering an Alternative Investment Market (AIM) listing. However, he has some concerns. During a recent meeting with his accountant, Gordon commented: 'I have done some preliminary reading around obtaining an AIM listing, and I know that if we offer some shares to the public there are governance implications for how we run the company, which will increase our responsibilities towards a wider group of stakeholders. I am particularly concerned that we will not be able to take the same risks in our approach to business. I'm worried our results will suffer, even if we do have better access to finance for research'.

Explain the impact that an AIM listing is likely to have on HH and the likely changes that are going to be required to the company's governance and risk management processes.

8.7 Governance of government, public and non-profit organisations

This section applies to the following:

- **Government** – areas like defence and the law, which are the responsibility of the nation state.

- **Public** – the provision of health, transport, energy and other services which may be the responsibility of the state or may have been privatised, depending on the political views of the government.

- **Not-for-profit** – institutions that work for the common public good but are independent of the state – for example, charities, trusts and similar institutions.

In profit-oriented organisations, the board's minimum responsibilities are established by statute, regulation and case law. Many corporate boards also assume broader responsibilities in other key areas, such as health and safety or environmental practices. No similar set of legal minimum responsibilities exists for non-profit organisations' boards. Many of the issues are the same but there are some that are of specific importance to these sectors:

- **Accountability:** This is fundamental to the corporate governance of public bodies, and in recent years, the voluntary sector with regard to both the proper stewardship of public and donated funds and the increasing demand for service users to be involved in decision-making.

- **Stakeholders**: Whilst commercial companies are primarily accountable to the shareholders, organisations in the public and voluntary sectors are accountable to a wide range of stakeholders, including service users, the general public, funders and national government. Issues of accountability are not clear-cut and conflicts can arise, eg charity trustees have a legal duty to act in the interests of their beneficiaries, but if the charity is a membership body this may conflict with the wishes of members.

- **Openness and transparency**: There is a demand for open government and a distrust of decisions taken 'behind closed doors'. Voluntary organisations also face calls for transparency.

- **Governance/board structures**: The unitary board is not common in these sectors. Boards, or their equivalent, may be directly elected or appointed, and are often volunteer-based.

- **Monitoring performance**: In recent years a major emphasis in the public sector has been on performance measurement and evaluation. Increasingly voluntary organisations are beginning to look at ways of measuring outcomes.

Each group involved in a not-for-profit organisation – its board, management, staff, volunteers, donors and others – plays a part in its governance system. The board's role and activities can be examined in terms of five distinct areas:

1. **Responsibilities and mandate**: In profit-oriented organisations, the board's minimum responsibilities are established by statute, regulation and case law. No similar set of legal minimum responsibilities exists for NFP boards. The board bears the ultimate responsibility, though it usually delegates the authority to run the organisation to a CEO and a management team. The board's primary role is to oversee management and ensure that the NFP's affairs are being conducted in a way which achieves the organisation's objectives. NFP boards should have responsibility for:

   - Strategic planning for the organisation
   - Risk identification and management
   - Management effectiveness and succession
   - Communications with stakeholders, and
   - Internal control and management information systems.

2. **Structure and organisation**: The structure and mandates of the board and each of its committees should be documented, to help ensure that board members, management and the NFP's stakeholders clearly understand the board's role. The board should also consider the qualifications it requires of individual board members in order for them to help carry out the board's responsibilities.

3. **Processes and information**: Processes of decision-making and consultation should be open and will need to conform to procedures laid down in statute law (eg planning applications) or in accordance with procedures laid down by the organisation itself. Information must be provided to interested parties and may be subject to various legal duties of disclosure.

4. **Performance assessment and accountability**: Boards of directors are accountable for their actions, and board members of all organisations are exposed to a growing personal liability resulting from the actions of the board and the organisation as a whole. Even though NFP board members are volunteers, their liability is the same as that of remunerated members of corporate boards. The responsibilities of board members include:

   - Acting in good faith, in the best interests of the NFP
   - Avoiding conflicts of interest
   - Being diligent with regard to board meetings and obtaining information, and
   - Obtaining a degree of confidence regarding the CEO's integrity and ability.

5. **Organisational culture**

   A key development for the corporate governance of the UK public sector was the Nolan Committee on Standards in Public Life.

The Nolan Seven Principles of Public Life include:

- **Selflessness**: Holders of public office should take decisions solely in terms of the public interest. They should not do so to gain financial or other material benefits for themselves, their family or their friends.

- **Integrity**: Holders of public office should not place themselves under any financial or other obligation to outside individuals or organisations that might influence them in the performance of their duties.

- **Objectivity**: In carrying out public business, including making public appointments, awarding contracts or recommending individuals for rewards and benefits, holders of public office should make choices on merit.

- **Accountability**: Holders of public office are accountable for their decisions and actions to the public and must submit themselves to whatever scrutiny is appropriate to their office.

- **Openness**: Holders of public office should be as open as possible about the decisions and actions that they take. They should give reasons for their decisions and restrict information only when the wider public interest clearly demands.

- **Honesty**: Holders of public office have a duty to declare any private interests relating to their public duties and to take steps to resolve any conflicts arising in a way that protects the public interest.

- **Leadership**: Holders of public office should promote and support these principles by leadership and example.

Summary

Business Strategy

Structure follows strategy (Chandler)

Top down

Bottom up

Strategy emerges from and conditioned by structure

Governance

Organisation structure

Consists of:
– Staff roles
– Primary grouping into teams
– Departments and divisions
– Supervisory and management teams
– Control systems
– Corporate board and governance

– Constitution of board
– Reward structure
– Risk profiles

Divisionalisation

or Hybrid
– Functional
– Geographic
– Product/brand
– Customer/market segment

Centralisation

How authority/ decision making diffused

Centralised
– Control
– Co-ordination
Decentralised
– Motivation
– Quicker

Span of control

Matrix

Functions

Markets

Mintzberg organisations

Strategic apex

Technostructure

Middle line

Support staff

Operating core

Configuration
– Simple
– Machine bureaucracy
– Professional bureaucracy
– Divisionalised form
– Adhocracy

Divisionalised form

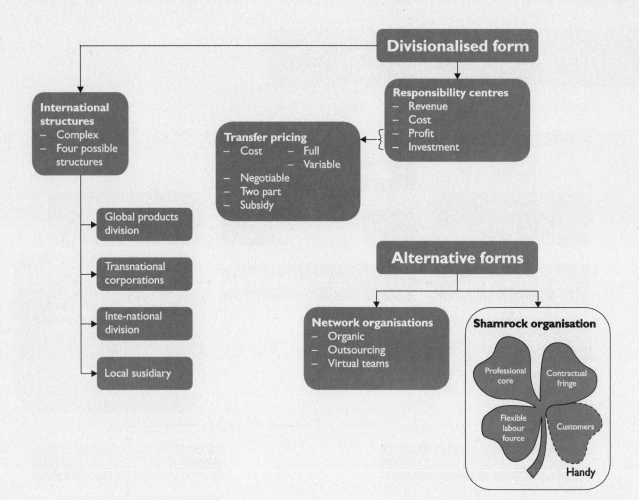

Divisionalised form

International structures
– Complex
– Four possible structures

Global products division

Transnational corporations

Inte-national division

Local susidiary

Transfer pricing
– Cost   – Full
              – Variable
– Negotiable
– Two part
– Subsidy

Responsibility centres
– Revenue
– Cost
– Profit
– Investment

Alternative forms

Network organisations
– Organic
– Outsourcing
– Virtual teams

Shamrock organisation

Professional core

Contractual fringe

Flexible labour fource

Customers

Handy

Self-test

Answer the following questions.

1   Greenleaf Ltd has grown from a small entrepreneurial company of five staff to a larger organisation of thirty-five. The growth, though welcome, has thrown Greenleaf into chaos. No-one is sure what they should be doing and mistakes are beginning to be made.

    Recommend, with reasons, a suitable organisation structure and suggest the mechanism required to co-ordinate the various parts of the organisation.

2   Suggest two ways in which a company can ensure corporate governance processes are incorporated into the organisation structure.

3   What is a professional bureaucracy? Give two examples of organisations that would suit this form of structure.

4   What is meant by a matrix organisation structure?

5   Compare and contrast centralisation and decentralisation.

6   How do 'the location and complexity of the work' and 'the degree of delegation possible' influence the span of control?

7   Travel Fast Ltd is an established bus company. Its organisation chart shows a three-tier structure of directors, managers and drivers.

    What factors will influence the span of control of the managers?

8   A substantial architectural practice designing and managing the construction of various buildings is likely to be best suited to a matrix organisational structure.

    Why?

9   Within a manufacturing business an excerpt from the organisation chart is as follows.

The chief accountant is collating budget information for the coming year and the production managers (after reference to the chart) are unwilling to supply figures, saying they report to the production director.

Explain why the problem has arisen and how it can be solved.

10 In the context of international structures, explain the difference between a 'global product division' and a 'local subsidiary' and suggest when each might be appropriate.

11 **Byron Tuffin**

    Byron Tuffin is the owner of four hotels. Three of these have been recently acquired; one is in London, one in the Lake District (Ambleside) and the third in the Clifton area of Bristol. The original hotel is the Imperial, outside Brighton. The Imperial has been in the Tuffin family for fifty years and was bequeathed to Byron by his father.

    The Imperial has forty rooms. Five of these are de-luxe suites with lounge/ante-room, bedroom and bathroom. Twenty are double bedrooms and the remainder are single rooms. The hotel has a beautiful location in ten acres of landscaped gardens and, being on a small hill, the rooms at the top command impressive views over Sussex. The hotel makes good returns and has good all-year-round occupancy rates. Much more comes from special events like weddings and as a stopover for honeymooning couples before departure elsewhere the next day.

The Regent in Clifton and The Orangery in the Lake District are similar to The Imperial. The former has 30 rooms while the latter has only 20 double rooms. The Serpentine hotel in London has 55 rooms, ie 30 double, 5 de-luxe suites and 20 single rooms.

Byron bought the hotels from an old family friend. Each of the hotels needs some refurbishment. Byron has ten years' experience in managing The Imperial but realises that a four-hotel group is a different matter. As a consultant brought in by his bankers (who helped in the acquisitions) you have been called in to assist Byron in developing the company. During the course of your investigations you conduct many interviews: details from some of these are given below.

Carolyn Reeder (Finance manager, The Imperial)

'I'm a bit overqualified for this job. I'm an ACA with four years' post-qualification experience. I've been here for two years and, although the job is fairly easy, the people here are great to work with. Byron is absolutely superb with customers: he checks their file (if they have one) before they arrive and he makes them feel really special. They love him. On the other hand he does not want to be concerned with detail. He forgets about decisions and he has trouble taking decisions without consulting everyone else first. He thinks about "direction of the hotel" etc, so I suppose he's more strategic. He does interfere sometimes though, by ordering my staff about or bypassing me to get information from them.'

Rick Fowler (Facilities manager)

'There's a fair amount to do here with the hotel being a grade II listed building. This is a "special" occasion hotel and I love the "pre-war" feel to it. I've an excellent team of tradesmen under me who are all qualified. They take pride in their work but there isn't always enough to keep them occupied. Byron is a good enough man but on occasion he's difficult to pin down. He does occasionally annoy me. He gives his opinion on how one of my staff should carry out a repair. He orders them about too, overriding my authority. One instance will suffice. Last month he ordered Angus (a joiner) to repair his office door when I'd told Angus to refit a bathroom door in Room 22. This door would not close. We had a particularly stroppy customer who wanted a room change. When I remonstrated with Byron his response was "...why didn't you tell me you'd scheduled Angus for elsewhere ...". That's not the principle. Byron should only take decisions like that following consultation with me. I go to Peter (Unwaring) for decisions on most things.'

Peter Unwaring (Operations manager)

'I look after the day-to-day operations of the hotel – bookings, staffing, etc. I only involve Byron if there is a problem. We have our weekly manager meetings which are fairly easy going. Byron is a good man to work for – he does think "big" though. He's always coming up with ideas for the hotel. He's also astonishing to watch with our regular customers. They adore him.'

Alexandra Thorpe-Watson (Manager, The Regent)

'The acquisition was good news for us. The hotel needs some refurbishment – at the moment it has a little too much "faded gentility". Byron from The Imperial seems an enthusiastic person. We've agreed that this hotel needs to be re-positioned. I've been here a year, and before I joined the hotel was losing its direction.'

Niall Gallagher (Manager, The Serpentine)

'This is a good hotel with a good occupancy rate. Our clients are mostly business people in London for a few days. We also get tourists, which we need to encourage as our weekend occupancy needs improving. Byron seems to be fairly open-minded in terms of ideas for the direction of the group. I'll be interested in what he comes up with.'

Byron Tuffin (Group owner)

'I'm really excited about our future. The group now has different hotels. We now have different coverage geographically and in terms of markets. We'll need to invest in refurbishment, though. I have no problem with that. I fully understand and believe in the importance of the client. You have to make each guest feel that he is the most important person in the hotel.'

Requirements

Prepare a memorandum covering the following.

(a) An appropriate organisation structure for the group together with reasons for your recommendation and the advantages your structure would bring. **(9 marks)**

(b) A review of Byron's management style and your reasoned suggestions for a new management structure, indicating the advantages of the new structure. **(9 marks)**

(18 marks)

12 Goddess plc

Goddess plc is a manufacturer of kitchen appliances. The chairman and chief executive is Barbara Best, whose father, Sid, originally set up the business 14 years ago. The company has a good reputation for the production of up-market refrigerators for built-in kitchens, following an invention by Sid of a fan to run at low speeds and keep food fresher for far longer than conventional products. The refrigerators have always sold at premium prices, but in the last 18 months demand has levelled off as the market sector has become saturated. The main customers have been department stores and electrical retailers. Due to Goddess plc being a relative newcomer to the kitchen appliances market, it has had to give retailers a 60% trade discount on the price sold to the consumer, in order to obtain floor space in stores.

The company floated on the stock market five years ago. Initially the share price rose as sales exceeded expectations, but recently the price has fallen due to the decrease in demand for the fridges. Barbara and her family own 40% of the share capital, and a further 45% is owned by institutional investors, which have been critical of the underperformance of the share price. The institutional investors have also been unhappy about Barbara's domineering managerial style, and her refusal to allow non-executive directors on the board despite support for such a move from other executive directors.

Barbara feels that, as her father set up the company and developed many of the initial products, the board should always agree with her views. She does not believe that the other directors are as committed to the company as she is, and so insists on being involved in all decisions. She believes that she has always made the right decisions for the company as she has a vested interest arising from her shareholding. She has imposed her views by removing two of the directors in the past who have voted against her proposals. She is now aware that she needs the support of the other directors to help turn the company around.

The company has tried to counter criticisms regarding trading and the falling share price by entering a new market. The development has just been completed of a new style machine that washes twice the volume of a traditional washer, but in half the time. It has taken a lot of time and expense to create the new machine, called the Spin-King, but initial reaction by both retailers and consumers has been favourable. A new division will be set up to produce and market the Spin-King.

At a board meeting on 3 February 20X4 the finance director revealed the following projections for the Spin-King division.

	£
Annual factory rent	944,000
Material costs per unit	80
Production labour per unit	72
Advertising costs per annum	350,000
Initial investment in machinery	4,500,000

It is estimated that the Spin-King will be launched in April 20X4. The new machinery has an expected lifespan of five years with no residual value. Goddess plc does not have sufficient cash to buy the new production machinery, but the board is hoping to persuade institutional investors to support a new share issue that will raise funds to finance the capital expenditure. The manager of the new division will be paid a bonus based on the return on investment.

Market research analysis indicates that demand for Spin-Kings will be 60,000 units per annum at a trade price of £200 per unit, and 112,000 units per annum if the trade price is £160 per unit.

The purchasing director is confident that he can obtain a 15% discount on all material costs for the Spin-King if Goddess plc is buying materials for more than 100,000 units per annum.

Requirements

(a) (i) Spreading the cost of the new machinery evenly over the life of the asset, determine the annual output required for the Spin-King division to achieve break-even profit each year at both the suggested price points.

(ii) Comment on the significance of these calculations to Goddess plc. **(7 marks)**

(b) Discuss the merits of Goddess plc appointing non-executive directors. Explain the benefits of Barbara pursuing a less authoritarian role in the running of the company, and how as a consequence the board could be made a more effective group for decision making.

(10 marks)

(17 marks)

13 Read the scenario of the **June 2014 Business Strategy** paper in the Question Bank entitled Best Fresh Bakeries Ltd, referred to at the beginning of the chapter. Draft an answer for requirement (b) concerning transfer pricing and requirement (c) on governance issues.

14 Read the scenario of the **June 2011 Business Strategy** paper in the Question Bank entitled *Henford plc,* referred to at the beginning of the chapter. Draft an answer for requirement (b) on organisational structure.

15 Read the scenario of the **June 2009 Business Strategy** paper in the Question Bank entitled *Evara Electrical Engineers Ltd*. Draft an answer for requirement 2a and 2ci and ii on appropriate organisation structure.

16 Go online at The Times 100 Business Case Studies and read the Coca Cola case study 'Creating an effective organisational structure' at: http://businesscasestudies.co.uk/coca-cola-great-britain/creating-an-effective-organisational-structure

Now, go back to the Learning objectives in the Introduction. If you are satisfied that you have achieved these objectives, please tick them off.

Answers to Interactive questions

Answer to Interactive question 1

(a) Adhocracy

(b) Professional bureaucracy

Answer to Interactive question 2

The bank basically serves two markets: the personal sector and the corporate sector. However, it would perhaps be ill advised to organise the bank **solely** on that basis because:

(a) The banking needs of customers in the personal sector are likely to be quite distinct. This market is naturally segmented geographically. Users of the telephone banking service, for example, will want to speak in their own language. Also, despite the Single European Market, the competitive environment of financial services is likely to be different in each country (eg credit cards are widely used in France, but hardly used at all in Germany).

For the personal sector, a geographic organisation would be appropriate, although with the centralisation of common administrative and account processing functions and technological expertise, so that the bank gains from scale economies and avoids wasteful duplication.

(b) For the corporate sector, different considerations apply. If the bank is providing sophisticated foreign currency accounts, these will be of most benefit to multi-nationals or companies which regularly export from, or import to, their home markets. A geographical organisation structure may not be appropriate, and arguably the bank's organisation should be centralised on a Europe wide basis, with the country offices, of course, at a lower level.

Answer to Interactive question 3

Answer to Interactive question 4

(a) Profits and losses – Transfer price based on existing basis

	Manufacturing Division £m	Retail Division £m
Estimated retail sales	–	30
Estimate sales/purchases (at 60% of retail sales)	18	(18)
Variable costs	(12)	(5)
Fixed costs	(7)	(3)
Loss/profit	(1)	4

(b) Transfer price set on break-even basis

Sales needed to break-even = £19m (£12m+£7m)

19m ÷ 30m = 0.633

Transfer price needs to be Retail price less 36.66%

Answer to Interactive question 5

(a) Division B would **reject** the offer as there is a negative contribution of – £5 (30 – 20 – 15).

(b) If A has **surplus capacity**, it is acceptable to the company, as contribution is £5 (30 – 15 – 10).

If A is at **full capacity**, there is a lost external sales contribution in A of £10.

Therefore, for the company, contribution = – £5, thus reject. (B may also lose contribution.)

Answer to Interactive question 6

(a) **Company**: transfers recommended, as contribution = £5 (40 – 20 – 15).
(b) **Selling division**: transfers not recommended, as contribution = – £6 (40 – 31 – 15).

Answer to Interactive question 7

		A	B	
(a)	Actual recharge	$\dfrac{£18,000}{6,000} \times 4,000$	$\dfrac{£18,000}{6,000} \times 2,000$	
		= £12,000	= £6,000	£18,000
	Expected recharge (per kwh)			
	$£1 + \dfrac{£10,000}{10,000} = £2/kwh$	4,000 × £2	2000 × £2	
		£8,000	£4,000	£12,000
		£	£	
(b)	Proportion of budgeted fixed cost according to budget usage	4,000	6,000	
	Standard variable cost of actual usage	4,000	2,000	
		8,000	8,000	£16,000

In power plant £(18,000 – 16,000) = £2,000 adverse variance remaining uncharged due to inefficiency.

Answer to Interactive question 8

Performance related bonuses. Directors may be paid a cash bonus for improving the performance of the company. Performance related bonuses can be effective in aligning the interests of the directors with those of the shareholders, as improved company performance may help to trigger bonus payments. The danger with performance related bonuses is that if not adequately controlled, directors may be incentivised to take short term decisions to improve performance to the detriment of the company's longer term performance in order to trigger bonus payments. To guard against excessive payouts, some companies impose limits on bonus plans as a fixed percentage of salary or pay.

Transaction bonuses tend to be much more controversial. Some chief executives get bonuses for acquisitions, regardless of subsequent performance, possibly indeed further bonuses for spinning off acquisitions that have not worked out. The danger with such schemes is that it may encourage directors make acquisitions simply for the sake of it and not because it benefits the company. Again, such behaviour may be to the detriment of the company if bonuses are being paid in respect of acquisitions which do not workout.

Share options give directors the right to purchase shares at a specified exercise price over a specified time period in the future. If the price of the shares rises so that it exceeds the exercise price by the time the options can be exercised, the directors will be able to purchase shares at lower than their market value. Such schemes can be effective in encouraging directors to stay with the company over the longer term as share options act as an incentive for directors to work harder at improving the company's performance. It is likely that share options will influence the level of risk that the directors are prepared to take as the pursuit of high risk strategies may reflect negatively on the company's share price, which may diminish the potential return the directors may be able to realise when they exercise their options. Share options may also help to ensure that directors focus on the company's share price as opposed to focusing solely on profit measures.

[The UK Corporate Governance Code states that non-executive directors should not normally be offered share options, as options may impact upon their independence.]

Answer to Interactive Question 9

Governance and risk management as a result of listing

Happy Harvesters Ltd is currently 100% family-owned. By listing on AIM it will become a part publicly-owned company with a wider range of range of shareholders. This may give rise to possible agency issues as the owners and managers of HH will no longer necessarily be the same individuals.

Institutional shareholders are likely to have expectations concerning the corporate governance of HH – where corporate governance is about the relationship between the HH board and external stakeholders. Companies listed on the Alternative Investment Market are not required to comply with the UK Corporate Governance Code. However, pursuing good corporate governance practice will likely increase investor confidence.

HH may benefit by going beyond minimum regulatory requirements and adopting a positive approach to corporate governance, HH is likely to be more successful in satisfying the needs of stakeholders which may help to improve the company's competitive advantage especially if this helps to attract more investors.

As HH has been a growing business to date, it is likely that the company will have already put in place some form of internal controls and management information systems to help the company meet its objectives and create a culture of innovation. When HH lists the company should ensure that the corporate governance provisions surrounding the principles of leadership and effectiveness are adopted. Such provisions will require the separation of the roles of the Chairman and CEO. The Chairman should be solely responsible for running the board and the CEO responsible for running the company.

HH should also look to appoint some independent non-executive directors to ensure that the board has the necessary skills to govern the effectively.

Risk management

Gordon is concerned that by taking HH onto AIM that he will not be able to take the same types of risk. Clearly, in order to continue the company's success the directors will need to give consideration to the risks attached to the strategic decisions they make. External shareholders need to have confidence that the board is aware of the risks HH faces and have systems in place for monitoring them. As a result Gordon will need to ensure that there are systems in place to identify the strategic, operational, financial and hazard risks faced by the business. The scale of the risks can then be assessed, and appropriate priorities determined for risk mitigation. Risks can then be dealt with according to the TARA model – transfer, avoidance, reduction or retention.

For example HH could take steps to reduce the reputational risks that may arise as a result of the high levels of emissions that the company's combine harvesters currently emit.

Given the nature of HH's business the board and management will need to take into account any legal requirements such as health and safety in the manufacturing process.

1   Recommendation – functional (bureaucratic)

Reasons:

- Formal job descriptions
- Clear reporting lines
- Formal procedures

Co-ordinating mechanism – standardisation of work.

2   • Appoint both executive and non-executive directors to the board
- Establish an audit committee to oversee the board
- Create an internal audit function

3   An organisation where the main building block is the operating core (professionally skilled staff) and the controlling mechanism is the standardisation of skills.

Suitable organisations:

- Solicitors' practice
- GP practice
- Accountants' practice

4   The matrix structure involves overlaying a second set of hierarchical connections over the first but at right angles to it. As an example consider a county council.

In this structure service supervisors for roads, education, health, etc in accounting, economics and marketing report to the head of services. Borough executives report to the head of boroughs. Each carries equal weight in terms of authority.

An individual (X above) who is part of Borough 3 may at the same time be part of the team responsible for roads. Thus the individual reports two ways – to the service supervisor and to the borough executive, and is subject to two lines of authority.

5   A centralised structure is a condition where the upper levels of an organisation's hierarchy retain the authority to make most decisions. The authority of lower levels to make decisions is very limited.

A decentralised structure is a condition where authority to make most decisions is passed down to lower levels of the hierarchy.

Upper levels of the hierarchy tend to set organisation objectives and strategies; lower levels are left to decide about detailed operational plans and take day-to-day decisions.

Decisions are taken quicker and are often better than in centralised systems as they are made by people with the relevant skills/knowledge. Delegation is part of decentralisation because authority must be delegated for decentralisation to occur.

6 • **The location and complexity of the work**: If the work is technically sophisticated, requiring a range of technical expertise or is physically widely distributed, then the smaller should be the span of control.

 • **The degree of delegation possible**: The degree to which authority can be delegated to subordinates to carry out their tasks, which in turn is influenced by the ability of the subordinates. The less supervision required, the more the subordinates who can be controlled, eg an audit team.

7 The following factors influence the span of control.

(a) Drivers should understand what is required of them without much guidance, eg sticking to a set timetable with fixed stopping points.

(b) Face to face contact is not often necessary.

(c) Objective measures can be used to evaluate performance, eg

 (i) Bus mileage
 (ii) Takings per trip
 (iii) Customer complaints

The managers' span of control is likely to be fairly large.

8 A single design director or project management director is unlikely to be able to control all the projects of the practice at one point in time.

This overall directorship role would be allied with individuals or teams controlling individual jobs, eg

Design director	Project management director
Project 1	
• Designer A	
• Manager B	
Project 2	
• Designer C	
• Manager D	

9 The problem arises from two aspects of the organisation chart.

(a) It completely ignores the 'information flows' around a business – in this case budgets and management accounts.

(b) The chart can encourage staff to interpret their roles very narrowly; in reality the responsibilities of the production managers would necessarily include budget information.

The solution to the problem would be moving 'up' the organisation chart, and then back down again, ie the finance director (and the managing director if necessary) ensuring that the production director explains the importance of budget information to the business as a whole.

A combination of organisation chart and detailed job description, one of which would be communicating budget details to the chief accountant, would also be of assistance.

10 International businesses can follow a multi-domestic strategy where activities are located in individual national markets and products/services tailored to local needs, or a global strategy where standardised products are developed and produced centrally.

Thus international structures vary depending on the extent of global coordination and the amount of local independence/responsiveness required.

A **global product division** is typical for a company following a global strategy, which will have separate world-wide divisions for soft drinks, alcoholic beverages etc. This gives high global coordination but limited local responsiveness.

A **local subsidiary** is geographically based in the individual national market and operates independently. Local management has a high degree of autonomy, hence local responsiveness is high and global coordination is low. This is appropriate for a business following a **multi-domestic strategy**.

11 Byron Tuffin

Memorandum

To	The Imperial Hotel Group Ltd
Prepared by	ABC Consultants
Date	July 20X4
Subject	Management and organisation structure

1 Organisation structure

Current structure

The current structure is functional. This can be shown as follows.

This structure is perfectly suitable for a single hotel. However, despite the acquisitions being in the same area of business (hotels), this structure is no longer available for the following reasons.

(a) Decision-making will take too long due to

- The sheer volume of information being made available
- Different geographical coverage

(b) Centralised decisions will not make individuals react quickly enough to changes in the market.

(c) It may stifle initiative and creativity of the individual hotel managers who may well have very good marketing ideas.

Recommended structure

For the reasons outlined above and below we would recommend the adoption of a divisional structure.

This would be as follows.

The following are the advantages of such a structure.

(a) It is now much easier to assess the performance of each hotel and its manager.

(b) Group services can set standards for the whole group

  –   In maintenance
  –   In service

(c) The group may benefit from purchasing economies, eg

  –   In cleaning services
  –   Laundry arrangements

(d) Individual managers feel more motivated because they are directly responsible for the performance of their hotel.

(e) They can adapt more quickly to any changes in their respective markets.

(f) Group services can usefully redirect and re-allocate funds to the hotel needing it most.

This structure will also facilitate any potential growth. With group support services in place, extra hotels could be added as new divisions.

2   **Management style and structure**

Current style of structure

Byron Tuffin's current management seems to vary between authoritarian and decentralised.

At times he interferes with decisions taken by individual managers (see the comments of R Fowler).

Conversely, he distances himself from detail and is only interested in top-level considerations and decisions.

This ambiguity leads to inconsistent attitudes. Staff need to know exactly to whom to report and the precise extent of their own authority.

Recommended style and management structure.

We recommend that Byron introduce a management structure as outlined in the diagram above, ie

•   A board of directors comprising the group service directors and directors of the other three hotels plus at least one non-executive director.

•   The adoption of a decentralised management style.

The advantages of these two simple changes are numerous and include the following.

(a) Clear and unambiguous reporting line – it is very important that the exact extent of the decentralisation is established. The limits should be defined in terms of spending limits, hire/fire of staff, etc.

(b) It allows individual hotel managers to exercise initiative in running the hotels.

(c) This delegation of authority will improve/maintain motivation of the hotel managers. They are aware that their performance is to be assessed on the basis of the performance of the individual hotel.

(d) It allows Byron to stay away from the 'detail' and thus to focus on group direction/strategy.

(e) The board is now responsible for group direction; this is preferable to having Byron dictate the direction and action of individual hotels. The Serpentine, for example, taps a different market from the other hotels in the group and so requires a knowledge of a different market. It is thus important that the board take decisions at this level. The non-executive directors will provide a check on the activities of the directors.

12 Goddess plc

(a) Break-even

	Price 1 £	Price 2 £
Sales price	200	160
Variable costs		
Labour	72	72
Materials	80	68
Contribution	48	20
Fixed costs		
Machinery depreciation	900,000	900,000
Advertising	350,000	350,000
Factory rent	944,000	944,000
Total	2,194,000	2,194,000
Break-even	2,194,000 ÷ 48	2,194,000 ÷ 20
	45,708 units	109,700 units

Comments on significance of calculations

Benefit of bulk discount on higher sales volume outweighed by greater contribution at higher price.

At price of £200 the safety margin is far higher than at £160.

If the company adopts a low price strategy, then extra marketing may be required to obtain the significantly higher sales volumes required. This would further increase the advertising spending.

If lower volumes were produced, excess factory capacity could be used to produce other goods.

(b) Merits of appointing non-executives

Improves the perception of independence between the board and the shareholders.

Removes the ability of directors to set their own pay and create an efficient executive remuneration scheme.

Acts as a buffer between the auditors and the board.

Brings experience to the board from other posts held by these non-executives.

Reduces the ability of a chief executive to dominate the board of directors.

Assists appointment of new directors on a merit basis.

Can also act as a voice piece for the interests of stakeholders.

Merits of less authoritarian role and improving board effectiveness

Barbara is reluctant to delegate any element of decision making and decisions are imposed.

Other directors are demotivated by threat of the sack. They may be choosing not to give their opinions as a result and decisions may be made by Barbara without all the knowledge held by individual directors.

Barbara is likely to lack the time and knowledge to make all decisions effectively.

By taking a less authoritarian role, Barbara could create a more participative environment and encourage discussion of issues. This is likely to lead to better decisions.

Such an environment would encourage open decision making, by removing fear of dismissal for disagreeing with Barbara's views.

Barbara should split the board into teams to work on individual tasks and projects.

She should encourage consensus decision making, rather than the use of votes of individual members of the board.

Institutional investors would welcome more openness and are likely to be reassured by the move.

Increased delegation/participation is likely to free up Barbara's time to concentrate on the strategic direction of the business and the relationships with key stakeholders.

13 Refer to the answer to parts b and c of Best Fresh Bakeries Ltd in the Question Bank.

14 Refer to the answer to part b of Henford plc in the Question Bank.

15 Refer to the answer to parts a and c of Evara Electrical Engineers Ltd in the Question Bank.

16 There is no answer to this self-test, as it is designed just to help you increase your business awareness.

CHAPTER 10

Risk management

Introduction

Examination context

Topic List

    1   Risk and uncertainty

    2   Introduction to risk management

    3   Risk appetite

    4   Risk identification

    5   Risk analysis

    6   Evaluating and addressing risk

    7   Risk monitoring, reviewing and reporting

    8   Risk and uncertainty in decision-making: sensitivity and break-even analysis

    9   Probability, expected values and decision trees

    10 Risk management and business continuity planning

Summary and Self-test

Answers to Interactive questions

Answers to Self-test

Learning objectives

- Explain what is meant by risk in a business context

- Explain the elements of a risk management strategy

- Identify the risks attached to a given situation or proposed course of action

- Identify strategies for managing risk and recommend appropriate treatments of risks to reduce the overall risk of a business

- Explain and demonstrate how a business can use management accounting techniques to evaluate its proposed strategies, including the risk associated with forecasts

Specific syllabus references for this chapter are: 1f, 2d, 2g, 2j, 3d.

Syllabus links

Some of the risks associated specifically with IT/IS will be covered in Chapter 14.

The concept of risk and risk management was introduced in the Business & Finance paper.

There is a distinction between management of business risks and management of financial risks. While you need to be generally aware of financial risk management for Business Strategy, this topic is dealt with primarily in the Financial Management paper, which also deals in more detail with methods of handling risk and uncertainty in decision making.

Risk management is an important topic and is taken forward at Advanced level.

Examination context

The issues involved in analysing risk, for example in the context of the external environment, have already been discussed in previous chapters. This chapter discusses attitudes to those risks and how an organisation can manage such risks.

In Q2 September 2010 (*e-Parts Ltd*) the scenario contains information about the company's business, competitors and brand. As an online retailer, it is very reliant on its website functioning effectively. The first two requirements are:

'(a) Explain the relevance of risk management to the business as a whole and identify the main factors that would be covered in EP's business continuity plan. **(6 marks)**

(b) Identify the key risks arising for EP as a result of its reliance on IT (other than those relating to business continuity) and recommend how they can be managed. **(8 marks)**'

As well as applying the principles of risk management to the business's particular situation, these requirements also cover how to keep the business going if there is a problem with the website, and what particular problems the business faces given its reliance on IT. There is a danger of being repetitive when preparing an answer to these two requirements; it is important to distinguish clearly between them.

It is particularly important that you appreciate how to use financial data to assess the types of risk facing an organisation featured in an exam question. Questions may require you to analyse the level of risk by conducting sensitivity analysis to determine an entity's breakeven point.

A question in the June 2013 exam (Up 'n' Over) focused on a manufacturer of low cost garage doors. Candidates were required on the basis of the information in the Exhibit, to determine:

(i) The expected variable cost per garage door for 2013; and

(ii) The break-even level of sales by volume for UnO in each of the years ended 31 December 2011 and 31 December 2012.

and to briefly comment on the implications for operating risk of these calculations.

The examiner commented that a number of candidates mixed up the figures used in their calculations, using the revenue and cost figures provided in respect of the wrong years. The discussion of operating risk was not well dealt with.

Candidates are encouraged to draw upon knowledge obtained from earlier studies when considering the financial implications associated in making business decisions. The examiner has highlighted that there have been a number of occasions when candidates have failed to correctly identify which calculations are required when answering the numerical element in questions. Common mistakes involve the mixing up of terms such as profit and contribution, and including figures which are not relevant to decision making.

1 Risk and uncertainty

Section overview

- Risk arises when there may be a variety of possible outcomes.

- Risk management is concerned with the positive and negative aspects of risk. A business may look to minimise its downside risk while leaving open the potential to share in any upside.

- The term 'risk' is often muddled with 'uncertainty' which is strictly-speaking different because the latter cannot be quantified.

- Modern thinking suggests that all future outcomes are subject to uncertainty which ranges from a 'clear enough future' to one of 'true ambiguity'.

- Therefore risk management requires management to treat risks that it can forecast but also to take courses of action to cope with risks it cannot forecast.

1.1 What is risk?

It is usual to consider risk as negative, and in the field of safety this is certainly true since there is no gain if things go right- just a loss if they go wrong. As a result, safety risk management concentrates on the prevention or minimisation of harm. In most other spheres, however, risk implies variability which may work in the favour of the business (**an opportunity**) or against it (**a risk**).

Risk is more than probability. It includes consequences. The chances of flipping a coin and getting heads is 50%. It only becomes a risk if we gamble on the outcome. The larger the amount at stake, the bigger the risk, but the probability stays the same.

Risk is also different from uncertainty, which arises due to a lack of information about the future.

Definitions

Risk: The possible variation in outcome from what is expected to happen.

Uncertainty: The inability to predict the outcome from an activity due to a lack of information.

Downside risk (pure risk): The possibility that the outcome will be worse than expected ie something will go wrong (the worst case scenario).

Upside risk (speculative risk or opportunity): The possibility that something could go better than expected (best case scenario).

Risk management is increasingly recognised as being concerned with both the positive and negative aspects of risk and looks to control risk from both perspectives.

For example, a person buying a house with a loan may decide to fix the interest rate for a period. They are eliminating two kinds of risk: the downside risk that their loan would become more expensive if the interest rate rose but also the upside risk that it could have become cheaper if the interest rate had fallen.

Businesses may look for ways to manage their downside risk, whilst at the same time leaving open the potential to share in any upside, although this flexibility may come at a price premium. In the context of our house purchase example, a capped rate loan would offer such an opportunity.

1.2 Risk and uncertainty

There is a technical distinction between risk and uncertainty:

- Risk is a quantification of the potential variability in a value based on past data (eg when a coin is tossed the outcome will either be heads or tails).

- Uncertainty on the other hand, is non-quantifiable (whether a key customer will be retained for the next two years).

Strictly speaking, risk should therefore be defined as a measure of the variability in the value of a factor that is capable of statistical or mathematical evaluation.

For the purposes of risk management, risk can be defined as the combination of the likelihood of an event and its consequences:

Definition

Risk = Likelihood × Impact

Given that we are mainly interested in the financial impact of risk this can be stated as:

Risk = Likelihood × Financial consequences

In practice, the distinction between risk and uncertainty is blurred. Huge losses by insurance underwriting syndicates show that assessments of risk used in insurance have been compromised by unanticipated events such as flooding and hurricanes from climate change and claims for industrial injury resulting from asbestos and stress.

Despite using terms like risk, many business strategies are actually taking place in situations of uncertainty. A management team that only undertakes strategies in which the likelihood of success or failure can be precisely quantified would launch no new products, enter no new markets, and research no new technologies.

Courtney *et al* (*Strategy Under Uncertainty*) describe four classes of uncertainty.

1. **Clear enough futures**: The future can be assessed with reasonable accuracy because it follows on from the past without major change. Eg the forecasts of bread sales made by management of a bakery.

2. **Alternative futures**: Outcomes depend on an event, eg the value of rights to make national football team merchandise depends on whether they qualify for the World Cup or not.

3. **Range of futures**: Outcome varies according to a number of variables that interact, eg hotel operator's forecasts of sales of holiday accommodation depend on level of temperature, prices of flights, levels of disposable income etc.

4. **True ambiguity**: Very high uncertainty due to the number and unpredictability of the variables influencing the outcome, eg investment in emerging economies where the outcome will be determined by political events, global economic developments, natural and man-made disasters, cultural and religious change etc.

The first two of these could be quantified with tolerable accuracy perhaps. The second two are much more uncertain.

Therefore risk management requires management to treat risks that it can forecast but also to take courses of action to cope with risks it cannot forecast.

1.3 Why manage risk?

Corporate governance was covered in Chapter 9. Corporate governance standards encourage organisations and public sector bodies to adopt good practices in risk assessment and risk management. The board's role is to provide entrepreneurial leadership of the organisation within a framework of prudent and effective controls which enables risk to be assessed and managed.

A risk based management approach is required for all UK listed companies under the **UK Corporate Governance Code**, which sets out the following principles on the management of risk:

- The board is responsible for determining the nature and extent of the significant risks it is willing to take in achieving its strategic objectives and should maintain **sound risk management and internal control systems**.

- The board should, at least annually, conduct a **review of the effectiveness of the company's risk management and internal control systems** and should report to shareholders that they have done so. The review should cover all material controls, including **financial, operational and compliance controls**.

The Code recommends following the **Turnbull Guidance** on **internal controls,** which emphasises that the Board of Directors must:

- Ensure the company has an effective system of internal control, covering financial, operational and compliance controls as well as risk management systems.

- Review the effectiveness of the internal control system in addressing the risks that the Board has identified face the company.

- Report on the internal control system every year (covered later in the chapter).

Shareholders of a company need to feel confident that the Board of Directors are aware of the risks facing the company and has a system in place to monitor and control them. Thus the Board should seek not only to adopt risk controls but also to make the deployment of such controls transparent and visible.

The Risk Management Standard issued by the Institute of Risk Management sets out the **responsibilities of the directors** in this respect:

'The Board has responsibility for determining the strategic direction of the organisation and for creating the environment and the structures for risk management to operate effectively.

The Board should, as a minimum, consider, in evaluating its system of internal control:

- The nature and extent of downside risks acceptable for the company to bear within its particular business

- The likelihood of such risks becoming a reality

- How unacceptable risks should be managed

- The company's ability to minimise the probability and impact on the business

- The costs and benefits of the risk and control activity undertaken

- The effectiveness of the risk management process

- The risk implications of board decisions

Risk management should be embedded within the organisation through the strategy and budget processes.'

Whether a business thrives or fades is determined partly by how it manages risks and exploits opportunities. Thus risk management is not just a regulatory requirement or a defensive tactic to avoid losses but is integral to seeking and exploiting **competitive advantage.**

2 Introduction to risk management

Section overview

- Effective risk management should involve the implementation of a risk management policy involving all levels of management and staff in the identification, reporting and treatment of risk.

2.1 What is risk management?

Definition

Risk management: The process of identifying and assessing (analysing and evaluating) risks and the development, implementation and monitoring of a strategy to respond to those risks.

A risk management strategy involves the selection, implementation, monitoring and review of suitable risk treatments for each risk identified.

Effective risk management enables a business to:

- Reduce business threats to acceptable levels
- Make informed decisions about potential opportunities

This allows stakeholders (investors, lenders, customers, suppliers, employees etc) to have confidence in the business and its future prospects.

2.2 Risk management policy

In business, risk is unavoidable and the strategy must be to reduce risks to acceptable levels. The effect of risk management should be to reduce the probability and/or consequences of any failure whilst retaining, so far as possible, the benefits of successes.

Central to the risk management strategy, therefore, will be the organisation's risk management policy describing its approach to and appetite for risk, along with any legal requirements the business faces such as health and safety legislation.

In order to implement correctly any risk management strategy there will need to be an effective system for risk management, risk reporting and communication involving all levels in the business:

- **The board** – who are in a position to take an overall business view and has the authority to demand policies be implemented and adhered to.

- **Managers of the business units** – who are in a position to assess risks from a business unit perspective but also must ensure that risk management policies are implemented.

- **Individuals** – who may need to be aware of or be responsible for managing certain risks.

Risk management strategy needs to be a top-down process to ensure it is integrated across the entire business. In so far as it is possible, the risk treatments should be embedded within the businesses' culture and systems so that it becomes an integral part of the operations and financing of the business. Senior management must translate the risk management strategy into tactical and operational objectives, with managers and employees given the responsibility and authority to deal with such matters.

Examples of risk management policies for a large corporation would include:

- **Corporate codes of conduct**: Regulates how managers and staff relate to each other and to outsiders and will seek to control risks from discrimination, bullying, bribery, anti-social behaviour.

- **Environmental policies**: Issues such as energy use, emissions, recycling, waste disposal etc.

- **Health and Safety policies**: Requiring H&S officers at all levels, setting up committees, requirement for routine testing and risk assessments, fire procedures.

- **Financial controls**: Budgetary control to safeguard earnings and spending, capital expenditure authorisation procedures, financial accounting systems, credit control procedures, cash management procedures, insurance of assets.

- **Information systems controls**: Creation of information officers at all levels, regulations on use by staff, password and access controls, requirements for back-ups and stand-by systems, institution of firewalls and other security programmes.

- **Personnel controls**: Policies on identity and background checks on new recruits, discipline and grievance procedures, door entry controls and conventions on wearing of ID, attendance monitoring. Appraisals of staff and management can provide early warnings of stress or potential inability to perform vital tasks.

- **Internal audit processes**: In addition to its familiar role in assuring financial systems in relation to the requirement for a statutory audit, many internal audit functions have an expanded business assurance remit which will report on the adequacy of the controls above.

Many of these policies fulfil other functions too. Here we are concerned with how they are used to mitigate the danger of financial loss to the organisation.

Such financial loss can arise from:

- Litigation from persons injured by the activities of the organisation and its staff

- Fines from regulatory bodies

- Loss of assets due to theft or damage

- Costs of making up for errors, eg replacing lost data, apologising to injured parties, restoring lost corporate reputation

- Revenues lost due to breakdowns, eg factory burned down, operations temporarily grounded by authorities

- Loss of reputation: customers, suppliers, investors etc lose faith in management

Interactive question 1: Risk management policy of your training provider

[Difficulty level: Easy]

You are probably taking classroom tuition as part of your preparation to pass this exam. Therefore having you on its premises represents one part of the risks being managed by the college or training firm offering you the classes.

Suggest the elements of a risk management policy that your college should adopt to treat the risks of having you in its classrooms.

See **Answer** at the end of this chapter.

2.3 Risk management models

The management of risk is an ongoing business process involving continuous identification, assessment, treatment, monitoring and review.

Risk management models are designed to show that risk management is continuous and that it is a logical process. They aim to demonstrate the **interaction and comparison** of risks, as well as the **assessment of individual risks**. Risks change and compliance must be continuous. The management of risk is an ongoing business process involving continuous identification, assessment, treatment, monitoring and review. Though it is most convenient to discuss it as a linear process, it is in reality a circular one with the results of any monitoring and review feeding back into the process to refine the identification, assessment and treatment processes:

This framework will be used for the rest of this chapter.

3 Risk appetite

Section overview

- Risk appetite considers the extent to which an organisation is prepared to take on risk to achieve its objectives.

- Miles and Snow provide a useful characterisation of firms' attitudes to risk and how it influences their strategies (Defenders, Prospectors, Analysers and Reactors).

- Attitudes to risk will also be influenced by shareholder expectations, the regulatory framework and national and cultural factors.

3.1 What is risk appetite?

An organisation's risk management approach will depend on the appetite it has for bearing risks, which should link in with its business objectives and strategy.

Definition

Risk appetite is the extent to which a company is prepared to take on risks in order to achieve its objectives.

In broad terms we can distinguish **risk averse** attitudes, **risk neutral** attitudes and **risk seeking** attitudes.

Management responses to risk are not automatic but will be determined by their own attitudes to risk, which in turn may be influenced by shareholder attitudes and cultural factors.

3.2 The influence of Managerial culture – Miles and Snow

Miles and Snow undertook an in-depth cross-industry analysis of a sample of large corporations from which they developed a theory that there are four strategic types of business, defined by the orientations of their management to strategic challenges.

(a) *Defenders*. Firms with this culture like low risks, secure markets, and tried and trusted solutions. These companies have cultures whose stories and rituals reflect historical continuity and consensus. Decision taking is relatively formalised. (There is a stress on 'doing things right', that is, efficiency.)

(b) *Prospectors* are organisations where the dominant beliefs are more to do with results (doing the right things, that is, effectiveness), and therefore prospectors take risks.

(c) *Analysers* try to balance risk and profits. They use a core of stable products and markets as a source of earnings to move into innovative prospector areas. Analysers follow change, but do not initiate it.

(d) *Reactors*, unlike the three above, do not have viable strategies. Arguably, they do not have a strategy at all, unless it is simply to carry on living from hand to mouth, muddling through. Unlike the other three, which may exhibit superior performance the Reactor, is sub-optimal in its performance.

Their findings suggest that to be superior, there must be a clear and direct match between the organisation's mission/values, the organisation's strategies, and the organisation's characteristics and behaviour.

3.2.1 Defenders – low risk tolerance

Defenders are specialist providers of a specific product or service and concentrate on a single core technology which is often vertically integrated. They tend to have a stable structure and strong finances. They also have highly efficient processes giving them a competitive advantage and they seek to maintain this advantage through intensively incremental improvements.

They have a narrow area of operations with top managers who exhibit significant expertise in these areas. They do not tend to look for business opportunities outside their sphere of expertise, seeking to protect their market position through efficient production, strong internal controls, continuity and reliability.

Defenders tend to perform best in stable markets with high barriers to entry where they can look to protect their market position through high cost-efficiency and the utilisation of bespoke standardised processes.

The basic strategy adopted by defenders is to aggressively maintain their market share in their chosen market segment. They ignore developments outside of their sphere of expertise, preferring to seek to increase the depth of their expertise within their current markets. They look to grow cautiously and incrementally. The risk tolerance of such businesses is consequently quite low.

3.2.2 Prospectors – risk seeking

Prospectors are at the opposite end of the spectrum from defenders. They are proactive and pursue an aggressive strategy towards addressing new market opportunities. They adopt an entrepreneurial attitude and are almost continually searching for new products/markets and seeking potential responses to emerging trends. They demonstrate a willingness to take on the risks associated with new developments and maintain a flexibility to respond to change. Such organisations are innovators and their innovations cause change and uncertainty to which their competitors must respond. As such, prospectors are risk seekers, looking to benefit from taking on the entrepreneurial risk.

As a result of their way of operating, prospectors tend to be less efficient than defenders due to their continually changing structure and technology. They may utilise many technologies in their broad range of operations and regularly prototype potential new products.

As a result of the uncertainties regarding any innovations they may make and how the market may react, their planning tends to be quite broad and less intensive. The resultant business/management structure tends to be a product based one where management is results-orientated and where managers are appraised by reference to managers in similar organisations.

3.2.3 Analysers – balanced attitude to risk and return

Analysers operate somewhere between prospectors and defenders, balancing the risk-avoidance attitude of the defenders and the risk-seeking attitude of prospectors. They are less innovative than prospectors, waiting to see the markets reaction to new developments then carefully analysing the key success factors of any new opportunity before committing themselves. Once a product is developed, analysers will then establish formalised structures and processes to achieve a high level of efficiency in order to build and maintain market share, similar to defenders, and it is these products which tend to be the major revenue generators.

Analysers therefore effectively operate in two different product/market areas, one relatively stable, the other innovative and constantly changing. In the stable areas analysers operate like defenders, using formalised structures and processes to achieve a high level of efficiency. In the changing area they operate like prospectors, looking to innovate, keeping a close eye on their competitors and rapidly adapting to any promising changes.

Analysers therefore tend to exhibit moderate levels of efficiency overall, being highly efficient in the stable areas but less so in the more volatile areas. Their key business functions are marketing, applied research, and production.

3.2.4 Reactors – inconsistent attitude to risk

Reactors are businesses that respond inconsistently or are unable to respond effectively to changes and developments in their business environment, seldom making changes of any sort until forced to do so.

Reactors do not have any consistent or clearly defined strategy and consequently lack consistency within their business structure.

Reactors tend to make one of the following strategic mistakes:

- Management fails to develop a viable organisational strategy

- Management develops an appropriate strategy, but technology, structure, and process are not appropriately linked to that strategy

- Management adheres to a particular strategy/structure relationship that is not relevant to the business environment

3.3 Other influences on risk appetite

Miles and Snow indicate the role of managerial culture in determining a firm's attitude towards the risks of strategic ventures.

Management may be responding to other factors shaping the risk appetite of the organisation. These include:

- **Expectations of shareholders**: If a firm has a long history of stable and unremarkable performance it will attract investors requiring 'blue chip' performance rather than sudden lurches into the unknown.

- **Organisational attitudes:** Management may be influenced by significant losses in the past, changes in regulation and best practice, or even changing views of the benefits risk management can bring.

- **National origin of the organisation**: Some national cultures exhibit uncertainty avoidance. Surveys suggest that attitudes to risk vary nationally according to how much people are shielded from the consequences of adverse events. National culture is a matter to consider when trying to establish an organisation-wide risk culture: a highly procedural approach, say, that is quite acceptable in the country where the head office is based, may be difficult to implement in other countries.

- **Regulatory framework**: Investment firms and banks are required to maintain prudent reserves to display capital adequacy to their regulators. They cannot afford to get involved in too many gambles.

- **Nature of ownership**: The management of state-owned enterprises stand to gain little from successful but risky ventures but they will lose much from unsuccessful ones. Similarly a family firm may be prevented from risk taking by the influence or dependence of family members on the 'family firm' and the potential shame of failure.

- **Personal views**: Surveys suggest that managers acknowledge the emotional satisfaction from successful risk-taking, although this is unlikely to be the most important influence on appetite. This has been attributed in part to the fact that, unlike shareholders, they will not suffer a loss of their investment if the decision doesn't pay off.

4 Risk identification

Section overview

- Risks are categorised for ease of identification according to their origins, into strategic, operational, hazard and financial risks. These can be identified with reference to the *International Risk Standard*.

- Risks may be identified by reference to **risk sources**, ie risk factors which can lead to variability of outcomes, or **risk events**, ie events which are known in the industry and for which the contributory factors can be identified and treated.

- A risk description should be prepared for each risk to which the firm is subject.

Risk identification sets out to identify an organisation's exposure to risk.

This requires knowledge of the organisation, the market in which it operates and the legal, social, political and cultural environment in which it exists.

4.1 Types of risk

Ultimately, all business risks will be reflected in financial risk. In 2014, ebay's website was compromised by hackers who accessed databases containing customer information. The attack led to a fall in the company's share price.

For the purpose of managing risk it helps to break risks down further into their origins.

Business risk is the variability of returns due to how a business trades or operates, its exposure to markets, competitors, exchange rates etc. This business risk itself can be sub-analysed into:

- **Strategic risk**: Risks associated with the long-term strategic objectives of the business, potential variability of business returns arising as a result of the company strategy and its strategic position with respect to competitors, customers, reputation, legal or regulatory change, political change. Strategic risk also encompasses knowledge management, ie the effective management and control of the knowledge resources including key personnel, intellectual property and production technology.

  Note: The risks associated with information systems and knowledge management are dealt with in more detail in Chapter 14.

- **Operational risk**: Variability arising from the effectiveness of how the business is managed and controlled on a day to day basis, the accuracy and effectiveness of its information/accounting systems, its reporting systems and its management and control structures. Operational risk also encompasses compliance with issues such as health and safety, consumer protection, data protection etc.

- **Hazard risk**: The exposure a business may have to natural events and their impacts, the actions of employees, the consequences of accidents etc, be it on the business, its trading partners or customers.

- **Financial risk** is the risk arising as a result of how the business is financed – its level of gearing or leverage, its exposure to credit, interest rates and exchange rates, liquidity risks. Financial risk tends to amplify the inherent business risk at low levels of gearing, and at higher levels may directly contribute to the risk of business failure. Interest and exchange rates, taxes, and the state of the economy will bear more heavily on firms with operations limited to one country than they will upon a transnational operator.

- **Compliance risk** is the risk arising from non compliance with laws or regulations. This includes breach of laws/regulations by the company, or breaches by a stakeholder (eg customer or supplier) which may have consequences for the company. It may relate to financial laws/regulations (eg contracts, tax, financial reporting, pensions and social security, company law etc) or to non-financial laws/regulations (eg health and safety, employment law etc).

- **Internal risks** are risks arising from factors internal to the company, factors over which the company can exercise complete control whether it does so or not.

- **External risks** are risks arising from factors outside of the control of the business, factors that the company may be subject to but that it has no influence over, eg natural disasters.

The tools discussed in earlier chapters for analysing the internal position of a business and its external environment (SWOT, PESTEL, Porter's 5 forces) may be useful in identifying risk.

Overall risk

The *International Risk Standard* pulls these sources together into diagram.

Source: *Institute of Risk Management – A Risk Management Standard*

4.2   Risk identification techniques

Management must identify the types of risk faced by its business. Risk identification must be a continuous process so that management can quickly identify new risks and changes that affect existing risks.

There are two broad approaches:

- **Risk sources:** The cause of potential problems, things (people/activities/events) that may give rise to risk that may trigger an event. These risk sources may be either internal or external to the business as discussed above. Management deals with the source.

- **Risk events (problems):** Specific identified threats or events themselves. Management can attempt to deal with the problem.

Worked example: Print works

A printing company is conducting a risk assessment of its operations. A fire officer is looking at the machine room:

- Risk source approach: The fire officer sees machine minders smoking and also sees piles of loose discarded paper. Both are risk sources.

- Risk event approach: The fire officer knows that fires in machine rooms are a major cause of loss.

Seeing risks from both ends is complementary. It is obvious that an employee carelessly discarding a cigarette butt into a pile of paper may cause a fire. Using both approaches together will yield insights that neither alone would:

- **Risk source**: There are more risks arising from smoking than just fire. For example to the health of the employee and to passive smokers, using machines one-handed, triggering respiratory attacks in colleagues. Firms could face litigation from the effects of any of these. In fact, in the UK and many other European countries it is now illegal to smoke in any work place or public place. Similarly, loose paper or can cause people to slip over, conceal health hazards, offer potential for good work to be thrown out along with scrap in a hasty tidy-up.

- **Risk event**: Fires are caused by more than physical sources and their effects depend on how they are handled. The officer might consider whether evacuation procedures are in place, whether extinguishers are regularly tested, whether smoke vents have been fitted to the roof. This assessment would enable management of risks arising from more than smoking such as electrical faults causing fires or poisonous fumes from chemical spillages.

4.3 Risk description

A risk description table can be used to facilitate the identification and assessment of risks and should include:

- Description of the risk
- Scope of the risk – description of the events and impacts of the risk
- Nature of the risk – ie financial, strategic, operational, hazard
- Parties affected – both internal and external parties and how they will be influenced
- Quantification of the risk – the probability and scale of any losses or gains, possibly including Value at Risk assessments
- Risk tolerance/appetite – level of risk considered acceptable for this matter
- Risk treatment and control – the means by which the risk is managed at present and an assessment of the current risk controls in force
- Potential action for improvement – recommendations about further risk reduction options
- Strategy and policy developments – identification of function responsible for developing strategy and policy

Note: Only the first four of these can be completed at this risk identification stage, the remainder are completed as the process continues.

5 Risk analysis

Section overview

- Once risks have been identified, the organisation needs to understand and assess the scale of the risk. This can be done by risk assessment and profiling.

- The organisation's likely exposure to loss can be assessed by quantitative or non-quantitative methods for risk assessment and prioritisation.

- The result of this should be a risk profile of the firm which management can use to set priorities for risk mitigation.

5.1 Risk assessment

Definition

Risk assessment is establishing the financial consequences of each risk event (severity) and its likelihood of occurrence (frequency).

In many cases the financial consequences are easy to measure, eg the value of lost inventories or the cost of rebuilding premises, although it may not be until after an event that the full cost of a loss can be recognised.

Some consequences may be more awkward, particularly where loss of life is concerned.

The assessment of the probability of occurrence is often more problematic, particularly for the less likely events such as natural disasters.

Worked example: Railtrack

The UK railway infrastructure provider Railtrack was accused of foregoing maintenance leading to loss of life in several appalling crashes and derailments in recent years. This created expensive rush repairs with consequent compensation payments to train operators suffering loss of rail passengers, poor service, low reliability, loss of corporate reputation and loss of subsidies. Ultimately, this resulted in insolvency and its compulsory purchase by the state at a price of the state's choosing together with the destruction of the individual reputations of the directors several of whom lost lucrative non-executive roles on other boards in the years that followed.

Risk estimation can be quantitative, semi-quantitative or qualitative in terms of the

probability of occurrence and the possible consequence.

Quantitative risk assessment involves the determination of measured figures for probabilities and consequences producing a specifically quantified measure of likelihood and of impact.

Some types of risk lend themselves to this process. Insurance companies have detailed statistical information on the occurrence of many risk events. They also have detailed estimates of the cost of repairing the insured loss, of say a car or house.

Others are very difficult to assess. For example, the impact of an event on the reputation of a business is much harder to quantify, and from this perspective risk assessment is more subjective.

Worked example: Buying new aircraft

In 2007 many transnational airlines needed to replace or expand their fleets. The investments were worth billions of pounds and the lifetime of the aircraft they were buying was 25 years. At the time of the purchase the industry was looking at a number of developments that would affect their decisions, but none was certain in its likelihood of introduction nor its impact. Each nation could choose different policies and rates of charges, and some varied from airport to airport within a country according to the power of local stakeholders. Potential developments were:

- National carbon taxes on airlines according to the CO_2 emissions from the planes

- The possibility that they could buy or sell licences to pollute

- Locally decided restrictions on noise where each would get a certain number of noise units per airport

- The possibility that surplus noise units could be bought and sold

The rival planes on offer differed in their noise, fuel use and emissions. Choosing the wrong plane imposed financial risk from less flights, increased costs, lost opportunities to sell permits, defection of ecologically concerned passengers and exclusion from some countries.

One major airline based its decision on an NPV calculation into which the cost increases and savings etc of each potential risk had been entered based on a subjective assessment of the likelihood of its occurrence in each country, its timing, and its potential financial impact. This was constructed as a model on an Excel spreadsheet with cost lines for each of the 120 destinations the airline intended to serve reflecting the assumptions it had made about the likelihood and impact of the carbon and noise taxes at that destination.

It conducted the same exercise for its 150 existing planes to decide which to phase out first.

5.2 Risk profiling

The result of the risk analysis process is an overall risk profile detailing each of the risks along with an estimate of the risk to the company. This risk profile ranks each identified risk so as to give a view of the relative importance, forming the primary tool for prioritising and addressing risks.

One way of doing this is to use a severity/frequency matrix (also known as a likelihood/consequences matrix).

		Severity	
		Low	High
Frequency	*Low*	Loss of small suppliers	Loss of senior or specialist staff Loss of sales to competitor Loss of sales due to macroeconomic factors
	High	Loss of lower-level staff	Loss of key customers Failure of computer systems

This profile can then be used to set priorities for risk mitigation. Clearly risks categorised as high frequency and high severity should be prioritised and dealt with first.

The risk profile will

- Describe the risk and the business area affected

- Describe the primary control procedures in place

- Indicate areas where the level of risk control investment might be increased, decreased or reapportioned

The similarity of this to the techniques used in auditing a company's accounts will be obvious to you. This is because audit risk is an example of the sorts of more general risks discussed in this chapter.

Interactive question 2: Identification of risks facing an airline
[Difficulty level: Exam standard]

As a consultant specialising in risk management, you have been appointed by the Director of Corporate Development (DCD) to undertake a comprehensive review of the risks facing SkyWays Airlines (SWA) as a precursor to the latest strategic planning process.

You are told that the extended supply chain of SWA makes it reliant on suppliers of fuel, aircraft parts, air traffic control etc. SWA has increased its borrowings this year and its liquidity ratio has fallen below one and it has negligible retained earnings. It has also experienced increased dissatisfaction from employees as a result of voluntary redundancies arising from moving to a new more efficient terminal and, apparently, the loss of control over them by the decline in influence of the Trades Unions.

The Engineering Director has advised that the International Civil Aviation Organisation has shown a preference for the International Risk Standard developed by the Institute of Risk Management.

Requirements

From the information provided and your knowledge of the industry, prepare a report identifying the range of externally driven risks to which SWA is subject and any internally driven risks. Suggest appropriate improvements to controls for the risks you identify.

See **Answer** at the end of this chapter.

6 Evaluating and addressing risk

Section overview

- Risks are evaluated according to significance. The most significant and most probable risks will be prioritised for treatment.

- The possible strategies for dealing with a risk are avoidance, reduction, transfer or retention.

- The chosen response is likely to depend on the significance of the risk and the specific risk appetites of management.

6.1 Risk evaluation

Definition

Risk evaluation: The process by which a business determines the significance of any risk and whether those risks need to be addressed.

Risk evaluation should be carried out both for:

- New business proposals and changes to operations
- Existing business operations

Once risk analysis has been completed for these operations and the businesses risk tolerance established and accounted for, management should compare the identified risks to the risk criteria established by the business. This will allow them to make decisions about the significance of the risks to the organisation and whether each specific risk should be accepted or treated.

This risk criteria is liable to include a consideration of such factors as costs and benefits, legal requirements, socioeconomic and environmental factors, concerns of stakeholders, etc.

Interactive question 3: Risk assessment of outsourcing cleaning
[Difficulty level: Intermediate]

The management of a state-funded hospital is considering outsourcing the cleaning of its premises. This will mean private firms taking over as employers of existing cleaning staff and assuming responsibility for the cleaning of the areas around beds, corridors and communal spaces.

Increases in incidents of infections during hospital stays by patients, some resulting in death, has been widely attributed by the media to poor hospital hygiene. Several legal cases for compensation have been decided against hospitals on the grounds of negligence by management.

What factors should management consider in evaluating the proposal to outsource its cleaning?

See **Answer** at the end of this chapter.

6.2 Addressing risk

Addressing risk involves the selection of procedures to monitor, control and mitigate the effects of risk. The possible approaches to the treatment of risk are:

- Avoidance
- Reduction
- Transfer
- Retention

The ideal use of these strategies may not be possible, however, as some of them may involve trade-offs that are not acceptable to the business making the risk management decisions.

Risk response can be linked into the severity/frequency matrix, discussed earlier and also the organisation's **appetite** for risk-taking.

Severity

		Low	High
Frequency	Low	**Accept** Risks are not significant. Keep under view, but costs of dealing with risks unlikely to be worth the benefits.	**Transfer** Insure risk or implement contingency plans. Reduction of severity of risk will minimise insurance premiums.
	High	**Control or reduce** Take some action, eg enhanced control systems to detect problems or contingency plans to reduce impact	**Abandon or avoid** Take immediate action, eg changing major suppliers or abandoning activities.

6.2.1 Risk avoidance

Risk avoidance means not undertaking or terminating an activity that carries risk. Examples of this would be not entering a contract with many contingencies, or not buying a business to avoid any potential tax consequences. Avoidance may seem to be the obvious answer to all risks, but avoiding risks also means losing out on the potential return or profit associated with it.

6.2.2 Risk reduction

Risk reduction means retaining the activity in the business whilst undertaking actions to constrain the risk to acceptable levels, establishing systems and procedures to mitigate the effects or probability of any risk. Risk reduction examples include alarm systems to warn of a fire or sprinkler systems to reduce its effects.

Mitigating controls include:

- **Preventative controls**: Controls designed to minimise the probability of occurrence of an undesired event. Many of the usual business internal controls such as segregation of duties, authorisation limits etc fall into this category. A non financial example is that no smoking rules reduce the probability of fires.

- **Corrective controls**: Controls designed to correct the effects of an undesired event, such as the fire sprinkler system.

- **Directive controls**: Controls designed to ensure a particular outcome is achieved, especially in the context of security or Health and Safety. For example protective clothing may be obligatory when undertaking certain tasks.

- **Detective controls**: Detective controls are designed to identify the occurrence of risk events. Examples would include alarm systems for fire and security purposes, financial reconciliations, inventory checks.

6.2.3 Risk transfer

Risk transfer is the transfer of the risk to a third party either contractually or by hedging. Insurance is a contractual method of transferring risk as are many outsourcing contracts. Financial risks, on the other hand, tend to be hedged through the use of offsetting derivatives positions or contractual arrangements.

6.2.4 Risk retention

Risk retention involves tolerating the loss when it arises. All risks that are not avoided or transferred fall into this category. Many business risks are tolerable without any further action being taken. Risk retention is a viable strategy for small risks where the cost of insuring against the risk would be greater than the total losses sustained over time. This may be described as **self insurance**.

Risk retention is also the only treatment for some uninsurable risks such as the effects of war. In this situation, the decision to tolerate the risk may, however, be supplemented by contingency planning to mitigate its effects.

Furthermore, for most insured risks there is an excess which counts as a retained risk, as would any amount of a potential loss in excess of the insured sum

6.2.5 Other considerations

Any system of risk treatment should, as a minimum, provide:

- Effective and efficient operation of the organisation
- Effective internal controls
- Compliance with laws and regulations

The effectiveness of an internal control can be assessed based on the degree to which it will either reduce or eliminate the associated risk. It is important, however, that the control put in place is proportional to the risk. The cost effectiveness of internal control, therefore, relates to the cost of implementing the control compared to the risk reduction benefits expected.

Compliance with laws and regulations is not optional; legal or regulatory breaches may result in severe penalties for a business. An organisation must understand the applicable laws and must implement a system of controls to achieve compliance.

Interactive question 4: Managing risks in an oil company

[Difficulty level: Intermediate]

A multinational oil company is considering exploiting the gas and oil reserves in a country where the national government has a history of suddenly seizing control of foreign assets and of introducing taxes to ensure all the profits are taken away.

Prepare a risk register for what you consider to be the THREE most significant political risks to the oil company. Use a table with three columns, for each risk which explains:

- The nature of the risk
- The possible impact of the risk and likelihood of it occurring
- Possible risk management procedures

See **Answer** at the end of this chapter.

7 Risk monitoring, reviewing and reporting

Section overview

- The nature of risks and the adequacy of the risk management strategies will change over time.

- For this reason management should not treat risk management as a one-off exercise but instead set up systems to regularly monitor, review and report on risk (embedded risk management).

- Managing risk requires that organisations have procedures to detect lessons and to learn from them.

7.1 Systems to monitor, review and report on risk

Management must establish systems for the monitoring and review for two important reasons:

- To monitor the effectiveness of the current risk management processes
- To monitor whether the risk profile is changing or not

Processes should be put in place to review whether risks still exist, whether new risks have arisen or whether the likelihood or impact of a risk has changed. These processes should report significant changes that impact on risk priorities. These should be embedded into the normal reporting procedures of the company so risk management is regularly reported alongside other reporting practices such as monthly management accounting reports (embedded risk management).

In addition, the overall risk profile should be reviewed on a regular basis to give assurance that there are appropriate controls in place for the organisation's current activities and that the controls are understood and followed.

7.2 Examples of risk monitoring processes

Examples of risk monitoring processes include:

- Regular review of projects against specific costs and completion milestones

- Systems of notification of incidents (eg accidents at work, near misses of aircraft)

- Internal audit functions (eg financial, systems security, compliance with health and safety)

- Employment of compliance monitoring staff

- Skills assessment and medical examinations of staff and managers to assure competence and fitness to work

- Practices and drills to confirm readiness (eg fire drills, evacuations, disruption to operations)

- Use of embedded IT 'intelligent agents' to monitor risks (eg bad debts, unusual costs or revenue entries, attempts to access restricted files)

- Intelligence gathering on occurrences elsewhere (eg experiences of frauds, equipment failures, outcomes of legal cases)

- Monitoring of the regulatory framework of the industry to ensure compliance

The monitoring and review process should also establish whether:

- The controls adopted achieved the desired result

- The procedures adopted and information gathered for undertaking the assessment were appropriate

- Improved knowledge would have helped to reach better decisions, identifying what lessons could be learned for future assessments

Interactive question 5: Risk monitoring in a fast-food restaurant

[Difficulty level: Intermediate]

What risk monitoring systems should be established by the management of a global fast-food restaurant chain?

See **Answer** at the end of this chapter.

7.3 Feedback, communication and learning

Organisations are dynamic and operate in dynamic environments. Changes in the organisation and the environment in which it operates must be identified and appropriate modifications made to systems. Thus communication and learning is not a separate stage in the risk management process, rather it is something that must be in place and operating effectively at every stage of the process.

- **Learning from experience:** It is important that the effectiveness or otherwise of the planned risk management process is thoroughly reviewed and critically appraised so that risk plans can be revised as necessary in the light of anything learned, eg an IT department learning from restoring systems after a breakdown, an office learning from regular fire drills, emergency services learning from actual or simulated call-outs.

- **Constant updating:** In a dynamic business the risks will be in a state of continuous flux. Management must ensure systems exist to identify any new risks or changes in risks As a result, the risk management process must be a continuous ongoing one where risks are continuously being assessed and plans continuously refined (especially in light of the occurrence of any risk events) eg money laundering practices change continuously as do the penalties for infringement of the law. The experiences of different divisions or offices must be shared.

Effective and efficient communication is vital for the business as it is essential that:

- Everyone in the risk management process is fully familiar with its importance to the business, the risk priorities of the business and their role within the process. Without this, risk priorities may be misinterpreted and risk controls may not be correctly integrated into business systems.

- Knowledge gleaned from any new risks identified by one area of the business or any lessons learnt from risk events is transferred to all other areas of the business in a considered and consistent manner, so that it can be correctly incorporated into the business-wide risk management strategy.

- All levels of management are regularly updated about the management of risk in their areas of responsibility, to enable them to monitor the adequacy and completeness of any risk plans and controls.

- There are procedures in place for escalation of any issues arising.

7.4 External considerations

No organisation operates in isolation; they all have trading partners/customers/suppliers.

Communication of risk issues with business partners is essential, especially when one business is dependent on another. Differing risk priorities mean that a partner may not have the requisite policies and systems in place to satisfy our own risk appetite. Management must gain assurance that its major partners have implemented an adequate and appropriate risk management strategy.

All business stakeholders are concerned by risk and so it is important that the business communicates the way it is managing risks. It is equally important that any business manages stakeholders' expectations on the subject of risk management through regular communication.

7.5 Reporting on risk management

The UK's Turnbull report stated that the board should disclose as a minimum in the accounts, the existence of a process for managing risks, how the board has reviewed the effectiveness of the process and that the process accords with the Turnbull guidance. The board should also include:

- An acknowledgement that they are responsible for the company's system of internal financial control and reviewing its effectiveness.

- An explanation that such a system is designed to manage rather than eliminate the risk of failure to achieve business objectives, and can only provide reasonable and not absolute assurance against material misstatement or loss.

- A summary of the process that the directors (or a board committee) have used to review the effectiveness of the system of internal financial control and consider the need for an internal audit function if the company does not have one. There should also be disclosure of the process the board has used to deal with material internal control aspects of any significant problems disclosed in the annual accounts.

- Information about those weaknesses in internal financial control that have resulted in material losses, contingencies or uncertainties which require disclosure in the financial statements or the auditor's report on the financial statements.

The system recommended by the Turnbull report is notable because of the following.

- It is forward looking.

- It is open, requiring appropriate disclosures to all stakeholders in the company about the risks being taken.

- It does not seek to eliminate risk. It is constructive in its approach to opportunity management, as well as concerned with 'disaster prevention'. To succeed companies are not required to take fewer risks than others but they do need a good understanding of what risks they can handle.

- It unifies all business units of a company into an integrated risk review, so that the same 'language' of risk (risk terminology) is applied throughout the company.

- It is strategic, and driven by business objectives, particularly the need for the company to adapt to its changing business environment.

- It should be re-evaluated on a regular basis.

- It should be durable, evolving as the business and its environment changes.

- In order to create shareholder value, a company needs to manage the risks it faces and communicate to the capital markets how it is carrying out this task. Communication of risks helps shareholders make informed decisions – remember shareholders are prepared to tolerate risk provided they receive an acceptable level of return. It will also provide more confidence in the company and hence lower the required return of shareholders and lenders. However this will be balanced against the need to avoid excessive disclosures to competitors.

Interactive question 6: Ferry [Difficulty level: Exam standard]

You are a senior manager in the internal audit department of Ferry.

In July 20X0, Ferry purchased exclusive rights to operate a car and passenger ferry route until December 20X9. This offers an alternative to driving an additional 150 kilometres via the nearest bridge crossing. There have been several ambitious plans to build another crossing but they have failed through lack of public support and government funds.

Ferry refurbished two 20-year old roll on, roll off ('Ro-Ro') boats to service the route. The boats do not yet meet the emission standards of Environmental Protection Regulations which come into force in two years' time, in 20X6. Each boat makes three return crossings every day of the year, subject to weather conditions, and has the capacity to carry approximately 250 passengers and 40 vehicles. The ferry service carried 70,000 vehicles in the year to 31 December 20X3 (20X2: 58,000; 20X1: 47,000).

Hot and cold refreshments and travel booking facilities are offered on the one hour crossing. These services are provided by independent businesses on a franchise basis.

Ferry currently receives a subsidy from the local transport authority as an incentive to increase market awareness of the ferry service and its efficient and timely operation. The subsidy increases as the number of vehicles carried increases and is based on quarterly returns submitted to the authority. Ferry employs 20 full-time crew members who are trained in daily operations and customer-service, as well as passenger safety in the event of personal accident, collision or breakdown.

The management of Ferry is planning to apply for a recognised Safety Management Certificate (SMC) in 20X5. This will require a ship audit including the review of safety documents and evidence that activities are performed in accordance with documented procedures. A SMC valid for five years will be issued if no major nonconformities have been found.

Requirements

(a) Identify and explain the business risks facing Ferry which should be assessed. **(12 marks)**

(b) Describe the processes by which the risks identified in (a) could be managed and maintained at an acceptable level by Ferry. **(13 marks)**

(Total = 25 marks)

See **Answer** at the end of this chapter.

8 Risk and uncertainty in decision-making: sensitivity and break-even analysis

Section overview

- Business decisions are based on estimates and forecasts which are subject to varying degrees of uncertainty.

- The business can increase its confidence in a decision by trying to reduce uncertainty, using techniques such as sensitivity analysis and break-even.

- Scenario building can be used to develop contingency plans to cope with risks and as a prediction technique.

8.1 Techniques for dealing with uncertainty

A business can build confidence into its decisions by reducing uncertainty.

Techniques for dealing with decision making under situations of risk and uncertainty include:

- Making prudent estimates of outcomes to assess the worst possible situation, eg at what level of sales would the business become loss-making (break-even)

- Assessing the best and worst possible outcomes to obtain a range of outcomes

  Thus in assessing a business plan received from a company seeking finance, the bank or investor may want to consider the best and worst possible scenarios.

- Using sensitivity analysis to measure the impact of changes in forecast estimates eg by considering for example how much fixed costs could increase before the business failed to meet its profit target, or by measuring the margin of safety associated with the current level of operations (see below)

8.2 Sensitivity analysis

In its simplest form sensitivity analysis involves changing the value of one variable in order to test its impact on the final result. The sensitivity could be with respect to the break even position, but this need not be the case.

Sensitivity analysis is an attempt at priority setting. By looking at how sensitive results are to changes in assumptions, it allows an organisation to ascertain which parameters will have the biggest impact on a decision and therefore which ones need to be forecast most accurately.

Various mathematical techniques exist for performing sensitivity analysis. Eg in Financial Management you will look at sensitivity in the context of project evaluation and net present values.

On a practical level however, sensitivity analysis can be seen as a technique that allows an organisation to consider the range of possible outcomes by asking 'what if?' type questions. Eg

- What will happen to profits if the price of components increases by 10%?
- What would happen to demand and profit if the selling price were to be increased by 15%?
- What would happen to sales revenue if the business's market share drops by 5% etc?

Using sensitivity analysis a business can only consider changes in one variable or parameter at a time and therefore it does not allow for the interaction between variables. Techniques such as simulation remedy some of the shortcomings of sensitivity analysis by allowing the simultaneous change of values for key variables in the decision.

In determining whether to go ahead with a new product, or whether to create a new overseas subsidiary, the business may want to consider how much margin of safety exists between planned and break-even sales.

Worked example: Sensitivity analysis

Sensivite Ltd has estimated the following sales and profits for a new product which it may launch on to the market.

		£	£
Sales	(2,000 units)		4,000
Variable costs:	materials	2,000	
	Labour	1,000	
			3,000
Contribution			1,000
Less incremental fixed costs			800
Profit			200

Requirement

Analyse the sensitivity of the project.

Solution

(a) If incremental **fixed costs** are more than 25% above estimate, the project would make a loss.

(b) If **unit costs of materials** are more than 10% above estimate, the project would make a loss.

(c) Similarly, the project would be sensitive to an **increase in unit labour costs** of more than £200, which is 20% above estimate, or else to a drop in the **unit selling price** of more than 5%.

(d)   The **margin of safety**, given a breakeven point of 1,600 units, is (400/2,000) × 100% = 20%.

Management would then be able to judge more clearly whether the product is likely to be profitable. The items to which profitability is most sensitive in this example are the selling price (5%) and material costs (10%). Sensitivity analysis can help to **concentrate management attention** on the most important factors.

Weaknesses of sensitivity analysis include:

- It only examines the risks relating to one variable at a time. Changes in more than one variable are likely to occur simultaneously, particularly where they are interrelated.

- It measures the extent of the change needed before break even is reached, but not the probability of this occurring. In the above example, to reach break even it would take a 20% movement in sales volume, but only a 10% movement in material cost. Nevertheless, a 20% movement in sales volume may be far more likely to occur than the 10% movement in material cost and may therefore be the greater risk.

8.3   Break even analysis and margin of safety

A simple method of evaluating one aspect of risk is break-even analysis. This technique is, in essence, a measure of the sensitivity of profit to changes in output.

The breakeven point occurs where total sales revenue equals total costs. The below chart shows the relationship between the different kinds of costs, revenue, profits and losses.

Break-even point: $\dfrac{\text{Fixed costs}}{\text{Sales revenue per unit} - \text{variable costs per unit}}$

The bottom part of this formula, sales revenue-variable costs, is known as the **contribution per unit.**

The **margin of safety** is the extent to which the planned volume of output or sales lies above the breakeven point.

The relationship between contribution and fixed costs is known as **operational gearing**. An activity with high fixed costs compared with its variable costs is said to have high operational gearing. Increasing the level of operational gearing makes profits more sensitive to changes in the volume of activity.

The calculations are derived as follows:

Total contribution – Total fixed costs	=	Profit
Total contribution	=	Contribution per unit × output

At the break even point:

Total contribution	=	Total fixed costs

Thus:

Contribution per unit × output	=	Total fixed costs

Therefore:

Break even output $=\dfrac{\text{Total fixed costs}}{\text{Contribution per unit}}$

To achieve a required level of profit (say £10,000) then:

Required output $=\dfrac{\text{Total fixed costs} + £10,000}{\text{Contribution per unit}}$

Margin of safety $=\dfrac{\text{Planned sales} - \text{Breakeven sales}}{\text{Planned sales}}$

The greater the margin of safety, the less sensitive the profits to a sudden fall in sales.

Worked example: Break even

Selling price per unit	£10
Variable cost per unit	£6
Fixed costs	£10,000 per month

Requirements

(a) Calculate the break even volume per month.
(b) Calculate the volume of output needed to achieve a profit of £2,000 per month.
(c) Calculate the margin of safety if planned sales are 4,000 units per month.

Solution

(a) Contribution per unit $=$ £4

Breakeven $=\dfrac{£10,000}{£4}$

$=$ 2,500 units

(b) Output $=\dfrac{£10,000 + £2,000}{£4}$

$=$ 3,000 units

(c) Margin of safety $=\dfrac{4,000 - 2,500}{4000}$

$=$ 37.5%

8.3.1 Popularity and weaknesses of break-even analysis

Break-even analysis provides useful insights into the relationship between an organisation's fixed costs, variable costs and level of activity. It is a widely-used and popular planning tool.

There are, however, three main problems associated with breakeven analysis.

- **Non-linear relationships**. Breakeven assumes linear (straight line) relationships. This is unlikely in real life.

- **Stepped fixed costs**. Most fixed costs are not fixed over **all** volumes of activity and are more likely to be stepped.

- **Multi-product businesses**. Most businesses offer more than one product or service. It may be hard to identify which fixed costs belongs to which product, and the effect that the sale of one product may have on the sales of another.

8.4 Scenario building

Scenario planning is discussed in Chapter 4.

Scenarios are used in two situations.

1. **To develop contingency plans** to cope with the arrival of threats or risks which, although they may arise at any time, are of indeterminable probability. For example, a chemicals company may develop a scenario of a major spillage at one of its plants and then set up emergency routines to cope with it. They cannot assess how likely the spillage is to occur in actual practice.

2. **As a prediction technique**: A series of alternative pictures of a future operating environment are developed which are consistent with current trends and consistent within themselves. The impact of each different scenario upon the business is assessed and specific risks highlighted. Contingency plans are drawn up to implement in the event of a given scenario coming true, or to implement now to give protection against the scenario.

Approaches to choosing scenarios as a basis for decisions are as follows:

Assume the most probable: This would seem common sense but puts too much faith in the scenario process and guesswork. Also, a less probable scenario may be one whose failure to occur would have the worst consequences for the firm.

Hope for the best: A firm designs a strategy based on the scenario most attractive to the firm. Wishful thinking is usually not the right approach.

Hedge: The firm chooses the strategy that produces satisfactory results under all scenarios. Hedging, however, is not optimal for any scenario. The low risk is paid for by a low reward.

Flexibility: The firm plays a 'wait and see' game. This means that the firm waits to follow others. It is more secure, but sacrifices first-mover advantages.

Influence: A firm will try to influence the future, for example by influencing demand for related products in order that its favoured scenario will be realised in events as they unfold.

9 Probability, expected values and decision trees

Section overview

- Probability is a measure of likelihood, and expected values are weighted average values based on probabilities. These calculations and values are incorporated into decision trees to illustrate the possible choices and outcomes of decisions.

Decision trees can be very helpful tools for making strategic and operational decisions. Each branch of the tree represents the different outcomes that may occur. In order for the decision tree to be useful, each outcome should be assigned a probability and an expected value. This is so that we can evaluate how likely each outcome is to occur, and what will be achieved should that outcome actually occur. Let us first recap the basic concepts of probability and expected values before we go on to look at how these can assist decision making by incorporating them into decision trees.

9.1 Probability

Probability is a measure of **likelihood** and can be stated as a percentage, a ratio, or more usually as a number from 0 to 1. It is a measure of the likelihood of an event happening in the long run, or over a large number of times.

$$\text{Probability of achieving the desired result} = \frac{\text{Number of ways of achieving desired result}}{\text{Total number of possible outcomes}}$$

Mutually exclusive outcomes are outcomes where the occurrence of one of the outcomes excludes the possibility of any of the others happening, for example, you can't roll one dice and score both five and six simultaneously.

The probability of mutually exclusive events occurring can be calculated by adding the probabilities together. For example, the probability of rolling a dice once and scoring either a five or a six can be determined by adding together the probability of rolling five and the probability of rolling six.

$1/6 + 1/6 = 2/6$

Independent events are events where the outcome of one event in no way affects the outcome of the other events. For example, simultaneously rolling a dice and tossing a coin. The probability of both throwing a five and getting heads on the coin can be found by multiplying the probabilities of the two individual events.

$1/6 \times 1/2 = 1/12$

The **general rule of addition** for two events, A and B, which are not mutually exclusive, is as follows.

Probability of (A or B) = P (AUB) = P(A) + P(B) – P(A and B)

For example, in a standard pack of 52 playing cards, what is the probability of selecting an ace or a spade?

Ace = 4/52

Spade = 13/52

Ace of spades = 1/52

Therefore the probability of selecting an ace or a spade is:

$4/52 + 13/52 – 1/52 = 16/52 = 4/13$

Dependent or **conditional** events are events where the outcome of one event depends on the outcome of the others. The probability of two dependent events occurring is calculated by **multiplying** the individual probabilities together. **Contingency** tables can be useful for dealing with conditional probability.

For example, the probability of rolling a six, followed by another six is

$1/6 \times 1/6 = 1/36$

Probability is used to help to calculate **risk** in decision making. The higher the probability of an event occurring, the lower the associated risk will be.

Risk involves situations or events which may or may not occur, but whose probability of occurrence can be calculated statistically and the frequency predicted.

Uncertainty involves situations or events whose outcome cannot be predicted with statistical confidence.

A popular quote that illustrates an element of the distinction between risk and uncertainty was given by the United States ex Secretary of Defence, Donald Rumsfeld

'There are known knowns; there are things we know that we know.
There are known unknowns; that is to say there are things that, we now know we don't know.
But there are also unknown unknowns – there are things we do not know, we don't know.'

9.2 Expected values

An **expected value** (or **EV**) is a weighted average value, based on probabilities. The expected value for a single event can offer a helpful guide for management decisions.

Although the outcome of a decision may not be certain, there is some likelihood that probabilities could be assigned to the various possible outcomes from an analysis of previous experience.

If the probability of an outcome of an event is p, then the expected number of times that this outcome will occur in n events (the expected value) is equal to n × p.

The concepts of probability and expected value are vital in **business decision-making**. The expected values for single events can offer a helpful guide for management decisions.

- A project with a positive EV should be accepted.

- A project with a negative EV should be rejected.

- When choosing between options the alternative which has the **highest EV of profit** (or the **lowest EV of cost**) should be selected.

Where probabilities are assigned to different outcomes we can evaluate the worth of a decision as the **expected value**, or weighted average, of these outcomes. The principle is that when there are a number of alternative decisions, each with a range of possible outcomes, the optimum decision will be the one which gives the highest expected value.

Expected values can be built into decision trees in order to aid decision making. The amount of expected profit is likely to be conditional on the result of various decisions. We will look at this in more detail below. First, let us briefly consider some limitations of using expected values as a basis for decisions.

9.2.1 Limitations of expected values

Evaluating decisions by using expected values has a number of limitations.

(a) The **probabilities** used when calculating expected values are likely to be estimates. They may therefore be **unreliable** or **inaccurate**.

(b) Expected values are **long-term averages** and may not be suitable for use in situations involving one-off decisions. They may therefore be useful as a **guide** to decision making.

(c) Expected values do not consider the **attitudes to risk** of the people involved in the decision-making process. They do not, therefore, take into account all of the factors involved in the decision.

(d) The time value of money may not be taken into account: £100 now is worth more than £100 in 10 years' time.

Probabilities and expected values can be represented diagrammatically using **decisions trees** in order to aid decision making.

9.3 Structure of decision trees

Decision trees are diagrams which illustrate the choices and possible outcomes of a decision.

A **decision tree** is a pictorial method of showing a sequence of interrelated decisions and their expected outcomes. Decision trees can incorporate both the probabilities of, and values of, expected outcomes.

Decision trees provide a clear and logical approach to problem solving by:

- Showing all possible **choices** as **branches** on the tree (squares)
- Showing all possible **outcomes** as **subsidiary branches** on the tree (circles)

Decision trees begin with a decision point, usually represented by a **square**, and the various choices branch off from this, flowing from left to right.

If the outcome for any of those choices is certain, then the branch of the decision tree for that alternative is complete.

If the outcome of a particular choice is uncertain, then the various possible outcomes must be shown. This is done by inserting an **outcome point** on the branch. This is symbolised by a **circle**. Each possible outcome will then branch out from that outcome point. These are known as **subsidiary branches**.

The **probability** of each outcome occurring should be written on the branch of the tree that represents that outcome.

Sometimes a **decision taken now** will lead to **other decisions** being taken in the future. When this situation arises, the decision tree can be drawn as a **two-stage tree**, as shown below.

In this tree, either a choice between A and B or else a choice between C and D will be made, depending on the outcome which occurs if Decision X has previously been chosen.

The decision tree should be in chronological order from left to right.

9.3.1 Evaluating decisions with a decision tree

The EV of each decision option can be evaluated, using the decision tree to help with keeping the logic properly organised. Once the basic decision tree (ie choices, outcomes and probabilities) has been drawn from left to right chronologically, the basic rules for attaching values to the decision process are as follows.

(a) We start on the **right hand side** of the tree and **work back** towards the left hand side and the current decision under consideration. This is sometimes known as the '**rollback' technique** or '**rollback analysis**'.

(b) Working from **right to left**, we calculate the **EV of revenue, cost, contribution or profit** at each outcome point on the tree.

Consider the decision tree below which has been prepared for a new product that has been developed. The decision is whether the new product should be test marketed or abandoned. The outcomes are high, medium or low demand and are dependent on whether the result of the test marketing is positive or negative.

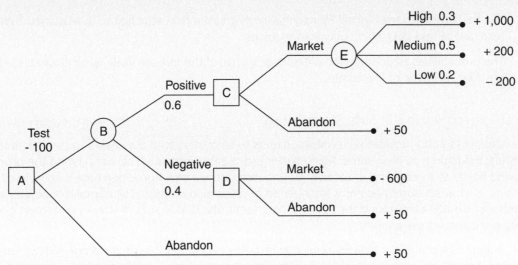

The right-hand-most outcome point is point E, and the EV is as follows.

	Profit X £'000	Probability p	px £'000
High	1,000	0.3	300
Medium	200	0.5	100
Low	(200)	0.2	(40)
		EV	360

This is the EV of the decision to market the product if the test shows a positive response. It may help you to write the EV on the decision tree itself, at the appropriate outcome point (point E).

(a)   **At decision point C**, the **choice** is as follows.

   (i)   Market, EV = +360 (the EV at point E)
   (ii)   Abandon, value = +50

   The choice would be to market the product, and so the EV at decision point C is +360.

(b)   **At decision point D**, the **choice** is as follows.

   (i)   Market, value = – 600
   (ii)   Abandon, value = +50

   The choice would be to abandon, and so the EV at decision point D is +50.

The second stage decisions have therefore been made. If the original decision is to test market, the company will market the product if the test shows positive customer response, and will abandon the product if the test results are negative.

The evaluation of the decision tree is completed as follows.

(a)   **Calculate the EV at outcome point B.**

   0.6 × 360 (EV at C)
   +0.4 × 50 (EV at D)
   = 216 + 20 = 236.

(b)   **Compare the options at point A**, which are as follows.

   (i)   Test: EV = EV at B minus test marketing cost = 236 – 100 = 136
   (ii)   Abandon: Value = 50

The choice would be to test market the product, because it has a **higher EV of profit**.

Evaluating decisions by using a decision tree has a number of limitations:

•   The time value of money may not be taken into account.

•   Decision trees are not suitable for use in complex situations (eg probabilities could be continuous in the form of a normal distribution, rather than only two possible outcomes).

- The outcome with the highest EV may have the greatest risks attached to it. Managers may be reluctant to take risks which may lead to losses.

- The probabilities associated with different branches of the tree are likely to be estimates, and possibly unreliable or inaccurate.

Interactive question 7: Safe Storage Ltd [Difficulty level: Exam standard]

Safe Storage Ltd (SS) provides secure storage units to customers who are unable to store all of their personal belongings at their home. Many customers use the company's services during the process of moving house as an easy way of securely storing items until a new home purchase is completed. On average, customers store their items for a period of six to nine months. The company operates a number of storage sites around the country. At present, the direct costs of storing customers goods are £202 per customer per annum.

SS is unique as it provides a delivery service to its customers of items held in storage. Customers can have their goods delivered to any UK location without charge for up to the first three deliveries. Customers pay a £50 subscription per month for the use of the storage service. The company currently has 28,000 customers on average per year which generates revenue of £11m.

SS has recently been approached by a large retailer, Furniture World plc, to enter into a contract to store furniture for the company over the next 12 months, after Furniture World's main depot was recently destroyed in a fire. Furniture World has requested a fixed price arrangement which would see SS hold inventories of furniture, with up to three deliveries over the course of the year being made to each of its 1,050 UK stores. Each store is to be treated as an individual customer as part of the arrangement. Although unlikely, in the event that more than three deliveries per store are needed Furniture World has agreed that its own fleet of trucks will collect furniture from SS and arrange delivery to store. Furniture World is renowned for driving a hard bargain and wants to receive a discount on all contracts it enters into, usually at 25% of the standard prices charged.

SS currently has spare capacity at some of its storage sites to hold furniture for Furniture World. The MD of SS has estimated that the probability of deliveries being needed over a 12 month period to Furniture World stores would be:

Number of requests	0	1	2	3
Probability	5%	10%	40%	45%

At present SS's average delivery costs are £32 per delivery made. Each delivery attracts an administration cost of £10, this relates to the processing of the delivery at the respective storage site. SS's current fixed costs amount to £143,000, however this would increase by £162,000 to £305,000 should the company accept the contract with Furniture World as additional storage sites would need to be rented at locations where SS has no spare capacity.

Requirements

A discussion of how the discount requested would affect the profitability of the Furniture World contract. Show supporting calculations including a break-even price.

See **Answer** at the end of this chapter.

10 Risk management and business continuity planning

Section overview

- Risk can be mitigated by management having plans to deal with problems if they occur.

Definition

Business continuity planning: A process through which a business details how and when it will recover and restore any operations interrupted by the occurrence of a rare, but massive, risk event.

Because all businesses must accept some level of residual risk, business continuity planning has been developed to deal with the consequences of any realised residual risks. These are likely to be the unpredictable one-off events such as building fires, acts of terrorism, regional incidents like earthquakes, or national incidents like pandemic illnesses.

Factors that must be considered include:

- Securing interim management and staff
- Inventory replacement
- Restoration of data and other IT systems
- Securing interim premises
- Management of the PR issues

Though events bringing a business's existence into jeopardy do not arise on a regular basis, they do, nevertheless, arise occasionally and business continuity planning is concerned with crisis management and disaster recovery if an event of this magnitude occurs.

Summary

Definition of risk
'the combination of the likelihood of an event and its consequences'.
Risk = Likelihood x Impact
(or financial consequences)

Risk
- Quantifiable
- Based on past occurrences

Risk management strategy

Uncertainty
- No statistical basis of assessment

Types of business risk
- Strategic
- Operational
- Hazard

Approaches
- Risk sources
- Risk problems

Identify risks

Identification techniques
- Objective-based
- Scenario-based
- Taxonomy-based
- Common risk checking
- Risk charting

Risk description
- Description of the risk
- Scope of the risk
- Nature of the risk
- Parties affected
- Qualification of the risk
- Risk tolerance/appetite
- Risk treatment and control
- Potential action for improvement
- Strategy and policy developments

Risk appetite of management (Miles and Snow)
- Defenders – risk averse
- Prospectors – risk seeking
- Analysers – balanced attitude
- Reactors – oblivious to risk

Risk appetite of stakeholders
- Investors
- Customers
- Regulators
- Owners

Assess risk

Quantitative measures
- Non-quantitive assessments

Address risk

Risk treatments
- Avoidance
- Reduction
- Transfer
- Retention

ICAEW

Self-test

Answer the following questions.

1   Risk = ... × ....

2   Distinguish between risk and uncertainty.

3   Explain the two general approaches to risk identification.

4   Identify four general strategies for risk management.

5   Identify two sources of risk to which multinational firms in particular are exposed.

6   State the four classes of externally driven risks identified by the IRM Risk Standard.

7   Identify the four descriptions of management attitudes to strategic risk identified by Miles and Snow.

8   **Ferien plc**

Ferien plc is a small listed company which sells country cottage and camping holidays in France and Italy. It was founded 17 years ago and floated on the London Stock Exchange 7 years later, much of the additional capital then raised being used to purchase camp sites abroad. The company has no long term fixed interest debt, and 55% of the equity is still in the hands of the three families which set up the business.

After flotation the company's revenue and pre-tax profits grew steadily, reaching £100 million and £10 million respectively in the year ended 31 December 20X4. However, with three quarters of the revenue coming from sales of holidays in France, pre-tax profits declined to £7 million in 20X5, when fine summer weather in the UK, the high value of the French franc relative to sterling, and a decline in the popularity of French country cottage holidays adversely affected trading. Performance in 20X6 showed some recovery but was still disappointing, notwithstanding a steady weakening of the French franc against the pound, with pre-tax profits totalling £8 million. Early bookings in 20X7 have shown little improvement and the board has recently met to consider various strategies that might be pursued to maintain the growth momentum experienced in the early 20X0s.

Ferien plc purchases its country cottage holidays in advance each year and, under an agreement with the agents representing cottage owners, the company pays half the amounts due on 1 February and the balance six months later on 1 August.

The industry profile

About half the 24 million foreign holidays taken by Britons each year are sold as packages, of which two thirds are supplied by three companies ('the Big Three'). The remainder are sold by some 100 independent (and overwhelmingly privately owned) firms, many of which specialise in particular types of holiday.

The dominant position of the Big Three is reinforced by vertical integration, eg as owners of hotels, charter airlines and cruise liners, through their control of the three leading travel agencies, which together sell well over half of all package holidays, and through the included tied holiday insurance contracts as part of the package deals. The commission structure of the travel agencies has led to accusations that they unfairly promote packages offered by their associated operators. After an extensive study of the situation the Competition and Markets Authority decided that they should make clear to customers their relationships with the operators.

Profits are not only determined by the volume of holidays sold, but also by avoiding having to sell off surplus holidays at knock-down prices. Another factor is a growing tendency for customers to put together their own packages from flight and accommodation offers made via direct selling organisations. Other key variables are the changing preferences of customers, and shifts in taxes and exchange rates. In particular, it is desirable for travel companies to immunise themselves from the latter as prices are set some months in advance of the actual travel dates. This is usually done by currency hedging and by charging supplements to reflect costs at the date of travel.

It is also necessary for companies selling package holidays to be able to forecast annual sales volumes with some accuracy – which will depend on the sensitivity of demand to both prices and customer incomes – otherwise they can find themselves overcommitted. To the extent that companies get their budgets wrong, reported profits will tend to be highly volatile; this is evident from the records of the largest operators, as well as from the experience of their smaller counterparts.

Another feature of the industry is the need to manage cash flows and the highly seasonal patterns of business. With respect to the former, it is necessary to pay deposits up front to hoteliers, air charter and ferry companies. This in turn means that operators ask customers for deposits on booking in order to minimise the strain on their working capital requirements. As for seasonal patterns of trading, there are clearly advantages in trying to spread business over twelve months, eg by offering skiing holidays, short breaks and long-haul packages, as well as popular summer holidays at European destinations.

Clearly the largest companies have the advantage of diversification, backed up by vertical integration, which reduces their exposure to risk and smoothes demand on working capital. Nevertheless, even the biggest operators can overreach themselves, and at the smaller end of the market there is a steady stream of failures, some 5-10 independent companies collapsing each year. However, customers paying deposits in advance are generally protected by the existence of industry-backed guarantees, although such schemes may encourage reckless operators to offer cut-price deals in the hope of generating sales volume, but with a reduced risk of losing customers. On the other side, in seeking to unload surplus holidays the big operators usually publicise massive discounts (often recouping some of the lost revenues through tied insurance and 'hidden' supplements), knowing full well that around 30% of bargain-hunting customers book at the last minute.

The options facing Ferien plc

At the board meeting convened to consider the strategic options facing Ferien plc, the managing director argued that it was necessary to try to reduce the volatility of profits and cash flows. In particular, he felt it would be helpful to diversify the interests of the company. He suggested that the company should try to arrange villa and camping holidays in Spain and Portugal; and villa holidays further afield in Greece and Cyprus.

The marketing director generally agreed that this strategy should be pursued, but he felt it would also be useful to reduce dependence on sales and summer holidays and on camping and cottage and villa holidays. He argued that the company should offer skiing holidays in the French and Italian Alps and the Pyrenees, while at the same time entering the long-haul holiday market.

The finance director was in general agreement with his fellow directors, but he suggested that the expansion envisaged would require considerable new investment. He was aware that the founding families would find it difficult to subscribe to a share issue to finance such expansion and still retain majority control of the company. A debt issue was a possibility but, apart from the camp sites, the company could offer few assets as security and, given the risks inherent in the travel business, he would anticipate high interest rates. In the circumstances he felt that it would be necessary for the diversification strategy to be phased in gradually.

Requirements

As an assistant to the finance director, prepare a memorandum to the board of Ferien plc which examines the strategic options available to the company. It should deal only with the following matters.

- Risks inherent in the travel and overseas holiday industry

- Risks specific to Ferien plc

- The advantages and disadvantages to Ferien plc of diversifying the types and locations of holidays offered to customers

(20 marks)

9   Read the scenario of the **September 2010 Business Strategy** paper in the Question Bank entitled *e-Parts Ltd,* which we mentioned at the beginning of this chapter. Draft answers for requirements (a) and (b) on risk management and risks arising from reliance on IT.

10   Read the scenario of the **March 2011 Business Strategy** paper in the Question Bank entitled *Family Entertainment Company*. Draft answers for requirements (b) and (c) on risk, break-even and sensitivity.

11   Read the scenario of the **June 2013 Business Strategy** paper in the Question Bank entitled *Up 'n' Over plc*. Draft answers for requirement (a) which cover expected variable cost calculations and break-even analysis.

12   Go online at The Times 100 Business Case Studies and read the Eurostar case study 'Calculating and managing risk' at: http://businesscasestudies.co.uk/eurostar/calculating-and-managing-risk

Now, go back to the Learning objectives in the Introduction. If you are satisfied that you have achieved these objectives, please tick them off.

Answer to Interactive question 1

Elements of a risk policy for a training provider offering classroom courses would include the following:

Policies to control admission

The training provider probably has door entry and identification systems to ensure only those entitled to attend classes can do so. This provides protection for its assets and its revenues. It can also stop undesirables disturbing students and staff. How tightly these are monitored, for example whether you are asked to wear photo-ID at all times, whether student passes are inspected, how often door entry codes are changed and whether security staff are available to eject undesirables, presumably depends on the training provider's attitudes to risk and the its assessment of the likelihood of trouble.

Health and safety policies

This will include whether staff are instructed in how to spot safety hazards (trailing wires, badly stacked furniture, loose fitments etc.) and whether they have a mechanism for reporting risks. It will also cover whether there are staff on site who can deal with medical emergencies and whether they have a first aid kit. Does the training provider have a dedicated senior member of staff on site responsible for Health and Safety to make sure these things are done? Is there someone senior at head office overseeing Health and Safety and conducting regular training and visits to classrooms? Is anyone responsible for ensuring your desk is adequately lit, of the right height for the chair, safe and secure etc? Who sees to it that the electrical equipment above you, or the IT you may use and the sockets you plug it into has been tested? Who is responsible for ensuring toilets are hygienic and dry or that the vending machines are safe and the contents suitable to eat?

Identity and data security

Your name is on electronic records. Who ensures they don't get given to the wrong people? If someone calls asking if you are attending class today who has trained staff to decline the information in case someone you'd rather not meet would be waiting outside? How does the training provider ensure that attendances, results and comments entered on your personal record are accurate and fair?

Course quality

This course is supposed to improve your chances of passing the exam. What processes and policies are in place to make sure that materials you study are right and that tutors know what they are talking about? Is the marking of your progress tests and mock exams fair and giving you the right messages to improve your performance? What policies and plans does the training provider operate to ensure a suitably qualified and up-to-date tutor will appear in your class at the start of your lesson?

Answer to Interactive question 2

Report

To	Director of Corporate Development, SkyWays Airlines
From	Financial Analyst
Date	XX.XX.XXXX
Subject	Risks faced by SWA

Terms of reference

This report has been commissioned by the Director of Corporate Development to illustrate the risks facing SWA and to identify appropriate controls. The Risk Management Standard developed by the Institute of Risk Management has been utilised as a framework for this.

Introduction

Risk has been defined as 'a condition in which there exists a quantifiable dispersion in the possible outcomes from any given activity'. This report does not attempt to quantify the risks faced by SWA. Rather it seeks to identify the origins of such risk and, for each, suggest suitable controls to manage that risk.

Financial risks

Interest rate risk: A change in the interest rate can affect the cash flows of the company where there are debts owed by the company at variable rates. Similarly any incomes related to interest rates, such as from short-term deposits or where passenger or freight volumes are affected by interest rates, will also be subject to risk.

This risk can be managed in a variety of ways:

- Avoidance of floating rate debt by switching funding to equity or fixed rate debt or interest hedging. (It might be noted however that fixed rate debt changes the type of risk but may not eliminate it altogether. Hedging avoids the cash flow risk in future interest payments but transfers risk into a fair value risk in term of the susceptibility of the value of the bond to market interest rate changes.)

- Deliberate purchase of floating rate debt such that the fall in earnings from business operations as rates rise can be offset by the increase in returns from the investments.

- Development of lines of business where earnings are negatively co-variant to those of SWA with respect to interest rates, ie internal diversification.

Foreign exchange risk occurs when exchange rates change and affect the cost of servicing debts denominated in foreign currency, the receipts from payments denominated in foreign currency and the changes in the volumes of business as the foreign currency costs of tickets changes.

Methods of managing this risk include:

- Denomination of debts and sales in domestic currency where possible

- Exchange rate hedging

- Development of streams of earnings and expenditures that are matched for each currency. For example if SWA needs to pay sterling for meals supplied on return journeys from London it should consider using the ticket revenues from sales in UK to pay this. If these are insufficient then a sterling denominated airline shop should be considered

- Diversification of operations across several currency zones

Credit risk is the disruption to revenue streams by delayed payments from debtors or from bad debts.

This risk can be managed by:

- Credit control procedures
- Debt factoring

Operational risks

Regulation risk refers to the costs of complying with changes in aviation regulations, fines for non-compliance and of disruption to operations if aircraft are grounded.

This risk can be managed by:

- The creation of mechanisms for consultation and advance warning with regulators. The experience and contacts of SWA's Engineering Director will be an important part of this.

- Compliance with regulations. SWA will need to have robust procedures for all operations that can be inspected and verified by regulators.

- Transfer of sensitive operations outside the business. Outsourcing maintenance, staffing, catering etc. means that the expertise of the provider may reduce some of the risk but also that they will bear the costs of changes to regulation or fines for non-compliance. Loss of earnings due to disruption of these activities can be recovered by SWA through legal action.

Culture risk deals with the danger of commercial failure, reputation damage, or disruption to operations due to mismanagement of cultural interfaces in the business. Examples include the adverse effects of staffing or advertising decisions, poor product or service provision. At the highest level it can include the fall-out from national cultural clashes for the firms in those nations.

This risk can be managed by:

- **Taking appropriate advice on cultural issues**: Many consultancies will provide SWA with practical advice on doing business in particular countries to avoid damaging cultural sensibilities.

- **Business partnerships with local operators**: These will be more experienced in dealing with differences.

- **Diversity policy**: SWA could take deliberate action to ensure that the breadth of cultures that it deals with are represented within its staff at all levels. Staff could also be given culture awareness training such as BA did with cabin staff to make them aware of the variability of dietary conventions, body language, name conventions, forms of address etc that will be encountered by a global airline.

- **Organisational development**: SWA could take the decision to shift from a national to a global organisation by a transformational change involving restructuring, recruitment and changing the perspective of existing staff towards persons from other cultures.

Board composition: To avoid operational risks the board should have representatives of main operational areas such that the operational implications of board decisions receive proper consideration and that operational concerns receive a proper airing.

This risk can be managed by key operations having board representation.

Hazard risks

Contracts: The extended supply chain of SWA makes it reliant on suppliers of fuel, aircraft parts, air traffic control etc. Particular contract risks in SWA's present situation are its employment contracts with staff, and potential contracts with the makers of new aircraft. Risks arise where a counterparty is unable or unwilling to fulfil their obligations under the contract, such as a threat to strike or to withdraw service, or where SWA wishes to vary the terms of the contract but cannot without penalties.

Management of this risk can be assisted by:

- Proper procedures for supplier selection.
- Development of dedicated procurement and contracts function within SWA.
- Multisourcing of inputs to avoid excessive reliance on one.
- Financial redress for non-performance of contract such as penalty payments.

Relationship building with counterparties to develop trust and commitment. Regular meetings to air concerns and address grievances will assist and will also provide SWA with early warnings of potential risk from the contracts.

Natural events: For airlines this includes hurricanes, snow, rain and fog. These lead to cancellations and diversions of flights resulting in displaced passengers and aircraft with subsequent costs of relocation (buses, alternative flights, empty flights), compensation and lost revenue. Such events can also affect demand for air services such as a lack of snow reducing demand for flights to skiing resorts or the tragedy of a Tsunami making tourists unwilling to visit island and low lying coastal resorts.

Management controls that can be used include:

- Contingency plans for dealing with disruptions such as alternative schedules, stand by arrangements with other transport providers and airports.

- Advance warning such as use of weather forecasts.

- Contractual clauses limiting SWA's liability for costs of losses due to natural events and *force majeure.*

- Risk assessment of airports used to assess vulnerability to fog, flood etc.

Suppliers: These are risks arising from the collapse or poor performance of suppliers or aggressive action on their part such as levying of increased prices.

Many of the management controls for contract risk discussed above apply here too. Additional controls would include:

- Engagement of suppliers in long-term contracts.

- Creation of parallel sourcing strategies to ensure suppliers remain competitive and sourcing approach (eg a sole reliance on agents or e-trading) is not an additional source of risk.

Management controls include:

- Development of relationship with key stakeholders (eg governments, environmental groups, local warlords etc).

- Improvement of physical security of operations.

- Improvement of information available by environmental scanning and creation of knowledge management within SWA.

Strategic risks

Competition: This imposes the commercial risk of reduced profits through lower prices and volumes and increased costs of participation in the industry (service quality, promotion etc).

Management controls include:

- Competitor monitoring and analysis

- Development of competitive advantage such as brand or unique access or technology

- Pre-emptive action such as developing 'flanker' businesses. Faced with challenges from low cost airlines many full service airlines developed cheaper second brands (eg in 2013 Aeroflot the Russian national carrier announced plans to launch Dobrolet, a low cost airline offering flights from St Petersburg to other Russian cities). Ryanair moved in the opposite direction by seeking to acquire the Irish long-haul operator Aer Lingus. In 2013 Ryanair's bid to acquire Aer Lingus was blocked by European competition authorities

- Diversification of business to reduce expose to particular competitors

- Negotiation of understandings with competitors (potentially unethical and illegal)

- Acquisition of competitors

Customer changes includes loss of key customers, failure of key target customers, or sharp changes in customer demand patterns. An example is the successful publicity by economy airlines to name and shame corporations who refuse to use them and hence expend shareholders' money on flying staff with expensive full-service airlines.

Management controls include:

- Operation of a flexible fleet able to be adapted to serve a variety of customer types and destinations.

- Provision of a portfolio of ticket prices and service levels (eg BA offer First, Business, Premium economy and economy classes).

- Avoidance of reliance on one or a few main clients or destinations.

- Good quality customer information to detect changing tastes or defections to rivals.

Industry changes: This includes the arrival of new competition, merger of rivals and the failure of rivals. These change the nature of competitive pressure. For example a merger may create greater economies of scale for the larger firm, a threat to SWA, but may also reduce capacity in the industry and so relieve price pressure, an opportunity for SWA.

Management controls include:

- Environmental information on potential industry changes.

- Ability to launch pre-emptive action such as appeals to regulatory authorities or to mount counter-bids.

- Leasing some aircraft to enable reduction or changes in fleet composition.

Customer demand refers to fluctuations in demand. These are inevitable for airlines as a consequence of the strategic choice to be an airline. Their profits and survival will depend on developing strategies to cope with these changes in demand. For example, in 2014 Ryanair reported a fall in net profit – the first drop in five years. In recent years Ryanair had become renowned for poor customer service and charges on excess baggage, an image the company is now working hard to revise. Travel Weekly reported that the 2012 London Olympic games had a positive impact on BA, with the airline reporting a 4.6% and 8% increase in the number of leisure and premium passengers using its services compared to the same period the year before. Management controls include:

- Use of flexible staffing (part-time, contract etc) to cope with peaks and troughs in passenger volumes.

- Dynamic pricing to raise or lower prices to shift demand towards unfilled seats.

- Flexible service and maintenance schedules which allow planes to be pressed into service during peaks and rested during troughs.

- Variety of plane sizes to enable low demand routes to have small planes and so re-deploy larger planes to busy routes.

- Multi-skilled staff able to cope with changes of aircraft on their route (in particular pilots who must be able to switch flight decks) or being asked to work a different route and so be familiar with passenger demands and able to give information on customs formalities etc.

Internally driven risks

These are ones that result from the operations of management. The Risk Management Standard makes clear that some of these risks are incurred as a response to particular external risks, such as the investment of funds in R&D to gain strategic advantage to reduce strategic risk. Other internal risks leave the firm exposed to external risk, such as poor liquidity and cash flow leaving a firm exposed to the financial risks from higher interest rates or banks withdrawing credit. The internally driven risks that can be identified in SWA are discussed below.

Liquidity and cash flow: Borrowing increased during the latest financial year. SWA has a liquidity ratio below 1. This means that any interruption to its business and cash flows could potentially leave it unable to pay its creditors. Moreover it has insufficient retained earnings to meet its present operating capital needs, hence the increased borrowing in the last year despite a modest increase in business activity, and so may not be able to repay any loans falling due in the near future. Any fall in liquidity may make SWA unable to maintain its dividend and hence jeopardise its share price.

Employees and supply chain: Both internal risk drivers are present with the increased dissatisfaction of employees with the voluntary redundancies resulting from the new terminal and, apparently, the loss of control over them by the decline in influence of the Trades Unions.

Public access is an inherent risk for all airlines. Admitting passengers and relatives to airport buildings, airplanes etc also means admitting potential illnesses (such as the avian flu virus) or terrorists.

Intellectual capital: The customer and flight information held by SWA is of high commercial value, yet under the codeshare arrangement, is sometimes shared with potential rivals. The board should remember the scandal that engulfed BA when it was revealed that its seat reservation system, leased to other airlines for their use too, was being used to break into the passenger details held by Virgin Atlantic for the purposes of poaching customers – the so-called 'dirty tricks' campaign. The damage to BA's reputation and the commercial damage to Virgin Atlantic from this episode illustrates the risks inherent in high dependence of IT/IS.

Conclusions

This report has identified the range of risks present in SWA's environment and also those to which it is subject from its own internal structure and operations. It has been noted that at present there is no board position responsible for implementing and monitoring a risk management strategy at SWA. Some appropriate management controls have been suggested.

Recommendations

SWA should establish a role at board level for risk management by creating a new post or by extending the portfolio of an existing director. The first task of this role holder should be to assess internal controls at SWA and, on the basis of this, present a risk analysis to the board.

ICAEW

Tutorial note

You will note that despite the highly limited information originally offered in the question it is possible to construct a reasonably thorough report based on your general knowledge.

Answer to Interactive question 3

The list of factors will be very large. It will include:

Costs and benefits from outsourcing

- Fees charged by contactors

- Cost presently incurred by using own staff

- Financial returns from transfer of assets to contractor (floor polishing machines, vacuum cleaners etc)

- Potential redundancy costs of staff not transferred

- Costs of writing and agreeing suitable contracts and service level agreements

- Costs of monitoring compliance of contractors with service agreements

Risks from outsourcing

- Financial stability and robustness of the contractor

- Track record of contractor in delivering suitable service elsewhere

- Availability of controls over performance (eg whether staff will take instructions from hospital managers, performance indicators, regular meetings, legal redress mechanisms)

- Potential staff and media criticism of decision

- Extent of proof of link between hospital cleanliness and acquired infections

- Extent of public hostility to outsourcing as a source of increased infections

- Will legal liability for negligence claim pass to the contractor or stay with the hospital?

Risks from continuing to provide cleaning in-house

- Operational risks from cleaners not being available (eg strike action)
- Employment risks of having own staff (eg claims for industrial injury, discrimination etc)
- Rising wages and other employment costs
- Legal costs of negligence claims resulting from poor cleaning
- Potential fines for inadequate monitoring of staff (work permits, benefit fraud, health and safety)

Risk environment and appetite

- Potential changes in government policy resulting in contract penalties

- Extent of pressure on hospital to cut costs

- Management's previous experience of outsourcing agreements

- Relative risks of other cost-cutting measures under consideration

- Degree of support management enjoys from influential stakeholders (eg media, governors, doctors, nurses)

- Potential personal consequences for management of bad decision (eg personal liability, career impact, stress of dealing with problems)

Answer to Interactive question 4

Risk	Impact and likelihood	Risk management
Loss of profits due to government seizing assets or imposing stringent taxes	Potentially high significance (however will be determined by the size of the oil company's operations) High likelihood due to government's past behaviour of taking over assets belonging to privately owned companies	Risk avoidance. Don't invest in the country Risk reduction. Insist on written assurances from the government that they will not intervene or tax.
Loss of expensive resources (drilling equipment, pipelines leading out of the country and knowledge) if government takeover the company's assets	High significance and likelihood as the government is unlikely to reimburse the oil company for any resources assumed	Risk reduction. Retain as many of the venture's assets as possible outside the country. Or, invest small amounts incrementally.
A government takeover of the company's assets or operations may put the organisation as a whole under financial distress possibly causing bankruptcy.	Potentially highly significant with high likelihood depending on the global spread and size of the oil company's operations.	Risk transfer. Set up the venture as a separate company with own sources of finance. Or, use local sources of financing the assets (preferably government sources where possible). Sell the rights to the oil to third parties as soon as possible so they adopt the risk.

Other risk management strategies which you could have mentioned include:

Risk reduction

- Ensure the firm has other sources of oil and gas and of earnings
- Seek to influence the policy of the government by political lobbying
- Invite the government to be part owner of the venture

Risk transfer

- Insure the assets
- Invite involvement and investment from other oil firms or pipeline owners
- Obtain assets using operating leases
- Sell the rights to the oil to third parties as soon as possible so they adopt the risk
- Enter into joint ventures

Risk retention

Accepting the remaining loss if and when it occurs

Note: This solution deals with only the political risks from the project. It has not dealt with other risks such as explosions, fall in the price of oil and gas, unexpected cost overruns, poor weather hampering production, industrial action, laws being passed to discourage use of fossil fuels to quote some of numerous examples.

Answer to Interactive question 5

At store level risk monitoring should be established for:

- Temperature of chilled and frozen foods such as alarm bells or luminescent strips that are activated if temperatures rise

- Compliance with food hygiene procedures such as visual inspections and questions to staff

- Compliance with customer service standards such as by mystery shoppers

- Financial integrity such as by close reconciliations between ingredients supplied and totals from sales data and wasted stock

- Staff integrity such as by existence checks on names and personal tax references, confirmations of employment from past employers.

At national level risk monitoring should be established for:

- Compliance with laws on hygiene, employment, food labelling
- Impact of the competitive strategies of rivals
- Changes in the costs of ingredients, staffing or premises costs
- Impact of potential legislation
- Social attitudes towards the firm, its activities and its products
- Stability and performance of business partners

At global level monitoring should be established for:

- Changes in cost of capital resulting from market sentiments or interest rate movements

- Development of new country markets

- Developments in trading relations between host and home country that may affect access and earnings repatriation

- International pressure group activity aimed at the industry or firm

Answer to Interactive question 6

Ferry

(a) **Business risks**

Rights to operate

The exclusive rights to operate are **only effective** for **another five and a half years**. Depending on the likelihood of these rights being renegotiated this raises questions about the ongoing viability of the business.

The right to operate may have been granted provided that **certain conditions** are met. If Ferry does not continue to satisfy these terms its operational existence may be called into question.

Future competition

Profitability could be affected by **future competition**. This might be the case if a new bridge is constructed or if the rights were no longer exclusive to Ferry.

Age of the ferries

It is likely that **running costs** will be higher than those for newer ships.

Fuel consumption is likely to be **higher** as the engines will be less efficient. This is of particular concern in periods when **fuel prices are volatile**. Ongoing maintenance is also more likely to be required.

Emission standards

The company will be required to meet the emission standards which come into force in 20X6. If the necessary modifications are not made the company could incur **substantial penalties**.

Custom may be lost due to the potential disruption caused to services during the period in which the modifications are made to the ferries.

Surplus capacity

The ferries are currently only operating at **40% capacity**

2 boats × 40 vehicles × 6 crossing × 365 days = 175,200

70,000/175,200 = 40%

As a high proportion of the cost of each trip is likely to be fixed (ie fuel), consideration needs to be given as to whether the business is **viable** at this level. The company is also likely to be sensitive to any downturn in business (for example, due to general economic conditions).

Franchise arrangements

The **quality of outsourced services** are outside the direct control of Ferry. Ferry may receive complaints and ultimately lose customers if services are poor.

Subsidy

Ferry may **depend on the subsidy** to continue in business. Cash flow problems could arise if the subsidy stopped (ie it may only be awarded for a given period or be dependent on certain quality standards being maintained.)

If sufficient controls are not in place returns may be **submitted late** or may include **inaccurate information**. **Cash flow problems** could result due to late or non-payment.

There is a risk that details on the return might be **deliberately inflated** to increase the payment received.

Health and safety

Ferry may **not be awarded its Safety Management Certificate** if it fails to meet the performance and documentation standards.

Ferry will find it difficult to **find and retain staff** if working conditions do not comply with health and safety regulations.

Litigation

Ferry may be **sued by customers** for personal injury and damage to, or loss of, property. In the case of serious injury or death damages could be substantial.

Serious incident

A catastrophic incident could lead to a **loss of assets** which may threaten the operations in the short and long term.

(b) **Rights to operate**

It is unlikely that the business is in a position to change the situation regarding the period for which the rights have been granted and therefore is a risk that the **business has to accept**. Management should be aware of any **conditions** which will affect the renewal of rights and take steps to ensure that these are complied with.

Relevant staff should be made aware of any **contractual conditions** and their responsibility for ensuring that these are met. Compliance should be **reviewed** and **monitored** by an appropriate level of management.

Future competition

Management should **monitor any plans** which would introduce new competition, for example the building of a new bridge. Management should also consider how it can **maintain its competitive advantage** by ensuring that its service meets the needs of its customers.

Age of the ferries

Running costs should be **adequately budgeted** for and **cash flows monitored** to ensure that these can be met.

Price structures should be **flexible** to allow increased fuel costs to be passed on to the customer.

Forward contracts could be **used to hedge** against the effect of changing oil prices.

Emissions standards

Management should **familiarise** themselves with the **Environmental Protection Regulations**. Funds should be made available and the work scheduled to ensure that the deadline for compliance is met.

Plans should be made to **minimise the inconvenience** to **the customer** eg changes in the schedule should be advertised, the work should not be planned for peak periods in the year.

Surplus capacity

Management need to be aware of the **capacity** required to ensure that revenue at least covers costs (ie breakeven point). This should be **reviewed and monitored** on a continual basis.

Marketing strategies should be used to **encourage bookings and maximise revenues,** for example discounts for regular users and different price structures for peak and off peak travel.

Franchise arrangements

The **performance of other businesses/franchisees should be monitored** by Ferry through the press, observation etc.

Franchise agreements should stipulate **minimum quality standards** and should include **penalties/termination clauses** for consistent unsatisfactory performance.

Subsidy

Management should be aware of the conditions attached to the payment of the subsidy and ensure that **these targets** are met. If the subsidy is available for a limited period plans should be made to ensure that the business can remain viable by a long-term review of revenues and benefits.

Controls such as checking by other staff should be implemented to ensure that **returns are accurate** and completed on time. Checks by **Internal audit** may provide management with added assurance.

Fraudulent completion of returns is likely to be performed with the knowledge of management. The **seriousness of this risk depends** largely on the **integrity** of the individuals involved.

Health and safety

Management should **monitor activities** and the **completion of safety documents**. This function could be performed by internal audit.

Litigation

Liability should be limited where possible (eg telling passengers they leave valuables in unattended vehicles at their own risk).

Staff training should emphasise public safety. Safety drills should be practised regularly.

The company should have adequate public liability insurance.

Serious incident

The ships should be maintained to a high standard and regular checks should be made to ensure that safety equipment is in working order, eg life boats.

The ships should be fitted with up to date equipment to prevent or deal with serious incidents. This equipment should be tested and maintained regularly.

Answer to Interactive Question 7

Factors affecting profitability

Calculation of the contract price:

Number of deliveries	0	1	2	3
Probability	5%	10%	40%	45%
Prob x number of deliveries	0	0.1	0.8	1.35

EV deliveries per store = 2.25

Incremental costs:

Direct storage costs (£202 × 1,050 stores)	£212,100
Delivery costs (£32 per delivery × 1,050 stores × 2.25 prob)	£75,600
Administration costs (£10 admin charge × 1,050 × 2.25 prob)	£23,625
Additional fixed costs	£162,000
Total costs	£473,325

Therefore, assuming that costs for the contract are comparable to those for existing customers, SS needs revenue of £473,325 to break-even on the contract.

The break-even contract price = £473,325. This equates to breakeven prices of £450.79 per annum per store (£473,325/1,050 stores) or £37.57per month per store.

SS's normal standard price for individual customers is £50 per month or £600 per annum.

Therefore, if SS charged £50 per store per month, SS would receive £630,000 per year from Furniture World, making £156,675 profit on the contract (£630,000 – £473,325). The maximum discount SS could offer on the standard price would be £156,675/£630,000 = 24.9%, but it would then only break-even.

Furniture World has asked for a discount of 25%, ie a charge of £37.50 would result in revenue of £472,500, which based on original costs would result in a loss of £825 (being £472,500 – £473,325).

On the balance of the information provided it would be advisable for SS to not enter into a contract with Furniture World on the terms currently being requested.

1 Risk = Likelihood × Impact

2 **Risk:** The possible variation in outcome from what is expected to happen

Uncertainty: The inability to predict the outcome from an activity due to a lack of information

3 **Risk sources:** The cause of potential problems, things (people/activities/events) that may give rise to risk that may trigger an event. These risk sources may be either internal or external to the business. Management attempt to deal with the source.

Risk events (problems): Specific identified threats or events themselves. Management can attempt to deal with the problem.

4 • Risk avoidance – not undertaking the relevant activity
  • Risk reduction – taking steps to reduce the severity of the impact
  • Risk transfer – passing the risk to a third party through hedging or insurance
  • Risk retention – accepting the loss, if and when it occurs

5 Two of:

  • Political risk
  • Currency risk
  • Cultural risk
  • Trading risk

6 • Hazard risk
  • Strategic risk
  • Financial risk
  • Operational risk

7 • Prospectors
  • Defenders
  • Analysers
  • Reactors

8 **Ferien plc**

Memorandum

To	Board of directors, Ferien plc
From	Assistant to the Finance Director
Date	Today
Subject	The strategic options available to Ferien plc

1 **Risks inherent in the travel and overseas holiday industry**

The risks inherent in the industry in which Ferien plc operates include the following.

  • Risk of fewer people holidaying overseas due to better weather in the UK (global warming?), a recession in the UK economy and/or fluctuations in exchange rates, especially a weakening of the pound. A company could reduce its exposure here by selling UK holidays as well.

  • Risk of wrongly estimating demand for different destinations and having to cut prices to sell off surplus holidays. As tastes become more sophisticated and costs lower, customers want increasingly exotic holidays. Companies can limit their exposure here by offering holidays to destinations all around the world.

  • Risk of wrongly estimating costs and hence mispricing holidays. Costs may vary due to inflation in different countries and to exchange rate fluctuations. Some of these variations can be limited by fixing prices with suppliers in advance and some can be recovered through supplements charged to customers.

- Business risk due to high fixed costs. Vertically integrated firms in particular will have a high proportion of fixed costs.

- Risk of reduced revenue due to more and more customers delaying their purchase to the last minute to get discounts.

- Risk of further intervention by the Competition and Markets Authority.

- Risk of more people deciding not to go via travel/holiday companies but choosing to design their own holidays. With the increase in availability of information on figures, hotels, etc and the ease with which these can be booked, for example, over the Internet, this is a significant threat to the long-term future of the industry.

- Risk of cash flow problems due to having to pay most costs up front before the bulk of income is received. This structure, coupled with the very seasonal nature of the business has resulted in many firms going into liquidation.

2   Risks specific to Ferien plc

Of the risks detailed in section 1, Ferien plc is particularly exposed to the following.

- Given that Ferien plc sells holidays only in France and Italy it is particularly vulnerable to people deciding to holiday in the UK rather than overseas and to people switching between different countries (eg Turkey rather than Italy).

- Selling only cottage and camping holidays exposes Ferien plc to the problem of customers becoming more sophisticated and not wanting what could be perceived as old-fashioned holidays.

- Selling summer holidays only in Europe makes the volatility of Ferien plc's cash flow much greater than that of companies offering holidays through the year.

- Owning camp sites presumably gives Ferien plc more control of these costs but it is still exposed to changes in travel costs and cottage costs.

- The increased ease in which people can travel to France (eg via the Channel tunnel) may leave Ferien plc more exposed than most to the risk of customers choosing the 'DIY' alternative.

3   Diversification

The advantages and disadvantages of diversifying the types and locations of holidays offered to customers include the following.

Advantages	Disadvantages
- Diversification of risk, ie not all of the eggs in one basket. - Reduces the impact of customers switching to other countries. - Ferien plc has experience of offering cottage and camping holidays. This could be used to develop similar in Spain, Portugal, Greece and Cyprus. - Winter holidays will smooth out Ferien plc's cash flow. - Ferien plc already uses French and Italian speaking reps who could also be employed for the winter season.	- Merely extending the range of summer holidays offered would place even greater demands on cash flow. - Ferien plc has little or no experience of the skiing holiday market. It is unlikely to be able to match the low costs of the Big Three or the knowledgeable personal service of specialised skiing operators. Without expenditure to get such expertise, Ferien plc would be left without a competitive advantage. - People who go skiing are not necessarily going on cottage or camping holidays in the summer. Thus the Ferien plc brand name is unlikely to count for much in this market. - Problems with finance. - The best villas and hotels in new locations are probably already booked up by other operators. This could be a significant barrier to expansion.

4 Conclusion

Ferien plc operates in a highly competitive, high-risk industry. Due to its narrow focus and hedging policies it is more exposed to some of these risks than many other firms so it is critical to Ferien plc's survival that these risks be reduced.

To obtain the greatest benefits of diversification, Ferien plc should look to winter holidays as well as expanding summer camping and cottage/villa deals.

Unfortunately this is the area where it is most difficult for the company to extend its existing competitive advantage. A possible solution would be to look to take over or merge with a specialist skiing company that is also looking to diversify.

9   Refer to the answers to parts a and b of e-Parts Ltd in the Question Bank.

10   Refer to the answers to parts b and c of Family Entertainment Company in the Question Bank.

11   Refer to the answer to part a of Up 'n' Over plc in the Question Bank.

12   There is no answer to this self-test, as it is designed just to help you increase your business awareness.

CHAPTER 11

Methods of development

Introduction

Examination context

Topic List

Summary and Self-test

Answer to Interactive question

Answers to Self-test

Learning objectives

- Identify and evaluate methods of further developing a specific business which adjust existing strategies or implement new strategies to take account of changing position and risk

☐

- Choose for a given scenario, a strategy, or combination of strategies, which will best achieve the business's objectives, taking account of known constraints, including stakeholder risk preferences

☐

Specific syllabus references for this chapter are: 2a, 2g, 3d.

Syllabus links

The concept of different forms of business alliance will be familiar to you from your Business and Finance studies.

The discussion of acquisition and mergers here complements the studies you will be taking in Financial Management concerning business valuations.

Examination context

Having decided on a strategy for growth, an organisation must consider how that growth is to be achieved. This chapter considers the options available to a business that wishes to expand. In the exam you will be expected to apply the knowledge covered in this chapter to the scenario, in order to advise an organisation on the most appropriate method of expansion. This is a popular exam topic.

In Q3 September 2010 (*Marcham plc*) the scenario contains information about a supermarket's plan to develop its own major new banking product rather than to 'buy in' to another party's by means of a partnership. The third requirement is:

'(iii) Discuss the relative merits of Marcham's intention to expand into banking via organic growth rather than having an established bank as a business partner.   **(8 marks)'**

As ever the key thing to remember is to apply your knowledge of the various methods of expansion to the scenario itself, as marks are limited otherwise.

1 Methods of growth

Section overview

- Many organisations pursue **growth**, which can be defined in many ways such as increases in profits or market share. Growth may be achieved organically, or through a link to another firm. Once a firm has made its choice as to which strategies to pursue it needs to choose an appropriate mechanism:
    - Develop the business from scratch
    - Acquire or merge with an already existing businesses
    - Co-operate in some way with another firm

1.1 What is growth?

An organisation's growth may be expressed in a number of ways, for example:

- Sales revenue (a growth in the number of markets served)
- Profitability (in absolute terms, and as a return on capital)
- Number of goods/services sold
- Number of outlets/sites
- Number of employees
- Number of countries

Chapter 7 looked at Ansoff's four directions (or vectors) of growth available to the business. Growth may be achieved by a number of mechanisms:

- Develop the business from scratch
- Acquire or merge with an already existing business
- Co-operate in some way with another firm

The main issues involved in choosing a method of growth are these.

- A firm may not be able to go it alone, or it may have plenty of **resources** to invest.

- Two different businesses might have **complementary skills.**

- Does a firm need to **move fast**?

- A firm might wish to **retain control** of a product or process.

- Is there a potential acquisition target or joint venture partner with compatible **people and organisation culture**?

- **Risk**: A firm may either increase or reduce the level of risk to which it is subject.

1.2 Expansion method: Lynch

Lynch summarised possible expansion methods in the matrix below.

Company → New location ↓	Internal development	External development
Home country	Internal domestic development	Joint venture Merger Acquisition Alliance Franchise/licence
Abroad	Exporting Overseas office Overseas manufacture Multinational operation Global operation	Joint venture Merger Acquisition Alliance Franchise/licence

2 Organic growth

Section overview

- **Organic growth** is expansion by use of internal resources (internal development).

- Its advantages are the maintenance of overall control, and the fact that managers can concentrate on product-market issues, rather than concerns of organisation structure.

- Its drawbacks are that it can be slow and there may be barriers to entry preventing organic growth.

Definition

Organic growth: Expansion of a firm's size, profits, activities achieved without taking over other firms.

2.1 Benefits of organic growth

Firms pursue organic growth for a number of reasons.

- The **process of developing** a new product gives the firm the best understanding of the market and the product.

- It might be the only sensible way to pursue **genuine technological innovations**.

- There is **no suitable target for acquisition**.

- It can be planned and financed easily from the company's **current resources** and the costs are spread over time.

- The same **style of management** and corporate culture can be maintained so there is less disruption.

- **Hidden or unforeseen losses**, common in acquisitions, are less likely with organic growth.

- It provides **career development** opportunities for managers otherwise plateaued in their present roles.

- It could be **cheaper** because assets are being acquired without additional payments for goodwill (eg future earnings foregone by the persons selling their business or shares).

- It is less risky. In acquisitions the purchaser may also take on liability for the effects of decisions made by the previous owners (eg underpaid tax, liability to employees for health and safety breaches and so on).

2.2 Drawbacks of organic growth

- It may **intensify competition** in a given market compared to buying an existing player.

- It is too **slow** if the market is developing very quickly.

- The firm does **not gain access to the knowledge and systems** of an established operator so it can be more risky.

- It will initially lack economies of scale/experience effects.

- There may be prohibitive barriers to entry in new markets.

3 International expansion

Section overview

- International expansion is a big undertaking and firms must understand their reasons for it, and be sure that they have the resources to manage it, both strategically and operationally. The decision about which overseas markets to enter should be based upon assessment of market attractiveness, competitive advantage and risk.

3.1 Reasons for overseas expansion

Some of the reasons management cites for expanding overseas are the following:

- **Chance**: A company executive may recognise an opportunity while on a foreign trip or the firm may receive chance orders or requests for information from potential foreign customers.

- **Life cycle**: Home sales may be in the mature or declining stages of the product life cycle. International expansion may allow sales growth since products are often in different stages of the product life cycle in different countries.

- **Competition**: Intense competition in an overcrowded domestic market sometimes induces firms to seek markets overseas, where rivalry is less keen.

- **Reduce dependence**: Many companies wish to diversify away from an over-dependence on a single domestic market. Increased geographic diversification can help to **spread risk**.

- **Economies of scale**: Technological factors may be such that a large volume is needed either to cover the high costs of plant, equipment, R&D and personnel or to exploit a large potential for economies of scale and experience. For these reasons firms in the aviation, ethical drugs, computer and automobile industries are often obliged to enter multiple countries.

- **Variable quality**: International expansion can facilitate the disposal of discontinued products and seconds since these can be sold abroad without spoiling the home market.

- **Finance**: Many firms are attracted by favourable opportunities such as the following:

    - The development of lucrative emerging markets (such as China and India)
    - Depreciation in their domestic currency values
    - Corporate tax benefits offered by particular countries
    - Lowering of import barriers abroad

- **Familial**: Many countries and companies trade because of family or cultural connections overseas.

- **Aid agencies**: Countries that benefit from bilateral or unilateral aid often purchase goods which normally they would not have the money for.

3.2 Involvement overseas

- **Reasons supporting involvement overseas**

  - **Profit margins** may be higher abroad.

  - Increase in **sales volume** from foreign sales may allow large reductions in unit costs.

  - The **product life cycle** may be extended if the product is at an earlier stage in the life cycle in other countries.

  - **Seasonal fluctuations** may be levelled out (peak periods in some countries coinciding with troughs in others).

  - It offers an opportunity of **disposing of excess production** in times of low domestic demand.

  - International activities **spread the risk** which exists in any single market (eg political and economic changes).

  - **Obsolescent products** can be sold off overseas without damage to the domestic market.

  - The firm's prestige may be enhanced by portraying a **global image**.

- **Reasons for avoiding involvement**

  - Profits may be unduly affected by factors outside the firm's **control** (eg due to fluctuation of exchange rates and foreign government actions).

  - The **adaptations** to the product (or other marketing mix elements) needed for success overseas will diminish the effects of economies of scale.

  - Extending the product life cycle is not always **cost effective**. It may be better to develop new products for the domestic market.

  - **Opportunity costs** of investing abroad – funds and resources may be better utilised at home.

  - In the case of marginal cost pricing, **anti-dumping duties** are more quickly imposed now than in the past.

3.3 Issues for management to consider

3.3.1 Strategic issues

- Is the venture likely to yield an acceptable financial **return**?

- Does it fit with the company's overall **mission** and objectives?

- Does the organisation have (or can it raise) the **resources** necessary to exploit effectively the opportunities overseas?

- What is the impact on the firm's **risk** profile?

- What **method of entry** is most suitable?

3.3.2 Tactical issues

- How can the company get to **understand customers' needs** and preferences in foreign markets?

- Does the company know how to **conduct business** abroad, and deal effectively with potential partners there?

- Are there **foreign regulations** and associated hidden costs?

- Does the company have the necessary **management skills** and experience?

Such tactical issues may mean overseas expansion is more easily achieved through some form of acquisition or shared arrangement, rather than by organic growth.

4 Mergers and acquisitions

Section overview

- A merger is the integration of two or more businesses. An acquisition is where one business purchases another. This offers speedy access to new technologies and markets, but there are risks: only about half of acquisitions succeed.

- The mechanics of financing and undertaking a merger or acquisition are essential to its success and will be covered in the Financial Management syllabus.

4.1 The motives for acquiring companies

Definitions

A **merger** is the joining of two separate companies to form a single company.

An **acquisition** is the purchase of a controlling interest in another company.

Some acquisitions are dressed up to look like mergers (ie a combination of equals) because it suggests agreement and may ease the integration of cultures.

In financial reporting, IFRS do not permit the concept of a merger. Nevertheless, strategically and in terms of financial arrangements, a merger may best describe a business combination, rather than being forced to identify an acquirer.

The classic reasons for mergers/acquisitions as a part of strategy are as follows.

Reason	Effect on operations
Marketing advantages	<ul><li>New product range</li><li>Market presence</li><li>Rationalise distribution and advertising</li><li>Eliminate competition</li></ul>
Production advantages	<ul><li>Economies of scale</li><li>Technology and skills</li><li>Greater production capacity</li><li>Safeguard future supplies</li><li>Bulk purchase opportunities</li></ul>
Finance and management	<ul><li>Management team</li><li>Cash resources</li><li>Gain assets</li><li>Tax advantages (eg losses bought)</li></ul>
Risk-spreading	<ul><li>Diversification</li></ul>
Retain independence	<ul><li>Avoid being taken over by acquiring predator by becoming too big to buy</li></ul>
Overcome barriers to entry	<ul><li>Acquired firm may have licences or patents</li></ul>
Outplay rivals	<ul><li>Stop rival getting the target</li></ul>

4.2 Diversification

Diversification means a change of both products and markets from the company's present base. Because of the extent of the change there is clearly more risk involved than in expansion, so we must consider the reasons why firms nevertheless diversify:

- **Objectives can no longer be met without diversification**. This would be identified by the gap analysis. The reason for the dissatisfaction with the present industry might be due to poor return caused by product decline, with little chance of technological innovation in the same field, or due to a lack of flexibility, eg unavoidable dependence on a single customer or a single product line.

- **The firm has more cash than it needs for expansion.** Whether it prefers to invest this outside the business or to seek opportunities for diversification will depend on the relative rates of return obtainable (in general the return from operations exceeds the return from outside investments, but of course more risk is involved) and management preference (management have to balance the internal flexibility achieved by keeping reserves in liquid form with external flexibility offered by diversification).

- **Firms may diversify even if their objectives are being or could be met within their industry**, if diversification promises to be more profitable than expansion.

Related and conglomerate diversification were covered in detail in Chapter 7.

4.3 Porter's attractiveness tests

An acquisition at a bargain price is unlikely to make up for a long-run lack of profits due to a flawed industry structure. For reasons of cost, the ideal acquisition is in an industry not yet attractive but capable of being made attractive.

Porter proposes two tests:

1. **The 'cost of entry' test**

   Unfortunately attractive industries tend to have high costs of entry. Premiums likely to be paid for the acquisition of companies are an important consideration.

2. **The 'better off' test**

   The acquisition must do something for shareholders that they cannot do for themselves. Diversification for its own sake will not increase shareholder wealth. Asset stripping brings only one-off benefits and is not a sound basis for long-run investment.

Worked example: Morrisons buy Safeway

Family controlled supermarket operator Morrisons became the UK's fourth largest supermarket retailer in 2004 as a result of the acquisition of larger rival Safeway for £3bn. Originally an offshoot of the US group of the same name, Safeway was established as an independent company in 1987. Its fortunes were bumpy to say the least over the next 10 years, but the group finally found its feet in 2001 with the appointment of a new CEO and an emphasis on fresh food and aggressive pricing. In a bold move to become a national operator, regional group Morrisons agreed a deal to acquire Safeway in 2004, despite fierce competition from a number of other, more powerful supermarkets that also bid for Safeway once Morrisons' offer was made. These later bidders were precluded by the Competition Commission from buying the company, but their interventions had the effect of making Safeway more expensive.

Integration of the two businesses proved far more difficult than Morrisons had anticipated, forcing the group to issue an almost unprecedented total of five profit warnings in just the first six months of 2005.

The integration problems included:

- Rationalisation of competing stores: This was required by the UK Competition Commission as a condition of allowing the acquisition to proceed and led to the sell-off of 113 stores.

- Rationalisation of depots and distribution systems: This led to a threatened strike by the logistics team and in Morrisons having to pay more to achieve the rationalisation.

- Cultural issues: Morrisons was headquartered in Bradford, Yorkshire (Northern England) and had a reputation for bluff dealing. Safeway was managed from Hayes, Middlesex (Southern England) and carried over many of the cultural styles from the US. Morrisons' Chairman Sir Ken Morrison made his distain for 'soft southern ways' abundantly clear and the job losses of the early months were principally born by Safeway management. This had the effect of removing a cadre of management with the knowledge of how Safeway and its systems operated.

- Integration of IT systems: Safeway operated an industry standard People-Soft system and had just introduced new accounting systems. Morrisons had a bespoke system which relied on manual inventory recording and reconciliations. They struggled for a year to integrate the systems, admitting in April 2005 that they had lost control over the table of accounts and could not assess store profitability in the acquired business, before switching off the superior Safeway system and reverting to the original, and inferior, Morrisons system.

- Changes to stores: Morrisons stores featured narrower aisles and higher shelving than Safeway to give better yields, they had a different name, they had different product ranges. The stores were gradually converted from the more up-market Safeway to the value-positioned Morrisons.

- Joint ventures between Safeway and petrol retailers to set up convenience stores on forecourts were abandoned.

- The autocratic and hands-on style of the Chairman of the group and grandson of the founder irked investors who forced the appointment of NEDs against his wishes. Following the 5th profit warning in 6 months he resigned his Chair of the operating board in May 2005 but retained the overall Chair of the company. The share price did not fall on this announcement.

Morrisons appeared to be back on track by the end of 2006 and since then has continued to grow the business by attracting new customers and gaining market share. The supermarket chain has since scooped a number of industry accolades, including Grocer Gold employer of the year 2013 and Meat and Fish retailer of the year 2012.

4.4 Acquisitions and risk

Acquisitions provide a means of entering a market, or building up a market share, more quickly and/or at a lower cost than would be incurred if the company tried to develop its own resources.

Corporate planners must however consider the level of **risk** involved. Acquiring companies in overseas markets is more risky, for a number of reasons.

The acquirer should attempt an evaluation of the following.

- The prospects of technological change in the industry
- The size and strength of competitors
- The reaction of competitors to an acquisition
- The likelihood of government intervention and legislation
- The state of the industry and its long-term prospects
- The amount of synergy obtainable from the merger or acquisition

4.5 Synergy as a motive for acquisitions

Definition

Synergy: The benefits gained from two or more businesses combining that would not have been available to each independently. Sometimes expressed as the 2 + 2 = 5 effect. Synergy arises because of complementary resources which are compatible with the products or markets being developed and is often realised by transferring skills or sharing activities.

Worked example: Marriott group

The US-based Marriott group provides a good example of skill transfers. The group initially began in the restaurant business. One of its major skills was the use of standardised menus and hospitality routines. Much of its initial business was in the sale of takeaways to customers on the way to the airport. Accordingly it diversified in turn into airline catering, in-house catering, family restaurants, gourmet restaurants, hotels, cruise ships, travel agents and theme parks. Interestingly some areas, such as gourmet restaurants and travel agents, where skills were not easily transferred, were subsequently divested.

Synergies arise from four sources:

1. **Marketing and sales synergies**

   - Benefits of conferring one firm's brands on products of another
   - Use of common sales team and advertising
   - Ability to offer wider product range to the client

2. **Operating synergies**

   - Economies of scale – in purchasing of inputs, capital equipment etc
   - Economies of scope – including use of distribution channels and warehousing
   - Rationalisation of common capacity (eg logistics, stores, factories)
   - Capacity smoothing (eg one firm's peak demand coincides with the other's slack time)

3. **Financial synergies**

   - Risk spreading allows cheaper capital to be obtained
   - Reduction in market competition if firms in similar industry
   - Shared benefits from same R&D
   - Possibly more stable cash flows
   - Sale of surplus assets

4. **Management synergies**

   - Highly paid managers used to fix ailing firm rather than administer successful one
   - Transfer of learning across businesses
   - Increased opportunity for managerial specialisation in a larger firm

Worked example: Rolls-Royce and Vickers

Rolls-Royce has a strong business in defence aerospace, and, according to the company's website, it is the world leader in military transport aircraft.

With aerospace a maturing market, Rolls-Royce has looked for new expansion opportunities. Since its acquisition of Vickers in 1999, it has built a strong presence in marine markets. In 2013 Rolls Royce reported that marine operations accounted for 16% of group revenue. More than 4,000 customers use Rolls-Royce equipment with Rolls-Royce products powering ships in 70 navies. Its global presence makes this possible: Rolls-Royce Naval Marine Inc deals with the US Navy as a US-registered company. The reasons for its expansion are:

- The marine industry is looking to increase engine power for both passenger and freight ships.
- The marine industry is under pressure to meet demanding emissions regulations.

The products acquired as a result of the Vickers takeover were market leading marine brands that expanded Rolls-Royce's route to market and made it a world leader in marine systems, from vessel design and control, to winch manufacture and steering gear.

4.6 The mechanics of acquiring companies

Management will wish to assess the value of an acquisition since the price to be paid is critical in determining whether the acquisition is worthwhile. A number of share valuation techniques are available and there are different ways of paying for an acquisition (cash, shares, loan stock). These topics will be covered in your Financial Management syllabus.

Broadly speaking, there are two types of acquisition approaches:

1. **Agreed bids**: Here there have been discussions beforehand between the boards of the two companies and their significant investors and a price and management structure agreed. The bid is announced and the board of the target recommends acceptance to the shareholders.

2. **Hostile (contested) bids**: The predator has either been turned down by the board in discussions or did not approach them to begin with, preferring to build a shareholding over the months beforehand at lower prices before announcing a bid to the market through the financial media.

4.7 Reasons for failure of acquisitions

Takeovers benefit the shareholders of the acquired company often more than the acquirer. According to the Economist Intelligence Unit, there is a consensus that fewer than half of all acquisitions are successful, if seen from the point of view of the buyer's shareholders.

Worked example: Nike and Umbro

Nike agrees £285m Umbro deal

The following worked example focuses on Nike's purchase of UK sportswear manufacturer Umbro in 2007 and it's subsequent decision to divest it's investment in 2012. The following example consists of news reports written during the respective periods.

Nike purchases Umbro: 2007

Nike will somersault Adidas to become the biggest brand in world football if its £285m bid for the UK's Umbro is successful.

The American sportswear company, the biggest in the world, on Tuesday outlined an agreed 195p-a-share cash offer for Umbro, whose rhombus logo adorns the England football team's shirt.

Nike would meet early its stated goal of becoming the biggest kit sponsor in world football by the time of the South African World Cup in 2010.

The Umbro shareholders will receive 193.06p a share. They will also receive the declared interim dividend of 1.94p a share bringing the total to 195p a share. That represents a premium of 61 per cent to Umbro's closing price of 120p on October 17, the day before it announced it had received an approach.

Umbro shares jumped 15.3 per cent to 190¼ p.

Over the past decade, Nike has been snapping at the heels of Adidas, the German sportswear giant which has strong ties with FIFA, the world football governing body.

'Umbro is a brand with a powerful heritage and deep experience in the world's most popular sport and the world's biggest football market [the UK],' said Mark Parker, Nike chief executive.

Nike has won the backing of The Football Association, which could have been a stumbling block because of a change in ownership clause in the contract between the sport's governing body in England and Umbro.

'We are delighted that the proposed acquisition will allow us to continue our strong historical relationship with Umbro while benefiting from the marketing expertise and financial strength of Nike,' said Brian Barwick, FA chief executive.

Nike has agreed that Umbro will keep its headquarters in the UK, that the brand will retain the Umbro name and its focus on football above all other sports. The deal is Nike's first acquisition outside north America, and follows the pattern of its previous deals for Converse, Cole-Hann, Hurley and Bauer brands.

'This is an excellent deal for all our stakeholders,' said Steve Makin, Umbro chief executive. 'We look forward to taking Umbro to new levels with Nike's support.'

The 'key unknown' at this stage would be the intention of Sports Direct and JJB Sports, which control 15 per cent and 10 per cent of Umbro respectively.

The two sports retailers are expected to want assurances that supplier terms will not deteriorate under Nike control. JJB has stated publically it wants a 'seat at the table' as Umbro's future is thrashed out.

Kate McShane, footwear analyst at Citi Investment Research, said she expected Nike to be able to significantly expand Umbro's sales in Asia, which currently accounts for only around 15 per cent of its sales.

23 October 2007, *Financial Times*

Nike to divest Umbro brand: 2012

Nike, the UK sportswear group, said on Thursday that it would divest its Umbro and Cole Haan brands in an effort to focus on its core brand and other faster-growing business lines.

'Divesting of Umbro and Cole Haan will allow us to focus our resources on the highest-potential opportunities for Nike Inc to continue to drive sustainable profitable growth for our shareholders,' said Mark Parker, Nike chief executive.

Umbro, the UK-based football brand, sponsors the England team kit and its diamond logo appears on sportswear around the world. Nike took Umbro private in 2008 for £285m, as the Oregon-based company sought to increase its football revenues, which it said at the time had reached $1.5bn annually.

However, Umbro failed to perform under Nike. Revenues of $276m in 2006 fell to $224m last year. Nike did not indicate if it would seek to relist Umbro or sell it.

'Although Umbro's financial performance for fiscal 2009 was slightly better than we had originally expected, projected future cash flows had fallen below the levels we expected at the time of acquisition,' the company said in last year's annual report.

'This erosion was a result of both the unprecedented decline in global consumer markets, particularly in the United Kingdom, and our decision to adjust the level of investment in the business.'

31 May 2012, *Financial Times*

The reasons for the poor performance of acquisitions include:

- Acquirers conduct financial audits but, according to research by London Business School, only 37% conducted anything approaching a management audit.

- Some major problems of implementation relate to human resources and personnel issues such as morale, performance assessment and culture. If key managers or personnel leave, the business will suffer.

- A further explanation may be that excessive prices are paid for acquisitions, resulting in shareholders in the target company being rewarded for expected synergy gains.

- Lack of actual strategic fit between the businesses.

- Failure of new management to retain key staff and clients.

- Failures by management to exert corporate governance and control over larger business.

4.8 Reasons acquisitions still occur

- Many acquisitions and mergers are successful.

- Evidence of a loss of value resulting from a merger doesn't consider whether a worse outcome might have occurred if the firms had not combined.

- Vested interests of corporate financial advisors in pressing for the acquisition, ie commissions and fees.

- Weak corporate governance allows domineering CEOs or boards to pursue personal agendas with shareholder funds (eg 'empire building').

- Short-term need for boards to give impression of strategic action to convince investors that business is growing.

As the following example illustrates however some mergers and acquisitions are successful.

Worked example: Disney-Lucasfilm

In 2012, the American entertainment company Disney announced it was acquiring Lucasfilm, the production company behind the Star Wars films. The deal cost Disney $4.05bn (£2.5bn) and consisted of cash and share based payments. Following the announcement of the acquisition, Disney's CEO Robert Iger confirmed plans to develop a new Star Wars film ready for release in 2015, owing to substantial demand from fans for the franchise to continue.

Early signs for the new venture look positive with Lucasfilm's founder George Lucas continuing to serve in the capacity as a creative consultant. Josh Dickey, film editor at Variety magazine commented that the acquisition represents a 'great fit' between both companies, adding that 'they're (Disney) so good at branding and brands. They're so good at working with existing intellectual property and making it resonate with fans and marketing it very well.' This is not Disney's first large scale acquisition having previously purchased Pixar and Marvel; both of which have lead to a number of highly successful films.

Source: 'Disney buys Star Wars maker Lucasfilm from George Lucas', 31 October 2012, BBC

5 Joint ventures, alliances and franchising

Section overview

- These are other types of arrangement whereby businesses pool resources.

5.1 Choosing business partners

The following factors should be considered in choosing business partners for joint ventures, alliances and franchising.

Drivers	What benefits are offered by collaboration?
Partners	Which partners should be chosen?
Facilitators	Does the external environment favour a partnership?
Components	Activities and processes in the network.
Effectiveness	Does the previous history of alliances generate good results? Is the alliance just a temporary blip? For example, in the airline industry, there are many strategic alliances, but these arise in part because there are legal barriers to cross-border ownership.
Market-orientation	Alliance partners are harder to control and may not have the same commitment to the end-user.

5.2 Joint ventures

Definitions

Consortia: Organisations that co-operate on specific business prospects. For example the consortium of Bechtel, Almabani General Contractors, Consolidated Contractors Company and Siemens have been appointed to design and build a railway line in Riyadh, Saudi Arabia.

Joint ventures: Two or more organisations set up a third organisation or co-operate in some other structured manner to share control. For example American companies Greenbrier and Watco established GBW Railcar services, a 50:50 joint venture aimed at creating a network of rail repair shops in North America.

A joint venture: is a contractual arrangement whereby two or more parties undertake an economic activity which is subject to joint control.

Joint ventures are especially attractive to **smaller or risk-averse firms**, or where very expensive new technologies are being researched and developed. Other advantages of joint ventures are:

- They permit coverage of a **larger number of countries** since each one requires less investment.

- They can reduce the risk of **government intervention**.

- They can provide close **control** over operations.

- A joint venture with an indigenous firm provides **local knowledge**.

- They can also be a **learning exercise**.

- They provide funds for expensive **technology and research** projects.

- They are often an alternative to seeking to buy or build a wholly owned manufacturing operation abroad.

- Core competences, which are not available in one entity can be accessed from another venturer.

The major disadvantages of joint ventures are:

- Major **conflicts of interest** over profit shares, amounts invested, the management of the joint venture, and the marketing strategy.

- Problems in each party protecting **intellectual property** such as proprietary product designs, process methods.

- Danger that a **partner may seek to leave joint venture** if its priorities change (eg shortage of funds) or it is acquired by another firm.

- **Lack of management interest**: The JV will be seen as a secondment outside of the main career hierarchy of the parent firms.

- Exit routes may be unclear, including sharing of the assets generated in the venture.

- Contractual rights may be difficult to enforce across geographical borders or regulatory boundaries.

Worked example: Starbucks plans Indian joint venture

In January 2012 Starbucks announced plans to bring its coffee shops to India via an $80m joint venture with Tata Global beverages, one of the world's largest coffee plantation companies. As part of the agreement Tata was to provide coffee beans for use in the new outlets. Although formally established as Tata Starbucks Ltd it was agreed that all coffee shops would operate under the Starbucks livery. The first Starbucks outlet opened in Mumbai in late 2012. In January 2013 it was reported by The Hindu newspaper that Tata Starbucks had opened two new outlets at Indira Gandhi International airport. Since this time the venture has gone from strength to strength. By June 2014, Starbuck's website reported that it had 45 outlets in operation in India.

Source: The Hindu & Starbucks

5.3 Alliances

Some firms enter long-term **strategic alliances** with others for a variety of reasons:

- They share development costs of a particular technology.

- The regulatory environment prohibits take-overs (eg most major airlines are in strategic alliances because in most countries there are limits to the level of control an 'outsider' can have over an airline).

- Complementary markets or technology.

Such alliances tend to be a looser contractual arrangement than a joint venture and no separate company is formed. There may be less commitment than to a joint venture so the benefits whilst similar, may not be so great. Strategic alliances only go so far, as there may be disputes over control of strategic assets.

Alliances have some **limitations**:

- **Core competence**: Each organisation should be able to focus on its core competence. Alliances may not enable it to create new competences.

- **Strategic priorities**: If a key aspect of strategic delivery is handed over to a partner, the firm loses flexibility. A core competence may not be enough to provide a comprehensive customer benefit.

5.3.1 Information systems based alliances

The cost of major Information system (IS) based methods of working, combined with their inherent communications capability have made alliances based on IS a natural development. There are four common types:

- **Single industry partnerships**: For example, UK insurance brokers can use a common system called IVANS to research the products offered by all of the major insurance companies.

- **Multi-industry joint marketing partnerships**: Some industries are so closely linked with others that it makes sense to establish IS linking their offerings. A well-known example is holiday bookings, where a flight reservation over the Internet is likely to lead to a seamless offer of hotel reservations and car hire.

- **Supply chain partnerships**: Greater and closer co-operation along the supply chain has led to the need for better and faster information flows. Electronic data interchange between customers and suppliers is one aspect of this improvement, perhaps seen most clearly in the car industry, where the big-name manufacturers effectively control the flow of inputs from their suppliers.

- **IT supplier partnerships**: A slightly different kind of partnership is not uncommon in the IT industry itself, where physical products have their own major software content. The development of these products requires close co-operation between the hardware and software companies concerned.

5.4 Licensing agreements

A licence grants a third-party organisation the rights to exploit an asset belonging to the licensor.

Licences can be granted over:

- The use of brands and recipes (eg an Australian beer brewed 'under licence' in the UK)

- A patent or technology (eg an IT firm may be licensed to install and maintain some given software application)

- A particular asset (eg a drinks firm may buy a license to exploit a mineral water source or a media firm will license the rights to produce and sell a particular film, book or recording in its country)

Licensees will pay an agreed proportion of the sales revenue to the licensor for the right to exploit the license in a given geographical area or for a given range of products.

Licence agreements will vary considerably in the constraints the place on the licensee. Some will dictate branding, pricing and marketing issues. Others will leave there decisions to the licensee.

A very common form of licensing is the franchise.

5.5 Franchising

Franchising is a method of expanding the business on less capital than would otherwise be possible. Franchisers include IKEA, McDonald's, Starbucks and Pizza Hut.

Franchising can be a method of financing rapid growth without having to raise as much capital as conventional business structures. The International Franchising Association provides prospective franchisors with a directory of current global franchise opportunities. Companies including American car repair business AAMCO offer franchises in Africa, while Dairy Queen are looking for investors in their domestic US market.

The mechanism

- The franchiser grants a licence to the franchisee allowing the franchisee to use the franchiser's name, goodwill, systems.

- The franchisee pays the franchiser for these rights and also for subsequent support services which the franchiser may supply.

- The franchisee is responsible for the day-to-day running of the franchise. The franchiser may impose quality control measures on the franchisee to ensure that the goodwill of the franchiser is not damaged.

- Capital for setting up the franchise is normally supplied by both parties. The franchiser may help the franchisee in presenting proposals to suppliers of capital; presenting a business plan based on a successful trading formula will make it easier to obtain finance. Thus far, the franchiser needs less equity capital than other business structures.

- The franchiser will typically provide support services, including national advertising, market research, research and development, technical expertise, and management support.

Advantages for the franchiser

- Rapid expansion and increasing market share with relatively little equity capital, since franchisees will put in some capital. Strategically, the franchiser will be able to pursue an aggressive expansion policy to cover all geographical areas and establish brand dominance which otherwise could not be afforded.

- The franchisee provides local knowledge and unit supervision. The franchiser specialises in providing a central marketing and control function, limiting the range of management skills needed.

- The franchiser has limited capital in any one unit and therefore has low financial risk.

- Economies of scale are quickly available to the franchiser as the network increases. Hence supply of branded goods, extensive advertising spend are justifiable.

- Franchisee has strong incentives.

The advantages for the franchisee are mainly in the set-up stages, where many new businesses often fail. The franchisee will adopt a brand name, trading format and product specification that have been tested and practised. The learning curve and attendant risks are minimised. The franchisee usually undertakes training, organised by the franchiser, which should provide a running start, thus further reducing risk.

Disadvantages

- A franchisee is largely independent and makes personal decisions about how to run his operation. In addition, the quality of product, customer satisfaction and goodwill is under his control. The franchiser will seek to maintain some control or influence over quality and service from the centre, but this will be difficult if the local unit sees opportunities to increase profit by deviating from the standards which the franchiser has established.

- There can be a clash between local needs or opportunities and the strategy of the franchiser. For example, in the late 1980s McDonald's pursued a strategy of widening the usage of outlets, in particular by encouraging breakfast trade and family groups in the evenings. As part of this it was determined that ideal locations would be in pedestrian areas, near to schools, hospitals, office centres. A franchisee in an industrial town may disagree with this strategy and want to locate on a busy approach road to an industrial estate.

- The franchiser may seek to update/amend the products/services on offer, while some franchisees may be slow to accept change or may find it necessary to write off existing inventory holdings.

- The most successful franchisees may break away and set up as independents, thereby becoming competitors.

5.6 Agency arrangements

These can be used as the distribution channel where local knowledge and contacts are important, eg exporting. The agreements may be restricted to marketing and product support. Other situations where agents are used include:

- Sales of cosmetics
- Holidays
- Financial services, eg insurance

The main problem for the company is that it is cut off from direct contact with the customer.

Interactive question: Ponda
[Difficulty level: Exam standard]

Ponda plc is the second largest vehicle manufacturing firm in Europe. The board was recently concerned about the lack of 'infant' products in the firm's portfolio, and so decided to launch an electric car – the Greencar. Early research has shown that the demand is expected to be much higher in the US market than in the European market. This is at least partially due to the well publicised failure of a similar vehicle in Europe launched in the 1970s, having a top speed of only 30 mph and requiring recharges at the rate of at least three per hour.

For the initial trial launch Ponda has decided to distribute the car using the American dealer Envirofriend Inc. The firm was keen to participate in the venture to bolster its environmental credentials in the market. If the launch proves to be successful, the arrangement will be reviewed. If the new product proves to be as popular as the board of Ponda hopes, it may be necessary to enlist additional distribution networks. However, the managing director has assured Envirofriend that the networks will include Envirofriend (so long as the Greencar continues to be sold in American markets).

Ponda had originally wanted to invoice Envirofriend in sterling, but reluctantly agreed to do so in dollars, on the understanding that all the cars would be paid for, whether sold or not. Envirofriend accepted this risk, as the car's remarkable technical properties were expected to result in near certain sales (according to research).

If the car is popular in the initial market, Ponda has decided to penetrate the mass market as quickly and efficiently as possible by setting up a manufacturing subsidiary in the US. It has never been the intention of the firm to distribute its own products; Ponda will continue to do so via third parties. Franchising is currently being considered as part of the distribution mix.

Ponda's strategic planning department has investigated the possible effect of US Government policy on the Greencar venture. You have been given a rough draft of the research.

(1) It is likely that indigenous firms will be awarded preferential taxation treatment, such as 100% capital allowances, on research-related expenditure.

(2) Government grants for the purchase of the robotic machinery required for the manufacture of the electric cars are to be awarded to firms buying from US companies.

(3) Legislation is currently being planned to increase redundancy payments required in the hi-tech manufacturing industries. It is felt that this may lead to firms investigating ways in which to utilise their spare capacity.

(4) Unfortunately for Ponda the potential competitors are all government suppliers.

(5) The regulatory bodies in the US are likely to bring severe pressure to bear on Ponda – particularly with regard to price and environmental performance indicators.

(6) The Government has already decided to buy a large number of electric motorbikes for the state education sector, to provide free transport to children from low income families (as an alternative to public transport). The scheme has proved extremely popular in rural areas. The US supplier has profited considerably from the deal, and is considering diversification into related areas.

(7) Import tariffs are to be levied on all 'environmental' goods manufactured by firms which are not resident in the US.

(8) A network of 'recharging points' is to be set up by the US Government, designed for use by all types of 'electric vehicle'. The government is keen to set up the system as quickly as possible, and is therefore planning to develop a system ensuring compatibility with the first firm offering marketable vehicles.

(9) Output tax is to be levied on petrol, but not on electricity obtained from the 'recharging network'.

Apart from political research Ponda has also commissioned research into the environmental movement in the US. There is a board consensus in favour of electrically-powered vehicles, particularly in urban areas. The main lobby against such products argues that the switch from petrol engines to electrical engines merely transfers the pollution problem from the car to the power station. Ponda is finding it difficult to judge which lobby will win the greater support in the long term.

The technology associated with the Greencar is far superior to that developed by other manufacturers to date: the electric car is no longer the poor relation of the petrol car. In fact, the Greencar has consistently outperformed its 'petrol using' rivals in respect of

- Miles per $ of 'fuel'
- Top speeds
- Quietness inside the car
- Reliability of the engine
- Servicing frequency required
- Environmental pollution

Ponda is concerned about the expected speed of competitive reaction if the car causes the revolution in the industry which its performance specification would merit. Unfortunately, a patent could not be obtained for the design, so Ponda is expecting its rivals to introduce 'copycat' versions a year or so after the initial launch. One strategy, currently under serious consideration, would be to sell the manufacturing technology to allow production of the Greencar under licence. In any case the directors are sure of the need to establish a strong brand image as quickly as possible, so that the generic product – the electric car – becomes strongly identified in the mind of the consumer with the brand name Greencar, rather as the generic product 'vacuum cleaner' is strongly associated with the brand 'Hoover'.

Requirements

Write a memorandum to the managing director of Ponda concerning the strategic aspects of the Greencar project.

Your memorandum should include the following.

- US Government policy

- A discussion on whether the manufacturing plant should be constructed by Ponda or acquired or whether manufacturing should be licensed

- Consideration of the appropriateness of franchising as a distribution strategy for the Greencar

(20 marks)

Summary and Self-test

Summary

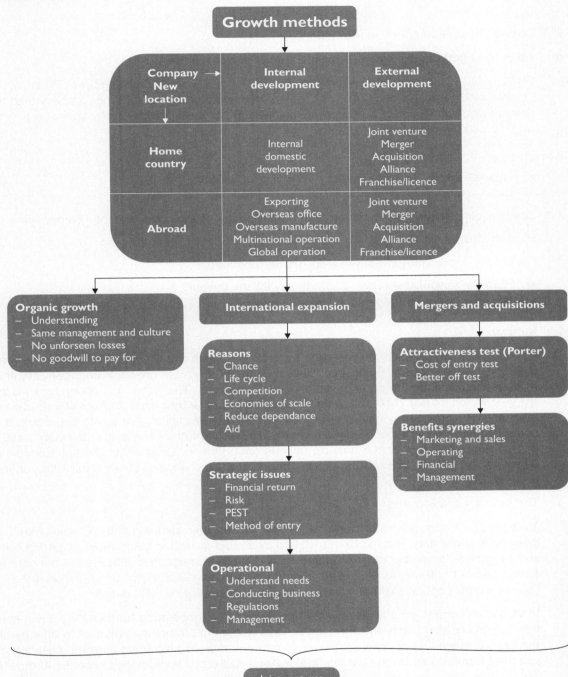

Growth methods

Company New location	Internal development	External development
Home country	Internal domestic development	Joint venture Merger Acquisition Alliance Franchise/licence
Abroad	Exporting Overseas office Overseas manufacture Multinational operation Global operation	Joint venture Merger Acquisition Alliance Franchise/licence

Organic growth
– Understanding
– Same management and culture
– No unforseen losses
– No goodwill to pay for

International expansion

Reasons
– Chance
– Life cycle
– Competition
– Economies of scale
– Reduce dependance
– Aid

Strategic issues
– Financial return
– Risk
– PEST
– Method of entry

Operational
– Understand needs
– Conducting business
– Regulations
– Management

Mergers and acquisitions

Attractiveness test (Porter)
– Cost of entry test
– Better off test

Benefits synergies
– Marketing and sales
– Operating
– Financial
– Management

Joint ventures
Alliances
Franchises/licences

Self-test

Answer the following questions.

1 What is the primary method of growth for most organisations?

    A   Acquisitions
    B   Organic growth
    C   Merger
    D   Franchising

2 Distinguish a merger from an acquisition.

3 **Fill in the blanks** in the statement below, using the words in the box.

(1) .... provide a means of entering a (2) .... or building up a (3) .... , more quickly and at a lower (4) .... than would be incurred if the company tried to develop its own (5) .... Corporate planners must however consider the level of (6) .... involved.

• risk	• cost	• market
• market share	• resources	• acquisitions

4 Define a joint venture. What are the chief disadvantages of a joint venture for a company?

5 Fill in the blanks.

Particularly important questions in a buyout decision are:

- Can the buyout team .... to pay for the buyout?
- Can the bought out operation generate enough ....?

6 **Kultivator Ltd**

Kultivator Ltd was founded ten years ago by Jamie Dimmock and Charlie Oliver, when they opened their first garden centre in Hampshire. Since then the business has grown, both organically and through the acquisition of other privately-owned businesses. The largest acquisition took place in the year ended 31 July 20Y0, following an injection of capital by a small number of institutional investors, who now own 15 per cent of the company's share capital. As a result, Kutivator Ltd currently operates a chain of 25 garden centres across the south of England, employing 1,250 staff. In order to expand further, it is now considering raising more capital, either through borrowing or by converting to a plc and floating on the London Stock Exchange to obtain a full listing or floating on the AIM.

The industry background

Over the past fifteen years a growing proportion of consumer spending in the UK has been devoted to gardening. This has been matched by a rapid growth in the number of garden centres and an increasing number of TV programmes and 'lifestyle' magazines dedicated to the pastime. Today, two out of three people in Britain admit to gardening as a hobby, which makes it the country's most popular pastime, and the industry now employs 60,000 people.

Most garden centres are privately-owned businesses, usually operating from one site. Frequently they buy in bedding plants and specialist services, sometimes franchising retailers to offer particular services (eg mower repairs and garden equipment sales; garden furniture; fencing; greenhouses and huts; fountains and water garden facilities; etc). Others have developed expertise in growing certain types of plants and trees, which has enabled them in part to capture a niche in the market and partially integrate their production activities into one or more retailing outlets.

Despite the rapid growth in this part of the consumer market, amongst large companies only a few DIY chains have ventured into the field. A major inhibiting factor appears to have been the general lack of horticultural skills amongst potential employees. Such skills, however, are often possessed by the owners of smaller, locally-based businesses. Some of these – such as Kultivator Ltd – have been able to expand successfully, either growing organically by opening up new outlets, or – more usually – by acquiring other ready-made family businesses. This has enabled them to take advantage of economies of scale in retailing (eg in providing deliveries), and their buying power when dealing with larger specialist suppliers (eg of plants and trees and of garden equipment).

The flotation option

A merchant bank consulted by Kultivator Ltd has estimated the most likely flotation value of the business, once it has converted to become a plc, would be £94,200,000. This is based on the estimated 20Y0/20Y1 pre-tax profit growing at 4 per cent per annum over the next three years and thereafter at 2 per cent per annum.

The bank has proposed that the company should either be floated on The London Stock Exchange to obtain a full listing or be floated on the AIM. This means that Jamie Dimmock and Charlie Oliver will together receive over £20 million for part of their holding in the business, but still leave them with a controlling interest of 63%.

The views of the owners of Kultivator plc

Jamie Dimmock is disappointed with the merchant bank's advice. He believes that it is unduly pessimistic to assume that the growth rate in pre-tax profits will be as low as 4 per cent per annum over the next three years, falling thereafter to a mere 2 per cent. After all, in recent years profits have grown faster than the increase in revenue, reflecting the company's ability to reap the rewards of economies of scale, while at the same time being able to exercise greater bargaining power when negotiating with suppliers. He believes that the merchant bank's rather pessimistic forecasts are based on an unrealistic assumption that the large DIY groups will take a growing share of the market at the expense of independents such as Kultivator Ltd. Already they face an effective barrier to entry inasmuch as they are having difficulty in employing skilled horticulturalists. Customers are increasingly anxious to have appropriate advice, and the existing well-rewarded staff at Kultivator Ltd have the appropriate expertise. In the circumstances, he would prefer either to rely on further bank borrowing or to seek advice from another merchant bank.

Charlie Oliver does not entirely agree. She is not so sure that the barriers to entry facing the large DIY groups are that high, and anyway she cannot quite see what competitive edge companies such as Kultivator Ltd have over these groups when it comes to recruiting skilled personnel. Equally, she would favour growth by pursuing an alternative production strategy rather than only by expanding retail sales. This could be achieved if Kultivator Ltd were to grow its own plants and shrubs or sought a tie-up with a nursery or seed merchant. Capital could also be used to increase holdings of inventories and reduce short-term borrowings, thus strengthening the company's working capital position.

Requirements

As an assistant to a partner in the firm of accountants which advises Jamie Dimmock and Charlie Oliver, draft a memorandum for them which deals briefly with the following issues:

- An assessment of how floating the company might affect the objectives of the company, even though Jamie Dimmock and Charlie Oliver would still control the business.

- The validity of the assumptions which appear to underlie the growth projections implicit in the merchant bank's calculation of the company's flotation value, dealing in particular with:

  - Barriers to entry and the threat of competition from large DIY groups
  - Whether growth should be via vertical integration or horizontal expansion

- Whether organic growth should be preferred to expansion via acquisition.

Note: Ignore taxation.

(15 marks)

7 Read the scenario of the **September 2010 Business Strategy** paper in the Question Bank entitled *Marcham plc*, which we mentioned at the start of the chapter. Draft an answer for requirement (a)(iii) on organic growth versus acquisiont.

8 Read the scenario of the **December 2009 Business Strategy** paper in the Question Bank entitled *Total Equipment Hire Ltd*. Draft an answer for requirement (c) on the joint venture.

9 Re-read the scenario of the **September 2008 Business Strategy** paper in the Question Bank entitled *DT Ltd,* which was referred to in Chapter 7. Draft an answer for requirement (b) on the two different proposals for expansion (franchising or new investment).

10 Go online at The Times 100 Business Case Studies and read the Burmah Castrol case study 'Building a joint venture in an emerging market' at: http://businesscasestudies.co.uk/burmah-castrol/building-a-joint-venture-in-an-emerging-market

Now, go back to the Learning objectives in the Introduction. If you are satisfied you have achieved these objectives, please tick them off.

Answer to Interactive question

Answer to Interactive question

Ponda plc

Memorandum

To	The Managing Director, Ponda plc
From	F Smith
Date	Today
Subject	The strategic aspects of the Greencar project

Government policy

According to research present policy favours the US firms over foreign competition. Import tariffs for non-resident companies in the sector, preferential taxation treatment relating to R&D expenditure, grants to aid the purchase of equipment from US firms, and heavy government expenditure on Ponda's competitors all mean that Ponda has an inherent disadvantage compared to the US competition. The extent of the government support is well illustrated by the government contract to buy electric motorbikes for the state sector. This has resulted in the supplier making large profits, and thus being able to finance new developments internally, which may include the production of a Greencar-like product.

The planned legislation concerning increasing the redundancy payments in the high-technology sector effectively acts as an exit barrier, as firms will incur high costs if they attempt to close down manufacturing plant. Therefore, excess capacity in the industry is to be expected. Some firms may use this spare capacity to produce rival products to the Greencar. Alternatively, Ponda can use this resource to 'contract out' its productions.

The output tax treatment of electricity from the recharging network (at 0%) gives the electric car product an advantage over its petrol-engine rivals. This is an advantage for the entire industry, but is most significant for Ponda, which, as the pioneering manufacturer, will be the first to realise the benefits. Similarly, the government-funded recharging network will prove advantageous to Ponda, particularly as the technical capability (with Ponda) will inevitably force Ponda's rivals to alter their designs.

The manufacturing plant

The manufacturing facility, whether acquired or constructed, will only be required if the initial sales go well. This is expected because of the extraordinary technical specification of the Greencar. Therefore, given a successful result in the test market, the company should proceed with a 'fast growth' strategy in order to capture the mass market before the competition has a chance to enter the market. Ponda could achieve this by

(i) Buying an existing manufacturing firm (bearing in mind that the process of adoption may be onerous and lengthy)

(ii) Allowing other firms to manufacture the Greencar under licence (essentially a joint venture)

(iii) Setting up its own plant

The case in favour of Ponda setting up its own plant is weak: to build up the necessary capacity quickly by internal means could be difficult. However, the overwhelming case against Ponda setting up its own plant is found in the US Government policy of favouring US firms. Because of increased redundancy payment legislation, many suitable firms will have spare capacity that they are anxious to use. It should be possible to enter into a very favourable joint venture with a US firm. (It is assumed that if a US firm were taken over by Ponda, it would lose its favoured position as a US firm.)

Franchising as a possible distribution a strategy

Assuming that the test market is a success, the firm should attempt to reach the mass market as soon as possible. Assuming that Ponda has arranged sufficient production capacity to achieve this, distribution networks must be set up quickly. The main choice appears to be between established dealers and franchisees (since Ponda has expressed an intention not to set up its own networks). There is an additional constraint: under either scenario Envirofriend must be included in the distribution mix.

Franchising is an arrangement whereby a company distributes products – usually of a 'famous' brand type (as Greencar is expected to become). For the privilege the franchisee pays a capital sum (at the start of the arrangement) plus a stream of royalty payments, dependent on the success of the franchise.

Franchising would be a suitable component of distribution for Ponda for the following reasons.

- The arrangement typically involves tight control over the marketing elements of the business such as brand name, unique selling points to employ, in-store promotions, etc. A unified marketing effort across the outlets is essential for the firm to penetrate the market, and this is arguably easiest to achieve by franchising.

- The franchisees are strongly motivated to sell a high volume of cars (since their success depends on it).

- Ponda does not have to invest in any capital (this is provided by the franchisee), thus the strategy is low risk (for Ponda) if the project fails no capital has been wasted, whereas if the project succeeds the franchisees suffer (and Ponda is not affected).

- Franchise systems have been associated with a high rate of growth (eg McDonald's in the 1980s) – ideal for Ponda.

The disadvantages include the following.

- Selection of the franchisees may be difficult (given the new type of products).

- Since the Greencar has no track record, setting the balance between the initial fixed capital and the variable royalty payments could be difficult.

- The time spent in training the franchisees could result in a drain on resources.

Nevertheless, these disadvantages are not insurmountable, and therefore the franchising strategy is to be recommended.

Answers to Self-test

1   B

2   A merger is the joining of two separate companies to form a single company.
    An acquisition is the purchase of a controlling interest in another company.

3   (1) Acquisitions (2) market (3) market share (4) cost (5) resources (6) risk

4   A joint venture is an arrangement where two firms (or more) join forces for manufacturing, financial and marketing purposes and each has a share in both the equity and the management of the business. The major disadvantage of joint ventures is that there can be conflicts of interest.

5   Particularly important questions in a buyout decision are:

    •   Can the buyout team afford to pay for the buyout?
    •   Can the bought out operation generate enough earnings to pay the interest on the borrowings?

6   **Kultivator plc**

    Memorandum

To	AN Other & Co
From	Assistant to A Partner, AN Other & Co, Chartered Accountants
Date	Today
Subject	Objectives, assumptions and growth

    An assessment of how floating the company might affect the objectives of the entity, even though the existing majority shareholders would still control the business

    Clearly at the present time Jamie Dimmock and Charlie Oliver, as controlling shareholders of Kultivator Ltd, can run the business in a way which suits their own private objectives.

    These might include maximising revenue, expanding the business, and/or maximising their directors' salaries.

    However, as soon as outside shareholders take a stake in the company the interests of Jamie Dimmock and Charlie Oliver will be constrained to some degree, even if they retain a controlling stake in the business.

    In fact, Jamie Dimmock and Charlie Oliver will almost certainly already be constrained to some extent, given that institutions have taken a 15% stake in the business.

    It is unlikely that they will have done this without having some say in the way in which the company is managed eg by appointing a director to the board.

    It is also probable that the bank will also have placed restrictions on the way in which the directors may operate if it has lent money to the business.

    However, in the absence of any contractual constraints, in company law the fact that Jamie Dimmock and Charlie Oliver would still own more than 50% of the share capital of Kultivator plc would effectively mean that they could do very much as they pleased.

    This follows from the 'majority rule' principle established in *Foss v Harbottle* in 1843.

    The main constraint imposed by company law is that Dimmock and Oliver will no longer have a 75% majority of votes, which would enable them to pass a special resolution.

    But once a company becomes a plc there is an implied assumption that the directors must run a business in the best interests of all the shareholders, presumably meaning that the overriding goal is to maximise the value of the company.

    This is now formally recognised with respect to quoted companies in the Combined Code on Corporate Governance that is included in The Stock Exchange's Listing Agreement.

    Nevertheless, despite the introduction of the Code on corporate governance of listed companies, the majority owners of a business exercise considerable power.

Consequently one could regard the overriding goal of shareholders' wealth maximisation as being severely constrained in the case of Kultivator plc by the fact that Jamie Dimmock and Charlie Oliver would still in large part be able to pursue their own private objectives, even if this might lower the value of the business to the detriment of the minority of shareholders.

However, Dimmock and Oliver will no longer be able to determine their directors' salaries immune from criticism.

The validity of the assumptions which appear to underlie the growth projections implicit in the merchant bank's calculation of the company's flotation value

(a) **Barriers to entry and the threat of competition from large DIY groups**

With respect to the growth rates assumed, these depend on a number of factors.

These include the growth in demand in the industry and the level of competition (which will affect both the volume of sales and the prices and profit margins that can be charged).

Estimates of the former will depend in part on the forecasts for the economy as a whole and on consumer tastes and habits.

The level of competition, however, will depend on a number of factors (eg the rate of technological change and how easy it is for rivals to enter the industry if it appears to be profitable).

It is the latter issue that is to be addressed here, ie are there significant barriers to entry?

Jamie Dimmock apparently takes the view that the merchant bank's assumption that the growth rate in pre-tax profits over the next three years will only be 4% per annum and thereafter 2% per annum is far too pessimistic.

He bases this assessment on the fact that in recent years profits of Kultivator Ltd have grown faster than the increase in revenue reflecting the company's ability to reap the rewards of economies of scale as it has expanded, while at the same time using its greater bargaining power when negotiating with suppliers.

Nevertheless, he believes that there is still potential for further profitable growth.

This is because he does not believe that the large DIY groups will take a growing share of the (expanding) market at the expense of independents because they face an effective 'barrier to entry'.

In particular, they do not possess one of the key 'core competences' possessed by Kultivator, namely horticultural expertise. Moreover, these groups are finding it difficult to employ personnel with the necessary skills, which is a severe disadvantage when customers are anxious to have appropriate advice.

Further, he believes independents (such as Kultivator) have an in-built advantage here because they pay well qualified staff appropriately.

However, as Charlie Oliver seems to be suggesting, there is nothing to stop the large DIY groups matching these pay scales, so that alone is unlikely to be an effective 'barrier'.

Only if there is some other factor that enables independents to hold on to the scarce supply of skilled labour will such a 'barrier' be effective.

(And then presumably only in the short term as the labour market adjusts, more individuals train as horticulturalists or where appropriately trained personnel are recruited from abroad.)

In fact, there are several other possible barriers to entry that may thus far have prevented DIY firms entering the industry, quite apart from the fact that they may not anticipate growth prospects to be sufficiently attractive.

These include:

- The fact that existing garden centres have strong bargaining power with suppliers and/or are vertically integrated, giving them a competitive edge

- Garden centres enjoy the maximum economies of scale, so DIY firms could not beat them on efficiency grounds

- DIY stores are typically located at relatively expensive city centre or edge-of-town sites, whereas garden centres are usually to be found out in the country.

Another difference is that DIY stores typically use the 'shed' format, as this facilitates rapid throughput and the use of JIT inventory replenishment systems. By contrast, garden centers tend to carry large ranges of plants, shrubs and trees, many of which will be slow moving.

Garden centres also often emphasise their ambience, tending to focus on a positive 'shopping experience' (eg by offering refreshment facilities). In other words, DIY stores and traditional garden centres appear to be catering for different niche markets.

On the other hand, DIY firms enjoy certain advantages, suggesting that there would be synergies if they decided to expand their garden centre activities (eg they already stock garden furniture, decking, huts, tools and garden equipment).

(b) Whether growth should be via vertical integration or horizontal expansion

Charlie Oliver appears to think that independents such as Kultivator may enjoy another competitive advantage, namely through vertical integration by growing their own plants and shrubs or seeking a tie-up with a nursery or seed merchant.

If this is so, it would provide an alternative means of expanding to horizontal integration, where more and more garden centres are set up or are acquired.

(However, it should be recognised, of course, that the two means of growth are not mutually exclusive.)

The main disadvantage of vertical integration is that it reduces flexibility and tends to increase operational gearing.

On the other hand, there should be opportunities to cut costs (eg by reducing the levels of inventories of plants, shrubs and trees held at individual garden centres, although such savings are likely to be minimal).

Another potential advantage, which may be important for Kultivator, is that it should be easier to exercise quality control (potentially important where customers are likely to want plants which grow vigorously and flower profusely).

The main benefits of horizontal integration are that it should provide opportunities to exploit economies of scale, while at the same time slightly reducing risk exposure as a result of diversification.

More generally, if Jamie Dimmock and Charlie Oliver really feel that the merchant bank has undervalued their business, they could raise finance to expand the business in other ways.

Whether organic growth should be preferred to expansion via acquisition

In a perfect market there should be little to choose between expansion via organic growth rather than via acquisition, regardless of whether the proposal involves horizontal or vertical integration.

The additional costs that will be incurred setting up a business from scratch, including the greater risks being taken, should be matched by the higher price one might expect to pay to acquire a 'going concern' where someone has already taken those risks.

In practice, however, other strategic considerations are likely to determine which option will be preferred.

Thus, for instance, if speed is of the essence to secure a competitive advantage in a market, expansion via acquisition is likely to be preferred.

Indeed, sometimes two independent entities will see it as being in their mutual interest to engage in a defensive merger, in which case both sides should benefit by sharing the potential synergistic gains.

However, at other times, where speed is not of the essence, it may be preferable for a business to grow organically, particularly where it has an in-built competitive advantage (eg because it has a technological superiority, backed up by patents).

In the circumstances relating to Kultivator, the main justification for opting for expansion via acquisition, rather than via organic growth, would be to establish a strong position in the market.

Given the fact that the DIY groups are an ever-present threat, there may be a strong case for trying to expand as quickly as possible via acquisition, even though this may mean that a large part of the potential synergistic gains may have to be paid for 'up front'.

7   Refer to the answer to Q3a(iii) of the September 2010 Business Strategy paper in the Question Bank.

8   Refer to the answer to Q3c of the December 2009 Business Strategy paper in the Question Bank.

9   Refer to the answer to Q3b of the September 2008 Business Strategy paper in the Question Bank.

10 There is no answer to this self-test, as it is designed just to help you increase your business awareness.

CHAPTER 12

Evaluating performance and strategies: data analysis

Introduction

Examination context

Topic List

Summary and Self-test

Answers to Interactive questions

Answers to Self-test

Introduction

Learning objectives

Tick off

- Show, in a given scenario, how a business chooses from competing strategies in order to maximise the achievement of its key objectives, including those relating to corporate responsibility and sustainability

- Choose, for a given scenario, a strategy or combination of strategies which will achieve the business's objectives, taking account of known constraints, including stakeholder risk preferences

- Identify the implications for stakeholders, including shareholder value, of choice between strategies

- Assess a business's current position and performance from both a financial perspective and a non-financial perspective, using management information and data analysis

- Explain and demonstrate how a business can collect and analyse financial and other data in order to provide relevant information for strategic decision making at an appropriate level within the business

- Explain and demonstrate how a business can use management accounting techniques to evaluate its proposed strategies, including the risk associated with forecasts

- Explain and demonstrate how financial and non-financial data, including budgets and other management information, can be analysed in order to implement and manage a business's strategy and to monitor the performance of its projects, divisions and other strategic units

Specific syllabus references for this chapter are: 1g, 2b, 2c, 2e, 2g, 2j, 3g.

Syllabus links

The techniques covered in this chapter were introduced in your Business and Finance and Management Information papers at Professional Stage.

Earlier chapters in this text have looked at a variety of techniques that can be used to analyse data for risk analysis and other purposes. This chapter attempts to draw these techniques together and to provide guidance on how to tackle data analysis requirements in the exam. In the Business Strategy paper there is coverage of both financial and non-financial data analysis. The analytical skills covered at Professional level will help you to develop necessary skills in preparation for Advanced level.

Examination context

This chapter looks at two key technical areas: evaluation of strategies and performance measurement. It also looks at a key skills element in the exam: data analysis.

At least one of the exam questions will include data analysis. Data may be presented in different forms (and in more than one question) in order to assist your understanding and strategic analysis of a particular situation. When you are presented with data in a question you are expected to use it in forming your answer. It is particularly important that you draw upon this data even if you are not presented with a separate numbers requirement.

The key issue is that the data analysis you perform should be linked to the wider strategy, position or issue in the scenario. Numbers will form part of the analysis but it is important to recognise that the numbers are a peg on which to hang discussion: you must demonstrate an understanding of the story behind the numbers. Explanation of your numerical analysis is thus an important element of data analysis.

In Q2 March 2008 (*Kraftvagen Gmbh*) the scenario gives data on **the car manufacturer's sales by location of market and by location of production, plus additional data on sales volumes in a particular market and of a particular type of product.** The first requirement is:

'(a) Using the data provided, evaluate the relative product and market positioning of KV. Identify, with reasons, any other information that would be necessary to make a more complete assessment of KV's competitive position and performance. **(10 marks)'**

This is a fairly typical 'data analysis' requirement, in which you have quite a lot of numbers to play with and are asked to make both comparisons and judgements. It is also fairly common to be asked to identify what further information would be useful for your analysis, since recognising the limitations of the data you have (in terms of either content or accuracy) is an important skill.

1 Choice of strategic options

Section overview

- Strategic choices are evaluated according to their suitability (to the organisation and its current situation), their feasibility (in terms of usefulness or competences) and their acceptability (to relevant stakeholder groups).

- Using these criteria a strategy can be selected and then be broken down into functional strategies to be implemented.

1.1 Recap of the rational approach

The rational model was described in Chapter 2.

If the business is facing a gap, then devising strategies to fill the gap is a two-step process:

1. Option generation: creative thinking to generate options.

2. Evaluation and selection: assessment of options against goals of the business and commitment to some and not to others.

In Chapters 7 and 11 we considered how a business might develop strategic options, using models such as Ansoff.

Evaluation of these options in order to decide which of the options to implement occurs as the second phase of **strategic choice**.

In the next section we will look at how the business can use strategic control systems to monitor the success of the strategy and its impact on performance, once implementation has taken place.

1.2 Evaluation criteria: SFA

Johnson, Scholes and Whittington (*Exploring Corporate Strategy*) provide a checklist for assessing options:

- **Suitability**: Is this option appropriate considering the strategic position and outlook of the business?

- **Acceptability**: Will this option gain the support of the stakeholders essential for the success of the strategy and the organisation as a whole? Will the option antagonise significant powerful stakeholders that could thwart its success or that of management as a whole?

- **Feasibility**: Does the firm have the resources and competences required to carry the strategy out? Are the assumptions of the strategy realistic?

1.3 Suitability

Suitability relates to the **strategic logic** and **strategic fit** of the strategy. The strategy must fit the company's operational circumstances and strategic position. Does the strategy:

- **Exploit** company strengths and distinctive **competences**?
- Rectify company **weaknesses**?
- **Neutralise** or deflect environmental **threats**?
- Help the firm to seize **opportunities**?
- **Satisfy the goals** of the organisation?
- **Fill the gap** identified by gap analysis?
- Generate/maintain **competitive advantage**?

1.4 Acceptability (to stakeholders)

The **acceptability** of a strategy relates to people's expectations of it and its expected performance outcomes. This includes consideration of:

- Returns – the likely benefits that stakeholders will receive, and
- Risk – the likelihood of failure and its associated consequences.

It is here that stakeholder analysis, described in Chapter 3, can also be brought in.

- **Financial considerations**: Strategies will be evaluated by considering how far they contribute to meeting the dominant objective of increasing shareholder wealth, using measures such as:
    - Return on investment
    - Profits
    - Growth
    - EPS
    - Cash flow
    - Price/Earnings
    - Market capitalisation

- **Customers** may object to a strategy if it means reducing service, but on the other hand they may have no choice.

- **Banks** are interested in the implications for cash resources, debt levels etc.

- **Government**: A strategy involving a takeover may be prohibited under monopolies and mergers legislation. Similarly, the environmental impact may cause key stakeholders to withhold consent.

Considerations of **ethics and corporate responsibility** are included here.

1.5 Feasibility criteria

Feasibility asks whether the strategy can in fact be implemented.

- Is there enough **money**?
- Is there the **ability** to deliver the goods/services specified in the strategy?
- Can we deal with the likely **responses that competitors** will make?

- Do we have access to **technology, materials and resources**?
- Do we have enough **time** to implement the strategy?
- Will the strategy deliver results within an appropriate timeframe?

Strategies which do not make use of the existing competences, and which therefore call for new competences to be acquired, might not be feasible.

- Gaining competences via organic growth takes time
- Acquiring new competences can be costly

1.6 Strategy selection and implementation

After evaluating the various strategic options for suitability, acceptability, feasibility, the business must make a decision as to which strategy(ies) to implement. It may be the case that some of the strategies are mutually exclusive. Others may be implemented in parallel.

To implement the chosen strategy, it needs to be broken down into the relevant functional strategies (marketing, operations, human resources, finance etc). This is considered further in Chapter 13.

2 Strategic control

Section overview

- A business's planning and control cycle is designed to ensure its mission and objectives are met by setting plans, measuring actual performance against plans, and taking control action.

- Control at a strategic level means asking the question: 'is the organisation on target to meet its overall objectives, and is control action needed to turn it around?'

- The existence of an annual budgeting process compels planning and enables the establishment of a system of control by comparing budgeted and actual results.

2.1 Strategic control systems

Steps in setting up formal systems of strategic control:

Step 1
Strategy review: Review the progress of strategy.

Step 2
Identify milestones of performance (**strategic objectives**), both quantitative and qualitative (eg market share, quality, innovation, customer satisfaction).

- Milestones are identified after critical success factors have been outlined.

- Milestones are short-term steps towards long-term goals.

- Milestones enable managers to monitor actions (eg whether a new product has been launched) and results (eg the success of the launch).

Step 3
Set **target achievement levels**. These need not be exclusively quantitative.

- Targets must be reasonably precise.
- Targets should suggest strategies and tactics.
- Competitive benchmarks are targets set relative to the competition.

Step 4
Formal **monitoring** of the strategic process. Reporting is less frequent than for financial reporting.

Step 5

Reward: for most systems, there is little relationship between the achievement of strategic objectives and the reward system, although some companies are beginning to use measures of strategic performance as part of the annual bonus calculations.

2.2 Budgets and budgetary control

2.2.1 Short-term planning and budget preparation

A budget is a plan expressed in financial terms. Short term plans attempt to provide short-term targets within the framework of longer-term strategic plans. This is generally done in the form of a budget.

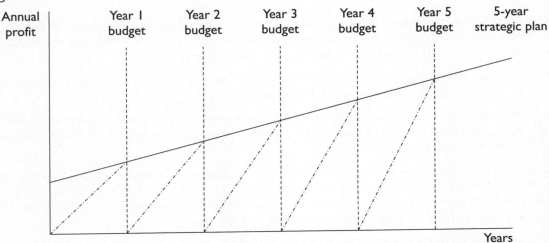

The diagram shows that the five-year strategic plan is to grow annual profits. This gives annual profit milestones and these are taken as the starting point for each annual budget.

2.2.2 Budgets, long term plans and corporate objectives

Budgets are an important planning tool for the organisation and are directly related to the mission, objectives and business strategy of an organisation.

A budget is a business plan for the short term, usually one year. It is likely to be expressed in financial terms and its role is to convert the strategic plans into specific targets. It therefore fits into the strategic planning process as follows.

- The mission sets the overall direction
- The strategic objectives illustrate how the mission will be achieved
- The strategic plans show how the objectives will be pursued
- The budgets represent the short-term plans and targets necessary to fulfil the strategic objectives

These budgets will then have to be **controlled** to ensure the planned events actually occur and is therefore a key element in assessing the effectiveness of the business strategy. This is as much a part of the budgeting process as actually setting the budget.

A budget is a **plan** not a forecast. You plan to meet the targets in the budget, a forecast is a prediction of future position. Forecasts are helpful to budget setters and planners.

A **periodic budget** is a budget covering a period, eg a year.

A **continual**, or **rolling budget**, is continually updated.

Different budgets are prepared for each specific aspect of the business, and the contents of the individual budgets are summarised in **master budgets**. The contents of each of the individual budgets affect, and are influenced by, the contents of the others; they are linked together.

The sales budget is usually the first budget prepared as the level of sales determines the overall level of activity for the period and therefore most of the cost budgets.

Planning (including budgeting) is the responsibility of managers, not just accountants. Although management accountants help by providing relevant information to managers and contributing to decision making.

2.2.3 Benefits of budgets

There are five main benefits of budgets.

1. **Promotes forward thinking.** Potential problems are identified early, therefore giving mangers time enough to consider the best way to overcome that problem.

2. **Helps to co-ordinate the various aspects of the organisation.** The activities of the various departments and sections of an organisation must be linked so that the activities complement each other.

3. **Motivates performance.** Having a defined target can motivate managers and staff in their performance. Managers should be able to relate their own role back to the organisational objectives, seeing as the budgets are based on these objectives.

4. **Provides a basis for a system of control.** Budgets provide a yardstick for measuring performance by comparing actual against planned performance.

5. **Provides a system of authorisation.** Allows managers to spend up to a certain limit. Activities are allocated a fixed amount of funds at the discretion of senior management, thereby providing the authority to spend.

These five uses may however conflict with each other. For example, a budget used as a system of authorisation may motivate a manager to spend to the limit even though this is wasteful. This is particularly likely where the budget cannot be rolled over into the next period. In addition to this, budgets have some other limitations that could potentially arise.

(1) Employees may be **demotivated** if they believe the budget to be unattainable
(2) **Slack** may be built in by managers to make the budget more achievable
(3) Focuses on the **short-term results** rather than the underlying causes
(4) Unrealistic budgets may cause managers to make decisions that are **detrimental** to the company

2.2.4 Using budgets for control

Budgets are useful for exercising **control** over an organisation as they provide a yardstick against which performance can be assessed. This means finding out where and why things did not go to plan, then seeking ways to put them right for the future.

If the budget is found to be unachievable, it may need to be revised. Only realistic budgets can form the basis for control, and therefore they should be adaptable.

Budgets enable managers to manage by exception, that is focus on areas where things are not going to plan (ie the exceptions). This is done by comparing the actual performance to the budgets to identify the **variances.** We will look at variances later in this chapter.

2.2.5 Making budgetary control effective

Successful budgetary control systems tend to share the same common features.

- **Senior management** take the system seriously. They pay attention to, and base decisions on, the monthly variance report. This attitude cascades down through the organisation.

- **Accountability.** There are **clear responsibilities** stating which manager is responsible for each business area.

- **Targets** are **challenging but achievable.** Targets set too high, or too low, would have a de-motivating effect.

- **Established data collection, analysis and reporting routines** which involve looking at actual versus budgeted results to calculate and report variances. This should be done automatically on a monthly basis.

- **Targeted reporting.** Managers receive specific rather than general purpose reports so that they do not have to wade through information to find the relevant sections.

- **Short reporting periods**, usually a month, so that things can't go too wrong before they are picked up.
- **Timely reporting.** Variance reports should be provided to managers as soon as possible after the end of the reporting period. This is so they can take action to prevent the same problems occurring in the next reporting period.
- **Provokes action.** Simply reporting variances does not cause change. Managers have to act on the report to create change.

2.2.6 Behavioural aspects of budgets

Budgets can be very effective in motivating managers. In particular, budgets have been found to

- Improve performance
- Be most effective when they are demanding, yet achievable. Though if they are unrealistically demanding performance may deteriorate
- Are most effective when the managers have participated in the setting of their own targets

2.2.7 Informal control

Many companies do not define explicit strategic objectives or milestones that are regularly and formally monitored as part of the ongoing management control process.

- Choosing one objective (eg market share) might encourage managers to ignore or downgrade others (eg profitability), or lead managers to ignore wider issues.
- Informality promotes flexibility.
- Openness of communication is necessary.
- Finite objectives overlook nuances especially in human resource management. In other words, an objective like 'employee commitment' is necessary for success, but hard to measure quantitatively.

Informal control does not always work because it enables managers to skate over important strategic issues and choices.

2.3 Guidelines for a strategic control system

The characteristics of strategic control systems can be measured on two axes.

- How formal is the process?
- How many milestones are identified for review?

As there is no optimum number of milestones or degree of formality, Goold and Quinn (*Strategic Control*) suggest these guidelines.

Guideline	Comment
Linkages	If there are linkages between businesses in a group, the formality of the process should be low, to avoid co-operation being undermined.
Diversity	If there is a great deal of diversity, it is doubtful whether any overall strategic control system is appropriate, especially if the critical success factors for each business are different.
Criticality	Firms whose strategic stance depends on decisions which can, if they go wrong, destroy the company as a whole (eg launching a new technology) need strategic control systems which, whether formal or informal, have a large number of milestones so that emerging problems in any area will be easily and quickly detected.
Change	Fashion-goods manufacturers must respond to relatively high levels of environmental turbulence, and have to react quickly. If changes are rapid, a system of low formality and few measures may be appropriate, merely because the control processes must allow decisions to be taken in changed contexts.

Guideline	Comment
Competitive advantage	• Businesses with few sources of competitive advantage – control can easily focus on perhaps market share or quality with high formality.
	• Businesses with many sources of competitive advantage – success over a wider number of areas is necessary and the firm should not just concentrate on one of them.

2.4 Using CSFs for control

In Chapter 6 we considered Critical Success Factors (CSFs) as the areas that are vital if the business is to achieve competitive advantage. CSFs focus management attention on what is important. The advantages of building a control system based around CSFs are:

- The process of identifying CSFs will help alert management to the things that need controlling (and show up the things that are less important).

- The CSFs can be turned into Key Performance Indicators (KPIs) for periodic reporting in the same way as conventional budgetary control might focus on, and report costs against standard costs.

- The CSFs can guide the development of information systems by ensuring that managers receive regular information about the factors that are critical to their business.

- They can be used for benchmarking organisational performance internally and against rivals (benchmarking was also discussed in Chapter 6).

3 Measuring performance

Section overview

- Effective performance measurement helps a business ascertain whether it has achieved its strategic and operational objectives.

- This section reminds you of some of the key performance measures you have studied in previous papers:
    - Profitability, liquidity and gearing
    - Economy, Efficiency, Effectiveness (the 3 Es)
    - CSFs and KPIs

- Performance measurement is only effective if there are yardsticks against which to compare.

- The 3 Es is an approach widely used in the public sector and by NFP organisations to measure Value for Money.

- Sections 7 and 8 of this chapter give guidance on how to approach performance measurement in the context of a data analysis question in the exam.

3.1 Measuring performance

Actual performance follows on from setting objectives and developing plans and targets.

Performance measurement is a fundamental part of the control process as it allows the business to consider how it has performed in comparison to those plans and to take corrective action where necessary.

Performance can be measured in different ways:

- **Financial performance** can be measured in terms of growth, profitability, liquidity and gearing.

- **Resource use** can be measured in terms of effectiveness, economy and efficiency.

- **Competitive advantage** can be measured by identifying critical success factors (CSFs) and then measuring achievement via appropriate key performance indicators (KPIs).

All of these approaches were introduced in the Business & Finance and Management Information papers and are summarised here as a reminder.

Remember that a performance measure is only useful if it is given meaning in relation to comparatives such as budgets or targets, trends over time and benchmarks from within or outside the business.

3.2 Measures of financial performance

3.2.1 Measures of growth

An organisation's growth may be expressed in a number of ways, for example:

- Sales revenue (a growth in the number of markets served)
- Market share
- Profitability
- Number of goods/services sold
- Number of outlets/sites
- Number of employees
- Number of countries in which the business operates (sales and/or production)

3.2.2 Measures of profitability

A company should be profitable, and there are obvious checks on profitability.

- Whether the company has made a profit or a loss on its ordinary activities.
- By how much this year's profit or loss is bigger or smaller than last year's profit or loss.

It is probably better to consider separately the profits or losses on exceptional items if there are any. Such gains or losses should not be expected to occur again, unlike profits or losses on normal trading.

Common measures of profitability include **gross profit margin** and **net profit margin** (measured in relation to revenue) and **gross profit mark up** (measured in relation to cost of sales). Profitability can also be measured in terms of return, via the **return on capital employed**.

3.2.3 Measures of liquidity and gearing

These are used to consider the financial health of the business.

The availability of short term cash and working capital can be considered using the **current ratio** and ratios such as **inventory turnover** and **receivable/payable days**.

The longer term financial structure can be assessed by considering **gearing ratio** and **interest cover**.

These measures of performance are covered in more detail in Management Information and Financial Management.

3.3 Economy, efficiency and effectiveness

Organisations need to ensure that the resources they employ are put to optimum use and that they are achieving an effective ratio of outputs to inputs. One way of doing this is to consider the 3 Es:

Economy – is a measure of the actual resources used (inputs) eg cost of labour per employee or the rent per square metre.

Efficiency – is a measure of productivity. It considers the relationship between the goods or services produced (outputs) and the resources used to produce them (inputs) eg output per person or per £ of labour, sales per square metre.

Effectiveness – is a measure of the impact achieved and considers outputs in relation to objectives. It looks at the extent to which the processes used by the business deliver the right results, eg percentage of products delivered without faults, market share.

The 3Es can be used to measure performance of support functions eg when assessing the performance of the IT department, the organisation could consider:

Economy – the total cost of the IT function

Efficiency – the amount spent on IT per user

Effectiveness – the competence of the users (measured for example by a survey or via an online assessment)

The 3Es are often used as an approach for measuring 'Value for Money' (VFM) in the public and not-for-profit sectors.

3.4 Critical success factors and KPIs

Once the business has identified its CSFs, it must set performance standards to be achieved in these areas. This is done by identifying appropriate KPIs. For example if quality is important, the business first needs to ascertain the quality expected by customers and then set appropriate targets which might include the percentage of products returned; the amount spent on warranties etc.

Some examples of KPIs which can be used to measure the effectiveness of different areas of the organisation and which cover both financial and non-financial criteria are outlined below.

Activity	Key performance indicators
Marketing	Sales volume
	Market share
	Gross margins
Production	Capacity utilisation
	Quality standards
Logistics	Capacity utilisation
	Level of service
New product development	Trial rate
	Repurchase rate
Sales programmes	Contribution by region, salesperson
	Controllable margin as percentage of sales
	Number of new accounts
	Travel costs
Advertising programmes	Awareness levels
	Attribute ratings
	Cost levels
Pricing programmes	Price relative to industry average
	Price elasticity of demand
Management information	Timeliness of reports
	Accuracy of information

3.5 Strategic performance measures

Desirable features of strategic performance measures are shown below.

Role of measures	Comment
Focus attention on what matters in the long term	For many organisations this might be shareholder wealth.
Identify and communicate drivers of success	Focus on how the organisation generates shareholder value over the long term.
Support organisational learning	Enable the organisation to improve its performance.
Provide a basis for reward	Rewards should be based on strategic issues not just performance in any one year.

Characteristics of strategic performance measures:

- Measurable
- Meaningful
- Defined by the strategy and relevant to it

- Consistently measured
- Re-evaluated regularly
- Acceptable

4 Divisional performance measurement

Section overview

- Return on Capital Employed and Residual Income are two methods of measuring divisional performance.

4.1 Return on Capital Employed (ROCE)

ROCE is also called Return on Investment (ROI or Return on Net Assets (RONA). This divisional performance target is calculated as:

$$\frac{\text{Pr ofit for the period} \times 100\%}{\text{Average capital employed during the period}}$$

The economic principle behind this measure, developed by Du Pont in the early 1900s, is that the return derived should be in excess of the cost of capital of the firm in order to provide a suitable return to investors.

In practice this measure has achieved popularity because:

- It can **lead to a desired group ROCE** ie if all divisions return a 15% ROCE then, assuming all central costs and assets are charged back to divisions, the group as a whole will make 15%. Improvements in group ROCE can also feed into the EPS of the group and so into the share price.

- It **enables comparisons** to be made between divisions of different sizes for the purposes of identifying where group value is being created or destroyed and also for the identification of high and low performing divisional managers.

- It is **readily understood by management** due to its similarity to an interest rate or other yield on assets.

- It is **cheap to calculate** given that the financial reporting system will be calculating profits and asset values already.

4.2 Residual Income (RI)

This measure was developed in 1950s by GE to avoid a dysfunctional consequence of ROCE/ROI, namely that managers who are evaluated and rewarded against ROCE improvements may choose to forego investments which are actually in the investor's interest.

Worked example: XYZ Corporation 1

XYZ Corporation has a cost of capital of 10% which is the rate that all new investments are expected to achieve as a minimum (the 'hurdle' rate), and so is the minimum benchmark for divisional performance.

Division A presently has profits of £158m on assets of £610m.

A proposed capital investment of £60m will yield net cash flows of £13m pa for the next 10 years after which the asset will be worthless.

Will management of Division A undertake the project?

According to the NPV approach to project appraisal they should

ie £12m for 10 years at 10% = £12 × 6.145 = £73.74m

NPV = (£73.47m – £60m) £13.47m

But the division's present ROI is £158/£610 = 26% whilst the project has an ROI of only £13/£60 = 22%

It will drag the divisional ROI down to (£158 + £13)/(£610 + £60) = 25.5%

The board of XYZ Corporation would not know this valuable project had been foregone. The decision is dysfunctional and so potentially is the use of ROI as a divisional performance measure.

Definition

Residual income is calculated as

Divisional profit – (Net assets of division × required rate)

Worked example: XYZ Corporation 2

Returning to the example of XYZ Corporation above:

Present divisional residual income is:

	£m
Profit	158
Cost of assets (£610 @ 10%)	(61)
Residual income	97
Divisional residual income with new project	
Profit (£158 + £12)	170
Cost of assets (£610 + £60) × 10%	(67)
New residual income	103

Residual income is theoretically superior to ROI for the reasons shown above. However it is not widely used because:

- It is conceptually more complex than a simple percentage yield.

- It doesn't allow easy comparison of divisions of different sizes.

- It requires that a required rate be assessed and this may be different between divisions according to risk.

- It lacks the clear link to the ROCE of the group. Although **in financial theory** the market capitalisation of the firm will be the NPV of all its business units rather than being influenced by one year's ROCE and EPS, the fact remains that, for all its shortcomings, ROCE is still closely monitored by the investment analysts who determine share prices with their buy/sell recommendations.

4.3 Problems of using ROCE/RI

Problems of both ROCE/ROI and RI in the evaluation and control of business divisions are:

- **Short-termist**: Being based on annual profit figures both disregard the future earnings of the division. Using BCG terminology from Chapter 6, a cash cow might present a high ROI and a star a low one which would be a misleading guide their true financial value if assessed as the NPV of future earnings.

- **Discourage investment in assets**: To boost ROI or RI assets with low book values will be used in preference to new assets. This could reduce the prestige of the organisation (eg shabby fittings) or lead to risk (eg leaking vessels). It may also lead to inappropriate outsourcing to avoid having the assets required to provide the service on the division's balance sheet.

- **Lack of strategic control**: Unless the corporation is acting merely as a super financial controller (eg as defined by Goold and Campbell) it will wish to co-ordinate and integrate operations of its divisions to gain group synergies. Financial control measures alone cannot do this.

Interactive question 1: ROI
[Difficulty level: Easy]

An asset costs £100,000, has a life of four years, and no scrap value. It generates annual cash flows of £34,000. Depreciation is calculated on the straight-line basis.

Requirements

(i)   Calculate annual ROI using opening carrying amount.
(ii) Calculate annual ROI using historic cost.
(iii) Comment on any problems identified by these calculations.

See **Answer** at the end of this chapter.

Interactive question 2: Asset disposal
[Difficulty level: Easy]

A manager has the following data.

	Year 1	Year 2	Year 3	Year 4
Profit	20	15	10	5
Historic cost	100	100	100	100
ROI	20%	15%	10%	5%

Manager's target ROI = 12% per annum.

Requirements

When would the manager dispose of the asset and what problem might this cause?

See **Answer** at the end of this chapter.

Interactive question 3: ROI or RI?
[Difficulty level: Easy]

A division manager has the following data.

Target ROI	20%
Divisional profit	£300,000
Capital employed	£1m

Requirements

Would the division manager accept a project requiring capital of £100,000 and generating profits of £25,000, if the manager were paid a bonus based on ROI?

Would the decision change if the manager's pay were based on RI?

See **Answer** at the end of this chapter.

Interactive question 4: Comparing divisions

[Difficulty level: Easy]

A company has two divisions.

Target ROI = 20%

	Division 1	Division 2
Capital	£1m	£100k
Profits		
Year 1	£200k	£20k
Year 2	£220k	£40k

Requirements

Which division is performing better

(a)   Using RI?
(b)   Using ROI?

See **Answer** at the end of this chapter.

4.4   Other considerations in divisional assessment

When assessing divisional performance, the following issues must also be considered:

- The division manager should only be held accountable for factors within his/her control. The divisional profit figure may be distorted by arbitrarily allocated Head office costs and thus performance measurement should focus on traceable profit.

- Where there is inter-divisional trade, careful consideration should be given to any transfer pricing mechanism in place, which may under or over-state the profits of a particular division.

- Divisions operating in different marketplaces and facing differing levels of competition cannot be expected to produce similar returns. Thus in addition to comparing one division against another, external comparisons should be made via benchmarking, eg to industry leader.

- Wider strategic issues need to be taken into account such as any interdependence between divisions eg shared distribution systems, shared customers, the impact that a division has on the portfolio of the business and its brand.

- In assessing the future strategic direction of the business it is not just the historic performance of the division but also its future potential that is relevant.

- Focus on a narrow set of financial measures is unlikely to give a true picture of performance (see section 5 below).

5   Balanced scorecard

Section overview

An approach that tries to integrate the different measures of performance is the balanced scorecard, where key linkages between operating and financial performance are brought to light. This offers four perspectives:

- Financial
- Customer
- Innovation and learning
- Internal business processes

5.1 Financial measures of performance

There are a number of limitations where management rely solely on financial performance measures.

- **Encourages short-termist behaviour**: Focusing on hitting monthly, quarterly and annual targets may be inconsistent with longer term strategic business development.

- **Ignores strategic goals**: Financial control cannot enable senior management to affect other important determinants of commercial success such as customer service and innovation.

- **Cannot control persons without budget responsibility**: Operative and other staff cannot be controlled by financial targets if they have no responsibility for financial results.

- **Historic measures**: Financial measures of performance are essentially **lagging indicators** of competitive success ie they turn down after competitive battles have been lost. Management needs **lead indicators** of where problems are occurring to avoid losing such battles.

- **Distorted**: Financial measures can be distorted by creative accounting. Also some of the conventions of financial reporting mean that internal financial control measures are of limited value for decision-making, eg lack of valuation of intangibles such as brands, failure to value inventory and transactions at opportunity cost and so on.

In section 4, we discussed divisional performance measures. The research of Goold and Campbell revealed the practice by the boards of divisionalised firms to utilise a **strategic control style** that combined financial and non-financial performance measures.

5.2 The origins of the balanced scorecard

Kaplan and Norton's **balanced scorecard** was developed in the early 1990s following research into performance measures in high-performing US firms, notably in the IT industries of Silicon Valley, Northern California.

According to their research these firms conducted regular assessments of **four different perspectives**, as follows.

Perspective	Question	Explanation
Customer	What do existing and new customers value from us?	Gives rise to targets that matter to customers: cost, quality, delivery, inspection, handling and so on.
Internal business	What processes must we excel at to achieve our financial and customer objectives?	Aims to improve internal processes and decision making.
Innovation and learning	Can we continue to improve and create future value?	Considers the business's capacity to maintain its competitive position through the acquisition of new skills and the development of new products.
Financial	How do we create value for our shareholders?	Covers traditional measures such as growth, profitability and shareholder value but set through talking to the shareholder or shareholders direct.

Performance targets are set once the key areas for improvement have been identified, and the balanced scorecard is the **main monthly report**.

Kaplan and Norton claimed that the scorecard is **balanced** in the sense that managers are required to think in terms of all four perspectives, to **prevent improvements being made in one area at the expense of another**.

A decade later and the BSC was being proposed as more than a performance measurement system. In *The Strategy Focused Organization* Kaplan and Norton state that the setting of performance measures in the four areas can drive strategic change (a topic returned to in Chapter 15).

5.3   Developing a balanced scorecard

Kaplan (*Advanced Management Accounting*) offers the following 'core outcome measures'.

Perspective	Core outcome measure
Financial	Return on Investment Profitability Revenue growth/revenue mix Cost reduction Cash flow
Customer	Market share Customer acquisition Customer retention Customer profitability Customer satisfaction On-time delivery
Innovation and learning	Employee satisfaction Employee retention Employee productivity Revenue per employee % of revenue from new services Time taken to develop new products
Internal business	Quality and rework rates Cycle time/production rate Capacity utilisation

Kaplan and Norton suggest the following process for setting the BSC.

1.   Senior executives decide strategy.

2.   Budgets and information systems are linked to the measures in the BSC. This allows divisional and operational management to monitor the performance of their areas of responsibility.

3.   Personal scorecards are developed and, through performance management (described in Chapter 13) become the basis for staff development and incentive payments.

4.   Collaborative working occurs as many targets require team work to achieve.

5.   Therefore strategy is 'operationalised' through being turned into day-to-day operations.

Kaplan and Norton recognise that the four perspectives they suggest may not be perfect for all organisations: it may be necessary, for example, to add further perspectives related to the environment or to employment.

A balanced scorecard for a computer manufacturing company

PERFORMANCE EVALUATION

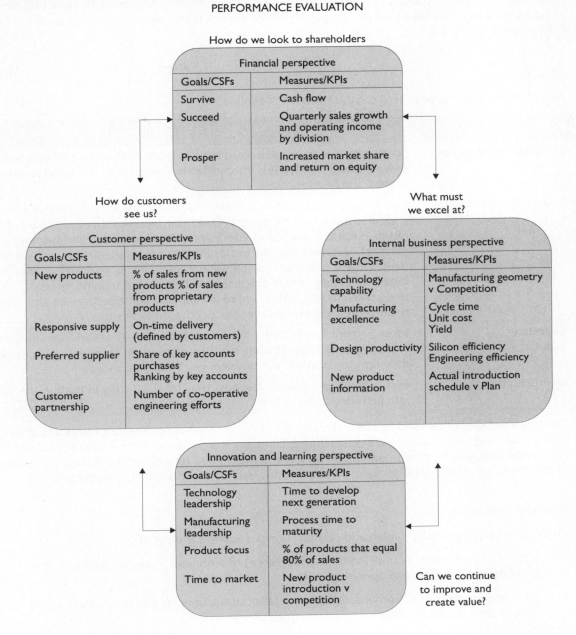

5.4 The vertical vector

Kaplan and Norton's original perspectives may be viewed as hierarchical in nature, with a **vertical vector** running through the measures adopted.

Perspective	Measures
Financial	ROCE
Customer	Relationships and loyalty
Internal business	Quality, efficiency and timeliness
Innovation and learning	Skills and processes

The balanced scorecard only measures performance. It does not indicate that the strategy is the right one. 'A failure to convert improved operational performance into improved financial performance should send executives back to their drawing boards to rethink the company's strategy or its implementation plans.'

5.5 Problems

As with all techniques, problems can arise when it is applied.

Problem	Explanation
Conflicting measures	Some measures in the scorecard such as research funding and cost reduction may naturally conflict. It is often difficult to determine the balance which will achieve the best results.
Selecting measures	Not only do appropriate measures have to be devised but the number of measures used must be agreed. Care must be taken that the impact of the results is not lost in a sea of information. The innovation and learning perspective is, perhaps, the most difficult to measure directly, since much development of human capital will not feed directly into such crude measures as rate of new product launches or even training hours undertaken. It will, rather, improve economy and effectiveness and support the achievement of customer perspective measures.
Expertise	Measurement is only useful if it initiates appropriate action. Non-financial managers may have difficulty with the usual profit measures. With more measures to consider, this problem will be compounded.
Interpretation	Even a financially-trained manager may have difficulty in putting the figures into an overall perspective.

The scorecard should be used **flexibly**. The process of deciding **what to measure** forces a business to clarify its strategy. For example, a manufacturing company may find that 50% – 60% of costs are represented by bought-in components, so measurements relating to suppliers could usefully be added to the scorecard. These could include payment terms, lead times, or quality considerations.

Worked example: Oil company's use of balanced scorecard

An oil company (quoted by Kaplan and Norton, *Harvard Business Review*) ties:

- 60% of its executives' bonuses to their achievement of ambitious financial targets on ROI, profitability, cash flow and operating costs.

- 40% on indicators of customer satisfaction, retailer satisfaction, employee satisfaction and environmental responsibility.

5.6 Using the balanced scorecard

- Like all performance measurement schemes, the balanced scorecard can influence behaviour among managers to conform to that required by the strategy. Because of its comprehensive nature, it can be used as a wide-ranging driver of organisational change.

- The scorecard emphasises **processes** rather than **departments**. It can support a competence-based approach to strategy, but this can be confusing for managers and may make it difficult to gain their support.

- Deciding just what to measure can be particularly difficult, especially since the scorecard **vertical vector** lays emphasis on customer reaction. This is not to discount the importance of meeting customer expectations, purely to emphasise the difficulty of establishing what they are.

The scorecard can be used both by profit and not-for-profit organisations because it acknowledges the fact that both financial and non-financial performance indicators are important in achieving strategic objectives.

5.7 Developments in the balanced scorecard

The original balanced scorecard of Kaplan and Norton was initially developed as a measurement and control tool for managers. Essentially, its focus was 'strategic control' rather than 'management control'. It has, however, been developed over time in terms of both its design and application.

The **second generation** balanced scorecard attempted to develop further the guidance on how the measures should be selected (filtered) and linked to the overall objectives of the organisation. It also began to look at more complex linkages and causality between the perspectives (sometimes called a 'strategic linkage model'). As a consequence, the balanced scorecard evolved from an improved measurement system to a core management system.

More recently, what has been termed a **third generation** balanced scorecard, has been developed. This involves enhancing the links between the balanced scorecard and the strategic objectives to be achieved within a given timeframe. This has been reflected in a 'destination statement' which sets out in some detail what the organisation is trying to achieve. Its purpose is to check the extent to which the objectives, targets and measures chosen, have been attained after a given period of time. It has also supported the development of multiple balanced scorecards in complex organisations.

6 Measuring performance in NFP organisations

Section overview

- Measuring the performance of NFPs can be challenging.

- Traditional financial measures of performance may not apply and outcomes and outputs may be harder to measure or quantify.

Measuring the performance of NFPs can be more challenging because they tend to have a more diverse set of stakeholders and therefore a wider set of objectives. Also the traditional financial measures of performance may not apply in the absence of a meaningful bottom-line profit figure. Thus the outcomes or outputs may be harder to measure or quantify.

If we consider a school for example, performance at a very basic level could be measured by considering the pass rates in external examinations.

However if the school is felt to have a wider role, eg in developing non-academic talents, or in preparing children for independent lives, then progress towards these objectives also need to be measured.

Since many NFP organisations have to deal with limited resources, the concept of 3Es is particularly relevant.

7 The data analysis element of the exam

Section overview

- At least one of the questions in the exam will include data analysis.

- These questions may include financial data or alternatively they may include some management data which may require analysis and some supporting argument or judgement to comment on the situation.

- The key issue is that the data analysis should be linked to the scenario and the strategy.

- This section looks at the types of requirement you may have to deal with, the key skills you need to develop and the mistakes to avoid in order to be successful.

7.1 What does data analysis involve?

A key requirement in the Business Strategy exam is to be able to interpret financial and other data provided in the question (such as non-financial performance indicators) and relate it to the business's strategy, its environment and others factors that may have influenced the scenario.

Typically this analysis may cover:

- The financial position of the business eg basic groups of key financial ratios (profitability/liquidity/gearing)

- The performance of the business – financial and non-financial (eg KPIs/balanced scorecard)

- The use of resources – economy, efficiency, effectiveness

- Product/market positioning eg market growth/share/BCG/ life cycle

- Risk eg break-even calculations, best and worst case scenarios, sensitivity analysis, expected values

- The financial impact of a new project or strategy eg analysing the effect by considering incremental contribution

- Evaluating the overall impact of a strategy in both financial and non-financial terms

- Operational and resource data over time (eg units of output, number of branches, floorspace, number of employees)

- Forecasts and budgets – forward looking data which, for example, may reflect the expected impact of a strategy or be used to monitor a strategy after implementation.

7.2 Data analysis skills required

The examiners are looking for you to demonstrate the following skills:

- Choosing analytical tools that are appropriate in the context of the question eg financial ratios, KPIs, BCG analysis, break-even calculations

- Carrying out the relevant calculations

- Interpreting the resulting information to demonstrate an understanding of the story behind the numbers and communicating that analysis succinctly

- Exercising judgement to draw conclusions and/or produce sensible recommendations

- Looking beyond the information provided at what additional information may be useful to generate a better analysis/understanding and at any reservations regarding the data/techniques/assumptions applied

- Linking different pieces of data to explain trends or outcomes

- Highlighting weaknesses or omissions in the data provided

- Analysing cause and effect relationships – eg identifying underlying causes of changes in the data

7.3 Key weaknesses in candidate scripts

The following list highlights the weaknesses most commonly identified in exam answers and suggests ways to address these:

1. Restating facts or numbers without applying them to the context of the question. A common failing is to explain **what** has happened rather than **why**, eg stating that sales have grown by 15% in the period but not indicating why they have done so.

    Solution: Use the '**because rule**' to add value.

    In most cases a good answer passes the 'because' test, eg 'Market share has fallen from 35% to 29% **because** of the entry of a new lower-cost competitor.'

    Including the word 'because' in your answer changes the 'what' into a 'why'.

The 'why' should be related to specific information in the scenario, demonstrating that you have understood the relationship between the financial/quantitative information and the business issues.

2. Failure to use the additional information from the scenario in formulating answers resulting in generic answers that could apply to any company rather than the one in question.

    Solution: Make specific points, focusing on the particular organisation and relating to the circumstances in the scenario.

    Eg 'falling R&D expenditure may be a problem for XYZ Ltd because it has built market share on the basis of innovative products.'

3. Interpreting figures/results in isolation

    Solution: Link the figures/analysis, eg if market share has increased but gross margins have decreased, the company may have made a decision to reduce the selling price as part of a market penetration strategy.

    Eg a company is considering outsourcing production as a result of rising raw material prices. This might be expected to lead to a decrease in gross margin if the company is unable to pass on the price increase to customers or a loss in sales/market share if, as a result of passing on the price increase, the company's product is no longer competitive. Outsourcing may also lead to a reduction in fixed costs and hence lower operating gearing (risk), but this would depend on the nature of the outsourcing contract.

4. Focusing on a narrow range of measures

    Financial measures alone will not provide the full picture and are often the result of other factors, not the cause.

    Solution: In addressing performance issues your answer should, where possible, address a variety of performance indicators. Consider using the balanced scorecard headings to help you cover a wider range of measures. Remember that these measures will often help you understand what is causing the strategy to succeed or fail.

5. Failure to use numerical analysis elsewhere to support your answer

    Often the data analysis element is one of the first requirements. Conclusions that you draw from this will help in answering later parts of the question.

    Solution: Consider where else in your answer the analysis may be relevant/how you can 'make the numbers talk'.

    Eg if you have been asked in another requirement to assess the suitability/feasibility/acceptability of a strategy being considered, you can refer to earlier calculations of profitability and other measures in your assessment of returns and/or break-even calculations when looking at risk.

    Eg if the data analysis shows that the business is currently loss making and that sales and profitability are forecast to decline further, then the business cannot afford to do nothing. Any new strategy that is expected to address this decline or increase returns should be acceptable to the shareholders.

6. Failure to explain trends in the data by identifying **cause and effect relationships**. This may, for example, include analysing information into ratios or percentages based on the data provided.

    Eg where sales revenues are growing by (say) 10% per year but the number of branches/outlets is growing by 15% per year then calculating the sales per branch/outlet will show that sales per branch are, on average, falling. Growth in overall sales revenue may therefore be due to greater investment (ie more outlets) rather than generic growth in sales per branch because of improved efficiency or stronger market conditions

    Eg an alternative analysis of sales revenue growth might be in relation to volume growth, changes in selling prices and changes in sales mix. Analysis of this data may reveal the relative causes (quantitatively) of sales revenue growth from each of these underlying factors.

7. Failure to get a **reasonable balance** between numerical analysis and descriptive analysis. Some weak answers are almost entirely descriptive, while other weak answers go to the opposite extreme, producing reasonable numbers but descriptive analysis that is little more than briefly stating which numbers have gone up and which have gone down.

Solution: Both numerical and descriptive analysis are important and need due emphasis. Two approaches by candidates in this respect are:

(1) To set out a comprehensive numerical analysis at the beginning of the answer with workings (eg in a table) then produce the descriptive interpretation of these numbers; or

(2) To mix the numerical analysis with the descriptive analysis by producing calculations as each issue arises.

In general approach (1) tends to produce better answers with a more systematic evaluation of the issues. Specifically, with approach (1) the numerical analysis tends to be more comprehensive and better thought out with clearer workings.

7.4 Additional information required

The examiner may ask you to highlight any additional information that might be necessary for a more meaningful analysis and on occasion you may be required to specify possible data sources. Even if this is not part of the requirement, a comment about the limitations of your analysis and any additional information required will demonstrate higher skills. It is important however that requests for additional data are realistic, relevant and obtainable.

- Information in the scenario is likely to be in the form of a summary.

  More detailed information may be required, eg a breakdown by product, country, business unit. If you have been provided with historic information for analysis purposes, eg at five-yearly intervals, data for the years in between would help assess the trend more accurately. If average figures have been given, then actual prices/volumes/data would be necessary to properly identify which products/business units are under-/over-performing for instance.

- The source of information can be both external as well as internal.

  In order to properly interpret performance it is necessary to make comparisons. Comparisons may be made between:

  - Current results and past results/budgets
  - One business unit and another
  - Industry/sector information
  - Market leader/other competitors

  Thus any data obtainable on the industry and competitors will help benchmark the performance of the business.

- Set out any assumptions made and explain any limitations of these.

  In order to carry out break-even analysis for example you will have to make certain assumptions about the split of costs between fixed and variable, and about the sales price and costs remaining constant.

8 Developing an approach to data analysis questions

Section overview

- In order to help you develop an approach and a range of skills for exam questions, this section leads you through a sample question 'The Legume'. The intention is to demonstrate the thought processes to be adopted when tackling such a question and the attributes of an answer that will score well in the exam.

- Once you have worked through this section, you should attempt the question Waltex at the end of this chapter.

- You will find further examples of data analysis questions in each of the past exam papers contained in the Business Strategy revision question bank.

8.1 Recommended approach to data analysis

The following is a suggestion for the approach to adopt when tackling questions:

Step 1: Initial review (of scenario and requirements)

Step 2: Decide on appropriate analysis to undertake

Step 3: Produce the necessary calculations (to form the appendix)

Step 4: Interpret your analysis

Step 5: Identify additional information required

8.1.1 What-How-Why-When-SoWhat analysis

The parts that cause most problems are Steps 3 and 4. It is difficult to produce a universal approach but one tool which draws together many of the issues already noted above is: **What-How-Why-When-SoWhat analysis** (WHWWsW), which includes both numerical and descriptive elements.

- **What** – looks at WHAT has happened overall (eg revenue has increased by 10.5%).

- **How** – attempts to analyse the available data in more detail to obtain a better understanding of HOW the WHAT element occurred (eg sales prices have risen by 10% and monthly sales volumes have risen by 10% following the price change).

- **Why** – looks for the underlying causes of the HOW element, which may be part of the story or strategy provided in the question (eg there have been significant product improvements introduced during the year with additional features compared to competitors which has enabled a higher price to be charged but also an increase in demand despite this increased price).

- **When** – in assessing the impact of changes in strategy over time or in making comparisons it is important to know WHEN changes occurred. Thus, for example, in assessing the impact of a price change it is important to know when during the year the price change took place. If the price change occurred, for example, half way through the year, then the impact on the current year may be reduced, but may be more significant on next year's trading. For example, using the above numbers if the change in the product, the price and the sales volumes only occurred half way through the year it would only impact on two of the four quarters resulting in a sales revenue increase of only 10.5%, rather than the 21% that might be expected for a full year.

- **SoWhat** – the above steps analyse and interpret the nature of the data provided and attempt to identify and explain the underlying causes of any changes in the data. This step goes to the next stage by attempting to ask the question 'SO WHAT are the consequences of our analysis for deciding on the future business strategy'? (Eg what are the consequences for profit of the 10% increases in sales price and sales volume after considering the variable cost increases arising from the product improvements and volume increases? How have competitors responded with price changes and improvements in their own products which may make the consequences next year different from those which occurred this year?)

Worked example: Snowdon Ltd

This is an example with a very simplified application of WHWWsW analysis.

Snowdon Ltd is the sole UK importer of a branded cast iron cooker. In order to penetrate the market it reduced its selling prices by 5% on 30 June 20X5. There have been no changes in total fixed costs or variable costs per unit. Prior to the change in price, monthly demand had been constant for some time. The Snowdon board is attempting to assess the impact of this change in strategy for the year ended 31 December 20X5 and provides the following data:

	20X5 £'000	20X4 £'000
Sales	21,400	20,000
Cost of sales	(11,000)	(10,000)
Gross profit	10,400	10,000

Requirement

Analyse the change in performance of Snowdon in 20X5.

Solution

What: gross profit has increased by £400,000 in absolute terms, but gross margins have fallen from 50% in 20X4 to (10,400/21,400) = 48.6% in 20X5.

How: sales revenues have risen by 7%. This includes a 5% price reduction so there must have been a significant increase in sales volumes to compensate and cause an overall increase in sales revenue. Note: there is only one product, so sales mix is not a factor in explaining HOW the change occurred. Also, see the WHEN question below, as the price change only occurred halfway through the year.

Why: sales prices have been reduced in order to sell greater volumes to pursue a strategy of penetrating the market.

When: as the price change only occurred half way through the year the impact is restricted to this period. Given we are told that the first half the year was similar to 20X4 we could do some analysis to isolate the second half effect in 20X5. If we take the first half of 20X5 as similar to half of 20X4 and strip this out we obtain the following:

	Actual full year 20X5 (A)	Half of 20X4 (ie first half of 20X5) (B)	Imputed second half 20X5 (A) – (B)
	£'000	£'000	£'000
Sales	21,400	10,000	11,400
Cost of sales	11,000	5,000	6,000
Gross profit	10,400	5,000	5,400

This table enables us to compare the two half years of 20X5. This shows that sales revenues have risen by 14% from £10m for six months to £11.4m. Given prices have fallen by 5% this implies that sales volumes have risen by 20% (ie 1.14/0.95 = 1.2). This 20% is consistent with the increase in cost of sales. (Note: this is because Snowdon is a retailer and hence cost of sales are variable costs. If Snowdon had been a manufacturer then cost of sales would not increase in a linear relationship with output as there would an element of fixed costs.)

SoWhat: More information is needed to assess the impact of this strategy in the longer term (eg market share). The response of competitors needs to be assessed. Snowdon's price reduction may not have been immediately followed but if the company is taking market share then competitors may decrease prices after a delay. In extrapolating the consequences of the price change forward care therefore needs to taken in allowing for different market conditions. Also price penetration is a temporary policy, but if competitors follow the price decrease of Snowdon it may be more difficult to increase them in future.

Summary

It is too early to judge the new strategy yet but in terms of short term financial performance there appears to have been a benefit in higher absolute profit despite the fall in percentage margin.

Note however that any tool needs to be used flexibly. In this case the HOW and WHEN questions could have been dealt with jointly.

The following is a longer question with more detailed analysis and shows that an understanding of the issues is needed and that any tool needs to be applied to purpose. It should not dominate thought and application to the scenario.

Worked example: The Legume

The business profile

'The Legume' is a prize-winning vegetarian restaurant located near the centre of Barchester, a cathedral city with a population of 100,000.

The restaurant was opened in January 20X0 by its proprietors, John and Eleanor Bold, who share responsibility for preparing the food and managing the restaurant. The staff comprises a full time chef, a kitchen assistant, four full-time and two part-time waiting staff.

'The Legume' seats 60 customers and is open six days a week, both at lunchtimes and in the evenings. It is licensed to sell alcohol and has established a reputation for having good wines.

Business is traditionally best at weekends, but activity is seasonal. Sales are above average in the four weeks in the year when there are meetings at the local racecourse, and the restaurant is equally busy before Christmas and during the summer tourist season.

The history of the business

John Bold commenced the business after investing £50,000 that he had inherited from his parents. Located on the ground floor of a Georgian building near the cathedral close, the restaurant attracted customers from among the many tourists visiting the city, but in addition its clientele included a small core of regular customers, local business people and shoppers.

Up until 20X5 the business was doing well, turning in good profits. However in 20X6 there was a 20% decline in the number of overseas tourists visiting Barchester as a result of a strong UK pound. In addition the local economy suffered when one of the city's largest employers decided to move its production overseas and was forced to lay off sizeable numbers of staff.

Although there was some revival in the number of overseas tourists visiting Barchester in 20X7, this coincided with a gradual erosion of the popularity of 'The Legume' amongst its local clientele. This was largely because rival restaurants and pubs had begun to include vegetarian dishes on their menus, but also because a new and inferior chef had been appointed, the decor was becoming rather faded, and the novelty value of the restaurant had worn off. Another factor, however, was the closure of the city's two cinemas, which were replaced by two multi-screen complexes sited in new out-of-town shopping centres.

As a result, there was a further sharp fall in trade in 20X7, forcing John Bold to turn to the bank for increased funding in the form of an increased overdraft facility. Initially support was forthcoming, since it was widely assumed that the setback would be temporary, and the bank took a second mortgage on the Bold's home as security. However, results in 20X8 were only slightly better and the Bolds were forced to cut their drawings significantly to keep the overdraft within reason.

Extracts from the management accounts for 'The Legume' restaurant over the last four years:

	20X5 £	20X6 £	20X7 £	20X8 £
Sales				
Food	170,000	149,750	155,400	154,000
Drink	85,000	74,875	81,400	87,500
Total	255,000	224,625	236,800	241,500
Cost of sales				
Food	68,000	59,900	62,160	61,600
Drink	42,500	35,940	36,630	35,000
Total	110,500	95,840	98,790	96,600
Gross profit				
Food	102,000	89,850	93,240	92,400
Drink	42,500	38,935	44,770	52,500
Total	144,500	128,785	138,010	144,900
Other costs				
Wages	74,000	71,000	74,000	76,000
Rent	14,000	15,000	15,000	15,000
Depreciation	3,000	3,000	3,000	3,000
Interest	0	3,000	4,000	2,000
Other expenses	17,000	22,000	20,000	24,000
Total	108,000	114,000	116,000	120,000
Net profit	36,500	14,785	22,010	24,900

	20X5 £	20X6 £	20X7 £	20X8 £
Average spend per customer				
Food	£10	£10	£10.50	£11
Drink	£5	£5	£5.50	£6.25
	£'000	£'000	£'000	£'000
Non-current assets at NBV	21	18	15	12
Bank overdraft	1	14	18	10
Drawings	33	30	25	20

The Bolds' dilemma

Somewhat belatedly the Bolds have begun thinking about how they might turn the business round. John Bold has been considering various options, each of which would be feasible under the existing 25-year rental agreement for the premises and under the current licensing arrangements:

Options

1. The restaurant could be converted into a wine bar serving hot and cold vegetarian and fish dishes. This might attract a younger clientele which at present largely patronises the local pubs and fast food restaurants.

2. By redesigning the layout a fast food, but vegetarian, menu could be offered at lunchtimes, while in the evenings the restaurant could revert to its more traditional role. However, in order to try to increase the volume of trade, prices would be cut and further discounts offered for regular customers, those eating midweek, and those starting their meals before 7pm.

As part of the reorganisation, the restaurant would have to be redecorated and new kitchen equipment installed. Option 1 would make it possible to dispense with full-time waiting staff and – apart from the chef – only employ part-time staff. Likewise, Option 2 would make it possible to dispense with one of the full-time waiting staff and instead employ two part-timers at lunch times.

The Bolds estimate that their pre-tax joint income in alternative employment would total £35,000 a year.

Any additional finance requirement would be provided by a loan from Eleanor Bold's family.

Requirements

You are a business consultant. The Bolds have asked for your help in assessing the current situation and deciding on a new strategic direction for The Legume:

(i)   Using the data and other information provided, explain how the business has performed since 20X5;

(ii) State what additional information would be useful to provide a more detailed assessment of performance; and

(iii) Evaluate the risk and potential rewards associated with the strategic options being considered.

Solution

Step 1: Initial review

Read the requirements and then read through the question. As you read, you should be thinking about:

*   Context
*   Requirements
*   Key issues
*   Purpose of analysis
*   Additional information

Context

You have been employed as a business consultant by the owner managers of the restaurant.

Requirements

Part (i) requires an analysis of performance since 20X5. The phrase 'using the data and other information provided' indicates the need to include both quantitative analysis and information drawn out of the scenario (see key issues) in formulating your answer.

In part (ii) you are required to state additional information that might be useful to you. Jot down anything that comes to mind as you read through the scenario.

Part (iii) asks for an evaluation of the strategic options being considered under the heading of risks and rewards. This evaluation will need to be undertaken in the light of your answer to (i). Thus if your performance analysis identifies issues such as a lack of sales volume or high fixed costs then it will be important to evaluate whether the options address this.

Key issues

- As a prize-winning vegetarian restaurant The Legume appears to be operating a focused differentiation strategy.

- Whilst initially profitable it now appears to lack competitive advantage (inferior chef, faded décor, other competitors offer vegetarian food etc).

- The business is highly seasonal and also very dependent on the state of the economy and the level of tourist trade.

- The high level of fixed costs, combined with falling sales volumes, have led to deteriorating profitability.

- The two key stakeholders could earn more elsewhere (£35k) than they are currently earning from the business. Also their home is at risk as a result of the bank taking a second mortgage.

- A new strategy is urgently needed for the business to survive.

- As a small business, sources of finance are presumably limited and if Eleanor's family are unable/unwilling to provide the necessary funds, the bank will need convincing of the Bolds' ability to turn the business round.

Purpose of analysis

Here we are told in the scenario, and we can see clearly from the accounts extracts, that in terms of profitability, the business performance has deteriorated since 20X5. The analysis should seek to address the underlying reasons for the decline and identify areas that need to be addressed by the new strategic proposals.

Additional information

The information provided is mainly financial, in the form of an income statement and a few highlights from the statement of financial position. We also have figures for average spend by customer.

There is little by way of non-financial performance indicators and no external information on competitors/the market sector.

Step 2: Decide on appropriate analysis to undertake

Much of the WHAT analysis is already provided in the question but in answering the HOW question and in deciding on what analysis to undertake and which calculations to perform it is important to consider the following:

- How does the analysis help to identify the issues the company is facing?
- How does the analysis demonstrate an understanding of the scenario?

If we look at the information from the income statement extract, the following analysis should help to confirm the reasons behind the declining performance:

- Sales mix
- Sales volumes (using the information on average customer spend)
- Sales growth
- Margins
- Operating gearing (level of variable costs in relation to fixed costs)

We might also want to analyse the other financial information provided:

- Non-current assets
- Drawings
- Bank overdraft

Finally there is sufficient information to undertake a break-even analysis, which would help to quantify the risk of the business becoming loss making. Operating gearing is also a good measure of risk; if a high proportion of total costs are fixed, any reduction in activity takes the business closer and closer to being loss-making.

Step 3: Produce the necessary calculations

This will form the appendix to your answer.

Appendix 1:

	20X5 %	20X6 %	20X7 %	20X8 %
Sales mix				
Food	66.7	66.7	65.6	63.8
Drink	33.3	33.3	34.4	36.2
Sales growth				
Food	n/a	-11.9	+3.8	-0.9
Drink	n/a	-11.9	+8.7	+7.4
Total	n/a	-11.9	+5.4	+2.0
Gross profit margin				
Food	60	60	60	60
Drink	50	52	55	60
Total	56.9	57.5	58.4	60.0
% Increase in fixed costs	n/a	5.6	1.8	3.4
Net profit margin	14.3	6.6	9.3	10.3
Operating gearing %	49.4	54.3	54.0	55.4
Other analysis				
No. of customers served (Sales/average spend)	17,000	14,975	14,800	14,000
Reduction in customers		11.9%	11.7%	5.4%
Average contribution per customer (GP/no of customers)	£8.50	£8.60	£9.33	£10.35
Breakeven number of customers (Other costs/average contribution)	12,706	13,256	12,440	11,594

Step 4: Interpretation

In conducting the WHY analysis it is important to look at the reasons behind the performance. Here are a number of areas that you might find it useful to consider:

- Trend in revenue – mix/volume/price. How achieved if rising /cause if falling?

- Pattern of costs against revenue – rising or falling; are they fixed or variable?

- Is the business seasonal? Does this place a strain on cash flow or lead to periods of under-capacity and a lack of recovery of fixed overheads?

- What is the level of operating gearing? Is this an issue for the business, eg because of the seasonality of sales or in view of falling demand?

- Is the level of profit satisfactory/stable/increasing/decreasing?

- Is the company earning an appropriate return for its stakeholders? Is it paying this out in the form of dividends?

- What is the organisation's long-term finance strategy and is it appropriate for the business?

- What are the strategic implications of the level of investment in R&D/HR and training, marketing and non-current assets? Is this consistent with the organisation's generic strategy, eg if a company is following a differentiation strategy it is likely to need to invest in at least some of these areas.

Interpreting the analysis from Step 3

This will form the text of your answer to requirement (i).

Sales growth/volumes

Sales growth figures indicate that sales have fallen by almost 12% between 20X5 and 20X6 and then risen by 5% and 2% respectively in the following two years. It is important to recognise that these movements could be the result of a price or volume change or a combination of the two.

Here we can use the figures provided on average spend per customer to deduce that the drop in revenue between 20X5 and X6 must be due to a loss of customers, because the average spend in the period remained constant.

In fact we can go a step further and calculate the number of customers served in the year, which allows us to see that the number of people served fell from 17,000 to 14,975. This is consistent with the information in the scenario which explains that there was a 20% decline in the number of overseas tourists visiting Barchester as a result of a strong UK pound. In addition the redundancies at the large local company are likely to have had an impact on the volume of local business.

The growth in sales in the following two years came at a time when the number of customers continued to fall. Although the volume of tourists increased, The Legume is unlikely to have benefited because of a loss of its competitive edge/differentiating factors (faded décor/inferior chef etc). It will also have suffered as a result of the reduction in customers due to the new out-of-town cinemas. Thus the overall increase in revenue in this period must be down to an increase in the average spend per customer.

Pricing and margins

Average food spend per customer, which was constant in 20X5 and 20X6, increased by approx 5% pa in each of 20X7 and 20X8. This could be because customers were buying more eg having a starter or dessert in addition to a main course, or it could be that the Legume is now charging more for the same food. If this has led to The Legume charging more than other restaurants in the town it could explain some of the loss of business.

Food margins have remained constant at 60%, which could be a result of good control of purchasing/wastage etc. Alternatively it may be that The Legume's pricing policy is to charge a fixed mark up on costs incurred.

The average spend on drinks has followed a similar trend although the increases have been higher at 10% and 14% respectively. Again this could be that the price of the drinks has increased or that, attracted by the reputation of The Legume's wines, customers are buying higher quality bottles of wine.

The margins on drinks have increased from 50 to 60% over the period. This may be because the more expensive wines can be sold at higher margins or might reflect better purchasing policies which have led to reduced costs.

The sales mix appears to have remained relatively constant over the period, with a marginal increase in the significance of drinks sales (33% in 20X5, increasing to 36% in 20X8).

In 20X8 the margins on both products were the same at 60% so the sales mix is irrelevant to profitability. However if the trend for increasing margins in the drinks side of the business continues, then increasing the sales mix in favour of drinks will have a positive effect on profits.

Other costs

The fixed costs have been increasing both in total and as a proportion of the total cost base.

This means the business has high and increasing operating gearing (moved from 49.4% fixed costs in 20X5 to 55.4% in 20X8) and as a result has profits that are more risky.

The restaurant is open twice a day, six days a week, and can seat 60 people.

Hence the maximum number of people eating per week is 720 which, assuming it is open 50 weeks of the year, amounts to a total potential volume of 36,000 customers pa.

Clearly with 14,000 customers in 20X8 it is operating significantly below capacity but despite the downturn in business, the restaurant is unable to reduce its cost base significantly, since it only has two part-time staff.

There are other clues in the question that operating gearing might be an issue:

- The seasonality of trade

- The new suggestions for reducing the number of full-time staff and increasing the level of part-timers, thus attempting to make the cost base more flexible. (Note: in other questions companies may be attempting to do this by outsourcing either production or services.)

Investment in the business/returns to the owners

The question states that the Bolds could together earn £35k pa in alternative employment.

The profits of the business in all but 20X5 have been considerably less than this, forcing the owners to overdraw in both 20X6 and 20X7, presumably in order to maintain their personal lifestyle. The total drawings taken over the four year period amount to £108k which exceed the £98,195 profits made.

Thus none of the profits have been reinvested in the business and after the initial £50k investment it does not appear that the Bolds have provided any further capital. This may explain the state of the restaurant and the lack of investment in non-current assets.

As a small business, sources of finance are presumably limited. If the Bolds are unable to invest further in the business and if Eleanor's family are unwilling to provide the necessary funds, then the bank will need convincing of the Bold's ability to turn the business round.

Any new strategy will need to generate better returns or the Bold's might be advised to consider closing the restaurant. Having said that, It may be that the owners are prepared to sacrifice some of this alternative income as a result of the benefits they perceive from being their own boss, so it would be useful to ascertain the minimum level of income they need to live off.

Risks

Having signed a second mortgage the Bold's house is at risk if the business fails or the bank withdraw the overdraft facility.

The breakeven analysis indicates that a further 17% drop in sales (14,000 – 11,594/14,000) would cause The Legume to become loss making.

Conclusions

The high level of fixed costs, combined with the fall in the volume of business, has sharply cut into profits so that earnings are below what the owners could earn outside.

The reduction in the volume of business is not just a result of reduced consumer spending but appears to be a result of a change in the competitive environment. Other restaurants now offer similar food to the Legume, which appears to have lost its competitive advantage by not maintaining its differentiating factors.

In addressing the SO-WHAT question we can conclude that, if the business is to survive, it urgently needs to improve performance by:

- Reducing fixed costs or finding ways to convert these to variable costs
- Increasing the volume of trade
- Addressing the finance requirement

Note: In applying WHWWsW analysis, the WHEN question is implicit here in the wide time span of the data provided, so intra-year analysis is not really required.

Step 5: Additional information

This will form the text of your answer to requirement (ii).

The following is indicative of the type of information that might help better assess the performance to date and indicate which of the proposals are likely to be more successful:

- Split of sales revenue by midweek/weekend/month/lunchtime/evening and between food and drink at these times. Also mix of meals and drinks served (eg sales of wine split by price range:

under £10/bottle; £10 – £15; over £20). This may help identify which of the new proposals is more suitable; for example it may be that the lunchtime trade is typically food only, whereas in the evenings more drink is sold.

- Analysis of capacity utilisation/throughput of customers, ie covers served v available tables at different times in the week and at different points in the year. The Bolds might be able to save money by closing the restaurant on certain days or at certain times of the year when trade is normally slow. Alternatively this may indicate when to implement special offers.

- The figures quoted are for average spend per customer. This is likely to vary between lunchtime and evening and by type of customer, eg business v tourist. A breakdown of the average spend by lunchtime and evening would be helpful, as well as details of any discounts offered at off-peak times.

- Whether the spend per customer has increased as a result of Legume increasing prices or whether they are trading up the sales eg by persuading more customers to buy a coffee at the end of the meal.

- Competitor information regarding prices charged, average spend per customer, number of customers (although not all of this will be easily available).

- Data regarding the total potential customers, their demographics and spending habits eg number of tourists visiting the town's restaurants each year, number of business customers, average age of local population, to help assess market share and suitable target markets.

- Minimum income level required for the Bolds to live off.

- Maximum overdraft limit.

- Cash flow showing the pattern of receipts/payments during the year to help better assess the short- and long-term financing requirement.

Step 6: Sample answer for (iii)

This will form the text of your answer to requirement (iii).

(ii) Strategic options for the business

Option 1: Conversion to a wine bar

Rewards

- Will capitalise on the good name built up for the wine cellar and it may be harder for others such as pubs to compete with this strategy

- May increase profitability since margins earned on wines have increased to 60% in 20X8

- The addition of fish to the menu may increase trade by attracting non-vegetarian customers

- The business will not be totally reliant on vegetarian meals. However there will be still no meat dishes on the menu

- It may reduce reliance on the tourist trade and lessen the effect of uncontrollable factors such as the exchange rate

- Only having part-time waiting staff should reduce operating gearing and hence profit volatility

Risks

- If Barchester has an ageing population then this approach may not generate more trade ie without cinemas etc there may be nothing to attract young people to Barchester in the first place

- The Legume may alienate its existing clientele by changing the décor/music/menu etc to appeal to young people

- This strategy may simply replace one type of clientele with another, rather than generate additional trade. Alternatively it may increase the sales of drinks but reduce the sales of food as customers purchase snacks to go with their wine, rather than full meals

- The wine bar image may be more suitable to evening trade only and still leave the restaurant empty at lunchtimes during the week

- The Legume may not be able to change its image sufficiently to appeal to its target clientele

- Running a successful wine bar rather than a restaurant may require different skills

- The strategy may lead to a loss of the good name built up amongst its existing clientele

Option 2: Offering fast food at lunchtime and varying prices

Rewards

- There should be little impact on the existing trade, which is likely to be mainly evening based

- It is consistent with the existing reputation for vegetarian food and the Bolds have the necessary experience

- It is in line with business customers need for fast food at lunchtime

- By varying the pricing some attempt is made to address the seasonality and offering discounts may increase the trade at off-peak times

- There will be some reductions in staffing levels and by employing part-timers more of the costs become variable

Risks

- There is a possibility that their evening clientele may not approve of the lunchtime operations

- The fast food concept may be seen as cheaper and detract from the image of a prize winning restaurant

- The business will be entering a highly competitive lunchtime market, one it knows little about

Conclusion

The additional information noted in (ii) above will help identify whether it is appropriate to increase lunchtime/evening trade and which food and drinks items on the menu are more profitable.

The Bolds should undertake some market research to assess the size of the potential customer base for each option and the forecast returns, before a decision can be made.

Whichever option is chosen, The Legume need to replace the inferior chef and improve the décor of the restaurant in order for it to address its current lack of competitive advantage.

Summary

Evaluation criteria

Suitability
– Strategic logic
– Strategic fit

Acceptability
– Financial
  risk/return
– Customers
– Investors
– Government

Feasibility
– Finance
– Competitor
  response
– Technology
– Time

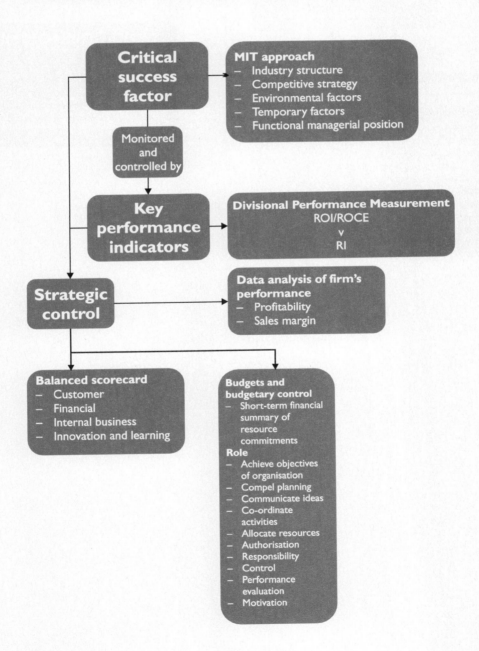

Critical success factor

MIT approach
– Industry structure
– Competitive strategy
– Environmental factors
– Temporary factors
– Functional managerial position

Monitored and controlled by

Key performance indicators

Divisional Performance Measurement
ROI/ROCE
v
RI

Strategic control

Data analysis of firm's performance
– Profitability
– Sales margin

Balanced scorecard
– Customer
– Financial
– Internal business
– Innovation and learning

Budgets and budgetary control
– Short-term financial summary of resource commitments

Role
– Achieve objectives of organisation
– Compel planning
– Communicate ideas
– Co-ordinate activities
– Allocate resources
– Authorisation
– Responsibility
– Control
– Performance evaluation
– Motivation

DATA ANALYSIS

- Financial position
- Performance
- 3Es
- Product/market positioning
- Impact of strategy/projects
- Risk
- Data

SKILLS

- Choosing analytical tools
- Calculations
- Interpreting results
- Conclusions/recommendations
- Looking beyond the information given
- Linking data/explaining trends
- Highlighting weaknesses/ omissions in the data provided

ADDITIONAL INFORMATION REQUIRED

- More detailed information
- Data for prior years
- Missing data
- Actual figures (if given estimates)
- Other data from the industry
- Market leader data
- Think of all information you may need, from internal and external sources

To interpret data properly, you need to make comparisons

APPROACH

1 Initial review
2 Decide on appropriate analysis
3 Perform calculations
4 Interpret your analysis
5 Additional information required

AVOID COMMON MISTAKES

- Use 'because'
- Relate to scenario
- Be specific
- Link the figures/analysis
- Use financial AND non-financial indicators
- Identify cause and effect relationships

Self-test

Answer the following questions.

1   What do the 3 Es stand for?

2   What are the four perspectives associated with the balanced scorecard?

3   What are the Johnson, Scholes and Whittington's criteria for evaluating individual strategies?

4   Identify the role that CSFs can play in strategic control and performance measurement.

5   A firm's ROCE is the product of which two ratio?

6   Define four liquidity ratios.

7   List four limitations of relying on financial measures alone to manage divisional performance.

8   **Cottingham City University**

Cottingham City University, in the city of Cottingham, has only recently been awarded the status of university; previously it had been a polytechnic. This government-led move, although giving the institution the potential for greater flexibility and increased control over its operations, has also meant that, due to the removal of local authority control, the university has lost an annual £3m 'topup' fund.

Since becoming a university it has been rationalised from the previous five sites to three sites, all within walking distance of each other. At the same time the university is increasing its number of students. Also in Cottingham is the Further Education College, which offers a wide range of courses ranging from pre-'A' level stage to some post-'A' level courses, such as accountancy and business studies.

The City University

The university's stated objective is 'to become an enterprising, accessible and highly regarded university, with strong continental and regional links, with the aim of having 5,000 students by 20X5'.

It has been reorganised into five faculties across the sites.

Campus A	Business School
	Science
Campus B	Art
	Catering/Leisure Management
Campus C	Social Sciences

Due to the low number of students attracted to the Arts and Science faculties it has been proposed that these be closed. However, this would result in an overall staff reduction of 15%. Courses at the university range from sub-degree through to post-graduate and post-experience courses, such as the Master of Business Administration (MBA) and Diploma of Management Studies (DMS). The latter courses have been popular.

There are currently some 3,400 students at the City University, 75% of whom live within a ten-mile radius of Cottingham. Due to the great demand for places on the business courses, the Cottingham Business School was formed from the previous business faculty. Over 50% of all students are on a business or business related course, and 70% of all students take some kind of business subject irrespective of the course taken.

The business school also boasts a strong financial position, generating a profit of £4m in 20X0/X1, contributing to an overall profit of £2m for the university as a whole. The university already has close links with a number of European countries (eg France, Germany, Holland) through its highly popular and successful European Business Studies course. For this degree course students spend two periods of six months studying in a foreign country.

Accommodation

Halls of residence both on and off campus provide accommodation for less than half of the students, the rest having to find rooms in a variable and contracting private rental market. The problem is not helped by the restricted land available for development on campus.

A further problem highlighted by the Student Union is the difficulty faced by students, particularly those who are part-time, in gaining access to computer and library facilities. The computer facilities were last reviewed four years ago when students numbered only 2,000. The difficulties arise from all first-year students being required to study Information Technology, and from many lecturers requiring reports to be word processed.

Opening hours	Library	Monday – Friday	8.30 am — 9.00 pm
		Saturday	9.00 pm — 12.30 pm
	Computer rooms		As above
Timetable hours	Full-time	Monday – Friday	9.00 am — 5.00 pm
	Part-time	Monday – Friday	6.00 pm — 9.00 pm

Teaching and staffing

Recently, a process of restructuring administration and ancillary staff was undertaken. The administration side was centralised into one building on each campus, the departmental structure being replaced by a faculty structure. This has, however, resulted in a number of redundancies and demotions, but few promotions. It is hoped that things will change in the next few years as management settle into their new role.

In 20X2 there were seven senior staff responsible for research; this has now fallen to two. Staff have been told that no promotional posts will be available for the foreseeable future. Moreover, the latest pay talks only resulted in a 3% offer, with a £500 bonus for signing new contracts. The union is totally dissatisfied with the offer and has advised its members neither to accept the pay rise nor to sign the new contract, and a number of one-day strikes have been proposed.

Requirements

As a local management consultant prepare a memorandum for the senior lecturers at the business school covering the following.

(a) Perform a SWOT analysis on Cottingham City University and suggest a possible strategy (or strategies), fully explaining your reasons, and also any problems which need to be overcome to achieve those strategies.

(15 marks)

(b) In the light of the strategies highlighted above, suggest a range of performance measures which might help to assess the success of the university. You should give reasons why you think each measure to be appropriate.

(15 marks)

(30 marks)

9 Greens Ltd is a growing firm providing organic fruit and vegetables for delivery via phone or Internet order. It has decided to measure performance for the coming year using the balanced scorecard approach. Suggest two measures in each of the four areas covered by the scorecard.

10 **Maysize Ltd**

Maysize Ltd owns a department store located in a prime site in a regional city in the UK. The store has 16 different departments, selling such diverse items as shoes, fabrics and children's toys, and it has an accounts office for administration. The store is run by a store manager and there is a manager for each department within the store. Selling margins are set by the store manager, although there is scope to flex the margin after consultation with departmental managers. All suppliers are paid by the accounts office. Each departmental manager is responsible for product sales, employee costs and any sale events (eg the January sales).

Management reporting

The management reporting system is very simple. The accounts office prepares a monthly cash flow statement, balance sheet and cumulative income statement. The income statement and balance sheet are compiled from the 16 departmental income statements and balance sheets. The departments prepare their income statements by calculating cost of goods sold by reference to the selling margins.

Maysize Ltd is now in the process of changing to a computerised management reporting system. This system will be able to generate reports in as much detail as is necessary for management.

The managing director has come to you for advice about the new reporting system. She would like to know what financial and non-financial performance indicators should be generated by the new reporting system so that she can monitor in more detail and improve the profitability and liquidity of the department store.

Requirements

Prepare a memorandum for the managing director suggesting the six most useful performance indicators that the new system should generate for the departments. For each performance indicator which you recommend, specify what information it should contain, its frequency and why it would be useful for the managing director. **(10 marks)**

11 Old and New

In 20X2 the divisional manager of the household products division of Rogers Industries plc, George Old, announced to the board of directors that he intended to retire at the end of 20X4. In view of this an assistant manager, Ian M New, was recruited in 20X3 with the intention that he should take over when Old retired. As part of his responsibilities New was given the task of preparing the budget for 20X4 onwards. It was felt that this would allow him to become acquainted with the way in which the division operated and introduce him to one of the jobs he would have to do when he became divisional manager.

As a divisionalised company Rogers Industries plc gives each division a fair degree of autonomy. Divisional budgets are reviewed by the central finance committee but rarely amended. Any capital investment decisions are made jointly by the finance committee and divisional manager; it is the responsibility of the divisions to implement the investment programmes. Rogers Industries plc assesses performance of divisions and their managers by reference to return on capital employed. Cash is controlled centrally. The figures below show the performance of the household products division for the years 20X3 to 20X5 and the budgets for 20X5 and 20X6. These budgets have been approved by the finance committee which agreed with New that there was no need to amend the 20X6 budget in the light of 20X5 performance.

Household products division

	Actual			Budget	
	20X3	20X4	20X5	20X5	20X6
	£'000	£'000	£'000	£'000	£'000
Sales	2,000	3,000	3,600	4,000	4,800
Variable costs					
Materials	200	300	360	400	480
Labour	300	450	540	600	720
Overheads	40	60	70	80	96
Repairs	100	150	90	200	240
Divisional fixed costs					
Staff training	60	70	40	80	90
Advertising	10	15	10	20	24
Maintenance	100	110	90	120	140
Depreciation	240	320	310	400	410
Rent	160	205	220	250	250
Other costs	20	25	30	30	35
Total divisional costs	1,230	1,705	1,760	2,180	2,485
Net profit	770	1,295	1,840	1,820	2,315
Divisional net assets					
Non-current assets	3,200	5,180	5,500	6,700	7,550
Receivables	200	300	350	400	480
Inventory	400	600	550	800	960
Payables	(300)	(450)	(750)	(600)	(720)
Divisional investment	3,500	5,630	5,650	7,300	8,270
Return on capital employed	22%	23%	32.5%	25%	28%

Requirements

(a) Comment on the performance of Ian M New during 20X5, calculating those extra ratios you feel are important and including a note on the areas of Mr New's responsibility for the household products division. **(8 marks)**

(b) Suggest what changes might be made in either the responsibilities of the divisional managers or the method of assessing their performance. **(6 marks)**

(c) Set out possible reasons why Rogers Industries plc might wish to be organised on divisional lines and the possible disadvantages of such a corporate structure. **(6 marks)**

(20 marks)

12 Waltex

Assume that the current date is December 20X7

Waltex Ltd (Waltex) is a large, unlisted company which manufactures watches. Its shares are held equally by three groups: the Waltex family, venture capitalists and employees. Customers are jewellers shops which are located throughout Europe and the Far East, although 90% of Waltex's sales are in the UK.

Company history

Waltex was established in Wales in 1924 as a manufacturer of watches, positioned in the low to medium price range. It has maintained a good reputation as a manufacturer of traditional style mechanical watches. Waltex has not copied many of the larger watchmakers which have moved to making quartz watches and have adopted sports or fashion stylings. Moreover, Waltex does not try to compete with the major watchmakers of international quality and reputation, which use precious metals and support their brands with significant advertising. The brand image that Waltex has tried to promote has been a good value, classic style and traditional mechanical mechanism that appeals mainly to the over 45s age group.

All watches are currently sold under the Waltex brand name. There are 59 different product lines (ie types of watch) which are sold to retailers in the price range £35 to £100. Retailers normally have a 30% mark-up on cost when selling to the public.

The UK watch market

The UK watch market generates retail sales of around £1,100 million per year. Wrist watches dominate the market, but there are three main types: quartz digital, quartz analogue and traditional mechanical watches. There is very high market penetration with around 70% of adults in the UK owning a watch.

There is a trend in the UK market for consumers to buy cheaper watches. This is partly due to 'watch wardrobing', whereby consumers own different watches for different occasions. This has given rise to the role of watches as accessories. The success of cross-branding (a marketing approach to enhance two brand names of different companies by associating them with each other) and seasonal collections from the major suppliers have encouraged this trend.

The market for watches is fragmented, with a significant number of suppliers and retailers. In watch retailing, the entry of large market participants (for example supermarkets and clothing chains) has increased the competition in recent years for traditional retailers such as jewellers and, as large retailers, supermarkets have significant buying power. The Internet, through on-line sales of watches, has created competition for traditional retailers and has also generated greater transparency in the market, as it is easier for consumers to make comparisons before buying.

The UK market for watches, in sales value terms, will probably experience a decline in the next few years, caused by continuing selection of cheaper watches; slower growth in the UK economy; and competition from other products in the leisure and consumer electronics markets.

Strategies for change

The poor performance of Waltex in recent years has caused some concern amongst shareholders and in September 20X7 some of the executive directors, who did not own shares, resigned, with a new chief executive and finance director being appointed almost immediately. After a period of evaluation, several strategies for change were identified. These are not mutually exclusive.

Strategy 1

Increase the advertising expenditure from £1 million in 20X7, to £2 million in 20X8, in order to promote the brand and increase sales.

Strategy 2

Launch a new range of watches with a new brand name. These would be ladies' quartz watches, branded with the name *Splash!* They would have a fashion orientation and a distinctive pink and yellow striped design. This would be part of a joint venture with a well-known fashion company, Kuchi plc, who would adopt the same design for their matching *Splash!* range of women's clothes. The *Splash!* watches and clothes would be jointly marketed to the same retailers, which would be fashion clothing and accessories shops, none of which have been previously used by Waltex. No separate joint venture company would be set up, but contractual obligations would be entered into to produce adequate volumes to match approximately the other venturer's production. Additional joint advertising obligations would also be needed to support the cross-branding (this would be independent of the £2 million commitment in strategy 1). The *Splash!* watches are expected to retail at £90, while the matching Kuchi clothing would retail at an average of around £250. Initial cash costs of £10 million would be incurred by Waltex to set up a quartz watch production line. Incremental annual fixed costs (in addition to the initial cash outlay) of £3 million would be incurred in manufacture. Variable costs are expected to be £40 per watch in the expected range of output, although sales volumes are very uncertain.

Strategy 3

Accept an offer from a large UK supermarket, Yarmack plc, to buy 40,000 watches in 20X8 with the possibility there would be a further contract in 20X9 if sales went well. These watches would normally have a price to jewellers of £45, but Yarmack is only willing to pay Waltex £36 per watch. Yarmack would then sell the watches for about £46. Yarmack is not currently a customer, but this contract would make it Waltex's largest customer.

The board meeting

A meeting of the new board was held to discuss the proposed strategies for change.

The **marketing director** spoke first: 'I would undertake all three of the strategies for change. From a marketing perspective we need to grow sales volumes and all three of these proposals achieve that.'

The **finance director** responded: 'The company has performed poorly in the past few years, as shown in the preliminary data I have provided for the UK market and the company (see **Exhibits 1 and 2**). However, I am not yet sure whether the poor performance is because of a difficult market or because there has been internal mismanagement. I agree that there needs to be change, but we first need to establish what has been going wrong. I have provided some information from a marketing survey to help us (**Exhibit 3**). However, it is not just about making sales, we need to look carefully at our costs.'

The **production director** also expressed some concerns: 'There is some spare capacity in the factory at the moment, but we need to make sure that we can supply all these new sales initiatives. I reckon our annual capacity is currently 1.2 million units. If we set up the quartz production we will probably lose factory floorspace and cut annual production capacity of existing mechanical watches to around 1.1 million units.'

Exhibit 1

UK Watch Market data

	20X3	20X4	20X5	20X6	20X7 (Estimate)
Total UK retail sales (£m)	998	1,049	1,112	1,125	1,100
UK media advertising expenditure on watches (£m)	26.5	27.2	28.9	27.0	26.5

Exhibit 2

Waltex data

	20X3	20X4	20X5	20X6	20X7 (Estimate)
Revenue £m	49.5	44	42.5	42.75	45
Fixed operating costs £m	20	20	20	20	21
Total variable operating costs £m	27	24	25.5	28.5	30
Operating profit/(loss) £m	2.5	0	(3)	(5.75)	(6)
UK media advertising expenditure (£m)	0.8	0.8	0.90	0.96	1.0
Units sold (watches millions)	0.90	0.80	0.85	0.95	1.00
Number of product lines	45	47	53	57	59

Exhibit 3

Marketing survey (in 20X7)

	Waltex	UK Industry Average
Age (percentage of sales to over 45s)	62%	29%
Higher Socioeconomic groupings (percentage of sales to groups A and B)	19%	24%
Gender (women's watches as a percentage of total sales)	54%	51%
Gender (percentage of watch purchases made by females, including gifts)	60%	53%
Average wholesale price	£45	£50

Requirements

(a) (i) Using the data in Exhibit 1 and Exhibit 2, prepare a memorandum which provides a preliminary analysis to help explain the performance of Waltex over the period 20X3-20X7. Show supporting calculations where appropriate.

   (ii) Indicate any further data that you would reasonably require for a more detailed performance report, including any additional breakdown of the existing data. Ignore the proposed strategies for change and the marketing survey. **(11 marks)**

(b) With respect to *Strategy 1* explain:

   (i) The types of advertising that would be appropriate to each of the market segmentation groups (ie age, socioeconomic and gender) identified in the market survey in Exhibit 3.

   (ii) How you would evaluate the impact of the proposed advertising campaign (assuming that the evaluation would take place in January 20X9). Use the data provided to support your arguments.

   Ignore the other proposed strategies for change. **(11 marks)**

(c) For each of *Strategy 2* and *Strategy 3*, identify the potential risks and benefits, and give a reasoned recommendation of whether the strategy should be undertaken in each case.

   (11 marks)

   (33 marks)

13 Read the scenario of the **March 2009 Business Strategy** paper in the Question Bank entitled *CWI International Ltd*. Draft an answer for requirement (a) on the data analysis.

14 Read the scenario of the **June 2009 Business Strategy** paper in the Question Bank entitled *Kemmex Ice Cream plc*. Draft an answer for requirement (c) on performance analysis and price reduction.

15 Go online at The Times 100 Business Case Studies and read the Anglo American case study 'Adding value through asset optimisation' at: http://businesscasestudies.co.uk/anglo-american/adding-value-through-asset-optimisation.

Now go back to the Learning objectives in the Introduction. If you are satisfied you have achieved these objectives, please tick them off.

Answer to Interactive question 1

ROI using opening carrying amount:

Year 1 34 – 25 ÷ 100 = 9%
Year 2 34 – 25 ÷ 75 = 12%
Year 3 34 – 25 ÷ 50 = 18%
Year 4 34 – 25 ÷ 25 = 36%

ROI improves despite constant annual profits thus divisional managers might hang on to assets for too long.
(RI would also improve, giving the same problem.)

ROI using historic cost:

Years 1– 4 34 – 25 ÷ 100 = 9%

(RI would also be constant under these circumstances.)

ROI using historic cost overcomes the increasing return problem of using the carrying amount. However, it is not perfect.

Answer to Interactive question 2

The manager would dispose of the asset after two years, ie she might get rid of the asset too quickly. (The same problem occurs with RI with interest at 12%.)

Answer to Interactive question 3

Divisional ROI pre-project	=	$\dfrac{£300k}{£1m}$
	=	30%
Divisional ROI post-project	=	$\dfrac{£325k}{£1.1m}$
	=	29.5%

Although the project ROI is acceptable to the company (25%), the manager would not be motivated to accept a project which lowers divisional ROI. In this particular circumstance, RI would lead to the right decision as the absolute figure for the division would increase.

RI pre project	300,000 – 20% (lm)	=	£100k
RI post project	325,000 – 20% (1.1 m)	=	£105k

Answer to Interactive question 4

Residual income

	Division 1	Division 2
Year 1		
200k – 20% (1m)	–	
20k – 20% (100k)		–
Year 2		
220k – 20% (1m)	20k	
40k – 20% (100k)		20k

Return on investment

	Division 1	Division 2
Year 1		
200k/1m	20%	
20k/100k		20%
Year 2		
220k/1m	22%	
40k/100k		40%

It is much easier for the larger division to generate a further £20k of residual income; hence using RI to compare divisions of different sizes is misleading. ROI gives a better indication of performance.

Answers to Self-test

1 Economy, Efficiency, Effectiveness

2
- Financial
- Customer
- Innovation and learning
- Internal business processes

3 Suitability, feasibility and acceptability

4 CSFs identify the areas that an organisation must excel at if it is to gain competitive advantage. Having identified its CSFs a business can determine suitable KPIs to measure the achievement of those CSFs. These can be used as part of the strategic control system and for performance measurement.

5 Profit margin × asset turnover = ROCE

6 Current ratio: current assets/current liabilities
Quick ratio: (current assets less inventories)/current liabilities
Receivable days: trade receivables/revenue × 365
Payable days: trade payables/cost of sales × 365

7 Four of:

- Encourages short-termist behaviour
- Ignores strategic goals
- Cannot control persons without budget responsibility
- Historic measures
- Distorted

8 **Cottingham City University**

Note: 'Not for profit' organisations are only examinable at a basic level and all relevant information would be given in an examination question.

Memorandum

To	Mr A Lecturer
From	M Consultant
Date	Today
Subject	Cottingham University – The future

(a) **Analysis and strategy**

Findings

The stated objective of Cottingham University is 'to become an enterprising, accessible, and highly-regarded university, with strong continental and regional links, with the aim of having 5,000 students by 20X5'. The words 'enterprising', 'accessible' and 'highly-regarded', are somewhat intangible, thus making it difficult to quantify their success. However, in order to look at a strategy(ies) for achieving this goal, it is necessary to look first at the resources which the university has to offer.

Resources available

There are a number of valuable resources which the university has to offer, including three easily accessible sites, an excellent business school, links with continental countries (providing potential for growth) and a good location in the town.

In order to understand the situation fully, it is necessary to perform a SWOT analysis which highlights strengths, weaknesses, opportunities and threats to the university.

CHAPTER

12

SWOT analysis

The important points are that the opportunities need to be turned into strengths, and the weaknesses need to become opportunities. This is the basis of the following strategy.

Formulation and evaluation of alternatives

In order to turn opportunities into strengths, a number of alternative strategies are suggested

Strengths

- Strong reputation of business school
- Location in town
- Links with continent

Opportunities

- Change of status from polytechnic to university allows greater competition for university students
- Students from College of Further Education
- Development of old sites into halls of residence
- Development of courses, such as the MBA
- Growth in continental ties
- Increased emphasis on business facilities
- Part-time students

Weaknesses

- Accommodation problems
- Low staff morale
- Time tabling problems

Threats

- Lack of funding
- Teaching staff leaving
- Competition from other local educational institutions
- Effect on potential students of teachers' strikes

(i) Develop other related professional courses, such as CIMA, ACCA and banking examinations. This will be in direct competition with the College of Further Education but the business school's reputation will help in attracting students.

(ii) Due to the problems with accommodation, a further strategy would be to develop existing land, which the university owns, into halls of residence. Obviously the costs of such a project would be high in the short term but in the long term the benefits gained from attracting new students will outweigh the costs. Before going ahead with such a scheme, a thorough financial analysis must be carried out.

(iii) Courses such as MBA and DMS have proved very popular in the past and should be developed and strengthened. This will probably increase the number of part-time students, which is another possible growth area for the university.

(iv) Growth in continental ties is probably more of a long-term strategy, especially if the university wishes to broaden its horizons to countries further afield. In the short to midterm, continental students provide the potential for developing business strategies abroad. Before this can be done, however, extensive market research into the needs and expectations of foreign students must be carried out.

Obviously the above are only some options to be considered and hopefully lecturers will be encouraged to put forward ideas of their own.

It is clear, in any case, that the business school is the key area to be developed if the university's objective is to be achieved.

Problems to overcome

There are a number of problems to be faced before considering the best way to implement the strategies suggested.

(i) Competition from other institutions: The University of North Midlands is also expanding and may be in direct competition for local students.

(ii) Staff disruptions: Problems caused by staff pay deals, leading to strikes, will deter potential students.

(iii) Poor accommodation: Non-local students will be put off by the lack of accommodation both in the university and in the town.

(iv) Lack of funding: Now that the university is self-funding, it must turn around the £2m loss made by the non-business faculties.

From the above discussion it is suggested that the following strategies be considered.

To concentrate the university's resources towards the business school by

• Improving the range of courses offered
• Increasing ties with the continent
• Encouraging part-time students and local professional students

In order to achieve this objective it must

• Overcome teacher problems
• Create better accommodation facilities

Summary

Cottingham City University has reached an important point. Recent events indicate that the University is facing some challenging times. As universities are essentially 'people focused' knowledge-driven ventures, factors affecting individuals connected with the institution will need to be well managed to avoid damaging its future success.

The lack of student accommodation and the proposed strike by staff is likely to have a detrimental impact on the student experience. This is a particular concern given the increase in competition among Higher Education providers to attract students.

The recent award of full university status is likely to be positive in the long term given the increased flexibility and control that has been gained by removing the local authority's control. This however, has been tempered with the loss in funding which will need to be addressed.

The University would appear, based on the above analysis, to be well placed to overcome these challenges, due to its strong reputation and connections with European Universities. Increasing demand for business-related subjects which are being delivered by the business school, is a particular opportunity, and the business school is in a strong financial position. Although potentially a difficult time, the proposal to close down the Arts and Science faculty due to low student numbers, indicates that management are prepared to respond to changes in the Higher Education market, which is particularly promising.

(b) **Performance measures**

In order to assess the success of the above strategies, a number of performance indicators can be used.

Financial indicators

(i) **Profitability (by department)**

In 20X1 the university contained 3,400 students and had a profit of £2m.

The business school contained 1,700 students and had a profit of £4m.

Therefore, the other four faculties were making a £2m loss.

In future it will be possible to assess the profitability more accurately because there will be fewer departments.

(ii) **Profitability (per student)**

In 20X1 the university contained 3,400 students and had a profit of £2m.

Profit per university student = £588

In 20X1 the business school contained 1,700 students and had a profit of £4m.

Profit per business school student = £2,353

A number of variations on this measure might be used, depending on the statistics available (eg profitability per foreign student and profitability per non-degree student).

There are also a number of non-financial performance measures which may be equally useful.

Non-financial performance measures

(i) **Increase in number of students**

As one of the main aims of the university is to increase its student numbers to 5,000, an important way of assessing the performance of the implemented strategy is to monitor the increase in the number of new students.

This can be split into a number of categories.

- Part-time students: These are obviously an important sector for the university and it will be advantageous to create more places in this area.

- Non-degree students (ie MBA, DMS, CIMA, ACCA, etc): This is also an important growth area for the university, particularly where there is direct competition from the local college. Therefore, if the university can attract students in this area, this will indicate confidence in the institution.

- Overseas students: This is a clear aim for the university, which can be monitored by the increase in overseas students.

(ii) **Achieving objective**

As previously mentioned the stated objective contains a number of intangible goals (ie 'enterprising', 'accessible' and 'highly-regarded').

Obviously it will be difficult to measure the achievement of such goals, but the following points may be useful.

Accessibility could be achieved by making as many courses available to as many students as possible. Therefore, a measure of accessibility could be the number of non-local students at the university. Accessibility could also be measured by the variety of students (eg age ranges, mixtures of degree, non-degree and other students).

Reputation could be measured by the calibre of students attracted to the university. Traditionally, universities attract students with high grades, but if the university can compete against the University of North Midlands for students, then it will gain a high regard amongst both students and academics.

A further performance measure is the calibre of staff attracted to the university and their research record (number and quality of papers published). A good research reputation should attract funds and grants from the various educational research councils.

Recommendations

From the above discussion and analysis, it is clear that there is a need for change and reorganisation if the university is to achieve its objective.

(i) The university should concentrate its efforts on its most successful department, namely the business school.

(ii) To widen its operations and increase its numbers, it should compete for students from other local institutions in other business-related courses.

(iii) A wide range of student needs should be recognised and catered for (ie part-time, post degree, professional, etc).

(iv) In order to increase overseas ties, the problems of accommodation and teaching staff dissatisfaction need to be overcome.

9 Financial perspective

Increase in revenue
Market share

Customer perspective
Time taken from order to delivery
Freshness of products (measured in terms of days since harvesting)

Internal business process perspective
Time taken to process an individual order
Speed with which product availability updates register on the website

Innovation and learning perspective
Number of different products in the range offered
Geographical areas covered by delivery teams

10 Maysize Ltd

Memorandum

To	Managing director, Maysize Ltd
From	AN Consultant
Date	1 January 20X2
Subject	Departmental performance indicators

This memorandum considers the new computer management reporting system for Department Store X. As requested six specific performance indicators for departments are identified as being of critical importance.

The relative importance of each of these indicators will vary over time as organisational priorities change (eg if liquidity were to become more important than profitability).

The specific indicators identified are, as requested, local in nature. Global considerations, such as market share and capital expenditure, will also be of relevance but are not discussed in this report. In each instance the reporting system should incorporate information on prior period and (flexed) budgetary comparatives, and be analysed between individual departments and the store as a whole. Where possible, appropriate industry averages should also be incorporated (eg in margin analysis or area utilisation).

Suggested indicators are as follows.

(1) Customer feedback summaries

Content

A summary of customer feedback, including details of the number and nature of complaints. These should include feedback received at the customer service desk, and a log of matters noted by store and department managers.

Frequency

Periodically (monthly – depending on the extent and gravity of matters arising).

Benefits

Levels of service quality will be critical to the success of the store. Weaknesses in customer relations management need identification to ensure that the appropriate client culture is adopted.

(2) Sales margins

Content

Gross profit margins should be calculated, expressing gross departmental profitability as a percentage of departmental revenue.

Frequency

Margins should be calculated periodically (probably weekly). In the event of specific queries, further detailed analyses could be provided on demand (eg a summary of exceptional margins for product lines relating to a specific department).

Benefits

Since authority to fix margins is delegated to the store manager (and in some cases department managers), some control will be vital.

Weak margins may indicate poor purchasing policies, or highlight high or low profitability for specific departments that may warrant a reallocation of resources.

Margins will also be relevant when considering strategic pricing policies (eg price wars). High level review should also facilitate overall goal congruence, eg one area targeting economy purchases (low margin), with another targeting the other end of the market.

(3) Area utilisation

Content

A measure of departmental revenue against space occupied should be prepared. [If possible a more elaborate measure of departmental profitability by floor space would provide further benefit.]

Frequency

Periodically (monthly) or even as sales seasons change.

Benefits

Store space is a key scarce resource; maximising returns from available space will be critical to success.

Measures yielding higher utilisation of existing space, once identified, could also be replicated within other departments.

Potential improvements in profitability from devoting more space to areas yielding the highest return will need to be balanced with interdependencies between the departments. Shoppers may, for example, be using the store primarily for convenience food shopping, but may make additional impulsive purchases while on the premises.

(4) Staffing

Content

A simple calculation of departmental turnover against head count should be performed.

Frequency

This should be produced on a periodic basis (monthly).

Benefits

Staff costs will represent a significant determinant of profitability. Given the extent of delegation of responsibilities, they are also an important resource.

The measure should highlight areas of possible over/under staffing and may assist in staff planning.

An 'equitable' allocation of the workload should also avoid demotivating the staff and reduce staff turnover (training costs, etc).

(5) Inventory holding

Content

Average inventory holding days by department calculated as

$$\frac{\text{Average inventory of finished goods}}{\text{Annual cost of sales}} \times 365$$

Frequency

Periodically (possibly monthly) with fuller analyses of individual product lines available on demand in the event of exceptional inventory holdings.

Benefit

Inventory will be the key element of working capital. Inventory levels may also have a direct impact on sales levels (eg if shelves are bare).

A simple comparison of inventory levels between departments will identify excessive or minimal inventory levels, assisting in the review of purchasing policies, or handling of slow moving inventory lines and the use of sales.

Inventory counts may also be modified to allow investigation of unusual inventory levels, which may have been a result of inventory losses or inaccuracies in the recording of inventory movements.

(6) Purchasing efficiency

Content

Value of trade and settlement discounts, in both absolute and relative (as a percentage of purchases) terms.

Frequency

Periodically (monthly), with the option of specific exception reporting (eg discounts over £1,000).

Benefits

The ability to purchase quality goods at a reasonable price will be a key factor in the success of the store.

The organisation of purchasing responsibilities between departments and a central purchasing department will be particularly relevant.

A review of discounts obtained may assist in consideration of strategic purchasing policy (central buying from key suppliers giving rise to potential economies of scale) and a consideration of payables management issues.

Conclusion

The new system offers the opportunity for a review of the full range of operational and tactical management information. The six indicators suggested have considered measures that may have more strategic relevance. I would be happy to offer further advice on other information enhancements at your instruction.

11 Old and New

(a) Performance evaluation

It would appear at first sight that Mr New has achieved much in his first year as divisional manager. Return on capital employed has risen by nearly 10% on the previous year and is well up on budget. The growth in net profit seen under Mr Old's management has been sustained under Mr New and the division's net profit percentage has cleared 50% (W1). However, when one examines how this has been achieved, Mr New's performance looks less spectacular, in particular with respect to the following points.

(i) Sales are down on budget (down £400,000 or 10% on budget and the chances of achieving the 20X6 budget seem remote).

(ii) Repair costs are down (other variable costs have maintained their normal relation to sales but repair costs have dropped off markedly) (W2).

(iii) Discretionary fixed costs are below budget (previously-made commitments to staff training, advertising and maintenance have been cut by 25% or even 50%).

(iv) Depreciation is below budget (perhaps as a result of reduced investment – see below).

(v) Non-current assets are £1.2 million below budget (capital investment programmes have not been carried out).

(vi) Receivables and inventory levels are down on budget (the first could be attributable to the low level of sales, the latter to efficient working capital management, though there could be problems of meeting future sales).

(vii) Payables have increased dramatically (this could be called good credit management or perhaps an attempt to manipulate figures used for divisional assessment).

Each of these items, of which items (ii) to (vii) are controllable by Mr New, have moved in such a way as to improve the division's reported return on capital employed. However, in the case of most of the controllable items, they could be said to have changed in a way that has improved short-term profitability whilst seriously jeopardising longer-term performance. The fall in repair costs, training and maintenance must put a question mark over whether the division can continue to be run efficiently. The cuts in non-current assets, inventory and advertising make it unlikely that sales will be maintained, even at their current level.

(b) **Changes in responsibility and evaluation**

Although the responsibilities that appear to have been assigned to Mr New, particularly the responsibility for producing regular budgets, are in line with what one would expect of a divisional manager, some changes need to be implemented.

(i) There is a need for managers' budgets to be more critically reviewed. Questions should be asked as to how certain budgetary targets can be attained.

(ii) Divisional managers must be fully committed to any capital investment programmes following joint discussions with the finance committee.

Major improvements, however, can be made in the method of appraising divisional performance.

(i) The extent to which a division might contribute towards the company's profit would be better measured by residual income (an absolute measure of profitability) rather than by return on capital employed (a relative measure).

(ii) Subsidiary ratios should be used such as asset/turnover; gross profit percentage; inventory, receivables and payables periods – though these may be open to the sort of 'window-dressing' carried out by Mr New.

(iii) Other performance measures could be introduced to establish whether discretionary costs have been cut back too far. Examples would be machine downtime and staff turnover ratios.

(iv) Using a balanced scorecard approach would involve assessing success from a financial, customer, innovation and learning and internal business perspective. Other useful measures might then include market share, dissatisfied customer orders, number of new products launched.

The important steps are to change the main evaluation measure used and to support it with other measures that aim to examine every facet of 'performance'.

(c) **Reasons for and disadvantages of decentralisation**

(i) Reasons why Rogers Industries plc might wish to be organised along divisional lines might include the following.

(1) Size – it is useful to split a large organisation into smaller manageable units.

(2) Specialisation and complexity – central management may not have sufficient skills to be responsible for the day-to-day control of certain specialised tasks.

(3) Uncertainty and unpredictability – in uncertain trading conditions local management will be able to react to changes more quickly than central management.

(4) Motivation – by assigning responsibility for a section of the business to one divisional manager, that manager might be encouraged to ensure that the division's performance is enhanced. The division also presents the manager with a degree of independence and acts as a training ground for him to develop his management skills.

(5) Economic – a geographical separation of divisions might allow advantage to be taken of local investment grants and favourable tax rates. Such geographical dispersion also allows a firm to be closer to markets or sources of supply.

(6) Freeing central management – being released from day-to-day responsibilities for some operations of the business allows central management to concentrate more on longer-term strategic planning and control.

(ii) Though these may be valid reasons for a firm decentralising, there are certain disadvantages of such a policy.

(1) Interdependencies – complete separation of divisions is probably impossible, since divisions may be engaged in supplying each other with goods or services or selling complementary or substitute products. Each makes demands on centralised resources, especially cash.

(2) Cost – the advantages gained from economies of scale may well be lost by decentralisation, with divisions each requiring certain types of assets or other resources which might otherwise be shared.

(3) Loss of goal congruence – divisional managers may make decisions which, whilst in the best interest of their own division, are not in the best interest of the organisation as a whole.

(4) Loss of control – central management will need to learn to delegate responsibility, co-ordinate divisional activities and control their performance.

12 Waltex

Memorandum

To	Board of Waltex Ltd
From	Accountant
Date	Today
Subject	Analysis of data

(a) (i) **Analysis of basic data**

	20X3	20X4	20X5	20X6	20X7
Average price per unit	£55	£55	£50	£45	£45
Market share (revenue x 90%)/ industry sales	4.5%	3.8%	3.4%	3.4%	3.7%
Advertising expenditure as % of industry	3.0%	2.9%	3.1%	3.6%	3.8%
Average variable cost per unit	£30	£30	£30	£30	£30
Break even (units)	0.8m	0.8m	1m	1.33m	1.4m
Contribution per unit	£25	£25	£20	£15	£15

Sales revenues

The volume of sales has increased by 100,000 units (11.11%) over the period 20X3-20X7 while, at the same time, sales revenues have fallen by £4.5m (9.09%) over the same period.

The sharp fall in the average selling prices of £10 (18.2%) appears to explain at least some of this difference. However more information is needed to determine the cause of the underlying fall in selling prices. Specifically, each of the following factors may be relevant:

(1) Prices of individual items may have been reduced in order to maintain or increase the volume of sales.

(2) The selling prices of individual items may not have changed substantially but there may have been a change in the mix of sales, with an increase in the proportion of lower priced items being sold within the price range of £35 to £100. This explanation is consistent with the 'trend in the market for consumers to buy cheaper watches'. The new product lines introduced may also have been at the bottom end of the product range.

A less important effect may also be a change in exchange rate on overseas sales, but these only make up 10% of sales.

Sales volumes

As already noted, sales volumes have increased significantly (11.1%) although not enough to compensate for the reduction is sales prices.

While more information is needed, the possible reasons for the increase may be:

- The reductions in selling prices may have increased demand.

- There may have been a change in the market desire to purchase traditional mechanical watches in general, and Waltex watches in particular.

- Increased advertising in absolute terms has increased. This may be important as watches are competing with 'other products in the leisure and consumer electronics markets'. However the levels of advertising in these industries would need to be assessed in order to provide evidence of whether the increase is sufficient to persuade customers to buy watches in preference to other consumer products.

- Increased advertising relative to the industry average. This is important to improve market share. However, despite the increased advertising compared to the industry average, the market share of Waltex has fallen. Care needs to be exercised here however as market share is in sales value terms, where Waltex has not performed well. Market share in volume terms may have increased, and more information is needed in this respect.

In terms of profitability, the company has performed poorly over the period 20X3-20X7 with a £2.5m operating profit turning into a £6m operating loss. Other costs such as financing costs may make these figures worse, although tax effects may moderate the decline.

Revenue factors have already been considered but costs are relevant to any analysis of performance.

Costs

Variable costs per unit have remained constant over a long period. A number of factors might have caused variable costs to change but may have acted in opposite directions.

- Variable costs might have been expected to fall as output increased with longer production runs (this would depend however on how much of the new output was due to the new product lines).

- Fixed costs remained constant, except in 20X7 when they increased to £21 million.

- Inflation may have been expected to increase costs (eg wage inflation).

(ii) **Further information**

Further information that is needed in respect of sales and marketing would be:

- Analysis of sales volumes for each type of product to evaluate whether there has been a shift in the mix from high value to low value

- A listing of selling price changes on individual products

- Prices of the new product lines compared to existing product lines

In order to assess the performance on costs the following information would be needed:

- Detailed analysis of costing for each product

- Split of overseas and UK costs to examine if overseas sales, at only 10% of the total revenue (and made to many different countries) are viable

- Impact of inflation of costs compared to underlying efficiency gains

- Identification of cost drivers to consider activity based costing and the viability/ performance of each of the 59 different product lines

(b) (i) **Demographic – age**

- Advertising in magazines that are read mainly by over 45s

- Radio and TV – day-time slots are cheaper and a proportion of over 45s may be retired and not working

- TV advertising during programmes which are popular with the over 45s

- Use of actors and images which are recognised and valued by over 45s age group

- Appearance of shops, packaging and staff that would appeal most to over 45s

Socioeconomic

- Advertising in newspapers and magazines read by middle income groups
- Direct mail – to occupations known to be in middle to low income ranges
- Selective use of Satellite TV for programmes popular with middle income groups
- Public transport – is used disproportionately by low-middle income groups
- Internet – identify commonly used web sites for middle income groups

Gender

- While females make up the largest proportion in this group, the male purchasers are also substantial and target marketing on a gender basis may not be sufficiently focused on a significantly large majority of customers

- Segmentation in this case may mean (rather than focusing on one gender group) advertising to each gender in different ways to attract consumers to the different features of male/female watches

- There is a difference between the consumer (male/female watches) and the customer (the retailers in the case of Waltex and for the retailers themselves it is the person who buys the watch)

- Promoting a female image of the watches to excess may make the watches less attractive to male customers

- To the extent that market segmentation is followed, then this may be similar to the above but on the basis of gender:

  – Female magazines

  – TV and radio programmes popular with females

  – Packaging and shop appearance that would have a feminine preference (but not at the cost of putting off male customers/consumers)

(ii) Identifying the impact of the advertising campaign would depend on the type of advertising and its objectives. Any evaluation should therefore be in comparison to the related objectives.

If the objective of advertising is to promote long term recognition of the brand, or a particular image of the brand, then the effects in terms of sales may not be noticed by January 20X9. Additional market research may therefore be needed to assess the impact in terms of customer recognition (eg questionnaires, interviews etc). This may determine whether there is increased recognition of the brand before advertising (pre test) and after advertising (post test) or, more directly the extent to which people can remember the advert or other form of promotion.

If the objective is more short term, such as promotion of a particular offer, or to stimulate sales of a particular product line, then sales figures could be examined before and after the adverts. The problem is that other factors are also changing (eg price, fashions etc) so changes in sales may not be entirely due to advertising.

In addition, retailers could be asked to give customer feedback on why they purchased a watch (eg as part of filling in the guarantee on the watch which is then submitted to Waltex)

Note:

- In each case significant sales are made outside the segmental target groups and it may be appropriate not to ignore these entirely

- The above are single variable segmentations. It may be appropriate to identify multivariable segmentation eg females over 45

(c) **Strategy 2 – Cross-marketing Joint Venture**

Risks

- This is a new venture that requires a new investment of £10 million. If the venture fails then there is a risk that exit costs may be high. However, as the investment is mainly in machinery to manufacture quartz watches, they are not specific to this venture and may be utilised in alternative product and market strategies in manufacturing quartz watches.

- There is a core competence in mechanical watch making. It is not clear that this competence could be readily transferred to quartz technology. It is the same watch market but largely a different industry, or at least a different production technique.

- Break even. The higher fixed costs may mean that break even will increase annually. The annual break even is £3m/(£90 – £30) = 50,000 units (or £450,000 or revenue). However, this ignores the depreciation on the initial outlay which will increase the break even.

- The contractual joint venture depends on a new partner Kuchi. Waltex is therefore at risk from the actions of the partner in terms of reputation, fulfilment of contract terms and acting reasonably in dealing with Waltex.

- The venture is based on a particular fashion design which may be short term. There is therefore a risk of sustainability of the market which is the subject of the joint venture.

- There is a risk that in focussing on ladies' watches in the new venture that the Waltex brand will be identified as a feminine brand and lose sales of men's watches.

- The contractual obligations of the joint venture may give rise to problems of meeting supply requirements under the arrangements.

- The selling price of £90 is low in comparison to the joint partner's average revenue of £250. The costs of the JV should therefore be considered on this basis of disproportionate benefits. If the cost are shared equally then this would present an additional risk.

- Even if break even can be attained in the short term, there needs to be a sustainable revenue in order to recover the initial outlay of £10 million over the life of the project.

- Some customers may switch from traditional to quartz watches, thus sales could be replacement rather than incremental.

- The production director appears to be concerned that the new production line might have a negative impact on existing capacity.

- As this is a new venture it is likely to require significant management time which could cause them to take their eye off the core business.

- As well as the extra operating gearing, funding the investment is likely to result in increased financial gearing. In addition there may be further WC requirements beyond the initial £10m, particularly if the business is expanding.

Benefits

- The venture may change the image of the company as well as that of the specific products in the venture.

- It diversifies out of mechanical watches, which have particular market attributes. Quartz watches may appeal to a different market.

- This is a high margin product at £60 per unit. If sales exceed the break even level then additional profits will be made. The break even level needs to be assessed as to whether it is attainable using market research but, at 50,000 units, it is low by comparison to existing output.

Recommendation

There are some concerns which need to be addressed before entering into the agreement. These include the following:

- The terms of the joint venture need to be established clearly so Waltex does not incur a disproportionate share of the costs.

- Market research needs to be completed to establish whether the break even is likely to be attained over the life of the project.

- The reputation and benefits of the joint venture partner need to be considered in terms of the benefits of cross marketing. Any alternative partners who can deliver a better package of benefits and costs of cross marketing may be considered.

Subject to these concerns there seems to be merit in investigating the venture further.

Strategy 3 – Yarmack offer

Risks

- Additional fixed costs may be incurred in addition to the variable costs.

- There may be some opportunity costs in terms of lost sales to the extent that people buy Waltex watches from Yarmack rather than other retailers. To the extent that this occurs, then there is a lost contribution of £9 per watch (see working) for each item purchased in this manner.

- The contract is short term and thus may fail to deliver benefits in the long term.

- The contract may reinforce the downmarket image of Waltex.

- If the contract is undertaken alongside Strategy 2, then there is no spare capacity in the factory to benefit from increased output – particularly if additional advertising is undertaken in Strategy 1.

- As a large and powerful buyer Yarmack may put further pressure on Waltex eg delayed payment, more stringent quality requirements.

Benefits

- Potential additional sales of 40,000 watches generating a contribution of £240,000.

- Yarmack may improve the exposure of Waltex and thus improve the promotion of the product.

- The contract may be renewed, perhaps at an increased volume, in future years if they sell well in the first year of the contract.

Recommendation

The benefit of the increased sales needs to be weighed against the lower margin and the risk to existing sales from lost sales and lowering of reputation.

Subject to these concerns, there seems to be merit in entering into the contract this year provided there is minimal substitution of sales, since there is a contribution of £6 and the potential increase in volume is 4% of existing output.

WORKING

Sales to jewellers:

	£
Original sales price	45
Less VC per unit	(30)
Contribution	15
Sales price to Yarmack	36
Less VC per unit	(30)
Contribution	6

Thus contribution lost by Waltex if customers buy from Yarmack instead of jeweller = £9

13 Refer to the answer to CWI International Ltd in the Question Bank.

14 Refer to the answer to Kemmex Ice Cream plc in the Question Bank.

15 There is no answer to this self-test, as it is designed just to help you increase your business awareness.

CHAPTER 13

Business planning and functional strategies

Introduction

Examination context

Topic List

Summary and Self-test

Answers to Interactive questions

Answers to Self-test

Learning objectives

- Evaluate, in a given scenario, the functional strategies necessary to achieve a business's overall strategy

- Draft a simple business plan, or extracts there from, which will achieve given or implied objectives

- Evaluate the form and content of an entity's business plan

Specific syllabus references for this chapter are: 3a, 3e, 3f.

Syllabus links

The development of operational plans to implement corporate strategy received brief coverage in your Business & Finance exam.

Examination context

There are two key elements in this chapter. Firstly, in the exam you might be expected to draft elements of a business plan for a client or to identify weaknesses and omissions in a given business plan and suggest improvements. Secondly, the chapter looks at functional strategies. These would normally be examined in the context of the overall objectives and strategy of an organisation. So for example you might be expected to look at how the organisation could develop an HR strategy to better support its generic strategy of differentiation.

In Q3 September 2008 (*DT Ltd*) the scenario contains information about the company's development of a driving simulator and its need to prepare a business plan for the next stage of its expansion. The third requirement is:

'(c) David has asked for your help in producing a business plan to attract potential franchisees.

Write the sections of the plan which cover:

(i)   DT's business model
(ii)   The basis of DT's competitive advantage
(iii) The benefits for a franchisee. **(12 marks)**'

The point to note is that you need to combine you knowledge and skills of competitive advantage and the nature of franchising with the ability to communicate in the particular form of a business plan that is intended to attract and inform a particular audience, namely the potential franchisees.

In Q2 December 2013 (The Foto Phrame Company) the scenario focused on a manufacturer of mid-market cameras based in Germany which had global sales. The nature of the company's business means that the technology that customers demand from digital cameras is constantly changing. Part (b) required candidates to evaluate the factors to be considered in respect of two procurement and supply chain issues identified in the scenario. Interactive Question 6 in this chapter is closely based upon Q2 in December 2013.

1 Business planning

Section overview

- Business planning converts longer-term business strategies into actions to be taken now.

- Business plans are also used to apply for funding and are a critical document for a potential investor.

- In the exam you must be able to critically appraise a business plan provided by a client, recognising weaknesses and omissions and making recommendations for improvement.

1.1 Planning

Chapter 2 covered strategic planning as a way of determining the long-term success of the business.

This chapter looks at planning as an activity concerned with implementation of strategy.

The long-term corporate plan serves as the long-term framework for the organisation as a whole, but for operational purposes it is necessary to **convert the corporate plan into a series of short-term plans relating to sections, functions or departments**, perhaps covering one year.

Business planning may assist with:

- Co-ordinating the activities of different functions behind the achievement of the strategic goals for the year

- Putting the case for finance to funding sources (eg small businesses may approach a bank with a business plan or a charitable organisation will approach potential donor organisations)

- Gaining the approval of the Board (eg a national car dealership requires the manager of each showroom to submit an annual business plan for its approval)

- Winning contracts where the potential client wishes to be convinced that the firm will fully support the product or service being offered

- The development of the annual budget

Worked example: Planning at an airline

A major global airline operates two levels of planning.

Strategic planning: This considers the development of the business over the coming 10 to 15 years, a long period coinciding with the lifespan of its major capital investments. Here management will consider the development of emerging markets, the airline's market position, issues such as carbon and noise pollution and consolidation in the airline industry.

Business planning may concern the coming 12 months and is driven by route planning, ie which planes will fly which routes and where route schedules will be increased or cut-back. From this route-planning will come estimates of staffing needs, the number of aircraft required, fuel and maintenance requirements and the number of passengers, and the promotional activity to be undertaken. These will then form the basis of the annual budget of costs and revenues.

The annual business plan is in effect an annual instalment of the airline's strategic plan. Of course, given the inherent uncertainties of the industry, the strategic plan is very flexible.

1.2 Creating the business plan

The process of creating a business plan from a bigger picture strategy leads to questions being asked, and issues raised, which require detailed resolution.

Frequently business plans are created using a pro-forma supplied by the approving body, say a bank or government development agency.

Worked example: Small business plan template

The Small Business Administration website provides the following template and advice to users:

'There may only be one sure-thing in starting your own business, and that is that you will not get a loan without a complete business plan. No plan – no loan – no business.'

Here, from the Small Business Administration, is a suggested outline for a business plan.

Elements of a business plan

1. Cover sheet
2. Statement of purpose
3. Table of contents

    (i)   The business

        (a)   Description of business
        (b)   Marketing
        (c)   Competition
        (d)   Operating procedures
        (e)   Personnel
        (f)   Business insurance
        (g)   Financial data

    (ii) Financial data

        (a)   Loan applications

        (b)   Capital equipment and supply list

        (c)   Statement of financial position

        (d)   Breakeven analysis

        (e)   Pro-forma income projections (forecast income statements)

            – Three-year summary
            – Detail by month, first year
            – Detail by quarters, second and third years
            – Assumptions upon which projections were based

        (f)   Pro-forma cash flow

            – Follow guidelines for letter (e)

    (iii) Supporting documents

- Tax returns of the business and owners for last three years

- Personal financial statement (all banks have these forms)

- In the case of a franchised business, a copy of franchise contract and all supporting documents provided by the franchisor

- Copy of proposed lease or purchase agreement for building space

- Copy of licences and other legal documents

- Copy of resumes of all owners and senior managers

- Copies of letters of intent from suppliers, etc

Small businesses frequently request the help of their accounting advisers in the preparation of these business plans.

Interactive question 1: Aldine Computers & Training   [Difficulty level: Exam standard]

A new client, Aldine Computers & Training (Aldine), has approached you for assistance in preparing a business plan to obtain bank funding. Aldine have drafted the following business plan and have requested your comments on its viability and on how it might be improved to maximise the chance of the bank giving them funding.

Requirements

Draft a report assessing the viability of the business proposal and making recommendations on how the document may be supplemented to improve the chances of Aldine securing funding.

BUSINESS PLAN

for

Aldine Computers & Training

May 20X0

For South East Bank plc

INDEX

1   Summary of Business Plan

   (a)   Introduction to Aldine Computers & Training & Co
   (b)   Product: Computer Sales
   (c)   Product: Training Services
   (d)   Critical success factors which will make Aldine succeed
   (e)   Financial Summary

2   Management

   (a)   Proprietor: Employment Record
   (b)   Junior Partners: Brief Summary
   (c)   How and Why the Business Started

3   Product/Service

   (a)   Computers Sales
   (b)   Printer Sales
   (c)   Training Sales

4   Marketing

   (a)   The Market Size
   (b)   Future Growth
   (c)   Market Sector
   (d)   Expected Client Profile
   (e)   Competitors

5   Sales

   (a)   Advertising
   (b)   Promotion
   (c)   Who will Sell
   (d)   The Unique Selling Points
   (e)   Setting the Price

---

6 **Operational**

    (a) Location
    (b) Equipment and Costs To-date
    (c) Equipment Required
    (d) Staff

7 **Short-Medium Term Trading**

    (a) Objectives Short and Medium-term
    (b) What if ? – contingency plans

8 **Financials**

9 **Contact Details**

Summary of Business Plan Page 1

Introduction to Aldine Computers & Training

Aldine Computers & Training (Aldine) was established in March to trade on a regional basis. There are currently two partners: Peter Stone (27) and Kate Schofield (26). Both have extensive experience of computers and training.

Product: Computer Sales

Peter Stone has been building computers for five years for the well known firm PCNow.com and can use his contacts from there to obtain computer parts at favourable prices. Aldine will aim its computers at the corporate market and will aim to sell them with service contracts as an add-on. They may also offer leasing facilities.

Product: Training Services

Kate Schofield has spent the past five years in computer training with the last two years as an independent consultant. Kate's area of expertise is in the most modern cutting edge technology. The planned courses will run for two – three days, with quarterly one-day progress and update courses to keep those under training up to date with the latest technology. It is intended that corporate clients will pay for an initial training course for a group of employees with an annual fee payable to entitle members of this group to attend update courses and also to receive technical e-bulletins.

Critical success factors which will make Aldine succeed

Peter and Kate will make a good team. Peter worked for the family manufacturing firm for four years as an office manager in a small company and has demonstrated strong managerial skills. These will compliment Kate's ability to easily master new technology and her proven skills in technology training. Further, both bring existing business and network contacts and both believe that they could increase their own business areas by 200% within 6 – 12 months if they could delegate some of the more day-to-day activities in their current work schedules to a team within the expanded Aldine business.

Financial Summary

Initial forecasts suggest mark-up will be 40% and will yield expected profits of £90,00 in the first year. Peter and Kate have, between them, £20,000 capital to invest in the company. They require a further £40,000 in funds from a lender – secured on Peter's home. An overdraft facility of £15,000 is also required to finance larger than expected growth if cash flow is limited due to increased costs.

Proprietor: Employment Record

Peter Stone – CV attached

Aged 37, Peter holds a City & Guilds qualification in Computer Studies (2003), and has always held responsible positions in his past career. Peter worked for his family's manufacturing company as office manager for five years up to 2004 where his interest in computers began. Since then Peter worked for PCNow.com as Computer Services Manager. He gained much experience of 'blue chip' requirements. Peter has been married for four years and has two young children.

Kate Schofield – CV attached

Aged 26, Kate has three A Levels in English, History and Art. Kate has always sought positions that allow her to use her skills as a communicator and organiser. Kate worked for the leading firm APB Training Systems for three years before branching out as a successful independent training consultant for the past two years.

Other: Brief Summary

Peter Stone's father, Andrew Stone, will be assisting with the initial setup of the manufacturing outlet. He retired four years ago after running his own successful manufacturing business for 40 years. He has promised to be available as an ongoing source of help and advice.

Two other suitable individuals have been sounded out for management positions and are keen to be involved with this venture.

How and Why the Business Started

Peter and Kate met about a year ago whilst working for the same client. Peter later used Kate's services on an in-house training need at PCNow.com. Both came to believe that actively sourcing business for each other as a combined service will give them 'first sight' of opportunities.

Computer Sales

Three models of computers will be built:

- RS 01 800 MHz 4MB 6.4GB 15' Screen
- RS 02 1066 MHz 44MB 4GB 15' Screen
- RS 03 2 MHz 8MB 8GB 17' Screen

Each machine can have a number of specified add-ons: CD-RW, DVD-RW, Modem, Network Card. The machine will built in Aldine's own manufacturing unit, with service for the first year at the client's site. Thereafter an additional service contract will be offered which will feature a back-to-base repair service.

Servers will be purchased externally, as required to the specifications of the client.

Printer Sales

A number of leading laser and ink jet printers will be available, with the anticipated service contracts as a major source of continuing income.

Training Sales

Four levels of training will be available:

1	Trainee:	Up to 8 persons with no, or little, computer experience
2	Basic:	Up to 8 persons with basic computer skills
3	Intermediate:	Up to 8 persons who have a good working knowledge of computer systems
4	Advanced:	Up to 4 persons who understand technical computer systems

Market Outlook

Corporate computer sales are rising at 8% per quarter. It is expected to continue at that rate for another two years at which point the forecast economic slowdown may reduce sales growth to 4%. This will also be affected by the availability of new applications requiring corporations to upgrade their IT equipment. The ability to configure and give service support to virtual networks of computers to facilitate remote (home) working will be an important requirement.

Future Growth

The growth of PCs took place in the past decade to a point that penetration of the UK corporate market is complete. The market is saturated. However new applications require larger memory capacity and higher processing (and co-processing) speeds. It seems likely that concerns over data security will make future applications less PC based and instead require much greater reliance on access to the corporate networks for data and applications.

This will create a further wave of PC spending as corporations upgrade to the new 'portal' technologies.

Market Sector

Based in Runcorn, North-West England, the need for computer hardware and training is always available. SME Office space is increasing by 10% per annum. There are currently 95,000 SME's within a 50 mile radius of Runcorn.

Expected Client Profile

- Small Medium Enterprise (SME) Computer Sales
- Medium to Large Companies for Training Services
- Commerce and Industry
- Revenue £2m +
- Initially: Manchester and Districts
- Prefer client to be computer literate

Competitors

Computers

Three main companies have been identified as true competitors ie computer and peripheral sales and service direct to corporate clients on-site.

- **PowerShed Computers (Liverpool):** Established six years, revenue £0 (not known), six staff, no growth in past two years

- **Kato & Son PCs (Cheadle):** Established four years, revenue £2m, 10 staff, specialist computer systems, steady growth

- **Solutions.com (national company):** Established two years, revenue £7.5m, 40 staff, mainly top end clients, always stretched

Summary

Service complaints are common with all competitors, and hardware upgrades are long overdue. Solutions.com is looking to revamp their national operation in the spring.

Training

Two companies currently service the above client profile in computer training.

- **TrainLine (Runcorn):** Established 15 years, revenue £900,000, computer training staff four, no plans for rapid growth

- **SolutionsTraining.com (National Company – sister firm to Solutions.com):** Established eight years, revenue £6.5m, computer training staff 35, no local office

Summary

At present demand exceeds resources. No effective competition is challenging the top companies, who offer only limited cutting edge technology training skills.

Advertising

An advert has been placed in:

- The *Computer Sales* and *Training* sections of local telephone directories

- The Tuesday business section of the syndicated regional newspapers covering Runcorn, Manchester and Liverpool (this appears each week and is booked to the end of the present calendar year)

- *Computing* magazine – classified advertisement for Aldine in each issue of this weekly trade newspaper for IT specialists (available on free subscription)

Promotion

- Targeted mail shot within three months of receipt of funding to SMEs within 50 miles radius of Runcorn

- Telesales company to start promotion within one month of receipt of funding

- Two regional computer shows booked – 1st in two months, 2nd in six months

Who will Sell?

Both Peter and Kate are competent sales negotiators

The Unique Selling Points (USPs)

- Dual capability of hardware supplier and training provider
- Latest technology training package
- Availability within seven working days

Setting the Price

Computers

PC computers:

Prices include one year on-site total cover

- RS 01 800 MHz 4MB 6.4GB 15' Screen £650.00
- RS 02 1066 MHz 44MB 4GB 15' Screen £800.00
- RS 03 2 MHz 8MB 8GB 17' Screen   £950.00

PC Service contracts are:

- £150 per annum for one PC and then £85 for each additional PC

Printers will be leased and serviced:

- £50 per annum for one, then £30 for each additional unit. This excludes consumables (paper, cartridges etc) which will be sold at cost + 30%

Training

- £110 Per Day **Trainee**:   Up to 8 persons with no, or little, computer experience
- £135 Per Day **Basic**:   Up to 8 persons with basic computer skills
- £180 Per Day **Intermediate**: Up to 8 persons, a good working knowledge of computer systems
- £295 Per Day **Advanced**:   Up to 4 persons who understand technical computer systems

20% reduction for in-house training

CHAPTER

13

Location

New office-warehouse development on Industrial Estate located three miles from Runcorn town centre. Development has three meeting/conference rooms of high standard.

Three-year lease – no payment for first three months, then £3,000 per quarter in advance.

Equipment and Costs To-date

£

Office

4 × Tables	475
4 × Chairs	350
4 × Filing cabinet	210
2 × Computer (at cost)	875
1 × Laser printer	375
1 × Ink jet printer	300
1 × Photocopier	1,200
1 × Fax	250
1 × Answer phone	100
2 × Phone lines (installation)	150
Stationery and printing	1,100
Sub Total	5,385

Warehouse

4 × Work bench	2,000
6 × Stack shelving	1,500
Lighting	750
Sub Total	4,625

Inventory

Computer parts	3,750

Total 13,860

Staff

A mature office manager, and a trainee computer assembler will be sufficient for the initial three months – between three and nine months two training staff (to cover Trainee and Basic training) and a junior office clerk will be employed. At nine months a review of staff will need to take place.

Short – Medium Term Trading

Objective Short-term

Computers

An average of five computer sales per week, and two service contracts. The trainee assembler to be competent at assembly within six months, and to service a computer on site within 9 months.

Training

Kate training for average of three days per week within three months. New training staff to be working an average of four days per week by nine months.

At the 12 month plus period, a number of Kate and Peter's tried and tested ex-colleagues and friends will be approached to join the company with equity available.

What if ? – Contingency Plans

Both Peter and Kate are confident (with good reason) that a contingency plan is unlikely to be needed. However, Peter has contacts who can provide him with computer fitting and servicing without notice, and likewise Kate has her training contacts.

In a real emergency, say, Peter or Kate became ill, it is anticipated that the new staff could continue with 'basic' computer servicing or training – the requirement of a mature Office Manager is a strategic and important position.

Financials

Monthly Income Statement – projected for two years

- 20X1 to 20X2 Net Profit £90,000
- 20X2 to 20X3 Net Profit £175,000

As you can see from the Income Statement the business is expecting to make a net profit of £90,000 in the first year. The figures include the salary of the full compliment of staff as outlined on page 6 (c) above. The second year shows a net profit of £175,000: if this does happen they will purchase their own premises for £180,000. The total compliment of staff at the end of 20X2 is 25.

Statement of financial position projected for two years

- 20X1 to 20X2 Net Assets £130,000
- 20X2 to 20X3 Net Assets £260,000

The projected figures show the anticipated reinvestment of all profits for the first two years: this trend will continue. Inventory at the end of the second year is high but the discounts on bulk purchase is a profitable option in the computer industry, if technology allows.

Monthly Cash Flow Forecast for two years

- 20X1 to 20X2 Year-end Net Cash Flow £25,000
- 20X2 to 20X3 Year-end Net Cash Flow £120,000

In the first year the cash flow will remain positive unless an opportunity to buy bulk computer parts presents itself. Likewise the entire second year is planned to be in the black and consideration will be given at that time as to the purchase of assets.

Contact Details		End Page
Peter Stone		**Kate Schofield**
0XXXX 9876543	**Office**	0XXXX 9876543
	Unit 3 The Trading Estate	
	The Avenue	
	Runcorn WA7 4SA	
019671 3546387	**Home**	01234 1234567
09876 1234567	**Mobile**	017790 9876544
96 Avenue Hill	**Home Address**	12 High Road
Runcorn WA7 5RR		Runcorn WA7 3AA

See **Answer** at the end of this chapter.

2 Implementing strategy

Section overview

- Implementation requires the corporate strategy to be broken down into functional strategies and operational plans.

- The business's choice of competitive strategy (cost leadership or differentiation) has implications for its functional strategies.

To implement the chosen corporate strategy, the business's competitive, investment and financial strategies need to be broken down further into functional strategies and operational plans.

The operational plan sets out what is expected of each function of the business and how actions will be taken to meet those expectations.

2.1 The finance department and strategic planning

The role of finance is three-fold.

1. Finance is a resource, which can be deployed so that objectives are met.

2. A firm's objectives are often expressed in financial or semi-financial terms.

3. Financial controls are often used to plan and control the implementation of strategies. Financial indicators are often used for detailed performance assessment.

As a planning medium and tool for monitoring, financial management makes a variety of strategic contributions.

- Ensuring that resources of finance are available. Issues of raising equity or loan capital are important here. The amount of resources that the strategy will consume needs to be assessed, and the likely cost of those resources established. Cash flow forecasting will also be necessary.

- Integrating the strategy into budgets for revenues, operating costs and capital expenditure over a period. The budgeting process serves as a planning tool and a means of financial control and monitoring.

- Establishing the necessary performance measures, in line with other departments for monitoring strategic objectives.

- Establishing priorities, if, for example, altered conditions make some aspects of the strategy hard to fulfil.

- Assisting in the modelling process. Financial models are simplified representations of the business. It is easier to experiment with models, to see the effect of changes in variables, than with the business itself.

2.2 Functional strategies and competitive advantage

In Chapters 6 and 7 we considered how competitive advantages can be gained by a business. We examined the concept of the value chain and discussed how a business can create and sustain competitive advantage using cost or value drivers. The business's choice of competitive strategy determines whether the focus of the chain should be cost (cost leadership) or value (differentiation).

This has implications for the organisation when it is implementing its functional strategies.

The rest of this chapter will discuss functional strategies for:

- Marketing
- Human resources
- Research and development
- Operations/production
- Purchasing

3 Marketing planning

Section overview

- Marketing planning is one way by which corporate strategy is implemented.
- This requires a detailed plan of implementation and also of control.

3.1 The marketing plan

The main concepts and tools of marketing received detailed coverage in Chapter 8.

The implementation and control of the marketing effort might take the form of a **marketing plan**:

Section	Content
The executive summary	This is the finalised planning document with a summary of the main goals and recommendations in the plan.
Situation analysis	This consists of the SWOT (strengths, weaknesses, opportunities and threats) analysis and forecasts.
Objectives and goals	What the organisation is hoping to achieve, or needs to achieve, perhaps in terms of market share or 'bottom line' profits and returns.
Marketing strategy	This considers the selection of target markets, the marketing mix and marketing expenditure levels.
Strategic marketing plan	• Three to five (or more) years long • Defines scope of product and market activities • Aims to match the activities of the firm to its distinctive competences
Tactical marketing plan	• One-year time horizon • Generally based on existing products and markets • Concerned with marketing mix issues

Section	Content
Action plan	This sets out how the strategies are to be achieved. The Marketing mix strategy should cover the 7 Ps discussed in Chapter 8. The mix strategy may vary for each segment.
Budgets	These are developed from the action programme.
Controls	These will be set up to monitor the progress of the plan and the budget.

3.2 Corporate strategy and marketing strategies

So, what is the relationship between marketing and overall strategic management? The two are closely linked since there can be no corporate plan which does not involve products/services and customers.

Corporate strategic plans aim to guide the overall development of an organisation. Marketing planning is subordinate to corporate planning but makes a significant contribution to it and is concerned with many of the same issues.

- The **strategic** component of marketing planning focuses on the direction which an organisation will take in relation to a specific market, or set of markets, in order to achieve a specified set of objectives.

- Marketing planning also requires an **operational** component that defines tasks and activities to be undertaken in order to achieve the desired strategy. The **marketing plan** is concerned uniquely with **products** and **markets**.

The process of corporate planning and the relationship with marketing strategy is shown in the following table.

	Corporate	Marketing
Set objectives	For the firm as a whole: eg increase profits by X%.	For products and market: eg increase market share by X%; increase revenue.
Internal appraisal (strengths and weaknesses)	Review the effectiveness of the different aspects of the organisation.	Conduct a marketing audit: a review of marketing activities. Does the firm have a marketing orientation?
External appraisal (opportunities and threats)	Review political, economic, social, technological, ecological factors impacting on the whole firm.	Review environmental factors as they affect customers, products and markets.
Gaps	There may be a gap between desired objectives and forecast objectives. How to close the gap.	The company may be doing less well in particular markets than it ought to. Marketing will be focused on growth.

	Corporate	Marketing
Strategy	Develop strategies to fill the gap: eg diversifying, entering new markets.	A marketing strategy is a plan to achieve the organisation's objectives by specifying: • Resources to be allocated to marketing • How those resources should be used In the context of applying the marketing concept, a marketing strategy would: • Identify target markets and customer needs in those markets • Plan products which will satisfy the needs of those markets • Organise marketing resources, so as to match products with customers
Implementation	Implementation is delegated to departments of the business.	The plans must be put into action, eg advertising space must be bought.
Control	Results are reviewed and the planning process starts again.	Has the firm achieved its market share objectives?

The following diagram summarises the relationship of marketing planning to the corporate plan.

Marketing and corporate planning

3.3 Controlling marketing activities

Once marketing strategies are implemented, there needs to be **control** and **performance measures** in place to support the purpose of the plan. **Marketing strategies** are developed to satisfy corporate objectives and may reflect the results of the marketing audit.

The **marketing control process** can be broken down into four stages.

- Development of objectives and strategies
- Establishment of standards
- Evaluation of performance
- Corrective action

Part of the corrective action stage may well be to adjust objectives and strategies in the light of experience.

The marketing control process

Typical quantitative performance levels might be as follows.

- Market share, perhaps by comparison with a major competitor.

- Operational targets may also be relevant to marketing performance, for example having the right products available.

- Other measures can include measures of customer satisfaction, if these are regularly monitored.

Performance is evaluated by comparing actual with target. Control action can be taken.

3.4 The marketing audit

A marketing audit is a wide ranging **review of all activities associated with marketing** undertaken by an organisation.

In order to exercise proper strategic control a marketing audit should satisfy four requirements:

- It should take a comprehensive look at every product, market, distribution channel and ingredient in the marketing mix.

- It should not be restricted to areas of apparent ineffectiveness such as an unprofitable product, a troublesome distribution channel, or low efficiency on direct selling.

- It should be carried out according to a set of predetermined, specified procedures.

- It should be conducted regularly.

Worked example: Tesco

In 2014, Marketing Week published an article titled 'Tesco looks to end frivolous promotions with £200m price investment'. The article followed a review by senior management at the UK's largest retailer which highlighted the volatility of price promotions among the major supermarkets. Tesco managing director Chris Bush says the retailer is shifting investment in promotions to 'lower, more stable pricing'. He adds that while Tesco will not be stopping promotions altogether, it will look to offer more focused, relevant deals underpinned by its Price-Promise price matching service'.

According to Marketing Week, 'Tesco last launched a big price initiative in 2011 with its £500m 'Big Price Drop'. Then the supermarket was criticised for having a one-dimensional approach to marketing and was forced to rethink its approach. Tesco CEO Philip Clarke admits that 'was not executed well' but says it will focus this time on service, quality and range as well. We are focused on sharper prices, improved quality, stronger ranges, better service'.

In July 2014, it was announced that Phillip Clarke would be stepping down in October. The announcement followed Tesco's latest profit warning.

Source: *Marketing Week*

Interactive question 2: Marketing plan   [Difficulty level: Intermediate]

(a) What is a SWOT analysis and how does it lead to an understanding of realistic market opportunities?

(b) Explain the importance of marketing planning for a new consumer product to be launched in your country.

(c) Using examples, identify the main steps involved in the marketing planning process.

See **Answer** at the end of this chapter.

---

4 Human resources planning

Section overview

- **Human resource management (HRM)** is the process of evaluating an organisation's human resource needs, finding people to fill those needs, and getting the best work from each employee by providing the right incentives and job environment – with the overall aim of helping achieve organisational goals.

- This requires planning resource needs for the future and succession planning for existing staff.

- Staff appraisals are a vital part of this process.

4.1 Scope of human resource management (HRM)

Definition

Human resource management (HRM): 'A strategic and coherent approach to the management of an organisation's most valued assets: the people working there who individually and collectively contribute to the achievement of its objectives for sustainable competitive advantage.' (Armstrong)

4.1.1 Goals of strategic HRM

- Serve the **interests of management**, as opposed to employees.
- Suggest a **strategic approach to personnel issues**.
- Link **business mission to HR strategies**.
- Enable **human resource development to add value** to products and services.
- Gain **employees' commitment** to the organisation's values and goals.

The HR strategy has to be related to the business strategy.

Worked example: HR issues in the airline industry

Most airlines are trying to become global companies to avoid dependence on one country.

Business planning and functional strategies   457

Business strategy	HR implications	Airline example
What business are we in?	What people do we need?	Air transportation requires pilots, cabin crew, ground crew etc.
What products/markets, level of output and competitive strategy, now and in future	Where do we need people, what are they expected to do, and how many? Location and size of workforce? Productivity expected and output?	The airline is going global and therefore it needs cabin crew who are skilled in languages and are sensitive to cultural differences.
What is the culture and value system? Is it the right one?	The need to change culture and values.	A cultural change programme; recruiting people to fit in with the right value system; attitudinal assessments.
Tomorrow's strategies, demands and technologies	Tomorrow's personnel needs must be addressed **now**, because of lead times. New technology requires training in **new skills**.	Recruitment, training, cultural education.
Critical success factors	How far do these depend on staff?	Service levels in an aircraft depend very much on the staff, so HRM is crucial.

4.2 Human resources planning

HR must keep a **balance** between the **forecast supply** of human resources in the organisation and the organisation's **forecast demand** for human resources.

Forecast internal supply

- Numbers of people
- Skills/competences
- Experience
- Age/career stage
- Aspirations
- Forecast natural wastage

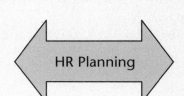

HR Planning

Forecast demand

- New skills required
- New attitudes needed
- Growth/contraction in jobs/roles
- New technologies

Assessed from:
- Human resource audits
- Staff appraisals
- Historical records of staff turnover
- Forecasts of economic outlook (lose staff in boom)

Derived from:
- Business strategy
- Technological developments
- Competitor behaviour
- Outlook for the industry

4.3 Closing the gap between demand and supply: the HR plan

The HR plan is prepared on the basis of personnel requirements, and the implications for productivity and costs. The HR plan breaks down into subsidiary plans.

Plan	Comment
Recruitment plan	Numbers; types of people; when required; recruitment programme
Training plan	Numbers of trainees required and/or existing staff needing training; training programme

Plan	Comment
Redevelopment plan	Programmes for transferring, retraining employees
Productivity plan	Programmes for improving productivity, or reducing manpower costs; setting productivity targets
Redundancy plan	Where and when redundancies are to occur; policies for selection and declaration of redundancies; re-development, re-training or re-location of redundant employees; policy on redundancy payments, union consultation
Retention plan	Actions to reduce avoidable labour wastage

The plan should include budgets, targets and standards. It should allocate responsibilities for implementation and control (reporting, monitoring achievement against plan).

4.4 Succession planning

Succession planning should be an integral part of the HR plan and should support the organisation's chosen strategy. The developed plan should also be compatible with any changes that that are foreseen in the way the organisation operates. It is likely that strategic objectives will only be obtained if management development proceeds in step with the evolution of the organisation.

4.4.1 Benefits of succession planning

- The development of managers at all levels is likely to be improved if it takes place within the context of a succession plan. Such a plan gives focus to management development by suggesting objectives that are directly relevant to the organisation's needs.

- Continuity of leadership is more likely, with fewer dislocating changes of approach and policy.

- Assessment of managerial talent is improved by the establishment of relevant criteria.

4.4.2 Features of successful succession planning

- The plan should focus on future requirements, particularly in terms of strategy and culture.

- The plan should be driven by top management. Line management also have important contributions to make. It is important that it is not seen as a HR responsibility.

- Management development is as important as assessment and selection.

- Assessment should be objective and preferably involve more than one assessor for each manager assessed.

- Succession planning will work best if it aims to identify and develop a leadership *cadre* rather than merely to establish a queue for top positions. A pool of talent and ability is a flexible asset for the organisation.

4.5 The human resource (HR) cycle

A relatively simple model that provides a framework for explaining the nature and significance of HRM is Devanna's human resource cycle.

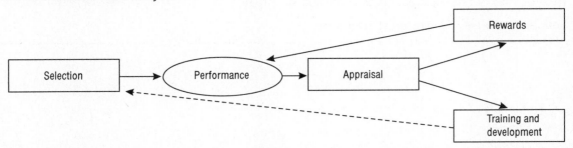

Selection is important to ensure the organisation obtains people with the qualities and skills required.

Appraisal enables targets to be set that contribute to the achievement of the overall strategic objectives of the organisation. It also identifies skills and performance gaps, and provides information relevant to reward levels.

Training and development ensure skills remain up-to-date, relevant, and comparable with (or better than) the best in the industry.

The **reward system** should motivate and ensure valued staff are retained.

Performance depends upon each of the four components and how they are co-ordinated.

4.5.1 The role of staff appraisals

The setting up of a systematic approach to staff appraisal (otherwise called a performance review) is essential to good human resources management. It has the following benefits.

- A forum for agreeing objectives for the coming year that ensure the individual pursues goals that are congruent with the business strategy

- An opportunity to outline or respond to difficulties affecting the individual's performance

- Provision of feedback will motivate and develop the individual

- Identifies personal development needs of the individual, eg for future roles

- Identifies candidates for succession and development

Worked example: Google

The following example highlights the importance of effective Human Resource Management.

In 2014, Google was named the 'Best Company to Work For' by Fortune magazine. Speaking to the CBS network, Fortune Managing Editor Andy Serwer highlighted that the list is based on more than the benefits and pay a company offer. 'Obviously, pay and benefits are all really important, but perks demonstrating corporate citizenship and an effort to create an appealing work environment are as important.'

An article on the recruitment industry website ere.net notes 'winning a spot on the 100 Best Companies to Work For List is not an easy job. Many companies actively campaign to earn top scores, but all must submit to a rigorous series of surveys of employees and managers, and onsite inspections by The Great Place to Work Institute. The end result is a Trust Index measuring what the Institute believes are the cornerstones of a great place to work: Credibility, Respect, Fairness and Pride, and Camaraderie.'

Google's focus on corporate citizenship is evident in the way the company conducts its business. Google is renowned for 'giving back' to the communities it interacts with, running a 'Donations for Doers' programme aimed at getting its employees (referred to as 'Googlers') involved in supporting good causes. An article on greatrated.com highlights that the company donates '$50 for every five hours a Googler volunteers with an approved non-profit organisation'. The article highlights 'not only do Googlers take tremendous pride in their work, but 99 percent say they enjoy special and unique benefits. In its efforts to attract and retain top talent, Google's famous employee-friendly perks include onsite cafes, dry cleaners and bowling alleys, all designed to encourage collaboration and help Googlers working around the clock.'

Serwer notes that 'you look at Google: They get the best talent in America. Young people are killing to work there. It's super competitive to get a job there and they continue to innovate and a lot of that is because they get the best people to come and stay there'.

Sources: www.ere.net & us.greatrated.com

ScannerTech is a fast growing hi-tech company with expertise in electronic scanners. It has 100 employees and aims to double in size over the next three years. The company was set up by two researchers from a major university who now act as joint managing directors. They are intend leaving ScannerTech once the growth objective is achieved and it is large enough to be sold.

ScannerTech makes sophisticated imaging devices used by the airline security and health industries. These two markets are very different in terms of customer requirements but use the same basic technology. Because of growing sales from exports the current strategic plan anticipates a foreign manufacturing plant being set up within the next three years. Present managers are staff who joined in the early years of the company and have their expertise in research and development. Further growth will require additional staff in all parts of the business, particularly in manufacturing and sales and marketing.

Olivia Marcuse is HR manager at ScannerTech. She is annoyed that HR is the one management function not involved in the strategic planning process shaping the future growth and direction of the company. She feels trapped in a role traditionally given to HR specialists, that of simply reacting to the staffing needs brought about by strategic decisions taken by other parts of the business. She feels it is time to make the case for a strategic role for HR at ScannerTech to help it face its challenges.

Requirements

Prepare a short report for Olivia Marcuse to present to ScannerTech's board of directors on the way a Human Resource plan could link effectively to its growth strategy.

See **Answer** at the end of this chapter.

5 Research and development planning

Section overview

- Research and development is essential for product and process improvement.
- The need to ensure that R&D has a commercial application forms a link between R&D and other disciplines such as Marketing, Operations and Finance.

5.1 Product and process research

Research may be intended to improve **products** or **processes**. R&D should support the organisation's strategy, be properly planned and be closely co-ordinated with marketing.

Many organisations employ **specialist staff** to conduct research and development (R&D). They may be organised in a separate functional department of their own. In an organisation run on a product division basis, R&D staff may be employed by each division.

There are two categories of R&D.

Product research – new product development

The new product development process must be carefully controlled; new products are a major source of competitive advantage but can cost a great deal of money to bring to market. A screening process is necessary to ensure that resources are concentrated on projects with a high probability of success.

Process research

Process research involves attention to how the goods/services are produced. Process research has these aspects.

- **Processes** are crucial in service industries (eg fast food), as part of the services sold.
- **Productivity**: Efficient processes save money and time.
- **Planning**: If you know how long certain stages in a project are likely to take, you can plan the most efficient sequence.
- **Quality management** for enhanced quality.

R&D should be closely co-ordinated with marketing

- Customer needs, as identified by marketers, should be a vital input to new product developments.

- The R&D department might identify possible changes to product specifications so that a variety of marketing mixes can be tried out and screened.

Worked example: R&D at Nestlé

An example of the relationship of R&D to marketing was described in an article in *The Financial Times* about the firm Nestlé, which invested £46m a year in research and approximately £190m on development. Nestlé had a central R&D function, but also regional development centres. The central R&D function was involved in basic research. 'Much of the lab's work was only tenuously connected with the company's business... When scientists joined the lab, they were told "Just work in this or that area. If you work hard enough, we're sure you'll find something."' The results of this approach were:

(a)   The research laboratory was largely cut off from development centres.
(b)   Much research never found commercial application.

As part of Nestlé's wider reorganisation, which restructured the business into strategic business units (SBUs), formal links were established between R&D and the SBUs. This meant that research procedures have been changed so that a commercial time horizon is established for projects.

5.2 Strategic role of R&D

Despite the evident costs and uncertainties of R&D expenditure its strategic importance can be understood by reference to some of the strategic models discussed earlier:

- **Porter's generic strategies**: Product innovation could be a source of **differentiation**. Process innovation may enable differentiation or **cost leadership**.

- **Porter's value chain**: R&D is included within the support activities of **technology development**. It can be harnessed in the service of lower costs or improved differentiation.

- **Ansoff matrix**: R&D supports all four strategic quadrants. Strategies of Market Penetration and Market Development can be served by product refinement. Product Development and Diversification will require more significant innovations to product.

- **Industry and product lifecycles**: The obsolescence of existing products can be accelerated by product R&D and so R&D is required to provide the firm with replacements.

6   Operations planning and management

Section overview

- Operations management is concerned with the transformation of 'inputs' into 'outputs' that meet the needs of the customer.

- It is characterised by the four Vs of volume, variety, variation in demand, and visibility.

- Capacity planning and some of the modern IT/IS applications supporting them are reviewed.

- Quality assurance and TQM are essential components of many modern manufacturing approaches.

6.1 Formulating operations strategy

Definition

Operations management is concerned with the **design, implementation** and **control** of the **processes** in an organisation that transform inputs (materials, labour, other resources, information and customers) into output products and services.

In broad terms, operational planning will include many of the following concepts.

- Setting **operational objectives** that are consistent with the overall business strategy of the organisation.

- Translating **business strategy** or **marketing strategy** into **operations strategy**, by means of identifying key competitive factors (referred to perhaps as order-winning factors or critical success factors).

- Assessing the relative importance of different **competitive factors**.

- Assessing current operational performance by **comparison** with the performance of **competitors**.

- Using the idea of a 'clean-slate' or 'green-field' approach to strategy selection. Managers are asked to consider how they would ideally design operations if they could **start again from scratch**. The ideal operations design is then compared with actual operations, and important differences identified. Strategy decisions are then taken to move actual performance closer towards the ideal.

- Formulating strategy could be based on other types of **gap analysis**, such as comparing what the market wants with what the operation is actually achieving, and taking decisions aimed at closing the significant gaps.

- Emphasising the iterative process of strategy selection: Strategies should be **continually reviewed, refined and re-developed** through experience and in response to changes in the environment.

Six items that should be incorporated into an organisation's operations strategy:

Item	Comment
Capability required	What is it that the organisation wants to 'do' or produce?
Range and location of operations	How big does the organisation want to be – or can it be? How many sites and where should they be located?
Investment in technology	How will processes and production be performed?
Strategic buyer-supplier relationships	Who will be key strategic partners?
New products/services	What are the expected product life-cycles?
Structure of operations	How will staff be organised and managed?

6.2 Operations: the four Vs

In Business & Finance you will have learnt about the **four Vs** of operations: **volume, variety, variation** in demand and **visibility**. These affect the way in which an operation will be organised and managed.

	High	Low
Volume	A high volume operation lends itself to a capital-intensive operation, with specialisation of work and well-established systems for getting the work done. Unit costs should be low.	Low-volume operations mean that each member of staff will have to perform more than one task, so that specialisation is not achievable. There will be less systemisation, and unit costs of output will be higher than with a high volume operation.
Variety	When there is large variety, an operation needs to be flexible and capable of adapting to individual customer needs. The work may therefore be complex, and unit costs will be high.	When variety is limited, the operation should be well defined, with standardisation, regular operational routines and low unit costs.
Variation in demand	When the variation in demand is high, an operation has a problem with capacity utilisation. It will try to anticipate variations in demand and alter its capacity accordingly. For example, the tourist industry takes on part-time staff during peak demand periods. Unit costs are likely to be high because facilities and staff are under-utilised in the off-peak periods.	When demand is stable, it should be possible for an operation to achieve a high level of capacity utilisation, and costs will accordingly be lower.
Visibility	Many services are highly visible to customers. High visibility calls for staff with good communication and inter-personal skills. They tend to need more staff than low-visibility operations and so are more expensive to run. When visibility is high, customer satisfaction with the operation will be heavily influenced by their perceptions. Customers will be dissatisfied if they have to wait, and staff will need high customer contact skills. Unit costs of a visible operation are likely to be high.	When visibility is low, there can be a time lag between production and consumption, allowing the operation to utilise its capacity more efficiently. Customer contact skills are not important in low-visibility operations, and unit costs should be low. Some operations are partly visible to the customer and partly invisible, and organisations might make this distinction in terms of front office and back office operations.

6.3 Capacity planning

Various types of capacity plan may be used.

- **Level capacity plan** is a plan to maintain activity at a constant level over the planning period, and to ignore fluctuations in forecast demand. In a manufacturing operation, when demand is lower than capacity, the operation will produce goods for inventory. In a service operation, such as a hospital, restaurant or supermarket management must accept that resources will be under-utilised for some of the time, to ensure an adequate level of service during peak demand times. Queues will also be a feature of this approach.

- **Chase demand plan** aims to match capacity as closely as possible to the forecast fluctuations in demand. To achieve this aim, resources must be flexible. For example, staff numbers might have to be variable and staff might be required to work overtime or shifts. Variations in equipment levels might also be necessary, perhaps by means of short-term rental arrangements.

- **Demand management planning**: Reduce peak demand by switching it to the off-peak periods such as by offering off-peak prices. Price discrimination is discussed in Chapter 8.

- **Mixed plans**: Capacity planning involving a mixture of level capacity planning, chase demand planning and demand management planning.

6.4 Capacity control

Capacity control involves reacting to actual demand and influences on actual capacity as they arise. IT/IS applications used in manufacturing operations include:

- **Materials requirements planning (MRP I)**: converts estimates of demand into a materials requirements schedule.

- **Manufacturing resource planning (MRP II)**: a computerised system for planning and monitoring all the resources of a manufacturing company: manufacturing, marketing, finance and engineering.

- **Enterprise resource planning (ERP)** software: includes a number of integrated modules designed to support all of the key activities of an enterprise. This includes managing the key elements of the supply chain such as product planning, purchasing, stock control and customer service including order tracking.

6.5 Just-in-time systems

Definition

Just-in-time: An approach to planning and control based on the idea that goods or services should be produced only when they are ordered or needed. Also called lean manufacturing.

6.5.1 Three key elements in the JIT philosophy

Element	Comment
Elimination of waste	Waste is defined as any activity that does not add value. Examples of waste identified by Toyota were: • Overproduction, ie producing more than was immediately needed by the next stage in the process. • Waiting time: Measured by labour efficiency and machine efficiency. • Transport: Moving items around a plant does not add value. Waste can be reduced by changing the layout of the factory floor so as to minimise the movement of materials. • Waste in the process: Some activities might be carried out only because there are design defects in the product, or because of poor maintenance work. • Inventory: Inventory is wasteful. The target should be to eliminate all inventory by tackling the things that cause it to build up. • Simplification of work: An employee does not necessarily add value by working. Simplifying work reduces waste in the system (the waste of motion) by eliminating unnecessary actions. • Defective goods are quality waste. This is a significant cause of waste in many operations.
The involvement of all staff in the operation	JIT is a cultural issue, and its philosophy has to be embraced by everyone involved in the operation if it is to be applied successfully. Critics of JIT argue that management efforts to involve all staff can be patronising.
Continuous improvement	The ideal target is to meet demand immediately with perfect quality and no waste. In practice, this ideal is never achieved. However, the JIT philosophy is that an organisation should work towards the ideal, and continuous improvement is both possible and necessary. The Japanese term for continuous improvement is *kaizen*.

6.5.2 JIT purchasing

With JIT purchasing, an organisation establishes a close relationship with trusted suppliers, and develops an arrangement with the supplier for being able to purchase materials only when they are needed for production. The supplier is required to have a flexible production system capable of responding immediately to purchase orders from the organisation.

Interactive question 4: Lean manufacturing at Toyota

[Difficulty level: Intermediate]

Japanese car manufacturer Toyota was the first company to develop JIT (JIT was originally called the Toyota Production System). After the end of the world war in 1945, Toyota recognised that it had much to do to catch up with the US automobile manufacturing industry. The company was making losses. In Japan, however, consumer demand for cars was weak, and consumers were very resistant to price increases. Japan also had a bad record for industrial disputes. Toyota itself suffered from major strike action in 1950.

The individual credited with devising JIT in Toyota from the 1940s was Taiichi Ohno, and JIT techniques were developed gradually over time. The *kanban* system for example, was devised by Toyota in the early 1950s, but was only finally fully implemented throughout the Japanese manufacturing operation in 1962.

Ohno identified wastes and worked to eliminate them from operations in Toyota. Measures that were taken by the company included the following.

(a)   The aim of reducing costs was of paramount importance in the late 1940s.

(b)   The company should aim to level the flow of production and eliminate unevenness in the work flow.

(c)   The factory layout was changed. Previously all machines, such as presses, were located in the same area of the factory. Under the new system, different types of machines were clustered together in production cells.

(d)   Machine operators were re-trained.

(e)   Employee involvement in the changes was seen as being particularly important. Team work was promoted.

(f)   The *kanban* system [production on demand] was eventually introduced, but a major problem with its introduction was the elimination of defects in production.

Requirements

Can you explain how each of the changes described above came to be regarded as essential by Toyota's management?

See **Answer** at the end of this chapter.

6.5.3 JIT and service operations

The JIT philosophy can be applied to service operations as well as to manufacturing operations. Whereas JIT in manufacturing seeks to eliminate inventories, JIT in service operations seeks to remove queues of customers.

Queues of customers are wasteful because:

*   They waste customers' time.
*   Queues require space for customers to wait in, and this space is not adding value.
*   Queuing lowers the customer's perception of the quality of the service.

The application of JIT to a service operation calls for the removal of specialisation of tasks, so that the work force can be used more flexibly and moved from one type of work to another, in response to demand and work flow requirements.

Worked example: JIT in a postal service

A postal delivery has specific postmen or postwomen allocated to their own routes. However, there may be scenarios where, say, Route A is overloaded whilst Route B has a very light load of post.

Rather than have letters for Route A piling up at the sorting office, when the person responsible for Route B has finished delivering earlier, this person might help out on Route A.

Teamwork and flexibility are difficult to introduce into an organisation because people might be more comfortable with clearly delineated boundaries in terms of their responsibilities. However, the customer is usually not interested in the company organisation structure because he or she is more interested in receiving a timely service.

In practice, service organisations are likely to use a buffer operation to minimise customer queuing times. For example, a hairdresser will get an assistant to give the client a shampoo to reduce the impact of waiting for the stylist. Restaurants may have an area where guests may have a drink if no vacant tables are available immediately; such a facility may even encourage guests to plan in a few drinks before dinner thereby increasing the restaurant's revenues.

6.6   Quality management

Definitions

Quality assurance focuses on the way a product or service in produced. Procedures and standards are devised with the aim of ensuring defects are eliminated (or at least minimised) during the development and production process).

Quality control is concerned with checking and reviewing work that has been done. Quality control therefore has a narrower focus than quality assurance.

6.6.1   Cost of quality

The **cost of quality** may be looked at in a number of different ways. For example, some may say that producing higher quality output will increase costs – as more costly resources are likely to be required to achieve a higher standard. Others may focus on the idea that poor quality output will lead to customer dissatisfaction, which generates costs associated with complaint resolution and warranties.

The demand for better quality has led to the acceptance of the view that quality management should aim to **prevent** defective production rather than simply detect it because it reduces costs in the long run.

Most modern approaches to quality have therefore tried to assure quality in the production process, (quality assurance) rather than just inspecting goods or services after they have been produced.

6.6.2   Total Quality Management (TQM)

Total Quality Management (TQM) is a popular technique of **quality assurance**. Main elements are:

- **Internal customers and internal suppliers**: All parts of the organisation are involved in quality issues, and need to work together. Every person and every activity in the organisation affects the work done by others. The work done by an internal supplier for an internal customer will eventually affect the quality of the product or service to the external customer.

- **Service level agreements**: Some organisations formalise the internal supplier-internal customer concept by requiring each internal supplier to make a **service level agreement** with its internal customer, covering the terms and standard of service.

- **Quality culture within the firm**: Every person within an organisation has an impact on quality, and it is the responsibility of everyone to get quality right.

- **Empowerment**: Recognition that employees themselves are often the best source of information about how (or how not) to improve quality.

7 Purchasing

Section overview

- Purchasing is a major influence on a firm's costs and quality.

- Sourcing strategy is developing from the use of many suppliers to get a better price to the fostering of strategic procurement relationships with just a few.

- E-procurement systems can help to improve the efficiency of the process and reduce costs.

Definition

Purchasing is the acquisition of material resources and business services for use by the organisation.

7.1 The importance of purchasing

Cost: Raw materials and subcomponents purchases are a major cost for many firms.

Quality: The quality of input resources affects the quality of outputs and the efficiency of the production function.

Strategy: In retailing, buying goods for resale is one of the most important activities of the business.

7.2 The purchasing mix

The purchasing manager has to obtain the best purchasing mix.

7.2.1 Quantity

The size and timing of purchase orders will be dictated by the balance between two things:

- Delays in production caused by insufficient inventories

- Costs of holding inventories: tied up capital, storage space, deterioration, insurance, risk of pilferage

A system of inventory control will set optimum reorder levels (the inventory level at which supplies must be replenished so as to arrive in time to meet demand) to ensure economic order quantities (EOQ) are obtained for individual inventory items.

7.2.2 Quality

The production department will need to be consulted about the quality of goods required for the manufacturing process, and the marketing department about the quality of goods acceptable to customers. Purchased components might be an important constituent of product quality.

7.2.3 Price

Favourable short-term trends in prices may influence the buying decision, but purchasing should have an eye to the best value over a period of time – considering quality, delivery, urgency of order, inventory-holding requirements and so on.

7.2.4 Delivery

The lead time between placing and delivery of an order can be crucial to efficient inventory control and production planning. The reliability of suppliers' delivery arrangements must also be assessed.

7.3 Sourcing strategies

There are a range of possible strategies open to an organisation when deciding who they will purchase their supplies from.

Supply sourcing strategies	
Option	**Comment**
Single supplier	**Advantages** • Stronger relationship with the supplier. • Possible source of superior quality due to increased opportunity for a supplier quality assurance programme. • Facilitates better communication. • Economies of scale. • Facilitates confidentiality. • Possible source of competitive advantage. **Disadvantages** • Vulnerable to any disruption in supply. • Supplier power may increase if no alternative supplier. • The supplier is vulnerable to shifts in order levels.
Multiple suppliers	**Advantages** • Access to a wide range of knowledge and expertise. • Competition among suppliers may drive the price down. • Supply failure by one supplier will cause minimal disruption. **Disadvantages** • Not easy to develop an effective quality assurance programme. • Suppliers may display less commitment. • Neglecting economies of scale.
Delegated	A supplier is given responsibility for the delivery of a complete sub-assembly. For example, rather than dealing with several suppliers a 'first tier' supplier would be appointed to deliver a complete sub-assembly (eg a PC manufacturer may delegate the production of keyboards). **Advantages** • Allows the utilisation of specialist external expertise. • Frees-up internal staff for other tasks. • The purchasing entity may be able to negotiate economies of scale. **Disadvantages** • First tier supplier is in a powerful position. • Competitors may utilise the same external organisation so unlikely to be a source of competitive advantage.

Interactive question 5: PicAPie Ltd   [Difficulty level: Intermediate]

Gourmet PicAPie Ltd employs a total quality management program and manufactures 12 different types of pie from chicken and leek to vegetarian. The directors of PicAPie are proud of their products, and always attempt to maintain a high quality of input at a reasonable price.

Each pie has four main elements:

• Aluminium foil case
• Pastry shell made mainly from flour and water

- Meat and/or vegetable filling
- Thin plastic wrapping

The products are obtained as follows.

- The aluminium is obtained from a single supplier of metal related products. There are few suppliers in the industry resulting from fall in demand for aluminium related products following increased use of plastics.

- The flour for the pastry shell is sourced from flour millers in four different countries – one source of supply is not feasible because harvests occur at different times and PicAPie cannot store sufficient flour from one harvest for a year's production.

- Obtaining meat and vegetables is difficult due to the large number of suppliers located in many different countries. Recently, PicAPie obtained significant cost savings by delegating sourcing of these items to a specialist third party.

- Plastic wrapping is obtained either directly from the manufacturer or via an Internet site specialising in selling surplus wrapping from government and other sources.

Requirements

(a) Explain the main characteristics of a Total Quality Management (TQM) programme.

(b) Identify the sourcing strategies adopted by PicAPie and evaluate the effectiveness of those strategies for maintaining a constant and high quality supply of inputs. Your answer should also include recommendations for changes you consider necessary.

See **Answer** at the end of this chapter.

7.4 Strategic procurement

The traditional supply chain model (see diagram below) shows each firm as a separate entity reliant on orders from the downstream firm, commencing with the ultimate customer, to initiate activity.

The disadvantages of this are:

- It slows down fulfilment of customer order and so puts the chain at a competitive disadvantage.

- It introduces possibility of communication errors delaying fulfilment and/or leading to wrong specification products being supplied.

- The higher costs of holding inventories on a just-in-case basis by all firms in chain.

- The higher transactions costs due to document and payment flows between the stages in the model.

Strategic procurement is the development of a true **partnership** between a company and a supplier of strategic value. The arrangement is usually long-term, single-source in nature and addresses not only the buying of parts, products, or services, but product design and supplier capacity.

This recognises that increasingly, organisations are recognising the need for and benefits of establishing **close links** with companies in the supply chain. This has led to the **integrated supply chain** model (the second model in the following diagram) and the concept that it is **whole supply chains** which compete and not just individual firms.

Traditional and integrated supply chain models

Traditional supply chain

Integrated supply chain

The integrated supply chain shows that the order from the ultimate customer is shared between all the stages in the chain and that the firms overlap operations by having integrated activities as business partners. This is consistent with the idea of a **value system** and the concept of **supply chain networks** discussed in Chapter 6.

Interactive question 6: Beau Ltd   [Difficulty level: Exam standard]

Beau Ltd is a medium sized maker of specialised components which are used in the manufacture of tablet computers. It has three major customers, each of which are major players in the global personal tablet market. The three customers are very demanding, and constant advances in tablet technology mean that Beau Ltd invests heavily in R&D to keep the components it produces at the cutting edge of technology.

Beau Ltd purchases the parts it uses in production from a supplier in China, Xu Co. Xu Co sends deliveries from its factory in China to Beau Ltd's production facility in the UK. Xu Co is in daily communication with Beau Ltd's procurement staff regarding quantities. Recently, there have been delays in supply, so Beau Ltd has taken to holding 20 days worth of parts in inventory. Xu Co charges high prices; the company's MD explains that this reflects Xu Co's focus on improving product quality and service delivery.

Beau Ltd is currently in the process of updating the main component that it sells, the POD52. The POD52 is regarded as being 'state of the art' technology. The updated version will be launched next year and is expected to be highly sought after by the three customers.

Beau Ltd has identified two issues in respect of its procurement and supply chain management:

Issue 1: Beau Ltd is unsure whether to procure parts for the mass production of POD52 from (i) one supplier, Xu Co; or (ii) a range of seven new suppliers, producing similar parts for the POD52 component. One of the suppliers would be Xu Co, three would be American, and three would be German.

Issue 2: POD52 is constructed from 37 individual parts. In a bid to reduce costs, Beau Ltd is undertaking an assessment of its procurement activities. It is looking to review all of its direct 'Tier 1' suppliers in order to improve efficiencies. The Head of Procurement at Beau Ltd has mentioned the need to review the company's own supplier's suppliers (Tier 2) to ensure that they are being cost efficient.

Requirements

(i) Issue 1

Outline the main advantages and disadvantages to Beau Ltd of using one supplier or more than one supplier for the components needed to manufacture POD52. You should recommend a course of action.

(ii) Issue 2

Review the Head of Procurement's comment that Beau Ltd should conduct a Tier 2 inspection of its supplier's suppliers. You should recommend whether a Tier 1 or Tier 2 supplier review would be most appropriate.

See **Answer** at the end of this chapter.

7.5 Suppliers and e-procurement

E-procurement involves using technology to conduct business-to-business purchasing over the Internet.

There are huge savings to be had, especially for large corporate organisations with vast levels of procurement. Siemens believes that, since it embarked on its fully-integrated e-procurement system, this purchasing strategy saved $15 million from material costs and $10 million from process costs in the one year alone, close to a 1,000% increase in savings from the previous year and only the second year into implementation.

7.5.1 Advantages of e-procurement for the **buyer**:

- Facilitate cost savings
- Easier to compare prices
- Faster purchase cycle
- Reductions in inventory
- Control indirect goods and services
- Reduces off-contract buying
- Data rich management information to help reduce costs and predict future trends
- Online catalogues
- High accessibility
- Improved service levels
- Control costs by imposing limits on levels of expenditure

7.5.2 E-procurement from a supplier's perspective

Traditionally the business of supplying goods has been about branding, marketing, business relationships, etc. In the expanding e-procurement world the dynamics of supplying are changing and, unlike the expectations of companies implementing e-procurement systems for cost savings, suppliers are expecting to feel profit erosions due to the e-procurement mechanism.

Nevertheless, there are obvious advantages to suppliers:

- Faster order acquisition
- Immediate payment systems
- Lower operating costs
- Non-ambiguous ordering
- Data rich management information
- 'Lock-in' of buyers to the market
- Automate manufacturing demands

7.6 Ethical aspects of purchasing and procurement

Many firms seek to fulfil their own CSR commitments by demanding similar commitments from their suppliers. This gives rise to **ethical procurement** which is examined in more detail in Chapter 16.

Summary and Self-test

Summary

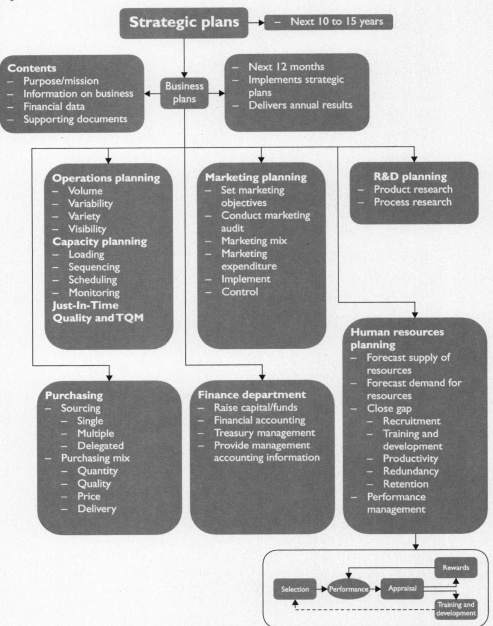

Strategic plans — Next 10 to 15 years

Business plans

Contents
- Purpose/mission
- Information on business
- Financial data
- Supporting documents

- Next 12 months
- Implements strategic plans
- Delivers annual results

Operations planning
- Volume
- Variability
- Variety
- Visibility

Capacity planning
- Loading
- Sequencing
- Scheduling
- Monitoring

Just-In-Time

Quality and TQM

Marketing planning
- Set marketing objectives
- Conduct marketing audit
- Marketing mix
- Marketing expenditure
- Implement
- Control

R&D planning
- Product research
- Process research

Human resources planning
- Forecast supply of resources
- Forecast demand for resources
- Close gap
  - Recruitment
  - Training and development
  - Productivity
  - Redundancy
  - Retention
- Performance management

Purchasing
- Sourcing
  - Single
  - Multiple
  - Delegated
- Purchasing mix
  - Quantity
  - Quality
  - Price
  - Delivery

Finance department
- Raise capital/funds
- Financial accounting
- Treasury management
- Provide management accounting information

Selection → Performance → Appraisal → Rewards / Training and development

ICAEW

Self-test

Answer the following questions.

1   Here are four characteristics of long-term planning information. List the corresponding characteristics of short-term planning information.

    A   Used by top management
    B   Broad in scope rather than deep in detail
    C   External
    D   Looks to the future and lacks certainty

2   List the ten purposes of using budgets.

3   Which of the following is not a use of budgetary control?

    A   To define the objectives of the organisation as a whole
    B   To ensure that resources are used as efficiently as possible
    C   To provide some central control when activities are decentralised
    D   To provide the basis for the preparation of future budgets

4   What is the main intention behind R&D?

5   What are the elements of the purchasing mix?

6   What is the role of the production function?

7   Define marketing.

8   How does the finance function relate to strategic planning?

9   What are the four main objectives of HRM?

10   Six factors that should be taken into account when devising an operations strategy are:

- Capacity
- Range and location of operations
- Investment in technology
- Strategic buyer-supplier relationships
- New products/services
- Structure of operations

Requirements

Briefly describe what each of the six factors identified above mean in the context of operations strategy.

Illustrate your answer with examples related to a retail supermarket chain.   **(15 marks)**

11   The recently appointed HR manager in a medium sized accounting firm is struggling. The Senior Partner of the firm is unconvinced about the benefits of appraisal systems. He argues that accountants, through their training, are self-motivated and should have the maximum freedom to carry out their work. His experience of appraisal systems to date has shown them to lack clarity of purpose, be extremely time consuming, involve masses of bureaucratic form filling and create little benefit for the supervisors or their subordinates. He refuses to have his own performance reviewed through an appraisal system.

The HR manager is convinced that performance management and an appraisal system are integral elements in helping the firm achieve its ambitious strategic growth objectives. This reflected her experience of introducing an appraisal system into the corporate finance unit for which she was responsible. The unit had consistently outperformed its growth targets and individual members of the unit were well motivated and appreciative of the appraisal process.

Requirements

(a)   Evaluate the extent to which an effective appraisal system could help the accounting firm achieve its goals.   **(12 marks)**

(b)   Assess the contribution of performance management to the strategic management process.
    (8 marks)

    (20 marks)

12 Defence Lamination Ltd

Defence Lamination Ltd (DLL) has been trading for many years making specialist glass products for military uses. Its main customers have been manufacturers in the defence sector which need glass that can withstand special conditions, such as windscreens in jet fighter aeroplanes. By 20X2 annual sales had grown to £22 million with net profits of around 9% after tax.

The current position

Over the past two years DLL has found its customer base eroded by the end of the Cold War. Sales have fallen to a likely £14 million in 20X6 and, although some cost savings have been possible, the company lost £500,000 in 20X5.

DLL has the advantage of very modern computer-controlled equipment which allows it great flexibility and enables the company to pursue new markets by applying expertise gained in the (now rapidly shrinking) defence sector.

Staff and management have become very anxious but are loyal and keen to change the direction of the company. Managers see themselves as experienced, yet modern.

The industry environment

Customers are historically defence based but, as DLL has realised, these are fewer in number. New customers would include private sector firms such as high street banks, which need security glass. Major customer potential exists overseas, but here the twin problems of bad debt risk and uncertain cash flow are key factors.

Rivals are largely niche operators, except for a few big companies such as Pilkington, but tend to be small because each customer has a unique problem to solve. Product quality and innovative design are crucial elements but branding is not important.

Technology is continually evolving but pricing is not a major problem because customers value quality above all, and are prepared to pay a premium for new technology that can (for example, with bomb-proof glass) save them a fortune.

Suppliers are plentiful, except that key skilled staff are highly sought after.

With the breakdown of the Iron Curtain political barriers are few but nationalism and terrorist activity mean that many opportunities exist for DLL globally.

The proposal

The managing director of DLL, Peter Hobbs, has proposed to the board that a bold expansion programme is implemented. He believes that DLL has the skills to attack the private sector financial services sector and diplomatic protection market. To fund the sales team and working capital, he proposes to use National Factors plc (NF) which should advance up to 80% of current receivables, yielding about £2.8m, which will be adequate to fund growth. He also proposes to change the company name to Security Glass Ltd.

The board's response

DLL has a non-executive director, James Greening, who convinces the board that a proper business plan is needed. He argues that NF will only agree to the proposal if such a plan is produced. However, he is unsure how to go about this and advises that DLL's accountants become involved.

Requirements

As a member of staff of DLL's accountants, write a memorandum to Peter Hobbs which explains the steps required to create, implement and review a business plan. You need not specify detailed strategies but must identify the critical factors for successful implementation of the plan.

(15 marks)

13 Eavesdrop Ltd

Company history

Eavesdrop Ltd was incorporated 25 years ago. It was founded by Eric Oppenheimer, a specialist in telecommunications, and produces specialist/mobile phones, fax machines and bleepers. The first three years of business proved to be very profitable and saw very rapid growth in each of the markets.

Eric started the company with a small inheritance from a distant aunt. As the business took off Eric asked a close ex-university friend of his, Braniac Shultz, to join the company as a co-director.

Braniac was an expert in physics and electronics, and was put in charge of research and development – an essential part of the business if Eavesdrop Ltd was to remain competitive in this industry of rapid technological progress.

Eavesdrop Ltd makes most of its sales and profits from mobile phones of which it makes two different models: the Nakia 18C which is very small and light but has a range of only 100 miles, and the larger, more sophisticated Nakia 25F which can operate anywhere in the UK and also act as an answering machine. Originally Eric bought in the required components for both models but, following the recruitment of Braniac, the firm is itself producing more and more of the necessary parts.

The market

Demand for the special mobile phones comes primarily from three distinct markets and sales for the forthcoming year are expected to be as follows.

	Nakia 18C (units)	Nakia 25F (units)
Private consumers	5,000	5,000
Businessmen	7,000	3,500
Public sector	48,000	21,500
	60,000	30,000

There are few but large customers within the public sector – usually in the form of local government authorities, hospitals, education, etc – whereas in the other two markets each consumer generally orders only one unit.

Over the last two years the market for mobile phones (in particular) but also fax machines and bleepers has become very competitive. Whereas in the early days of incorporation Eric was able to increase his share of the market without paying too much attention to pricing, costs, marketing, advertising and research, the situation has now turned around completely. New firms producing very similar products – often with more facilities and of a better quality – are emerging from within the UK and from abroad, particularly from Japan.

Eric has very little interest or knowledge of financial and marketing matters, while Braniac considers both functions to be a nuisance which interferes with his research and development activities.

Unfortunately, a major competitor, Nippon Telecommunications of Japan, has just invented a micro-printed circuit so small that it will be able to produce portable phones of half the size and weight of Eavesdrop's Nakia 18C but with an international usage range. Obviously this new product, although much more expensive than the Nakia 18C or Nakia 25F, poses a very serious threat to the future sales of Eavesdrop's products. Braniac, though full of admiration for his adversaries in Tokyo, believes it will be at least another nine months before he is able to give birth to an equally sophisticated and competitive product. To develop the micro-printed circuits necessary to compete with the Japanese technology, an additional £0.5m will need to be invested each year in research and development. As an alternative, the firm could abandon its challenge to the Japanese technological advancements, reduce its investment in research and development, and try to hold on to as large a slice as possible of its current market by cutting the selling prices of its existing models.

Eavesdrop Ltd – statement of financial position as at 31 March 20X4

	£'000	£'000
Non-current assets		1,000
Current assets		
Inventory		1,125
Receivables	287	
Cash	188	
		1,600
		2,600
Current liabilities		
Payables		(1,000)
Net assets		1,600
Financed by		
Share capital		500
Reserves		600
		1,100
Bank loan – repayable 31 March 20X5		500
Capital employed		1,600

If the firm abandons its research into micro-printed circuits it is expected that sales of the Nakia 18C will fall by 50% in the forthcoming year and to zero in the following year, unless large reductions are made in the selling price. Sales of the Nakia 25F are unlikely to be affected by this competition as it is a specialist phone of a different nature.

Eric and Braniac are the only two directors of the firm. There was a financial director in the early years but he was sacked by Eric when he threatened to reduce the cash available to Braniac for research unless Braniac could justify and account for the money. Braniac considered this to be an unacceptable constraint on his development flair and threatened to resign – hence the departure of the finance director.

Neither Eric nor Braniac has much interest in accounts and try to get by with maintaining as little documentation as possible. There is no particular management structure in place within the firm and accounting data is minimal.

Requirements

In your capacity of management consultant to the firm, write a memorandum to the two directors outlining the present position of the company and suggest strategies which the company could adopt to achieve self preservation and growth. In doing so use the following headings.

- Current position

- Strategic options

  - Financing
  - R&D
  - Personnel
  - Systems
  - Products/markets

- Recommendations   **(23 marks)**

14 Read the scenario of the **September 2008 Business Strategy** paper in the Question Bank entitled *DT Ltd,* mentioned at the beginning of this chapter. Draft an answer for requirement (c) on the business plan.

15 Go online at The Times 100 Business Case Studies and read the Cummins case study 'Using effective recruitment to retain competitive advantage' at http://businesscasestudies.co.uk/cummins/using-effective-recruitment-to-retain-competitive-advantage

Now, go back to the Learning objectives in the Introduction. If you are satisfied you have achieved these objectives, please tick them off.

Answer to Interactive question 1

Report

To	Aldine Computers & Training
From	An Accountant
Date	Today
Subject	Evaluation of business plan and application for funding

Terms of reference

We have been asked to comment on the viability of the business proposal by Aldine Computers & Training (Aldine) to secure funding for an extension to its business and to propose improvement to the proposal document.

Disclaimer

This report is based on the information given us by the management of Aldine and its accuracy is restricted to the accuracy of that data. No opinion is expressed on the accuracy of that data. This report is intended solely for the management of Aldine and is not for any third parties. The authors cannot be held liable for any loss incurred by third parties relying on this report.

1   **Introduction**

Aldine has been established three months and is trading. We understand that some initial capital investment has taken place and that premises have been secured. The business plan therefore is to secure funding for the expansion of the business.

2   **The business model**

Business proposals should be evaluated according to the criteria of suitability, acceptability and feasibility.

Suitability concerns the strength, weaknesses, opportunities and threats of the business and the industry in which it operates.

The **strengths** of Aldine include:

- Relevant experience of management in the proposed areas of business
- Industry links with suppliers and corporate customers

The **weaknesses** of Aldine are:

- Very high reliance on its principal managers, Peter and Kate for both direct making and provision of training and also for business development and client prospecting

- Relatively small size will deny Aldine economies of scale in the purchasing of components compared to larger PC makers like PCNow and Dell

- Its inability to offer a national coverage for servicing and training means it will not be able to gain access to national corporate clients

- Low brand and business profile compared to established PC providers

- Many aspects necessary to run its business have not been considered in its business plan (see section 3 below)

The **opportunities** for Aldine include:

- Continued sales of PCs encouraged by new applications and the desire by firms to encourage flexible working

- The perceived service failings and backlogs of rival providers

The **threats** facing Aldine include:

- Competition in the PC construction market from larger firms able to access cheaper manufacturing resources overseas

- Development of more sophisticated computer-based training and virtual learning which will reduce demand for the face to face training proposed by Aldine

- Increased outsourcing of IT by firms will reduce the demand for Aldine's services

- Forecast economic slowdown in two years will reduce demand for PCs and hence leave Aldine with excess capacity and costs.

In summary its business model poses significant risks to Aldine. By focusing on SMEs it is possible that it may access a market segment overlooked by larger rivals but at the expense of high marketing to sales costs and it will be serving markets where low IT literacy will necessitate considerable and costly support.

Acceptability means that the business proposal should meet approval from key stakeholders.

Kate and Peter are clearly in favour of the business proposal. There is no research presented to help us form a judgement about client attitudes to the services proposed and to dealing with Aldine. The remaining key stakeholder will be the bank. The present report will need some modification before it will secure the banks agreement to lend the money (see section 4 below).

Feasibility means the ability of the business to carry out its strategic initiatives. This will depend on a combination of internal resources and external factors.

The production plan seems well-thought through. However questions must be raised over the feasibility of the 40% markup behind the forecast first year profit of £90,000 which implies a revenue of £225,000 (100/40 × £90,000) supporting the two founders, the mature office manager and the trainee assembler as well as the actual costs of production and service provision. Margins in a competitive industry like IT are likely to be lower and it is an industry with a high failure rate amongst start-ups like Aldine.

The other issue of feasibility seems to be Aldine's reliance on supplier relations build up by Peter whilst at PCNow. Faced with competition from Aldine there is a danger that PCNow would pressurise its suppliers for preferential terms over Aldine.

In summary the business model is potentially viable but the founders need to satisfy themselves, and the bank, on the issues above.

3   **Critique of the business plan**

The main omissions from the business plan are:

- A statement of the legal entity: It is not clear whether Aldine is to be a company or a partnership.

- Detailed financial workings to back up the ambitious forecasts on page 8: The business mix between sales, service and training is not clear and nor are the volumes and costs of each. These should be included as an appendix together with a sensitivity analysis of profits against price, costs and volumes.

- The purposes for which the money is required: The initial equipment has been detailed and purchased. What is not clear is what the further £40,000 is required for inventory, working capital, marketing etc. It is not clear. A bank will wish to ensure it is adequate and will not be impressed by the £15,000 additional commitment it is being asked to pledge.

- Any evidence of demand for its services or the preferential supply terms: These are key elements in the business model and so letters of reference and indications of willingness to buy/supply should be included.

- Job roles: Aldine intends to employ office staff, trainees etc. It is not clear what they will do.

- Security: Details of the assets to be pledged by Peter should be included.

- Market information: It is not appropriate to leave details of competitors at the level they are. Evidence is needed of their size, strengths and weaknesses and also their likely responses to Aldine's arrival in the market.

- The proposals for the loan: The business plan does not indicate the likely timing for take-up of the borrowing nor the repayment proposals.

- Plans beyond 20X3: The plan ceases at the year the economic slowdown is forecast to begin. There is no indication on how Aldine intends to develop its business then. Most business plans will be for five years.

- Detailed operational information such as how clients will be prospected and dealt with.

4 Suggested improvements to the business plan

As indicated above, there are several elements of the business plan that need improvement.

As a minimum Aldine should include:

- A cash flow forecast broken down by month indicating the likely timing for take-up of the borrowing and the repayment proposals.

- Evidence of supplier and client intentions.

- Details of the security being offered for the loan.

- A better strategic analysis utilising the SWOT analysis in section 2 of this report and indicating how the weaknesses and threats may be addressed.

- Better competitor analysis.

- Job descriptions for the roles being recruited and also how work will be allocated to cover the manufacture and servicing of the PCs.

5 Conclusions

Providing the above issues are addressed we believe that Aldine will be successful in business and in the application for its loan.

If there are any questions on this report, or further assistance is required, please revert to the author.

Answer to Interactive question 2

(a) A **SWOT analysis** identifies the strengths and weaknesses of the organisation relative to the opportunities and threats it faces in its marketing environment. The SWOT analysis leads to an understanding of **realistic market opportunities** through the process of a detailed **marketing audit**, covering market and environment analysis, competitor and supplier analysis, customer analysis and internal analysis.

This analysis will highlight potential market gaps, new customer needs, marketing channel developments, competitor strategies and their strengths and weaknesses. The organisation can evaluate market opportunities against its strengths and weaknesses and identified threats and determine what actions to take to exploit the opportunity.

(b) To successfully launch a new customer product into the UK market the organisation needs to have clear and realistic **objectives**, and identification and understanding of its **target market segment**. Its channel of distribution, branding, packaging and communications activity need to be in place to support the launch. Forecasts of future demand, and return on investment need to be assessed and projected.

A formalised **marketing planning system** that involves all departments, customers, agents and suppliers, the complexity and timing of activities is required to support the launch to prevent lack of coordination, resource and ultimate failure. A **monitoring system** is also required to evaluate the effectiveness of the launch and take actions as required. A successful launch requires a planning process that pulls all the people and activities together, co-ordinates what is done, by who, when and with what resource.

(c) Marketing planning involves the following stages.

(i) **Market analysis**: This phase involves establishing an audit process that assesses the macro and micro market environment, market segment analysis, customers, competitors and development strategy. Without a clear understanding of these issues it is difficult to set objectives and develop strategy.

(ii) **Objective setting**: Once the issues arising from market analysis have been understood, objectives can be set. Objectives should be consistent with the overall mission of the organisation and goals, and they must be realistic.

(iii) **Strategy development**: This phase can begin once the objectives have been agreed. In this process alternative strategic options will be evaluated to determine the best way forward for the organisation. Strategy evaluation should consider the organisation's current strengths and weaknesses, market attractiveness, resource requirements, and profitability.

(iv) **Implementation**: This is frequently the hardest part of the marketing planning process. Effective implementation requires co-ordination between different organisations, people and departments. An organisation structure and culture should support this co-ordination, provide good communication and access to information and appropriate levels of resources. In reality, many issues, conflicts and trade offs occur within organisations that act as barriers to effective implementation.

(v) **Evaluation and control**: The final phase of the process involves setting an effective system of monitoring and control to measure and evaluate performance.

Answer to Interactive question 3

Report

From   Olivia Marcuse: HR Manager, ScannerTech
To   Board of Directors: ScannerTech
Date   Today

Human resource planning and strategy

ScannerTech's strategy calls for the company to double in size over the next three years. This will require the employment of extra staff, particularly in marketing, sales and manufacturing. The ambitious planned rate of growth and the high technology base of ScannerTech's business mean that these extra staff must be of very high quality. Human resource (HR) management is thus an **essential component** of the company's business strategy and so should be **integrated with its development**. The alternative is increased potential for serious shortages of staff and mismatches between job requirements and staff availability. The establishment of a foreign manufacturing plant will complicate all HR issues significantly and will demand very careful consideration.

Human resource planning follows a logical sequence, echoing the rational model of strategy. This is not necessarily linear and some of the activities involved in establishing a satisfactory plan can overlap chronologically. There will also be occasions where the various activities influence one another, as, for example, when the persistence of staff shortages in important areas leads to a change in reward policy.

An **audit of existing staff** should reveal those with potential for promotion or employability in new specialisations. It would also indicate where shortages already exist.

Concurrently, an analysis of **likely future staff requirements** could be carried out. We anticipate the need to employ more staff in the areas already mentioned, but we do not really know how many will be required, whether other functions will need to be increased in size or if more support and administrative staff will be needed. There are also the related and sensitive issues of **management succession** and **internal promotion** to consider. In particular, we must consider the eventual replacement of our existing joint Managing Directors, who are likely to leave once the current growth objective has been achieved.

These two studies should enable us to identify the gaps that we need to fill if we are to have the staff required for our overall strategy.

Recruitment, in the sense of attracting applicants, and **selection** from within the pool of applicants are the logical next steps. This work is often **outsourced** and it will be necessary to decide whether the **expertise** and **economies of scale** offered by outsourcing outweigh the need for deep familiarity with our operations on the part of the recruiters.

Reward policy must be considered. At the moment, ScannerTech's staff profile is heavily biased towards people with a background in research and development. Different types of people will be required in the future and their expectations must be expected to show some differences. A doubling in size to, say, 200 employees is likely to take the company into an area of HR complexity in which a formal reward policy and structure is required. Informal decisions about pay and benefits will not be satisfactory. It may be necessary to establish a more formal scheme of **employee relations**, possibly along the lines of a works council.

Increasing size is also likely to require the establishment of a policy on **appraisal and performance management**. This should be linked to a programme of **training and development**. No doubt ScannerTech will continue to hire well-qualified technical staff, but there will be a need for development of staff in other functions and for management development in particular.

Answer to Interactive question 4

(a) **Cost reduction**: Toyota was losing money, and market demand was weak, preventing price rises. The only way to move from losses into profits was to cut costs, and cost reduction was probably essential for the survival of the company.

(b) **Production levelling**: Production levelling should help to minimise idle time whilst at the same time allowing the company to achieve its objective of minimum inventories.

(c) The **change in factory layout** was to improve the work flow and eliminate the waste of moving items around the work floor from one set of machines to another. Each cell contained all the machines required to complete production, thus eliminating unnecessary materials movements.

(d) With having **cells of different machines**, workers in each work cell would have to be trained to use each different machine, whereas previously they would have specialised in just one type of machine.

(e) A **change of culture** was needed to overcome the industrial problems of the company. Employee involvement would have been an element in this change. Teamwork would have helped with the elimination of waste: mistakes or delays by one member of a team would be corrected or dealt with by others in the team. The work force moved from a sense of individual responsibility/blame to collective responsibility.

(f) The *kanban* system is a 'pull' system of production scheduling. Items are only produced when they are needed. If a part is faulty when it is produced, the production line will be held up until the fault is corrected. For a *kanban* system to work properly, defects must therefore be eliminated.

Answer to Interactive question 5

(a) In a nutshell, **Total quality management** (TQM) is a management philosophy, aimed at **continuous improvement** in all areas of operation.

A TQM initiative aims to achieve continuous improvement in quality, productivity and effectiveness. It does this by establishing management responsibility for processes as well as output.

Principles of TQM

(i) **Prevention**
Organisations should take measures that prevent poor quality occurring.

(ii) **Right first time**
A culture should be developed that encourages workers to get their work right first time. This will save costly reworking.

(iii) **Eliminate waste**
The organisation should seek the most efficient and effective use of all its resources.

(iv) **Continuous improvement**
The Kaizen philosophy should be adopted. Organisations should seek to improve their processes continually.

(v) **Everybody's concern**
Everyone in the organisation is responsible for improving processes and systems under their control.

(vi) **Participation**
All workers should be encouraged to share their views and the organisation should value them.

(vii) **Teamwork and empowerment**
Workers across departments should form team bonds so that eventually the organisation becomes one. Quality circles are useful in this regard. Workers should be empowered to make decisions as they are in the best position to decide how their work is done.

Note: This is a question that may appear daunting at first, but if you go through and deal with each element in turn it should not prove too difficult to earn a pass. Ensure you provide justification for the changes you recommend.

(b) **Aluminium foil** is obtained from a single supplier – a sourcing strategy termed '**single sourcing**'. The advantages of this strategy include:

* Easy to develop and maintain a relationship with a single supplier – which is especially beneficial when the purchasing company relies on that supplier.

* A supplier quality assurance program can be implemented easily to help guarantee the quality of products – again mainly because there is only one supplier.

Economies of scale may be obtained from volume discounts.

However, the **disadvantages** of this strategy are:

* PicAPie is dependent on the supplier – providing significant supplier power. Issues such as quality assurance may not be addressed quickly because the supplier is aware that there are few alternative sources of supply.

* PicAPie is vulnerable to any disruption in supply.

Given that there are few suppliers in the industry this strategy may be appropriate. However, there is no guarantee that the current supplier will not go out of business so the directors of PicAPie could look for alternative sources of supply to guard against this risk.

The **pastry shell flour** is obtained a number of suppliers – a strategy known as **multi-sourcing**. The advantages of this strategy include:

- Ability to switch suppliers should one fail to provide the flour. Having suppliers in different countries is potentially helpful in this respect as poor harvests in one country may not be reflected in another.

- Competition may help to decrease price.

Disadvantages include:

- It may be difficult to implement a quality assurance program due to time needed to establish it with different suppliers.

- Suppliers may display less commitment to PicAPie depending on the amount of flour purchased making supply more difficult to guarantee.

PicAPie appears to have covered the risk of supply well by having multiple sources of supply. The issue of quality remains and PicAPie could implement some quality standards that suppliers must adhere to in order to keep on supplying flour.

A third party is given the responsibility for obtaining **meat and vegetables** – this is termed **delegated sourcing**. Advantages of this method include:

- Provides more time for PicAPie to concentrate on pie manufacture rather than obtaining inputs. Internal quality control may therefore be improved.

- The third party is responsible for quality control checks on input – again freeing up more time in PicAPie. Where quality control issues arise, PicAPie can again ask the third party to resolve these rather than spending time itself.

- Supply may be easier to guarantee as the specialist company will have contacts with many companies.

Disadvantages are:

- Quality control may be more difficult to maintain if the third party does not see this as a priority.

- There will be some loss of confidentiality regarding the products that PicAPie uses, although if there are no 'special ingredients' then this may not be an issue.

Given the diverse sources of supply, PicAPie are probably correct using this strategy.

The **plastic film** is obtained from two different sources utilising two different supply systems. This is termed **parallel sourcing**. The advantages of this method include:

- Supply failure from one source will not necessarily halt pie production because the alternative source of supply should be available.

- There may be some price competition between suppliers.

Disadvantages include:

- PicAPie must take time to administer and control two different systems.

- Quality may be difficult to maintain, and as with multiple sourcing, it will take time to establish supplier quality assurance programmes. Given that some stock is surplus to requirements from other sources, quality control programmes may not be possible anyway.

The weakness in the supply strategy appears to be obtaining film from the Internet site – in that quality control is difficult to monitor. Changing to single sourcing with a supplier quality assurance programme would be an alternative strategy to remove this risk.

Answer to Interactive Question 6

Issue 1

The key issues:

(1) Whether to have one supplier or many
(2) Whether to continue solely with a current supplier or to engage with new suppliers

One supplier: Xu Co

*   The arrangement with Xu Co represents strategic procurement.

*   This relationship can be beneficial as Beau Ltd and Xu Co can establish close links in the supply chain through introducing EDI facilities to reduced the need for daily communication.

Advantages to Beau Ltd from single sourcing from one supplier:

*   Consistent parts from a sole supplier

*   Should make monitoring quality easier

*   Xu Co may be dependent on Beau Ltd for income, and therefore more responsive to Beau Ltd's needs

*   Collaboration in working together on new components is mutually beneficial

*   Beau Ltd already has a relationship with Xu Co

Disadvantages to Beau Ltd from single sourcing from one supplier:

*   Disruption to Xu Co's output will impact on Beau Ltd. Could damage relations with the three highly demanding customers if orders are not fulfilled on time. Furthermore, Beau Ltd is already having to hold higher levels of inventory than it might otherwise hold to overcome current problems.

*   Xu Co may not to be able to support increases in demand.

*   Xu Co may attempt to exploit relationship with Beau Ltd by increasing prices if a long-term supply agreement is entered into.

Advantages to Beau Ltd of having seven suppliers:

*   Beau Ltd can encourage competition among suppliers to reduce prices.
*   The costs of switching supplier are reduced.

Disadvantages to Beau Ltd of having seven suppliers:

*   Increased scope for suppliers to lack commitment to supply as less revenue is generated per supplier from serving Beau Ltd

*   Increase in costs and management time of communicating with seven suppliers

*   Reduced economies of scale

*   Still have long lead times if parts are being delivered from China and the US in particular. Increases the uncertainty of delivery

Recommendation

Beau Ltd is advised to continue using existing supplier Xu Co due to the relationship that the two have already established. This approach helps increase Beau Ltd's buying power as the company will be better placed to negotiate on price. The threat of losing Beau Ltd altogether to other suppliers may incentivise Xu Co to improve its current terms of supply.

Issue 2

An integrated supply chain approach highlights that the supply chain of an organisation and it's suppliers should be viewed as a whole. The desire for information about Beau Ltd's own suppliers (Tier 1) and its supplier's suppliers (Tier 2) is a feature of this approach.

In theory, if Tier 2 suppliers can find efficiencies and reduce costs these can be passed onto Tier 1 suppliers, which should result in lower purchase prices for customers, in this case the likes of Beau Ltd. Sound supply chain management is needed to attain such benefit.

Beau Ltd's supply chain review is focused on upstream supply chain management as there is no focus on its own customers, with the main emphasis being on realising cost efficiencies.

Beau Ltd as a customer does not have a legal right to request an inspection of its suppliers processes. However, it should be noted that such a review may help to improve transparency and the degree of openness between the parties. Suppliers for whom Beau Ltd is a major customer may be more inclined to participate in the review for fear of damaging existing relations.

Tier 2 suppliers have no legal obligations to participate in Beau Ltd's review as the two parties do not have any direct contractual obligations to one another. However, Tier 2 suppliers may be motivated to allow Beau Ltd to investigate their own operations due to the fact that Beau Ltd could cease to make purchases from a Tier 1 supplier, which in turn would result in fewer purchases from Tier 2 suppliers.

Recommendation

Attempts to manage costs throughout the supply chain are in line with best practice in supply chain management. A focus on Tier 1 suppliers is most likely to be more value adding to Beau Ltd as these are the third parties which most closely interact with the company's own value chain.

1   A   Used at a lower level by those who implement plans
    B   Detailed
    C   Internal
    D   Definite

2   • Ensure the achievement of the organisation's objectives
    • Compel planning
    • Communicate ideas and plans
    • Co-ordinate activities
    • Allocate resources
    • Authorisation
    • Provide a framework for responsibility accounting
    • Establish a system of control
    • Provide a means of performance evaluation
    • Motivate employees to improve their performance

3   C   To provide some central control when activities are decentralised.

4   To improve products or processes and so support the organisation's strategy.

5   • Quantity
    • Quality
    • Price
    • Delivery

6   To control the necessary activities to provide products (or services) creating outputs which have added value over the value of inputs.

7   'The management process which identifies, anticipates and satisfies customer needs profitably'. Chartered Institute of Marketing

8   • Ensuring that resources of finance are available
    • Integrating the strategy into budgets
    • Establishing the necessary performance measures
    • Establishing priorities
    • Assisting in the modelling process

9   • To develop an effective human component for the company
    • To obtain, develop and motivate staff
    • To create positive relationships
    • To ensure compliance with social and legal responsibilities

10 • **Capacity required**: Any operations strategy will be influenced by what it is that the organisation does.

    For example, a supermarket chain sells food and other items to consumers.

    • **Range and location of operations**: The operations strategy will be affected by the scale and geographical spread of the organisation's operations.

    For example, a supermarket chain with say 10 outlets in one region of a country will face different operation strategy issues than a nationwide chain.

    • **Investment in technology**: Technology will impact upon operations and therefore operations strategy as it has the potential to change the processes associated with operations.

    For example, a supermarket chain operating using an EFTPOS system linked to their stock (logistics/warehousing systems will operate differently to a chain relying on less-automated systems).

- **Strategic buyer-seller relationships**: Who key strategic partners are will affect operations strategy.

  For example, a supermarket may have a preferred supplier for canned food items. Operations may then be designed to help facilitate this relationship. Relationships with 'buyers' (consumers) may be developed using loyalty card schemes – and operations changed based on what the scheme reveals.

- **New products/services**: This relates to how long the business will be able to do what it is currently doing (in the same way).

  A supermarket may find it also needs to offer on-line shopping and home delivery. It could also decide to move into non-traditional areas such as consumer electronics – or even consumer insurance or finance. These types of changes require changes to operations strategy.

- **Structure of operations**: Operations strategy will also be influenced by how staff are organised and managed.

  For example, will 'regional managers' have responsibility and complete control over all stores in one region – or will one national strategy apply?

  Issues such as staff levels, shift patterns and human resources policies will also affect operations strategy. For example, will stores be open 24 hours – and if so how will this be staffed?

11 (a) The Senior Partner and the HR manager emphasise the aspects of appraisal schemes that **support their own favoured policies**. Such schemes should support the organisation's overall objectives without incurring excessive administrative and management costs.

In an organisation such as an accounting practice, the professional staff should indeed be highly **self-motivated**, able to judge the effectiveness of their own performance and bring to their work a commitment to high professional standards. On the other hand, it is inevitable that their **talents and performance will vary** and they will need **guidance and help with their future development**. Dealing with these issues would be the role of an appraisal scheme.

The overall aim of such a scheme would be to **support progress toward the achievement of corporate objectives** and it would do this in three ways: performance review, potential review and training needs review.

Performance review: Performance review should provide employees with an **impartial and authoritative assessment of the quality and effect of their work**. Individuals should have personal objectives that support corporate goals via intermediate objectives relevant to the roles of their work groups. A reasoned assessment of performance can have a **positive motivating effect**, simply as a kind of positive, reinforcing feedback. It can also provide an opportunity for analysing and addressing the **reasons for sub-optimal performance**.

Potential review: Any organisation needs to make the best use it can of its people; an accountancy practice is typical of many modern organisations in that its people are its greatest asset and its future success depends on managing them in a way that makes the best use of their skills and aptitudes. An important aspect of this is **assessing potential for promotion and moves into other positions of greater challenge and responsibility**.

Training needs review: A further aspect of the desirable practice of enabling staff to achieve their potential is the provision of training and development activities. The appraisal system is one means by which **training needs can be assessed** and training provision initiated.

The appraisal system: An appraisal system must be properly administered and operated if it is make a proper contribution to the organisation's progress.

The appraisal cycle: Formal appraisal, with interviews and written assessments, is typically undertaken on an **annual cycle**. This interval is commonly regarded as too long to be effective because of the speed with which individual roles can evolve and their holders can develop, so the annual appraisal is often supplemented with a less detailed review after six months. Sometimes the procedure is sufficiently simplified that the whole thing can be done at six monthly intervals. Much modern thinking on this topic is now suggesting that any frequency of periodic appraisal is unsatisfactory and that it should be replaced by a **continuous process of coaching and assessment**.

Objectivity and reliability: Appraisal involves an element of direct personal criticism that can be stressful for all parties involved. If the system is to be credible its outputs must be seen to be objective and reliable. This requires proper **training for appraisers**, the establishment of appropriate **performance standards** and, preferably, input into each appraisal from **more than one person**. Having reports reviewed by the appraiser's own manager is one approach to the last point; 360 degree appraisal is another.

Setting targets: Past performance should be reviewed against **objective standards** and this raises the question of the type of objective that should be set. Objectives set in terms of **results** or outcomes to be achieved can encourage **creativity** and **innovation** but may also lead to **unscrupulous**, **unethical** and even **illegal choice of method**. On the other hand, objectives designed to maintain and improve the quality of output by **encouraging conformity** with approved procedure and method may stifle the creativity and innovation widely regarded as a vital source of continuing competitive advantage.

(b) **Performance management** involves the establishment of clear, agreed individual **goals and performance standards**, continuous leadership action to both **motivate and appraise subordinates** and a **periodic review** of performance at which the goals and performance standards for the next cycle are set.

Performance management is an application of the **rational model** of strategic management, in that individual goals are intended to form the lowest echelon of a **hierarchy of objectives** that builds up to support the **overall mission** of the organisation. It is an essential aspect of the system that individual goals should be **agreed and internalised** so that true **goal congruence** is achieved.

This overall approach was first described (as is so often the case) by Peter Drucker, in 1954, and is seen most clearly in the system of **management by objectives** (MbO). MbO as a management system has fallen somewhat from favour with the rise of quality management methods that emphasise processual and procedural conformance rather than the attainment of overall performance goals. Nevertheless, it has much to offer.

Under a formal MbO system, the process of setting goals is part of the **implementation phase** of strategic management and follows consideration of resources, overall objectives and SWOT analysis. Top level subordinate goals are agreed for heads of departments, divisions or functions: these goals should be specific, measurable, attainable, relevant and time-bounded (SMART). It is particularly important that the achievement of a goal can be established by objective **measurement**. There may be different timescales for different objectives, with short-term goals supporting longer-term ones.

Departmental heads then agree SMART goals for their subordinates in discussion with them, that support their own personal goals, and so on down the hierarchy to the level of the individual employee. All members of the organisation thus know what they are expected to achieve and how it fits into the wider fabric of the organisation's mission.

Periodic **performance review** is based on the objective appraisal of success against agreed goals, the agreement of goals for the next period and an assessment of the resources, including training, that the reviewee may require to reach those goals. The MbO system thus closes the **feedback loop** in the corporate control system.

12 Defence Lamination Ltd

Memorandum

To   Peter Hobbs Esq, Managing Director, Defence Lamination Ltd
From   A Smith, on behalf of Taylor & Co, Chartered Accountants
Date   31 October 20X6
Subject Proposed business plan

The planning process

Broadly this covers

- Creation
- Implementation
- Review

Creating the plan involves a position analysis for DLL which would include the following.

- The company mission, which could be changed to include civilian private sector markets. The name change will help this.

- Shareholder analysis, which would highlight the anxiety of staff and the need to return DLL to profit.

- Internal strengths and weaknesses of DLL such as its high product quality. See below for critical success factors.

- External pressures and future events, including rivalry, political changes, new technology, and economic forecasts.

Implementing the plan involves two steps.

- Setting objectives that are measurable, specific and realistic. You need targets at which to aim, but these will presumably include sales and profit measures, as well as cash flow. In addition, I suggest qualitative targets such as customer satisfaction and product quality.

- Deciding on a strategy. This is up to you, although it will involve debt factoring. It would be helpful to have a unique selling proposition to put to National Factors plc (NF) and I imagine sales and language expertise must be part of the team. You ought to set a timetable for implementation.

Reviewing the plan means that you must assess three factors.

- Is the plan consistent? Does it fit in with the position analysis that you have done?
- Is the plan sufficient? Does it meet your objectives previously set?
- Is the plan feasible? Do you possess the resources necessary?

It would be sensible for the review to be done independently, perhaps by James Greening.

Critical success factors

I believe that success depends on six factors.

(1) DLL's ability to adapt to new markets. This should be possible, given that you have high quality flexible production facilities. If you can make any type of glass in any size, then you should penetrate new markets.

(2) Finding new customers in the non-defence sector. Your brand name counts for very little and potential customers must be convinced that you are serious. Your ability to meet their exact requirements will evidence this, but you have to diversify into a new customer base or face closure.

(3) Providing top quality and specific solutions. Each customer is a new challenge and, if you are to compete with other niche rivals, you must offer excellent quality and innovation. Do you have product testing facilities?

(4) Retention of key employees as your rivals perceive a threat and try to poach them.

(5) DLL's willingness to tackle overseas markets. If you are to be successful, you need to be prepared to travel, employ interpreters and take some risks in unknown markets.

(6) Bad debt and foreign exchange risks. If you achieve overseas sales, you will be exposed to these risks, but NF may provide some stability and credit insurance for a fee.

13 Eavesdrop Ltd

Memorandum

To	Company Directors, Eavesdrop Ltd
From	Management Consultant
Date	Today
Subject	Future corporate strategic options

1 Current position

The company is technologically sound with an established clientele and reputation for quality. This is mainly the result of the background in electronics of the two directors.

The company has established a strong foothold in the market and is exceptionally profitable. However, this has in the past been achieved with innovative research.

The rapid growth of the mobile phone market has stimulated the emergence of competitive firms wishing to take advantage of this opportunity.

The future for the company looks very doubtful should the directors fail to perceive the need to identify and adopt a suitable strategy for growth and self preservation in the light of the threat from emerging competition and technology from Japan.

There appears to be no effective communication network in existence and no management structure. There is no financial director and no marketing or selling expertise within the firm.

The firm is a classic example of insufficient breadth of management skills. This is often seen in companies where the founder is the current managing director and where there has been rapid growth due almost entirely to technical excellence.

The management structure has failed to develop to accommodate the increased size and complexity of the business. Strengthening the management team is now a priority. Professional help is urgently required in the fields of finance and marketing. Both directors will need to accept that such professional managers must be free to make their own decisions in those fields where they are the experts, without interference from existing directors. If they are continually overruled or not consulted they will leave of their own volition.

2 Strategic options

Financing

The latest statement of financial position shows that Eavesdrop Ltd has a serious liquidity problem pending, as it has a bank loan of £0.5m due to be repaid in twelve months' time.

However, the firm does have security in the form of non-current assets and should have little difficulty in re-negotiating another loan.

The current level of gearing is not high and, provided the company is successful in developing a competitive form of technology to meet the threat from Japan, profit prospects for the future are encouraging.

At the moment the firm's current ratio looks weak at 1,500:1,600 (treating the £0.5m bank loan as a current liability) but this will fall to 1,000:1,600 once the loan is re-negotiated.

It may be necessary to examine more closely the inventory control procedures in force at the firm as the current inventory figure seems to be excessively high.

R&D

It is suggested that the research into new technology be continued and that suitable expert technicians and scientists be recruited by the firm to assist Braniac in his development work. A failure to do so will result in the company becoming uncompetitive with an outdated range of products.

If the company therefore is to grow and sustain profits in the future, it will need to update and develop its own range of products. The firm is in a healthy position in this respect in that it already manufactures most of the components required by its products, has very little reliance on outside suppliers and has the expertise to move forward and develop the required technology.

The existing production and research methods appear to have operated successfully in the past, although it is clear that Braniac requires more assistance.

Personnel

In addition to recruiting suitable management expertise in the financial and marketing/selling fields, along with telecommunications technicians and scientists, it is recommended that Mr Oppenheimer become chairman of the company and be prepared to relinquish the day-to-day management of the company.

Systems

A comprehensive accounting system providing financial information for the management team, probably on a monthly basis, needs to be installed.

A review of the accounting records and procedures should also be carried out.

Products/markets

Opportunities exist in the form of product development and product diversification. The individual private customer market looks relatively untapped, and a programme of market research to determine customer needs and demands should be carried out if this opportunity is to be exploited.

At the moment too much reliance is being placed on the public sector; a complete review of budgeted future demand for products from this market sector needs to be carried out. In particular the consequences of privatisation need to be considered. With the adoption of the correct marketing and product development this threat could be turned into a fresh opportunity for further market expansion.

3   **Recommendations**

- The existing managing director, Mr E Oppenheimer, to become chairman.

- A new managing director, marketing director, finance director and personnel director to be recruited forthwith and allowed to manage their respective fields without hindrance from above.

- A small team of technicians/communications experts to be recruited to assist Braniac in his R&D activities.

- Research into the required new technology to be expanded and financed with a medium/long-term secured debt.

- A complete overhaul of inventory control procedures to be enacted with a view to reducing inventory levels and improving cash flows.

- Negotiate new medium/long-term debt in the region of £1.5m – £2m.

14   Refer to the answer to part c of DT Ltd in the Question Bank.

15   There is no answer to this self-test, as it is designed just to help you increase your business awareness.

CHAPTER 14

Strategies for information

Introduction

Examination context

Topic List

Summary and Self-test

Answers to Interactive questions

Answers to Self-test

Learning objectives

- Explain how a business collects, analyses and distributes information in order to manage its strategy and measure the performance of its projects, divisions and other strategy units ☐

- Explain and demonstrate how a business can use a management information system to implement, monitor and modify a strategy in order to create or sustain competitive advantage ☐

- Identify the risks associated with use of information technology and the controls available ☐

Specific syllabus references for this chapter are: 1f, 2d, 3g, 3h.

Syllabus links

You will have been introduced to the provision and use of financial information in your Management Information and Business and Finance studies.

The strategic value of IT/IS is a new topic that complements earlier chapters on strategy.

Examination context

In the examination you are unlikely to get a whole question focussing on information systems. Instead you may be required to comment upon the information available for decision making in a scenario question – is there enough information available? What other information is needed? Where might the business source relevant information? Is the information system adequate to fulfil the functions required of it by the business? How can the organisation use information to generate competitive advantage?

In the context of the exam, a key aspect of information strategy is that it should provide the appropriate type and amount of information needed by management to select, implement and control its chosen business strategy. The information strategy therefore needs to match the business strategy in terms of the types of information available. Also, the level of detail, the form of the information and its timing should be appropriate to the role of the person(s) who receive it.

In Q3 September 2009 (*Somborne Zoological Park*) the scenario contains information about the park's efforts to be sustainable. The fourth requirement is:

'(d) Explain how the zoo could use an information system to assess the success of its sustainability initiative and suggest some appropriate performance measures that could be used for each of the four areas identified by the IZF. **(10 marks)**

In answering this question an applied approach is needed, plus the ability to incorporate knowledge and skills in relation to information systems in the context of sustainability and performance measurement. A close reading of the scenario gives clues as to the way this answer should be structured however.

In Q1 March 2014 (Emelius Ltd) the scenario focused on a company which offers paper document storage and management services. The company had recently developed a new digital data capture service whereby paper documents could be scanned in and then made available on an electronic platform. The second requirement asked:

'(b) Explain four key drivers in the value chain for Emelius' new digital data capture service.

(12 marks)'

As the examiner noted 'this was a slightly different take on the normal value chain requirement, as a detailed value chain diagram was already provided. Better answers discussed their answer in the context of Emelius' generic strategy using value chain terminology; identified and explained a range of both cost and value drivers; and brought out the importance of linkages in the value chain'.

The examiner's comments again highlight the importance of being able to apply your knowledge to the scenario. Although not directly a requirement about information strategy, this requirement considers how IT can be used to develop an organisation's competitive advantage and the implications that reliance on IT may have for other activities in the value chain. In this case Emelius' competitive advantage centres on the speed, security and reliability of access to digital information, once captured. Analysis of the value chain showed that, as might be expected with digital data, Emelius makes heavy use of technology throughout the chain to address these critical success factors.

1   The role of information

Section overview

Information takes many forms and has many roles within the organisation. It comes from **internal** and **external** sources.

Organisations require information for a range of purposes.

- Planning
- Controlling
- Recording transactions
- Performance measurement
- Decision making

Organisations require different types of information system to provide different levels of information in a range of functional areas, supporting the distinction between strategic, tactical and operational decision making.

1.1   Why do organisations need information?

A modern organisation requires a **wide range of systems** to hold, process and analyse information. Organisations require different types of information system to provide different **levels of information** in a range of functional areas. **Strategic planning, management control** and **operational control** may be seen as a hierarchy of decisions. This is sometimes called the Anthony hierarchy, after the writer Robert Anthony. One way of portraying this concept is shown on the following diagram.

Types of information systems

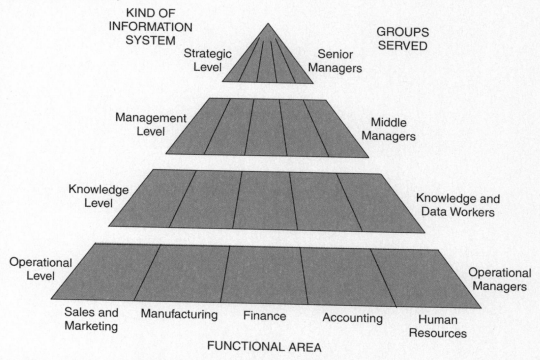

The point to note from the above diagram is that the higher level applications such as managerial information depend to a great extent on skimming data from the operational systems maintained by the different functional departments for their own purposes.

Strategic information	Tactical information	Operational information
Derived from both internal and external sources • Summarised at a high level • Relevant to the long term • Concerned with the whole organisation • Often prepared on an *ad hoc* basis • Both quantitative and qualitative • Uncertain, as the future cannot be accurately predicted	• Primarily generated internally (but may have a limited external component) • Summarised at a lower level • Relevant to the short and medium term • Concerned with activities or departments • Prepared routinely and regularly • Based on quantitative measures	• Derived from internal sources • Detailed, being the processing of raw data • Relevant to the immediate term • Task-specific • Prepared very frequently • Largely quantitative

Worked example: An evening newspaper

- Operational information will include supplies and returns from vendors to support invoicing, costs of production, controls over inventories of paper, ink etc, hours worked by staff to support payroll, health and safety compliance.

- Managerial information will include levels of sales to plan production runs of each edition (up to seven a day in some cities), the quality of stories and likely interest in them to plan production runs, advertising sales and success of special editions, supplements etc, the weather on the day and its effects on sales. Clearly the main information that will be used at this level will be the articles and stories themselves and the editorial team will decide inclusion and position of each.

- Strategic information includes the plans of rival newspaper owners, the policies of the press watchdogs, potential sources of new advertising revenues, new printing technologies, the costs and efficiency of the various printing plants operated by the firm potential new markets for newspapers (eg morning free papers).

1.2 The qualities of good information

The **qualities of good information** can be summarised by the mnemonic **Accurate**: **A**ccurate, **C**omplete, **C**ost-beneficial, **U**ser-targeted, **R**elevant, **A**uthoritative, **T**imely and **E**asy to Use.

1.3 Information requirements in different sectors

Sector	Information type	Example(s)	General comments
Manufacturing	**Strategic**	Future demand estimates New product development plans Competitor analysis	The information requirements of commercial organisations are influenced by the need to make and monitor profit. Information that contributes to the following measures is important:
	Tactical	Variance analysis Departmental accounts Inventory turnover	• Changeover times • Number of common parts

Sector	Information type	Example(s)	General comments
	Operational	Production reject rate	• Level of product diversity
		Materials and labour used	• Product and process quality
		Inventory levels	
Service	**Strategic**	Forecast sales growth and market share	Organisations have become more customer and results-oriented over the last decade. As a consequence, the difference between service and other organisation's information requirements has decreased. Businesses have realised that most of their activities can be measured, and many can be measured in similar ways regardless of the business sector.
		Profitability, capital structure	
	Tactical	Resource utilisation such as average staff time charged out, number of customers per hairdresser, number of staff per account	
		Customer satisfaction rating	
	Operational	Staff timesheets	
		Customer waiting time	
		Individual customer feedback	
Public sector	**Strategic**	Population demographics	Public sector (and non-profit making) organisations often don't have one overriding objective. Their information requirements depend on the objectives chosen. The information provided often requires interpretation (eg student exam results are not affected by the quality of teaching alone).
		Expected government policy	
			Information may compare actual performance with:
			• Standards • Targets • Similar activities • Indices • Activities over time as trends
	Tactical	Hospital occupancy rates	
		Average class sizes	
		Percent of reported crimes solved	
	Operational	Staff timesheets	
		Vehicles available	
		Student daily attendance records	

Sector	Information type	Example(s)	General comments
Non-profit/ charities	Strategic	Activities of other charities	Many of the comments regarding public sector organisations can be applied to not-for-profit organisations.
		Government (and in some cases overseas government) policy	
		Public attitudes	Information to judge performance usually aims to assess economy, efficiency and effectiveness.
	Tactical	Percent of revenue spent on admin	A key measure of efficiency for charities is the percentage of revenue that is spent on the publicised cause (eg rather than on advertising or administration).
		Average donation	
		'Customer' satisfaction statistics	
	Operational	Households collected from/approached	
		Banking documentation	
		Donations	

Interactive question 1: Strategic decision making　　　　[Difficulty level: Intermediate]

Decision making at the strategic level in organisations needs to be supported by information systems that are flexible and responsive.

Requirements

(a)　Describe the characteristics of information flows at the strategic level.

(b)　Describe the sources of information required for strategic decision making and the characteristics of an information system used to provide strategic information.

See **Answer** at the end of this chapter.

2　The strategic value of IT/IS in business

Section overview

* Business analysis views the information system in the context of the organisation's operations and strategy.

* As the importance of information has increased, organisations have realised that information systems and information technology can be used as a source of competitive advantage.

2.1　The benefits of a proposed information system

The benefits from a proposed information system should be evaluated against the costs. To quantify the benefits, several factors need to be considered.

* **Increased revenue**

   Improved data collection, storage and analysis tools may indicate previously unknown opportunities for sales. Such tools may include **data-mining** software which allows relationships to be discovered between previously unrelated data.

- **Cost reduction**

  New technology can be used to automate previously manually intensive work. This saves staff time and may result in a smaller workforce being required.

  Systems such as stock control can benefit as losses from obsolescence and deterioration are reduced.

- **Enhanced service**

  Computerised systems that create a more prompt and reliable service will increase customer satisfaction. In some cases it may be a source of **competitive advantage**.

- **Improved decision making**

  Providing decision makers with the most accurate and up-to-date information that is possible can have substantial benefits. The main areas of benefit are:

  - **Forecasting**

    Models can be created to forecast sales trends and the likely affect on costs. Organisations that can make accurate forecasts are in a better position to plan their structure and finances to ensure long-term success.

  - **Developing scenarios**

    Organisations facing uncertain times, or those which operate in dynamic, evolving environments, need to make complex decisions (often quickly) to take advantage of opportunities or to avoid threats. Scenario planning models enable a wide range of variables to be changed (such as inflation rates or sales numbers), the overall effect on the business to be identified and a business plan to be constructed.

  - **Market analysis**

    Modelling can be extended into the market that the organisation operates in. Trends such as sales volumes, prices and demand can be analysed. Relationships between price and sales volume can be identified. These can be used by an organisation when deciding on a pricing strategy. Setting the best price for a product can help drive up sales and profitability.

  - **Project evaluation**

    Organisations will benefit from improved decision making where systems can accurately evaluate a wide range of projects. Investment decisions often involve large capital outlays and if the system prevents bad decisions it can prevent the organisation wasting large sums of money.

Systems can also prevent an organisation agreeing 'bad' deals. Tenders for suppliers or other long-term contracts can prove costly if the wrong choice is made.

2.2 Strategic implications

When formulating an overall information technology strategy the following aspects should be taken into consideration:

- What are the key business areas which could benefit most from an investment in information technology, what form should the investment take, and how could such strategically important units be encouraged to use such technology effectively? Will maintenance of the new system be provided in-house or be outsourced?

- How much would the system cost in terms of software; hardware; management commitment and time; education and training; conversion; documentation; operational manning; and maintenance? The importance of lifetime application costs must be stressed – the costs and benefits after implementation may be more significant than the more obvious initial costs of installing an information technology function.

- What criteria for performance should be set for information technology systems. Two areas can be considered: the technical standard the information system achieves and the degree to which it meets the perceived and often changing needs of the user.

- What are the implications for the existing work force – have they the requisite skills; can they be trained to use the systems; will there be any redundancies? The decision to automate existing processes through the use of IT often underlines the need for business leaders to possess effective change management skills. A good change management process is likely to be critical in overcoming any resistance that may arise from those individuals affected by the introduction of a new IT system.

2.3 Earl's systems audit grid

Earl suggests a **grid** to analyse an organisation's current use of information systems

	High	Renew	Maintain, enhance
Business			
Value			
	Low	Divest	Reassess
		Low	High

Technical quality

- A system of poor quality and little value should be **disposed of** (divest).

- A system of high business value and low technical quality should be **renewed** (invested in). An important system of low quality carries a high business risk.

- A system of high quality but low business value should be **reassessed**. Is the system meeting an information need? Why is it under-utilised?

- High quality systems with a high business value should be **maintained** to preserve the high quality, and if possible **enhanced** in the quest for competitive advantage.

Establishing where to place systems on the grid is the difficult part. Consultation with system users and those for formulating and implementing information system strategy would be undertaken to form an opinion of each system. Again, judgements are subjective.

2.4 Information systems and competitive advantage

Porter identified three generic strategies that an organisation can use to compete and depending on the chosen strategy, IT can be used in different ways to enhance the business's competitive advantage.

This if the business has chosen cost leadership, IT can be used within the supply chain to improve scheduling and thus reduce the costs of inventory.

A differentiator may use IT to make the customer ordering process as easy and flexible as possible.

A business that focuses on a particular niche market may use IT to capture data electronically via a loyalty card and use it to generate information about customer preferences and buying habits.

Value chain analysis, also covered in Chapter 6 can be used to assess the impact of IS/IT, and to identify **processes where IT could be used to add value**.

IT can be used to **automate** and improve physical tasks in the **manufacturing** sector. It also provides **extra information** about the process.

2.4.1 Operations

- **Process control**: Computer systems enable tighter control over production processes.

- **Machine tool control**: Machine tools can be automated and, it is hoped, be made more precise.

  - **Numerical control**: Information to operate the machine tool is prepared in advance to generate a set of instructions.

  - **Computer numerical control** is where the computer produces the instructions.

- **Direct numerical control** is where the computer is linked directly to the machine tool.

- **Robots** can automate some of the process.

- **Computer aided manufacturing** (CAM) involves a variety of software modules such as:

    - Production control, supervisory systems

    - Materials requirement planning (MRP 1) and Manufacturing Resources Planning (MRP II). These are automated component ordering and automated production scheduling systems respectively

    - Capacity requirements planning

- **3D printing** involves producing a three-dimensional object using a 3D printer. This technique uses a robotic printer laying successive layers of material on one another, and these are then etched into a three dimensional shape using light. The increasing publicity surrounding the commercial benefits of using 3D printing has attracted interest from various industries, including clothing manufacturers and even the construction industry.

- **Computer Integrated Manufacturing** (CIM) integrates all aspects of an organisation's manufacturing activities. 'IT cannot solve basic organisational problems, but the essence is the use of the IT to provide integration though communication, effectiveness and efficiency'. Flexible manufacturing systems include:

    - Machine tools
    - Materials handling conveyor sets
    - Automatic guided vehicles

- **Enterprise Resource Planning** (ERP) systems take MRP II systems a step further, and are not restricted to certain types of organisation. ERP systems are used for identifying and planning the **enterprise-wide** resources needed to record, produce, distribute, and account for customer orders.

2.4.2 Logistics

In both **inbound** logistics and **outbound** logistics IT can have an impact.

- The use of IT in **inbound logistics** includes stock control systems such as MRP, MRPII, ERP and IT.

- **Warehousing**: The use of barcodes can increase knowledge about the quantity and nature of stock in hand.

- It is possible to create computer models, or **virtual warehouses**, of stock actually held at **suppliers**. For example an organisation with several outlets might have each connected to a system which indicates the total amount of stock available at different sites.

2.4.3 Marketing

Marketing and services can be made more effective by **customer databases** enabling market segmentation.

- Buying and analysing a mailing list is a more precise method of targeting particular groups of consumers than television advertising.

- A variety of market research companies use IT to **monitor consumers' buying habits**.

- Supermarkets can use automated **EPOS** systemsto have a precise hour-by-hour idea of how products are selling to enable speedy ordering and replenishments.

Furthermore, many large organisations have redirected their marketing effort through social media ie Facebook and Twitter, as a means of achieving competitive advantage.

Worked example: Benefits of Social Media Marketing

An article published on the Forbes website highlights the increasing use of social media marketing and information systems by businesses looking for a 'big return' on their investment in marketing activities. The article highlights a number of good reasons for organisations to turn to social media marketing.

Brand recognition

Social media can be used a means of brand-building. 'With consistent effort and great content, you can build a reputation for your brand around your company's values, benefits, and advantages.'

Community

Social media is particularly effective at creating a community. 'When your followers become part of your community, you gain instant access to them. That means you can find out what challenges they are facing and what they like and don't like about your offerings. You can engage in ongoing dialogue that can be more valuable than any kind of paid market research.'

Repeat Exposure

Forbes notes that social media provides organisations with the opportunity to 'remind followers over and over again about what companies have to offer, which can shorten the sales cycle dramatically'.

Influence

By building a social media following, this can create a 'snowball effect'. In essence, the greater the social media audience the greater scope for attracting new 'customers, media interviews, joint venture partnerships, and all kinds of other opportunities'. Forbes highlights that effective social media marketing through sharing posts, videos and other content can lead to an increased 'hit' rate on a company's websites.

Big Wins

'While many businesses large and small are trying to justify the cost and time investment for managing social media marketing, an important benefit often gets overlooked: Big Wins. For example, if someone from LindedIn connects your business with a significant government contract, then that would certainly qualify as a Big Win. If a major media outlet finds your business on Twitter and interviews the MD for a national article, then that is also a Big Win – one that you can't measure based on revenues directly generated.'

Source: Adapted from 'The hidden benefits of social media marketing', by Stephanie Chandler, December 2013, Forbes [online]

2.4.4 Service

Customer relationship management (CRM) describes the methodologies, software, and usually Internet capabilities that help an enterprise manage customer relationships.

For example, an enterprise might build a database about its customers that described relationships in sufficient detail so that management, salespeople, service staff, and maybe the customer, could access information, match customer needs with product plans, remind customers of service requirements and know what other products a customer had purchased.

CRM consists of:

- Helping an enterprise to identify and target their best customers, manage marketing campaigns with clear goals and objectives, and generate quality leads.

- Assisting the organisation to improve telesales, account, and sales management by **optimising information shared**, and streamlining existing processes (for example, taking orders using mobile devices).

- Allowing the formation of relationships with customers, with the aim of improving customer satisfaction and maximising profits; identifying the most profitable customers and providing them with the highest level of service.

- Providing employees with the information and processes necessary to know their customers, understand their needs, and effectively build relationships between the company, its customer base, and distribution partners.

2.4.5 Support activities

As far as **support** activities are concerned IT has some impact.

- **Procurement**: IT can automate some purchasing decisions. Paperwork can be saved if the organisation's purchase systems are linked directly to the sales order systems of some suppliers (eg by electronic data interchange) and costs can be reduced through the use of internet based marketplaces (see following worked example).

- **Technology development**. Computer automated design (**CAD**) is, in a number of areas, an important influence.

    - **Drafting**: CAD produces engineer's drawings, component design, layout (eg of stores, wiring and piping) and electronic circuit diagrams in complex systems.

    - **Updating**: It is easy to change design in CAD systems and to assess ramifications of any changes. Some CAD systems have archive data (eg for reference).

    - CAD enables modelling to be **checked** without the necessity of producing working prototypes. Some 'stress testing' can be carried out on the model.

- There is perhaps less impact on **human resources**. However, the HR applications include the maintenance of a skills database, staff planning (eg using network analysis), computer based training, time attendance systems, payroll systems, pension systems.

Worked example: Alibaba

Alibaba is the world's largest e-commerce company which predominantly operates in China. According to the company's website its mission is to 'make it easy to do business anywhere'. Alibaba was set up in 1999 by a Chinese English teacher (Jack Ma), with the aim of helping small Chinese businesses trade globally. As Linda Yueh, the BBC's Chief business correspondent explains, Alibaba is effectively a 'combination of eBay and Amazon. It is an online company with multiple revenue streams that are more conventional than a social network site. Alibaba.com is a B2B, or business-to-business, website. It links up businesses around the world looking for suppliers. For instance, they link wholesalers to distributors around the world, from the UK to China to the US'. Businesses can trade almost anything from olive oil to computer components.

Source: Alibaba & BBC

3 Knowledge management

Section overview

- Knowledge management is a key element in this chapter. Effective use of information requires knowledge. Knowledge is seen as a strategic asset and organisation-specific knowledge, which has been built up over time, is a core competence that cannot easily be imitated.

- Knowledge management (KM) refers to the process of harnessing ICT and other systems to develop and disseminate relevant knowledge throughout the organisation.

- KM is a source of competitive advantage because it encourages process improvement and innovation and helps the organisation identify ways to meet customer needs better than the competition.

- Capturing the knowledge is insufficient. Competitive advantage is achieved by acting on the knowledge and using it to make effective decisions.

3.1 Knowledge management programmes

Definitions

Knowledge is the potential for action based on data, information, intuition and experience.

Explicit knowledge is knowledge that the company knows that it has. This includes facts, transactions and events that can be clearly stated and stored in management information systems.

Tacit knowledge is personal knowledge and expertise held by people within the organisation that has not been formally documented.

Knowledge management describes a range of strategies and tools that capture all the knowledge that is valuable to an organisation, and deliver it to the people in such a way that it can be acted on quickly, to the competitive advantage of the business.

In an age of information and in the face of increasing environmental change, organisations have begun to focus on the importance of exploiting their **intangible assets**, one of which is knowledge. The **effective use of information** requires knowledge.

Knowledge management programmes extend beyond any particular piece of IT/IS and embrace changing the attitudes of management and staff towards sharing information. They concern:

- Designing and installing techniques and processes to create, protect and use **explicit knowledge**.

- Designing and creating environments and activities to discover and release **tacit knowledge**.

- Capturing good quality information from outside the business as well as within eg intelligence on competitors.

Tacit knowledge is a difficult thing to manage because it is **invisible** and **intangible**. We do not know what knowledge exists within a person's brain, and whether he or she chooses to share knowledge is a matter of choice. Tacit knowledge may be difficult to express or communicate to others but is also invaluable because it is a unique asset that is very hard for other organisations to copy.

Collaboration between employees helps to transform tacit knowledge into explicit knowledge.

The **motivation to share** hard-won experience is sometimes low; the individual is 'giving away' their value and may be very reluctant to lose a position of influence and respect by making it available to everyone.

Organisations should encourage people to share their knowledge. Electronic tools such as online bulletin boards, web logs (blogs) and wikis (editable web pages designed for groups of users) all facilitate knowledge sharing.

However, whilst technology can help unlock knowledge, corporate culture is more important. Collaboration can be encouraged through a culture of openness and rewards for sharing knowledge and information.

3.2 Systems that aid knowledge management

Information systems play an important role in knowledge management, helping with **information flows** and helping formally **capture** the knowledge held within the organisation.

Worked example: How to facilitate knowledge sharing

An article by Forbes (2012) highlighted the findings from research which suggests that the typical person will receive data equivalent to reading 174 newspapers every single day over the course of a year. To combat the perils of data overload many companies actively attempt to manage knowledge throughout the organisation. The article argues that good knowledge management systems are central to success by helping to:

- Facilitate decision-making
- Build the learning organisation
- Stimulate cultural change and innovation

Facilitates decision-making

Companies that have cultures that **encourage best practice sharing** can unlock the rich stores of knowledge within each employee: sharing promotes overall knowledge, and facilitates further creativity. World-class companies are innovatively implementing best practice sharing to shake them of out of the rut of 'the way it's always been done.' Programs such as General Electric's Corporate Executive Council (CEC) provides the company's executives with the opportunity to cut out so called 'noise' (being unnecessary data). Forbes highlight that 'the CEC is composed of the head's of GE's fourteen major businesses and the two-day sessions are forums for sharing best practices, accelerating progress, and discussing successes, failures, and experiences'.

Equally, Wal-Mart's famous Saturday meetings help employees challenge conventions and suggest creative new ideas that drive process improvement, increased efficiency, and overall, **a stronger bottom line**.

Builds learning organisations

The fundamental goal of **knowledge management** is to capture and disseminate knowledge across an increasingly global enterprise, enabling individuals to avoid repeating mistakes and to operate more intelligently – striving to create an entire **learning organisation** that works as efficiently as its most seasoned experts.

Forbes highlights the words of David Garvin who notes 'to move ahead, one must often first look behind'. 'The U.S, Army's After Action Reviews (AAR's) are an example of a knowledge management system that has helped build the Army into a learning organisation by making learning routine...after every important activity or event, Army teams review assignments, identify successes and failures, and seek ways to perform better the next time.'

Stimulates cultural change and innovation

Positive management of knowledge by may help organisations to stimulate innovation through the free flow of ideas. Best Practices' recently updated report, *Knowledge Management of Internal Best Practices*, profiles innovative methods used by world-class companies to communicate best practices internally. The study provides recommendations for how to create a best practice-sharing culture through all levels of the organisation, how to use both external and internal sources to find best practices and how to capture that knowledge and communicate it to all employees.

Best Practices, LLC contacted over fifty leading companies at the vanguard of knowledge management to compile its report. Some of the vital issues these thought leaders addressed include **measurement and management of intellectual assets**, best practice identification and recognition systems, best practice prioritisation systems, communication of best practices, and **knowledge sharing through**

technology. For example, in the area of best practice communications, the report examines how General Electric spreads best practices with **regular job rotations**.

Fortune notes that 'Fortune 500 companies lose roughly $31.5bn a year by failing to share knowledge.'

Source: Adapted from 'Why knowledge management is important to the success of your company', written by Lisa Quast, August 2012, Forbes [online]

Interactive question 2: Information and knowledge management
[Difficulty level: Intermediate]

Increasingly the management of information sharing and group working ventures is a fundamental part of business management.

Requirements

(a) Discuss how the management of information might differ from the management of knowledge.
(b) How can an organisation develop a knowledge strategy?

See **Answer** at the end of this chapter.

3.3 Knowledge management as a source of competitive advantage

The resource based view of strategy, discussed in Chapter 2, is one of a successful organisation that acquires and develops resources and competences over time and exploits them to create competitive advantage.

The ability to capture and harness corporate knowledge has become critical for organisations as they seek to adapt to changes in the business environment, particularly those businesses providing financial and professional services.

Knowledge is seen as a strategic asset and organisation-specific knowledge, which has been built up over time, is a core competence that cannot easily be imitated.

Knowledge management can help promote competitive advantage through:

- The fast and efficient exchange of information

- Effective channelling of the information to:

    - improve processes, productivity and performance
    - identify opportunities to meet customer needs better than competitors
    - promote creativity and innovation

In Chapter 6 we discussed benchmarking. The process of identifying the outstanding qualities and practices of competitors allows an organisation to capture knowledge that can then be used internally to make improvements that will further its competitive advantage.

If knowledge management is about making sure that information flows efficiently through a company, competitive advantage is achieved by making sure that the knowledge is translated into decisions and actions.

Knowledge must be delivered in a form that can be quickly interpreted and acted on. There must also be a processes for learning from past experiences (successes or failures) and identifying opportunities to improve.

Thus competitive advantage is not necessarily achieved by those who have the best knowledge, but by those who use knowledge best.

Worked example: Tesco

Tesco, the UK's largest supermarket chain, uses information from its 'Clubcard' loyalty card to understand customers, their preferences and their purchasing behaviour. This enables it to plan promotions and target them to meet customer requirements. The success of this scheme is based on

Tesco's ability not only to capture information about customer preferences, but to analyse this data to support decisions on pricing and marketing.

An increasing number of companies around the world are turning to the widespread use of mobile technologies to collect data about their customers. American firm Front Flip has developed a special mobile phone application which acts as a loyalty card for users. An article by Forbes highlights that 'Front Flip distinguishes themselves from other mobile app loyalty card companies by creating profitable and long-term relationships with their customers through fun experiences and instant promotions. Front Flip also offers rich customer analytics and targeted mobile campaigns. Front Flip works with national businesses to help them see an increase in traffic and sales in the first 90 days'.

Front Flip works with a number of well known restaurant chains including KFC, McDonalds, Pizza Hut and Wendys. The system works by customers using their mobile phones at the point of sale to scan a 'Quick Response' (QR) code, which then allows users to access a 'digital scratch card' . The scratch card then reveals whether the user has won an instant prize. This enables businesses to send the customer a 'virtually wrapped mobile gift', for example a discount on certain products on their birthday or a gift aimed at getting customers who haven't visited an outlet for a while back in-store. The system is also a particularly useful way for businesses to capture data about their customers, as every time 'a customer scans a business's QR code, their data and the day and time of their visit is shared with the business'.

Source: Adapted from 'Front flip is a mobile loyalty program that helps drive customer engagement and frequency', written by Amit Chowdhry, July 2013, Forbes [online]

Interactive question 3: Kid A plc

[Difficulty level: Exam standard]

Kid A plc (KA) is a company that runs four pre-school nurseries for children aged two to four years old, and is planning to expand the business.

Industry background

Demand for pre-school nurseries has grown substantially in the UK since the start of the 19X0s. Changes in the labour market have resulted in a rise in the number of working women with dependent children. In 20X8, 52% of women whose youngest dependent child was under five years of age were working, compared to only 31% 10 years earlier. During this period unemployment in the UK fell significantly.

This has, however, coincided with a change in demographics in the UK and a drop in the birth rate, resulting in a falling population of children of pre-school age.

There has been an increased emphasis by the Government on the role of childcare and education in raising educational standards and enhancing children's social development. In the UK over the last 10 years, the number of day nursery places more than doubled as more nurseries were opened. Day nurseries are one form of pre-school childcare available in the UK, the other main ones being playgroups, childminders and the use of domestic nannies.

Most day nurseries operate independently from one another and are, in the main, owner managed. Demand for nursery places normally outstrips supply.

Since 20X1, all nurseries have been subject to government registration and inspection, and the inspectors' reports are available on the Internet for viewing by interested parties.

Company background

KA was formed in 20X2 by Thom Yorke, a former IT engineer, and Debra Curtis, who previously worked as a manager for another nursery. Both Thom and Debra have a close involvement in the day to day running of the nurseries, which have a maximum of 48 children on each of the premises at any one time.

The company has utilised modern technology to help address concerns of parents. All the children at the nurseries are given GPS (global positioning satellite) wristbands that are linked wirelessly to a series of webcams. Parents can call up the webcams from their workplaces to see the activities of their children.

Parents who have busy work commitments can also utilise a collect and return service whereby KA will pick up children and return them to their homes outside the normal nursery hours of 8am-6pm. This service, although popular with some parents, has attracted criticism from some commentators, who believe it results in disruption to the lives of children.

The KA nursery has a far greater emphasis on learning, especially via computers, than children of the same age-groups at other nurseries, and this has proved to be very popular with some parents. Parents can review the computer-based games and work undertaken by their children remotely via the Internet. These innovations have been praised in the government inspector reports on KA.

KA operates on a staff-to-child ratio that is far higher than the industry average, to ensure the children are given a more structured environment and personal attention. All staff members are NNEB (National Nursery Examining Board) qualified, unlike other nurseries which have a mixture of qualified and unqualified staff. Staff are paid a premium over the salaries of other nurseries. They are expected to have an understanding of the technology that is used within the nurseries and are given a list of tasks each day that they are expected to carry out. Tasks are reviewed by Thom and Joy each week to ensure they have been completed.

KA charge about 40% more than other nurseries, to reflect the extra services provided, but this has not prevented the nurseries being permanently full with a waiting list. Despite extra costs being incurred, KA has a higher profit margin than most other nurseries.

Latest developments

KA is now considering an expansion of the business and opening four more nurseries, with a view to opening additional nurseries if this proves to be a success. Thom and Debra have previously controlled the individual nurseries themselves. They now want to appoint managers to run the nurseries and to set budgets to ensure that they generate a return on the initial investment made, without compromising the standards of care and education offered to children. They are uncertain as to how to assess the managers in terms of how well they are running the individual nurseries.

Thom and Debra will dictate the initial layout of the individual nurseries in terms of building sizes and fixtures and fittings. The nursery managers would be responsible for advertising, bookings, staff, communication with parents and day-to-day running expenses.

Requirements

(a) Prepare a Porter's Five Forces model for the nursery industry as a whole.   **(10 marks)**

(b) Identify and explain the critical success factors that operate within the business of KA. Discuss how KA has used information systems and technology to add value and give competitive advantage.
(8 marks)

(c) As an external consultant, prepare a report to Thom and Debra that

    (i)   Explains the business risks that may arise as a result of expanding the business.

    (ii) Suggests how they could implement an effective budgeting process for the nurseries.

    (iii) Explains the strategic, tactical and operational information that Thom and Debra will need to assist in decision making and control.   **(20 marks)**

(38 marks)

4 Risks associated with IT/IS

Section overview

- The risks of IT/IS can be summarised as:

  - The **risk of inadequacy**: the failure by the firm to utilise IT/IS as effectively as its rivals will lead to loss of competitive advantage, eg inferior service, poorer products, excess costs.

  - The **risk of breakdown**: where the firm depends on IT/IS a breakdown in its operations threatens the business.

  - The **risk of excess expense**: IT/IS is a significant budget item. Botched projects, expensive contracts, inappropriate systems or non-adoption presents a direct financial risk.

- Risks are present at the system specification stage, and they carry through to implementation. There is also the risk of systems failure. Controls are therefore needed to protect data and information.

4.1 Development and implementation – what can go wrong

Problems that occur when implementing a new information system can usually be traced to deficiencies in the development and specification process. Some of these issues involve change management which is covered in Chapter 15.

The following table outlines some common mistakes that adversely affect the implementation process.

Stage/activity	Problems
Analysis	The problem the system is intended to solve is not fully understood.
	Investigation of the situation is hindered by insufficient resources.
	User input is inadequate through either lack of consultation or lack of user interest.
	The project team is unable to dedicate the time required.
	Insufficient time spent planning the project.
Design	Insufficient user input.
	Lack of flexibility. The organisation's future needs are neglected.
	The system requires unforeseen changes in working patterns.
	Failure to perform organisation impact analysis. An organisational impact analysis studies the way a proposed system will affect organisation structure, attitudes, decision making and operations. The analysis aims to ensure the system is designed to best ensure integration with the organisation.
	Organisational factors sometimes overlooked include:
	- Ergonomics (including equipment, work environment and user interfaces)
	- Health and safety
	- Compliance with legislation
	- Job design
	- Employee involvement

Stage/activity	Problems
Programming	Insufficient time and money allocated to programming.
	Programmers supplied with incomplete or inaccurate specifications.
	The logic of the program is misunderstood.
	Poor programming technique results in programs that are hard to modify.
	Programs are not adequately documented.
Testing	Insufficient time and money allocated to testing.
	Failure to develop an organised testing plan.
	Insufficient user involvement.
	User management do not review and sign-off the results of testing.
Conversion	Insufficient time and money allocated to data conversion.
	Insufficient checking between old and new files.
	The process is rushed to compensate for time overruns elsewhere.
Implementation	Insufficient time, money and/or appropriate staff mean the process has to be rushed.
	Lack of user training increases the risk of system under-utilisation and rejection.
	Poor system and user documentation.
	Lack of performance standards to assess system performance against.
	System maintenance provisions are inadequate.

A recurring theme when examining the reasons for information system failure is user resistance. Users may be management and staff, but for outward-facing systems equally could involve customers, suppliers and other partners.

The three types of theories to explain user resistance are explained in the following table.

Theory	Description	Overcoming the resistance
People-oriented	User-resistance is caused by factors internal to users as individuals or as a group. For example, users may not wish to disrupt their current work practices and social groupings.	User training. Organisation policies. Persuasion. User involvement in system development.
System-oriented	User-resistance is caused by factors inherent in the new system design relating to ease of use and functionality. For example, a poorly designed user-interface will generate user-resistance.	User training and education. Improve user-interface. Ensure users contribute to the system design process. Ensure the system 'fits' with the organisation.

Theory	Description	Overcoming the resistance
Interaction	User-resistance is caused by the interaction of people and the system.	Re-organise the organisation before implementing the system.
	For example, the system may be well-designed but its implementation will cause organisational changes that users resist eg reduced chance of bonuses, redundancies, monotonous work.	Redesign any affected incentive schemes to incorporate the new system.
		Promote user participation and encourage organisation-wide teamwork.
		Emphasise the benefits the system brings.

4.2 Risks from IT systems

- **Natural threats**: Fire, flood, electrical storms.

- **Human threats**: Individuals with grudges and other staff are a physical threat to computer installations, whether by spilling a cup of coffee over a desk covered with papers, or tripping and falling doing some damage to themselves and to an item of office equipment. Political terrorism is a major risk in the era of cyber-terrorism.

- **Data systems integrity**: These may include incorrect entry of data, use of out-of-date files, loss of data through lack of back-ups.

- **Fraud**: The theft of funds by dishonest use of a computer system.

- **Deliberate sabotage**: For example, commercial espionage, malicious damage or industrial action.

- **Viruses and other corruptions** can spread through the network to all of the organisation's computers. **Hackers** may be able to get into the organisation's internal network, either to steal data or to damage the system.

- **Denial of Service (DoS) attack**: A denial of service attack is characterised by an attempt by attackers to prevent legitimate users of a service from using that service.

- **Non-compliance with regulations**: The use of IT systems, and the data they contain, is subject to close legal supervision in most countries. In the UK relevant legislation includes the *Data Protection Act* for which penalties are imposed by courts if data is wrongly used or control procedures are not in place.

Worked example: Social media risks

In September 2013 accounting firm Grant Thornton published a report titled 'Social media risks and rewards'. The report explored the increasing use of social media by large companies and the new types of risk that such communication brings. The growing importance of social media among big business is evident from the reports findings:

- More than half of (55%) of the executives who responded to the survey feel that social media will be an important component of corporate marketing efforts going forward.

- Two thirds (66%) of respondents expected their company's use of social media to increase slightly or significantly over the next 12 months.

Social media risks

The report identifies four main risks of using social media:

(1) Damage to brand reputation
(2) Disclosure of proprietary and/or confidential information
(3) Corporate identify theft
(4) Legal, regulatory and compliance violations

'Nearly three quarters (71%) of executives surveyed were concerned about the potential risks involved in the use of social media, but believe the risks can be mitigated or avoided'.

The report highlights some memorable examples of companies which have failed to manage their social media communications effectively, including blunders by Gap and Netflix.

Gap

In 2012, Hurricane Sandy struck parts of America causing severe devastation, retailer Gap posted a tweet via Twitter which advised customers to 'stay safe, and perhaps shop at Gap.com'. Gap apologised shortly afterwards and removed the message.

Netflix

The US Securities and Exchange Commission (SEC) investigated Netflix in 2012 after the company's CEO, Reed Hastings, posted information on Facebook which boosted its share price.

Reed Hastings comment raises an interesting issue about social media communications and associated risks. As social media starts to play an increasing role in how businesses communicate careful consideration needs to be given to ensuring that private messages expressing personal opinions are not perceived as official corporate communications.

Source: Grant Thornton

4.3 Security controls

Definition

Security means the protection of data from unauthorised modification, disclosure or destruction, and the protection of the information system from the degradation or non-availability of services – in other words, system failure.

Security can be subdivided into a number of aspects.

- **Prevention**: It is in practice impossible to prevent all threats cost-effectively.
- **Detection**: Detection techniques are often combined with prevention techniques: a log can be maintained of unauthorised attempts to gain access to a computer system.
- **Deterrence**: As an example, computer misuse by personnel can be made grounds for dismissal.
- **Recovery procedures**: If the threat occurs, its consequences can be contained.
- **Correction procedures**: These ensure the vulnerability is dealt with (for example, by instituting stricter controls).
- **Threat avoidance**: This might mean changing the design of the system.

4.4 Combating IT risks and IT security

The international security standard, ISO17799 groups its recommendations under the following headings.

- **Business continuity planning**: This means that there should be measures to ensure that if major failures or disasters occur, the business will not be completely unable to function.
- **Systems access control**: This includes protection of information, information systems, networked services, detection of unauthorised activities and security when using the systems.
- **Systems development and maintenance**: This includes security measures and steps to protect data in operational and application systems and also ensuring that IT projects and support are conducted securely.

- **Physical and environmental security**: Measures should be taken to prevent unauthorised access, damage and interference to business premises, assets, information and information facilities and prevention of theft.

- **Compliance** with any relevant legal requirements and also with organisational policies in standards. There is no point in having them if they are not enforced.

- **Personnel security**: This covers issues such as recruitment of trustworthy employees, and also reporting of security-related incidents. Training is particularly important, with the aim that users are aware of information security threats and concerns and are equipped to comply with the organisation's security policy.

- **Security organisation**: It should be clear who has responsibility for the various aspects of information security. Additional considerations will apply if facilities and assets are accessed by third parties or responsibility for information processing has been outsourced.

- **Computer and network management**: This includes ensuring continuity of operations and minimising the risk of systems failures, also protecting the integrity of systems and safeguarding information, particularly when exchanged between organisations. Particularly important is protection from viruses.

- **Asset classification and control**: Information is an asset, just like a machine, building or a vehicle, and security will be improved if information assets have an 'owner', and are classified according to how much protection they need.

- **Security policy**: A written document setting out the organisation's approach to information security should be available to all staff.

Strategies for identifying and managing other risks faced by a business were discussed in Chapter 10.

Summary

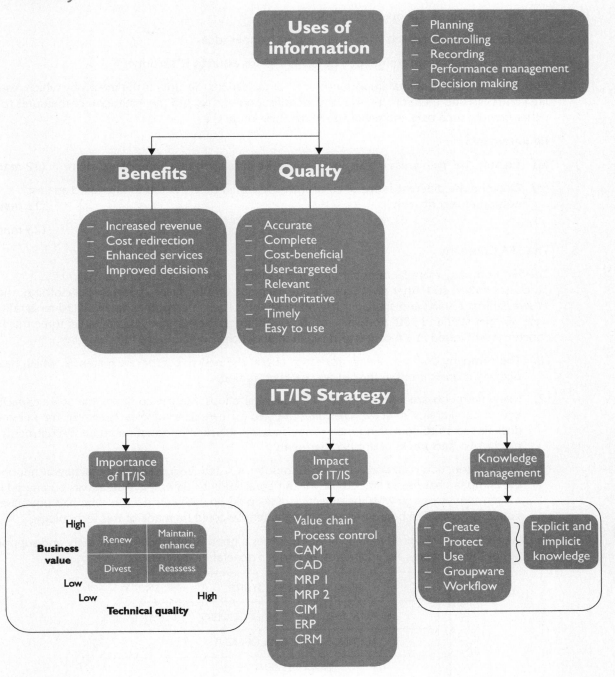

Self-test

Answer the following questions.

1   List five uses of information.

2   List five characteristics of strategic information.

3   List five characteristics of tactical information.

4   List five characteristics of operational information.

5   Distinguish between explicit knowledge and tacit knowledge.

6   Identify four controls recommended by ISO17799 for assuring IT security.

7   Computer security is of vital importance to all organisations. Security is the means by which losses are controlled and therefore involves the identification of risks and the institution of measures to either prevent such risks entirely or to reduce their impact.

    Requirements

    (a)   Identify the main areas of risk which may arise in relation to a computer system.   **(12 marks)**

    (b)   Describe the different forms of control which should be instituted to safeguard against computer security risks.   **(13 marks)**

                                                                                               (25 marks)

8   **The SFA Company**

    The SFA Company manufactures clothing and operates from one location in a major city. It purchases cotton and other raw materials and manufactures these into garments of clothing, such as sweatshirts, T-shirts and similar articles in its factory. There are approximately 20 administration staff, 30 sales staff and 300 production workers. Although the company is profitable, three major concerns were raised at a recent board meeting about the operations of the company:

    (1)   The company does not always appear to obtain the best prices for raw materials, which has decreased gross profit in the last few years of trading.

    (2)   Many garments are made to order for large retail shops, but the company has spare capacity and so it maintains an active salesforce to try to increase its total sales. However, the salesforce does not seem to be making many sales because of lack of information about the garments in production and stocks of finished garments.

    (3)   Some production is carried out using Computer Assisted Design and manufacture although the company has found limited use for this application to date. The system was purchased in a hurry two years ago with the objective of keeping up with competitors who had purchased similar systems. The board believes that greater use could be made of this technology.

    The Value Chain model produced by Porter provides a good summary of the primary and support activities of the company. An adaptation of Porter's general model follows.

The board of SFA is currently considering introducing some form of information system or systems, such as a MIS, into the company for all staff to use. Because of the perceived weaknesses in the current systems already mentioned, the directors are particularly interested in the areas of:

(1) Inbound logistics
(2) Marketing and sales
(3) Technology development

Requirements

(a) Explain what inputs will be needed for the information systems designed to support the operations of the business in the three areas mentioned above. **(14 marks)**

(b) Explain what outputs will be required from those information systems. **(6 marks)**

Note: Do **not** describe Porter's general model. **(20 marks)**

9 Read the scenario of Question 3 of the **September 2009 Business Strategy** paper in this text entitled *Somborne Zoological Park*. Draft an answer for requirement (d) on the information system and performance measures.

10 Go online at The Times 100 Business Case Studies and read the Canon case study 'Integrated information systems: seeing the whole picture' at http://businesscasestudies.co.uk/canon/integrated-information-systems-seeing-the-whole-picture

Now, go back to the Learning objectives in the Introduction. If you are satisfied you have achieved these objectives, please tick them off.

Answer to Interactive question 1

(a) **Long-term outlook**

Information flows at a strategic level will be geared towards information expected to impact on the long-term future of the business. There is a need for high quality information to enable sound long-term decisions to be made.

Flexible

Organisations are complex systems.

In order to maintain control in a constantly changing organisation the information flows and systems at strategic level need to be flexible and able to respond quickly to new demands.

For example, if a new competitor enters the market place, or environmental legislation is introduced affecting production processes or a trading opportunity arises in an overseas territory, then strategic decisions will be required to formulate the most appropriate response.

Good decisions can only be made when all the implications can be quantified with an acceptable degree of certainty. Management information systems must be flexible enough to provide concise, accurate and timely information relevant to the new environment.

Multi-directional

In a business organisation information flows both vertically and horizontally. The familiar pyramid hierarchy of an organisation sets out three levels of control and information.

Information flows at the strategic level facilitates decision-making that will affect the whole organisation and provide the framework for long term strategic plans. Internal information will flow from middle management up to senior management and *vice versa*.

Information also flows horizontally between different activities in a business. For instance overtime hours provided by the payroll section may be used by the production department, delivery lead times from warehouses may be used by the sales team and the level of future orders from the sales department will be used to forecast turnover and cash flows by the accounts department. The quality of these information flows will dictate both the efficiency of the business operations and will impact on the type and quality of information received by senior management.

The complex nature of strategic decisions makes information sharing vital.

An external component

Strategic level information flows will include information from external sources (eg government, suppliers, media etc). Strategic decisions are generally non-routine and require a high degree of judgement. The quality of information is critical at the strategic management level.

(b) Information used at a strategic level is often *ad hoc* – strategic decision making is non-routine and potentially risky.

Strategic information comes from both internal and external sources.

Internal sources

Most management information systems are now computer-based because of processing speed, accuracy and the ability to process large volumes of data. Internal data needs to be captured from day-to-day operations, processed into relevant information and made available in a suitable form at a strategic level.

Senior management information requirements should play a part in the development of information systems to ensure that the information required for strategic decision making is able to be produced.

Centralised systems are relatively powerful and usually controlled at senior level. However, a flexible response to non-routine problems may be lacking.

Decentralised systems may provide more flexibility, however central control and standard formats are often lacking.

Currently, popular solutions revolve around **networked and distributed** processing systems. These can provide information to different levels of management – often from the same database. They combine the advantages of local control, speed and ease of use with flexibility and the potential for standardised presentation of information.

Executive Support Systems (ESS) can be particularly useful in this area, providing summarised high-level information with the ability to view the underlying data if required.

The introduction of an ESS will also encourage senior management to consider which type of information is really relevant to the business.

An **intranet** may also be appropriate to encourage the sharing of knowledge and opinions relevant to strategic decisions (eg bulletin boards).

External sources

External information may be in the form of official reports, tax leaflets, technical updates, press updates and often just word of mouth.

Much of this information is now available via the **Internet. Intelligent agents** and **newsclipping services** can also be utilised on the Internet, to find user-defined information and forward it – usually via e-mail.

Some organisations are able to access external information through an **extranet** – allowing them to enter certain parts of another organisation's intranet.

Answer to Interactive question 2

(a) **Information management** entails identifying the current and future information needs, identifying information sources, collecting and storing the information and facilitating existing methods of using information and identifying new ways of using it. It should also ensure that the information is communicated to those who need it and not to those who are not entitled to see it.

Mayo defines **knowledge management** (KM) as 'the management of the information, knowledge and experience available to an organisation – its creation, capture, storage, availability and utilisation – in order that organisational activities build on what is already known and extend it further'.

More specifically, **knowledge** is interpreted in terms of **potential for action** and distinguished from **information** in terms of its more immediate link with performance. This interpretation is consistent with what the information systems philosopher and professor Charles West Churchman observed three decades ago in his pioneering work *The Design of Inquiring Systems*: 'knowledge resides in the user and not in the collection of information… it is how the user reacts to a collection of information that matters'.

Databases, or more correctly **knowledge bases**, need to be designed and developed to store the organisation's knowledge. This will be particularly difficult because of the **tacit** nature of much of the knowledge and also because it is largely inside the heads of individuals. Recording this knowledge will be very different to recording the fields and records of a traditional database. An **expert system** seems one way forward as this has a knowledge base made up of facts, rules and conditions. But much of this knowledge may have to be represented pictorially as images and 'knowledge maps'. An intranet that lends itself to full multimedia representation and intelligent searching may therefore be the way forward.

Knowledge-based companies will vary from industry to industry but there are some broad common principles about where knowledge resides and how to capture its value. The intellectual capital can be divided between human capital (the bodies that go home at night), and structural capital. Structural capital includes innovation capital (intellectual property), customer capital (address lists and client records), and organisational capital (systems for processing policies and claims). A number of organisations are creating knowledge management programmes for

protecting and distributing knowledge resources that they have identified and for discovering new sources of knowledge.

- One such programme is the identification and development of informal networks and communities of practice within organisations. These self-organising groups share common work interests, usually cutting across a company's functions and processes.

- Another means of establishing the occurrence of knowledge is to look at knowledge-related business outcomes eg, product development and service innovation. While the knowledge embedded within these innovations is invisible, the products themselves are tangible.

- Every day companies make substantial investments in improving their employees' knowledge and enabling them to use it more effectively. Analysis of these investments is a third way of making KM activities visible. For example how much technical and non-technical training are individuals consuming? How much is invested in competitive and environmental scanning, and in other forms of strategic research?

The process by which an organisation develops its store of knowledge is sometimes called **organisational learning**. A **learning organisation** is centred on the people that make up the organisation and the knowledge they hold. The organisation and employees feed off and into the central pool of knowledge. The organisation uses the knowledge pool as a tool to teach itself and its employees.

There are dozens of different approaches to KM, including document management, information management, business intelligence, competence management, information systems management, intellectual asset management, innovation, business process design, and so on. Many KM projects have a significant element of information management. After all, people need information about where knowledge resides, and to share knowledge they need to transform it into more or less transient forms of information.

(b)   A **knowledge management strategy** might take the form shown in the diagram below.

The stages may include the following.

(i)   Develop and determine a policy for owning, growing and sharing knowledge within the organisation.

(ii)   Identify critical knowledge functions within each department.

(iii)   Audit knowledge to determine its type, location, longevity and whether it is explicit or tacit.

(iv)   Document knowledge in a medium that best suits the purpose for which it will be used.

(v)   Store it in a repository where it can be easily updated and retrieved.

(vi)   Determine ways in which it can be grown and tracked.

(vii) Decide how the knowledge will be disseminated inside the organisation and possibly outside.

(viii) Ensure this valuable organisational asset is kept secure.

Answer to Interactive question 3

(a) **Porter's five forces**

Customers

- Parents individually have very little power/influence over the industry.

- This is because they have low buying power in relation to the size of the industry.

- Because demand exceeds supply of childcare places even if parents take their children elsewhere, it is unlikely to cause any problems for the industry as others will take their places.

- However, if there were a series of damaging reports into the industry, then parents may decide to use alternative forms of childcare. Their children are very precious to them and they would not be prepared to accept substandard levels of service.

- Switching costs are low in terms of money; however parents would have to consider issues such as distress to the children involved and the problem of finding a better alternative in the local vicinity due to the lack of supply.

- Overall influence: Low

Suppliers

- Supply of products to nurseries is likely to be quite diverse as individual nurseries will have different demands. The main issues would be the provision of food, clothing, nappies and toys for the children in the nurseries. The market for these products is likely to be competitive and therefore the bargaining power of individual suppliers is weak.

- However, given that the majority of nurseries themselves are relatively small, their bargaining power is also weak which will neutralise the above position.

- The other main supplier group will be skilled staff. Their power is likely to be low on an individual basis and they are unlikely to be unionised.

- Only if nurseries form groups or chains, to place volume orders, is the negotiating position likely to improve.

- Overall influence: Low

Substitutes

- Demand currently exceeds supply within the childcare industry. Substitutes exist in the form of domestic nannies, playgroups and childminders.

- These competitors individually have little power, although they may offer a service which is more convenient and local to that of nurseries, especially in the form of domestic nannies and childminders.

- Considerations such as the level of service offered by the competition would have an influence on whether they could take market share away from nurseries. Parents would be concerned about the level of regulation over the substitutes, due to the importance of high quality childcare to them.

- Overall influence: Medium

Competitors

- The majority of entities in the industry are small, owner managed businesses. As such competitors' power is low, as one nursery will not be able to significantly influence the behaviour of others.

- Even if individual nurseries set up close to one another, because demands outstrips supply there is potentially room for both to survive.

- If there were a number of chains of nurseries then they might be able to demonstrate some power, but there seems to be little evidence of this.

- Overall influence: Low/Medium

New entrants

- Set up costs are relatively low, as demonstrated by the large number of owner managed nurseries in existence. The main costs to be incurred would be premises and equipment, along with ensuring that staff were appropriately qualified and trained.

- The excess demand for childcare is likely to attract new entrants to the market. This may come from existing nursery staff who decide to set up businesses themselves.

- Government regulation and red tape may however act as a deterrent to new entrants.

- The other main restraint on new entrants would be the ability to find suitable premises from which to operate.

- Overall influence: High

(b) **Critical Success Factors**

Innovation

KA has a range of services and tools that distinguish it from competitors due to the company embracing modern technologies and applying them to the nursery model. This will help to attract new children as parents will be keen to take advantage of being able to see the activities their children undertake during the day.

This is coupled with flexibility in terms of offering services such as the collect and return service, which puts KA in a position of offering unique services that competitors are either unable or unwilling to provide.

This is likely to result in fewer children being removed from the nursery, and customers being willing to accept the higher pricing structure charged by KA.

Compliance with regulations

KA has a good reputation in the form of the positive feedback from the government reports. Independent approval from a third party is one of the considerations that parents would take when deciding where to send their children. This will keep parents satisfied that the level of care given to their children is appropriate.

Quality of staff

KA offers a more personal level of service to children, through having a higher staff-to-child ratio, with staff being qualified to a degree in excess of competitors. In addition one of the owners of the company has extensive experience of working in the industry and knows the concerns of customers. This will be a comfort factor to parents.

Use of information systems and technology

According to Porter Kid A is operating a differentiation strategy. Parents are prepared to pay a premium for the factors noted above and as a result KA can charge 40% higher fees and still have full nurseries with waiting lists.

Porter's value chain can be used to identify areas where IT could be used to add value.

KA makes use of IT in the following areas:

- The use of GPS wristbands linked to webcams allays parents concerns regarding the safety and welfare of their offspring. This may make them more likely to choose KA over other nurseries.

- Computers are used within the nursery for learning purposes. In addition parents are able to get feedback via the Internet on the computer based games and work that their children have been involved in. These have helped KA gain a good reputation in government reports which is likely to increase demand and retention rates.

- Staff are expected to have knowledge of the systems used and are paid more highly as a result. This may encourage better quality nursery nurses who are more able to communicate with parents.

(c) **Report**

To: The Directors of Kid A Limited
From: XYZ Consultants
Date: 21 June 20X8
Re: Expansion plans

1 Business risks caused by expansion

1.1 Loss of control

As the number of nurseries increases you will have to take a more strategic and hands off approach to running the business. This will require developing a new range of skills and provide new problems.

The managers recruited must be competent at the tasks that are being delegated to them. If not, the business could suffer damage to its reputation that would be difficult to repair.

Given the sensitive nature of the business, one poorly performing nursery could have a detrimental impact on the reputation of the whole business. There is also the potential conflicts that would arise between yourselves and new managers

1.2 Financial/economic risks

Fresh finance will be required to expand the business. Because you are running a small business this will have to come from your own savings or new borrowings. If you borrow money then the lenders will require security, either over the nursery properties themselves (if purchased as opposed to rented) or in the form of personal guarantees.

Interest on borrowings will eat into profit and is a fixed cost. If demand for nursery spaces falls then there is a risk that the interest payments may not be fulfilled.

To attract good nursery managers you may have to increase salaries, which will also have an impact on profitability.

A downturn in the economy could have a significant impact on the business. Higher unemployment could result in more families where both parents are not working, and therefore demand for nursery spaces may fall. Financial insecurity amongst the working population may mean that fewer families are willing to pay the premium prices charged by KA.

2 Budget issues

There are a variety of budget elements that could be adopted to make the process more effective:

2.1 Profit centres

Because you want to transfer responsibility for each individual nursery to the managers, consider making each nursery a profit centre. Here the managers are responsible for both revenues and costs within the nursery.

2.2 Controllable costs

Budgets and income statements should be produced for you to review on a regular (say monthly) basis for each nursery.

These should focus on controllable issues over which managers have influence (local advertising, recruitment, pay and day-to-day expenses). It is not appropriate to assess them on costs over which they have no control.

2.3 Delegation/participation

Managers should be involved in the budget setting process, rather than it being imposed by you. This is because managers will be motivated by the increased responsibility and their knowledge of local conditions may improve the budget.

2.4 Authorisation

Care must be taken however that managers do not build in slack into their budgets to make them too easy. It may therefore be useful to compare the different budgets prepared by individual managers and adopt one of them as the approved model.

Once the budget has been approved this will act as authorisation to the manager to incur expenditure. Budgets should be created by computer, as this will allow for greater sensitivity analysis.

2.5 Evaluation of performance

Actual performance should be compared to the budget plan, feedback provided to the managers and any necessary action taken. The budgets should be flexed to allow you to compare the performance of different sized nurseries operated by KA.

2.6 Rewards

Managers should be given rewards for achieving and exceeding budgets. This could be extended to their staff too.

3 Information for control and decision making

Strategic information

Thom and Debra will require strategic information to help with long term planning and assess whether objectives are being met. This information will be both external and internal:

- Information about the external environment would be useful to assess the future political, economic, social and technological changes that may impact on KA eg proposed changes to health and safety regulations, the government's inspection process.

- Market information to estimate future demand eg demographic information regarding the local population for each nursery – number of working parents with pre-school age children living or employed locally who might choose to use the nursery.

- Data about competitors might provide a benchmark against which the performance of individual nurseries and the business as a whole might be assessed. This should consider financial and non-financial factors eg the fees charged, government ratings, range of services offered, opening hours etc.

- Financial information to assess the overall profitability of the business and each nursery

- Information regarding fixed asset investments eg premises and capital structure/financing

Tactical information

This might focus on key performance indicators such as the utilisation of resources by each nursery, particularly in relation to staff requirements eg ratio of children to staff, fees earned per staff member, staff turnover rates, expenditure as a percentage of fees earned.

Thom and Debra should monitor customer satisfaction, eg by asking parents to complete a survey online.

They should monitor the number of parents who switch from them to other nurseries, the number of parents they attract from competitors.

They could monitor utilisation of capacity by considering nursery places filled as a percentage of places available and the waiting lists at each nursery. They can also monitor the ability of individual managers to convert enquiries into bookings.

It would be useful to monitor the take up of some of the additional services offered eg the number of parents who actually use the webcam, the number of times work is reviewed by parents on the Internet. This will help assess the demand for these services and the value being ascribed to them by parents.

KA should ensure that they generate and monitor performance indicators for the areas that the government inspection focuses on.

Operational information

This should be prepared very frequently to help track the specific day-to-day activities of the nursery:

Staff timesheets to monitor hours worked and sickness

Weekly task completion sheets

Weekly running costs in comparison to budget

Weekly attendance record for children

Fees invoiced/collected

1 Planning, controlling, recording transactions, measuring performance and making decisions.

2 Five of:

- Derived from both internal and external sources
- Summarised at a high level
- Relevant to the long term
- Concerned with the whole organisation
- Often prepared on an *ad hoc* basis
- Both quantitative and qualitative
- Uncertain, as the future cannot be predicted accurately

3 Five of:

- Primarily generated internally (but may have a limited external component)
- Summarised at a lower level
- Relevant to the short and medium term
- Concerned with activities or departments
- Prepared routinely and regularly
- Based on quantitative measures

4 Five of:

- Derived from internal sources
- Detailed, being the processing of raw data
- Relevant to the immediate term
- Task-specific
- Prepared very frequently
- Largely quantitative

5 Explicit knowledge is knowledge that an organisation already stores in formal systems. It includes facts, transactions and events that can be clearly stated and stored in information systems.

Tacit knowledge is expertise held by people within the organisation that has not been formally documented.

6 Four from:

- Business continuity planning
- Systems access control
- Systems development and maintenance
- Physical and environmental security
- Compliance
- Personnel security
- Security organisation
- Computer and network management.
- Asset classification and control
- Security policy

7 (a) The main areas of risk to which a computer system is exposed, and some of the factors which may lead to the exposure are as follows.

    (i) **Accidental destruction** or **loss of data** by operator or software error. The auditors should pay particular attention during their audit to recovery procedures. In addition the possibility of accidental destruction of programs or hardware, particularly the dropping of a disk pack, by an operator, and the consequences thereof, should not be overlooked.

    (ii) The **acceptance of inaccurate input data** due to inadequate edit or other checks is another frequent cause of loss of data.

(iii) A **complete systems failure** can lead to loss of data and may be caused by a failure in the power supply or possibly a failure of the air conditioning or other environmental controls.

(iv) **Theft of data** from a **batch processing system** by an operator copying or removing data files, particularly where these are on easily transportable media such as magnetic tapes.

(v) **Theft of data** from an **on line or real time system** by a person obtaining unauthorised access to the system via a remote terminal and either using passwords illegally or alternatively using a 'piggyback system' (in which a valid transmission is intercepted and the final 'logging off' operation stopped in transmission to permit the illegal operator to continue in operation masquerading as the authorised user).

(vi) **Theft of software** either by operators copying or removing the program file, and in the latter case possibly demanding a ransom from the rightful owner, or alternatively by programming staff copying and attempting to sell the source documentation, with or without the object program.

(vii) **Deliberate destruction of the hardware** has been known to occur, and where adequate protection has not been provided, such acts have also led to the simultaneous destruction of software and data. Similar results may occur as a result of fire or explosion either in the computer room or adjoining premises.

(b) The different forms of control which should be instituted may be sub-divided into three main headings.

Physical security

(i) **Strict control of access** to the computer area, using such devices as magnetic keys and alarm systems.

(ii) **Effective precautions** against **fire** or other **natural disruption** including alarm systems, automatic extinguishing systems and regular inspections.

(iii) Established and well-practised **emergency procedures** in the event of fire or other disorder and alternative power supply.

(iv) **Location of the computer** so that it is difficult for unauthorised personnel to have access with the minimum of entrances and exits.

(v) Possibility of **remote storage of security copies of data**.

(vi) Location of the computer room so that it is, if possible, **situated away from known hazards** such as flooding, radiation from X-ray equipment and radio systems and fire/explosion risks in adjoining premises.

Software security

(i) **Effective control** over the **preservation of information** contained on files by ensuring that before a file is to be overwritten a check is made on the file version.

(ii) **Prevention of unauthorised access** by the use of devices such as passwords.

Systems security

(i) **Strict control and verification** of all **input data**, where possible with control totals prepared outside the computer department.

(ii) All input should pass through an **'edit' program** as the first stage in being entered on to the computer files. This program clearly indicates all items accepted and rejected, the latter to be investigated by the user department.

(iii) Adequate controls should be in force to ensure that **amendments to programs** are properly **authorised, checked out** and **validated** before use.

(iv) There should be **adequate recovery, restart and standby procedures** in the event of power failure or machine breakdowns, which can be facilitated by a 'log' of all work performed and by frequent dumping of files.

(v) Controls should be instituted to ensure that **computer output** is **properly distributed**, especially confidential print-outs, payments and so on.

(vi) Proper control over **storage and issue of electronic media** with manual records being kept of physical maintenance performed. Such records frequently also record current status of the media and the details of the file(s) currently stored upon it.

8 (a) **The SFA Company**

Introduction

As a result of concerns raised at the recent board meeting a new Management Information System (MIS) is currently being considered. Output from the main transaction processing systems will form the input of the MIS.

The MIS manipulates this data into summary level information for control and decision-making purposes to support the monitoring and control of the key functions of the organisation. The MIS will require inputs relating to the three key primary activities of inbound logistics, marketing and sales and technology development.

Inbound logistics

The inbound logistics function aims to ensure the **right materials are available at the right price and at the right time**. A key element of this involves ensuring the best possible price for raw materials of the required quality is negotiated. Output from the Computer Assisted Design (CAD) and Computer Assisted Manufacture (CAM) systems will become inputs into the MIS. The MIS will manipulate and summarise this data, resulting in information that will enable the purchasing department to **plan** and meet its responsibilities in the most efficient manner. For example, negotiations with suppliers can be faced with **improved knowledge** of the quantities of raw materials required in the medium term which should help win **improved prices**.

Marketing and sales

The MIS can provide information on the activities of customers and salespeople, showing who is buying and selling what. Over time, useful **trends** should become apparent. The links with the CAM system will enable customers to be given accurate information relating to both orders in progress and finished goods. Forecast demand can be made available via the feeder systems to the MIS, and when matched with production scheduling information, instances of **spare capacity** should be able to be established and appropriate action taken.

Technology development

The new MIS should provide information that will allow the increased use of **Computer Assisted Design** (CAD) and **Computer Assisted Manufacture** (CAM). Use of CAD and CAM techniques will **improve efficiency**, resulting in the **faster** production of garments, and **improved garment quality**. **Prototypes** can be produced rapidly allowing customer feedback to be acted on at the design stage.

The MIS can **monitor sales and production** information and when necessary provide **control information** to ensure orders are delivered on time. One difficult area to predict in the clothing industry is future demand levels for fashion items, as a change in consumer taste can often be rapid and on the surface unpredictable. The MIS will therefore require information feeds from '**outward looking**' sources such as fashion show trends and market research.

(b) **Outputs required**

Outputs from the CAD/CAM systems should include **performance measures** that show whether the design, development and production activities are **achieving their targets**, and how these functions are contributing to the overall performance of SFA. The performance measures should be available for on-screen viewing, and be included in control reports that highlight areas in need of corrective action.

Reports from the MIS should also show supplier and buyer performance, including information on price, quantity and quality (including service quality). Marginal cost information should feed from the accounting system to the MIS, as this information is vital when negotiating prices relating to 'extra' production runs to utilise any spare capacity.

Conclusion

The proposed MIS will consolidate information from the main transaction processing systems. It will 'pull-together' information from the separate functions of SFA, allowing the **overall picture** to be seen more clearly. This will enable SFA to identify and respond quickly to circumstances that require action. The MIS will enable SFA to operate more **efficiently and effectively** and should be implemented as soon as possible.

9   Refer to the answer to Q3d of the September 2009 Business Strategy paper in this text.

10   There is no answer to this self-test, as it is designed just to help you increase your business awareness.

CHAPTER 15

Strategies for change

Introduction

Examination context

Topic List

    1   The need for change

    2   Strategic change in organisations

    3   Change and the individual

Summary and Self-test

Answers to Interactive questions

Answers to Self-test

Learning objectives

- Explain the levels of change in a business and the approaches used at each level, using appropriate examples

- Describe the key stages in a change management process

- Identify in a given situation the key issues which should be addressed by the management of a business during the planning and implementation of change

The specific syllabus reference for this chapter is 3i.

Syllabus links

This chapter involves the implementation of the strategies discussed in the preceding chapters. It has not been covered in the syllabus of previous examinations.

Examination context

Previous chapters concentrate on identifying the need for and the direction of change if an organisation is to remain successful. This chapter looks at the issues which need to be addressed by an organisation during the planning and implementation of such changes.

In exams so far, most candidates have demonstrated a reasonable knowledge of change management but a common mistake has been to provide a generic answer, repeating elements by rote from the learning materials.

In Q1 September 2008 (*Embury Ltd*) the scenario contains the leaking of information, by a newspaper, about possible redundancies at the company, a manufacturer of watering equipment.. The fourth requirement is:

'(d) Explain the change management problems that are likely to occur as a result of the newspaper article and the planned factory closures. Discuss how these problems might be addressed.

(11 marks)'

It can be easy to trot out models with change management, and to fail to apply them to the scenario. Stopping to think about the particular issues that arise when bad news is discovered in a newspaper and not via the proper channels highlights the particular change management challenges faced by the company.

1 The need for change

Section overview

- The sources of change are both internal and environmental.

- The range of impacts of a 'change trigger' will be felt as shock waves through the organisation and will affect staff and management at all levels.

- Change must be handled carefully to avoid the organisation being overwhelmed.

1.1 The need for an organisation to change or develop

The need for an organisation to change or develop could be caused (or 'triggered') by a number of factors:

- **Changes in the environment**: These could be changes in what competitors are doing, what customers are buying, how they spend their money, changes in the law, changes in social behaviour and attitudes, economic changes, and so on.

- **Changes in the products the organisation makes, or the services it provides**: These are made in response to changes in customer demands, competitors' actions, new technology, and so on.

- **Changes in technology and changes in working methods**: These changes are also in response to environmental change such as the advent of new technology and new laws on safety at work.

- **Changes in management and working relationships**: For example, changes in leadership style, and in the way that employees are encouraged to work together. Also changes in training and development.

- **Changes in organisation structure or size**: These might involve creating new departments and divisions, greater delegation of authority or more centralisation, changes in the way that plans are made, management information is provided and control is exercised, and so on. **Organisation restructuring** will be made in response to changes of the types discussed above.

- **Post–acquisition**: Incoming management will wish to improve and integrate the firm into the new parent's structure and systems. This will involve visible change to names and signage but also deeper changes to organisational structures, culture, job roles, staff numbers and management systems.

Case study: Ford Motor Company

Ford in trouble – 2006

'The Ford Motor Company could lose as much as $9bn (£4.8bn) this year (2006) as it undergoes a huge restructuring in a desperate attempt to halt its ongoing loss of market share in the US.

Ford announced yesterday [15 September 2006] it would cut a third of all salaried employees – 14,000 jobs – and offer voluntary redundancy to all of its 75,000 hourly paid workers. It also announced it would close two more manufacturing plants by the end of 2008, on top of 14 closures already announced this year.

Ford, which hopes the cuts will save it $5bn in operating costs, also admitted it would no longer reach profitability in 2008 as it had expected.

"These actions have painful consequences for communities and many of our loyal employees," said chairman Bill Ford, who this month stepped down as chief executive of the company founded by his great-grandfather, Henry Ford. "But rapid shifts in consumer demand that affect our product mix, and continued high prices for commodities, mean we must continue working quickly and decisively to fix our business."

The situation at the Michigan-based carmaker could be even worse than it admitted yesterday. *The Detroit News* reported on Thursday that an internal company report dated September 6 and prepared by chief finance officer Don Leclair's office projected that its worldwide automotive operations' losses would be nearly $6bn this year. Once restructuring costs were included, the report said, Ford's 2006 pre-tax loss could be between $8bn and $9bn.

The central cause of Ford's problems is that Americans are increasingly buying their cars from Japanese competitors such as Toyota. Ford has lost market share in the US for 10 successive years. It now has a share of only 16%, and said yesterday it expected that to drop to between 14% and 15%. Above all, it has been hit by falling sales of pick-up trucks such as the F-150 and sports utility vehicles (SUVs), once best-sellers that generated the bulk of profits, as petrol prices have hit $3 a gallon.

Ford yesterday revealed details of new, smaller, more fuel-efficient models that it hopes will help it to regain market share. It announced the launch of a new "crossover" (a cross between an SUV and a car). But analysts remain sceptical.

The problems faced by carmakers were underlined yesterday when DaimlerChrysler announced losses of $1.2bn for the third quarter, double previous forecasts.

Under Ford's previous restructuring plan announced in January, titled the Way Forward, Ford planned to cut 25,000–30,000 manufacturing jobs and close 14 plants by 2012. It has now decided to bring forward the plans by four years and complete the cuts by the end of 2008.

The voluntary redundancies at Ford are similar to a plan by General Motors earlier this year that succeeded in cutting 34,000 workers – or about a third of the hourly workforce – from the payroll. GM now employs 95,000 hourly workers, 39% of the number it employed 10 years ago.

Ford announced last month that it plans to sell Aston Martin, and there has been speculation about sell-offs of other parts of its Premier Automotive Group, which includes Land Rover and Jaguar. But it insisted yesterday that it had no plans to dispose of Jaguar. "Jaguar is not for sale," Mark Schulz, executive vice-president, said. Ford's announcement of its restructuring plans came days after Mr Ford stood down as chief executive. Mr Ford admitted at the time of his move that he was overwhelmed by the job, and he had been "wearing too many hats".

In his place he appointed Boeing's head of commercial aircraft, Alan Mulally, who is known as a turnaround expert. Mr Mulally was not involved in the plan announced yesterday, and whether the company will have to put together yet another restructuring once he has got his feet under the table remains to be seen. "We know our work is far from over," he said yesterday.'

Ford – the results of drastic change

Following years of turmoil, in 2012 a report on the company's website noted 'out of the worst of times came change, and a road map for survival. We have spent the last several years radically overhauling our production strategy from what was, in essence, that of a regional company to that of a fully globalised business. We simplified by making many drastic changes, but the results are paying dividends – both literally and figuratively.'

Through a series of workforce reductions, plant closures and reducing inefficiencies Ford has been able to make its manufacturing operations more flexible and leading to faster product development. Part of this process saw the 2008 sale of Land Rover and Jaguar to Tata Motors for £1.3bn, with Ford reducing the number of 'global vehicle nameplates' it manufactures from 97 in 2006 to 37 in 2011.

In 2013, The Guardian commented on a historic year for the company, with Ford reporting $7.2bn in profits boosted by US sales.

Ford's Focus, which was the world's best-selling car in 2013 has become a big hit in China. Last year (2013), sales of the Focus in China rose 50 percent to total 403,219. Ford says the key to its success in China, the world's largest automobile market has been its wide range of product offerings that allow it to effectively target first-time buyers. The U.S. auto giant's sales in mainland China jumped 45 percent year on year in the first quarter of 2014, making it one of the fastest-growing major international carmakers in the country. '[Chinese buyers] want different sized vehicles – small, medium and large – because they make a lifestyle choice with their decision,' Alan Mulally, CEO of Ford told CNBC on the sidelines of the Beijing auto show. 'We probably have the most complete line-up of vehicles anywhere in the world now.'

Sources: *The Guardian*, CNBC and Ford

1.2 Types of change

Change itself may be divided into two types, **incremental** and **transformational**, and so may the management approach to change be divided into **reactive** and **proactive**.

Definitions

Incremental change is characterised by a series of small steps. It is a gradual process.

Transformational change is characterised by major, significant change being introduced relatively quickly.

Step change describes an unexpected jump (upwards) or drop (downwards) in the pace of change. The step is caused by an unexpected event (eg environmental disaster, unexpected change in government etc).

Planned change involves following a series of pre-planned steps.

Emergent change views change as a series of continuous open-ended adjustments to the environment.

Johnson, Scholes and Whittington suggest the model of change shown below:

	Nature of change	
Management role	Incremental	Transformational
Pro-active	Tuning	Planned
Reactive	Adaptation	Forced

The importance of **proactive management** is that it implies that organisational change may be undertaken **before** it is imposed by events. It may, in fact, result from the process of forecasting and be a response to expected developments. **Forced change** is likely to be both painful and risky.

Interactive question 1: Types of change   [Difficulty level: Easy]

Classify and explain the following changes using Johnson, Scholes and Whittington model.

* Ford Motor Company's turnaround strategy
* Tesco's entry into the Indian market

See **Answer** at the end of this chapter.

1.3 Levels at which change efforts may focus

There are three main levels to which organisational development and change efforts may be directed:

* **Individual level** where the focus is on improving individual skill levels, attitudes and motivation. Techniques employed could include education and training, management development, coaching and counselling, team building activities, inter-group activities, role analysis, job re-design, planning and objective setting activities and process consultation.

* **Organisation structure and systems level**: The characteristics of the organisational situation in which people work (eg job redesign, reward systems, setting clear objectives) that help achieve organisational goals.

* **Organisational climate and interpersonal style levels**: The improvement of social and other informal processes among organisation members by creating a system with a wide climate of high interpersonal trust and openness and a reduction in the negative consequences of excessive social conflict and competitiveness.

2 Strategic change in organisations

Section overview

- Change management involves management of people's expectations and attitudes. This can range from the willingness of an operative to learn a skill or change a shift up to the willingness of the Board to authorise the necessary resources.

- Therefore most change models seek to describe stages of psychological transition.

- These stages may be the focus of planned change management initiatives.

2.1 Change processes

For an organisation to be innovative, and continually responsive to the need for change, a systematic approach should be established, for planning and implementing changes.

Although each situation should be considered individually, the following general steps can be identified in a major change initiative.

Step 1
Determine need or desire for change in a particular area.

Step 2
Prepare a tentative plan. Brainstorming sessions are a good idea, since alternatives for change should be considered.

Step 3
Analyse probable reactions to the change.

Step 4
Make a final decision from the choice of alternative options. The decision may be taken either by group problem-solving (participative) or by a manager on his own (coercive).

Step 5
Establish a timetable for change.

- 'Coerced' changes can probably be implemented faster, without time for discussions.

- Speed of implementation that is achievable will depend on the likely reactions of the people affected.

- Identify those in favour of the change, and perhaps set up a pilot programme involving them. Talk with any others likely to resist the change.

Step 6
Communicate the plan for change. This is really a continuous process, beginning at Step 1 and going through to Step 7.

Step 7
Implement the change.

Step 8
Review the change. This requires continuous evaluation.

2.2 The three-stage approach (iceberg model)

The Lewin/Schein three-stage **model of change** identifies key steps as **unfreeze**, **move** and **refreeze**.

UNFREEZE		**MOVE**		**REFREEZE**
Existing behaviour	→	Attitudinal/behavioural change	→	New behaviour

Step 1

Unfreeze is the most difficult (and in many cases neglected) stage of the process, concerned mainly with selling the change, with giving individuals or groups a motive for changing their attitudes, values, behaviour, systems or structures.

Unfreezing processes require four things:

- A trigger
- Someone to challenge and expose the existing behaviour pattern
- The involvement of outsiders
- Alterations to power structure

Step 2

Move is the second stage, mainly concerned with identifying what the new, desirable behaviour or norm should be, communicating it and encouraging individuals and groups to 'own' the new attitude or behaviour. This might involve the adoption of a new culture. To be successful, the new ideas must be shown to work.

Step 3

Refreeze is the final stage, implying consolidation or reinforcement of the new behaviour. Positive reinforcement (praise and reward) or negative reinforcement (sanctions applied to those who deviate from the new behaviour) may be used.

2.3 Adaptive change approach

Adaptive change occurs when an organisation's environment changes slowly. It is **change implemented in little stages,** and thus has the advantage of minimising the resistance faced at any one time.

2.4 Coercive change approach

Coercive change is enforced without participation. Change of culture and power structures is left to the end of the change process. There are several problems with a coercive approach:

- Underestimation of the forces of resistance
- Failure to muster forces in favour
- Failure to attack root causes of resistance
- Management shift their attention too quickly elsewhere
- Failure to ensure implementation

This approach is necessary in situations of **crisis** where there simply is no time to consult, or where decisions need to be taken quickly. Crisis has the effect of inducing panic – which managers must do what they can to minimise – but **it can also promote an immediate willingness to change**: it can be the necessary 'unfreeze' process before an organisational change.

An example is a sudden environmental shock that endangers the company's survival.

Most of the time, a **mixed approach between coercive change and adaptive change** is suitable. Adaptive change may be too slow, whereas coercive change is often resented and therefore not accepted.

2.5 Change agents

A change agent is an individual (sometimes called a **Champion of Change**), a group or external consultancy with the responsibility for driving and 'selling' the change.

The role of the change agent varies depending on the brief they are given. It may include:

- Defining the problem
- Suggesting possible solutions
- Selecting and implementing a solution
- Gaining support from all involved

To be effective a change agent should have the following skills and attributes:

- Communication skills
- Negotiation and 'selling' skills
- An awareness of organisational 'politics'
- An understanding of the relevant processes

The **champion of change model** recognises the importance of change being led by a **change agent**, who may be an individual or occasionally a group.

Step 1

Senior management are the change strategists and decide in broad terms what is to be done. There is a need for powerful advocacy for change at the strategic apex. This will only occur if senior management are themselves agreed on the need for change. This is a role requiring a clear vision of what the change is to achieve.

Step 2

They appoint a change agent to drive it through. Senior management has three roles:

- Supporting the change agent, if the change provokes conflict between the agent and interest groups in the organisation

- Reviewing and monitoring the progress of the change

- Endorsing and approving the changes, and ensuring that they are publicised

Step 3

The change agent has to win the support of functional and operational managers, who have to introduce and enforce the changes in their own departments. The champion of change has to provide advice and information, as well as evidence that the old ways are no longer acceptable.

Step 4

The change agent galvanises managers into action and gives them any necessary support. The managers ensure that the changes are implemented operationally, in the field. Where changes involve, say, a new approach to customer care, it is the workers who are responsible for ensuring the effectiveness of the change process.

It is important to realise that successful change is not something exclusively imposed from above. There is a sense in which middle and junior managers are **change recipients** in that they are required to implement new approaches and methods. However, they are themselves also **change agents** within their own spheres of responsibility. They must be committed parts of the change process if it is to succeed.

Worked example: ASDA

One company that exemplifies successful combinations of change styles is ASDA, the UK grocery chain. Archie Norman took over as CEO of ASDA in December 1991 when the retailer was nearly bankrupt. Norman laid off employees, flattened the organisation, and sold off loss making businesses – acts that usually spawn distrust among employees and distance executives from their people. Yet during Norman's eight-year tenure as CEO, ASDA also became famous for its atmosphere of trust and openness. It has been described by executives at Wal-Mart – itself famous for its corporate culture – as being 'more like Wal-Mart than we are'. With his opening speech to ASDA's executive team Norman indicated clearly that he intended to apply both soft and hard strategies in his change effort. He said: 'Our number one objective is to secure value for our shareholders and secure the trading future of the business. I intend to spend the next few weeks listening and forming ideas for our precise direction. We need a culture built around common ideas and goals that include listening, learning, and speed of response, from the stores upwards. [But] there will be management reorganisation. My objective is to establish a clear focus on the stores, shorten lines of communication, and build one team.' If there is a contradiction between building a high-involvement organisation and restructuring to enhance shareholder value, Norman embraced it.

In 1992 Archie Norman appointed Allan Leighton, from Mars' Pedigree Petfoods division, to the role of Group Marketing Director. Allan Leighton was appointed ASDA CEO in 1996. Leighton pioneered the idea of 'huddles' at ASDA in which teams of managers and staff, would get together to discuss the daily issues and find ways to resolve them.

In June 1999 ASDA was bought by Wal-Mart for £6.7bn having been worth only £500m five years earlier. Bolstered by the Wal-Mart takeover, ASDA experienced success in the early years of the new millennium. Almost immediately after the purchase ASDA adopted Wal-Mart's "price roll-back" program, thus igniting price wars among UK supermarkets. ASDA opened its first store under the Wal-Mart banner in 2000 and by 2003 it had usurped competitor J Sainsbury plc from its number two position in the U.K. food retailing market. In 2004 Asda replaced Marks & Spencer as Britain's biggest clothing retailer by volume. In 2005, ASDA's chief executive Tony De Nunzio left and was replaced by Andy Bond. In the same year it expanded into Northern Ireland by purchasing 12 Safeway stores from Morrisons.

In 2009 Wal-Mart 'sold' Asda for £6.9 billion to their Leeds-based investment subsidiary Corinth Services Limited. The deal was described as part of a 'group restructuring' and meant that Asda remained under Wal-Mart's control, since Contrith is also a subsidiary of Wal-Mart.

In May 2010, Asda announced it would buy all of Netto's UK operations in a £778 million deal allowing Asda to move into the smaller, more localised, store market with most Netto stores being only one-fifth the size of the average Asda supermarket. However, a ruling by the Office of Fair Training led to Asda's announcement in September 2010 that it would be forced to sell 47 of the existing 194 Netto stores. The rebranding of Netto stores to Asda began in early 2011. In February 2011, Asda announced the purchase of six stores from Focus DIY for conversion into supermarkets subject to approvals and local planning consents.

In early 2014 the Grocer magazine reported that Asda had moved to put 4,100 managerial store roles at risk of redundancy. Asda claim that the move will increase the number of section leader jobs in-store which will 'put more staff on the shop floor'. The company also plans to create up to 5,000 roles – a net benefit of 900 new jobs. Mark Ibbotson Asda's chief operations officer commented 'the only constant in retail is change – and whilst people will always be at the heart of our business, the jobs we were asking our colleagues to do five years ago – when we just operated shops and had a small Home Shopping business – are not the jobs they are actually doing today, and not the jobs we need to empower them to do over the next five years if we are to continue to grow and deliver our strategy for growth'. The Grocer highlights that this is part of Asda's plan to save £1bn over the next five years. Asda's announcement was followed by the news that during the first three months of 2014, the UK grocery market had experienced its slowest pace of growth in 12 years.

2.6 The Gemini 4Rs framework for planned strategic change

Management consultants Gouillart and Kelly describe a four-dimensional process for business transformation in their book *Transforming the Organisation*. Known as the Gemini 4Rs framework, this approach aims to cover all the important components of the organisation's identity.

Reframing involves fundamental questions about what the organisation is and what it is for:

- **Achieve mobilisation**: Create the will and desire to change.
- **Create the vision** of where the organisation is going.
- **Build a measurement system** that will set targets and measure progress.

Restructuring is about the organisation's structure, but is also likely to involve cultural changes:

- **Construct an economic model** to show in detail how value is created and where resources should be deployed.

- Align the physical infrastructure with the overall plan.

- Redesign the work architecture so that processes interact to create value.

Revitalising is the process of securing a good fit with the environment:

- Achieve market focus.
- Invent new businesses.
- Change the rules of competition by exploiting technology.

Renewal ensures that the people in the organisation support the change process and acquire the necessary skills to contribute to it:

- **Create a reward system** in order to motivate.
- **Build individual learning.**
- **Develop the organisation** and its adaptive capability.

Worked example: Royal Mail

The attached press release sets out the difficulties that faced the Royal Mail when the government announced that from 1 January 2006 any licensed operator would be allowed to deliver mail to business and residential customers, effectively ending the state-owned business's monopoly:

'Royal Mail [17 May 2005] today announced a record £537 million profit on its operations for 2004 – 05 with quality of service to customers now hitting the highest levels in a decade.

Royal Mail's Chairman, Allan Leighton, said: 'Postmen and women have achieved a fantastic turnaround. They will now deservedly each get a 'Share in Success' payment of £1,074, amounting to £218 million of the company's profit. It's one of the biggest profit shares with employees in UK corporate history.'

But Mr Leighton warned: 'There is still a huge amount to do. Transforming our operations, cutting our costs and, above all, winning the support of our people for the modernisation plan with its top priority being to improve customer service, has been Royal Mail's greatest achievement in decades.

But competing successfully in an open mail market is going to be even more difficult. We've a mountain to climb and we've only reached the base camp.

The greatest challenge now is to bring about a complete culture change in Royal Mail. We need everyone in the company focused on ensuring that we consistently deliver high quality, value-for-money services that customers need and want. Competition has arrived and customers have a choice; so we need to prove that Royal Mail is the best and our people are key to that' said Mr Leighton.

The company, he said, was also facing other daunting hurdles:

Royal Mail will have to generate sufficient profit to pay millions of pounds into its pension fund to tackle the £2.5 billion deficit, the 14,609-strong network of Post Office branches made a loss on its operations last year of £110 million. Its rural network of 8,037 branches is fundamentally uneconomic and needs an injection of £3 million a week to survive. However, with the current annual Government funding of £150 million due to end in 2008, Post Office Ltd cannot be expected to absorb extra costs at this level.

Royal Mail lags behind its major rivals in automated sorting technology. It needs to make a several billion pound investment if it is to compete successfully and that means being more profitable in order to invest. However, the 8.6% return on its domestic letters business last year compares with the 16.4% Deutsche Post makes in its home market, and 22.2% made by TNT Post Group.

Royal Mail's Chief Executive, Adam Crozier, also stressed the challenges ahead.

'The huge task now facing Royal Mail is to make the cultural change needed to succeed as a commercial business and to become the postal operator of choice for customers in an open competitive market.

Our vision remains to be demonstrably the best and most trusted mail company in the world. With the dedication and commitment of our people, we are confident we can achieve our goal. '

Source: Royal Mail Press Release 17 May 2005 (extract)

Since 2005 the Royal Mail has undergone some significant changes. In October 2013, the UK government controversially sold off the Royal Mail for £3.3bn. The flotation saw a significant number of Royal Mail employees (15,000) purchase shares in the company. In May 2014, it was reported by the Independent newspaper that Royal Mail was embroiled in a row with regulator Ofcom over the company's ability to meet its obligations to provide a 'universal postal-delivery service'.

The Independent reported that at the same time as she unveiled a 12 per cent rise in full-year operating profits to £671m, Royal Mail's chief executive, Moya Greene, warned that there is a prospect that Royal Mail will not be able to sustain a commercial rate of return if it maintains its commitment to deliver mail to all of the UK's homes six days a week.

A spokesman for Ofcom commented 'we do not believe there is presently a threat to the financial sustainability of the universal postal service. Royal Mail should take appropriate steps to respond to the challenge of competition, including improving efficiency'.

When the UK government sold off the Royal Mail in 2013 it guaranteed that the company would continue with its universal six day service.

A press release concerning the Royal Mail's 2013/14 financial results noted the following comments made by Moya Greene.

'Our performance was in line with our expectations. We delivered two per cent revenue growth, controlled operating costs and drove strong free cash flow. We are facing a couple of headwinds. The competitive environment on the parcels side is more intense. We are taking steps to remain the leader in this growing market. On the letters side, the headwind is direct delivery and we have strategies in place to counter its adverse financial impact. However, without timely regulatory action, direct delivery could undermine the economics of the Universal Service and our ability to generate sustainably a five to ten per cent EBIT margin in our reported business .

Our key value drivers of single digit revenue growth, margin expansion and underlying free cash flow growth remain the objectives for the Group for the 2014-15 financial year'.

Below are a selection of key highlights from the Royal Mail's press release:

- 'Group revenue increased by two per cent, due to parcel revenue growth. Parcels are the largest contributor to Group revenue, accounting for 51 per cent.

- Group operating profit before transformation costs grew to £671 million.

- Transformation costs of £241 million for the year include a provision of £104 million in relation to the management reorganisation programme, announced on 25 March 2014, which will be implemented in 2014-15.

- As previously indicated, the Board has recommended a final dividend of 13.3 pence per share, subject to shareholder approval at the Annual General Meeting, to be held on 24 July 2014.

- Based on our estimates of the impact of TNT Post UK's publicly-stated plans, direct delivery could reduce Royal Mail revenue by over £200 million in 2017-18.

Summary outlook

We are facing increasing challenges in the parcels and letters markets in the UK.

Royal Mail's annual report 2013/14 highlighted a number of initiatives the company has undertaken to boost its performance. It has acknowledged the decline in the number of letters now being posted, and has moved to streamline its operations, with plans to reduce the number of people it employs by 1,300 over the coming year (2014-15).

In May 2013, the company unveiled an agreement it has entered into with the Post Office to offer retailers and customers the option of having parcels delivered to a local post office ready for collection. The 'local click and collect' service has led Royal Mail to modernise a number of its operations.

Royal Mail also invested £70m in the year on improving its business mail operations. And it intends to introduce barcode technology to allow business customers to track their parcels prior to delivery.

Sources: Royal Mail Press Release 22 May 2014 and 2013/14 Annual Report & The Independent newspaper

---

Interactive question 2: Transforming the Royal Mail　　　　[Difficulty level: Intermediate]

Consider the cultural change described in the final paragraphs of the Royal Mail press release from 2005 and the steps taken to respond to the deregulation of the postal service.

Requirements

Apply the activities of the Gemini 4Rs approach to this change. Refer to the information provided in respect of the period 2013/14 where relevant for evidence of how successfullly the various elements of the 4 Rs framework were applied.

See **Answer** at the end of this chapter.

3 Change and the individual

Section overview

- Understanding the implications of change for the individual is essential to a change agent or other would-be 'midwife' of change.

- The way the individual views the change will be influenced by the manner of its introduction and the forces driving it and restraining it.

3.1 How change affects individuals

Change may affect individuals in several areas.

- **Physiological** changes: Pattern of shift-working, location of place of work

- **Circumstantial** changes: Unlearning previous knowledge and learning new ways of doing things, new work-mates, using new IT/IS

- **Psychological** changes: Feelings of disorientation, insecurity, changing relationships etc

3.2 Reactions to proposed change

The importance of staff support during a change programme should not be underestimated. We look here in more detail at the barriers to change they may cause to arise.

3.2.1 Cultural barriers

Structural inertia is the cumulative effect of all the systems and procedures the organisation has installed over the years to ensure consistency and quality. These act as barriers to change. For example, selection processes systematically select certain kinds of people; promotion processes regularly reward certain kinds of people.

Group inertia may block change where changes are inconsistent with team/departmental norms, or where they threaten to make skills and expertise of a particular professional or skill group less important or even redundant.

Power structures may be threatened by the redistribution of decision-making authority or resources, or the re-routing of lines of communication.

3.2.2 Personnel barriers

In addition to cultural barriers, there are also barriers which affect individuals and result in them seeing the change as a threat.

- Habit, because habitual ways of work are hard to change, and the new and unknown is often uncomfortable.

- Security is almost inevitably threatened – job security and the security of familiarity.

- Effect on earnings may be considerable: impact on promotion and income.

- Fear of the unknown reduces people's willingness and interest in learning new skills and processes; they may lack the confidence to take on a new challenge.

- Selective information processing results in employees choosing what to hear and what to ignore; they can then use their selected information to justify their position and ignore management argument for change.

3.2.3 The psychological contract

The psychological contract is the 'deal' between employer and employee. It covers the full set of expectations each party has of the other.

On either side of the contract, there are offers and wants.

EMPLOYER	EMPLOYEE
OFFERS:	**WANTS:**
Certain pay levels.	Certain pay levels.
Certain benefit levels.	Certain benefit levels.
Job design which offers particular opportunities for responsibility and learning.	Particular opportunities for responsibility and learning.
Availability of promotion.	Access to promotion/or not.
Working conditions of a certain quality.	Desire for particular level of conditions.
Opportunities for close relationships.	Desire for close working relationships.
Style of management.	Style of being managed.
WANTS:	**OFFERS:**
Particular skills, experience, attitudes.	Particular skills, experience, attitudes.
Particular level of commitment.	Capacity level of commitment.
Particular quality of contribution.	Capacity for contribution.

Match (between employer OFFERS and employee WANTS)

Match (between employer WANTS and employee OFFERS)

The contract works if offers and wants match. The selection process is the means both parties use to assess the initial match. The promotion process is the means used to check the ongoing match. In addition, both parties continuously monitor the match. The model is dynamic, any change in one part triggers changes in others. If a change programme threatens any item listed under employer offers, the employee will reconsider what they offer as their part of the deal. If the employee believes that their offers will be made wholly or partially redundant by the changes, they will anticipate that their wants will no longer be satisfied.

3.2.4 Identification of pressure points

Two important pressure points can develop in the psychological contract during times of change.

- **Lack of appropriate skill levels:** This can happen if the employer fails to reconsider how employee wants will alter as a result of changes, or if the employer fails to redesign their offers to ensure these attract and encourage the right kind of people needed in the new set-up.
- **Declining staff morale:** The driver of employee performance is the human emotions which underlie employee wants. These wants express personal motives, desires, ambitions and needs and determine people's commitment to the changes.

A change programme must be preceded by a review of:

- New competences and qualities required
- Selection processes to ensure they identify the above
- Promotion processes to ensure they identify the above

A change plan must include a staff development plan covering:

- Communication of implications for jobs
- Communication of required skills
- Discussions about individual development needs/options
- Learning and training opportunities
- Opportunities for making a contribution to changes

Worked example: Sainsbury's

It is interesting to set side by side the comments of Sainsbury's Director of Personnel and a senior official of the shop workers' union regarding the introduction of Sunday working. It isn't difficult to tell which is which!

- 'I have taken a close personal interest to ensure that in every branch the people who are working on Sundays are those who volunteered. Not working on Sunday is not going to affect promotion prospects, it is not going to affect people's pay, and it is not going to affect our attitude to them.'

- 'Retailers have ways of making Sunday working become the norm. Employers work through the ranks. First they approach the weakest, the people who have less than two years' experience and who have no rights for unfair dismissal, then they pick the starry-eyed people who think they are going to be managing director, then they pick the people who work low hours and need a few bob. Then they come to the resolute minority and say: "You are out of step".'

3.3 Introducing the change

Three factors for managers to consider when dealing with resistance to change.

- The **pace** of change
- The **manner** of change
- The **scope** of change

3.3.1 Pace

Given time, people can get used to the idea of new methods – can get acclimatised at each stage, with a consequent confidence in the likely success of the change programme, and in the individual's own ability to cope.

- Presenting the individuals concerned with a *fait accompli* may short-circuit resistance at the planning and immediate implementation stages. But it may cause a withdrawal reaction (akin to 'shock'), if the change is radical and perceived as threatening, and this is likely to surface later, as the change is consolidated – probably strengthened by resentment.

- **Timing** will also be crucial: those responsible for change should be sensitive to incidents and attitudes that might indicate that 'now is not the time'.

3.3.2 Manner

The manner in which a change is put across is very important: the climate must be prepared, the need made clear, fears soothed, and if possible the individuals concerned positively motivated to embrace the changes as their own.

- **Resistance should be welcomed and confronted**, not swept under the carpet. Talking through areas of conflict may lead to useful insights and the adapting of the programme of change to advantage. Repressing resistance will only send it underground, into the realm of rumour and covert hostility.

- **There should be free circulation of information** about the reasons for the change, its expected results and likely consequences. That information should appear sensible, clear, consistent and realistic: there is no point issuing information which will be seen as a blatant misrepresentation of the situation.

- **The change must be sold to the people concerned**: People must be convinced that their attitudes and behaviours need changing. Objections must be overcome, but it is also possible to get people behind the change in a positive way. If those involved understand that there is a real problem, which poses a threat to the organisation and themselves, and that the solution is a sensible one and will solve that problem, there will be a firm rational basis, for implementing change. The people should also be reassured that they have the learning capacity, the ability and the resources to implement the plan. It may even be possible to get them really excited about it by emphasising the challenge and opportunity by injecting an element of competition or simply offering rewards and incentives.

- **Individuals must be helped to learn,** that is, to change their attitudes and behaviours. Few individuals will really be able to see the big picture in a proposed programmed of change. In order to put across the overall objective, the organisation should use **visual aids** to help conceptualise. Learning programmes for any new skills or systems necessary will have to be designed according to the abilities of the individuals concerned.

- The effects of **insecurity,** perceived **helplessness,** and therefore **resentment,** may be lessened if the people can be **involved** in the planning and implementation of the change, that is, if it is not perceived to have been imposed from above.

3.3.3 Scope

The scope of change should be carefully reviewed. Total transformation will create greater insecurity – but also greater excitement, if the organisation has the kind of innovative culture that can stand it – than moderate innovation. There may be hidden changes to take into account: a change in technology may necessitate changes in work methods, which may in turn result in the breaking up of work groups. Management should be aware of how many various aspects of their employees' lives they are proposing to alter – and therefore on how many fronts they are likely to encounter resistance.

3.4 Force field analysis

There is a technique developed by Lewin to visualise the change process called **force field analysis** It is based on the idea that in any group or organisational situation there is an **interplay of restraining and driving forces that keeps things in equilibrium.**

Lewin's **force field analysis** maps the forces that are pushing **toward the preferred state** and the restraining forces, which are **pushing back to the current state.** They can then be presented in a chart.

The example below describes a public sector organisation whose management are introducing a performance review system. A group of workers are producing at 70% of the efficiency that might be expected on purely technical grounds. Their output can be visualised as a **balance** between two opposing sets of forces, ie **driving forces** which are propelling their output upwards and **restraining forces** which are preventing it from going beyond the 70% level.

The role of change management is to help

- Weaken the resisting forces
- Strengthen the driving forces

The Lewin/Schein three-step (iceberg) approach is one way to do this.

Driving forces (for change)	Current state	Restraining forces (resistance)	Ideal position

A requirement of new legislation — Cynicism about change 'another fad'

Existing systems are sufficient

Professional commitment to controlling the organisation — Trade Union concern over effects on jobs and working conditions

Requirement to report to external agencies — Complexity of producing such reviews

A concern for quality

Cost of carrying out reviews

Arrow sizes denote the relative strength of the forces.

Interactive question 3: Gerrard, Dudek & Smicer [Difficulty level: Intermediate]

Gerrard, Dudek & Smicer are a small long established firm of solicitors. They have recently appointed Eva, a new business development manager. She has suggested that the firm introduce electronic diaries as staff often don't know where to find each other. Secretaries also struggle to book meetings as the partners often keep their agendas with them, which has annoyed some key clients. However, the partners are extremely reluctant to consider such a departure from their current methods.

Using Lewin's force field model, analyse the above situation and suggest how the new manager could bring about the change she wants.

See **Answer** at the end of this chapter.

3.5 Communicating change

Stakeholder	Their needs	What they want to know	How to communicate
Shareholders	Reassurance	That there is well thought-through strategy. How the strategy will benefit them	The press Financial statements AGM Website
The press	A good story	What is happening, the rationale, and whether the changes are under control	Briefings
Suppliers	Information	How the changes will affect their working relationship	Meetings face-to-face with major suppliers Letters/email to small suppliers
Customers	Motivation	That the service will continue uninterrupted	The press Advertisements

Stakeholder	Their needs	What they want to know	How to communicate
Senior managers	Acknowledgement and involvement	How they will be involved and opportunities in the new structure. Reassurance over employment positions	One-to-one meetings
Staff	Help to adapt	Training and support Job security	Briefings One-to-one with line manager
Line managers	Involvement	Opportunities to be involved and opportunities to learn	Briefings One-to-one with senior manager/HR

Interactive question 4: Burgermania   [Difficulty level: Exam standard]

Company background

Burgermania plc (hereafter Burgermania) is the world's largest fast food chain. The company has 30,000 restaurants in over 100 countries, and has been committed to opening over 700 new restaurants each year in recent times. The company has benefited from consumers wanting quick and filling foodstuffs, and has met this need with its style of product for both adults and children. The company has also had many tie-in arrangements with sports and films, to encourage consumers to buy its product range. The range is very limited, focussing mainly on burgers, fries and soft drinks. There are occasional variations in some countries. This approach has proved popular with consumers who have conservative tastes and are happy to know that the food will be of a consistent quality wherever it is sold.

The company operates mainly via a combination of owned and franchised restaurants. Franchisees sign a 15-year deal in which they are given the right to use Burgermania trademarks, restaurant decor designs, formulae and specifications for menu items, use of Burgermania's inventory control systems, bookkeeping, accounting, marketing and the right to occupy the restaurant premises.

In return the franchisee agrees to operate the business in accordance with Burgermania's standards of quality, service, cleanliness and value. The company is anxious to avoid any negative publicity, so it employs 'secret shoppers' who randomly visit and assess restaurants on the above criteria. The company pays relatively low wages and has high staff turnover; this has prevented Burgermania being able to recruit high calibre staff, as the image of the jobs offered is poor.

Recent events

The company has had stagnant profits and sales growth in the last two years. The main reasons for this are increased health concerns in its major geographical markets. The company's products are high in both fat and carbohydrate content, and stories in the media about preventable obesity, heart disease, diabetes and cancer have caused turnover to falter. Furthermore, new style diets, whilst promoting meat consumption, have discouraged many consumers from eating bread or fries due to their high carbohydrate content. Initially Burgermania claimed that its products were nutritious and healthy, but this policy was deemed to be a failure as it did not reverse the stagnation of sales. Some high profile legal claims against the company from consumers claiming that Burgermania products caused health problems have also had a negative impact on the company's image.

The company has decided at board level to respond to this deterioration in its financial performance by introducing and promoting a healthier menu, with options that include burgers but no burger buns, chicken and fish based products, grilled rather than fried meats, salads, fruit and healthier drinks, as well as phasing out extra large portions of food on its menu. The directors want to give more autonomy to individual restaurant managers to offer a wider range of products that will vary between different locations.

In addition, the board intend to change the company name to 'Eatwise' to move away from the association with burgers and fries. The cost of changing all the company, logos, livery, advertising campaigns and cooking equipment is expected to be massive. Staff will also will have to be trained to use the new equipment and promote healthy eating to customers. The company is uncertain how the public and franchisees will respond to these changes in the business. Moreover, Burgermania is under pressure to deliver improved financial performance as its share price has underperformed that of the overall stock market by 20% in the last 18 months.

Requirements

(a) Identify the type of change that Burgermania is considering.   **(2 marks)**

(b) Outline the potential barriers to the proposed changes from:

    (i) Franchisees
    (ii) Restaurant staff
    (iii) Customers   **(9 marks)**

(c) Prepare a draft blueprint for submission to the board of directors of Burgermania that details how the company will deal with the changes of menus and name.   **(7 marks)**

(d) Suggest ways in which the company can communicate successfully the changes to customers, franchisees and shareholders.   **(3 marks)**

                                                                                    (21 marks)

See **Answer** at the end of this chapter.

Summary and Self-test

Summary

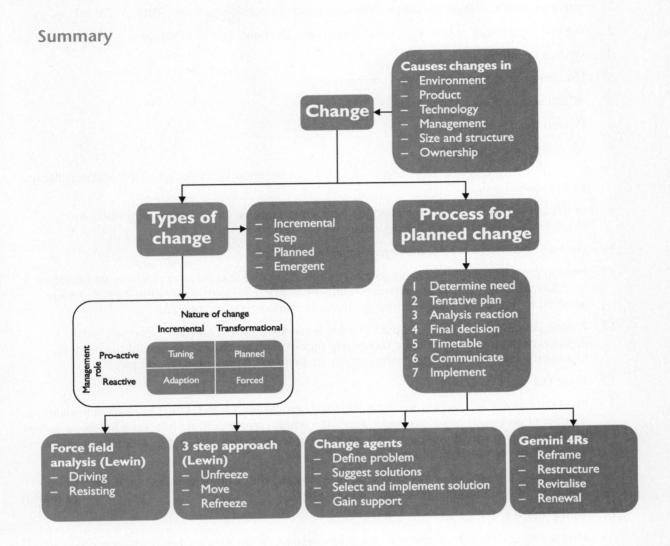

Change

Causes: changes in
- Environment
- Product
- Technology
- Management
- Size and structure
- Ownership

Types of change
- Incremental
- Step
- Planned
- Emergent

Process for planned change
1 Determine need
2 Tentative plan
3 Analysis reaction
4 Final decision
5 Timetable
6 Communicate
7 Implement

Nature of change

Management role		Incremental	Transformational
	Pro-active	Tuning	Planned
	Reactive	Adaption	Forced

Force field analysis (Lewin)
- Driving
- Resisting

3 step approach (Lewin)
- Unfreeze
- Move
- Refreeze

Change agents
- Define problem
- Suggest solutions
- Select and implement solution
- Gain support

Gemini 4Rs
- Reframe
- Restructure
- Revitalise
- Renewal

CHAPTER

15

Self-test

Answer the following questions.

1   List the three levels at which organisational development/change efforts may focus.

2   'An organisation enjoying good profitability should not consider change.' TRUE or FALSE?

3   List the three stages of Lewin's model for changing the behaviour of individuals.

4   What is meant by 'refreezing'?

5   List three possible problems with coercive change.

6   What causes resistance to change?

7   What is force field analysis?

8   Fill in the following blanks.

   C...................., c................... and c................... play important roles when introducing change to an organisation.

9   In the Lewin/Schein three-stage change management model, what general principle does management use to embed the desirable new behaviour?

10   List four areas that a project manager should be skilled in.

11   Herring plc is in crisis. Major changes in its culture, structure and working practices are needed if it is to survive. The effects of any changes made are highly uncertain. Identify the type of change involved for Herring plc and the best approach to managing such change.

12   Freddis plc has sold its single product in a single market segment for many years. It's only competitor has just brought out a technically superior and far cheaper version of the product. Outline the cultural barriers to change which are likely to be present in Freddis plc.

13   **Plant Ltd**

   Plant Ltd has just finished implementing a major cost cutting project which involved automating a number of previously paper processes across the whole company. The project did not go as well as had been hoped and at one point the telephone ordering system was out of action for over a week as a result of unexpected problems.

   Explain how this type of change could be categorised. What kind of investigation is likely to be instigated as a result of the problems that occurred?
   (2 marks)

14   **Timbermate Ltd**

   After a difficult few years trading, a new chief executive, Brian Parsons, has been appointed to the board of Timbermate Ltd. A large divisionalised company, it specialises in the production of wood-based products, from plywood and chipboard, to kitchens and conservatory windows.

   Parsons in his initial press interview made it clear that the costs incurred by the business were far too high and that efficiency and productivity were unacceptably low. He has made clear his intention to turn the business around. However, there have already been rumblings from the union to which most of the workers belong. They are not prepared to negotiate over wages or working conditions.

   Timbermate is a major importer of wood. Russian and Scandinavian joinery redwood, together with spruce from North America, make up a high percentage of imports. They also import from the Baltic States. Although sterling is strong against the dollar it has been struggling lately against the other currencies. There have been signs that some of Timbermate's overseas suppliers are considering expanding into the UK directly. There has also been an increase in the popularity of UPVC alternatives in a number of Timbermate's core business areas.

   A number of operational issues need addressing. Recently, complaints about quality and product specification have become more common. Additionally the delivery fleet has become less reliable and several key customers have been let down. However many of the senior managers do not seem unduly concerned. They often talk of the timber crisis of 1992 and how these problems are just part of the nature of the industry. They rarely stay at their desks after 5pm. There is little in the way of knowledge sharing and it is unusual for staff in any one division to even know the names of staff in the others.

One key pillar of Parson's plan is to introduce a fully integrated information system, covering (amongst others) stock control and e-procurement, computer aided design and manufacture, resource planning and management accounting. The system is to operate across all the divisions and allow potential cross-selling and better customer management.

Requirements

(a) Analyse the forces for and against change at Timbermate Ltd.   **(6 marks)**
(b) Recommend to Brian Parsons how he might best manage the change process.   **(8 marks)**

                                                                                    (14 marks)

15 Read the scenario of the **September 2008 Business Strategy** paper in the Question Bank entitled *Embury Ltd*. Draft answers for requirements (a), (b) and (d) on PESTEL, production and change management.

16 Go online at The Times 100 Business Case Studies and read the Corus case study 'Overcoming barriers to change' at http://businesscasestudies.co.uk/corus/overcoming-barriers-to-change

Now go back to the Learning objectives in the Introduction. If you are satisfied you have achieved these objectives, please tick them off.

Answer to Interactive question 1

Ford

Forced: They are continuing to react to external competitive and environmental changes and the results so far have lead to a significant changes in the way Ford is structured.

Tesco

Planned: It is proactive, aimed at seizing an opportunity, and given the size of the Indian markets it will change the character of Tesco in terms of size but also its global profile.

Answer to Interactive question 2

Reframing

The major reframing is the term 'commercial business' which implies making profits as the primary goal, or at least providing as good a service as competitors in a de-regulated environment.

The ensuing strong emphasis on profits and termination of loss-making activities underlines this.

The challenge for management would be to make this a goal that staff wished to support. In fact, Allan Leighton had hoped to issue shares to all Post Office staff to give them a stake in profits but was overruled by the UK Treasury. This was taken as a set-back for him but instead remuneration was linked to changes in value and staff were offered 'phantom shares', in effect non-tradable rights to shares of profits. The governments decision in 2013 to sell off the Royal Mail appears to have been well received by employees, with 15,000 choosing to purchase shares. This change in the ownership structure of the Royal Mail is likely to be positive in aligning the aims of the company with its employees.

Restructuring

None obviously stated in the 2005 press release although references to automated sorting suggest changes were required here. The points raised from the 2013/14 annual report indicate that Royal Mail is attempting to automate and enhance its current operations in response to changes in the demand for its services. In fact there has been major restructuring with closures of thousand of network post offices, the removal of twice daily post delivery and the closure of entire administrative and sorting offices.

Revitalising

In 2005, Allan Leighton recognised the challenge of adapting to the new competitive environment: 'Competing successfully in an open mail market is going to be even more difficult. We've a mountain to climb and we've only reached the base camp.' The 2013/14 annual report explains how Royal Mail is looking to increase it's use of technology to respond to the change in the nature of the marketplace and the increasing competition.

Renewal

The statements from 2005 are clearly inclusive and Allan Leighton emphasises the importance of gaining staff commitment… "with the dedication and support of our people". Royal Mail's change process in recent years has not been without its problems and 2007 saw several days of strike action as workers protested at the potential loss of jobs due to modernisation. To support the change there have been new financial control systems and new reward structures. The offer of shares to employees as part of the 2013 flotation might be seen as a further attempt to gain support from staff. In March 2014 however the Telegraph announced that Royal Mail had been threatened with strike action from postal unions after announcing its intention to cut 1,600 jobs. The newly privatised delivery company said in a statement that it was proposing a net reduction of 1,300, including the creation of 300 new jobs in a drive to achieve £50m of annualised cost savings.

Answer to Interactive question 3

Driving forces for change: Technological developments raising customer expectation, irritated customers, new innovative staff member.

Restraining forces: Partners' habits and possible fear of the unknown, possible concerns over expense.

Eva should strengthen the driving forces by stressing to the partners the level of clients' concerns and gain the support of the secretaries in encouraging the partners to consider the system.

The restraining forces should be weakened by producing costings, and explaining clearly how the system would work and what benefits would arise.

Answer to Interactive question 4

(a) **Type of change**

Burgermania is undertaking a change in the business that would be deemed revolutionary in terms of impact on the business. Both the process and the underlying paradigm of the company will have to change. The retraining and rebranding of the business suggests a low degree of predictability, as it will be difficult to anticipate the reaction of stakeholders, especially customers, to the proposed changes.

(b) **Barriers to change**

Franchisees

- Franchisees will fear that new system is too radical and may have detrimental impact on revenues of restaurants.

- They may fear that costs of changing name and livery of the restaurants will be recovered by Burgermania in the form of higher franchise fees.

- Franchisees will be reluctant to change to a new system of delivering food if they are happy with current products and procedures.

- They may lack initiative when it comes to introducing new products that they can add to the menu.

Restaurant staff

- Staff in fast food restaurants tend to be poorly paid and have short periods of employment. Therefore they may be reluctant to be retrained or adopt a pro-active policy with customers in terms of promoting the new healthier food lines.

- Staff may feel that if Burgermania is suffering then jobs may be lost – likely to cause demotivation.

- Staff may fear that management will use the change as a means of introducing new working practices that could reduce income, overtime, bonuses etc.

- Staff may lack the skills to adapt to the new nature of the business.

- The decision is likely to be enforced by coercion if necessary due to Burgermania's poor recent results, potential for conflict and resentment by staff.

Customers

- Customers are more concerned with being fed quickly than with the quality of what they eat, so may choose to go elsewhere. Many people have conservative tastes and so will be reluctant to try the new products on offer.

- They may feel that the new products are being forced on them and again vote with their feet by eating at other fast food restaurants.

(c) **Draft blueprint**

To   Board of directors, Burgermania plc
From   B. Cowie, consultant
Date   Today

Subject Blueprint for menu and name changes

Action required

- Introduction of healthier menus and local autonomy
- Launch of new name/brand for the company

Purpose

- The objective of the changes is as follows.

  - To reverse the decline in the company's performance.
  - To adapt to changes in consumer demands and tastes.
  - To promote the company as a family-friendly and healthy eating place.

Timing of changes

- Given the nature of the company's products and positioning in the market, a national change will have to be launched if it wants to maximise publicity for the changes. The company could try introducing the new menus on a trial basis in selected restaurants.

- The transformation will be very time-consuming given the global nature of the company and its products.

Responsibilities

- A committee needs to be formed to co-ordinate the changes, headed by a senior manager/director.

Evaluation

- Market research needs to be undertaken to establish public reaction to both the menu and name changes.

- Performance data can be produced to determine the popularity of the new food products on a trial basis in selected stores.

(d) **Communication of changes**

- Franchisees could be invited to a conference to see the new 'Eatwise' logos and product range.

- A major PR campaign, with TV, radio and press adverts should take place to coincide with the changes to advise customers. Perhaps special promotions relating to the new products could be used to encourage customers to try them out.

- Shareholders could be briefed via email and the company's website, together with press releases in the financial media.

1 Individual; organisation structure and systems; organisation climate and interpersonal style.

2 FALSE. Organisations should embrace change, and not wait until the obsolescence of their current practices leads to crisis.

3 Unfreeze, change (or move) and refreeze.

4 The final stage of the Lewin/Schein three-stage approach in which the desired new behaviour is consolidated.

5 Underestimating resistance; not coercing hard enough or long enough; failure to ensure implementation.

6 Attitudes, beliefs, loyalties, habits and norms, politics.

7 Lewin's analysis of the driving and restraining forces which underlie any group or organisational equilibrium.

8 Commitment, co-ordination and communication.

9 Reinforcement – both positive and negative.

10 Four of:

- Leadership
- Team building
- Organisation
- Communication
- Technical expertise
- Personal qualities

11 Revolutionary change

Approach – emergent, ie flexibility is essential.

12 Structural inertia – systems and procedures are likely to have been in place for many years.

Group inertia – production and marketing departments, for example, may resist change (probably used to doing things in the same way for many years).

Power structures – lack of pressure to change in the past may have resulted in clear lines of decision making authority and/or control over resources.

13 **Plant Ltd**

The change could be categorised as reconstruction – it affects the entire organisation, but does not appear to require a paradigm shift.

A post-project audit would be required. It would be carried out by an independent team who would review all elements of the project process in detail to identify why the problems arose.

14 **Timbermate Ltd**

(a) **Forces for and against change**

Forces for change

The forces for change in Timbermate appear to be both external and internal.

External factors would include:

- Overseas competitors: Current suppliers may be able to undercut Timbermate if they set up their own operations in the UK. It will be essential for them to bring down their own cost base to survive.

- Exchange rates: Weakening sterling will make imports more expensive, putting up Timbermate's costs still further.

- Growth in plastic alternatives may reduce demand in a number of key areas. Unless they can fight back, share will be lost, reducing economies of scale and brand strength.

Internal factors would include:

- Brian Parsons' determination to make the changes needed.

- Customers: Increasing dissatisfaction with the current standard of service has already given rise to complaint and may, if not addressed, lead to loss of current customers and brand image.

- Shareholders: A period of poor results cannot have been satisfactory for the shareholders which is presumably why they have appointed Parsons.

Forces against change

- Attitude of managers: The managers lack a sense of urgency and are therefore likely to resist any major change programme as unnecessarily disruptive.

- Attitude of staff: It is likely that the laid back culture permeates the whole organisation and staff may not understand the need for change. They will undoubtedly also be fearful for their jobs.

- Unions have already expressed their intention to resist any changes to wages or working conditions. This could lead to walk-outs and strikes.

(b) **Managing change**

A useful method of managing change was proposed by Lewin. This divides the process of change into three stages, unfreezing, changing and refreezing.

Unfreezing

The forces for change must be used to encourage the change, and the forces against it must be weakened. Methods might include:

Carrying out a PEST analysis to identify the exact nature of the threats from the outside environment (issues such as deforestation may also have potential impact and have been overlooked).

These issues and their consequences should then be stressed to the managers. Forecasts of market performance (and its impact on bonuses) if no change is made should be communicated. Workshops to involve senior managers in the process may help them to appreciate the urgency of the situation.

Consultation and negotiation with the unions will have to be entered into. They will need to be persuaded of the importance of change now to protect jobs in the future.

Change

The new information system must be introduced. Training in all aspects will be required – not just in how to use the system, but in its potential benefits, so that staff start to identify ways in which it could further improve business.

New working practices will need to be introduced. Some processes may need re-engineering.

Greater collaboration between different divisions needs to be encouraged.

Efforts must be made to change the culture of the organisation. Stories about problems being caused by economic cycles that can be ignored, rituals such as leaving work on the dot, and an organisation structure so rigid that there is little or no horizontal communication suggests a 'jobs worth' paradigm where bureaucracy has taken on all its worst characteristics. Whilst education may start the process, it may be necessary to remove those managers who are unwilling or unable to change.

Refreezing

This is the process of trying to ensure planned changes become the norm.

Reward systems should be developed to focus on issues such as cost management, customer satisfaction, productivity and innovation.

Continual training: The staff should be given regular training updates to deepen their understanding of the new system.

Communication: Interdivisional meetings should be scheduled on a monthly basis. The agenda should be shared problem solving and sharing of best practice. It may be that major customers should be provided with a single point of contact, who will then liaise with all divisions on their behalf (a matrix structure within the divisional one).

15 Refer to the answer to requirements a, b and d of Embury Ltd in the Question Bank.

16 There is no answer to this self-test, as it is designed just to help you increase your business awareness.

CHAPTER 16

Ethics, sustainability and corporate responsibility

Introduction

Examination context

Topic List

1 Strategy and ethics

2 Marketing and ethics

3 Ethical issues in manufacture and procurement

4 The concepts of sustainability and corporate responsibility

5 Sustainable development

6 Corporate responsibility

7 Monitoring and measuring sustainability

8 Developing an approach to ethics requirements of the exam

Summary and Self-test

Answers to Interactive questions

Answers to Self-test

ICAEW

Learning objectives

- Explain the ethical factors to be considered in determining the scope and nature of a business's objectives and its strategic analysis, having regard to the legitimate interests of all stakeholder groups ☐

- Evaluate the ethical implications of a business's strategies and operations, including those for the organisation and for individuals (including the accountant in business and others) ☐

- Identify sustainability issues that may impact on a business's performance and position ☐

- Evaluate the ethical implications of how a business chooses to implement and modify its strategies, suggesting appropriate courses of action to resolve ethical dilemmas that may arise

- Identify issues of Corporate Responsibility (CR) and the strategies available to discharge an organisation's CR ☐

- Show how a business chooses strategies to maximise the achievement of its objectives relating to CR and sustainability ☐

Specific syllabus references for this chapter are 1b, 1h, 2f, 3j.

Syllabus links

Some coverage was given in your Business and Finance paper to the policies that can be used to help ensure a business acts ethically, and issues of sustainability and corporate responsibility. The knowledge from B&F is developed further in Business Strategy and applied in the context of different business scenarios. At Advanced Stage ethics, sustainability and corporate responsibility are integrated into technical areas of the syllabus including Business Analysis and will involve making ethical judgements.

This chapter also considers how best to apply knowledge of ethics, sustainability and corporate responsibility in the exam, in the context of a specific scenario. This is an approach which will help you in developing the necessary skills to make ethical judgements at Advanced Stage.

Examination context

Ethics

At least one of the exam scenarios is likely to include an ethical issue or dilemma, possibly in the context of the ethics of an organisation or in relation to a professional accountant working in business. Between 5% and 10% of marks of the paper will be allocated to the appropriate discussion of such ethical issues, but they are often not clear cut. The important skills here are for you to develop a balanced argument, use appropriate ethical language and have regard to any relevant professional principles.

Scenarios might include topics such as:

- Conflict between the accountant's professional obligations and the responsibilities to the organisation

- Lack of professional independence eg personal financial interest in business proposals

- Conflicts of interest among stakeholders

- Attempts to intentionally mislead key stakeholders (by disclosure or non-disclosure of information)

- Doubtful accounting or commercial business practice

- Facilitation of unethical strategies

- Inappropriate pressure to achieve a result

- Actions contrary to law, regulation and/or technical and professional standards

In Q1 June 2010 (*Executive Travel Ltd*) the scenario contains information about some employees whose activities, in relation to accepting gifts and claiming travel expenses, were questionable. An employee who has recently resigned has contacted the finance director, Carol Gull, to 'blow the whistle'. The fourth requirement is:

'(d) Discuss the key ethical issues that arise from the letter sent to Carol Gull and explain what actions she should take. **(7 marks)**'

This requirement highlights that a requirement on ethics is always set very much in the context of the scenario. Although the question may indicate clearly that there is an ethical issue, it can be tricky to tease out the exact nature of it. The key to a good answer is also to appreciate that ethical issues are unlikely to be black and white and that a balanced argument rather than a definitive "right or wrong" answer is required.

CR and sustainability

Scenarios may consider how organisations create, embed and monitor a CR strategy. Areas that might be examined in the context of sustainability and CR include:

- The involvement of key stakeholders in identifying objectives, conflicts of interest, and communication with such stakeholders

- The development of appropriate strategy and governance structures to implement CR

- Determination of appropriate KPIs to measure performance of the CR strategy

In Q2 June 2010 (Hutton Haulage plc), a large UK road haulage company, is contracting to supply transport services for a large supermarket, Freshco. The second requirement is:

'(b) Prepare a memorandum for discussion by the HH board that explains:

(i) How the outsourcing arrangement with HH can improve the efficiency of Freshco's supply chain; and

(ii) The actions that HH can take in order to enhance the environmental sustainability in its activities for Freshco. **(12 marks)**'

1 Strategy and ethics

Section overview

- Morals and ethics involve doing the 'right' thing. This may not always be the same as 'best for the individual manager' or 'best for the organisation as a whole'.

- Some ethical imperatives may be enshrined in laws but ethics and law are not the same thing.

- Ethical issues exist at the level of the individual, the business and, at its widest, corporate responsibility.

- A professional accountant is required to comply with the five fundamental principles of The ICAEW Code of Ethics.

- The Code provides guidance for the professional accountant working in business on how to identify, evaluate and address any threats to those fundamental principles and the safeguards to implement.

- The desire by management to act ethically affects the scope of strategies adopted but also requires that management keep an eye on the ethical consequences of its operations.

- Section 8 of this chapter gives guidance on how to approach ethics in the context of an examination question.

1.1 Ethics and morals

The meanings of the words 'ethics' and 'morals' are intermingled and difficult to distinguish. For example, the Concise Oxford Dictionary offers the following two definitions:

- **Morals** are 'standards of behaviour or principles of right and wrong'.
- **Ethics** are 'the moral principles governing or influencing conduct'.

Morals or ethics will also differ depending on the beliefs, value systems and norms of a particular society or culture. So ethics might be considered as:

Definition

Ethics: A system of behaviour which is deemed acceptable in the society or context under consideration.

Another area in which ethics can be invoked is Corporate Responsibility (CR) which is discussed in more detail later in this chapter.

For present purposes the field can be simplified by suggesting that business ethics exist at three levels.

1. **Personal ethical behaviour**

    This relates to the way you as an individual conduct yourself. Bad behaviour would include bullying, stealing, discrimination against a colleague and giving away business secrets to a rival.

2. **Business ethics**

    This is the way a firm as a whole behaves. Bad conduct here would include offering bribes to win contracts, distorting the accounts, victimisation or discrimination against certain workers and telling lies to regulators.

3. **Corporate responsibility**

    This is the belief that a firm owes a responsibility to society and its wider stakeholders, as well as to shareholders. Examples of bad behaviour would include pollution, mass redundancies and dangerous products.

1.2 Ethical stance of corporation

An organisation can adopt a range of ethical stances:

- Meet minimum legal obligations and concentrate on short-term shareholder interests

- Recognise that long-term shareholder wealth may be increased by well-managed relationships with other stakeholders (corporate governance approach which was discussed in Chapter 9)

- Go beyond minimum legal and corporate governance obligations to include explicitly the interests of other stakeholders in setting mission, objectives and strategy. In this context issues such as environmental protection, sustainability of resources, selling arms to tyrannical regimes, paying bribes to secure contracts, using child labour etc would be considered

- Public sector organisations, charities, etc where the interests of shareholders are not relevant

The ethical stance taken by an organisation is often reflected in its mission statement.

Worked example: Innocent drinks

The following statement about ethics is contained on the Innocent Drinks website:

We sure aren't perfect, but we're trying to do the right thing.

It might make us sound a bit like a Miss World contestant, but we want to leave things a little bit better than we find them. We strive to do business in a more enlightened way, where we take responsibility for the impact of our business on society and the environment, and move these impacts from negative to neutral, or better still, positive. It's part of our quest to become a truly sustainable business, where we have a net positive effect on the wonderful world around us.

Our Strategy

sustainable **nutrition** sustainable **ingredients** sustainable **packaging** sustainable **production** sustainable **legacy**

Source: Innocent Drinks website 2013

1.3 Regulating ethical behaviour

Ethical business regulation operates in two ways:

1. **Forbidding or constraining certain types of conduct or decisions**: eg most organisations have regulations forbidding ethically inappropriate use of their IT systems. Similarly many will forbid the offering or taking of inducements in order to secure contracts.

2. **Disclosure of certain facts or decisions**: eg because the board sets its own pay they disclose it, and sometimes the reasons behind the awards, to shareholders in final accounts.

In other Professional Stage papers you will have been introduced to the following codes potentially binding on you as a trainee Chartered Accountant.

The Auditing Practices Board (APB)

- Ethical standards for Auditors – concerned with assuring their integrity and independence in the audit of financial statements and in how fees are levied.

- Ethical standards for Reporting Accountants – concerned with integrity and independence of accountants involved in writing investment circulars.

Five fundamental principles:

1. **Integrity**: Straightforward and honest in business and professional relationships.

2. **Objectivity**: Not allow bias, conflict of interest or influence of others to override professional or business judgement.

3. **Professional competence and due care**: Be aware of all prevailing knowledge necessary to give professional service and apply the same diligently to affairs of the client in accordance with technical and professional standards.

4. **Confidentiality**: Respect the confidentiality of information acquired as a consequence of professional or business engagements and not use the same for personal advantage or that of third parties.

5. **Professional behaviour**: Comply with laws and regulations and not to discredit the profession.

Interactive question 1: Why have ethical standards? [Difficulty level: Intermediate]

The Codes of the ICAEW and of the APB above seek to regulate the behaviour of accountants. Why do the bodies have these?

See **Answer** at the end of this chapter.

Below we consider in more detail the ICAEW code as it applies to **professional accountants working in business.**

1.4 ICAEW Code of Ethics for Professional accountants working in business

Investors, creditors, employers, the business community, government and the public may **rely** on the work of professional accountants in business in the context of

*   Preparation and reporting of financial and other information
*   Providing effective financial management
*   Competent advice on a variety of business-related matters

The more senior the position held, the greater the ability and opportunity to influence events, practices and attitudes.

A professional accountant in business is expected to **encourage an ethics-based culture** in an employing organisation, that emphasises the importance that senior management places on ethical behaviour.

1.4.1 Threats

The code outlines areas where there may be **conflict** for the professional accountant between furthering the legitimate aims of their organisation and their absolute duty to comply with the fundamental principles:

(a) **Self-interest** – Financial interests, loans or guarantees; incentive compensation arrangements; inappropriate personal use of corporate assets; concern over employment security; commercial pressure from outside the employing organisation.

(b) **Self-review** – Business decisions or data being subject to review and justification by the same professional accountant in business responsible for making those decisions or preparing that data.

(c) **Advocacy** – When furthering the legitimate goals and objectives of their employing organisations, professional accountants in business may promote the organisation's position, provided any statements made are neither false nor misleading. Such actions generally would not create an advocacy threat.

(d) **Familiarity** – A professional accountant in business in a position to influence financial or non-financial reporting or business decisions having an immediate or close family member who is in a position to benefit from that influence; long association with business contacts influencing business decisions; acceptance of a gift or preferential treatment, unless the value is clearly insignificant.

(e) **Intimidation** – Threat of dismissal or replacement of the professional accountant in business or a close or immediate family member, over a disagreement about the application of an accounting principle or the way in which financial information is to be reported; a dominant personality attempting to influence the decision making process, for example with regard to the awarding of contracts or the application of an accounting principle.

1.4.2   Safeguards

To comply with the Code, professional accountants are required to consider whether their actions or relationships might constitute **threats** to their adherence to the fundamental principles and where these are significant, to implement **safeguards.**

These safeguards might be generic, created by the profession or regulation or developed in the working environment by the individual or their organisation.

If effective safeguards are not possible, they are required to **refrain** from the action or relationship in question.

The Code sets out the types of safeguards in the **work environment** which might be applied to overcome these threats:

- The employing organisation's systems of corporate oversight or other oversight structures.

- The employing organisation's ethics and conduct programs.

- Recruitment procedures in the employing organisation emphasising the importance of employing high calibre competent staff.

- Strong internal controls.

- Appropriate disciplinary processes.

- Leadership that stresses the importance of ethical behaviour and the expectation that employees will act in an ethical manner.

- Policies and procedures to implement and monitor the quality of employee performance.

- Timely communication of the employing organisation's policies and procedures, including any changes to them, to all employees, and appropriate training and education on such policies and procedures.

- Policies and procedures to empower and encourage employees to communicate to senior levels within the employing organisation any ethical issues that concern them without fear of retribution.

- Consultation with another appropriate professional accountant.

1.4.3   Action required in unethical circumstances

In circumstances where a professional accountant in business believes that unethical behaviour or actions by others will continue to occur within the employing organisation, they should consider seeking **legal advice**.

In extreme situations where all available safeguards have been exhausted and it is not possible to reduce the threat to an acceptable level, a professional accountant in business may conclude that it is appropriate to **disassociate** from the task and/or **resign** from the employing organisation.

1.5   Other ethical codes

Other ethical codes impacting on businesses include the *Sarbanes-Oxley Act* requirement, policed by US Securities and Exchanges Commission (SEC), that public corporations filing returns in the US have a Code of Ethics and that this should be detailed in their annual filings. It is described by SEC as

A codification of standards that is reasonably necessary to deter wrongdoing and to promote:

1. Honest and ethical conduct, including the ethical handling of actual or apparent conflicts of interest between personal and professional relationships.

2. Avoidance of conflicts of interest, including disclosure to an appropriate person or persons identified in the code of any material transaction or relationship that reasonably could be expected to give rise to such a conflict.

3. Full, fair, accurate, timely, and understandable disclosure in reports and documents that a company files with, or submits to, the Commission and in other public communications made by the company.

4. Compliance with applicable governmental laws, rules and regulations.

5. The prompt internal reporting of code violations to an appropriate person or persons identified in the code; and accountability for adherence to the code.

Many firms use these headings to develop their own internal code of ethics for management.

For example BT, the UK and global telecoms corporation with securities issued under the regulations of the SEC has the following code for its senior finance staff:

Worked example: BT internal code of ethics for senior finance staff

The Chief Executive Officer, Group Finance Director and Director Group Financial Control & Treasury will:

*   Act with honesty and integrity, including ethically handling actual or apparent conflicts of interest between their personal relationships or financial or commercial interests and their responsibilities to BT

*   Promote full, fair, accurate, timely and understandable disclosure in all reports and documents that BT files with, or submits to, the US Securities and Exchange Commission or otherwise makes public

*   Comply with all laws, rules and regulations applicable to BT and to its relationship with its shareholders

*   Report known or suspected violations of this code of ethics promptly to the Chairman of the Audit Committee, and

*   Ensure that their actions comply not only with the letter but the spirit of this code of ethics and foster a culture in which BT operates in compliance with the law and BT's policies.

BT will take appropriate disciplinary action against any such officer who acts in contravention of these principles.

Interactive question 2: Ethical dilemmas

[Difficulty level: Intermidiate]

So far we have looked at the ethical considerations that relate to professional accountants working in business. This next question should serve as a refresher from your earlier studies as to how ethics and professional standards impact the work of accountants in different settings.

Russell Ltd

Your company has been acting as consultants to Russell Ltd providing advice about the need to cut costs and restructure the company's manufacturing operations. In a recent meeting with the Production Director of Russell Ltd you are made aware that the entire consulting team will be invited to the company's Christmas celebrations which run over the course of a weekend and are being held at an expensive Castle-Keep Hotel.

Ravencroft White plc

You are a manager in the audit firm of Swain Brothers. Mr Bootle has been the engagement partner for a client Ravencroft White plc for the last eleven years. He has excellent knowledge of the client and knows all of the directors of Ravencroft White exceptionally well.

Sole Records Ltd

Mr Minus, the principal consultant in the advisory firm for which you work, has been assisting a client Sole Records Ltd to help improve the company's performance. Mr Minus's son, David, recently joined the finance department of Sole Record's largest competitor.

Requirements

Explain the ethical threats which may affect the independence of the accountants/consultants featured in the three scenarios.

For each threat explain how it might be reduced.

See **Answer** at the end of this chapter.

1.6 Simple ethical tests for a business decision

Compliance with codes of conduct will be mandatory for members and employees subject to the codes.

Ethical tests enable managers to consider ethical consequences of decisions where

- The wording of codes may be imprecise
- Situations arise that are not covered in the codes

Initially at least the situation should be evaluated as to:

1. The facts of the situation and whether all relevant information is available for making the decision, and

2. Whether there is any possibility of illegality – if there is then seeking legal advice should be considered.

The *Institute of Business Ethics* offers three tests to then apply to situations to assess whether they raise ethical issues:

1. **Transparency:** Do I mind others knowing what I have decided? Would a third party construe it as honest and straightforward for instance?

2. **Effect:** Whom does my decision potentially affect or hurt? Have the interests of all stakeholders been considered?

3. **Fairness:** Would my decision be considered fair by those affected and by third parties?

1.7 Impact of ethics on strategy

In Chapter 2 we considered the points in the strategy process where ethics may have an impact:

- In the formulation of strategic objectives, some firms will not consider lines of business for ethical reasons.

- External appraisal will need to consider the ethical climate in which the firm operates. This will raise expectations of its behaviour.

- Internal appraisal: Management should consider whether present operations are 'sustainable', ie consistent with present and future ethical expectations.

- Strategy selection: Management should consider the ethical implication of proposed strategies before selecting and implementing them.

1.7.1 Conflict between ethics and business

Potential areas for conflict between ethics and business strategy include:

- **Cultivating and benefiting from relationships with legislators and governments:** Such relationships may lead politicians to ignore the national interest (eg of the people who elected them) to further their own personal interests.

- **Fairness of labour contracts**: Firms can use their power to exploit workers, including child labour, and subject them to unethical treatment in areas where jobs are scarce.

- **Privacy of customers and employees**: Modern databases enable tracking of spending for marketing purposes or to discriminate between customers on basis of their value. Staff can be subject to background checks and monitored through their use of email and the location of their mobile phones.

- **Terms of trade with suppliers**: Large firms may pay poor prices or demand long credit periods and other payments from weak suppliers. This has been a particular criticism of large retail food stores in North America and Europe who are blamed for the impoverishment of farmers at home and in developing countries.

- **Prices to customers**: Powerful suppliers of scarce products such as energy, life saving drugs or petrol, are able to charge high prices that exclude poorer individuals or nations. Examples here include anti-aids drugs to Africa or purified water to developing countries.

- **Managing cross cultural businesses**: Different countries of operation or different ethnic groups within the domestic environment can present ethical issues affecting what products are made, how staff are treated, dress conventions, observance of religion and promotional methods.

2 Marketing and ethics

Section overview

- Marketing is sometimes accused of having the same low ethics as some used-car dealers.

- Ethical issues begin with questioning whether marketing exists to sell people things they don't need and so wastes resources and cause envy and dissatisfaction.

- The nature of products, the means by which they are promoted, the level of prices and the selective way they are made available are also ethical issues.

- Marketers may defend themselves to some extent by noting that ethics are culturally relative and therefore, given that marketing seeks to identify and satisfy needs, it will follow and not lead ethical consciousness.

2.1 Ethical issues in the marketing concept

The most fundamental ethical issue facing marketing is the potential accusation that marketing wastes the world's resources by making things that people don't really need and then using promotion to convince people that they are not satisfied without them.

It is hard to accept this argument in the areas of essential products, but the destruction of clothes, electrical appliances etc on the basis that they are outmoded or have obsolete technologies, and the huge amount of paper used to advertise products and to direct-mail promotional material (junk mail) does lend weight to the argument.

The envy created by development and presentation of products that only some can have, such as personal digital players, mobile phones, expensive trainers etc also contributes to street crime. Sports shoe manufacturer Nike was caught-up in accusations that its slogan 'just do it' was encouraging street thefts of its shoes.

To tilt the argument back in favour of marketing the following points can be made:

- **Value judgements**: Phrases like 'things that people don't really need' are not helpful because if people will spend money and effort to get them, who is to say they don't need them?

- **Employment effects**: The production of goods and services creates jobs. This is an ethical good to come from marketing.

- **Proper target marketing may reduce waste.** Marketing tries to ensure that unwanted products and marketing effort is reduced. This saves resources.

- **Ethical marketing**: Marketing has been used to promote alternative and more ecologically responsible products and ways of life (eg quit smoking). This suggests that it is not the practice of marketing that is unethical but rather some of the ends to which it has been put.

2.2 Ethical issues and the marketing mix

The way that marketing is carried out may raise ethical concerns:

Product issues

Some products are dangerous but are sold without this being considered. Cigarettes and alcohol are obvious examples but increasingly processed foods are being criticised as leading to illness due to high fat, sugar and salt content.

Some products are wasteful of resources or lead to environmental pollution. The sports utility vehicle (SUV) has been a criticised example of this.

Decisions to cease provision of products, or never to offer them at all, can reduce the welfare of society and possibly inflict hardship. Pharmaceutical firms have been accused of suppressing drugs that could cure a condition in favour of continued sales of palliatives.

Price issues

Pricing products to maximise returns may mean pricing them out of the reach of many who want them. Where products are essential, such as life savings drugs or affordable homes, this has clear ethical implications.

Price discrimination remains discrimination. To charge higher prices to people in rural areas compared to towns because competition is less, or to charge people differently because of their gender or age seems unfair.

Pricing low to encourage usage may have the effect of increasing consumption to unhealthy levels. Two-for-one offers on alcohol, or multi-buy offers on confectionary are examples of this.

Promotion issues

The public has expressed concern that they are being 'brainwashed' by clever advertising techniques such as hidden messages in subliminal advertising (flashes of images too brief to be registered and filtered by the conscious mind). It is unlikely that these techniques work as feared but the broader principle that promotion manipulates behaviour remains an ethical issue.

Some images used in advertising and promotion may be offensive to some in society. A knitwear manufacturer using pictures of Aids victims to promote a global caring image was regarded as distasteful and exploitative.

Promotion has been blamed for causing anti-social behaviour. A soft drink advertisement was withdrawn following protests from schools that children were emulating a character in the advertisement by ambushing and slapping schoolmates so they could experience the 'burst of taste'.

Some advertising is upsetting to casual observers. Road safety advertisements showing slow motion footage of children being propelled over the top of speeding cars has shock value but is potentially very upsetting.

Place issues

The principal ethical issues here revolve around encouraging or denying access.

Stores have been accused of encouraging consumption of confectionery by mounting displays at children's eye levels at the check-out leading to parents being pestered.

The use of premium rate telephone lines for enquiries and service calls, often with substantial waiting times, has been criticised as a hidden charge. These are also common on children's phone-in quizzes and television shows.

Closures of branches to save cost leaves some customers with a lack of service and poorer quality of life. This has been a common criticism of banks.

Migration of customer service from the High Street to call centres and websites excludes those without IT access, credit cards or those put off by the impersonal contact.

2.3 Ethical marketing

Marketers defend their profession against the issues above in a number of ways.

- **Personal choice**: Providing the information given is clear about the content and effects of products it is for the buyer to decide for themselves their ethical priorities, rather than for the firm to decide it for them.

- **Codes of practice**: Most marketers abide by voluntary codes of practice in how they promote products and deal with customers. These are developed after taking a balanced view of the issues rather than accepting the assurances of the industry or the accounts of their critics.

- **Societal marketing concept**: Marketing is about meeting people's needs and expectations and not about leading them. If issues such as junk food are bothering society then effective marketing would reduce reliance on the product as demand fell and instead find refinements or new products. Demand has not fallen which suggests that it is not as widespread an issue as the popular media makes out. They will point to ethical investment funds, cosmetics and energy as examples of marketing following a genuinely widespread ethical issue and responding appropriately with new market offerings to meet the need.

Interactive question 3: Socially responsible marketing [Difficulty level: Intermediate]

Your senior partner has requested a memo for developing into a report to a global food manufacturer regarded as being a leading exponent of modern marketing practice.

(a) Explain what you understand to be the advantages of a marketing orientation to food consumers and food manufacturers.

In February 2013 UK retailers including Tesco, Asda, Co-op and Iceland were forced to remove vast quantities of frozen ready meals from their shelves after it was discovered that some products contained up to 60% horsemeat. The scandal caused outcry among consumers as food marketed as containing beef was found to contain horsemeat. This led to an investigation by the Food Standards Agency and required the company to issue an apology to customers.

(b) Identify some of the ethical and social responsibility issues that face contemporary marketers in the food manufacturing industry.

See **Answer** at the end of this chapter.

3 Ethical issues in manufacture and procurement

Section overview

- Organisations have a duty to ensure that production processes and products do not cause harm to workers, customers, the environment and wider society.

- Many firms seek to fulfil their own CSR commitments by demanding similar commitments from their suppliers.

3.1 Ethical issues in manufacture

The ethical issues in manufacture cover the duties of an organisation to ensure that products and production processes do not cause harm.

The issues raised include the following:

- Ethical relations between the organisation and the environment in terms of pollution, carbon emissions trading and environmental ethics.

- The manufacture, marketing and distribution of defective, addictive and inherently dangerous products and services (eg tobacco, alcohol, weapons, motor vehicles and some chemicals) that companies knew were harmful to the buyers of those products.

- The use of child labour often in hazardous jobs such as the manufacture of matches, fireworks and carpets.

- Ethical problems arising out of new technologies such as genetically modified food, mobile phone radiation and health.

- Product testing ethics concerning animal rights and animal testing and the use of economically disadvantaged groups (such as students) as test objects.

- The environmental impact of end-of-life cycle products such as discarded electric equipment or scrapped cars.

Consumers have moved towards products that are considered more environmentally and ecologically friendly and where people have not been exploited in their manufacture. Hence we now see a greater range of products labelled, for example:

- Organically grown
- Not tested on animals
- The manufacturer is a carbon neutral firm
- This paper is from recycled sources
- This wood is from sustainable forests
- The chemicals contained in this product are biodegradable

This may be used by a firm as a means of differentiation, in order to increase competitive advantage.

3.2 Ethical aspects of purchasing and procurement

Many firms seek to fulfil their own CSR commitments by demanding similar commitments from their suppliers. This gives rise to **ethical procurement**.

Ethical procurement impacts in several areas:

1. The human rights of workers within supplier firms.

   Many UK firms require that suppliers sign up to the Code of Practice of the *Ethical Trading Initiative*, a charity with representation from industry, government, non-governmental and voluntary organisations. This requires firms to ensure:

   - Employment is freely chosen (ie no forced, slave or prison labour)
   - Freedom of workforce association and collective bargaining are respected
   - Working conditions are safe and hygienic
   - No child labour used
   - Living wages are paid
   - Working hours are not excessive
   - No discrimination is practised
   - Regular employment is provided
   - No harsh or inhumane treatment is allowed

2. Proper health and safety standards are maintained in operations a they may affect employees and the general public.

3. Environmental protection.

4. Having fair contracting terms and conditions with suppliers.

   This involves fair prices, adherence to reasonable payment terms and have a grievance procedure to deal with suppliers grievances.

   Note: This is an undertaking by the procuring company to its suppliers and is an element of partnership in ethical procurement.

5. Transparency in negotiations with suppliers.

This includes making timescales for contract re-tendering clear and making awards and non-renewal of contracts in good time.

6. Fraud and corruption.

7. There will be zero tolerance of the offering of gifts and inducements by suppliers and also of conflicts of interest.

Worked example: O_2 ethical procurement policy

Mobile telephone operator O_2 has the following policy:

'Ethical procurement policy

Our policy is based on the standards adopted by the UN through the Universal Declaration of Human Rights, and the ILO Conventions [International Labour Organisation]. The standards we apply are as follows:

- The law is applied
- Employment is freely chosen
- Freedom of association and the right to collective bargaining are respected
- Working conditions are safe and healthy
- Child labour is eliminated
- Living wages are paid
- Working hours are not excessive
- No discrimination is allowed
- Regular employment is provided
- No harsh or inhumane treatment is allowed

We require all suppliers to comply with our policy and we reserve the right not to do business with companies where it can be demonstrated that significant violations of the policy exist. In particular, we will not bring companies on to our supplier list where there is evidence of underage workers; forced, bonded or involuntary prison labour; or where the supplier's workers are found to be subjected to potential life threatening working conditions or harsh inhumane treatment.

Environmental procurement

Our policy supplements O_2's internal efforts to help protect and sustain the environment, and is an integral part of our ISO14001 accredited Environmental Management System. Our aim is to drive our objectives for sustainable development deeper into the supply chain, and work with our suppliers to help minimise the impact of their activities.

Suppliers will be required to:

comply with all relevant environmental legislation (including but not limited to waste, emissions, and noise), acting in a preventative way to avoid pollution, implement corrective action plans and to have programmes in place for improving environmental performance.

Telefónica will look favourably upon suppliers who:

have an up-to-date, documented, Environmental Policy including commitment to environmental protection, prevention of pollution, compliance with environmental legislation, continuous improvement and procure in line with its policy;

have a documented Environmental Management System to ensure effective planning, operation and control of environmental aspects. This Environmental Management System shall satisfy the requirements of ISO 14 001 or other internationally recognised standards;

During the period of any contract we expect suppliers to make all reasonable efforts to support initiatives or targets that O_2 may from time to time introduce where the initiatives are relevant to their area of the O_2 supply chain, eg Energy consumption reduction targets.

Examples of where we work with suppliers range from sourcing recycled paper for all of our marketing material, through to energy saving initiatives with our major network equipment suppliers.'

Source: O_2 website 2012

4 The concepts of sustainability and corporate responsibility

Section overview

*   Sustainability is about maintaining the world's resources rather than depleting or destroying them. This will ensure they support human activity now and in the future.

*   Corporate responsibility: the actions, activities and obligations of business in achieving sustainability.

*   A commonly employed and useful way of thinking about sustainability issues is under three key headings: social, environmental and economic.

In Chapter 3 we discussed the fact that although the primary stakeholders of a company are its shareholders, increasingly there is a need for an organisation to consider other stakeholders and wider areas of social responsibility.

This is enshrined in the concept of corporate governance, covered in Chapter 9.

4.1 What is sustainability and corporate responsibility?

Definitions

Sustainability: The ability to 'meet the needs of the present without compromising the ability of future generations to meet their own needs' (the Bruntland Report).

Sustainable development is the process by which we achieve sustainability.

Sustainable enterprise: A company, institution or entity that generates continuously increasing stakeholder value through the application of sustainable practices through the entire base activity – products and services, workforce, workplace, functions/processes, and management/governance. (Deloitte: *Creating the Wholly Sustainable Enterprise*)

Corporate responsibility: The actions, activities and obligations of business in achieving sustainability.

Sustainability is about maintaining the world's resources rather than depleting or destroying them. This will ensure they support human activity now and in the future.

Sustainability is not limited to the environment. Interpretations of the scope of sustainable development have developed from a narrow interpretation which focuses on 'green issues' to broader interpretations which include concerns such as:

*   Increasing extremes of poverty and wealth
*   Population growth
*   Biodiversity loss
*   Deteriorating air and water quality
*   Climate change
*   Human rights

A commonly employed and useful way of thinking about these issues is under three key headings: **social**, **environmental** and **economic** (or **financial**).

Issues	Examples
Social	Health and safety, workers' rights (in the business itself and its supply chain), pay and benefits, diversity and equal opportunities, impacts of product use, responsible marketing, data protection and privacy, community investment, and bribery/corruption
Environmental	Climate change, pollution, emissions levels, waste, use of natural resources, impacts of product use, compliance with environmental legislation, air quality
Economic	Economic stability and growth, job provision, local economic development, healthy competition, compliance with governance structures , transparency, long-term viability of businesses, investment in innovation/NPD

To achieve sustainable success, these three issues must be addressed and balanced; not just the concrete issues such as raw materials or energy use, but also less tangible ones such as relationships with wider stakeholders and employees, whose goodwill is necessary to the long-term success of the business.

Sustainable development recognises the interdependence between business, society and the environment, since without the environment neither business nor society could exist. Thus businesses, in order to deliver value to their shareholders, must respond to the needs and priorities of their stakeholders and not exhaust the world's capital.

Corporate responsibility is a strategic business issue, since by addressing their social and environmental impacts, organisations can have a positive effect on their economic performance.

An organisation can adopt different **strategic approaches** to corporate responsibility:

Proactive strategy	A business is prepared to take full responsibility for its actions. Eg A company which discovers a fault in a product and recalls the product without being forced to, before any injury or damage is caused, acts in a proactive way.
Reactive strategy	This involves allowing a situation to continue unresolved until the public, government or consumer groups find out about it.
Defence strategy	This involves minimising or attempting to avoid additional obligations arising from a particular problem.
Accommodation strategy	This approach involves taking responsibility for actions, probably when one of the following happens. • Encouragement from special interest groups • Perception that a failure to act will result in government intervention

5 Sustainable development

Section overview

- This section reviews the mechanisms by which governments, businesses and other global organisations support and promote sustainable development.

The term 'sustainable development' originally appeared in literature on development economics, often as a contrast to the 'unsustainable development' of some countries that were receiving large inward investment from multinational corporations. This was believed to be destroying the social and ecological infrastructure and hence hampering the future development of the countries.

Following the Rio 'Earth Summit' of 1992 and ensuing political support in the USA and at the World Trade Organisation the need for 'sustainable development' has, amongst political initiatives, led to a focus on firms developing appropriate strategies and thereby becoming **'sustainable enterprises'**. The focus has moved from just host developing countries to include impacts on mature home economies too.

5.1 Global initiatives to promote sustainable development

There are a wide variety of UK, European and global initiatives to foster sustainable development, including steps taken by governments, business and other organisations. Such actions are shown to take the form of eight different mechanisms:

- **Corporate policies** whereby the perceived expectations of society convince organisations of the merits of adopting policies on sustainability and publishing information about the policies and their impact.

- **Supply chain pressure** by which the expectations of society drive purchasers to promote a desired standard of sustainable performance and reporting amongst suppliers and others in the supply chain.

- **Stakeholder engagement** enabling those with a particular interest to influence the decisions and behaviour of an organisation, to engage an organisation in ongoing dialogue and a process of feedback to and from stakeholders, supported by information flows about sustainable performance.

- **Voluntary codes** through which society encourages organisations to improve particular aspects of their sustainability performance, often requiring a statement for stakeholders regarding compliance or an explanation of non-compliance.

- **Rating and benchmarking** by which investors and others, or agencies working on their behalf, grade organisations through the use of benchmarks or ratings on the basis of information on sustainability policies and performance and thus influence the behaviour of organisations and stakeholders.

- **Taxes and subsidies** to incentivise organisations to operate in ways that contribute to sustainability, requiring information in the form of tax returns and grant claims.

- **Tradable permits** whereby governments ration allocations of scarce resources or undesirable impacts so as to improve sustainability, requiring information about quota utilisation and prices to support the operation of fair markets.

5.2 Perspectives on sustainability

- An **essential consideration** for which corporations must shoulder responsibility if the Earth is to avoid global tragedy.

- A **fad** pushed by elite political groups and which is now being alighted on by consultants and academics to generate research and consultancy incomes.

- **'Greenwash'** that large corporations can use as rhetoric whilst underneath they continue to conduct their usual disruptive activities.

6 Corporate responsibility

Section overview

- Corporate responsibility can be a source of both risk and opportunity.

- This section considers the reasons why organisations might choose to demonstrate CR, and the extent to which pursuing a CR strategy is congruent with delivering value to shareholders.

- The scope of CR varies with the nature of the organisation.

- Embedding sustainability and CR within an organisation requires the formulation, implementation and control of a strategic plan and the involvement of senior management.

6.1 Why consider corporate responsibility?

Corporate responsibility is no longer just a public relations exercise but is a strategically fundamental driver for business.

CR is both a source of **risk** – the reputational damage that can be done by 'bad' behaviour – and of **opportunity** – companies that are more efficient in their use of energy, for example, will make fewer emissions but will also have lower cost bases.

Attention to **social, environmental** and **economic** aspects of business activity and performance is increasing from customers, suppliers, investors, pressure groups and the community. In a sense each group's support gives a company a licence to operate. Without the support of these stakeholders a business will find its ability to operate effectively is impaired, thus damaging its performance over the long-term.

Firms that misbehave will find fewer and fewer trading partners, consumers will stop buying their products, host nations will withdraw licences or impose fines, local communities will withdraw their support and possibly become hostile and workers will become de-motivated and unproductive. In addition, investors will stop buying their stock, and existing shareholders will sell, banks will increase their lending rates and the cost of capital will increase.

Justifications offered for management seeking to demonstrate corporate responsibility outside a business's normal operations are:

- Self-regulation by the firm or industry now is likely to be more flexible and less costly than ignoring CR and facing statutory regulation later.

- It improves relations with key external stakeholders such as regulators, government and legislators.

- Donations, sponsorship and community involvement are a useful medium of public relations and can reflect well on the business and its brands.

- Involving managers and staff in community activities develops them more fully.

- It helps create a value culture in the organisation and a sense of mission, which is good for motivation.

- In the long-term, upholding the community's values, responding constructively to criticism and contributing towards community well-being might be good for business, as it promotes the wider environment in which businesses flourish.

Tangible benefits of adopting CR include:

- Firms may achieve a lower cost base through the efficient use of resources, which would help improve competitive advantage.

- CR may provide opportunities to enter new markets or attract new ethical customers eg Innocent drinks.

- Providing new solutions to existing business problems eg food waste from Budgens supermarkets which historically went to landfill sites is now delivered to an Anaerobic Digestion plant, where it is transformed into electricity that can be used on the national grid.

- A CR policy may help protect the company's licence to operate and its reputation eg Anglo American, the global mining company is committed to minimising any negative impacts of its operations on the environment and working with local communities to ensure that they benefit from its activities. The focus on safe and responsible extraction enhances its image and helps it retain a social licence to operate.

- CR offers an opportunity to build new core competences, eg Toyota's 'Prius' was the first mass-produced electric and petrol hybrid car.

- CR may enhance a firms reputation and hence attract more finance from ethical investors eg by gaining a listing on the FTSE4Good index of companies that meet globally recognised corporate responsibility standards.

Worked example: HSBC

We aim to be the world's leading and most respected international bank. We will achieve this by focusing on the needs of our customers and the societies we serve, thereby delivering long-term sustainable value to all our stakeholders. For HSBC, sustainability is about reaching a balance of positive economic, social and environmental outcomes. We seek to make good decisions and act with integrity to ensure we can deliver our strategic priorities and create sustainable long-term value.

Source: HSBC Holdings plc Sustainability Report 2013

Interactive question 4: Being socially responsible   [Difficulty level: Easy]

What are the implications in the

(a)   Short term
(b)   Long term

of a company acting in a socially responsible manner?

See **Answer** at the end of this chapter.

6.2   Scope of corporate responsibility

The scope of CR varies from business to business. Factors frequently included are:

- **Health and safety**: This includes workplace injury, customer and supplier injury and harm to third parties

- **Environmental protection**: Energy use, emissions (notably carbon dioxide), water use and pollution, impact of product on environment, recycling of materials and heat

- **Staff welfare**: Issues such as stress at work, personal development, achieving work/life balances through flexibility, equal opportunities for disadvantaged or minority groups

- **Customer welfare**: Through content and description of products, non-exclusion of customer groups, fair dealing and treatment

- **Supply-chain management**: Insisting that providers of bought-in supplies also have appropriate CR policies, ethical trading, elimination of pollution and un-recycled packaging, eliminating exploitative labour practices amongst contractors

- **Ethical conduct:** Staff codes for interpersonal behaviour, prohibitions on uses of data and IT, management forbidden from offering bribes to win contracts, ensuring non-exploitation of staff

- **Engagement with social causes:** This includes secondment of management and staff, charitable donations, provision of free products to the needy, involvement in the local community, support for outreach projects such as cultural improvement or education

Successful CR programmes focus on issues of most strategic **relevance** to an organisation which offer an opportunity to meet both shareholder and wider stakeholder expectations. Examples include:

- A service organisation might focus on a staff welfare programme to encourage retention

- A supermarket could stock ethically sourced food, and attract new customers as a result

- A software company might introduce a new programme designed for the elderly to tackle digital exclusion and create an additional revenue stream in the process

- A bank may allocate funds to invest in technology to combat climate change

Interactive question 5: Skin Care Company [Difficulty level: Exam standard]

You have recently accepted a position as a Chartered Accountant working for the Skin Care Company.

The Skin Care Company (SCC) specialises in making beauty products, predominantly for women. All products are made at the company's UK factory and are sold around the world. The company's founder was keen to introduce a range of ethically produced beauty products made from sustainable ingredients. The founder's vision was to source ingredients from farmers and growers in some of the world's most impoverished regions through establishing long term relationships with suppliers. As a result, SCC pays its growers higher prices for ingredients than competing beauty care companies. SCC's ethical stance helps the company command premium prices for its products and it remains well known among 'ethically minded' customers.

In the years since the founder's retirement, demand for SCC's products has continued to increase and the company has recently finalised plans to list on the London Stock Exchange. One week before the official listing you are accidentally copied in on an email from the company's MD to the Head of Production.

The e-mail reveals that one of the ingredients used in one of SCC's most popular skin care products has been found to contain a toxin which can cause nasty rashes on certain skin types. Although not illegal to use the ingredient in such products, several neighbouring countries have recently commenced an investigation into its safety. The UK government has yet to announce plans to conduct its own investigation.

The MD suggests in the email that because only he and the Head of Production are aware of the exact recipe for the product, they should not reveal this potential problem to the rest of the directors for fear of lowering the company's share price when it floats on the exchange the following week.

Describe the ethical and CSR related issues that should be considered upon discovery of the contents of this e-mail and suggest any appropriate actions that should be taken.

See **Answer** at the end of this chapter.

6.2.1 Achieving corporate responsibility

The management of the business must put CR at the centre of its activities by:

1. Identifying the sustainability corporate responsibility issues that are relevant to the organisation.

2. Developing an organisational strategy to embed corporate responsibility into the organisation's corporate policies.

As with all strategic management this involves the formulation, implementation and control of a strategic plan and the involvement of senior management.

The www.sustainabilityatwork.org.uk website sets out the key factors required for an organisation to **embed sustainability in its day-to-day operations:**

1. Board and senior management commitment

2. Understanding and analysing the key sustainability drivers for the organisation

3. Integrating the key sustainability drivers into the organisation's strategy

4. Ensuring that sustainability is the responsibility of everyone in the organisation

5. Breaking-down sustainability targets and objectives for the organisation as a whole into targets and objectives which are meaningful for individual subsidiaries, divisions and departments

6. Processes that enable sustainability issues to be taken into account clearly and consistently in day-to-day decision-making

7. Extensive and effective sustainability training

8. Including sustainability targets and objectives in performance appraisal

9. Champions to promote sustainability and celebrate success

10. Monitoring and reporting sustainability performance

Later in the chapter we look at how to ensure that organisations and their stakeholders have the information available to support the mechanisms that will enhance sustainability.

6.3 Sustainable development and CR in practice

The following extracts are taken from the sustainability section of the Thames Water Corporate Responsibility report 2012/13. They illustrate the link between sustainability and corporate responsibility.

'To deliver a service fit for future generations, we need to strike a balance between the level of service we provide to our customers, our impact on the environment and communities, the level of customer bills and future investment in the business.

Respecting the world we live in

Our business revolves around a precious natural resource, essential to all life. Whilst we are a regulated monopoly, we will ensure that our activities make a positive contribution to our customers and influence the future for our industry to deliver a sustainable future. We will remain flexible and adaptable to deliver essential services in what is an uncertain future, balancing environmental, social and economic needs'.

Thames Water sets out six areas with accompanying objectives it regards as being important in achieving sustainability in its operations, these focus on:

- Local community
- Employees
- Customers
- The environment
- Contractors and the supply chain
- Shareholders

Thames Water's website notes that during 2012/13 period the company maintained its platinum ranking in the Business in the Community Corporate Responsibility Index. The index provides insight into how big companies are driving responsible business practice.

Our approach to sustainability

Being truly sustainable and leading the sector on sustainability means doing the right thing for people, for the planet and for our own performance, both now and into the future. We need to make sure that what we do today is right for tomorrow and that we don't disadvantage future generations or store up problems for the future in the process.

We have continued to develop our approach to sustainability and look at how we can better embed sustainability into how we do business.

In 2009/10, we reviewed the sustainability and climate change commitments and practice of all of the contractors bidding to manage the engineering projects that make up our capital programme for 2010 –15.'

7 Monitoring and measuring sustainability

Section overview

- A sustainable development strategy needs to be implemented and regularly monitored.

- Monitoring involves measuring progress in terms of both processes and outcomes.

- The GRI reporting framework is a global, voluntary code for corporate responsibility and sustainability reporting. It provides a generally accepted framework that organisations can use to measure and report their economic, environmental, and social performance.

- A key principle is that strategically important financial and sustainability performance information should be reported in a way that demonstrates the strong interdependence between the two.

7.1 Monitoring process

It is not enough for an organisation to develop a sustainable development strategy. Delivery of the strategy needs to be implemented and regularly monitored:

As with any strategy the implementation and monitoring process involves:

- Identifying the key sustainability issues for the business and the factors that drive them – the social, environmental and economic framework discussed earlier can be used.

- Sustainability issues are not static. Changes to the activities and operations of the organisation may give rise to new issues, so one aspect of monitoring involves giving consideration to any new developments.

- Set targets and standards for sustainability objectives. The standards might originate from government guidance and policy, legislation, public commitments or commonly accepted industry or sector standards.

- Monitor progress towards sustainability objectives in terms of both processes and outcomes.

   Process – is the organisation doing the things that it said that it would to implement sustainability initiatives?

   Outcome – having implemented initiatives is the organisation achieving the outcomes towards which it is striving?

- Report progress and evaluate the implications for future decision making and performance (feedback).

An organisation will need to develop its management information systems to meet the requirements of sustainable development monitoring, reporting and evaluation. This may involve making better use of existing financial and non-financial information.

7.2 Reporting requirements

Effective reporting involves ensuring that the organisation is transparent in communicating with internal and external stakeholders.

In the public sector there are a number of organisations that have a role in evaluating the outcomes of sustainability initiatives. These include independent advisory bodies, notably the Sustainable Development Commission, and auditing committees and bodies such as the National Audit Office and the Audit Commission. The Sustainable Development Commission produces a detailed annual appraisal of the UK Government's performance against its own sustainability targets.

In the private sector, reporting of social and environmental impacts is not mandatory. In the case of quoted companies, directors are required to report on environmental matters, the company's employees and social/community issues. Many companies now produce Sustainability or Corporate Responsibility reports, recognising a need to engage key stakeholders on particular issues of public interest.

7.3 Performance measurement

7.3.1 Global Reporting Initiative

The Global Reporting Initiative (GRI) is the world standard setter in sustainability reporting, agreed through a multi-stakeholder approach. The reporting guidelines issued by the GRI are the best known example of a global, voluntary code for corporate responsibility and sustainability reporting.

The GRI reporting framework is intended to provide a generally accepted framework that organizations can use to measure and report their economic, environmental, and social performance.

Economic: concerns the organization's impacts on the economic conditions of its stakeholders and on economic systems at local, national, and global levels.

Economic Indicators illustrate:

- The flow of capital among different stakeholders; and
- The main economic impacts of the organization throughout society.

Environmental: concerns an organization's impacts on living and non-living natural systems, including ecosystems, land, air, and water.

Environmental Indicators cover performance related to inputs (eg material, energy, water) and outputs (eg emissions, effluents, waste). In addition, they cover performance related to biodiversity, environmental compliance, and other relevant information such as environmental expenditure and the impacts of products and services.

Social: concerns the impacts an organization has on the social systems within which it operates.

Social Indicators identify key performance aspects surrounding labour practices, human rights, society, and product responsibility.

- Labour practices Indicators look at employment; labour/management relations; Occupational health and safety; training and education; and diversity and Equal Opportunity.

- Human Rights performance Indicators require organisations to report on the extent to which human rights are considered in investment and supplier/contractor selection practices. Additionally, the Indicators cover training on human rights as well as non-discrimination, freedom of association, child labour, indigenous rights, and forced and compulsory labour.

- Society performance Indicators focus attention on the impact organisations have on the communities in which they operate, and disclosing how the risks that may arise from interactions with other social institutions are managed and mediated. In particular, information is sought on the risks associated with bribery and corruption, undue influence in public policy-making, and monopoly practices.

- Product responsibility performance Indicators address the aspects of a reporting organisation's products and services that directly affect customers, namely, health and safety, information and labelling, marketing, and privacy.

Examples of GRI core performance indicators include:

Economic	Environmental	Social
Revenues and costs	Materials used	Employee turnover and absenteeism
Wages, pensions, other employee benefits	Energy consumption	Diversity of workforce, incidents of discrimination
Retained earnings and payments to providers of capital	Water use	Employee health and safety
Taxes paid, subsidies and grants received	Greenhouse gas emissions	Child labour
Geographic analysis of key markets	Effluents and waste produced	Training undertaken
Return on capital employed	Significant spillages	Bribery and corruption
	Fines and penalties	Community relations
	Impact of activities on biodiversity	Complaints re breaches of customer privacy
		Standard of Product labelling

(Source: GRI 2006)

Worked example: GRI G4

In 2013 the Global Reporting Initiative revised existing GRI guidelines. Objectives of the 'GRI G4' guidelines include:

- Being user-friendly for beginner and experienced reporters
- Aligning with other international reporting references (frameworks)
- Leading to reports that cover material topics
- Offering guidance on how to link sustainability and integrated reporting

Guidance issued by the GRI makes it clear that 'GRI G4' is not about all possible sustainability related topics that an organisation could monitor, but is focused on the material ones. The updated G4 guidelines have resulted in the introduction and revision to some of the disclosure requirements that companies are expected to make, including standard disclosures concerning supply chain operations, governance issues, ethics and integrity, anti-corruption and emissions and energy.

The GRI requires all participating organisations with sustainability reports published after 31st December 2015 to be produced in accordance with the new G4 guidelines.

(Source: GRI 2013)

7.3.2   Accounting for Sustainability

The **Accounting for Sustainability** project was established by the Prince of Wales in June 2006 to provide organisations with the methodology and tools to enable them to embed sustainability into day-to-day processes and to report more effectively on their sustainability performance.

Through a wide consultation process including large public companies, investors, NGOs, accounting standard setters, accountancy institutes and accounting firms, a **'Connected Reporting Framework'** was developed for use both within an organisation and externally.

The key principle behind the framework is that strategically important financial and sustainability performance information should be reported in a way that demonstrates the strong interdependence between the two.

The Connected Reporting Framework has the following five key elements:

1. An explanation of how sustainability is connected to the overall operational strategy of an organisation and the provision of sustainability targets. The challenge is to ensure that in mainstream reporting the sustainability information included is strategically important. Targets are important to ensure and demonstrate that sustainability issues are taken into account when making investment decisions.

2. Five key environmental indicators, which all organisations should consider reporting are: greenhouse gas emissions, energy usage, water use, waste and significant use of other finite resources.

3. Other key sustainability information should be given where the business or operation has material impacts.

4. To aid performance appraisal, industry benchmarks for the key performance indicators should be reported when available.

5. An explanation of the up-stream and down-stream impact of the organisation's products and services: the sustainability impacts of its suppliers and the use of its products or services by customers and consumers.

In the private sector, the Connected Reporting Framework is being used, among others, by Aviva, BT, EDF Energy and HSBC.

Source: www.accountingforsustainability.org

Worked example: Marks and Spencer

In January 2007 Marks and Spencer launched 'Plan A', setting out 100 commitments on the most important social, environmental and ethical challenges facing its business, requiring an investment of £200m over five years. This has since been extended to 180 commitments to achieve by 2015, with the ultimate goal of becoming the world's most sustainable major retailer.

Marks and Spencer state that 'Through Plan A we are working with our customers and our suppliers to combat climate change, reduce waste, use sustainable raw materials, trade ethically, and help our customers to lead healthier lifestyles.'

During 2009, Plan A became cost positive whilst also succeeding in reducing carbon emissions by 18%, food packaging by 12%, food carrier bag usage by 83% and improving the efficiency of delivery fleets by 20%. M&S also worked with suppliers to open four eco and three ethical model factories.

In their 2012 'How we do business' report Marks and Spencer set out in detail its progress in the key areas identified in Plan A: Involving all customers in Plan A; Making Plan A how we do business; Climate change, Waste and recycling, Sustainable raw materials, being a Fair partner to everyone connected with the business and helping people choose a healthier lifestyle.

In 2013 it was reported that Plan A had generated savings in its operations of £135m on the previous year.

The company reports that, of the 180 commitments, 139 have been achieved.

Source: www.plana.marksandspencer.com

Interactive question 6: Ashdene Homes
[Difficulty level: Exam standard]

Ashdene Homes is a regional house builder, having considerable knowledge and experience in the South of England where the current UK housing shortage is centred. The company caters for the mid to lower end of the market, with prices normally below £500,000, on relatively small and individual sites which tend to be too large for the resources of local builders but too small for the high volume national house builders. Any mass release of land for development in the South East due to government initiatives is likely to be centred in one area. The development of any such land would take many years given delays within the planning process.

The company, worth £67 million has looked like a takeover target for a while but unfortunately, the company's reputation for internal control has been damaged somewhat by a qualified audit statement last year (over issues of compliance with financial standards) and an unfortunate internal incident which concerned an employee expressing concern about the compliance of one of the company's products with an international standard on fire safety. She raised the issue with her immediate manager but when she failed to obtain a response, she decided to report the lack of compliance to the press. This significantly embarrassed the company and led to a substantial deterioration in their reputation, especially as there have been more press releases about the company's failure to adhere to the high welfare, health and safety, financial, marketing and ethical standards that the founder practised when he started Ashdene Homes.

Requirements

(a) Outline the implications of poor ethical standards and damaged reputation on the relationship between the affected stakeholder groups and Ashdene Homes. **(5 marks)**

(b) What are the main issues concerned with corporate responsibility and why might Ashdene Homes choose to act, or at least claim to act, in a socially responsive way? **(10 marks)**

(c) Explain, with reference to Ashdene Homes as appropriate, the ethical responsibilities of an accountant both as an employee and as a professional. **(10 marks)**

(25 marks)

8 Developing an approach to ethics requirements of the exam

Section overview

- The intention of this section is to demonstrate the thought processes to be adopted when tackling a question involving ethics and the attributes of an answer that will score well in the exam.

- You will find further examples of requirements covering ethical issues in the past exam papers contained in the Business Strategy Question Bank.

8.1 What will the ethics requirement involve?

Between 5% and 10% of marks in the Business Strategy paper will be allocated to the appropriate discussion of ethical issues, possibly in the context of the ethics of an organisation or an individual working in business who may be a professional accountant.

Scenarios might include topics such as:

- The impact of ethics on strategies and strategic choice
- Conflicts of interest among stakeholders
- Attempts to intentionally mislead key stakeholders (by disclosure or non-disclosure of information)
- Doubtful accounting or commercial business practice
- Facilitation of unethical strategies
- Inappropriate pressure to achieve a result
- Conflict between the accountant's professional obligations and responsibilities to the organisation
- Lack of professional independence eg personal financial interest in business proposals
- Actions contrary to law, regulation and/or technical and professional standards

Such issues are often not clear-cut and it is important that you can develop a balanced argument, use appropriate ethical language and have regard to any relevant professional principles.

8.2 Recommended approach

The following is a suggestion for the approach to adopt when tackling questions involving ethical issues:

1. Do I have all the facts and/or information? For instance, if the information is from a newspaper report, is it credible?

2. Is there a legal issue (criminal or civil law)? For instance, are the persons in question directors who owe statutory duties to their companies?

3. Do any other codes or professional principles apply? For instance, is the individual with the ethical dilemma a professional accountant, or is the organisation with an ethical issue subject to its industry's particular code of conduct?

4. Which stakeholders does the decision/action impact?

5. If appropriate, consider implications in terms of :

    - Transparency?
    - Effect?
    - Fairness?

6. If this action/decision is NOT taken, what are the issues?

7. Are there any sustainability, corporate governance or corporate responsibility issues?

These steps will be illustrated using the worked example that follows.

Key weaknesses in answering ethical questions have been:

1. Failure to identify the ethical issue (eg transparency or fairness)

2. Failure to use ethical language

3.   Answering simply by asserting an opinion rather than applying balanced reasoning using ethical principles

4.   Failure to identify appropriate safeguards

5.   Application of professional accountants' ethical codes to individuals in the scenario who are not accountants

6.   Failure to distinguish between the ethical responsibilities of the individual and those of the organisation

It is important to note that not all ethical questions will necessarily draw upon transparency, effect and fairness. In order to produce a good answer when attempting an ethical question it is critical that you adopt a structured approach. In some cases, instead of considering transparency, effect and fairness, it may be worth considering ethics at a personal, business and corporate responsibility level. This technique, used in Interactive question 5, was appropriate in the June 2013 question 'Hire Value' which dealt with the personal use of the company's assets by directors.

Worked example: Pharmaceutical dilemma

Pharma Co is a highly successful global pharmaceutical company. Pharma's board has recently received advance warning of the likely results of a recent study which is not due to be completed for another 12 months. The study is being conducted by Pharma as part of on-going product testing for its drugs that are already available in the market place. Although the study is only 30% complete, the initial indications are that one of Pharma's leading drugs, which significantly improves the quality of life for sufferers of a long-term chronic illness, may cause harmful side-effects if taken at the same time as a newly available over-the-counter medicine that can be self-prescribed for pain relief. The board, mindful of the company's social responsibilities and the potential for bad publicity, is currently discussing what action to take in response to this discovery but is concerned about the harmful impact of any premature announcement on its share price.

Requirement

Discuss the ethical implications of this situation for Pharma and any potential for stakeholder conflict that arises as a result.

Solution

The following solution uses the questions in the recommended approach as a prompt to generate a balanced answer:

Ethical implications

1.   *Do we have all the facts and/or information?*

     The study is only 30% complete, so the possibility that in the end the situation may be better than it appears currently should be considered. It is also sensible to double check that correct information gathering procedures are being implemented in the study, and that the preliminary conclusion has been soundly arrived at.

2.   *Is there a legal issue (criminal or civil law)?*

     There is likely to be considerable UK and international legislation governing the pharmaceutical industry and the safety of drugs and medicines. This may dictate the responsibilities of Pharma's directors in relation to transparency and communication of any possible safety issues and the timing of any announcements.

3.   *Do any other codes or professional principles apply?*

     The pharmaceutical industry will almost certainly have its own code of conduct and guidelines to ensure members behave in an ethical and professional manner. As a highly successful player, Pharma is likely to have a high profile in the industry and will be expected to set high standards of responsible behaviour. Most drugs on the market carry warnings of possible side-effects. A key issue here is the timing of any announcement and the point at which the legislation and/or any professional code of conduct specifies that an announcement and warning of possible side-effects is necessary.

4. *Which stakeholders does the decision/action impact?*

Pharmaceutical companies are commercial organisations and it is reasonable to assume Pharma's long term objective is to maximise shareholder wealth. If the board announces the research findings and they subsequently prove to be unfounded, then Pharma's share price and shareholders are likely to have suffered unnecessarily. Also sufferers of the chronic illness who stop taking the drug immediately may have a lower quality of life as a result. However were the board not to announce preliminary findings and the tests went on to be conclusive, patients taking the drug may experience adverse side-effects in the meantime.

The issue here involves balancing the interests of the shareholders with Pharma's wider corporate responsibility to its other stakeholders and society.

A useful way to analyse the situation is to use the three tests from the Institute of Business Ethics:

5. Here it is appropriate to consider *the implications in terms of transparency, effect and fairness*

Transparency – would Pharma mind if it subsequently came to light that the company was aware of the potential safety issues but had chosen not to disclose their concerns until the results were conclusive?

The issue here would be whether a reasonable person would have expected disclosure of the results. Pharma may have grounds for believing that the initial results will not prove representative, given that the study is only 30% complete. If however it is likely that the final results will confirm the initial findings then Pharma would probably not want the fact that it was aware of the problem earlier but took no action ever to come to light.

Effect – whom does the decision affect/hurt?

The possible side-effects may affect a significant number of people if the new over-the-counter remedy is widely used. Any side-effects would also have financial consequences for Pharma in terms of compensation payments and legal costs, as well as reputational consequences – lost customers, knock on effect on image and possible withdrawal of any licence to produce the drug.

Fairness – would the decision be considered fair by those affected?

This partly depends on whether any action taken by the board is seen as a justifiable business decision, which might take into account cost/benefit analysis, risk assessment and normal practice within the industry. Potential drug users may feel it is fairer to be given the information and then be allowed to decide on an individual basis whether they are prepared to risk taking the drug in view of the benefits it confers.

6. *If this action/decision is NOT taken, what are the issues?*

Presumably the worst case scenario is that the warning will be proved correct and Pharma will be forced to make an announcement in 12 months' time regarding possible side-effects (or possibly even to withdraw the drug completely). Alternatively concerns may prove to be completely unfounded or the outcome may lie somewhere in between these two extremes, suggesting there is some cause for concern but perhaps one that can be dealt with regarding a side-effects warning rather than withdrawal of the product.

7. *Are there any sustainability, corporate governance or corporate responsibility issues?*

The sustainability of Pharma's reputation and its long term profitability could be significantly affected if it comes to light that the drug is harmful and that Pharma's board were aware of this in advance but delayed giving warnings.

Stakeholder conflict

Stakeholders are groups of people who are interested in what Pharma does. In the case of Pharma's approach to the safety of its products this would include internal stakeholders (employees, management), connected stakeholders (shareholders, customers) and external stakeholders (government/regulatory bodies).

Here the issue highlights the potential for conflict within and between various stakeholder groups.

Shareholders want profitability so some may prefer Pharma to limit the damage and keep the information confidential until it is forced by legislation and/or regulation to announce it. Users of the drug and regulatory bodies may value safety more highly however and prefer to be in possession of the relevant information in order to make an informed choice.

Conclusion

Which stakeholders' interests determine Pharma's actions will depend to an extent on their relative power. Clearly Pharma's primary focus is to maximise shareholder wealth. However the users of the drugs are very important to success and may choose to stop buying the product or look to other companies if they think their safety is being compromised. Also shareholders may acknowledge that going beyond the basic requirements and demonstrating a responsibility to wider society will enhance Pharma's reputation and ensure government and public support, giving it a competitive advantage and higher profits in the long term.

Summary

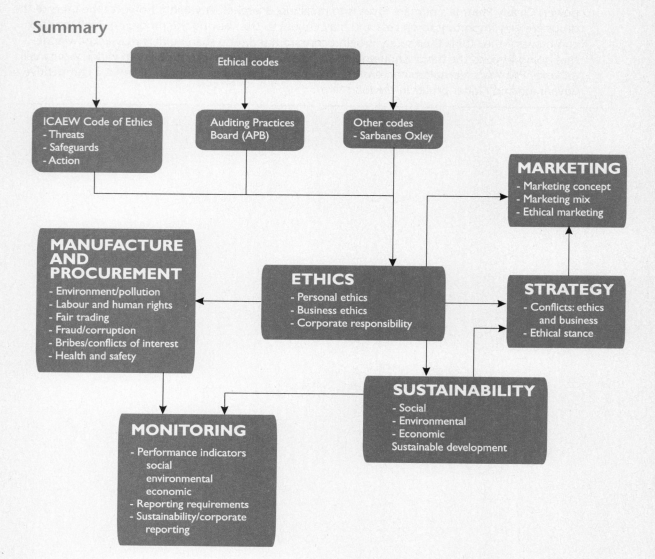

ETHICS
- 5-10% marks for discussion of ethical issues
- Often not clear - develop balanced argument

APPROACH
1. Legal (criminal or civil) issue?
2. Any other appropriate codes/professional principles?
3. Whom does decision/action impact?
4. Implications - transparency; effect; fairness
5. Issues if decision/action NOT taken
6. Sustainability issues

AVOID COMMON MISTAKES
- Properly identify ethical issue
- Use ethical language
- Apply balanced reason (not opinion)
- Identify appropriate safeguards
- Do not apply professional accountants' ethical codes to non-accountants
- Distinguish between ethical responsibilities of individual and organisation

Self-test

Answer the following questions.

1 Explain the three levels at which ethics can exist.

2 Give some examples of threats to self-interest that might arise for a professional accountant in business.

3 What are the sources of possible safeguards for a professional accountant working in business?

4 What action should a professional accountant take if threats cannot be reduced and safeguards have been exhausted?

5 What areas of a supplier contract may be affected by an organisation's ethical procurement policy?

6 What is meant by a sustainable enterprise?

7 Explain how questions of sustainability tie in with the short/long term debate?

8 What three areas of performance should be measured according to the Global Reporting Initiative?

9 Read the scenario of the **June 2010 Business Strategy** paper in the Question Bank entitled *Executive Travel Ltd*. Draft an answer for requirement (d) on the ethical issues.

10 Read the scenario of the **June 2010 Business Strategy** paper in the Question Bank entitled *Hutton Haulage plc*. Draft an answer for requirement (b)(ii) on enhancing environmental sustainability.

11 Go online at The Times 100 Business Case Studies and read the Tata Steel case study 'Business ethics and sustainability in the steel industry' at: http://businesscasestudies.co.uk/tata-steel/business-ethics-and-sustainability-in-the-steel-industry

Now go back to the Learning objectives in the Introduction. If you are satisfied you have achieved these objectives, please tick them off.

Answer to Interactive question 1

The ICAEW website explains the need for ethical standards as follows.

The work of the accountancy profession is crucial to the effective working of the capital markets (that is the mechanism for the provision of finance to business and the protection of those who supply it). Put very simply, investors may lose financially if their investment decisions are based on inadequate information and this would deter further investment. A loss of confidence in financial reporting could therefore undermine the economy.

Working to the highest standards of ethics and professionalism allows the public, investors and regulators to have confidence in the profession. Your ethical behaviour can protect not only your own reputation but that of the profession as a whole. We have a collective responsibility to apply principles, such as integrity and objectivity, that will enable high quality financial reporting, and effective financial management and business practices; to protect investors, businesses and the wider public interest.

Answer to Interactive question 2

Threat	Safeguards
Russell Ltd	
This involves a **self-interest threat** as the consultants' acceptance of the invitation to enjoy the lavish hospitality on offer increases the danger that the consulting team may be reluctant to raise any contentious matters as part of the cost cutting review.	Gifts and hospitality should not be accepted unless the value is trivial and inconsequential.
There is also a **familiarity threat** because involvement in social events with the client is likely to increase the consulting team's familiarity with client staff which may impair their ability to give impartial advice.	In this case it would be appropriate to decline the weekend away, so as not to impair the consulting firm's independence.
Ravencroft White plc	
This involves a familiarity threat because Mr Bootle has been the engagement partner for eleven years and his long association with the client could mean that he does not question judgements made by the client and does not exercise sufficient professional scepticism.	Mr Bootle should be rotated off the audit and another partner assigned to the client. Given that Ravencroft White is a public listed entity, the engagement partner should serve ideally for no more than five years before being rotated off.
	The five year term for a listed client engagement partner may be extended for an additional period of up to two years if the client's audit committee considers that this extension is necessary to safeguard the quality of the audit.

Threat	Safeguards

Sole Records Ltd

Given that the consultant's son works for Sole Records largest competitor there is a danger that a **confidentiality threat** could arise. Mr Minus may be tempted to pass on confidential information about Sole Records' operations to his son.

Mr Minus should be removed from the consulting team and replaced by an independent consultant.

An **intimidation threat** could also exist if the son tries to pressure his father into providing Sole Records with poor consulting advice in order to give his own employer a competitive advantage.

If it is felt that David does not have any influence over his father's work at Sole Records then it may be appropriate for Mr Minus to remain as the principal consultant. This illustrates the need for discretion and tact when assessing ethical issues as a perceived threat may not actually represent a threat at all.

It should however be noted that Mr. Minus's son has only taken up a very junior position with the competitor so in reality his degree of influence over his fathers work is likely to be insignificant.

Mr Minus may wish to disclose his connection with the competitor to avoid any perceived conflict of interest in his dealings with Sole Records Ltd.

Answer to Interactive question 3

Memorandum

To   Senior Partner
From   Accountant
Date   Today
Subject Marketing and responsibility issues

I shall outline the broader perspectives of marketing to food consumers and food manufacturers and consider the implications of these issues.

(a) **Benefits to business organisations, consumers and society**

Marketing touches everyone's life. It is the means by which a standard of living is developed and delivered to people and is a human activity directed at satisfying needs and wants through exchange processes. Marketing oriented companies combine many activities – marketing research, product development, distribution, pricing, advertising, personal selling and others – designed to sense, serve and satisfy consumer needs whilst meeting the organisation's goals. The core concepts of marketing are needs, wants, demands, products, exchange, transactions and markets that will benefit the individual, consumers and society at large, organisations and national and international governments. Marketers must be able to manage the level, timing and composition of demand from these different beneficiaries to satisfy their needs and wants. For instance, McDonald's have adopted the broader marketing concept on a global scale through understanding and responding to the changing needs of their customers.

Modern marketing is guided by a number of converging philosophies. The production concept holds that the consumer favours products which are available at low cost and that marketing's task is to improve production efficiency and bring down prices. The marketing concept holds that a company should research the needs and wants of a well defined target market and deliver the desired satisfactions, which is accompanied by long-run societal well being. In marketing-led organisations the entire workforce share the belief that the customer is all important and that building lasting relationships is key to customer retention. A company's sales are derived from satisfying existing customers and attracting new customers. This approach benefits the livelihoods of the employees and suppliers and their staff. Successfully adopting a marketing approach improves customer retention and minimises additional costs. A satisfied customer buys more, stays loyal longer, talks favourably to others, pays less attention to competing brands and is less price sensitive. These benefits are transferred into gains for consumers and ultimately society at large as success breeds success. McDonald's divert much of their energies to ensuring that customers repeatedly return to them satisfied and content with their offering.

(b) **Responsibilities of the modern marketer**

Marketing is seen as a social force which not only conveys a standard of living but also serves as a force that reflects and influences cultural values and norms. The boundaries of marketing extend beyond economic considerations. Marketing concepts and techniques are used to promote the welfare of society as a whole instead of the traditional approach of providing products that satisfy consumers' needs efficiently and profitably. They could encompass reduction in poverty, improved education and improved healthcare. For instance, marketing tools are used in promoting healthier lifestyles through better diets, encouraging leisure activities and pursuits and social behaviour. Social marketing suggests that a more ethical and moral orientation be incorporated into companies' marketing strategies: marketers should consider and incorporate the wider social implications of their products and services, such as natural conservation or labour exploitation in emerging countries.

Social marketing does not imply a replacement of the traditional marketing concept but it is an extension so as to recognise and encompass the wider needs of society at large. The criticisms of marketing generally focus on ethical issues and the extent to which marketing is responsible for a variety of social and environmental problems. Whatever the reasons, voluntarily or otherwise, marketers have to consider ecological, environmental and consumer welfare issues together with their wider social role more frequently in their marketing plans and activities.

Effective and aware marketers have responded to these developments in a number of ways, for instance, by producing recyclable products and packaging, reducing pollution generated by toxic products or from contamination and protecting consumers against harmful or hazardous products by modifying them or withdrawing them from sale.

Answer to Interactive question 4

(a) **Short term**

- Additional costs – using greener fuels, buying fairly traded products, rebuilding green areas, paying higher salaries

- Reduced income – no sales to unethical purchasers

- Distribution of wealth to non-shareholders – giving to charity

- Distorts focus – one more target for managers

(b) **Long term**

- Avoids legislative imperative – will otherwise fall to Government to enforce and measures may be more Draconian

- May avoid financial penalties where behaviour is covered by legislation

- Improves PR

- Attracts ethical investors

- Attracts ethical consumers

- Improves staff morale

Answer to Interactive question 5

Ethical issues

Personal ethical issues

(i) As an ICAEW chartered accountant you have a responsibility to follow the ethical code of ICAEW.

(ii) Just because a product contains an ingredient which is not illegal for use at the current time does not mean that it is ethical for consumers to use it if concerns over the products safety come to light. The fact that you became aware of the issue with the ingredient via an email which discusses non-disclosure to the other directors supports the need to act.

(iii) The first thing you should do is discuss the matter with your manager in the Finance Department, and then contact the ICAEW ethical department for advice.

Directors' ethical responsibilities

(i) The fact that both the MD and Head of Production are aware of the potential problem is a governance issue, and the fact that they are keeping it secret from the remainder of the board is a breach of their duties to the company as a whole and potential shareholders who may invest in SSC when the company floats.

(ii) The MD and Head of Production have not however, done anything that appears to be illegal. There is a difference between breaches of legislation and activities that appear to be unethical.

Corporate ethical responsibilities:

The Skin Care Company has a responsibility towards its customers and their wellbeing. Many corporate entities do have a code of ethics which covers all stakeholders, given SSC's historic approach to business it is highly likely that the company does have a code of ethics. Although the other directors are unaware of the issues relating to the ingredients in the product, it could be argued that this is due to poor internal controls, which should identify issues of this nature. The responsibility for maintaining a system of internal controls lies with the board as a whole, and so they could be collectively responsible for the failings to identify any health related concerns.

Answer to Interactive question 6

(a) When more than one stakeholder group has reason to question the otherwise good reputation of an organisation, the effect can be a downward spiral leading to a general lack of confidence which, in turn, can have unfortunate financial effects. In particular, however, poor ethical standards are likely to affect one or more of the organisation's interactions with:

- **Customers** – Customers will expect certain standards of health and safety and ethical behaviour from Ashdene Homes, especially regarding its treatment of employees. The recent damage to their reputation may reduce confidence among customers leading to reduced sales – with a subsequent impact on corporate profits.

- **Shareholders** – Investor confidence is important in public companies and any reputation risk is likely to be reflected in market value. Shareholders may invest in buying shares, or their wealth, tied up in pension funds, may be invested for them by investment firms. The growth in ethical funds management where investment firms guarantee their customers not to invest in ethically-unsound organisations has led to company directors addressing the issue in earnest rather than giving it cursory attention.

- **Senior management** – Poor ethical behaviour from them creates a poor perception of the organisation in the market. However, poor ethical behaviour from those below can also have a negative impact on such executives and make them wish to disassociate themselves from a failing enterprise; the loss of key talent may be sorely felt by those who remain.

- **Employees** – Although not directly affected, poor ethical standards may leave the employee feeling that they no longer have a worthy association with the firm, which may cause them to leave or be de-motivated as a result. Also, if the organisation exhibits poor ethical standards, employees may feel that they either can or even should follow suit, and a general decline in standards will follow.

- **Suppliers** – Also not greatly affected, but it may be the case that suppliers decide not to deal with Ashdene Homes because they feel that the poor ethical standards will in some way implicate themselves.

(b) Corporate responsibility (CR) is concerned with companies acting in a socially responsible and sustainable manner. It generally refers to business decision-making linked to ethical values, compliance with legal requirements, and respect for people, communities and the environment.

There is a growing view that the best-managed companies are those that are aware of their wider responsibilities to the social community and to the environment. In order to ensure that a company honours those responsibilities and protects its reputation, it is necessary to embed these core values into the policies, practices and programmes of the company's systems and decision-making processes.

The CR issues that affect companies vary according to the nature of the company but there are five broad areas where CR might be relevant:

- To treat employees fairly and with respect
- To operate in an ethical way and with integrity
- To respect human rights
- To sustain the environment for future generations
- To be a responsible neighbour in the community

There are several reasons why Ashdene Homes might choose to act in a socially responsible way:

- They might want to act voluntarily in order to avoid legislation. For example, to avoid excessive pollution of the environment in their methods of working and by buying materials locally to reduce transport use and avoid allegations of their suppliers adding to deforestation.

- They might want to act in an ethical and socially responsible way by making the houses eco-friendly, reducing carbon emissions, having rigorous health and safety checks on their building sites and incorporating recycled materials where possible into the buildings.

- They might want to respond to pressure from shareholders. Some institutional shareholders have a policy of investing only in socially responsible and ethical companies.

- To protect their reputation.

The risk to the company's reputation from adverse publicity about social and environmental factors is always difficult to assess. Ashdene Homes will be aware that adverse publicity can have a damaging effect on customer goodwill – and sales and profits. Management might need to consider CR as a strategic issue when evaluating their strategic options.

(c) **Ethical responsibilities of a professional accountant**

A professional accountant has two 'directions' of responsibility: one to his or her employer and another to the highest standards of professionalism.

Companies provide a Code of Ethics that all employees are expected to follow to maintain a culture of corporate ethics. Issues to be included in such a Code of Ethics are:

- Avoiding conflicts of interest

- Compliance with laws and regulations

- Rules about disclosure or avoidance of opportunities for personal gain through use of company property or their position in the company

- Confidentiality – extending to absolute discretion of all sensitive matters both during and after the period of employment

- Fair dealing with customers, suppliers, employees and competitors

- Encouragement to report illegal and unethical behaviour

The responsibilities also include the expectation that the accountant will act in shareholders' interests as far as possible and that he or she will show loyalty within the bounds of legal and ethical good practice.

In addition to an accountant's responsibilities to his or her employer, there is a further set of expectations arising from his or her membership of the accounting profession. In the first instance, professional accountants are expected to observe the letter and spirit of the law in detail and of professional ethical codes where applicable (depending on country of residence, qualifying body, etc).

In any professional or ethical situation where codes do not clearly apply, a professional accountant should apply 'principles-based' ethical standards (such as integrity and probity) such that they would be happy to account for their behaviour if so required. Finally, and in common with members of other professions, accountants are required to act in the public interest that may involve reporting an errant employer to the relevant authorities. This may be the situation that an accountant may find him or herself in at Ashdene Homes. It would clearly be unacceptable to be involved in any form of deceit and it would be the accountant's duty to help to correct such malpractice if at all possible.

1   **Personal ethical behaviour**

This relates to the way you as an individual conduct yourself.

Business ethics

This is the way a firm as a whole behaves.

Corporate responsibility

This is the belief that a firm owes a responsibility to society and its wider stakeholders, as well as to shareholders.

2   Threats to self interest include: Financial interests, loans or guarantees; Incentive compensation arrangements; Inappropriate personal use of corporate assets; Concern over employment security; Commercial pressure from outside the employing organisation.

3   Safeguards might be generic, created by the profession or regulation or developed in the working environment by the individual or their organisation.

4   In circumstances where a professional accountant in business believes that unethical behaviour or actions by others will continue to occur within the employing organisation, they should consider seeking **legal advice**.

In extreme situations where all available safeguards have been exhausted and it is not possible to reduce the threat to an acceptable level, a professional accountant in business may conclude that it is appropriate to **disassociate** from the task and/or **resign** from the employing organisation.

5   Contract terms might cover:

- The use of child labour
- Human rights
- Health and safety standards
- Working conditions
- Minimum wages
- Environmental protection
- Terms for contract negotiation and renewal
- Basis of contract price

6   Sustainable enterprise: A company, institution or entity that generates continuously increasing stakeholder value through the application of sustainable practices through the entire base activity – products and services, workforce, workplace, functions/processes, and management/governance. (Deloitte: *Creating the Wholly Sustainable Enterprise*)

7   The short term/long term debate refers to the trade off management must make between decisions with short-term impacts on the business and those with impacts on its longer term success. Here the assumption is that sustainability will have an adverse short-term impact on the business, for example due to the enhanced costs of compliance, but that it is essential to its long-term success in the face of mounting social and legal pressure to improve ecological performance.

Some writers suggest that there may be short-term benefits from sustainability, such as reduced costs from using less energy and other resources or attracting customers who will place contracts or buy the offerings of firms with better sustainability postures (eg 'carbon free').

8   **Economic**: the organization's impacts on the economic conditions of its stakeholders and on economic systems at local, national, and global levels.

Economic Indicators illustrate the flow of capital among different stakeholders; and the main economic impacts of the organization throughout society.

Environmental: an organization's impacts on living and non-living natural systems, including ecosystems, land, air, and water.

Environmental Indicators cover performance related to inputs (eg, material, energy, water) and outputs (eg, emissions, effluents, waste). In addition, they cover performance related to biodiversity, environmental compliance, and other relevant information such as environmental expenditure and the impacts of products and services.

Social: the impacts an organization has on the social systems within which it operates.

Social Indicators identify key performance aspects surrounding labour practices, human rights, society, and product responsibility.

9   Refer to the answer to requirement d of Executive Travel Ltd in the Question Bank.

10   Refer to the answer to requirement b(ii) of Hutton Haulage plc in the Question Bank.

11   There is no answer to this self-test, as it is designed just to help you increase your business awareness.

Sample paper

BUSINESS STRATEGY

This paper is made up of **THREE** written test questions (100 marks).

1. Ensure your candidate details are on the front of your answer booklet.

2. Answer each question in black ball point pen only.

3. Answers to written test questions must begin on a new page. Ensure that each question is clearly numbered. Use both sides of the paper in your answer booklet.

4. The examiner will take account of the way in which material is presented in the written test questions.

The questions in this paper have been prepared on the assumption that candidates do not have a detailed knowledge of the types of organisations to which they relate. No additional credit will be given to candidates displaying such knowledge.

DO NOT TURN OVER UNTIL YOU ARE INSTRUCTED TO BEGIN WORK.

1 Rugeley Tableware plc

Rugeley Tableware plc (Rugeley) is a niche manufacturer of quality ceramic tableware, based in the UK.

Company history

Rugeley was founded in 1779 by William Rugeley, a local businessman and entrepreneur. It specialises in the design and manufacture of exclusive ceramic tableware (sets of plates, bowls etc), which is sold direct to the hotel and restaurant industry and also to individual consumers. Rugeley's products are stocked by major retailers and can be purchased online via its website.

From the beginning, Rugeley created a reputation for manufacturing tableware of the highest quality which it originally sold to wealthy individuals. For more than two centuries, Rugeley tableware was used at dinner tables in sophisticated private houses and hotels and the brand name became associated with an elegant lifestyle. As a result of its innovative patterns and designs, Rugeley was recognised as a prestigious brand throughout Europe and the US and was sought after because of its quality and English heritage.

Rugeley enjoyed many years of profitability and was converted into a public limited company in 1989 at the peak of its success, when it became listed on the London Stock Exchange. 40% of the equity share capital remains in the hands of the Rugeley family, 45% is held by institutional investors and the remainder is owned by individual investors.

Declining fortunes

Several years after it was listed, Rugeley's results began to deteriorate. In 2000, Rugeley decided to outsource some of its manufacturing operations to Asia, in an attempt to reduce costs and to address competition from the following sources:

- Cheaper imports, which were almost entirely being produced in low labour cost countries.

- Large global retailers that had begun to introduce mass produced, own-label product ranges, designed to resemble high quality tableware.

- More diversified competitors in the tableware market that also offered glassware and table linen.

- Major international companies that were able to benefit from economies of scale by manufacturing a wider range of ceramics for use in the home (including bathroom sanitary ware, kitchen sinks, tiles and tableware).

These sources of competition have become more powerful since 2000 and sales and profits have continued to decline, despite the outsourcing decision. The most recent results (for the year ended 30 June 2009) show a fall in revenue of 15%, a fall in profit of 25% and negative operational cash flow. The business urgently needs to make changes if it is to avoid becoming loss making.

For nearly a year, institutional shareholders have been openly critical of the chairman and chief executive, Belinda Rugeley (a direct descendant of William). Belinda runs the company in an authoritarian manner. She has refused to appoint non-executive directors, on the basis that they would not be as committed to the company as its executive directors, whose remuneration is based on the financial performance of the business. Some institutional investors have suggested the company should consider seeking a buyer from among the major international manufacturers.

Future options

At a recent board meeting to discuss Rugeley's future strategic options, the following views were expressed:

Marketing director (Malcolm Enderby): 'For years we have set worldwide standards in tableware design and manufacturing, but people's attitudes to dining have changed. As formal dining has given way to more relaxed eating habits, so our traditional products have become unfashionable. As a result, our sales to individual customers are now concentrated on a very narrow market, consisting largely of customers over 40 years of age. What's more the recession is unlikely to help matters as it will inevitably depress sales of what is seen as a luxury item.

I think we have taken too narrow a view of Asia as the solution to our manufacturing. I believe we should also focus on Asia as a new sales market. There is an opportunity here to build a brand image of exclusive tableware, based on our English style and heritage.

We also need to target the new, younger generation who are unfamiliar with our products. The recession may work in our favour here, as more people choose to dine at home instead of eating out. We can exploit this by introducing a new range of everyday designer tableware. Melinda James, the famous chef, owns a well-respected design and marketing business and she has agreed to cooperate with us in a joint venture to launch such a product.'

Production director (Alex Rodin): 'I think the lack of sales is more about supply chain issues than anything else and these have impacted on our customer service capabilities. At the moment there is a mis-match between the high quality of our product and the level of service we are providing to customers. Although we carry very high levels of inventory, these are not always of the right product lines. Because of the lead times associated with overseas manufacturing, production and delivery times have increased and our level of overdue orders is unacceptably high.

The problem is exacerbated by the fact that all our key strategic and operational decision making is carried out by the board, so production is based on centrally produced sales forecasts and not driven by real customer demand. Our centralised management structure has given rise to inflexibility and slow response times. It has also stifled local sales initiatives and design innovations. I believe we need to address our supply chain issues and at the same time change our decision making structure so that more authority is delegated, and sales planning is undertaken by the local manager within each sales market.

A former colleague of mine now works at PCE plc, a company which manufactures portable consumer electronics such as digital radios, MP3 and DVD players. They have just completed a review of their own supply chain with amazing results, and they've published some of their data on this. I think we could learn something from what they have achieved.'

Chairman/chief executive (Belinda Rugeley): 'I really don't see how we can learn anything from PCE plc – they are in a completely different industry from us. Surely they don't know anything about the manufacture of ceramic tableware and any targets they set for their supply chain will not be a relevant benchmark for ours?'

Requirements

Acting as a consultant to the board of directors:

(a) Prepare a SWOT analysis of Rugeley's current strategic position, and highlight the key issues facing the company. **(8 marks)**

(b) Using Ansoff, analyse the proposals made by the marketing director. **(8 marks)**

(c) Evaluate the production director's proposals to decentralise decision making. Explain the change management issues that Rugeley would need to address if it were to go ahead with the proposed new decision making structure. **(10 marks)**

(d) Discuss the comments made by the production director and the chairman/chief executive in respect of PCE plc. **(7 marks)**

(e) Explain the principles of good corporate governance which would be relevant and the ways in which non-executive directors would be of benefit to the running of Rugeley. **(7 marks)**

(40 marks)

Pitstop Ltd (Pitstop) operates a well-known chain of roadside restaurants in the UK.

Company information

Pitstop's target market is road users, in particular business travellers and families with children, who want to break up a long journey and stop for refreshments. Pitstop has 65 restaurants, which occupy prime sites along major roads.

The restaurants all have the same internal design, décor, menu and prices. They are open 07:00 to 19:00 for 360 days in each year, and each has the capacity to seat 50 customers.

All procurement is done centrally and Pitstop sets strict guidelines regarding staff levels and the purchasing and preparation of food. Each restaurant is set a target for cost of sales of 68% of revenue so that waste is kept to a minimum and food and labour costs are carefully controlled.

All other costs incurred by Pitstop are fixed. These include the salaries of the restaurant managers, rent, marketing, procurement administration and other central costs. For reporting purposes, these are totalled and then divided equally across the 65 restaurants in the chain.

Key factors that influence performance for an individual restaurant are customer numbers and average amount spent by each customer. Pitstop's restaurants are all leased. Results have suffered recently as rents have increased considerably, whilst at the same time customer numbers have fallen.

The market is highly competitive and there is a variety of other outlets which cater for a similar need to Pitstop: petrol station forecourt shops, roadside facilities operated by regional and national chains, fast food outlets, coffee chains and local family friendly bar/restaurants. In addition, the volume of customers is highly affected by roadworks, the weather and the time of year.

The current focus on healthy eating has given rise to criticism that Pitstop's traditional menu places too much emphasis on fried food with a high fat content. In addition there have been changes in driving habits. The advent of in-car entertainment systems has made it easier for families to occupy children on a long journey. Many drivers prefer to purchase a snack that can be eaten quickly rather than stop for the time required to order and consume a meal.

Strategic proposals

Pitstop's board of directors has been discussing two possible strategies to improve profitability:

Strategy 1: Widen the appeal of the restaurant

Pitstop would attempt to increase customer volumes by a third in all its restaurants by:

- Targeting local families who could be encouraged to make regular visits to Pitstop as a neighbourhood restaurant

- Encouraging business executives to view the restaurant as a meeting point, by creating a special office area within each restaurant, with facilities for laptop computers and free internet access

- Attracting more road users with the introduction of a new snack menu. This would provide an alternative for customers who are short of time and wish to resume their journeys as soon as possible

The finance director is on long-term sick leave. In her absence, the sales director has produced a forecast of the likely impact of this strategy on an **average** Pitstop restaurant, which is set out in **Exhibit 1** along with actual results for an **average** restaurant in the year ended 31 July 2009. On the basis of these figures he is keen to implement the strategy across all Pitstop restaurants.

Exhibit 1: Strategy 1 projections for an average Pitstop restaurant

Year ended 31 July	Actual results 2009 £	Forecast strategy 1 2010 £
Revenue	486,000	648,000
Food costs	170,100	226,800
Labour costs	160,380	213,840
Cost of sales	330,480	440,640
Gross profit	155,520	207,360
Marketing	20,000	20,000
Rent	75,000	75,000
Other overheads	60,000	60,000
Profit before interest and tax	520	52,360
Average amount spent by each customer	£9.00	£9.00

Strategy 2: Reduce prices

This strategy would involve reducing prices by 15% to make Pitstop more competitive. Although gross profit margins would fall as a result, the sales director is confident that the increase in customers would more than compensate for this.

The operations director is concerned about the downside risk associated with this strategy. In particular he has pointed out that if the lower prices do not attract more customers, then the majority of Pitstop's restaurants will fail to break-even.

Risk assessment

To assist in assessing the risk of the two strategies, the operations director has provided some information about the variability of customer numbers, average spend and margins during the year ended 31 July 2009. This is set out in Exhibit 2, together with his estimate of the impact that Strategy 2 would have on gross profit margins.

Exhibit 2: Variability of Pitstop customer numbers, average spend and margins

	Worst performing restaurant	Average restaurant	Best performing restaurant
Year ended 31 July 2009 (actual)			
No of customers per day	95	150	245
Average amount spent by each customer	£7.50	£9.00	£10.50
Actual gross profit margin	30%	32%	34%
Year ended 31 July 2010 (estimate)			
Estimated gross profit margin with Strategy 2	18%	20%	22%

Requirements

(a) Using both exhibits and the other information provided:

    (i) Analyse Strategy 1 and evaluate its impact on an average restaurant.

    (ii) Assess the reasonableness of the sales director's forecast and assumptions as a basis for projecting the results for all Pitstop's restaurants.

    Show any additional calculations that are relevant. **(12 marks)**

(b) For Strategy 2:

    (i) Prepare calculations which demonstrate the increase in customers per day that would be required to maintain existing gross profits for an average restaurant.

    (ii) Discuss the likely impact of the proposed price reduction on the profitability of the company as a whole, showing any additional calculations. **(10 marks)**

(c) Explain any other factors that Pitstop should consider when making a decision about how to improve the company's profitability. **(5 marks)**

(27 marks)

3   Somborne Zoological Park Ltd

Somborne Zoological Park Ltd (Somborne) is a charitable, not-for-profit company. It is engaged in animal conservation and research and operates a well-known zoo in the UK. (Note: conservation is the securing of long-term populations of species in natural ecosystems and habitats wherever possible.) Somborne is home to more than 2,600 animals and attracts around two million visitors a year. In addition to income from visitors, the zoo receives financial support from corporate sponsors, grants for research, donations from benefactors and subscription income from its membership programme.

Governance and regulation

Somborne is managed by a board of trustees which has overall responsibility for the zoo's operations. Somborne is a member of The International Zoo Federation (IZF), a global industry body, which requires each member to achieve certain standards in conservation, education and animal care and to meet certain inspection criteria annually in order to maintain its licence to operate.

Staffing

Somborne has a staff of about 200 paid employees, and more than 1,500 volunteers. The zoo is led by a manager who is responsible for the maintenance and growth of the animal collection and who has overall responsibility for the staff. The day-to-day care of the animals is undertaken by zookeepers, supported by qualified vets. In addition Somborne employs a number of staff in catering and retail roles at the zoo's café and shop.

Aims and objectives

Somborne's mission is: 'To focus the zoo's resources on animal conservation and to support this through sustainable commercial activities, including managing the zoo as a first class visitor attraction.'

Somborne's strategic goals are stated as follows:

- To maximise the impact of our conservation activities and to undertake research activities which make contributions to conservation programmes both in captivity and the wild

- To promote and support the zoo through marketing and the provision of learning opportunities for the public

- To identify and develop alternative income streams to reduce dependency on visitor income

In addition, as part of a desire to gain accreditation for sustainability and environmental management from the IZF, the board has recently identified a fourth goal:

- To follow ethical principles to guarantee the well-being of our animal collection and to manage the operations and development of the zoo to ensure long term sustainability

A new chairman has recently been appointed to assist the board in implementing this sustainability initiative and has approached you, as a member of the zoo's finance department, for help:

'I think I am clear about the vision for the zoo but there appears to be a lack of detail on how the zoo intends to implement that vision. Please could you explain to me the relevance of strategic planning for a not-for-profit organisation such as ours, and give me some specific examples of detailed operational objectives that would allow us to meet our first three strategic goals.

As you are well aware we only have a finite budget and so the other thing I am concerned about is how to allocate the resources that we do have, between the various goals and projects that we could undertake.

In order to gain accreditation from the IZF we need to carry out an environmental audit to establish some baseline performance measures in four areas: financial, environmental, human resources and social. These measures will be used for monitoring during the first year of implementation of the sustainability initiative and subsequently. I have attached an extract of the guidance issued by the IZF on sustainability and environmental management in the **Exhibit** below which should explain more.'

Exhibit: Extract from the IZF report on 'Achieving Sustainability'

Achieving sustainability can be defined as reaching a state where all operations of a zoological institution are neutral in the environment.

All IZF members are expected to work towards sustainability by reducing their environmental impact and to lead by example, using green practices and educating staff and visitors about sustainable lifestyles.

An environmental management system (EMS) can provide a structured approach to implementing an environmental programme.

An EMS is a set of processes and practices that enables an organisation to reduce its environmental impacts and increase its operating efficiency.

An environmental audit measures and assesses the environmental impacts that a zoo's activities have on its surroundings. It considers all stakeholders and also takes into consideration historical and potential future impacts. An environmental audit is a first step in a successful EMS.

'The board of trustees has spent some time defining what sustainability means for the zoo in the four areas identified by the IZF:

- **Financial** – Somborne's income needs to match the zoo's growing expenditure. We want to ensure the application of environmental and ethical standards to our purchasing, sponsorship and investment.

- **Environmental** – Somborne must conduct activities in a way which minimises any negative impact on the environment (water, waste, energy, transport). Many zoo animals spend considerable periods of time in water and all rely on a plentiful daily supply for health and survival. The zoo intends to implement measures to reduce, reuse and recycle water. Our special exhibits, such as the reptile house, use lots of energy, and in addition to the volume of waste generated by visitors, care of the animals generates considerable natural waste. We need to reduce the amount of energy used and increase efficiency. We want to encourage staff to adhere to environmentally friendly principles and promote environmentally friendly methods of transport for staff and visitors.

- **Human resources** – We are committed to the management and development of talent and the application of ethical employment practices.

- **Social** – We are committed to extending the concept of corporate social responsibility to the wider community. Somborne will only use suppliers and contractors that follow ethical principles. In addition we are keen to increase our participation in the local community, in particular with local schools, to help educate the future generation about the need for sustainable living.'

Requirements

Prepare a report, in response to the chairman's request for help, which covers the following:

(a) (i) Explain the benefits of strategic planning for the zoo.

    (ii) Give two examples of specific objectives for each of the first three strategic goals identified in the scenario. **(8 marks)**

(b) Identify the issues that Somborne is likely to face in deciding how to allocate limited resources. **(6 marks)**

(c) (i) Explain the likely costs and benefits for the zoo of implementing a sustainability initiative.

    (ii) Assess the likely impact of such an initiative on the zoo's staff and one other key stakeholder. **(9 marks)**

(d) Explain how the zoo could use an information system to assess the success of its sustainability initiative and suggest some appropriate performance measures that could be used for each of the four areas identified by the IZF. **(10 marks)**

(33 marks)

Business Strategy

BUSINESS STRATEGY

ANSWERS

Examiner's commentary

Good candidates would be expected to identify most of the points listed in the marking plan. Markers are always encouraged to use discretion and to award partial marks where a point is either not explained fully or made by implication. More marks are available than could be awarded for each requirement. This allowed credit to be given for a variety of valid points made by candidates.

1   **Rugeley Tableware plc**

General comments

The scenario in this question looks at a listed company which is a niche manufacturer of quality ceramic tableware, based in UK. The company has attempted to address competition from cheaper imports by outsourcing some of its manufacturing operations to Asia, however this has not halted the decline in sales and profitability. The institutional shareholders have been openly critical of Belinda Rugeley (the Chairman and Chief executive) who runs the company in an authoritarian manner and has refused to appoint non-executive directors. The board is considering the future strategic options. The marketing director has suggested a strategy of both market and product development to attract a wider range of consumers. The production director on the other hand believes the lack of sales is a result of supply chain issues and the centralised management structure. He has identified a consumer electronics company that could be used to benchmark the supply chain and has also suggested changing the decision making structure of the company.

This question was the mini case and, at 40 marks, was the longest question on the paper. The requirements were broken down to help candidates in developing answer headings and assessing mark allocation. Overall candidates performed reasonably well, with good marks in the earlier requirements making up for relatively weaker attempts at parts (d) and (e).

(a)   (i)   **Swot analysis**

Strengths

- Long established business with a previously good record of growth and profitability

- Prestigious brand image and reputation and client base includes top hotels and restaurants

- High quality exclusive luxury product (may be recession proof as truly wealthy unaffected by credit crunch)

- Reputation for innovation (although not clear if this is still true today)

- Move to outsourcing is evidence that management are prepared to change

- Listed company therefore should have access to finance

Weaknesses

- Falling profits and negative operational cashflow are a cause for concern

- Unfashionable product, hence limited market with focus on older generation which restricts sales

- Poor customer service and high level of overdue orders may lose business

- High inventories lead to increased costs including obsolescence

- Long lead times due to overseas manufacturing will lead to dissatisfied customers

- Inflexibility and slow response times due to centralised structure and Belinda's authoritarian approach may mean alternative strategies are not fully considered

- More expensive than alternative products offered by cheap imports and retailers own brands

- Lack economies of scale of global ceramics manufacturers and presumably also can't match their marketing budget

- Not diversified so no spread of risk

- Lack of compliance with principles of good corporate governance
- Institutional shareholders have been openly critical of Belinda Rugeley which will undermine confidence in the company and its management.

Opportunities

- New product ranges eg designer everyday tableware
- New markets eg Asia, younger generation
- Expand into related products eg glassware, crystal, gifts
- Get taken over by one of global manufacturers
- Take over a competitor
- Re-engineer supply chain
- Change the structure of the company and the decision making

Threats

- Changing dining trends mean product has reached end of life cycle
- Credit crunch means further sales decline is likely
- High levels of competition from cheap imports, large global retailers and more diversified competitors may further reduce market share
- Liquidation as a result of poor cash position
- Dissatisfaction of institutional shareholders may cause them to force change

(ii) **Key issues**

The key issues are:

- The declining financial position raises questions over the long term viability of the business
- The long term change in dining habits which has significantly impacted on R's sales and means that its core product appears to be at the end of its life cycle, as a result R urgently needs to pursue other opportunities for growth
- Poor customer service which is inconsistent with premium product
- The centralised authoritarian structure and the dissatisfaction of the institutional shareholders which needs to be addressed as a matter of priority.

Examiner note:

In requirement (a) candidates were asked to prepare a SWOT analysis of Rugeley's current strategic position, highlighting key issues. Most candidates scored well here and it was pleasing to note an increase in the number of candidates providing explanations as to why a particular point was a strength or weakness etc. Some weaker candidates produced an imbalanced SWOT with a long list of strengths, when the weaknesses and threats were of far more concern in this scenario. A surprising number also made little effort to highlight the key issues, despite the specific requirement to do so. Those candidates that chose to include a summary at the end highlighting the need for Rugeley urgently to address the issues of declining demand, increased competition and negative cashflow, tended to score very well.

(b) **Strategic options proposed by marketing director**

The following matrix, developed by Ansoff, can be used to analyse the possible growth strategies available to Rugeley.

	Existing product	New product
Existing market	Internal efficiency and market penetration	Product development
New market	Market development	Diversification

(i)   Internal efficiency and market penetration involve attempts to reduce cost or further penetrate existing markets by taking market share from the competition. The outsourcing of some manufacturing in 2000 was presumably an attempt at increasing internal efficiency in order to match competitors through low cost manufacturing, but this does not appear to have generated additional sales. Thus to achieve market penetration, it may be better, as the marketing director suggests, to focus on differentiating itself from its competitors on a quality basis.

A marketing campaign aimed at emphasising the traditional English heritage might achieve this, although the problems identified by the SWOT analysis (and the marketing director) suggest that this approach may not be viable given the change in dining habits, the narrow customer base and the credit crunch. Indeed given that Rugeley are operating in a niche market, their market share/ level of penetration may already be high and there may be little scope to increase this, unless they can persuade customers to buy multiple dinner services for different occasions or increase penetration of sales to hotels and restaurants eg through links with Melinda James.

Hence increased sales growth is likely to necessitate other strategies.

(ii) Product development involves selling new products to existing customers and normally requires research and development expenditure.

The introduction of the Melinda James everyday designer tableware range could be said to represent product development, although it is also possible to view this as simply an extension of the existing product range.

The fact that R intends to introduce this by way of a joint venture would be deemed 'External domestic development' according to Lynch's expansion matrix. This shares some of the risk and may allow R to save on marketing as it will enjoy additional publicity from the association with Melinda.

Alternatively, as this product is not going to be targeted at existing customers, who are in the older age range and may not associate with the celebrity chef, it could be argued that it is a means of market development (see below).

Other possible product development opportunities include: increased R&D to make innovations in patterns and designs; own brand ranges for large retail chains; giftware, glassware and other associated items for dining.

(iii) Market development involves selling existing products to new customers and involves investment in marketing.

In this case the marketing director is proposing two elements of market development:

Domestic expansion in terms of targeting a new market segment of younger customers (discussed above).

Overseas expansion in the context of exporting to the Asian market. According to Lynch this could be achieved organically or through some form of JV/licensing agreement. The fact that the marketing director is keen to emphasise the English heritage may mean that use of a 'local' partner is inappropriate.

R could also consider overseas development of other markets eg India.

(iv) Diversification involves making new products for new markets. It can be vertical (backward or forward in the firm's existing production chain), horizontal (acquisition of competitors) or conglomerate (a move into a totally different area). R does not appear to be considering diversification at this point in time.

Possible diversification opportunities include wider ceramics manufacture for bathrooms and kitchens. As they have no experience of this, it would be sensible to use 201Cexternal development methods, eg JV/acquisition

Note: It is possible to argue that the JV with Melissa James (everyday tableware for the younger market) is related diversification (new product and new market)

(c) **Decentralisation and change management issues**

Decentralisation proposals

Currently it appears that Belinda Rugeley has adopted a very authoritarian, centralised management structure, with all key decisions being taken at Board level. The structure of the business does not appear to have changed despite growth.

The production director suggests that this has stifled innovation, and led to inflexibility and slow response times. He also implies that the sales forecasts produced centrally may have been inaccurate causing problems of overstocking and at the same time outstanding orders.

Decentralisation involves granting greater decision making powers and autonomy to a wider range of managers within the company.

Benefits of proposed changes:

- Increases speed of response to changes in local markets and local conditions.

- May facilitate supply chain changes and hence improved customer service. Individual managers are likely to have a better idea of customer requirements and can stock the products the customers actually require, reducing levels of incorrect inventory.

- Local knowledge and expertise eg in respect of sales planning might improve quality of information and decision making and allow production to be driven by demand.

- Less rigid structure may foster a different culture and promote innovation re methods and designs. This may help extend the product life cycle or attract a wider range of customers.

- Would free up the Board to focus on strategic rather than operational decision making, therefore allowing Belinda and the other directors to address the declining profitability.

- Increased responsibility may motivate more junior managers and create a career path/ on job training for senior management.

Disadvantages:

- Belinda and they other board directors may be reluctant to relinquish control.

- Lack of experience may lead managers to make incorrect decisions, exacerbating the issues of overstocking etc. May also lead to incongruent decisions if local managers have differing objectives.

- Would not reduce lead times as these are a result of basing production in Asia.

- Increased need for coordination and communication as decision makers will be spread across the business.

- Likely to require training of junior managers, some of whom may not want the added responsibility.

Change management issues

Type of change

The restructuring change here might be said by Johnson, Scholes and Whittington to be 'Adaptation' (incremental and reactive).

It is incremental in that it is likely to be a gradual process rather than a sudden major, transformational change. It is also reactive in the sense that it appears to be in response to continued declining results and poor customer service, so R is being forced to make adjustments to adapt to its environment.

The focus of the change is at the organisational structure and system level, since it involves redesigning the approach to planning and decision making to facilitate changes in the supply chain.

Given the recent poor performance, change may be fundamental to R's survival.

Barriers to change

Change management involves managing people's expectations and attitudes since all changes tend to be resisted by employees. The key staff affected here will be the Board and the management, rather than the general employees. The change will not be successful unless Belinda can be persuaded of the need for change.

(1) **Cultural barriers**

Power structures within R may be threatened. This will in particular affect senior management, who may be protective of their current decision making authority and be reluctant to implement changes which will be against their own interests.

Structural inertia: the existing systems of planning and decision making may act as a barrier to change to a new decentralised approach. It appears that Belinda has favoured an authoritative centralised approach in the past and the management may find it hard to believe that she will support a new structure.

Group inertia may block change where the changes are inconsistent with the norms of team working and departments, or where they threaten their interests. The local sales managers may feel that they lack the necessary skills or rewards to take on additional responsibility.

(2) **Personnel barriers**

There are also barriers which affect individuals and result in them seeing the change as a threat. Here habit and fear of the unknown may mean some individual managers are unwilling or reluctant to take on the additional responsibility involved.

Approach to change

A mixture of the adaptive and coercive approach is likely to be appropriate. Adaptive change alone may be too slow, and R's management may need to emphasise that it is vital that changes are made if the company is to survive. Some participation will be appropriate however, particularly given that the new structure is to involve more decentralisation.

Belinda will need to actively demonstrate a willingness to delegate and adopt a more hands off approach to the management of the company. Otherwise local managers may perceive that their involvement is simply a token and that the substance of decision making has not altered.

Managers will need educating that the existing systems are insufficient to allow successful improvements to the supply chain. R will need to provide local managers with training and support to increase their confidence in their ability to make sales planning decisions.

Conclusion

Decentralisation would appear to be sensible and is likely to help address the supply chain issues and facilitate growth of new markets, however this will only be successful if Belinda can be persuaded of the need for change.

(d) **Benchmarking**

By suggesting that Rugeley might use PCE's experience, the production director is referring to the activity of benchmarking.

Benchmarking is identifying, understanding and adapting business best practices and processes to lead to superior performance.

This can lead to changes which may improve productivity, reduce costs or increase competitive advantage. In Rugeley's case it appears that a key aim is to improve its supply chain in terms of responsiveness, reliability and relationships and hence improve customer satisfaction.

There are four bases for benchmarking:

- Internal – comparisons within the business over time, or between business units
- Competitive – comparisons with other firms in the same industry/sector
- Best in class/Activity – best practice in a completely different industry
- Generic – against a conceptually similar process

Internal and competitive benchmarking would involve making comparisons within R's own industry. To an extent R has done this in the past, as competitive benchmarking led it to outsource some of its manufacturing in 2000.

When a company or its whole industry is performing badly or losing out to other industries, there is a case for the wider perspective offered by 'best in class' and generic benchmarking. This would involve identifying suitable benchmarking partners.

The production director is thus correct that there may be lessons to learn from PCE's experience in re-engineering their supply chain and this would be in the context of activity/best in class benchmarking.

Whilst the industry is different, they both sell consumer products and the concepts of lead times, responsiveness, overdue orders and inventories would still apply. Also PCE may well have experience of outsourcing production to Asia.

The chairman's concerns that PCE operate in a different industry might in fact be an advantage rather than a constraint, as it could encourage R to think more widely and be more innovative in its approach, rather than being limited by the way things are normally done within the industry. This might lead to an approach which is different from competitors and hence generates competitive advantage (something that the outsourcing in 2000 appears to have failed to do).

One approach does not preclude the other, so R could identify the competitor with the best supply chain in the ceramics industry at the same time, although it may be harder to get the necessary information. PCE may be more inclined to share information as it will not feel the need to be protective of trade secrets and some data has already been published.

The Chairman is correct that PCE's targets may not be appropriate for R, but benchmarking is more than just collecting data or setting targets. R needs to identify the drivers of good performance. So comparisons with PCE might indicate the areas of the supply chain that R needs to focus on and may give R an insight into the problems that were experienced by PCE in managing the changes. This may help R obtain better results or facilitate the implementation of the change.

In addition to improving the efficiency of operations, benchmarking may also enable R to identify scope for improving its management structure and decision making processes eg the need to decentralise the system of sales planning and decision making.

A possible downside of benchmarking is that managers may feel their role is reduced to copying others and thus any benchmarking programme would need careful management.

Conclusion: R urgently needs to establish or regain its competitive advantage and benchmarking the supply chain against PCE may help it do so. It might also consider other forms of benchmarking and perhaps undertake a value chain analysis.

Examiner note:

In requirement (d) candidates had to discuss the differing views expressed in the scenario about the relevance of using a company (PCE) in a different industry to benchmark Rugeley's supply chain. Answers were varied. Some candidates failed to spot that this requirement was about benchmarking and limited their marks by discussing the potential comparison only in general terms. Better answers explained the different types of benchmarking available to Rugeley and went on to consider whether PCE plc was an appropriate choice for benchmarking. Many also provided consideration of supply chain issues. Candidates who discussed the use of value chain analysis as a means of identifying improvements to the supply chain and increasing competitive advantage were awarded credit.

(e) **Corporate governance and NEDs**

Corporate governance involves the set of rules which governs the structure and determines the objectives of a company and regulates the relationship between a company's management, its Board of directors and its shareholders. It is not about the day-to-day management of operations or the formulation of business strategy.

Key aspects of good corporate governance involve the transparency of corporate structure and operations; the accountability of managers and boards to shareholders; and corporate responsibility towards employees, creditors, suppliers and the local community.

The UK Corporate Governance Code 2010 issued by the FRC sets out best practice which R currently does not comply with:

- There should be a separate chairman and chief executive, whereas Belinda currently does both roles.

- The Board should consist of sufficient non-executive directors to prevent domination by the executive directors.

- Non-executive directors (NEDs) should establish a remuneration committee to decide on directors' remuneration and an audit committee to work with the external auditors. As there are no NEDs it is assumed that R does not have either of these currently.

The Code is only a legal requirement for premium listed companies so non-compliance by R in some ways is not an issue, as there is a 'comply or disclose' policy. Thus as a condition of its continued listing R is simply required by the Stock Exchange to disclose the areas where it has not followed the Code. However a bigger issue may be that the institutional shareholders are becoming increasingly unhappy with the situation.

Belinda would be advised to appoint NEDs and form a remuneration committee as this would protect her and the other executive directors from the criticism/accusation that the company is being run for their personal benefit.

NEDs would provide a better balance of power on the Board and may encourage Belinda to delegate some of the decision making to others.

NEDs could also help improve the efficiency and effectiveness of the remuneration system and act as a buffer between the Board and the auditors.

The benefit to Belinda of the NEDs is that they would be seen by the institutional investors and other shareholders as independent, which would improve the perception of the company.

In addition they may bring skills and experience that improves the quality of decision making which could lead to better performance. NEDs would also be able to help R appoint new directors should the need arise.

Overall the appointment of NEDs may increase institutional shareholder confidence in the running of the company, and if they are reassured by the move they are less likely to demand that the company seeks a buyer.

Examiner note:

Requirement (e) asked candidates to explain the principles of good corporate governance and the ways that non-executive directors (NEDs) might be of benefit to the running of the business. A disappointing number of candidates failed to explain the concept of corporate governance and restricted their answer to a discussion of NEDs. Better candidates considered corporate governance in the broader context of agency theory, talked about the applicability of the Code and the need for a separate Chairman and CEO, discussed the issue of directors' remuneration being linked to performance and highlighted the need for better governance given the concerns of the institutional shareholders.

2 Pitstop Ltd

General comments

Pitstop Ltd is a chain of 65 roadside restaurants, operating in an increasingly competitive market. The company has a good track record but increased site rental costs have led to a recent decline in financial performance. Two alternatives are being considered to improve profitability: Strategy 1 – widen the appeal of the restaurant in order to increase customer volumes by one third; Strategy 2 – reduce prices by 15% to become more competitive. As the finance director is on long term sick leave, the sales director has prepared forecasts of the likely impact of the two strategies. The operations director is particularly concerned about the downside risk associated with Strategy 2. Candidates were provided with two exhibits: the actual and forecast results for an average restaurant (Exhibit 1), together with some data on margins and average customer spend for the best and worst performing restaurants in the chain (Exhibit 2).

This, the data analysis question, was by far the least well attempted question on the paper and many attempts were marginal. Few candidates made use of the additional data in Exhibit 2 regarding the best, worst and average restaurants – those who did tended to score highly.

The question required candidates to analyse forecasts for two new strategies in relation to the current actual performance. Both forecast and actual data was provided in order to test candidates' ability to apply basic data analysis skills to data in a variety of forms but weaker candidates seemed unable to show flexibility in analysing forecast data. It appears from tutor feedback received, that some candidates may have been led by tutors to assume that there is a 'normal' data analysis question involving the analysis of only historic business performance. The learning materials are clear that this area is not limited in this way: 'the key requirement in the BS exam is to be able to interpret financial and other data provided in the exam and relate it to the business strategy'. In addition 'the ability to analyse the impact of a new project or strategy' is listed in the material as one possible area that might be examined, which includes the ability to analyse the reasonableness of forecasts.

(a) (i) **Evaluation of forecast for strategy 1**

Appendix 1:

	Actual 2009	Forecast 2010
Food as % of turnover	35%	35%
Labour % of turnover	33%	33%
Gross profit margin	32%	32%
Net profit margin	0.1%	8.1%
No of customers pa (Revenue/Ave spend)	54,000	72,000
No of customers per day (based on 360 days pa)	150	200
Turnaround of tables (daily customers/50)	3	4
Gross profit per customer (gross profit/no of customers)	£2.88	£2.88

	% Increase 2009 – 2010
Revenue	33.3%
Gross profit	33.3%
Overheads	Nil
Net profit	9,969%
Customers per day	33.3%
Ave spend per customer	Nil

Commentary: Impact on current position of an average restaurant

Currently the 'average restaurant' is making a contribution of £155,520 but only just breaking even (net profit of £520) after its allocated share of the rent, marketing and other overheads. This appears to be consistent with the suggestion that results have suffered as a result of significant rent increases.

Overall the new strategy would therefore appear to significantly improve the situation, with the 33% increase in customers generating a £51,840 increase in gross profit and hence PBIT.

Assuming there is no change in fixed costs, and that gross margins remain at 32%, any increase in customer volumes will increase capacity utilisation and hence lead to extra profit.

On the face of it, the sales director's forecasts suggest the proposal is a good one, however this depends on whether the sales director's forecast of both volumes and cost behaviour is realistic, and whether the increased customer numbers can be achieved across the chain in the manner suggested. Given the FD's absence, it is possible that the sales director lacks the necessary experience to produce accurate forecasts and this is examined further in a(ii) below.

(ii) **Reasonableness of forecast and assumptions for predicting company-wide results**

Customer numbers

The sales director has assumed that widening the target market will increase the number of customers by 50 per day or 33.3% overall. The implication is that these will come from the new target market.

This target seems quite ambitious and equates on average to an extra sitting a day, as the turnaround of tables increase from 3 to 4 times. Whether the planned increase is achievable will depend to an extent on the location of the restaurant and the competition in the surrounding area.

In reality the increase is unlikely to be spread evenly across the week – business customers are more likely to use the restaurant Monday-Friday, whereas local families may be more inclined to visit at weekends. The restaurant may encounter problems if, for example, the additional custom is all generated at lunch time, when the tables may already be full.

Also in view of the strong competition, if Pitstop continued with its existing strategy customer numbers may decline between 2009 and 2010, requiring even more customers to be generated from the new target market.

It would be helpful to break the forecast down, to more clearly identify the forecast revenue and customer numbers under both the existing and new strategies.

Average spend and margins

The forecast is based on average spend remaining constant at £9 per customer and gross margins continuing at 32% or £2.88 per customer. Thus the 33.3% increase in customers leads directly to a 33.3% increase in overall gross profit. The forecast does not appear to take account of the fact that the new target customers may have a different spending pattern. Business customers who use the restaurants for meetings are likely to occupy a table for longer but may spend less if they only purchase several cups of coffee.

The introduction of a new snack menu may attract increased volumes of travellers but is likely to lead to a reduction in the average spend. This type of food may require little preparation however, so it is possible that margins will increase on these menu items as there is less labour cost involved if the product is offered on a self service basis.

Average spend is thus likely to vary by type of customer and time of day and margins will vary by menu dish, thus more information would be required to make a more accurate prediction.

Overheads

The sales director has assumed that allocated overheads will remain constant. In reality overheads are likely to increase for the following reasons:

- Pitstop will need to raise awareness of its new strategy and menu. This will necessitate promotion to business customers and local families, and printing of new menus. Widening the target market will therefore involve increased marketing costs unless Pitstop believes that it can attract sufficient coverage via articles in local newspapers and word-of-mouth.

- Pitstop will incur capital costs to fit out part of the restaurant as an office area and ongoing IT costs to support and maintain this strategy.

- Certain costs may be subject to annual price increases eg rent and utilities.

Extrapolation of results company-wide

As the gross profit margin is broadly the same across all Pitstop restaurants and all other costs incurred by the business are split equally across the 65 restaurants, the only variables are customer numbers and average spend.

In order to properly predict the results for the chain as a whole, the customer numbers and average spend for each individual restaurant would be required and these could be amalgamated to create a group forecast.

In the absence of such information, the sales director's forecast for the average Pitstop restaurant could be extrapolated.

With the average restaurant only just breaking even after allocated overheads, the company's PBIT for year ended August 2009 could be estimated at £33,800 (65 × £520) which is unlikely to be a sufficient return for investors after interest and tax payments.

Leaving aside the inaccuracies noted above, then the overall forecast group PBIT for year ended August 2010 under Strategy 1 would be estimated at £3,403,400 (65 × £52,360) – a substantial improvement.

Range of possible results

To get a better idea of the variation in performance, the range of individual restaurant results could be considered:

Actual 2009

Gross profit:

Worst: 95 customers × 360 days × £7.50 × 0.32 = £82,080

Best: 245 customers × 360 days × £10.50 × 0.32 = £296,352

After deducting overheads at £155,000 this means PBIT in 2009 ranged from a loss of £72,920 in the worst restaurant to a profit of £141,352 in the best.

Forecast 2010

Assuming the worst and best restaurants were also forecast to increase their customer numbers by 33.3%, 2010 forecast profits under Strategy 1 would range from:

Gross profit:

Worst: £82,080 × 4/3 = £109,440

Best: £296,352 × 4/3 = £395,136

PBIT

Worst: £109,440 − £155,000 = Loss £45,560 (a reduction in the loss of £27,360)

Best: £395,136 − £155,000 = £240,136 (an increase of £98,784)

Thus the new strategy would increase profits in the average and best restaurants but would still result in Pitstop's worst restaurants being loss-making after the allocation of overheads.

The competition is likely to vary from one restaurant to another and this will affect the results and whether the planned 33% increase in customer numbers will be achievable uniformly across all Pitstop restaurants.

Also some restaurant locations may be more suitable for business/family trade than others. It may not be appropriate to convert all restaurants for business use for example.

Conclusion:

Strategy 1 may be feasible but requires more market research and competitor analysis. Pitstop could attempt to assess the impact of this strategy by running it as a trial in certain restaurants before phasing it in across the whole chain.

Examiner note:

Requirement (a)(i) asked candidates to analyse Strategy 1 and evaluate its impact on an average restaurant. Requirement (a)(ii) then asked candidates to assess the reasonableness of the sales director's forecast and assumptions as a basis for predicting the results for all the restaurants in the chain. Well-made points in a(ii) generally made up for poor analysis in a(i).

In a(i) weak candidates tended to avoid numerical analysis of the exhibits and concentrate on the suitability, feasibility and acceptability of Strategy 1, without reference to the sales director's forecasts, thereby failing to answer part of the requirement 'to assess its impact on an average restaurant'. Better candidates pointed out that the average restaurant was currently only just breaking even and therefore, on the face of it, the sales director's forecast indicated that the strategy would improve financial performance considerably. Given that fixed costs were forecast to stay the same, the strategy to increase customer volumes by one third whilst maintaining average spend and gross margins would, if it were achievable, increase capacity utilisation – and the additional volume would lead directly to additional profit. The better scripts identified that the crux of the matter was therefore whether the sales director's forecast of both volumes and cost behaviour was realistic, and whether the increased customer numbers could be achieved across the chain in the manner suggested.

In a(ii) most candidates provided a comprehensive discussion concerning the limitations of the sales director's assumptions regarding overheads, customer numbers and spend, and margins, although surprisingly few pointed out that, in the FD's absence, the sales director may lack the necessary experience to produce accurate forecasts. Disappointingly few candidates picked up on the other aspect of the discussion which was whether the situation could be considered on an average restaurant basis at all, given the wide variation of customer numbers and average spend between the worst and best performing restaurants.

(b) (i) **Strategy 2**

Customers required to maintain 2009 PBIT

Calculation of new contribution per customer

	Average restaurant £
Current average spend	9.00
New average spend (85% × current spend)	7.65
New contribution (20% × new spend)	1.53

Customers required to maintain profits:

	Average restaurant
Total 2009 Contribution	£155,520
New Contribution per customer	£1.53
Customers required per annum	101,647
Hence customers required per day	282
Increase in customers per day (282 – 150)	132

Alternative approach to calculations:

Contribution per customer

Gross profit per customer at existing prices (a(i))	£2.88
Reduction in gross profit due to price decrease	15% × £9.00 = £1.35
New contribution per customer	£2.88 – £1.35 = £1.53

No of customers required:

Lost contribution = lost revenue from price reduction = 150 × 360 × £9.00 × 15% = £72,900

Thus increase in customers required = £72,900 / £1.53 = 47,647 p.a. or 132 per day

(ii) **Likely impact of strategy 2**

Impact on average restaurant

Unless there are potential savings in staff and food costs, the 15% reduction in price causes the gross profit margin to fall from 32% to 20% for an average restaurant. The calculations in b(i) show that to compensate for this, the average restaurant would need to attract 282 customers per day. This is more than the best performing restaurant currently attracts and for an average restaurant represents an additional 132 customers per day (an increase of 88%).

This looks unobtainable and even if it were successful in doing this, the average restaurant would only be operating just above breakeven. In reality such additional volumes may also necessitate an increase in marketing expenditure or other fixed costs which would further reduce profitability.

Thus the sales director's confidence would appear to be misplaced unless demand is very price elastic.

Impact on the company as a whole

In 2009, using the existing pricing strategy, after allocating fixed costs, the worst restaurant made a loss of £72,920, the average restaurant was just breaking even, and the best restaurant made a profit of £141,352.

The operations director is worried about the downside risk of the price reduction strategy.

In the worst case scenario, if the price reduction failed to attract any additional customers, the calculations in Appendix 2 show that the worst and average restaurants would become loss making (£115,773) and (£72,380) respectively and the best restaurant would only make a small profit of £18,489. Thus the likely effect on the company as a whole is a significant deterioration in profitability, which would render it loss making.

Impact on breakeven point

An alternative way to assess the risk of the strategy is to consider the impact of the 15% price reduction on the breakeven point:

Compared to the actual number of customers in 2009, with the 15% price reduction the worst performing restaurant would need to generate an extra 280 customers a day just to break even – almost 3 times its existing customers and more than the number of customers of the best performing restaurant in 2009!

The average performing restaurant would require 131 customers and the best performing restaurant would have a margin of safety of 26 customers.

Conclusion

The price reduction of 15% proposed in Strategy 2 would not appear to be viable and without significant increase in numbers or major cost reductions is likely to increase the chain's losses. Rather than reducing all prices by 15%, Pitstop could consider implementing price discrimination strategies eg offering senior citizen or early bird discounts to smooth out the peaks and troughs of trade.

Appendix 2 of possible calculations:

	Worst	Ave	Best
New contribution per customer	£	£	£
Current Ave spend	7.50	9.00	10.50
New ave spend (85%)	6.375	7.65	8.925
New contribution (new spend × 18/20/22%)	1.147	1.53	1.963

Impact on profits of the price reduction if there were to be no increase in customer numbers:

	Worst	Ave	Best
Existing customers per day	95	150	245
New contribution per customer	£1.147	£1.53	£1.963
Annual Gross profit	£39,227	£82,620	£173,137
PBIT (after £155,000 overheads)	(£115,773)	(£72,380)	£18,137
Existing 2009 PBIT (see a(i))	(£72,920)	£520	£141,352
Reduction in profitability	(£42,853)	(£71,860)	(£123,215)

Impact of price reduction on breakeven point

	Worst	Ave	Best
Overheads	£155,000	£155,000	£155,000
New contribution per customer	£1.147	£1.53	£1.963
Break even no. customers	135,135	101,308	78,961
Breakeven customers per day	375	281	219
Actual customers per day 2009	95	150	245
Increase in customers required to break even	280	131	(26)

(c) **Additional considerations for future strategy**

Note: This answer includes a complete range of points for marking purposes and is far more than would be expected in the time available.

In order to decide on the future direction of the business Pitstop needs:

(i) To more accurately evaluate the proposed strategies

(ii) To assess the current position of each individual restaurant in order to identify the underperforming restaurants

(i) To assess the proposed strategies

Budgets – Predictions of customer numbers, average spend and overheads for 2010 if Pitstop continued with the existing strategy would be useful as a baseline to assess the impact of the new proposals.

Capital expenditure – More information is required regarding the cost of fitting out the restaurants as a business centre.

Competitor analysis – This needs to be done on an overall company and individual restaurant basis to establish the appropriate target market and strategy for each restaurant.

Market research – Pitstop needs to carry out some market research:

(1) Regarding the target market (local families, business users) and the new snack menu to accurately predict increased customer numbers and average spend for strategy 1.

(2) To assess the likely impact of reducing prices and the price elasticity of demand for Strategy 2. Each Pitstop restaurant should also compare their prices to those of the local competition.

(ii) **To assess underperforming restaurants**

Detail on individual restaurants

Pitstop's reporting system assumes constant gross profit margins and an equal allocation of overheads. In reality not all restaurants will successfully keep to the target for food and labour costs. Also the actual rents are likely to vary depending on the restaurant location eg those near London or on prime routes are likely to pay more rent than those in more rural areas. By allocating overheads evenly Pitstop is likely to be overstating the profit in some restaurants and understating others.

In order to assess each individual restaurant, a breakdown of revenue, costs and staffing levels is required. Pitstop also needs to make an attempt to split overheads between those that are traceable per restaurant eg rent, utilities and other premises costs, and those that are central costs eg marketing and management that need to be reallocated.

Seasonality

Trade is likely to be seasonal and the clientele is likely to vary at different times eg:

Time of year – the summer may be busier because of tourists

Time of week – more trade at weekends from families

Time of day – more business trade in the earlier part of the day

More information is required about the utilisation of the tables in order to assess when a restaurant needs to generate additional trade eg is the restaurant usually full on weekday lunchtimes but empty between 9.30am and 11.30am? This would help identify the type of clientele to be targeted.

Popularity and profitability of menu items

Some meals will be more popular than others and the profitability of the various menu items will differ. This information would help assess which menu items should be offered.

Comparative information

In order to interpret performance, information is needed regarding budgets and targets, competitors and industry norms, so that Pitstop can benchmark performance not just between its restaurants but against others in the industry. This would help Pitstop assess which restaurants are performing well and which are not, both currently and with respect to changes over time.

It is also important to distinguish the performance of the restaurant from the performance of the manager. A badly performing restaurant could be improved by changing the manager or it could be the inevitable consequence of its local market, additional competition or other non-controllable factors.

Multiple performance measures

Pitstop might consider using a wider set of assessment measures to identify the drivers of an individual restaurant's success or failure, including non-financial areas such as level of customer complaints, waiting times, staff turnover. One tool by which this can be achieved is the balanced scorecard.

Conclusion

Pitstop may be unable to return to profitability unless it has sufficient information to identify and either turn around or close underperforming restaurants.

Strategy 1 may be feasible but requires more market research and competitor analysis. The price reduction of 15% proposed in Strategy 2 would not appear to be viable and without significant increase in numbers or major cost reductions is likely to increase the chain's losses.

Other possible strategies to consider include:

- Offer takeaway or drive through service
- Get taken over by another chain
- Sell franchise to one of the fast food chains

3   **Somborne Zoological Park Ltd**

General comments

This scenario involves a charitable, not-for-profit company which is engaged in animal conservation and research, as well as operating a well-known zoo in the UK. The organisation has set itself a number of strategic goals including maximising the impact of its conservation activities, promoting the zoo and developing alternative income streams. It has recently decided to seek accreditation from the global industry body for sustainability and environmental management and has appointed a new Chairman to assist with this.

Candidates were not expected to have any specialist knowledge of these topics and additional information was provided in the scenario about the nature of environmental management and also to explain the zoo's aims for sustainability in four different areas: financial, environmental, HR and social.

NFP organisations and sustainability are far from being peripheral syllabus areas (a point suggested in tutor feedback), indeed both these topics are introduced in early chapters of the learning materials and are developed throughout. The concept of sustainable development is a key consideration for businesses today and for the ICAEW and its members.

There were some very good attempts at this question and no obvious evidence of time pressure. A sizeable number of candidates attempted the exam out of order and did this question first or second. Some candidates did start off badly however by failing to produce it in the required report format.

Report

To: Chairman of Somborne Zoo
From: A.N.Other
Date: September 2009
Re: Proposed Sustainability Initiative

(a) (i) **Strategic planning – benefits**

Strategic planning involves setting goals and then designing strategies to meet them.

Purpose and benefits of planning:

- To ensure Somborne meets the needs of its diverse stakeholders. A strategic plan will help communicate the purpose and values of the zoo to staff, visitors and sponsors, and help identify the priorities for the zoo.

- Attract and maintain funding and public support, avoiding over-reliance on any particular source of income. The availability of a plan may help sell the zoo to the public and sponsors in particular.

- Ensure optimum use of resources which, as with most NFP organisations, are likely to be limited.

- Ensure day-to-day operations are consistent with the long term goals of the zoo. As part of its strategic planning process Somborne has already identified four strategic goals. The strategic plan needs to set out in more detail how each of these goals will be pursued and will consider areas such as financial strategy and the raising of funds, marketing, visitor services, the organisation and scale of the site and exhibits, development of the animal collection, intentions for breeding, forming strategic partnerships for conservation and research.

- Guide the development and evolution of the zoo – coordinate the growth and ensure coherency of the site plan and exhibits. May help increase chances of gaining IZF accreditation.

- Relate the zoo to its external environment.

- Improve performance of zoo and its chances of survival.

- Help to identify and manage risks.

(ii) **Objectives**

Whilst the zoo's goals may be stated quite generally, the specific objectives need to be SMART (specific, measurable, achievable, relevant and with a timescale attached):

Goal: To maximise the impact of conservation and research activities

- Ensure at least five research papers are published during the year.

- Secure x number of new animals from threatened species within five years.

- Gain recognition from conservation bodies for activities eg be cited for or win awards, press coverage/media accolades within one year.

- Ensure x animals born per year under the zoo's breeding programme.

Goal: To promote the zoo and provide learning opportunities

- Increase the number of return visitors to 20% of total over three years.

- Increase admissions revenue by 15% per year.

- Complete the development of the panda exhibit by July 2010.

- Introduce a quarterly 'Friends of Somborne' newsletter in 2010.

- Upgrade the zoo's café and restaurant facilities by May 2010.

- Appoint a schools coordinator by Dec 2009 and visit 5 schools a month to promote the zoo's school programme.

- Ensure the zoo is featured in local press and current affairs programmes at least every month.

Goal: To develop alternative income streams

- Have approached 20 potential corporate/sponsors by Dec 2009.

- Attract five new benefactors in 2010.

- Increase the annual membership of the 'Friends of Somborne' by 15% by summer 2010.

- Promote the zoo as a venue for corporate events and hospitality such that this forms 10% of the income in 2010.

- Increase the sales of zoo merchandise by x%.

(b) **Allocation of resources**

In common with other not for profit (NFP) organisations, Somborne is likely to face the following issues in making decisions:

- Multiple objectives (driven by diverse stakeholder needs)
- Conflicts between stakeholders
- Need to take a long term view of the impact of short term decisions
- Not always easy to measure results or to quantify the impact of decisions
- Requirement for greater awareness of corporate responsibility and sustainability issues
- Financial and other resource constraints
- Operations in the public eye

In view of its limited resources, Somborne therefore needs to prioritise its goals, audiences, and activities.

In order to make a decision on how best to use resources and what projects the zoo can afford to carry out each year, Somborne first needs to identify the resources available, not just in terms of finances but also staffing and space. Potential projects will be constrained by any physical limitations of the actual site. Increasing Somborne's use of volunteers will help increase the resources available.

In making a choice as to which exhibits and programmes to allocate funds and space to, Somborne must strike a balance between the needs of the animals, visitors and staff.

Somborne's licence may require resources to be dedicated in certain areas and the desire for accreditation will affect the zoo's priorities. There may also be conditions attached to certain donations which restrict what the funds can be used for.

The mission statement acknowledges the dual role of the zoo as a visitor attraction and as an organisation engaged in animal conservation.

Thus it may appear that there is competition for resources between Somborne's revenue-producing activities and its conservation desires and needs eg the zoo may face a choice between dedicating more money for conservation and spending this on visitor facilities.

An improved entrance or a new exhibit may bring extra visitors and increase the number of returning visitors. This in turn may generate more funds for conservation and research activities.

Conversely good conservation or recognition of successful research may enhance the zoo's budget by attracting funding. This would then allow development of the zoo's visitor attractions.

Thus the two roles are not necessarily in conflict.

Having decided to spend money on either conservation/research or its commercial activities, Somborne still faces competing choices.

Resources for research are finite and must be carefully targeted. In choosing between potential research or conservation projects, priority must be given to research that has clear implications for saving species, populations and habitats.

If Somborne decides to spend money on new visitor features, then it will need to consider how best to spend this. Thus it may need to consider choice of location within the zoo, order of construction of exhibits, amount of space to be allocated to visitors/staff/animals.

There is also a distinction between short and long term goals. Somborne needs to focus on the ultimate goal of conservation, but also on meeting the immediate day-to-day needs of the living creatures for which it is responsible. Thus in allocating funds it needs to consider how to provide the best possible conditions for the animals in its care and whether funds will be available in future years for projects to continue.

One of the problems facing Somborne is how to measure the return on its investment. It is likely that the spending on projects within the zoo, rather than conservation research, will have a more direct impact which is easier to quantify. Eg If a new gorilla exhibit is created, Somborne can measure the impact in terms of number of visitors, press coverage, increased admissions revenue, adoption of the animals etc.

It may take much longer to assess the impact of conservation and research activities and this is also likely to be affected by wider and possible uncontrollable influences eg climate change, natural disasters eg fire and floods, other parties engaged in similar research.

Examiner note:

Requirement (b) asked candidates to identify the issues the zoo is likely to face in deciding how to allocate resources. Answers here were polarised. Most candidates identified the issue of limited resources in the context of funding and the need to choose between conflicting objectives, sometimes referring back to the wide range of goals identified in (a). Better candidates recognised the dual role of the zoo – as an organisation dedicated to conservation and as a visitor attraction – and the trade-off between allocating resources to animal welfare and research and spending on marketing and promotion to attract more visitors to the zoo. They also noted that the zoo's licence and its sponsors may impose certain constraints and that resources were not limited to cash but extended to labour, both paid staff and volunteers.

(c) (i) **Sustainability**

Costs and benefits of sustainability

Sustainability involves using natural resources in a way that does not lead to their decline. In the context of the zoo, sustainability has been identified as having an impact not just on the environment but also in other areas: financial, human resources and social.

Costs of implementing a sustainability programme

In the short term this may lead to:

- Increased costs eg using greener energy sources, buying fair trade products, paying higher wages to workers

- The environmental audit will take time and money, as may the accreditation process

- Increased admin time in screening suppliers and contractors, and reduced number of parties available

- Possible reduced income eg no donations from non-ethical sponsors

- Additional management considerations eg regarding the ethical HR policies

Benefits:

- Sustainable activities will help to improve the environment and will fulfil the zoo's moral obligation to be involved in such practices.

- Accreditation by IZF for its sustainable activities may enhance the reputation of the zoo particularly if, as a result, it qualifies for official awards and recognitions.

- If Somborne stresses sustainable activities as a basis for promotion and marketing it may become a more attractive option to visitors, donors, investors, and strategic partners and thus increase net income. Accreditation may help attract ethical investors.

- Green practices adopted by the zoo may lead to cost savings through eg reduced costs of utilities such as water and energy.

- This strategy will improve employees' awareness of environmental issues and responsibilities, enhance employee morale and help to ensure that Somborne is seen as a desirable employer.

- Somborne will stand as a model for sustainable practices, encouraging others, especially in the same community, and setting an example for 'greener' governance.

- The sustainability initiative will improve their image as champions for environmental responsibility, enhance compliance with environmental principles and, even better, help to inform and shape future legislation.

(ii) **Impact on staff and one other key stakeholder**

Stakeholder group	Area of interest	Impact
Staff	Financial	Will want the zoo to operate as a going concern to safeguard jobs.
	Environment	Can enhance sustainability through own personal convictions eg view on environment. May contribute to change and innovations or may resist change due to extra workload.
	HR	Will be interested in development opportunities, HR practices, Health and safety.
	Social	May feel rewarded through participation in educating the local schools and community.
Suppliers/ contractors and other business partners	Financial	Will be concerned about the potential impact on their contracts and working practices which could lead to additional costs.
	Social	May be concerned about the cost implications eg if required to use recyclable packaging.
		May welcome ethical procurement if it increases their chances of winning work or the price that they will receive.

Candidates may have instead analysed any of the following which were deemed to be key stakeholders:

Visitors	Environment Social	May have a genuine concern about the welfare of the animals ,the environment and the sustainability of the zoo's performance
Investors/ sponsors/ donors	Financial	May contribute if they believe that the zoo's activities and its financial position is sustainable.
		May want to ensure funds given are allocated for specific causes.

| Local community | Social | Will expect the zoo to provide socio-economic development through jobs, links with the schools, cooperation with local business. |

Examiner note:

Requirement (c)(i) asked candidates to explain the likely costs and benefits of implementing a sustainability initiative and (ii) to assess the likely impact of such an initiative on the staff and one other key stakeholder. Overall this was reasonably well done, although weaker candidates interpreted sustainability quite narrowly in terms of being 'environmentally friendly', failing to use the information provided in the scenario which extended this concept to ethical purchasing, sponsorship, and HR policies; staff development; and visitor education.

Stronger candidates referred to time lags and the potential in some cases for tangible benefits in the future arising from costs incurred today.

There were a number of other key stakeholders that could have been identified in (ii), including visitors, suppliers and sponsors. Better answers discussed the positive and negative impact that the initiative would have on the staff and one other group. Some candidates wasted time by discussing more than one stakeholder or alternatively failing to pick one that was 'key' – those candidates who talked about the impact on the animals or animal rights activists fell within this category!

(d) **Use of information to assess sustainability initiative**

Somborne needs to implement a system which provides the appropriate type and amount of information for managers to implement and control the sustainability initiative and assess its success.

The current information management system may need to be enhanced to allow collection of new types of data eg may need to first measure energy usage before can implement policies and procedures to reduce it.

In addition certain specific information may be required by IZF to demonstrate achievement levels and in order for Somborne to acquire accreditation. Thus S needs to establish any specific performance criteria that will be used by IZF in order to decide what indicators need to be measured and monitored in each of the four areas identified.

Some of the information that needs to be gathered may be qualitative as well as quantitative eg impact on visitors' willingness to adopt a sustainable lifestyle will be hard to measure and may be based on responses to surveys/conversations etc

Somborne may make use of exception reporting eg to highlight problem areas where energy or water usage has overrun, breaches of relevant guidelines

One purpose of an information system is knowledge management so that best practice with regard to sustainability can be shared. Staff may need training to formally record data/information necessary if such records have not been kept in the past.

Once the environmental audit has been conducted Somborne will have information about the current level of achievement in various areas. Baseline performance can be defined and targets set for future achievement.

On an ongoing basis performance can then be measured against these targets/budgets and deviations from the plan can be investigated. S may benchmark performance targets against other zoos (IZF may be able to provide appropriate information).

The zoo will need to undertake staff training, communicate the new system and establish procedures for cost control.

Baseline performance measures:

Overall impact

- Increase in positive zoo/conservation news stories or features.
- Increase in partnerships with other conservation bodies.

Financial

- % of revenue from zoo based activities.

- Retail revenue per visitor.

- Increase in number of visitors per month.

- Funds received from research and development activities.

- Donations received.

- Responses to pledges and petitions.

- Increased zoo membership numbers and increased sponsorship schemes, especially those prompted by support for conservation/sustainability.

- Deficit/surplus of income over expenditure.

- No. of suppliers/contractors subject to screening.

- No. of suppliers meeting sustainable criteria.

- % procurement from fair trade countries/suppliers.

Environmental

- Volumes of waste disposed of v recycled
- Monthly levels of energy consumption
- Monthly water usage
- Volume of recycled water
- Methods of visitor travel to and around zoo
- No. of fair trade and organic products in the shop and cafe
- No. of new environmentally friendly initiatives implemented
- CO_2 and other emissions
- % of energy from alternative sources

Human resources

- Staff and volunteer injury rate
- Hours and expenditure on sustainability training
- Number of certificates awarded to staff and others trained at the Zoo
- Percentage of staff receiving recognition from professional organisations
- Percentage of staff who have completed their professional development plan each year
- Percentage of staff walking/cycling or using car share schemes to get to work

Social

- Number of training programmes offered by Zoo staff covering topics related to sustainability

- Number of presentations and publications that connect and inform the general public and the professional community about sustainability

- Attendance figures at specific education projects

- Assessments of the educational effectiveness of different exhibits via surveys and questionnaires, observations of visitor behaviour, conversations

- Number of research programs, citations, no. of papers published

- Number of news stories that cover sustainability initiatives at the zoo

- Records of media coverage, and teacher feedback on formal programmes

- Records of sales of products in the zoo that have been associated with particular messages or campaigns

Examiner note:

In requirement (d) candidates were requested to explain how the zoo could use an information system to measure the success of its sustainability initiative and to suggest some appropriate performance measures that could be used. Candidates were obviously comfortable suggesting performance measures under the headings of finance, environment, HR and social, although to score well these needed to be related to the specific sustainability goals identified by the zoo. Most were less well-prepared to discuss information systems, a topic which came into the syllabus for the new Business Strategy paper and which has not yet been examined in any depth. A small minority made some good points about the need to design a system around the reporting requirements of the industry body (the IZF), the use of exception reporting to identify areas of underperformance and the benefits of introducing a knowledge management system to share information and experience.

Index

ICAEW

Notes

REVIEW FORM – BUSINESS STRATEGY STUDY MANUAL

Your ratings, comments and suggestions would be appreciated on the following areas of this Study Manual.

	Very useful	Useful	Not useful
Chapter introductions	☐	☐	☐
Examination context	☐	☐	☐
Worked examples	☐	☐	☐
Interactive questions	☐	☐	☐
Quality of explanations	☐	☐	☐
Technical references (where relevant)	☐	☐	☐
Self-test questions	☐	☐	☐
Self-test answers	☐	☐	☐
Index	☐	☐	☐

	Excellent	Good	Adequate	Poor
Overall opinion of this Study Manual	☐	☐	☐	☐

Please add further comments below:

Please return completed form to:

The Learning Team
Learning and Professional Department
ICAEW
Metropolitan House
321 Avebury Boulevard
Milton Keynes
MK9 2FZ
E learning@icaew.com